A GUIDE TO THE GOSPELS

KNOW YOUR BIBLE

A GUIDE
TO THE GOSPELS

W. GRAHAM SCROGGIE, D.D. (EDIN.)

Fleming H. Revell Company
Old Tappan, New Jersey

Printed in the United States of America

This edition is issued by
special arrangement with
PICKERING & INGLIS LTD.
the British publishers.

First published   -   1948
Reprinted   -   -   1952
,,   -   -   1958
,,   -   -   1962

TO MY WIFE
JOAN
ENCOURAGER AND HELPER IN
THE MINISTRY OF THE WORD

"*Then said the Interpreter (to Christian), Come in; I will show thee that which will be profitable to thee. So he commanded his man to light the candle, and bid Christian follow him. So he had him into a private room, and bid his man open a door; the which, when he had done, Christian saw the picture of a very grave person hang up against the wall; and this was the fashion of it:*

it had eyes lifted up to heaven,
the best of books in its hand,
the law of truth was written upon its lips,
the world was behind its back;
it stood as if it pleaded with men,
and a crown of gold did hang over its head."

JOHN BUNYAN

SYNOPSIS OF CONTENTS

DIVISION A

THE GOSPELS VIEWED SYNTHETICALLY

Part I—General

DIVISION B

THE GOSPELS VIEWED ANALYTICALLY

St. Mark

St. Matthew

St. Luke

2

St. John

DIVISION C

THE GOSPELS VIEWED CHRISTOLOGICALLY

INDICES

APPENDICES

MAPS

FEATURES

ARTICLES	NINETY
STUDIES	THREE HUNDRED AND FOURTEEN
QUESTIONS	SEVEN HUNDRED AND THIRTY-EIGHT
BOOK LISTS	THIRTY, and INDICES III, IV

A GUIDE TO THE GOSPELS

TO THE READER

1 As you begin this study of the Gospels resolve that you will be diligent in it, and will persevere until you get a real mental and spiritual grasp of their contents.

The design of this book is to supply the student with material, by means of which he may attain to a mastery of these priceless Memoirs which are called the Gospels.

2 Every time you turn to their pages, offer the prayer: ' Open Thou mine eyes, that I may behold wondrous things' (Psa. cxix. 18), and expect the Holy Spirit to do so.

3 Get a copy of each Gospel in good print; of a size that can easily be carried about. Open it up, and interleave it, and on the interleaves write the main divisions of the analysis of each, so that, whenever you read it you may see just where you are in the unfolding story.

4 Secure a note-book of reasonable size, about 6 in. by $4\frac{1}{2}$ in.; have it by you whenever you study, and make notes of things that impress you; of difficulties that arise in the course of your reading; of subjects you may wish to develop for class or pulpit use, and anything else of relevant interest. It would be well to number the pages, and make an index, so that you can readily turn to any subject on which you have a note. If you are likely to write much, let your note-books be all the same size, and number them.

5 Plan to spend so much time each week on this study. Arrange for it as you do for your meals, and keep to the arrangement. If possible, choose a time when you are not likely to be interrupted.

6 Make a point of speaking to somebody about your study, in order that you may create interest in another, and at the same time may impress your studies on your own mind. One of the best ways to learn is to teach; and, of course, in order to teach you must learn.

7 It will be well to assume ignorance of the Gospels rather than knowledge, because the more you study the more will you be convinced of the petty known and the vast unknown.

8 Realise that it is not irreverent to approach the Gospels, or any of the Scriptures, critically; that it is right and necessary to know what can be known about such matters as authorship, sources, style, etc., so that by such knowledge a foundation may be laid for a true appreciation of the finished product.

9 On the other hand, it should be recognized that critical study is not an end in itself, but only a means to an end. The sources of Matthew and Luke will continue to be matters of controversy, and various views will continue to be held, but the thing that finally matters is that we have the Gospels of Matthew and Luke, and that each is the Word of God to us, however it came into existence.

All examination should have experience for its end.

You should give to your work attention with intention, remembering that the benefit which can be derived from these studies will be in exact proportion to the attentiveness and industry of the student.

10 It is of supreme importance that the Gospels be read, and read, and read again. Nothing can be a substitute for the reading of the text itself. This should be done until mentally you can follow the outline of each Gospel and are able to refer easily to any passage you may want. Turn up every reference given, and ponder it.

A Parallel New Testament (Authorized and Revised Versions) will be most valuable for the purpose of comparison.

Do not use a Scofield, or any annotated Bible, with these studies, if you wish to keep your mind open and flexible.

11 But while the Gospels themselves are your study you should, as means and time allow, secure one or more of the best books on these Records. The titles of some useful books are given for your guidance, but they are not essential for the general mastery referred to, but an oft repeated reading of the text of the Gospels is absolutely necessary.

12 It would be well for you to carry a list of the questions, so that at odd moments, you can test your knowledge and make a mental note of what you need to look up in the studies.

13 Do not imagine that such work as this is too much for you. Do not underrate your ability, but with courage and confidence undertake something really big and worth while, and yours will be the joy of achievement.

14 Achievement means nothing less than that the spirit and truths of the Gospels are reincarnated in you in terms of character and service.

"To adhere to what is set down in them and appropriate to oneself what we can for moral strengthening and culture is the true edifying purpose to which we can turn the Gospels."

GOETHE

"Had our Gospels been unauthentic, they must inevitably have partaken of the characteristics which mark without exception every early fiction about the Saviour's life.

"The birth of Jesus had first been revealed by night to a few unknown and ignorant shepherds; the first full, clear announcement by Himself of His own Messiahship was made by a well-side in the weary noon to a single obscure Samaritan woman. Who would have invented things so unlike the thoughts of man as these?" F. W. FARRAR

A GUIDE TO THE GOSPELS

INTRODUCTORY

THE Four Gospels are not so much books as pamphlets, slender records of the life, work, death, and resurrection of Jesus of Nazareth, the Christ; pamphlets which can be read attentively in from eight to nine hours, and yet, in all the literature of the world there is nothing of comparable value with them. This value is not primarily literary, though in this respect the Gospels are impressive, but chiefly moral and spiritual. There is more wisdom in their pages than in all that all the philosophers have ever written.

There are various ways in which the Gospels can be studied, and probably among evangelicals, the prevailing way is devotional. These read and study the incomparable Story for spiritual illumination and refreshment, and there their interest largely ends. On the other hand there are those who, with less spiritual desire and purpose, perhaps, devote themselves to a critical examination of these Records, and with the results of their study their interest largely ends.

Now these two cases represent two things of momentous importance, and to take the second of them first, let it be said that critical examination of these and all Biblical Writings is not only permissible, but absolutely necessary. Belief in the inspiration of the Gospels is not a prerequisite for the study of them, but certainly it will be the result of such study, if it be properly done. After all, the thing of primary importance is not the inspiration of the Bible, but its revelation, because but for the revelation there would be no need of inspiration.

Critical study is, in the main, threefold: Textual, or Lower; Literary, or Higher; and Historical; and these lines of investigation must be honestly and earnestly pursued by anyone who would be a thorough student of these Records. Textual Criticism can be engaged in only by the scholar, by him who has the necessary *apparatus criticus*. Literary Criticism relates to such matters as authorship, style, and date, and may be pursued by anyone who can appreciate evidence, and the same may be said of Historical Criticism. But these lines of inquiry may easily become an obsession, and in pursuit of them one may miss what matters finally and forever.

The questions which criticism of the Gospels raises will always be subjects of controversy: such as, what are the designs of these Writings? who were their authors? when were they written? what is the relation of them to one another? how did they first come into being? what source or sources are drawn upon for their composition? what is their historical value? are they authentic and genuine? why are there four only? of what value are the Old Testament quotations and allusions in the Gospels? how are their parallels, omissions, and additions to be accounted for? are the recorded miracles credible? are historical references correct? can the presentation of Jesus be trusted? that is, is it a portrait, or a picture? These and other matters have been debated for more than a millennium and a half, and will continue to be, without approaching much nearer to agreement among students.

Why, then, it may be asked, are these inquiries pursued, and what profit is there in such investigations? Be it said that these difficulties should not foster scepticism, but rather should stimulate faith. Origen has said that the ' Divine Word ordered some stumbling blocks and stones of offence in the sacred records, that we might not be led away by the unalloyed attractiveness of the narration, and seek for nothing more Divine '; and Westcott has said: ' If there were no need for rigorous criticism, no reward for acute philology, no scope for philosophical inquiry, in the study of the Bible; if the text were uniform, the diction simple, and the connection obvious, we might neglect the consecration of our entire faculties to divine ends; while, as it is, we find in the human form, and the natural transmission of the sacred volume, the noblest field for our labours.'

What is wrong with the critical investigation of the Gospels is not the pursuit of it, but the spirit in which, too often, it is pursued. Much Biblical criticism is unscientific and unfair. Westcott says that ' many critics admit a fact on the testimony of Josephus, which they question if it rest on the statement of St. Matthew or St. Luke. They do not concede those privileges to the Evangelists which they yield to other historians in accordance with the received rules of evidence '; and this attitude is largely due to antecedent prejudices. ' Critical difficulties are too often in the first instance the excuse for a foregone conclusion, or at least, fall in with a definite bias.'

Believing that no line of critical inquiry is of no importance, not a little space in the following pages is given to matters which belong properly to this line of approach, but always, I hope, without dogmatism, irreverence, or unbelief.

Suppose it could be proved that Matthew's Gospel was not written by the Apostle of that name; that the Fourth Gospel was not written by the son of Zebedee, but by an Elder; that Matthew's and Luke's Gospels were not written until after, and, perhaps, long after the destruction of Jerusalem in A.D. 70; that the Synoptics and the Fourth Gospel are in hopeless disagreement with one another on many points; that there were primitive forms of the Synoptic Records, editions earlier than our canonical Gospels; that Matthew's Gospel was first written in Hebrew; that Mark abbreviated Matthew's Record; that much of Matthew and Luke is from a lost document which the critics call Q; that Mark's Gospel was written in Rome after Peter's death; that some of the quotations from the Old Testament are quite irrelevant; that some, at any rate, of the miracles are incredible; that much of what Christ is reported to have said was ' put into His mouth ' by the writers of the Records, especially in the Fourth Gospel. Suppose, I say, that these things could be proved, what would we have gained? Nothing whatever of spiritual significance. 'Source-Criticism,' and 'Form-Criticism' —the pursuit of the data behind the canonical Gospels—have a certain value, but both are speculative, and in quarters have become arbitrary and sceptical. (For these subjects see Dibelius, Baltmann, and Albertz).

So we are brought to the first of the two approaches to the Gospels, aforenamed, the devotional. I do not believe that we have to make a choice between the critical and the devotional study of the Gospels, but that the critical should be pursued devotionally, and the devotional, critically; but if a choice had to be made we ought not to hesitate. As some scientists believe that all human emotions can be resolved into chemical elements, so many students of the Gospels believe that these Records must finally be judged at the bar of human reason; but as there is a spiritual element in human experience, the faculty of faith is necessary for an understanding of the Gospels. Whatever secondary designs may be discerned in these Records, the primary design of each of them is to present a Saviour to sinful men; each of them leads to Calvary and points to the Redeemer of mankind; each of them proves the truth of Christ's claim: 'The Son of Man came not to be ministered unto, but to minister, and to give His life a ransom for many' (Matt. xx. 28).

As we do not need to know all the elements and processes which issue in a loaf of bread before we can eat it and be nourished by it, and as we do not need to understand the pigmentary art before we can appreciate and be inspired by a master-painting, so it is not necessary that we study the Gospels critically before we can experience the Saviourship of Christ. The value of the Gospels is independent of their authors and sources, their date and style; the issues vastly transcend the processes. We should know all we can about the processes, but such knowledge is as a millstone about our necks if it leaves us without a Saviour and Lord, without the spiritual experience of eternal life. The following pages are not chiefly devotional, except in spirit, but by exhibiting the critical and expository foundations of the Gospels, by assembling their immense detail, and by subjecting them to minute analysis, it is hoped that the student will be helped to see the grandeur of these Pamphlets, and will be led up from these foundations to devotion which is built on knowledge and not on fluctuating sentiment, and so, out of a full mind and heart, to say, ' my Lord, and my God ' (John xx. 28).

THE GOSPELS
VIEWED SYNTHETICALLY

PART I—GENERAL

Division A

THE GOSPELS VIEWED SYNTHETICALLY

Part I—GENERAL

PART I—GENERAL

I

KEY PLAN OF READING

THIRTY-FOUR STUDIES

EMPERORS OF ROME

B.C. 30—A.D. 180

1	AUGUSTUS	..	..	..	.. B.C. 30-A.D. 14
2	TIBERIUS	..	..	..	.. A.D. 14-37
3	CALIGULA	..	..	..	.. A.D. 37-41
4	CLAUDIUS	..	..	..	.. A.D. 41-54
5	NERO ..	..	..	..	.. A.D. 54-68
6	GALBA ..	..	..	..	.. A.D. 68-69
7	OTHO ..	..	..	..	.. A.D. 69 (3 months)
8	VITELLIUS	..	..	..	.. A.D. 69 (1 month)
9	VESPASIAN	..	..	..	.. A.D. 69-79
10	TITUS ..	..	..	..	.. A.D. 79-81
11	DOMITIAN	..	..	..	.. A.D. 81-96
12	NERVA	..	..	..	.. A.D. 96-98
13	TRAJAN ..	..	..	..	.. A.D. 98-117
14	HADRIAN	..	..	..	.. A.D. 117-138
15	ANTONINUS PIUS	..	..	..	A.D. 138-161
16	MARCUS AURELIUS	..	..	..	A.D. 161-180

3

CHURCH FATHERS

A S frequent reference will be made to Church Fathers in these Gospel Studies it will be well for the student to know who they are, when they lived, and any particulars which are of relevant interest. Whenever, in the Studies, any of the following names appear, refer back to this summary and refresh your memory of the person referred to.

1 IGNATIUS (A.D. 70-115).—Second bishop of Antioch in Syria. Said to have been appointed to this office by the Apostles. He wrote seven Epistles of unique importance, some of which his contemporary Polycarp quoted. These Epistles were written while Ignatius was travelling in chains from Syria across Asia Minor to Rome, where he was martyred, shouting: ‘ I am made happy by these wild beasts.’ When the Christians at Rome tried to hinder his martyrdom, he said: ‘ I am the wheat-corn of God; let me be ground by the teeth of wild beasts that I may become the pure bread of Christ.’

2 POLYCARP (A.D. 70-155).—Bishop of Smyrna. An outstanding figure of the early Church. Born, probably, in the year that Jerusalem fell. He knew the Apostle John, and other contemporaries of our Lord. He is an early and valuable witness to the teaching and organization of the Church in its earliest days, and to the Canon of the New Testament. There is extant an important letter of his in connection with the Epistles of Ignatius. He wrote an Epistle to the Church of Philippi in which he mentions Paul’s Epistle to that Church, and he shows a knowledge of at least seven other of Paul’s Epistles; and also he makes reference to sayings of our Lord.

He suffered martyrdom by burning. When invited to save his life by reviling Christ he made the famous answer: 'Fourscore and six years have I been His servant, and He hath done me no wrong; how, then, can I blaspheme the King who saved me?'

3 CLEMENT OF ROME (A.D. 92-99).—The first bishop of Rome (if the tradition that Peter was ever bishop there be set aside). The writer of a famous Epistle to the Church at Corinth, which is amongst the earliest non-canonical Christian Writings.

4 PAPIAS (A.D. 60-150).—Bishop of Hierapolis early in the second century. Tradition says that he was a pupil of the Apostle John. He wrote the *Exposition of the Oracles of the Lord*, in which he says what now is generally accepted, that Mark's is the earliest of the four Gospels, and that he drew his information from the Apostle Peter.

In this work is also found the famous statement, which will frequently be quoted in these pages, that Matthew wrote discourses of our Lord in the Hebrew tongue. On this statement is founded the *Logia*, or Q theory, which is explained in the section on the Synoptic Problem (page 83).

5 IRENÆUS (A.D. 120-200).—Bishop of Lyons. One of Polycarp's pupils. He is known as the author of two important works: *Against all Heresies*, and *In Proof of the Apostolic Teaching*. In the former, Irenæus bears witness to practically the whole of our New Testament Canon, especially to the Four Gospels.

The latter, known only in an Armenian translation, has been described as 'a sort of *vade mecum* for an intelligent Christian,' explaining his faith; or, as he calls it himself, 'a remembrancer of the more essential things.'

6 JUSTIN MARTYR (A.D. 100-165).—A Samaritan philosopher who embraced Christianity on the grounds of reason, and observation of the steadfastness of Christians. He addressed two *Apologies* to the Roman Emperor, defending the

Christians against charges of immorality and disloyalty.
His is the *Dialogue with Trypho*, setting before the Jewish
mind the justification of Christianity. He quotes the
Synoptists and John, and shows acquaintance with the
Epistles. He was a voluminous writer, and crowned his
faith by a martyr death.

7 TATIAN (A.D. 110-172).—An Assyrian rhetorician who was
won to Christianity by hearing Justin Martyr. He is the
author of the *Diatessaron* (*dia*, through; *tessaron*, four),
or, *Harmony of the Four Gospels*, ' a work of unique evidential value, the chief buttress of the authenticity of our
Four Gospels.' This work, long lost, was recovered by
Zahn. It contains 95 per cent. of John's Gospel.

8 TERTULLIAN (A.D. 160-222).—Born at Carthage, N. Africa,
of pagan parents. Trained as a lawyer. Converted ' in
mature manhood.' A Christian layman, the earliest Latin
Father of eminence, ' the first of that noble roll of names,
Tertullian, Cyprian, Hilary, Ambrose, Jerome, and Augustine, which no literature in any language can match.' He
was the author of many important works.

9 ORIGEN (A.D. 186-253).—One of the greatest of the theologians, though in many matters unorthodox. Much
given to allegorical interpretation. A prodigious worker,
he wrote commentaries on each book of the Bible. He is
regarded as the Father of Biblical Criticism, and he rendered
invaluable services to Biblical Textual knowledge.

10 CLEMENT OF ALEXANDRIA (A.D. 155-220).—Of the Gospels he
says that ' those that contained the genealogies were first
written.' Also, that Mark wrote his Gospel from matter
preached by Peter, which is now generally believed. Also,
that John ' last of all . . . wrote a spiritual Gospel.'

11 CYPRIAN (A.D. 200-258).—Born at Carthage, of heathen
parents, as was Tertullian, one of whose pupils he was.
He began life as a teacher of rhetoric. Became bishop of
Carthage. Was martyred in A.D. 258, uttering the words:
' Thanks be to God.'

12 ATHANASIUS (A.D. 296-373).—The greatest and most persistent of the early defenders of the Faith. Archbishop of Alexandria. The great champion of Christ's Divinity against Arius who denied it. To whom was due the affirmation of this doctrine at the Council of Nicæa, in A.D. 325. One of a group of great N. African theologians. Before he was twenty-two years of age he wrote his classic work *On the Incarnation of the Word of God.*

The Athanasian Creed sets forth most clearly of any of the priceless documents of primitive Christianity the faith for which Athanasius fought, though it was compiled at a later date to express what he taught, and was not written by him.

13 HILARY OF POICTIERS (A.D. 295-368).—A strong opponent of Arianism (see Athanasius). He wrote a commentary on St. Matthew. He believed some books of the Apocrypha to be canonical, *Wisdom,* and *Maccabees;* believed that the Lord's brethren were children of Joseph by a former wife; regarded Christian marriage as absolutely indissoluble. He was ' the first to excel in the composition of hymns.'

14 CYRIL OF JERUSALEM (A.D. 315-386).—A champion of the orthodox faith; an opponent of Arius (see Athanasius). A bishop.

15 GREGORY NAZIANZEN (A.D. 325-390).—Bishop of Constantinople (Istanbul). Life-long friend of Basil. Ordained by Athanasius. Opponent of Arian doctrines (see Athanasius). Jerome was one of his disciples.

16 BASIL THE GREAT (A.D. 330-379).—Reckoned one of the Four Doctors of the Eastern Church, the others being, Athanasius, Gregory Nazianzen, and Chrysostom. He wrote a great treatise on *The Holy Spirit,* and *Homilies on the Psalms.*

17 GREGORY OF NYSSA (A.D. 336-395).—A bishop. He, his elder brother Basil, and his friend Gregory Nazianzen, formed the great triumvirate of Eastern theologians in the fight with heresies as regards the Person of Christ, which established the triumph of orthodoxy against Arius.

18 AMBROSE (A.D. 340-397).—Bishop of Milan. Traditional author, with Augustine, of the *Te Deum*. To him Augustine owed his conversion.

19 CHRYSOSTOM (A.D. 347-407).—Bishop of Constantinople (Istanbul). One of the greatest preachers of any age, deservedly called ' the golden mouthed.' He wrote ' more abundantly than any other Greek Church writer.' Famous for his homilies on the Scriptures, especially those on the New Testament. He was ' one of the noblest, wisest, and most eloquent of the Fathers.'

20 JEROME (A.D. 342-420).—He has been spoken of as ' the least pleasing amongst early Christian saints, and as strangely full of contradictions as his learning is bright, shining, and supreme.' For 34 years he laboured at Bethlehem (A.D. 386-420). His inestimable contribution to Christian literature and worship is the scholarly edition of the Bible known as the Vulgate, the Latin translation of the Bible from the Hebrew of the Old Testament, and the Greek of the New Testament. For over 1000 years it was the sole form in which the Bible was known to Western Europe, and ' it remains to this day the Authorized Version of the Roman Church.'

21 AUGUSTINE (A.D. 354-430).—Bishop of Hippo, N. Africa. Had a saintly mother, Monica. Converted through Ambrose. Author of the *Confessions*, which is a classic of the soul. His greatest book is *The City of God*, which he took 14 years to write. In all, he wrote about 250 volumes. Harnack has described him as ' the Father of Roman Catholicism.' Farrar says he was ' the greatest of the Western Fathers, and the man who has exercised the deepest influence on the theology of the Church.'

We should have in view two other men, not Church Fathers, but historians, one Jewish, Josephus, and the other Christian, Eusebius, whose views, especially the latter's, are of considerable value for our study of the Gospels.

22 JOSEPHUS, Flavius (A.D. 37-100).—Jewish historian. He was born at Jerusalem seven years after Christ's Ascension: was one of the leaders of the great Jewish insurrection against the Romans in A.D. 66-67. After the capture of Jerusalem by Titus, in A.D. 70, he was taken to Rome where he settled down to literary work. He enjoyed the patronage of Vespasian, Titus, and Domitian, and was granted Roman citizenship. His two great works are *The Jewish War*, in seven books, which reaches from the time of the Maccabees to A.D. 73; and *Jewish Antiquities*, in twenty books, a comprehensive history of the Jewish people from the beginnings of Biblical history to the outbreak of the war in A.D. 66.

23 EUSEBIUS of Cæsarea (A.D. 260-340).—The greatest of Church historians, to whom we owe a vast store of knowledge of the early Church, the records of others which he preserved being a not less valuable legacy than the facts known to himself, or collected from eye-witnesses. Foremost amongst his writings must ever stand his great Ecclesiastical History which begins with the Preparation of the World for the Incarnation, supplements the canonical records as regards the earliest missionary work, and provides our chief store-house of knowledge of the sub-apostolic age, its persecutions, doctrinal disputes, and activities till the time of Constantine. Bishop Lightfoot says that 'no ancient ecclesiastical writer has laid posterity under heavier obligations than has Eusebius by his great erudition.'

24 MARCION (A.D. 140).—A heretic of the middle second century; intensely opposed to everything Jewish. He rejected the Old Testament and formed a canon of his own in which he admitted ten of Paul's Epistles, and a Gospel entitled 'Gospel of Christ.' It is now agreed that this last work is but a mutilated edition of Luke's Gospel, Marcion having cut out everything that directly contradicted his theory.

[Some of the foregoing dates are uncertain, but they may be taken to be approximately correct.]

QUESTIONS

1 Who was Ignatius: when, where, and how did he die?
2 Name a fact which distinguishes Polycarp, and quote his famous dying utterance.
3 What has made the name of Papias famous, and when did he live?
4 Who were Irenæus, and Justin Martyr?
5 What makes the name of Tatian famous?
6 Say what you know about Origen.
7 When did Athanasius live, and for what is he justly famous?
8 Name the four great Doctors of the Eastern Church.
9 Name two things which make Ambrose famous.
10 Who has been called ' the golden mouthed,' and ' one of the noblest, wisest, and most eloquent of the Fathers '?
11 When did Jerome live, and what is his inestimable contribution to Christian literature and worship?
12 When did Augustine live, and where; and what great books did he write?
13 Who is the earliest and greatest of Church historians?
14 Who was Josephus, and what did he write?

LITERATURE

'Ecclesiastical History' (2 vols.) - -	Eusebius
'Witnesses for Christ' - - - -	Backhouse and Taylor
'Handbook of the Early Christian Fathers'	E. Leigh-Bennett
'Lives of the Fathers' (2 vols.) - -	F. W. Farrar
	(very good)
'The Apostolic Fathers' - - - -	Bishop Lightfoot
'Mosheim's Ecclesiastical History' - -	———
'The First Five Centuries of the Church' -	J. Moffatt
'The Apostolic Fathers of the Second Century'	Wake and Burton
'The History of the Church' (2 vols.) -	P. Schaff
'The Church of the First Three Centuries'	T. A. Gurney
'The First Five Centuries' - - -	K. S. Latourette
'Patristic Study' - - - - -	H. B. Swete

The New Schaff-Herzog Encyclopædia of Religious Knowledge

Works on Church History, such as Neander's, Schaff's, etc.

Ante-Nicene Christian Library; Translations of the Writings of the Fathers down to A.D. 325.

Historical and Religious Background
of the Gospel Story

IT is absolutely necessary to realise that things are not taken
up by the New Testament from where the Old Testament
laid them down. When we turn from Malachi iv. to Matthew i.,
we must understand that about 400 years have come between,
and that in this period great changes have taken place. An
attentive reading of the New Testament will lead us to ask many
questions which, for the most part, can be answered only by
the Inter-Testament period.

We read of Cæsar Augustus. Who was he? And of Herod.
Who was he? In Palestine were cities bearing Greek names.
Whence these names? The language of the inhabitants of the
land was no longer Hebrew. Where did the new tongue come
from? In our Lord's time the official Council of the Jews was
the Sanhedrin. There were sects and parties in our Lord's
day which were unknown in the Old Testament: Pharisees,
Sadducees, Scribes, Essenes, Herodians. Who were these, and
when did they come into existence? John and James spoke of
the Dispersion. To what did they refer? In every Jewish city
there was a synagogue, or synagogues. Whence and why did
this institution arise? The temple of the time of Christ was not
the one which was in existence when we take farewell of the
Old Testament. Then when was it built, and by whom? Our
Lord was familiar with and quoted from a Greek Version of the
Old Testament Hebrew Scriptures. How and when did that
come into being?

The answer to these questions will furnish us, to a large extent,
with the historical background of the Gospels, which is necessary for a right understanding of them.

World Powers

At the end of the Old Testament the Persian Empire was in
power, and remained so until B.C. 333. Then, by the conquests

of Alexander the Great the Grecian Empire arose, and dominated from B.C. 333 until B.C. 167. During that period, after the death of Alexander in B.C. 323, his Empire was divided between four of his generals. Two of these were Ptolemy and Seleucus. Each of these inaugurated a dynasty, the former in Egypt, and the latter in Syria, and they contended with one another for the mastery of Palestine until B.C. 167, sometimes the one and sometimes the other being victorious.

Then came the struggle under the Maccabees for Jewish national independence, B.C. 167-141; and this was followed by the rule in Palestine of a family of Jewish Priest-Kings, descendants of the Maccabees known as the Asmonæans (a name derived from a Hebrew word meaning ' wealthy '), who remained in power for 78 years (B.C. 141-63), until, in B.C. 63, Pompey the Great conquered Palestine. This was the beginning of the domination of the Jewish people by Rome.

Now commenced a new and, for the Gospels period, a very important part of the story. The Herods were of Idumæan descent, and when, in B.C. 31, Augustus Cæsar overthrew Mark Antony at the battle of Actium, the first of the Herods sought and received from Augustus the Governorship of Judæa, Samaria, Galilee, Peræa, and Idumæa, and he was in power when Jesus was born (see ' The Herodian Family,' page 122).

Thus we see, in the period between the Testaments, world power passed from the Medo-Persians to the Greeks, and from the Greeks to the Romans, so that the Gospel Story opens under the ægis of Roman rule.

Sects and Parties

In the Gospels we read of Priests, and Levites, and Scribes, and Rulers; of Pharisees, and Sadducees, and Herodians; of Samaritans and Galileans; and we should know something about these, when they arose, and what they stood for. Some of them appear in the Old Testament, and some of them originated in the Inter-Testament period.

The Priests

The word, ' priest,' occurs in the Gospels a dozen times, and the word ' high priest,' or ' chief priests,' 84 times. The Jewish priesthood was ordained by God in the time of Moses, in the tribe of Levi, and the function of the priests was strictly religious; but after the return from Babylonian captivity, from the time of Ezra and Nehemiah, the civil power of the State passed into the hands of the priests, so that they were princes of the realm as well as ministers of religion; and the head of this order was the High Priest. In the time of Christ the priests, for the most part (cf. Luke i. 5), while religious in office, were carnal in spirit, were the persistent enemies of Jesus, and at last delivered Him to Pilate to be crucified (John xviii. 3, 35).

The Levites

The Levites were the descendants of Levi. They were accepted in the place of the first-born of the Israelites, and paid to Aaron their redemption price. They had charge of the tabernacle and its services, and were not numbered with Israel (Num. iii.). They are mentioned twice only in the Gospels (Luke x. 32; John i. 19).

The Scribes

In New Testament times the Scribes were the students, interpreters, and teachers of the Old Testament Scriptures, and were held in high esteem by the people. They were avowed opponents of Christ, and were publicly denounced by Him for making the Word of God of none effect by their traditions (Matt. xvi. 21; xxi. 15; xxiii. 2; (xxvi. 3); Mark xii. 28-40). They were also called lawyers (Matt. xxii. 35: Luke x. 25; xi. 45-52; xiv. 3).

The Rulers

Various officials are indicated by this word. It is used in John ii. 8, 9, of the governor of a feast (where the word is *architriklinos*, not *archōn*), and in John iii. 1 and vii. 26, of members of the Sanhedrin. The word is translated 'prince' seven times, six of which refer to the devil (the exception: Matt. xx. 25; cf. Mark iii. 22, *et al*); 'chief,' twice, once of the devil (Luke xi. 15; xiv. 1); 'chief ruler' (John xii. 42); 'magistrate' (Luke xii. 58); and 'ruler' ten times.

The Pharisees

The Pharisees (*separated*) arose in the time of the Maccabees, and were called 'separatists' in mockery by their enemies, because they 'separated' themselves from the ambitious political party in their nation. They were the exponents and guardians of the written and oral law, and, in belief, were the conservatives, in distinction from the Sadducees. But their religious orthodoxy was spiritually barren, and so they exposed themselves to the condemnation of Christ (Matt. xii. 1, 2; xxiii. 1-33; Luke vi. 6, 7; ch. xi. 37-54; ch. xii. 1), as well as to that of John the Baptist (Matt. iii. 7-12).

The Sadducees

This name, it is believed, is derived from Zadok, the high priest of Solomon's time (1 Kings ii. 35). They were the aristocratic and political party among the Jews, and the rivals of the Pharisees. In religious belief they were the 'modernists' of that day, denying the existence of spirits, the resurrection, and the immortality of the soul. They were the secularists of the Jewish faith, and would have paganized it. They came into prominence in the time of the Maccabees, and disappeared after the fall of the Jewish nation in A.D. 70. They came into collision with Christ, and were condemned by Him (Matt. xvi. 1-12; xxii. 23-33).

The Herodians

The Herodians were a political rather than a religious party. They took their name from the family of Herod, and derived their authority from the Roman Government. They were averse to any change of the political situation, and regarded Christ as a revolutionary character. This explains their approach to Him, and His condemnation of them (Mark iii. 6; viii. 15; xii. 13-17).

The Galilæans

This party rose in northern Palestine, and were the followers of one Judas of Galilee, who headed a rebellion against all foreign domination. They were insistent on their own rights, and reckless of the rights of others. They were political fanatics, and came into violent collision with Pilate (Luke xiii. 1-3). Christ's enemies tried to identify Him and His disciples with this party (Matt. xxvi. 69; Mark xiv. 70; Luke xxiii. 6).

The Samaritans

The Samaritans were a mixed race living in the province of Samaria. When, in 722 B.C., Sargon II took captive to Assyria the Israelites of the Northern Kingdom, he left many of the poorer and weaker people behind. Later, people from Babylon, Cuthah, Ava, Hamath, and Sepharvaim were sent to Samaria, and mingled with this remnant of Israelites, bringing with them their idolatrous forms of worship. Esar-Haddon of Assyria sent them a priest of the tribe of Levi, who dwelt at Bethel, and taught the people that they should fear the Lord. The result was that 'they feared the Lord and served their own gods.' When, in B.C. 535, the second temple was being built, the Samaritans offered their help, which was refused (Ezra iv. 1-3), with the result that an inveterate enmity sprang up between them and the Jews, which was in evidence in Christ's time (Matt. x. 5; John iv. 9). It is this feud which gives point to the story of the Samaritan leper (Luke xvii. 16), and to the parable of the Good Samaritan (Luke x. 30-37).

The Diaspora

The word *diaspora*, which occurs three times in the New Testament (John vii. 35; Jas. i. 1; Peter i. 1), is derived from two Greek words: *speirō*, to scatter, with a prefix *dia*, through, the two together meaning *scattered abroad*. It is used of the Jews. Moses had predicted that if they abandoned the law, they would be scattered (Lev. xxvi. 33-37; Deut. iv. 27-28; xxviii. 64-68), and this was fulfilled when the Israelites went into Assyrian captivity in B.C. 722, and the Jews into Babylonian captivity in B.C. 586. The mass of these did not return to Palestine, but settled in the cities of the Greek and Roman Empires (see Acts ii. 5, 9 11). Later on, when the persecution of Christians broke out, converted Jews were scattered abroad (Acts viii. 1, 4; xi. 19). The dispersion, though a penalty, became a blessing, for in captivity the Jews were cured of idolatry, and by the promul

4

gation of their faith countless numbers were led to turn to Israel's God, and these were known as *Proselytes*, a word which means *a convert to Judaism* (Matt. xxiii. 15; Acts ii. 10; vi. 5; xiii. 43). When Christianity began to spread, it found its earliest converts among the scattered Jews and these proselytes, and through them their heathen neighbours were reached.

Proselytes
(See under the DIASPORA)

The Synagogue

The two Greek words here brought together are *sun* and *agō*, which mean to assemble, to lead, bring, or come together; so *synagogue* refers to the place where Jews assemble, or to the Jews thus assembled.

The institution dates from the captivity in Babylon. The Jews there were under the necessity of gathering together in small groups, as they were no longer able to attend the Temple. This necessity would be felt by the Jews wherever scattered, and so everywhere synagogues were built. There they would gather for worship and religious instruction, and in this way the knowledge of the Law was kept alive in the minds of the Jews, and imparted to proselytes.

Our Lord was familiar with the synagogue service, and it was in the one at Nazareth that He began His ministry in Galilee (Luke iv. 14-30). The word ' synagogue ' occurs 34 times in the Gospels (see Matt. iv. 23; ix. 35; xii. 9; xiii. 54; John vi. 59). The Jews' attendance upon the synagogue has been maintained for over 2,400 years, and still, as long ago, it is a potent factor in the education of Jewish children.

The Septuagint

This is the Greek Version of the Old Testament Scriptures, and is called the *Septuagint*, the LXX, from the tradition that it was the work of *seventy* (seventy-two) Jews, who were brought from Palestine to Alexandria for the purpose. The tradition is spurious, but the translation was made at Alexandria in Egypt, between the years 285 and 130 B.C.

Read again the paragraphs on Diaspora and Synagogue, and you will see the need for and value of the Septuagint. The dispersed Jews were forgetting their native Hebrew, and the later Greek was becoming their mother tongue; it was, therefore, a great thing for them to have their Scriptures in Greek. This Version soon passed into general acceptance with the Greek-speaking Jews, even in Palestine, and its general circulation by their presence in the Greek cities paved the way for the spread of Christianity in the heathen world. The numerous quotations from the Old Testament in the New are, with few exceptions, taken from the LXX. Our Lord and His Apostles were, therefore, familiar with it. It is still the accepted Version of the Old Testament in the Greek Church.

The Sanhedrin

This is an interesting word. In Greek *hedra* means *a sitting place*, and *hedrion* is the diminutive form of *hedra*; *sun* means *together with*, so that *sunedrion* means *sitting together with*, or a council board; and it is used also of the council chamber, or place of session. The word occurs 22 times in the New Testament, of which 8 are in the Gospels, and is always translated *Council*.

The seed idea of this Body may be traced to the time of Jehoshaphat (2 Chron. xix. 8), or even to the time of Moses (Num. xi. 16, 17).

In the days of Christ the Sanhedrin consisted of:

(*a*) the Chief Priests or heads of the twenty-four priestly courses:

(*b*) the Scribes or lawyers; and

(*c*) the Elders, who were the representatives of the laity.

The Council had seventy or seventy-two members, the High Priest being the President, and they held their office for years, if not for life.

It was this Council before which Christ stood early that Friday (or Wednesday: see p. 569) morning, in the palace of the High Priest. This was an act altogether exceptional and illegal (Matt. xxvi. 57-68). The Sanhedrin had the right to pass sentence of death, but had not the power to execute it (John xviii. 31; xix. 7).

It was this Council before which Peter, and John, and Stephen stood (Acts iv. 1-7; vi. 12-vii. 1).

QUESTIONS

1 How long, approximately, was the interval between ' Malachi ' and ' Matthew '?
2 Of what significance is that interval for the Gospel Story?
3 What three Empires followed the Babylonian, and what are their dates?
4 Who were the Maccabees, and what was their period?
5 Who conquered Palestine in B.C. 63?
6 Who were the Herods, and of how many of them do we read in the Gospels?
7 State briefly what you know about the Priests, the Levites, and the Scribes.
8 Who were the Pharisees, the Sadducees, and the Herodians?
9 Who were the Samaritans?
10 What do you understand by the terms ' Diaspora ' and ' Proselyte '?
11 Where did the Synagogue originate, and what purpose did it serve?
12 What is the Septuagint, and what evidence is there of it in the Gospels?
13 What was the Sanhedrin, and where is it referred to in the Gospels?

LITERATURE

'Between Malachi and St. Matthew'	- G. M. Forde
'From Malachi to Matthew' - -	- R. W. Moss
'The Background of the Gospels' -	- W. Fairweather
'From the Exile to the Advent' -	- W. Fairweather
'Alexander the Great' - - -	- J. T. Wheeler
'The Story of Alexander's Empire' -	- J. P. Mahaffy
'First and Second Maccabees' - -	————
'The Age of the Maccabees' - -	- Henderson
'The Jews under Roman Rule' - -	- Morrison
'The Herods' - - - -	- F. W. Farrar
'Christ and the Pharisees' - -	- Baker
'The Pharisees and Jesus' - -	- A. T. Robertson
'The Rise of the Christian Religion' - -	- C. F. Nolloth

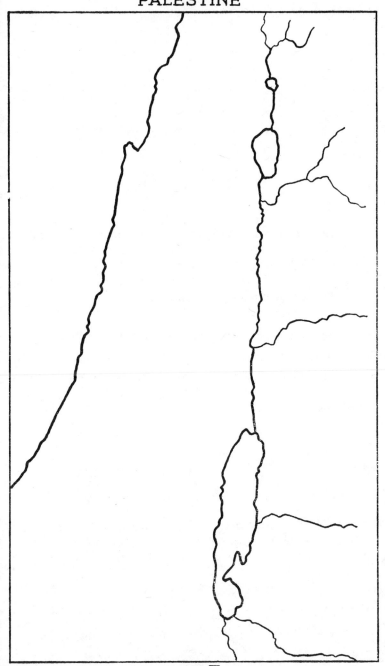

MAP I

FILL IN

The three provincial divisions of the Land in our Lord's
time.

The four great regions of Palestine.

The chief mountains, plains, valleys, seas, and rivers.

A selection of the principal places mentioned in the
Gospels. (pp. 51-59.)

Geographical Setting of the Gospel Story

PALESTINE

A GOOD map is essential for an understanding of this part of our subject.

1 Its Names

The country before us is variously named. It is the LAND (Ruth i. 1), the HOLY LAND (Zech. ii. 12), the LORD'S LAND (Hos. ix. 3), the GLORIOUS LAND (Dan. xi. 16, 41), the LAND OF PROMISE (Heb. xi. 9), the LAND OF ISRAEL (1 Sam. xiii. 19). It is also called CANAAN, perhaps because it was inhabited by the descendants of Canaan, the grandson of Noah (Gen. ix. 18), or, perhaps, because it means 'sunken' or 'lowland,' and may be used in opposition to the Lebanon highlands.

The usual, though not the oldest, name is PALESTINE, which occurs only once in the Bible (Joel iii. 4, A.V., cf. R.V.), and is derived from Philistia, the country of the Philistines which was the southern part of the coast along the Mediterranean.

2 Its Distinction

That Palestine should be the scene of the supreme revelation of God's redeeming grace in the person and work of Jesus Christ was not a mere incident, and certainly was not an accident. No other country in the world was so fitted for the purpose of preparing the chosen people to receive and preserve the revelations which issued in the manifestation of God in Christ.

Dr. George Adam Smith says that 'a vision of the Land in itself, and in its relations to the world, puts the whole Bible into perspective and atmosphere, and enables us to enjoy, possibly for the first time, a clear prospect of God's full purpose for the old and the new Israel, both in their discipline within Palestine and in their destiny of service across the world. Geography has

been called "the eye of history," and this is most true with regard
to the history of the Bible.'

3 Its Smallness

The geographical limitations of Palestine could never encourage
political ambitions and aspirations.

The Encyclopaedia Britannica (14th edition) says: "Palestine
stretches through only about 2 degrees of latitude, being roughly
140 miles long, and about 23 miles wide in the north, and about
80 miles in the south. Its area (excluding Transjordan) is just
over 9,000 square miles, being slightly larger than that of Wales"
(Vol. 17; p. 117).

Dean Stanley says: 'The breadth of the country from the
Jordan to the sea is rarely more than fifty miles. Its length from
Dan to Beersheba is about one hundred and eighty miles' (*Sinai
and Palestine*; p. 114).

Compared with surrounding lands of historic distinction, 'the
vast extent of the empires which hung upon its northern and
southern skirts,' Palestine is small, and this feature favoured
the end for which it was chosen, to be the training ground of
Israel.

4 Its Fertility

Another favouring feature was its productiveness, for it was
abundantly capable of supplying the needs of the chosen people.
It was a land of corn, and wine, and oil, of ' milk and honey,'
and was famous for its fruits—the olive, fig, orange, apricot,
pomegranate, grape, and walnut. It was rich also in trees—the
oak, the palm, the oleander, the cedar, the sycamore, and the
carob tree. This fertility was largely due to its wells and springs,
its rivers, its seas, and its rainfall. (See pp. 114, 115).

5 Its Seclusiveness

This geographical peculiarity of Palestine was conducive to
the safeguarding of Israel from their idolatrous neighbours.
In the land they were a nation set apart from the rest of the

world, ' haters,' it was said, ' of the human race,' and hated by
it in return.

The Land was bounded on the east by the desert, the hills of
Transjordan, and the deep fissures of the Jordan valley; on the
south by the ' great and terrible wilderness '; on the west by the
Mediterranean, and on the north by the mountains of Lebanon.
This geographical isolation had a moral intent, and what Israel
owed to it cannot be calculated.

6 Its Centrality

The relation of Palestine to the surrounding countries is noteworthy, and was of great importance long ago. Dean Stanley
says that ' Palestine, though now at the very outskirts of that
tide of civilization which has swept far into the remotest west,
was then the vanguard of the eastern, and therefore, of the
civilized world; and, moreover, stood midway between the two
great seats of ancient Empire, Babylon and Egypt. It was on
the high road from the one to the other of these mighty powers,
the prize for which they contended, the battlefield on which they
fought, the high bridge over which they ascended and descended
respectively into the deep basins of the Nile and Euphrates.'

This Land, remarkable in its isolation, was equally remarkable
in its centralization, lying, as it did, central to Egypt, Babylon,
Assyria, Persia, Greece, and Rome, the great nations and civilizations of antiquity.

Palestine has a place of its own in the history of revelation,
which only a Divine wisdom can have given it. In this land the
Son of Man, the Messiah, was born, lived, taught, worked, and
died; from it He ascended into heaven, and in all likelihood, to
it He will return.

Speaking generally, Palestine is divided into four great regions.

1 On the west is **The Maritime Plain**, stretching from Gaza, in the
south, to beyond Tyre in the north, embracing Philistia, Sharon,
and part of Phœnicia, moving from south to north.

2 Between the Maritime Plain and the Jordan Valley is what has been
called **The Central Range**. This includes **Judæa**, in the south,
Samaria, in the centre, and **Galilee**, in the north. South of Judæa
are Edom and the Arabian desert; north of Galilee are Syria and the

Lebanons; and cutting across, between Galilee and Samaria, reaching from the Mediterranean to the Jordan, are Mount Carmel, the Plain of Esdraelon or Megiddo, and the Valley of Jezreel.

3 On the east is **The Jordan Valley,** which reaches from Cæsarea Philippi in the north, to the Dead Sea in the south. The width of the Valley varies from 2 to 12 miles, becoming wider as it descends. In this some 104 miles are the Sea of Galilee, the Jordan River, and the Dead Sea.

4 On the eastern side of the Jordan is **The Eastern Range** which extends north and south from Mount Hermon to Mount Hor in Edom, and embraces Moab and Edom.

This land of Palestine is bounded on the north by Syria and Mesopotamia, on the west by the Mediterranean, on the south by the Peninsula of Sinai with Egypt west of it, and on the east by the Syrian desert, with Babylonia beyond. (The student of the Bible should fill in Map I of Palestine with these main divisions, and do so as he advances in his studies. (See Map I, page 53).

The Land is very varied and rich, and, of course, it is for ever sacred because it was the scene of the life and activities of the Redeemer of the world.

The following features should be placed in the blank Map I:

Mountains	-	Carmel, Ebal, Ephraim, Gerizim, Gilboa, Gilead, Hermon, Hor, Lebanon, Moriah, Nebo, Olivet, Pisgah, Tabor, and Zion.
Plains	-	Abel-shittim, Acre, Esdraelon, Gennesaret, Jordan, Philistia, Sharon, and Phœnicia.
Valleys	-	Ajalon, Baca, Beth-horon, Elah, Eschol, Jehoshaphat, Jordan, Rephaim, and Sorek.
Seas	-	Chinnereth or Sea of Galilee, the Salt or Dead Sea, and the Waters of Merom, i.e. Lake Huleh.
Rivers	-	Arnon, Cherith, Jabbok, Jordan, Kishon, and the Kidron.

PLACES MENTIONED IN THE GOSPELS

Ænon	-	A place near Salim, where John baptized (John iii. 23).
Bethabara	-	Reputed place of Jesus' baptism (John i. 28). Some MSS. read ' Bethany.'
Bethany	-	More than a mile east of Jerusalem, where Lazarus and his sisters lived; on the road to Jericho.
Bethesda	-	A pool with five porches at Jerusalem. A man healed here (John v. 1-9).

Bethlehem — Six miles south of Jerusalem. Birthplace of Jesus Christ.

Bethphage - A village on the road that runs from Jerusalem to Jericho. From hereabout Jesus sent two disciples to fetch the colt on which He entered Jerusalem on Palm Sunday (Luke xix. 28-35). About this place we know nothing, not even whether it was a village or a district, for it is not mentioned either in the Old Testament, the Apocrypha, or Josephus. The name occurs only in the Synoptic Gospels. It must have been on or near the Mount of Olives.

Bethsaida - Two miles from the Sea of Galilee. Native place of Peter, Andrew, and Philip (John i. 44; xii. 21). Near here Jesus fed a multitude.

Cæsarea Philippi - At the foot of Mount Hermon. Here Peter made the great confession (Matt. xvi. 13-20).

Cana — About 4 miles N.E. of Nazareth. Here Jesus performed His first miracle (John ii. 1, 11). Native place of Nathanael (John xxi. 2).

Capernaum — On the N.W. of the Sea of Galilee. The centre of Christ's labours. Matthew called to discipleship. Many miracles performed. Its destruction predicted. (Matt. iv. 13-16; viii. 5-13; ix. 1, 9-13; xi. 23, 24: Mark i. 21-31; ii. 1-13; ix. 33-37: Luke iv. 31; vii. 1-10: John iv. 46-54; vi. 17, 24, 59).

Chorazin - North of Capernaum, by the Sea of Galilee. Christ performed mighty works here. Denounced for unbelief (Matt. xi. 21; Luke x. 13).

Dalmanutha On the shore of the Sea of Galilee, near Magdala (Matt. xv. 39; Mark viii. 10).

Decapolis - A district consisting of ten cities (*deca-polis*), in the north-eastern part of Galilee, built by followers of Alexander the Great, and later rebuilt by the Romans. Consisted of Scythopolis, Damascus, Hippos, Philadelphia, Gadara, Pella, Dion, Gerasa, Kanatha, Raphana. From here many came to hear Jesus (Matt. iv 25; Mark v. 20; vii. 31).

Egypt - - Joseph and Mary took Jesus thither as an infant (Matt. ii. 13-15).

Emmaus - About 7½ miles from Jerusalem. On the way thither Jesus talked with two disciples, and on arrival ate with them, and revealed Himself to them (Luke xxiv. 13-32).

Ephraim - A city north-east of Jerusalem, to which Jesus and His disciples retired (John xi. 54).

Gennesaret A fertile plain on the western shore of the Sea of Galilee, about 3 miles long and 1 mile broad. Scene of healing miracles (Matt. xiv. 34; Mark vi. 53-56).

Gergesa - On the eastern shore of the Sea of Galilee. Near here two demon-possessed men were healed, and the demons entered into a herd of swine (Matt. viii. 28).

Gethsemane A garden, near the foot of Mount Olivet. Jesus often prayed here. The scene of His agony preceding His Passion (Matt. xxvi. 36-56; John xviii. 1, 2).

Golgotha - Aramaic word corresponding to ' Calvary,' outside the wall of Jerusalem, where Jesus was crucified (Matt. xxvii. 33-50).

Gomorrah - One of the cities of the Jordan valley destroyed by fire for its iniquity. Referred to by Jesus (Matt. x. 15).

Jericho - A city near the Dead Sea, about 900 feet below the level of the Mediterranean, and over 3000 feet below the level of Jerusalem. Two blind men were healed by Jesus (Matt. xx. 29). Zacchæus the tax-gatherer lived here, was converted, and entertained Jesus (Luke xix. 1-10).

Jerusalem - Called Jebus, Salem, Sion, Zion. From 2130 to 2570 feet above sea level. The Capital of the Jewish Theocracy. Saw much of the ministry of Jesus, Who was crucified outside its walls (Matt. xx. 18; Mark xi. 11; Luke ii. 43; xiii. 33; xix. 11; John iv. 45).

Jordan - The river of Palestine. It means 'the Descender.' Dean Stanley says that it takes its name from its swift descent as it leaves the Sea of Galilee; and he points out that the word for the 'coming down' of the waters of Jordan (Josh. iii. 16) is the same as that used in the singular for the river itself. (*Sinai and Palestine*: pp. 283-4). It rises at the foot of Mount Hermon, passes through the Sea of Galilee, and ends in the Dead Sea. From Mount Hermon to the Sea of Galilee is a distance of 39 miles, and between the two Seas 65 miles. At its highest sources the Jordan is 1700 feet above the level of the Mediterranean, and at its end it is 1292 feet below. In this river Jesus was baptized by John (Matt. iii. 5, 6, 13-17), and here He taught (Mark x. 1).

Kidron - Cedron. A ravine between Jerusalem and the Mount of Olives. It is crossed in going from Jerusalem to Gethsemane, Bethany, and Jericho (John xviii. 1).

Magdala - On the west shore of the Sea of Galilee, near Tiberias (Matt. xv. 39).

Nain - - About 5 miles south-east of Nazareth. Here Jesus raised to life a widow's only son (Luke vii. 11-17).

Nephthali - Naphtali. Mentioned with Zabulon as ' by the way of the Sea beyond Jordan, Galilee of the Gentiles ' (Matt. iv. 13, 15).

Nazareth - A city north of the plain of Esdraelon, about 20 miles south-west of Capernaum. Not mentioned in the Old Testament. The home town of Joseph and Mary, and of Jesus until He entered upon His public ministry. The inhabitants rejected Him (Matt. ii. 23; xiii. 54-58; xxi. 11; Mark i. 24; vi. 1-6; Luke ii. 39; iv. 16-30).

Nineveh - Capital of the Assyrian Empire. Preached to by Jonah. Prophesied against by Nahum. Referred to by our Lord (Matt. xii. 41; Luke xi. 32).

Olivet - A ridge on the east of Jerusalem, and separated from the City by the Kidron valley. It is 2641 feet above the sea level. The scene of some of the most sacred events in the life of Christ (Matt. xxiv. 3; Luke xxi. 37; xxii. 39; John viii. 1). From here He ascended into heaven, and to it He is to return (Zech. xiv. 4; Luke xxiv. 50, 51; Acts i. 9-12).

Salim - John baptized near here (John iii. 23).

Sarepta - The Old Testament ' Zarephath,' a town of Phœnicia, near Sidon. Referred to by Christ (Luke iv. 26).

Sidon - The Old Testament Zidon. A city of Phœnicia, north of Tyre. From here people came to hear Jesus (Mark iii. 8). Into this region Jesus withdrew with His disciples (Mark vii. 24, 31).

Siloam - A pool at Jerusalem. A man healed of blindness was sent thither to wash (John ix. 7). Probably here was the tower which fell on eighteen people (Luke xiii. 4).

Sodom - A city in the plain of the Jordan, where Lot resided. Destroyed by fire. Referred to by Christ (Luke x. 12; xvii. 29).

Sychar - A town on the eastern slope of Mount Ebal in Samaria; close to Jacob's well. To this place the Samaritan woman belonged (John iv. 5-7).

Tiberias - A city on the west of the Sea of Galilee, south of Magdala. The Sea is called ' of Tiberias ' (John vi. 1, 23; xxi. 1).

Tyre - - A city of Phœnicia, into the coasts of which Jesus went, and at or near which He healed the daughter of a Syrophœnician woman (Matt. xv. 21-28).

QUESTIONS

1 By what names is Palestine called in the Scriptures?

2 What is the origin of ' Canaan,' and the meaning of ' Palestine '?

3 What are the five outstanding features of the Holy Land?

4 Name some of the fruits and trees of Palestine.

5 By what geographical features was Palestine secluded from the rest of the world?

6 Show that Palestine was central to the ancient civilizations.

7 What are the approximate length and breadth of Palestine?

8 What were the four main divisions of Palestine in Christ's time?

9 What were the three parts of the second of these divisions?

10 Name six mountains, three plains, two seas, three rivers, and one valley in Palestine.

11 Name fifteen prominent places in Palestine, and tell of something in connection with ten of them.

12 What is said in the Gospels about Egypt and Nineveh?

LITERATURE

'Historical Geography of the Holy Land'	G. A. Smith
'The Land and the Book' (3 vols.)	W. M. Thomson
'The Bible Handbook'	Angus and Green
'Palestine in the Time of Christ'	Stapfer
'Sinai and Palestine'	Dean Stanley
'The Holy Land and the Bible' (2 vols.)	C. Geikie
'The River Jordan'	Nelson Glueck
'Palestine'	J. W. Clapham
'Sacred Sites of the Gospels'	W. Sanday
'Sacred Sites and Ways'	G. Dalman
'A Companion to the Bible' (pp. 133-156)	———
'Historical Atlas and Chronology of the Life of Christ'	Hodge

PALESTINE

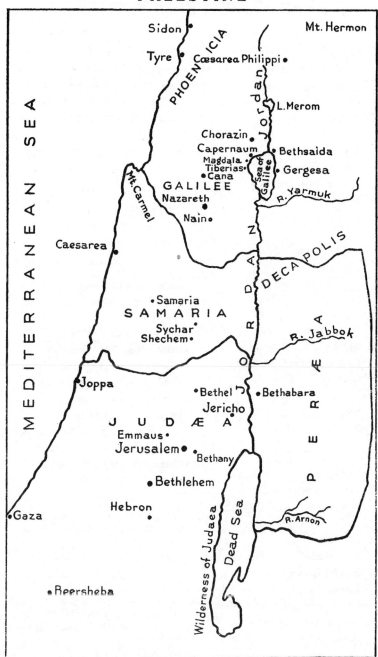

APPROXIMATE DISTANCES

Jerusalem to

Bethany, 1-2. Judæa.

Bethlehem, 6. Judæa.

Cæsarea, 57. Samaria.

Cæsarea Philippi, 105. Syria.

Capernaum, 85. Galilee.
(via Peræa, 100).

Emmaus, 7. Judæa.

Hebron, 20. Judæa.

Hermon Mt., 125. Syria.

Jericho, 15. Judæa.

Joppa, 33. Judæa.

Jordan, 21.

Mediterranean, 37.

Nazareth, 65. Galilee.

Samaria, 36. Samaria.

Capernaum to

Bethsaida, 6. Galilee.

Cæsarea Philippi, 27. Syria.

Cana, 16. Galilee.

Nain, 22. Galilee.

Nazareth, 20. Galilee.

Tyre, 35. Phœnicia.

Bethsaida to Gergesa, 7.

Jericho to Bethabara, 10.

Nazareth to Shechem, 35.

Lake of Galilee

Breadth (greatest), 6 - 7.

Length, 13 - 14.

Depth (greatest), 130 - 150 feet.

Surface, 112 square miles.

Below sea level, 680 - 696 feet.

Dead Sea

Breadth, $9\frac{1}{2}$.

Length, 48.

Depth, N.E., 1308 feet.
(2600 feet below sea level).

Depth, S., 8 - 14 feet.

Below sea level, 1292 feet (mean).

Lake of Galilee to Dead Sea, 65.

Mediterranean to Jordan—
in line with Nazareth, 37.
in line with Shechem, 45.
in line with Jerusalem, 56.

Heights of Mountains

Carmel, 1000 - 1810 ft. Galilee.
Samaria.

Ebal, 3077 feet. Samaria.

Gerizim, 2849 feet. Samaria.

Gilboa, 1500 - 1648 feet. Galilee.

Gilead, 3597 feet. Transjordan.

Hermon, 9000 - 9700 feet. Syria

Hor, 4360 feet. Edom.

Lebanon, 10016 - 10052 feet. Syria

Nebo, 2643 feet. Transjordan.

Olivet, 2680 - 2723 feet. Judæa.

Tabor, 1843 feet. Galilee

JERUSALEM, 2593 feet above sea level.

The numbers are in miles except where otherwise stated, and the distances are from point to point, not by travel routes.

6

Persons mentioned in the Gospels

I. In the Two Genealogies of Matthew and Luke

IN Matthew's Gospel 41 persons are named, and in Luke's, 74 persons. Of these, 19 are named in both genealogies:

ABRAHAM	ESROM	BOOZ	ZOROBABEL
ISAAC	ARAM	OBED	MATTHA(N)(T)
JACOB	AMINADAB	JESSE	JOSEPH
JUDA(S)	NAASSON	DAVID	JESUS
PHARES	SALMON	SALATHIEL	

Matthew's Genealogy goes back to Abraham; Luke's goes back to Adam. Matthew's traces the line from Abraham to Joseph; Luke's in the inverse order, from Joseph to Adam. Matthew's is Joseph's line of descent; Luke's is Mary's. (See 'The Two Genealogies,' p. 505).

II. Old Testament Characters

(Mentioned elsewhere than in the Genealogies)

ABEL	ELIJAH	JEREMIAH	NOAH
ABIATHAR	ELISHA	JONAH	RACHEL
ABRAM	ISAAC	LOT	SOLOMON
DANIEL	ISAIAH	MOSES	ZACHARIAS
DAVID	JACOB	NAAMAN	

III. Associated with Christ

I WOMEN

Anna - - A prophetess in Jerusalem, who declared the infant Jesus to be the Messiah (Luke ii. 36-38).

Elisabeth - The wife of Zacharias a priest, mother of John the Baptist, and kinswoman of the Virgin (Luke i. 5-45).

Joanna - The wife of Chuza, Herod's steward. She ministered to Jesus, and went to His tomb (Luke viii. 3; xxiv. 10).

Martha - The sister of Mary and Lazarus.

Mary - - The Virgin Mother of Jesus the Christ, and wife of Joseph (Matt. i. 18-25).

Mary - - The wife of Clopas, and mother of James the Less, and of Joses (Mark xv. 40).

Mary Magdalene Of Magdala, out of whom Jesus cast seven demons; a devoted follower of Him, and to whom He appeared in resurrection life (Mark xvi. 9; Luke viii. 2).

Mary - - The sister of Martha and Lazarus of Bethany (Luke x. 38-42; John xi. 1; xii. 1-3).

Salome - One of the women who travelled with Jesus, and ministered to Him of her substance (Mark xv. 40, 41). She was at the crucifixion, and also at the tomb on the resurrection morning (Mark xv. 40; xvi. 1, 2). Matthew xxvii. 56 identifies her with the wife of Zebedee, and, therefore, as the mother of James and John (cf. Matt. xx. 20-24; Mark x. 35-40). From John xix. 25 many infer that she was a sister of Mary, the mother of Jesus, which is most likely; and, in which case, Jesus and John would be cousins; but some dispute this inference.

Salome - The daughter of Philip and Herodias. (Josephus' *Antiquities*, xviii., v. 4). She danced before Herod, and got from him, at her mother's instigation, the head of John the Baptist. (See 'The Herodian Family,' p. 122).

Susanna - One who ministered to the needs of the Lord (Luke viii. 3).

2 THE APOSTLES

Andrew - Disciple of John the Baptist. Was directed to Jesus by the Baptist, and introduced his brother Simon Peter to Him. He was a fisherman, and lived at Bethsaida (Matt. x. 2; Mark i. 16-18; xiii. 3; John i. 35-42).

Bartholomew It is thought that this is the surname of Nathanael, who was brought to Christ by Philip (Matt. x. 3: John i. 45, 46).

James - Brother of John, son of Zebedee and Salome. With his brother, partner with Peter and Andrew in the fishing business. One of the first four disciples. The first martyr Apostle (Matt. iv. 21; Mark i. 19; Luke v. 10; Acts xii. 2).

James - Son of Alphæus and Mary. (Alphæus is also called Clopas, John xix. 25). Called James the Less, on account of his stature, or because he was younger than the other James (above). (Mark iii. 18; xvi. 1; xv. 40; Luke xxiv. 10). (See page 118).

John • • Son of Zebedee and Salome, brother of James, cousin of Jesus. A fisherman. One of the three favoured Apostles; 'the disciple whom Jesus loved.' Prominent in the early Church. Laboured in Ephesus. Banished to Patmos by Domitian. Wrote a Gospel, three Epistles, and the Revelation. Died in the reign of Trajan (Matt. xvii. 1; Mark i. 19, 20; Luke v. 10; John i. 35-40; xiii. 23, et al.; Acts iii. 1; Rev. i. 4, 9).

Judas - - Called Thaddæus, and Lebbæus (Matt. x. 3; Mark iii. 18; John xiv. 22).

Judas - - Son of Simon Iscariot, so that his surname was Iscariot. Treasurer to the Apostles. Sold Jesus for about £5. The traitor. Confessed his guilt and hanged himself (Matt. xxvi. 14-16, 47-50; xxvii. 3-5; Luke vi. 16; John xii. 6; Acts i. 18).

Matthew - Also called Levi. A tax-gatherer. Writer of the Gospel which bears his name (Mark ii. 14-17; Luke v. 27-32).

Peter - • Formerly called Simon. Son of Jonas. Native of Bethsaida. A fisherman. Always put first in the Apostolic lists. Made the great confession. Denied his Lord. Leader in the early Church. Wrote two Epistles. Tradition says he was crucified upside down (Luke iv. 38; v. 3, 10; vi. 13, 14; viii. 51: John i. 42, 44; xxi. 15: Acts i-xii).

Philip - Lived in Bethsaida. Brought Nathanael to Jesus (Matt. x. 3; John i. 43-48; xii. 20-22; xiv. 8-12; Acts i. 13).

Simon - The Zealot. Called 'Simon the Canaanite' (Matt. x. 4, 'Cananæan,' R.V.; Luke vi. 15).

Thomas - Called Didymus; both names meaning ' a twin ' (Matt. x. 3; John xi. 16; xiv. 1-6; xx. 24, 25, 26-29).

3 OTHERS

Alexander - A son of Simon of Cyrene who bore Jesus' cross (Mark xv. 21). (See Rufus).

Annas - Father-in-law of Caiaphas. Called 'High Priest' in Acts iv. 6. Our Lord was brought before him, and he sent Him to Caiaphas. It would seem that Annas continued to be called High Priest after he had been expelled from that position by Valerius Gratus, in A.D. 16. This would explain the fact that both Annas and Caiaphas are called High Priests at the same time (Luke iii. 2; John xviii. 13).

Barabbas - A robber and murderer; condemned to death; who was released that Jesus might be crucified (Matt. xxvii. 16-26).

Bartimæus - Son of Timæus. A blind beggar, whom Jesus healed (Mark. x. 46).

Cæsar Augustus - The first Roman Emperor. In his honour Herod the Great built Cæsarea. He was on the throne when Jesus was born.

Cæsar Tiberius - The son-in-law of Augustus, and followed him as Emperor. In his honour Herod Antipas built Tiberias, on the Sea of Galilee. He was Emperor when Jesus was crucified.

Caiaphas - (See under *Annas*).

Chuza - A steward of Herod Antipas. His wife, Joanna, ministered to Jesus of her substance (Luke viii. 3).

Cleopas - A disciple of Christ's to whom, with another, He appeared and talked on the way to Emmaus (Luke xxiv. 18).

Cyrenius - In R.V., Quirinius. A Roman Governor of Syria, who was in power when the census edict was issued which took Joseph and Mary from Nazareth to Bethlehem, where, at that time, Jesus was born (Luke ii. 1-5).

Herod the Great - Son of Antipater, an Idumæan, born B.C. 62; died B.C. 4. Was appointed Governor of Galilee by Julius Cæsar in B.C. 47. Later he ruled over nearly all Palestine. He had nine wives; was a cruel tyrant; massacred the infants at Bethlehem; and died a tragic death (Matt. ii). (See page 122).

Herod Philip - Son of Herod the Great and Mariamne (2nd). Herodias was his wife, and Salome was his daughter (Matt. xiv. 3, 6).

Herod Archelaus - Herod the Great's son, by Malthace. King in Judæa after his father's death, when Jesus was an infant (Matt. ii. 22).

Herod Antipas -   Son of Herod the Great, by Malthace. He was a Tetrarch (King), and, at the instigation of Herodias, murdered John the Baptist (Matt. xiv. 1-12; Mark vi. 14-28).

John Baptist   The son of Zacharias and Elisabeth. Elisabeth was cousin to the Virgin Mary. He was the predicted forerunner of Jesus, and he preached sin, judgment, and repentance. He baptized in the Jordan, and Jesus was baptized by him. His manner of living was austere. He was beheaded by Herod Antipas, at the instigation of Herodias. The last of the Hebrew prophets— Jesus said there was none greater (Matt. iii. 1-17; xi. 7-15; xiv. 1-12; Luke i. 5, 8-17; iii. 1, 2; John iii. 25-30).

Joseph -   The husband of Jesus' mother, Mary; a carpenter in Nazareth (Matt. i. 18-25; ii. 19-23; Luke iii. 23).

Joseph -   A member of the Sanhedrin; of Arimathæa; a secret disciple. He sought and received the body of Jesus, and placed it in a tomb which belonged to him (Matt. xxvii. 58-60; Mark xv. 43-46).

James, Joses, Jude -   Sons of Joseph and Mary, and brothers of Jesus. James and Jude wrote the Epistles which bear their names (Matt. xiii. 55; Mark vi. 3; John vii. 1-5).

Lazarus -   Brother of Martha and Mary, of Bethany. Was raised from the dead after having been in the grave for four days. He feasted with Jesus in the house of Simon (John xi; xii. 1-3, 10, 11).

Malchus   A servant of the High Priest, whose ear Peter cut off, and who was healed by Christ (John xviii. 10).

Nicodemus -   A Pharisee, and a member of the Sanhedrin. He came to Jesus by night, and a talk on the New Birth followed. He contended for the rights of Christ before the Sanhedrin; and he helped to embalm Christ's body for burial (John iii; vii. 50-52; xix. 39).

Pilate, Pontius -   A Roman, appointed Procurator of Judæa in A.D. 26 by Tiberius Cæsar. Jesus was tried before him, and condemned to death, against his wish and conscience, however. His wife warned him in consequence of a dream she had had about Jesus. Pilate finally was summoned to Rome, was banished, and at last took his own life (Matt. xxvii. 1-26; Luke xxiii. 1-24).

Rufus -   A son of Simon of Cyrene who bore Jesus' cross (Mark xv. 21). (See *Alexander*).

5

Simeon - A devout man who recognized the infant Jesus to be the promised Messiah (Luke ii. 25-35).

Simon - (See *Peter*).

Simon - The father of Judas Iscariot (John vi. 71).

Simon - A brother of Jesus (Matt. xiii. 55), son of Joseph and Mary.

Simon - A leper, who lived at Bethany, possibly the husband of Martha, Mary's sister (Matt. xxvi. 6-13; Mark xiv. 3-9; John xii. 1-8).

Simon - A Pharisee who entertained Jesus; in whose house a woman anointed Jesus' feet, and to whom He spake the parable of the Two Debtors (Luke vii. 36-50).

Simon - A Cyrenian, who was compelled to bear Jesus' cross to Calvary. The father of Alexander and Rufus (Matt. xxvii. 32; Mark xv. 21).

Observe that there are two Cæsars, four Herods, two Johns, three of James, two Josephs, three of Judas, six Simons, and four Marys.

These 54 characters in the Gospel Story should be studied one by one, all references to them sought out, and the lessons to be learned from them put down.

4 UNNAMED

In addition to these are a number of persons who are not named, such as the woman of Samaria, a nobleman, a paralytic, the woman who was a sinner, a blind man and his parents, a ruler, and others of not less importance than many who are named, and of more importance than some of them. Meet them, and listen to them.

QUESTIONS

1 How are the two Genealogies of Jesus to be explained?
2 Name ten Old Testament characters mentioned in the Gospels.
3 Name six women mentioned in the Gospels, and say something about three of them.
4 Name the Twelve Apostles, and say who were the three chief.
5 Who were Cyrenius, Annas, Nicodemus, Cleopas?
6 What Cæsars, and what Herods, appear in the Gospel Story?
7 Say what you know about John the Baptist.
8 How many Simons are mentioned in the Gospels, and who were they?
9 How are some unnamed people described?
10 How many Marys are mentioned in the Gospels, and who were they?
11 Is there any evidence that Jesus and the Apostle John were cousins?
12 Who were Joanna, Alexander, Chuza, Malchus, and Rufus?

LITERATURE
(PERSONS)

Dictionary of the Bible - - - -	Hastings
Dictionary of Christ and the Gospels - -	Hastings
International Standard Bible Encyclopædia -	———
'Our Lord's Characters' - - - -	Alexander Whyte
'Greater Men and Women of the Bible'	Hastings
'Men of the Bible' - - - - -	Various Authors
'Women of the Bible' - - - - -	Various Authors

7. HARMONISTIC READING SYLLABUS OF THE GOSPELS

BASED ON MARK'S GOSPEL

THE LIFE AND WORK OF JESUS THE CHRIST

PART ONE -   -   -   B.C. 5—A.D. 26

The Thirty Years of Preparation

	MARK	MATT.	LUKE	JOHN
(i) INTRODUCTORY				
Prologue of John's Gospel ...	—	—	—	i. 1-18
Preface to Luke's Gospel	—	—	i. 1-4	—
The Genealogies	—	i. 1-17	iii. 23-38	—
(ii) THE ANNUNCIATIONS				
To Zacharias ...	—	—	i. 5-25	—
To Mary ...	—	—	i. 26-38	—
To Joseph ...	—	i. 18-25	—	—
Mary's Visit to Elisabeth	—	—	i. 39-56	—
(iii) THE ADVENTS				
Of John the Baptist	—	—	i. 57-80	—
Of Jesus the Messiah	—	—	ii. 1-7	—
The Angels and the Shepherds	—	—	ii. 8-20	—
(iv) THE INFANCY OF JESUS				
The Circumcision ...	—	—	ii. 21	—
The Presentation ...	—	—	ii. 22-38	—
The Wise Men from the East	—	ii. 1-12	—	—
The Flight into Egypt ...	—	ii. 13-18	—	—
The Return from Egypt to Nazareth	—	ii. 19-23	ii. 39	—

69

HARMONISTIC READING SYLLABUS OF THE GOSPELS (*continued*)

	MARK	MATT.	LUKE	JOHN
PART FOUR - - A.D. 27. A Few Days				
The Samaritan Ministry				
The Departure from Judæa	i. 14	iv. 12	iv. 14	iv. 1-3
Discourse with the Woman of Samaria ...				iv. 4-26
Words to the Disciples on Sowing and Reaping ...				iv. 27-38
The Gospel in Sychar				iv. 39-42
PART FIVE - A.D. 27-29. About 22 months				
The Galilean Ministry				
PERIOD I.—From the Return to Galilee to the Choosing of the Twelve. A.D. 27-28. About 5 months				
(i) THE BEGINNINGS				
The Arrival in Galilee	i. 14	iv. 12	iv. 14	iv. 1-3
Commencement of the Galilean Ministry ...	i. 14, 15	iv. 12, 17	iv. 14, 15	iv. 43-45
The Healing of a Nobleman's Son at Cana ...				iv. 46-54
The First Rejection at Nazareth			iv. 16-30	—
Removal to Capernaum		iv. 13-16	iv. 31	—
(ii) THE FIRST PREACHING TOUR				
A Miraculous Draught of Fishes, and the Call of Four Disciples to Full-time Service	i. 16-20	iv. 18-22	v. 1-11	—
An Unclean Spirit Cast Out	i. 21-28	—	iv. 31-37	—
Peter's Mother-in-law Healed	i. 29-34	viii. 14-17	iv. 38-41	—
Preaching in Galilee with His Disciples ...	i. 35-39	iv. 23-25	iv. 42-44	—
A Leper Cleansed	i. 40-45	viii. 2-4	v. 12-16	—

70

(iii) GROWING HOSTILITY OF THE SCRIBES AND PHARISEES

	Mark	Matthew	Luke	John
A Paralytic Man Healed	ii. 1-12	ix. 1-8	v. 17-26	—
The Call of Matthew, and the Feast in his House	ii. 13-17	ix. 9-13	v. 27-32	—
The Question about Fasting and three Parables in Answer	ii. 18-22	ix. 14-17	v. 33-39	—
Healing of a Man at Bethesda on the Sabbath, and the Action Defended in a Great Discourse	—	—	—	v. 1-47
The Disciples Pluck Grain on the Sabbath, and the Following Controversy ...	ii. 23-28	xii. 1-8	vi. 1-5	—
Healing of a Man with a Withered Hand on the Sabbath, and the Following Controversy	iii. 1-6	xii. 9-14	vi. 6-11	—

PERIOD II.—From the Choosing of the Twelve to the Withdrawal into Northern Galilee

A.D. 28-29. About 12 months

(i) ORGANIZATION OF THE KINGDOM

	Mark	Matthew	Luke	John
The Widespread Fame of Jesus	iii. 7-12	xii. 15-21	vi. 12-16	—
The Choosing of the Twelve	iii. 13-19	—	vi. 17-49	—
The Sermon on the Mount	—	v. 1-viii. 1	—	—

(ii) THE SECOND PREACHING TOUR

	Mark	Matthew	Luke	John
A Centurion's Servant Healed	—	viii. 5-13	vii. 1-10	—
A Widow's Son Raised from the Dead ...	—	—	vii. 11-17	—
The Baptist's Inquiry and Jesus' Response ...	—	xi. 2-19	vii. 18-35	—
Woes upon the Cities of Opportunity ...	—	xi. 20-24	—	—
Christ's Prayer and Claim for Himself ...	—	xi. 25-30	—	—

HARMONISTIC READING SYLLABUS OF THE GOSPELS (*continued*)

	MARK	MATT.	LUKE	JOHN
(ii) THE SECOND PREACHING TOUR (*continued*)				
The Anointing of Jesus' Feet in the House of Simon, and the Parable of the Two Debtors	—	—	vii. 36-50	—
Christ's Companions on His Second Tour of Galilee	—	—	viii. 1-3	—
(iii) A DAY OF TEACHING				
Blasphemous Accusation of League with Beelzebub	iii. 19-30	xii. 22-37	—	—
The Scribes and Pharisees Demand a Sign	—	xii. 38-45	—	—
The True Kindred of Christ	iii. 31-35	xii. 46-50	viii. 19-21	—
The Parables of the Kingdom	iv. 1-34	xiii. 1-53	viii. 4-18	—
(iv) A DAY OF MIRACLES				
Jesus Stills the Tempest	iv. 35-41	viii. 18, 23-27	viii. 22-25	—
A Gerasene Demoniac Healed	v. 1-20	viii. 28-34	viii. 26-39	—
The Raising of the Daughter of Jairus ...	v. 21-24, 35-43	ix. 18, 19, 23-26	viii. 40-42 49-56	—
Healing of a Woman with an Issue of Blood	v. 25-34	ix. 20-22	viii. 43-48	—
Healing of Two Blind Men and a Dumb Demoniac	—	ix. 27-34	—	—
(v) THE THIRD PREACHING TOUR				
The Second Rejection at Nazareth ...	vi. 1-6	xiii. 54-58	—	—
The Third Tour in Galilee	vi. 6	ix. 35	—	—
The Mission of the Twelve	vi. 7-13	ix. 36-xi. 1	ix. 1-6	—
Death of John the Baptist	vi. 14-29	xiv. 1-12	ix. 7-9	—

	MARK	MATT.	LUKE	JOHN
(ii) JESUS AND HIS APOSTLES (continued)				
The Coming of the Son of Man	viii. 38-ix. 1	xvi. 27-28	ix. 26, 27	—
The Transfiguration near Cæsarea Philippi	ix. 2-8	xvii. 1-8	ix. 28-36	—
On the Way Down from the Mount ...	ix. 9-13	xvii. 9-13	—	—
Healing of a Demoniac Boy	ix. 14-29	xvii. 14-21	ix. 37-43	—
Christ Again Foretells His Death and Resurrection	ix. 30-32	xvii. 22, 23	ix. 43-45	—
(iii) IN CAPERNAUM AGAIN				
The Messiah Pays the Half-Shekel for the Temple	—	xvii. 24-27	—	—
Discourse on Humility as a mark of Greatness	ix. 33-37	xviii. 1-5	ix. 46-48	—
Discourse on Occasions of Stumbling	ix. 38-50	xviii. 6-14	ix. 49, 50	—
Discourse on Forgiveness	—	xviii. 15-35	—	—
Jesus Lingers in Galilee	—	—	—	vii. 1-9
PART SIX - A.D. 29. About 3 months				
The Later Judæan Ministry				
(i) ON THE WAY TO JERUSALEM				
Jesus' Departure from Galilee ...	x. 1	xix. 1, 2	—	vii. 10
Rejected by the Samaritans ...	—	—	ix. 51-56	—
The Cost of Discipleship ...	—	viii. 19-22	ix. 57-62	—
(ii) IN JERUSALEM				
At the Feast of Tabernacles ...	—	—	—	vii. 11-52
Story of an Adulteress Brought to Jesus	—	—	—	vii. 53-viii. 11

HARMONISTIC READING SYLLABUS OF THE GOSPELS (continued)

	MARK	MATT.	LUKE	JOHN
(i) WITHDRAWAL FROM JERUSALEM (continued)				
Discourse on the Cost of Discipleship ...	—	—	xiv. 25-35	—
Discourse on Seeking and Finding the Lost	—	—	xv. 1-32	—
Two Parables on Stewardship	—	—	xvi. 1-31	—
Concerning Offences, Forgiveness, and Faith	—	—	xvii. 1-10	—
Jesus Raises Lazarus from the Dead ...	—	—	—	xi. 1-44
Jesus Withdraws to Ephraim	—	—	—	xi. 45-54
(ii) THE LAST JOURNEY TO JERUSALEM BY WAY OF SAMARIA AND GALILEE				
The Healing of Ten Lepers	—	—	xvii. 11-19	—
Discourse on the Coming of the Kingdom	—	—	xvii. 20-37	—
Two Parables on Prayer	—	—	xviii. 1-14	—
(iii) IN PERÆA				
Teaching Concerning Divorce	x. 1-12	xix. 1-12	—	—
Christ and Little Children	x. 13-16	xix. 13-15	xviii. 15-17	—
The Rich Young Ruler and Teaching on Riches	x. 17-31	xix. 16-xx. 16	xviii. 18-30	—
Jesus Foretells His Death and Resurrection	x. 32-34	xx. 17-19	xviii. 31-34	—
The Selfish Ambition of James and John Rebuked	x. 35-45	xx. 20-28	—	—
(iv) TOWARDS JERUSALEM				
Blind Men Healed near Jericho	x. 46-52	xx. 29-34	xviii. 35-43	—
The Conversion of Zacchæus	—	—	xix. 1-10	—
The Parable of the Pounds	—	—	xix. 11-28	—
Jesus' Arrival at Bethany	—	—	—	xi. 55-xii. 1, 9-11

PART EIGHT - - A.D. 30.   One Week

The order of the Passion Week in this Harmony follows the traditional view of the Church, but is not necessarily on that account correct. (See article on 'The Day of the Crucifixion,' p. 569).

The Closing Events of Jesus' Ministry

(i) SUNDAY—THE DAY OF DEMONSTRATION				
The Triumphal Entry into Jerusalem	xi. 1-10	xxi. 1-9	xix. 29-40	xii. 12-19
Prediction over Jerusalem	—	—	xix. 41-44	—
Jesus in the City and the Temple, and Retirement to Bethany	xi. 11	—	—	—
(ii) MONDAY—THE DAY OF AUTHORITY				
A Fig Tree Cursed	xi. 12-14	xxi. 18, 19	—	—
Second Cleansing of the Temple ...	xi. 15-19	xxi. 12, 13	xix. 45-48	—
Jesus Works Miracles and Justifies the Praise of Himself	—	xxi. 14-17	—	—
(iii) TUESDAY—THE DAY OF CONFLICT				
The Fig Tree Withered and Jesus' Remarks thereon	xi. 20-26	xxi. 19-22	—	—
Controversy with the Priests, Scribes, and Elders about His Authority	xi. 27-xii. 12	xxi. 23-xxii. 14	xx. 1-19	—
Controversy with the Pharisees and Herodians about Paying Tribute to Cæsar	xii. 13-17	xxii. 15-22	xx. 20-26	—
Controversy with the Sadducees about the Resurrection	xii. 18-27	xxii. 23-33	xx. 27-40	—

HARMONISTIC READING SYLLABUS OF THE GOSPELS (continued)

	MARK	MATT.	LUKE	JOHN
(iii) TUESDAY—THE DAY OF CONFLICT (continued)				
Controversy with a Lawyer about the Commandments	xii. 28-34	xxii. 34-40	—	—
Christ's Unanswerable Question	xii. 35-37	xxii. 41-46	xx. 41-44	—
Denunciations of the Scribes and Pharisees	xii. 38-40	xxiii. 1-39	xx. 45-47	—
Jesus Commends the Liberality of a Poor Widow	xii. 41-44	—	xxi. 1-4	—
Greeks Desire to see Jesus, and Jesus' Following Discourse	—	—	—	xii. 20-36
The Jews' Rejection of Christ	—	—	—	xii. 37-50
Discourse concerning the Destruction of Jerusalem and the End of the Age ...	xiii. 1-37	xxiv., xxv	xxi. 5-38	—
Jesus Predicts His Death as at Hand ...	xiv. 1, 2	xxvi. 1-5	xxii. 1, 2	—
Anointing of Jesus by Mary of Bethany ...	xiv. 3-9	xxvi. 6-13	—	xii. 2-8
Judas Arranges to Betray Jesus	xiv. 10, 11	xxvi. 14-16	xxii. 3-6	—
(iv) WEDNESDAY—THE DAY OF SILENCE				
(v) THURSDAY—THE DAY OF PREPARATION				
Preparation for the Paschal Meal ...	xiv. 12-16	xxvi. 17-19	xxii. 7-13	—
Jesus Partakes of the Passover with His Apostles	xiv. 17	xxvi. 20	xxii. 14-16	—
Jesus Washes the Feet of the Apostles ...	—	—	—	xiii. 1-20
The Betrayer is Pointed Out	xiv. 18-21	xxvi. 21-25	xxii. 21-23	xiii. 21-30
The Apostles Warned Against Desertion ...	xiv. 27-31	xxvi. 31-35	xxii. 31-38	xiii. 31-38
Institution of the Lord's Supper	xiv. 22-25	xxvi. 26-29	xxii. 17-20	(1 Cor. xi. 23-26)

	Matthew	Mark	Luke	John
(v), THURSDAY—THE DAY OF PREPARATION *(continued)*				
Jealousy of the Apostles Rebuked ...	—	—	xxii. 24-30	—
Farewell Discourse to the Apostles in the Upper Room ...	—	—	—	xiv. 1-31
(vi) FRIDAY—THE DAY OF SUFFERING				
Discourse on the Way to Gethsemane ...	—	—	—	xv., xvi.
Christ's Intercessory Prayer ...				xvii.
Arrival at, and the Agony in Gethsemane ...	xxvi. 30, 36-46	xiv. 26, 32-42	xxii. 39-46	xviii. 1
The Betrayal and Arrest ...	xxvi. 47-56	xiv. 43-52	xxii. 47-53	xviii. 2-12
(a) THE JEWISH TRIALS				
First—Before Annas ...	—	—	—	xviii. 12-14, 19-23
Second—Before Caiaphas and the Sanhedrin ...	xxvi. 57, 59-68	xiv. 53, 55, 56	xxii. 54, 63-65	xviii. 24
Peter Thrice Denies his Lord and Repents	xxvi. 58, 69-75	xiv. 54, 66-72	xxii. 54-62	xviii. 15-18, 25-27
Third—Before the Sanhedrin, which Passes Sentence ...	xxvii. 1	xv. 1	xxii. 66-71	—
Remorse and Suicide of Judas ...	xxvii. 3-10	—	(Acts i. 18, 19)	—
(b) THE ROMAN TRIALS				
First—Before Pilate ...	xxvii. 2, 11-14	xv. 1-5	xxiii. 1-5	xviii. 28-38
Second—Before Herod Antipas ...	—	—	xxiii. 6-12	—
Third—Before Pilate Again ...	xxvii. 15-26	xv. 6-15	xxiii. 13-25	xviii. 39-xix. 16
Jesus Mocked by Roman Soldiers ...	xxvii. 27-30	xv. 16-19	—	—
On the Way to Calvary ...	xxvii. 31-34	xv. 20-23	xxiii. 26-33	xix. 16, 17

HARMONISTIC READING SYLLABUS OF THE GOSPELS (continued)

	MARK	MATT.	LUKE	JOHN
(c) CALVARY				
The First Three Hours on the Cross ...	xv. 24-32	xxvii. 35-44	xxiii. 33-43	xix. 18-27
The Second Three Hours on the Cross	xv. 33-37	xxvii. 45-50	xxiii. 44, 46	xix. 28-30
Phenomena Accompanying Christ's Death	xv. 38-41	xxvii. 51-56	xxiii. 45, 47-49	—
The Burial of Jesus' Body in Joseph's Tomb	xv. 42-46	xxvii. 57-60	xxiii. 50-54	xix. 31-42
(vii) SATURDAY—THE DAY OF ABSENCE				
The Watch of the Women by the Tomb	xv. 47	xxvii. 61-66	xxiii. 55, 56	—
PART NINE - - A.D. 30. About 6 Weeks				
The Forty Days of Confirmation				
(i) SUNDAY—THE DAY OF VICTORY AND EVENTS				
The Visit of the Women to the Tomb	xvi. 1	xxviii. 1	—	—
The Earthquake; the Tomb Stone Rolled Away, and the Fright of the Roman Watchers	—	xxviii. 2-4	—	—
The Message of Angels to Women at the Tomb ...	xvi. 2-8	xxviii. 5-8	xxiv. 1-8	xx. 1
Mary Magdalene and Other Women Report to the Apostles, and Peter and John Visit the Tomb ...	—	—	xxiv. 9-12	xx. 2-10

80

(ii) Appearances of Jesus on the Resurrection Day

	Mark	Matthew	Luke	John
First—To Mary Magdalene	xvi. 9-11	—	—	xx. 11-18
Second—To Other Women	—	xxviii. 9, 10	—	—
Some of the Guard Report to the Jewish Rulers	—	xxviii. 11-15	—	—
Third—To Two Disciples on the Way to Emmaus	xvi. 12, 13	—	xxiv. 13-32	—
Fourth—The Report of the Emmaus Disciples, and the News of the Appearance to Simon Peter	(I Cor. xv. 5)	—	xxiv. 33-35	—
Fifth—To Ten Apostles in a House	xvi. 14	—	xxiv. 36-43	xx. 19-25

(iii) Appearances of Jesus after the Resurrection Day

	Mark	Matthew	Luke	John
Sixth—To the Eleven Apostles in a House	—	—	—	xx. 26-31
Seventh—To Seven Apostles by the Sea of Galilee. A Miraculous Draught of Fishes	—	—	—	xxi. 1-14
Conversation of Jesus and Peter, and an Intimation of Peter's End	—	—	—	xxi. 15-25
Eighth—To Five Hundred Disciples in Galilee	xvi. 15-18	xxviii. 16-20	(I Cor. xv. 6)	—
Ninth—To James His Brother	(I Cor. xv. 7)	—	—	—
Tenth—To the Eleven in Jerusalem and on Olivet	—	—	xxiv. 44-49	—
The Last Commission and the Ascension	xvi. 19, 20	—	xxiv. 50-53	(Acts I. 3-12)

QUESTIONS

1 Into how many parts may the Life of Christ be divided, and how may they be denominated?
2 What five incidents are recorded in the period of Jesus' infancy?
3 What are we told of Jesus between the ages of twelve and thirty?
4 Name three great incidents in the Opening Events of Jesus' Ministry.
5 How many cleansings of the Temple were there, and when?
6 What in John's Gospel explains the evangelistic success recorded in Acts viii?
7 How many draughts of fishes were there, and when? Say what happened at each.
8 When, where, and why did Christ choose Twelve Apostles?
9 How many times was Jesus anointed; by whom, and where?
10 How many times did Jesus raise the dead? When, where, and who were they?
11 What two groups of persons did Jesus send on a mission, and why?
12 How many times did Jesus feed people, and where? Give details.
13 When, where, and why did Peter confess that Jesus was the Son of God?
14 What happened at the Transfiguration of Christ?
15 How many, and what Feasts did Jesus attend? Give references.
16 About how long did the Peræan Ministry last? Name some things which happened in that period.
17 How many publicans do we read of in the Gospels, and who were they? What was the work of a publican?
18 Write a brief outline of the happenings of the Passion Week.
19 How many Jewish, and how many Roman Trials of Jesus were there?
20 How many Sayings were there of Jesus when on the Cross, and what were they?
21 How many times did Jesus appear after His resurrection? Name five of them.
22 What was Christ's final commission to His Apostles?

LITERATURE

'Harmony of the Gospels in the American Standard Version' - - - - Kerr
'Harmony of the Gospels for Students of the Life of Christ' - - - - - A. T. Robertson
'Harmony of the Gospels for Historical Study' Stevens and Burton
'Harmony of the Gospels' - - - J. A. Broadus
'Harmony of the Synoptic Gospels' - Burton and Goodspeed
'A Combined Analysis of the Four Gospels' A. G. Secrett
'The Life and Teaching of Christ' - - Reginald Ponsonby

8

The Synoptic Problem

THAT there is such a problem is a fact, and everyone who is interested in the Gospels should know something about it. In detail it is a matter for the scholars, but the average student of these Records cannot afford to overlook it. Two opposite perils should be avoided:

(a) indifference to what can be known of the composition and construction of these Gospels; and

(b) such occupation with the pursuit of this inquiry that one's appreciation of and subjection to what is written is endangered.

All we can attempt here is to give a very general idea of what the problem is, and of the lines along which efforts have been made to solve it. This much is necessary for an understanding of references which will be made in the Analytical Division of the Guide.

We are in possession of three Gospels, Matthew, Mark, and Luke, which are called Synoptic, because they survey the life of Christ from a common viewpoint (*sun*, with; *opsis*, seeing). In these Gospels are resemblances and differences, and the problem consists in the harmonizing of these, and so of determining the relation of the Synoptics to one another. Anyone who will read a Harmony of the Gospels (Stevens' and Burton's, or A. T. Robertson's) will see at once these resemblances and differences. The following is a typical illustration:

THE TEMPTATION

MATTHEW iv. 1, 2	MARK i. 12, 13	LUKE iv. 1, 2
Then was JESUS LED up of the Spirit *into* the wilderness, to be tempted of the DEVIL. And when He had fasted forty days and forty nights HE afterward HUNGERED.	And straightway the Spirit driveth Him forth *into* the wilderness. And He was *in* the wilderness forty days, *being tempted* of Satan; and He was with the wild beasts, and the angels ministered unto Him.	And JESUS, full of the Holy Spirit, returned from the Jordan, and was LED by the Spirit *in* the wilderness during forty days, *being tempted* by the DEVIL. And He did eat nothing in those days, and when they were completed HE HUNGERED.

The capitals show agreements in Matthew and Luke which are not in Mark, and the italics show that the ' into ' (*eis*) of Matthew, and the ' in ' (*en*) of Luke, both occur in Mark, and that Mark and Luke have 'being-tempted' (Greek, *peirazomenos*, pres: part. pass.) implying that the temptation was spread over the forty days, whereas Matthew has 'to be tempted,' not necessarily covering the whole experience of those days.

The problem is how to account for such resemblances and differences throughout these Gospels. Such an inquiry is reasonable, and is neither irrelevant nor irreverent.

The phenomena lead to the supposition that these Records are compilations, and that behind them are sources upon which they have drawn. That the Gospels are so composed need occasion no surprise, because the use of sources is characteristic of the Scriptures. In the Old Testament reference is made to the Book of the Wars of the Lord, the Book of Jasher, the Book of Samuel the Seer, the Book of Nathan the Prophet, the Book of Gad the Seer, the Book of the Chronicles of the Kings of Israel and of Judah; and in the books of Nehemiah and Ezra are genealogies, letters of Persian Kings, and other documents. In the Book of the Acts a discourse of Paul's includes a quotation from a heathen poet, Aratus or Cleanthes, (xvii. 28), and in the Epistles are found snatches of song from an early Church hymn book, and summaries of credal statements which very early were in circulation. (1 Cor. xi. 23-25; Eph. v. 19, 14; Col. i. 13-20; 1 Tim. iii. 16; vi. 15, 16).

There are also at least two references in Paul's Epistles drawn from pagan sources. In 1 Cor. xv. 33, 'evil communications corrupt good manners,' is from an Attic drama, and is attributed to Menander (322 B.C.). In Titus i. 12, 'the Cretans are alway liars, evil beasts, slow bellies,' occurs in part, or the whole, in a hymn to Zeus by Callimachus, in Hesiod, and in a writing of Epimenides.

We need not, therefore, be surprised to find that the Gospels borrow material. For what reason the selections were made will become more evident when we consider why there are *four* Gospels; but what is now clear, as to the origin of these Records,

GALILEE

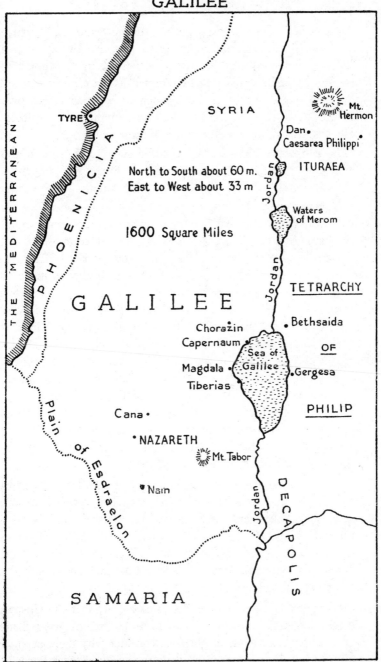

THE MEDITERRANEAN

P H O E N I C I A

TYRE

SYRIA

Mt. Hermon

Dan.
Caesarea Philippi

ITURAEA

North to South about 60 m.
East to West about 33 m

Jordan

1600 Square Miles

Waters of Merom

G A L I L E E

TETRARCHY

Chorazin
Capernaum

Bethsaida

OF

Magdala
Tiberias

Sea of
Galilee

Gergesa

PHILIP

Cana

NAZARETH

Mt. Tabor

Nain

Jordan

D E C A P O L I S

Plain of Esdraelon

S A M A R I A

Pages 53-59, 218, 219, 410, 411, 68-81

MAP III

is that they were produced independently, at different times, in different places, for different purposes; that they are compilations, and that, though they have their own characteristics of outlook and expression, yet they perfectly harmonize in their witness to Jesus the Messiah.

The present question is: What was there behind these Records which can account for them? The following are the main hypotheses which have been advanced.

1 The ORAL TRADITION Hypothesis

This theory 'assumes that each of the Evangelists wrote independently of the others, and derived the substance of his writing, not from written sources, but from oral narratives of sayings and doings of Jesus, which, through dint of repetition, had assumed a relatively fixed form.'

This oral tradition would have its rise in Jerusalem, and would be the teaching given in catechetical schools (Luke i. 4, R.V.); and, until written editions of it appeared (Luke i. 1), the truth would be ' intrusted to the trained memories of the Christian converts.'

That there were catechetical schools, and such oral instruction, are simply matters of fact, whether or not the theory solves the Synoptic Problem.

2 The MUTUAL USE Hypothesis

This is the view that the problem can be accounted for by assuming that the authors of these Gospels used each other's Writings, but there has never been agreement as to who the borrowers were, each in turn having been regarded as the source of the others, and there are six possible permutations. More need not be said about this as it has few advocates to-day.

3 The DOCUMENTS Hypothesis

This is the theory which almost all scholars hold at the present time, with differences of opinion as to how many such documents there were. Most scholars are agreed upon two such sources.

(a) Mark's Gospel.

(*b*)   A non-existent document which is called Q. The reasons for this 'Two Document' theory are as follows:

(i) *That Matthew and Luke drew largely from Mark.*

Of Matthew's 1068 verses (R.V.) about 500 are from Mark's 661 verses; and of Luke's 1149 verses (R.V.) about 320 are from Mark. Only from 50-55 verses of Mark are not to be found in Matthew and Luke. (See pp. 132, 140, 186, 253, 261).

(ii) That when the Marcan material is eliminated from Matthew and Luke, about 250 verses, common to both, consisting chiefly of sayings and discourses of Christ, show such close parallelism and similarity as to indicate a common source, and ' that this source is not oral tradition, but *a written Greek document.*'

This document is designated Q, from the German *Quelle*, which means ' source.'

Critics are not agreed upon the contents of Q. Dr. Moffatt gives details of no fewer than 16 varieties of opinion. Nor is there agreement as to how much of this hypothetical document each of these two Evangelists uses. Yet it is regarded as difficult to account for so many non-Marcan parallels in Matthew and Luke except by assuming some such document.

(iii) But when the Marcan material is eliminated from Matthew and Luke, and also the 250 verses which are common to both, which are supposed to be derived from Q, the 'Oracles' of Papias, or *Logia* of Matthew, there still remain in Matthew over 300 verses, and in Luke about 580 verses, to be accounted for.

These 300 verses in Matthew are of a special *Jewish* tone (see chaps. i.-ii; ix. 27-34; xiv. 28-33; xvii. 24 ff., *et al.*); and the 580 verses in Luke, after the Infancy stories, are of a definitely *Gentile* tone, including the best known parables, the Good Samaritan, the Prodigal Son, the Pharisee and the Publican, and others (see chaps. vii. 11-16, 36-50; x. 25 ff.; xvi.; xviii. 1-14, *et al.*).

The Synoptic Problem, therefore, has to account for

    (*a*) what is common to all the Gospels:
    (*b*) what is common to any two of them:
    (*c*) what is peculiar to each.

It is not possible for the average reader, or even the average student of the Synoptic Gospels, to go into all the intricacies of this problem, but no one should be wholly ignorant of the existence of it, but should know, in a general way, what the problem is, and what has been said about it. The above outline should, therefore, be carefully studied, but bear in mind that the Q hypothesis is a theory and not a certainty; and it has been well said that:

' The very fascination which such a theory must possess is a reason for meeting it with peculiar caution. It is hard to restrict the imagination to its true office in such inquiries. When once we have thought ourselves into a particular theory, a conviction of its truth is apt to be bred in the mind, which is altogether beyond the evidence, while inconvenient facts are ignored.' (V. H. Stanton. *Expositor*, Vol. vii., 1893).

Whatever may be the fate of the third of these theories, the first is historically established, and does not necessarily exclude the existence of some written records.

A saying of the early Rabbis was: ' Commit nothing to writing '; and Clement of Alexandria says: ' The Elders refrained from writing because they would not interrupt the care which they bestowed on teaching orally, by the care of composition, nor expend in writing the time required for the preparation of their addresses. Perhaps they felt that the functions of the speaker and writer were incompatible, and saw in books only the written confirmation for after time of the instruction which they conveyed at present.'

Bishop Westcott says: 'The evangelist was not the compiler of a history, but the missionary who carried the good tidings to fresh countries; the bearer, and not the author of the message.' And again: 'The primary Gospel was proved, so to speak, in life, before it was fixed in writing.'

For at least a score of years after the Ascension no need was felt of written records of the life and teaching of Jesus Christ, for ' the Old Testament was held to be the single and sufficient source of truth and wisdom, the reflection of divine knowledge, and the embodiment of hum an feeling' (Acts iii. 21, 24; xv. 15; xxviii. 23). And further, ┼hose who companied with Christ, who saw His deeds and heard His words, were still living, and could tell the people all they needed to know, in the way they were accustomed to learn, namely, by verbal instruction. This situation is clearly reflected in the New Testament. The teacher was the evangelist, and ' the place of instruction was the synagogue and the market-place, and not the student's chamber ' (Acts xv. 21). The men who had first-hand knowledge of the Messiah and who could speak with authority of the events which were bounded on one side by the appearance of the Baptist, and on the other side by the Ascension of Christ, were commissioned to bear their witness by word of mouth (Acts i. 8, 21, 22).

These men, we are told, gave themselves to ' prayer and the ministry of the Word' (Acts vi. 4); they ' spake the things which they had seen and heard ' (Acts iv. 19, 20). ' With great power gave the Apostles witness ' by word of mouth (Acts iv. 33). ' Philip preached the things concerning the Kingdom of God ' (Acts viii. 12); and Paul taught ' publicly and from house to house ' (Acts xx. 20).

What the content of the oral instruction was may be learned from the two cases where the message of Christianity was delivered in detail to those who were waiting for it. It was an outline of the ministry of Christ. Study carefully the message of Peter in the house of Cornelius (Acts x. 34-43), and that of Paul in the synagogue at Antioch (Acts xiii. 16-41). The address of Peter is a *précis* of the Second Gospel, or, to put it differently, Mark's Gospel is the extended statement of Peter's outline, and, be it remembered, ancient tradition is unanimous that Mark reported Peter. Papias said: ' Mark, being the interpreter of Peter, wrote down exactly whatever things he remembered, but yet not in the order in which Christ either spoke or did them;

for he was neither a hearer nor a follower of the Lord, but he was afterwards, as I (Papias) said, a follower of Peter.'

It seems clear, therefore, that behind the Gospel records was the Oral instruction which was given by the Apostles and those whom they taught. It is quite likely that at an early date some things were committed to writing, for example Matthew's *Logia*, certain *Testimonia* (pp. 253, 426), and other records (Luke i. 1), and that these were known to the Apostles, and, perhaps, later on were used by them; but while this is debatable, the fact of an orally delivered message is not. This fact by no means accounts for all that is in the Gospels, but it accounts for much.

Whatever the truth may be about the sources of these Gospels the thing that matters is the Gospels themselves as we now have them. Here are the finished products, the Spirit-directed records of the Redeemer and His redemption, each with its own value, and together recording for all time the sovereign revelation that 'God was in Christ reconciling the world unto Himself.'

I have carefully examined the views of seven scholars on the subject of what material in Luke is derived from Q, and what follows is the result. The scholars referred to are, Harnack, Holtzmann, Wellhausen, Wendt, Hawkins, Stanton, and Canon Redlich.

All seven agree on 107 verses in Luke; six agree on 56 verses; five agree on 31 verses; four agree on 43 verses; three agree on 31 verses; two agree on 31 verses; and one adds 216 verses to these.

When four in seven are in agreement that certain verses in this Gospel are derived from this Q source, we have a foundation for an examination of the matter.

The 107 verses on which all seven are agreed are: iii. 7; vi. 20-23, 27-36, 39, 40, 43-49; vii. 6-9, 18, 19, 22-28, 32-35; x. 2, 3, 5-7, 9, 12-15, 21-24; xi. 9-14, 19, 20, 24-26, 29-32, 39, 42, 44, 46-52; xii. 22-31, 39, 40, 42-46; xiii. 34, 35; xvi. 3, 4, 24, 26, 27, 33-35.

The 56 verses on which six of the scholars are agreed are: iii. 8, 9, 17; iv. 3-13; vi. 37, 38, 41, 42; vii. 2, 3, 20, 21; ix. 57-60; x. 4, 8, 11, 16; xi. 16, 17, 23, 34, 35, 41; xii. 2-9, 33, 51, 53; xiii. 20, 21; xiv. 26, 27; xvi. 16; xvii. 1, 6, 23, 37.

These verses are, of course, not instead of the 107, but in addition to them.

The 31 verses on which five are agreed are: iii. 16; vii. 4, 10; x. 10; xi. 2-4, 40; xi. 43, 45; xii. 34, 41, 52, 58; xiii. 18, 19, 24, 25, 28, 29; xiv. 11; xvi. 13, 17; xvii. 22, 25, 28-32; xix. 26.

The 43 verses on which four are agreed are: iv. 1, 2; vi. 24-26; vii. 1, 29; xi. 15, 18, 21, 22, 27, 28, 33, 36, 38; xii. 10, 32, 37, 38, 59; xiii. 26, 27; xv. 4, 5, 7; xvii. 2, 5; xix. 12-25; xxii. 30.

The other three reckonings need not concern us here. The aggregate of the four reckonings is 237 verses, which, let it be understood, are not in Mark, and which in Matthew and Luke are such close parallels, many of them being verbally exact, as to lead to the conclusion that both Evangelists had access to a document or documents which contained these utterances. The following illustrations speak for themselves:

MATTHEW	LUKE

The Messiah's Judgment

| Whose fan is in His hand, and He will throughly cleanse His threshing-floor; and He will gather His wheat into the garner, but the chaff He will burn up with unquenchable fire. iii. 12 | Whose fan is in His hand, throughly to cleanse His threshing-floor, and to gather the wheat into His garner; but the chaff He will burn up with unquenchable fire. iii. 17 |

Impossibility of Serving Two Masters

| No man can serve two masters: for either he will hate the one, and love the other; or else he will hold to one, and despise the other. Ye cannot serve God and mammon. vi. 24 | No servant can serve two masters: for either he will hate the one, and love the other; or else he will hold to one, and despise the other. Ye cannot serve God and mammon. xvi. 13 |

Illustration of the Lilies

| Consider the lilies of the field, how they grow; they toil not, neither do they spin: yet I say unto you, that even Solomon in all his glory was not arrayed like one of these. But if God doth so clothe the grass of the field, which to-day is, and to-morrow is cast into the oven, shall He not much more clothe you, O ye of little faith? vi. 28-30 | Consider the lilies, how they grow: they toil not, neither do they spin; yet I say unto you, Even Solomon in all his glory was not arrayed like one of these. But if God doth so clothe the grass in the field, which to-day is, and to-morrow is cast into the oven; how much more shall He clothe you, O ye of little faith? xii. 27, 28 |

MATTHEW	LUKE

Jesus and John the Baptist

Jesus began to say unto the multitudes concerning John, What went ye out into the wilderness to behold? A reed shaken with the wind? But what went ye out for to see? a man clothed in soft raiment? xi. 7, 8	He began to say unto the multitudes concerning John, What went ye out into the wilderness to behold? a reed shaken with the wind? But what went ye out to see? a man clothed in soft raiment? vii. 24, 25

The Lament Over Jerusalem

O Jerusalem, Jerusalem, which killeth the prophets, and stoneth them that are sent unto her! how often would I have gathered thy children together, even as a hen gathereth her chickens under her wings, and ye would not! Behold, your house is left unto you desolate. For I say unto you, Ye shall not see Me henceforth, till ye shall say, Blessed is He that cometh in the name of the Lord. xxiii. 37-39	O Jerusalem, Jerusalem, which killeth the prophets, and stoneth them that are sent unto her! how often would I have gathered thy children together, even as a hen gathereth her own brood under her wings, and ye would not! Behold, your house is left unto you desolate : and I say unto you, Ye shall not see Me, until ye shall say, Blessed is He that cometh in the name of the Lord. xiii. 34, 35

Dr. V. H. Stanton has pointed out that such close parallels as these ' amount in length to somewhat less than a third ' of the passages which are supposed to be derived from Q, and that ' in the remaining two-thirds the degree of verbal agreement is markedly less, and, speaking generally, is not at all close.'

If it be asked if such parallels are the only ground for postulating such a document as Q, the answer is, No. There is a famous saying of Papias, Bishop of Hierapolis (A.D. 130: see 'Church Fathers,' p. 39), to the effect that, 'Matthew composed (i.e. put together in writing) the Oracles (of Jesus) in the Hebrew (i.e. Aramaic language), and each one interpreted them as he was able.'

This tradition is confirmed by Irenæus in the second century, by Origen, in the third, and by Eusebius, in the fourth (see 'Church Fathers,' p. 39). These 'Oracles,' or *Logia*, as they are called, are supposed to have been a collection of the sayings and discourses of our Lord, together, perhaps, with a certain amount of connecting narrative, which Matthew compiled in Aramaic at a very early date, Sir William Ramsay thinks, ' while Christ still lived among men.'

The hypothetical Q document is generally identified with
the 'Oracles,' or *Logia*, referred to by Papias, that is with the
Logia of Matthew, and it is believed that when he wrote his
Gospel (our canonical Matthew) in Greek, he incorporated
much of what he had already written in Aramaic.

Students hold that evidence of this is found in five discourses
in the first Gospel, each of which ends with the formula, ' it
came to pass when Jesus had finished,' or its equivalent (vii. 28;
xi. 1; xiii. 53; xix. 1; xxvi. 1).

A certain amount of this material is found in Luke, but it is
widely scattered, and is presented in settings which are different
from those in Matthew. This fact, Dr. Stanton says, ' is highly
unfavourable to the idea that they both found this matter in the
same document,' yet the fact of these discourses in Matthew
has to be accounted for.

It is noteworthy that whereas Mark is chiefly *narrative*, Matthew is chiefly *discourses* and *sayings* of Jesus, and it is presump-
tive of such a collection as that of which Papias speaks that sayings
of Christ's are found outside the Gospels, for example, in Acts
xx. 35.

There is some evidence, also, that Paul was acquainted with
a collection of Christ's sayings; and further, in 1903 a Gospel
Fragment was found at Oxyrhynchus, in central Egypt, containing the conclusion of a discourse by Jesus, similar to a part
of the Sermon on the Mount. The sayings given in this Fragment are, for the most part, parallel to passages found in Matthew
and Luke.

The passages which Dr. B. H. Streeter assigns to Q, in Luke,
are: iii. 2a-9 (10-14), 16, 17, 21, 22; iv. 1-16a; vi. 20-vii. 10, 18-35;
ix. (51-56), 57-60 (61, 62); x. 2-16, (17-20), 21-24; xi. 9-52;
xii. 1b-12, 22-59; xiii. 18-35; xiv. 11, 26, 27, 34, 35; xvi. 13,
16-18; xvii. 1-6, 20-37; xix. 11-27. Brackets signify considerable
doubt. Unbracketed verses—272.

Perhaps as full a syllabus as can be given of Q in Luke (who,
in the main probably, preserves the original order of Q) and
Matthew, the parallels of which are at all close, is as follows:

	LUKE	MATTHEW		LUKE	MATTHEW
1	iii. 7-9, 16, 17	iii. 7-12	14	xi. 24-26	xii. 43-45
2	iii. 21, 22	iii. 16, 17	15	xi. 29-32	xii. 38-42
3	iv. 1-13	iv. 1-11	16	xi. 33-35	v. 15; vi. 22-23
4	vi. 41, 42	vii. 3- 5	17	xii. 2-12	x. 26-33; xii. 32; x. 19
5	vi. 47-49	vii. 24-27	18	xii. 22-34	vi. 25-33
6	vii. 1-10	viii. 5-10, 13	19	xii. 39-46	xxiv. 43-51
7	vii. 18-35	xi. 2-11, 16-19	20	xii. 57-59	v. 25, 26
8	ix. 57-60	viii. 19-22	21	xiii. 18-21	xiii. 31-33
9	x. 2-12	ix. 37, 38; x. 9-15	22	xiii. 34, 35	xxiii. 37-39
10	x. 13-15	xi. 21-23	23	xiv. 11	xxiii. 12
11	x. 21-24	xi. 25-27; xiii. 16, 17	24	xvi. 13	vi. 24
12	xi. 9-13	vii. 7-11	25	xvii. 1-6	xviii. 6, 7
13	xi. 14-23	xii. 22-30	26	xvii. 22-27, 33-37	xxiv. 26-28, 37-41, x.39

Write out these passages in parallel columns, as above, and observe their similarity, bearing in mind that they do not occur in Mark, that they were written by different men, at different times, in different places, and for different purposes, and the conviction will not be escaped that these passages came from a common document, the lost document Q.

Canon Redlich says: 'For such a short document as Q, the wealth of reference to nature, the animal world, the home life, and to details of daily interest is most striking. We find mention of the following: (1) wheat, harvest, grass, lilies, mustard seeds, reeds, figs, thorns, brambles, trees, sycamines, grapes; (2) foxes, serpents, vipers, birds of the air, ravens, lambs, sparrows, nests, wolves, eagles, moths, hens, chickens; (3) lightning, storms, clouds, winds, showers, scorching wind, streams, sand pits, rocks; (4) weddings, feasts, dinners, meals, loaves, fish, eggs, leaven; (5) axes, lamps, purses, mill-stones, houses, barns, bushels, sawdust, beams, cellars, house-tops, money, ovens, threshing, sandals, coats, clothes, wallets, cups and platters, chaff; (6) children's games, gifts to children, music on pipes.'

QUESTIONS

1 What is the meaning of the word ' synoptic,' and what is the Synoptic Problem?

2 What three hypotheses have been held to account for this Problem? Briefly summarize each.

3 What is to be understood by the designation Q, and what ground is there for the theory?

4 What is to be understood by the *Logia* of Jesus, and is there any connection between these and Q?

5 What is the famous saying of Papias on the subject of these *Logia*?

6 Is there any evidence of such a document as this in the canonical Matthew?

7 What three things has the Synoptic Problem to account for?

8 Name half a dozen passages in Matthew and Luke which, it is supposed, are derived from Q.

LITERATURE

'Oxford Studies in the Synoptic Problem '	
'The Students' Introduction to the Synoptic Gospels '	Canon Redlich
'Horæ Synopticæ '	Sir John Hawkins
'The Four Gospels. A Study of Origins '	Canon Streeter
'Cambridge Biblical Essays '	——
'Some Notes on the Gospels '	D. M. McIntyre
'Are the New Testament Documents Reliable?'	F. F. Bruce
The Standard Bible Dictionaries	——
'Some New Testament Problems'	A. Wright
'The Composition of the Four Gospels'	A. Wright
'Synopsis of the Gospels'	A. Wright
'The Common Tradition of the Synoptic Gospels'	Abbott and Rushbrooke
'Synopticon'	Rushbrooke
'Synopsis Evangelica'	Tischendorf
'The Formation of the Gospel Tradition'	V. Taylor
'Behind the Third Gospel'	V. Taylor
'An Aramaic Approach to the Gospels and Acts'	M. Black
'The Four Gospels in the Earliest Church History'	T. Nicol
'Gospel Parallels.' Revised Standard Version (1949)	

Diagrammatic View of the Gospels

THE following comparisons are general, but they are sufficiently distinctive to be important:

Matthew	Mark	Luke	John
E MIGHTY KING	THE LOWLY SERVANT	THE IDEAL MAN	THE DIVINE SON
n-like	Ox-like	Man-like	Eagle-like
the Jews	For the Gentiles	For the World	For the Church
phetical	Practical	Historical	Spiritual
ssianic	Realistic	Catholic	Christian
ver	Service	Sympathy	Wisdom
t	Present	Future	Eternity

Synoptical Matthew, Mark, Luke		Supplementary John	
Outward—Earthly—Galilean Public—Works—Human		Inward—Heavenly—Judæan Private—Words—Divine	

Official		Personal	
ng	Servant	Son of Man	Son of God

The Branch			
. xxiii. 5, 6	Zech. iii. 8	Zech. vi. 12	Isaiah iv. 2

Old Testament References in the Gospels

IT may be said that Old Testament references in the Gospels are of far greater importance than the average reader suspects, and that they raise many and difficult problems. All that is necessary for the present purpose is briefly to indicate this importance, and the nature of the problems.

How many Old Testament references there are in the Gospels is variously estimated. This is due to the fact that *references* embrace *quotations* and *allusions*; the quotations being sometimes more and sometimes less direct, and sometimes combined, and the allusions being sometimes more and sometimes less obvious.

Westcott and Hort estimate that there are in Matthew 94 references, in Mark 49, in Luke 80, and in John 20, making a total of 243. Of these the director formal quotations are, approximately, in Matthew 37, in Mark 32, in Luke 21, and in John 15, a total of 105. These figures, however, are too low, and it will be found that in each of the Gospels there are many more (see p. 146, and Division B, under each Gospel).

The sources of these references is a somewhat academic aspect of the subject, and need not be considered in detail by the student who has no knowledge of Hebrew and Greek, but certain facts are of general interest, and indicate the nature of the problems raised.

1 The two quotation sources are the Hebrew Old Testament and the Septuagint (LXX), the Greek Old Testament.

2 Some of these quotations conform to both the Hebrew and the Greek of the Old Testament; some conform to the Hebrew only; some to the Greek only; some vary from both the Hebrew and the Greek; some vary less from the Hebrew than from the Greek, and some vary less from the Greek than from the Hebrew.

3 In the great majority of cases the quotations are from the LXX.

4 Some of the quotations are introduced by the Evangelists (e.g., Mark i. 2, 3), but the great majority are in the sayings and discourses of Christ.

5 The quotations are introduced by formulas more or less fixed and uniform, such as: ' *that it might be fulfilled which was spoken by the Lord through the prophet,*' or '*then was fulfilled that which was spoken*' (Matt. i. 22; ii. 15, 17; iii. 3; iv. 14; viii. 17; xii. 17; xiii. 14, 35; xxi. 4; xxvi. 56; xxvii. 9); ' *it is written* ' (Matt. ii. 5; iv. 4, 7, 10; xi. 10; xxi. 13; xxvi. 31; Mark ix. 12; John vi. 45; viii. 17); '*as it is written*' (Mark i. 2; vii. 6; Luke ii. 23; John vi. 31, *et al.*); ' *it was said,*' or '*it hath been said*' (Matt. v. 21, 31, 33, 38, 43); ' *is it not written?*' (Mark xi. 17); ' *Moses wrote* ' (Mark xii. 19); ' *have ye not read in the book of Moses?* ' (Mark xii. 26); ' *David himself said* ' (Mark xii. 36; Luke xx. 42); and ' *that the Scriptures might be fulfilled* ' (Mark xiv. 49; John xix. 36).

These are not all the variations, and of those that are given these are not all the references, but they sufficiently illustrate the method whereby Old Testament passages are introduced.

6 Different estimates of the number of quotations in the Gospels are due, in part, to the fact that in places, two, or even three, quotations are combined, and by some are reckoned as one. Illustrations of this are: Matt. xv. 4: part from Exod. xx. 12 and part from Exod. xxi. 17. Matt. xxi. 13: part from Isa. lvi. 7 and part from Jer. vii. 11. Mark i. 2, 3: taken from Mal. iii. 1 and Isa. xl. 3. Luke x. 27: part from Deut. vi. 5 and part from Lev. xix. 18. Mark xiii. 24-27: the references here are traceable to at least six sources: Isa. xiii. 10; xxxiv. 4; Dan. vii. 13; Deut. xxx. 4; Zech. ii. 6, and Deut. xxviii. 64.

7 As our Lord commonly spoke Aramaic, the Greek reports of His conversations and speeches are translations.

7

The importance and value of the Old Testament references in the Gospels (and, of course, throughout the New Testament) may be said to be twofold: (a) they imply that the Old Testament Writings are an organic part of the progressive revelation of redemption; and (b) they indicate the estimate which Christ put upon the Old Testament Scriptures, and the way in which He interpreted them.

(a) THE OLD TESTAMENT WRITINGS ARE AN ORGANIC PART OF THE PROGRESSIVE REVELATION OF REDEMPTION

It is estimated that there are about 300 direct quotations from the Old Testament in the New Testament. This means that ' the New Testament writers regarded the Christian religion as having its roots in the Old Testament.' The New Testament would become practically unintelligible if what there is in it of the Old Testament were extracted. The two Testaments are one revelation; in both there is a single organic movement; the two dispensations are a unity (Mark vii. 6; Luke iv. 21; xx. 17; John iv. 37).

Further, and in close harmony with this fact is another, namely, that the Biblical movement was Divinely planned from the beginning. The Old Testament quotations in the New Testament make this clear. ' The Bible is one because the history out of which it grew is one. The history is one because God is in the history, and God is one.' This is made unmistakably plain in the Epistle to the Hebrews (i. 1, 2), and, indeed, but for this fact, the Epistle would completely lose its value.

Design and execution, prophecy and fulfilment, promise and realization constitute one whole. ' One mind, one will, and one central purpose are operating throughout the entire history which is, on the Divine side, the fulfilment of a plan complete in thought before it takes shape in events.' The greater part of the structure of the New Testament is reared on this fact (Matt. iv. 13-16; viii. 16, 17; Mark xiv. 27; Luke xxii. 37; John vii. 42).

This fact involves the recognition and acceptance of the Old Testament as authoritative, as being a real Word of God. Read tne Old Testament quotations in the Gospels in this light, and their deeper meaning and value will be apprehended (Matt. iv. 4; Mark vii. 10; Luke xix. 46).

The second thing of importance is that

> (b) THE OLD TESTAMENT QUOTATIONS IN THE GOSPELS INDICATE THE ESTIMATE WHICH CHRIST PUT UPON THE OLD TESTAMENT, AND THE WAY IN WHICH HE INTERPRETED IT

The Old Testament was our Lord's Bible. Certainly He read it in Greek, and it is more than probable that He read it in Hebrew also.

The majority of Old Testament quotations in the Gospels are in the reports of what Christ said. It is fashionable in quarters to affirm that, in places, the Evangelists attribute to Christ Old Testament quotations which He did not make. We reject this view, proof of which is entirely wanting.

Another view, promulgated by many, that Jesus was a true child of His age, and so shared its prejudices and fell into its errors, should be definitely rejected. Were this true, much of His teaching would be invalidated.

Believing, then, that He spoke the words attributed to Him, and that He had a knowledge of and insight into the Writings of the Old Testament, not only profounder than any others had, but which was absolutely true and authoritative, we should carefully examine all the passages which He quotes.

It is interesting and important to note what Old Testament Writings our Lord quotes. Of the 39 books which compose the Old Testament He directly quotes 14: Genesis, Exodus, Leviticus, Numbers, Deuteronomy, Samuel, Kings, Psalms, Isaiah, Jeremiah, Daniel, Hosea, Zechariah, and Malachi; and He makes many allusions to other Writings. Of those quoted from, He refers most often to Deuteronomy, Psalms, and Isaiah.

In His conflict in the wilderness all the quotations with which He met the assaults of the enemy were from Deuteronomy (Matt. iv. 1-11). With a passage from Isaiah He opened His ministry at Nazareth (Luke iv. 14-19), and to the Psalms He turned as He hung upon the Cross (Mark xv. 34).

Christ's interpretation of the Old Testament was original and authoritative. He did not follow the current interpretations and traditions (cf. Matt. v. 21-48). He plainly said that some of the Jewish teachers did not know the meaning of their own Scriptures (Matt. xxii. 29; Mark xii. 24, 27), and of others, that they did violence to these Scriptures (Matt. xv. 6; Mark vii. 13).

While recognizing the inadequacy of the Old Testament (Matt. v. 21-48), Christ always upheld its authority (Matt. v. 17-20; xxiii. 2, 3). That He believed Himself to be the fulfilment and the fulfiller of the Mosaic Law, and of the Messianic Prophecies of the Old Testament cannot be questioned. In its essence, the Law is an expression of the mind and will of God, and Christ repeatedly declared that He came to fulfil that will (Matt. iii. 15; v. 17-20; John iv. 34; v. 36; xvii. 4).

And Christ laid as great stress on His fulfilment of the Prophecies of the Old Testament as on the fulfilment of the Law, for both are declarations of the Divine purposes in human history, and these purposes He came to accomplish. Nor is it a few specific prophecies that He came to fulfil, but the prophetic Scriptures as a whole (Matt. xxvi. 54, 56; Mark xiv. 49; Luke xviii. 31; xxiv. 26, 27, 44-47; John v. 39). Attention will be called to specific quotations in the Gospels in which they occur, in the Analytical Division, but the particulars given here apply to all the Gospels, and should be carefully considered.

The benefit of the foregoing observations will be largely lost unless the student looks up all the references cited.

The bearing of Old Testament quotations in the Gospels, and throughout the New Testament, on the subject of inspiration, must be obvious.

Unless inspiration and authority are denied to the New Testament Writings, they cannot be denied to those Writings of which the New Testament makes such large use. Both Christ and His Evangelists and Apostles quote and refer to the Old Testament Scriptures in a way that plainly implies that they firmly believed in the plenary inspiration of those Scriptures. There is no need to select specific passages because all the references illustrate the fact.

QUESTIONS

1 Into what two classes may references in the Gospels from the Old Testament be divided?

2 How are Old Testament references in the Gospels introduced?

3 What two things do Old Testament references in the Gospels imply?

4 From what Old Testament books did Christ quote, and from which books most frequently?

5 What was Christ's attitude towards the Old Testament?

6 In what relation to the Old Testament did Christ claim that He stood?

7 What bearing have Old Testament references in the Gospels on the matter of inspiration?

8 How would you distinguish between the temporary and the permanent elements in the Old Testament?

9 In what sense, if in any, is the whole of the Old Testament prophetic?

10 Are Christ's interpretations of the Old Testament, for example, of Psa. cx, authoritative and unerring?

11 Is, or is not, the Old Testament more than the miscellaneous literature of a Semitic race?

12 Study carefully Christ's references to the Old Testament in Luke **xxiv.**

LITERATURE

'The Quotations of the New Testament from the Old' - - - - - - - F. Johnson

'Our Lord's Use of the Old Testament' (Cambridge Biblical Essays) - - - - A. H. McNeile

'New Testament Questions' - - - - E. F. Scott

'Quotations in the New Testament' - - - C. H. Toy

'The Old Testament in the New' - - - D. C. Turpie

'New Testament View of the Old Testament' - D. C. Turpie

'New Testament Quotations (compared with the Hebrew and the LXX)' - - - - Gough

'Jesus and the Prophets' - - - - - McFarland

The Authorized and Revised Versions

AFTER nearly four years of work (1607-1611) there appeared a Version of the Bible in 1611, with this title:

> 'The Holy Bible, conteyning the Old Testament and the New: Newly Translated out of the Originall Tongues; and with the former Translations diligently compared and reuised by his Maiesties speciall Commandement. Appointed to be read in "Churches." Imprinted at London by Robert Barker, printer to the King's Most Excellent Maiestie. Anno Dom. 1611 '

And after about ten and a half years of work there appeared a Version of the Bible in 1881, with this title:

> 'The New Testament of our Lord and Saviour, Jesus Christ, translated out of the Greek: being the Version set forth A.D. 1611 compared with the most ancient authorities, and revised A.D. 1881 '

Four years later, in 1885, the revision of the Old Testament was completed, and the whole Revised Bible bore the title:

> 'The Holy Bible Containing the Old and New Testaments, Translated out of the Original Tongues. Being the Version set forth A.D. 1611, compared with the most ancient Authorities and Revised. Printed for the Universities of Oxford and Cambridge, at the University Press, 1885.'

The first of these Versions is known as the *Authorized*, and the second, as the *Revised Version* of the Bible.

The need and warrant for a Revised Version in the nineteenth century was fourfold:

(1) Access to more ancient manuscripts than were available in the seventeenth century, notably the Codex Vaticanus, and the Codex Sinaiticus, both of which date from the fourth century;

(2) The greatly developed science of textual criticism, which teaches the value and the best methods of dealing with documents;

(3) Better acquaintance, on the part of scholars, with the Sacred Languages;

(4) The fact that, ' owing to the growth of the English language itself, many words in the Authorized Version have become obsolete, and some have completely changed their meaning.'

For the first time is combined in the Revised Version the help derivable from the sources of Manuscripts, Versions, and Church Fathers, and so its greater accuracy is inevitable, and the importance of comparing the two should be fairly recognized.

It is easy to understand why Bible readers cling to the Authorized Version, Tyndale's incomparable translation, so lucid and limpid, and so haunting in its phrases, yet the claims of greater accuracy must be respected even though we lose something of the fascination of the older style.

For the purpose of comparison we take the first fifteen chapters and a few other passages of Matthew's Gospel, in order to show some of the gains to be derived from a study of the Revised Version, and we suggest that the lines here followed, as well as others, be pursued by the student throughout the Gospels.

The points selected for illustration, are: the definite article; prepositions; tenses; more faithful rendering; clearing up of obscurities; correction of errors; and an illustration of comparative study.

(i) The Definite Article

By a proper recognition of the *article*, the R.V., or the Greek text, or both, make the sacred narrative much more graphic. The following are some illustrations of this fact :

(*a*) IN SOME PLACES IN THE A.V. IT IS WRONGLY INTRODUCED

Matt. ix. 13 -	'I came not to call (the) righteous (ones), but sinners.'
Matt. x. 21 -	'(The) brother shall deliver up (the) brother to death, and (the) children shall rise up against (their) parents.'
Matt. x. 24 -	'A disciple is not above his master, nor a servant above his lord.' The omission of the definite article indicates that no particular disciple or servant is meant, but that what is said is true of every disciple and servant.
Matt. xiii. 39 -	'The reapers are (the) angels.'
Matt. xiii. 44 -	'Which a man found,' instead of ' the which when a man hath found.'
Matt. xxvi. 74 -	'A cock crew.'

(*b*) MUCH MORE FREQUENTLY THE A.V. IS AT FAULT BY OMIT-
TING THE ARTICLE; AND WHERE THE R.V. SUPPLIES IT THE
GAIN IS EVIDENT

Matt.	i. 23 -	' *The* virgin shall be with child.'
Matt.	ii. 4 -	' Where *the* Christ should be born.'
		In the Gospels *Christ* is not a title, but indicates an office, *the Messiah*. In the Epistles the definite article is dropped, almost always.
Matt.	iv. 5 -	' *The* pinnacle of the temple '; a well-known one.
Matt.	v. 1; -	' *The* mountain '; a recognized feature of the
	xiv. 23 -	landscape.
Matt.	v. 15 -	' *The* bushel '; ' *the* lampstand,' ordinary utensils in every house.
Matt.	vi. 13;	' *The* evil one '; not evil generally, but the
	xiii. 19, 38 -	devil.
Matt.	vi. 25 -	' Is not the life more than *the* food, and the body than *the* raiment? '
Matt.	vii. 4 -	' *The* beam,' just referred to (3).
Matt.	vii. 6 -	' *The* swine.'
Matt.	vii. 24, 25	' *The* rock.' The A.V. rightly has ' the sand,' in verse 26.
Matt.	viii. 12;	' *The* weeping.'
	xiii. 42, 50	
Matt.	viii. 32 -	' Rushed down *the* steep '; perhaps the only one there.
Matt.	ix. 11 -	' *The* publicans and sinners '; conspicuous offenders.
Matt.	x. 27 -	' *The* darkness,' and ' *the* light.'
Matt.	xii. 41 -	' *The* judgment.'
Matt.	xii. 35 -	' *The* good man.'
Matt.	xiii. 42 -	' *The* furnace of fire.'
Matt.	xiii. 3 -	' *The* sower.'
Matt.	xiii. 44 -	' *The* field.'
Matt.	xiv. 19, 22	' *The* disciples,' instead of 'his.'
Matt.	xv. 11, 20	' *The* man.'
Matt.	xv. 26 -	' *The* dogs.'
Matt.	xviii. 17 -	' *The* Gentile and *the* publican.'

(ii) **Prepositions**

For an understanding of much of the New Testament the
meaning and use of its prepositions is of great importance. This
Guide is not written for students of Greek, but those who know
no Greek can learn with little effort to appreciate the value of
the New Testament prepositions. Dr. A. T. Robertson has

truly said: 'There are pictures in prepositions if one has eyes to see them.'

Though we are here concerned, for illustrative purposes, only with the prepositions in Matthew's Gospel, it will be well to get a general idea of the meaning of the seventeen prepositions which occur in the New Testament, as we may refer later to those employed in the other Gospels.

Make a chart, as is done in Newberry's Bible, by which you can view the prepositions according to the idea of geometrical relationship.

Draw a large circle. In the centre of the circle draw a cube showing back, front, top, bottom, and two sides.

In this simple diagram the prepositions can be so placed as to show their main meaning. They are:

1	*epi*	- upon, over		10	*dia*	- through, on account of
2	*en*	- in, by		11	*ana*	- up
3	*eis*	- into, unto		12	*kata*	- down, against, during
4	*ek*	- out of, from (interior)		13	*meta*	- with (association), after
5	*pros*	- towards, to		14	*sun*	- with (co-operation)
6	*apo*	- away from (exterior)		15	*para*	- alongside of, from
7	*huper*	- above		16	*pro*	- before, in front of
8	*hupo*	- under, by		17	*anti*	- over against, instead of
9	*peri*	- around, concerning, about				

Now, place these in your chart as follows:

Put *epi* on the top of your cube, and *en* inside it, with their meanings.

On the left of the cube, inside the circle, put *eis*, and its meaning, and on the right of the cube, inside the circle, put *ek*, and its meaning, in both cases with an arrow pointing to the right.

On the left of the circle, and outside of it, put *pros*, and its meaning, and on the right of the circle, and outside of it, put *apo*, and its meaning, in both cases with an arrow pointing to the right.

Above the cube, inside the circle, put *huper*, and its meaning, and below the cube, inside the circle, put *hupo*, and its meaning.

Somewhere on the rim of the circle, and outside of it, put *peri*, and its meaning.

Inside the circle, slantwise, from left to right, draw an arrow, making it to pass through the cube, and at the left hand end of it write *dia*, and its meaning.

On a level with the bottom of the circle, outside of it on the left-hand side, draw an arrow pointing up, and write by it *ana*, and its meaning.

On the opposite side, on a level with the top of the circle, outside of it, draw an arrow pointing down, and write by it *kata*, and its meaning.

Twelve prepositions have now been placed. The remaining five may be put at the foot of your diagram, below one another, with their meanings, *para, anti, pro, sun, meta*.

It should not take more than a couple of hours to master this prepositional chart, and by doing so the English reader will have access to the wealth of New Testament teaching which is resident in these words.

Sometimes the R.V. follows the A.V. translation of a preposition, without indicating which of two words is employed in cases where both have a similar meaning. The following examples will make clear which of the prepositions is used, within the limits chosen for illustration.

The following nine examples are a selection only, but each of them throws light on the passage in which it occurs.

1 APO (ἀπό) FROM

Apo and *ek* both mean ' from,' but *apo* indicates the point of departure, from the exterior outward, and *ek* indicates source or origin, from the interior outward. You will now see why *apo* and not *ek* is used twice in chap. vii. 16, 'grapes *from* thorns; figs *from* thistles '; in xi. 29, ' learn *from* Me '; in xiv. 26, ' they cried out *from* fear,' that is, *on account of* it, or because of it, as in xviii. 7, *on account of* the offences.

This preposition appears in our word *apo*stasy (*apo-stasia*, away from standing, revolt), Acts xxi. 21; 2 Thess. ii. 3.

2 EK (ἐκ) FROM, OUT OF

See under *apo* how that preposition differs from this one, and you will appreciate the occurrence of the latter in such passages as iii. 9, ' God is able *from* (out of) these stones to raise up children to Abraham '; and iii. 17, ' A Voice *from* (out of) the heavens '; not *apo*, from the heavens as a point of departure, but from within the heavens the Voice came. Compare *apo* in verse 16.

This preposition appears in our word, *ec*centric, out of, i.e. *from* the centre.

3 ANTI (ἀντί) OVER AGAINST

This preposition illuminates chap. v. 38, 'eye *over against* eye, and tooth *over against* tooth.' It is found in many English words with the idea of over against, or opposite; e.g., *anti*podes, having the feet opposite one another; *anti*dote, given against, as of medicine, to counteract poison.

4 DIA (διά) THROUGH

The importance of this preposition in the following passages (*et al.*) must be apparent (i. 22; ii. 5, 15, 23; iv. 14; viii. 17; xii. 17), because it shows that the prophets were not the *originators* but only the *agents* of their messages; the word came, not *from*, but *through* them. See also, x. 22; xiv. 3, 9; where it means '*on account of* My name'; '*on account of* Herodias'; '*on account of* the oaths.'

This preposition appears in our word *diameter*, a straight line passing *through* the centre of a figure, dividing it into two equal parts.

5 EIS (εἰς) INTO, UNTO

This is the opposite of *ek*, and often indicates motion. In chap. vi. 26, read, 'look at (or *unto*) the birds of the heaven'; chap. vi. 34, ' Be not anxious *for* the morrow ' (lit., project not your anxieties *into* the morrow). In iii. 11, read, ' I indeed baptize you *in* (*en*) water *unto* (*eis*) repentance.

The prepositions in chap. xxi. 19 are illuminating. ' Seeing one fig tree *by* (*epi*, upon) the way, He came *to* (*epi*, upon) it, and found nothing *on* (*en*) it except leaves only, and He saith to it, "Let there be no fruit *from* (*ek*) thee *for* ever (*eis*, unto the age)." ' In chap. xxviii. 19, read, ' Baptizing them *into* (*eis*) the name ——.'

6 EN (ἐν) IN, BY

For illustration of the use of this preposition see chap. i. 20:
' That which is begotten *in* her '; chap. viii. 6, ' my servant
lieth *in* the house '; chap. v. 34, 35, 36, ' *by* the heaven, *by* the
earth, *by* the head '; chap. xi. 22, ' more tolerable *in* the day of
judgment'; chap. xiii. 49, ' so shall it be *in* the consummation
of the age'; chap. ix. 34, '*by* (not *through*) the prince of the
demons; chap. xiv. 13, ' *in* a boat,' instead of ' by ship.'

This preposition appears in our word *en*grave, to bury

7 EPI (ἐπί) ON, UPON

In chap. iv. 4, read, ' man shall not live *upon* bread alone ';
chap. vi. 10, not ' *in*,' but ' *upon* the earth '; chap. ix. 16, not
' *unto*,' but ' *upon* an old garment.'

8 PERI (περί) ABOUT, CONCERNING

In chap. vi. 28, read, ' why are ye anxious *concerning* raiment?';
chap. ix. 36, ' He was moved with compassion *concerning* them.'
In these passages the preposition refers to the object of thought.
Chap. xi. 10, ' this is He *concerning* whom it is written.'   Chap.
xv. 7, ' *concerning* you.'   Chap. viii. 18, ' Jesus saw great multitudes *around* (or *about*) Him.   Chap. iii. 4, ' a girdle of leather
around (or *about*) his loins.'

9 PARA (παρά) BY THE SIDE OF, FROM

This preposition is used in chap. xiii. 1, 4, 19.   In chap.
xxi. 42, read, ' this was *from* the Lord.'   The preposition is in
the word ' *Comforter*,' of the Holy Spirit, literally, *Para*clete,
one called *alongside of* (John xiv. 16).   It is also in the word
parable, which means *a placing side by side* (Heb. ix. 9, ' which
(is) a parable ').

(iii) **Tenses**

For a right understanding of numerous passages in the New
Testament, it is of the utmost importance to distinguish certain
tenses.   The four which are seen to greater advantage in the
R.V. than in the A.V. are the *present*, the *imperfect*, the *perfect*,
and the *aorist*.

(a) THE PRESENT TENSE

This generally denotes a state of action as now existing, though, in places, it has other significances. Chap. ii. 22: 'Archelaus *was reigning*,' not 'did reign.' Chap. iii. 1: 'In those days *cometh* John,' not 'came.' Chap. x. 12: 'As ye enter into the house,' literally, '*entering into* the house, salute it.'

(b) THE IMPERFECT TENSE

This denotes continued action in past time. Chap. iii. 14: not 'forbade him,' but '*would have hindered*,' or '*was hindering* him.' John laboured for a time to avoid baptizing Jesus. Chap. v. 2: neither the A.V. nor the R.V. brings out the meaning of the imperfect tense in this verse, which is, 'He opened His mouth, and *proceeded to teach* them.' This indicates that it was *a course of instruction*. Chap. xxiv. 1, '*was going* on His way,' not 'departed.'

(c) THE PERFECT TENSE

This denotes an action or event as now complete. Chap. ii. 20, '*they are dead*,' or '*they have died*.' Chap. v. 10: not, 'that are persecuted,' but '*that have been persecuted*.' Chap. *i*. 32: neither of our Versions gives the force of the last verb in this verse. The A.V. is nearer its meaning with 'that is divorced,' than the R.V., with 'when she is put away'; but it is a perfect participle, passive, and means, '*who has been put away*,' denoting a completed action.

The perfect tense does not occur often in Matthew's Gospel.

(d) THE AORIST TENSE

This tense is of great importance for interpretation. Its force is that of simply indicating that a certain thing *happened*, or *occurred, once for all, in past time*.

It differs from the imperfect in that it points to *momentary occurrence*, whereas the imperfect indicates *continuance*, or *duration*.

The aorist differs also from the perfect tense. The latter denotes a past act, the consequences of which remain, but the aorist has not this element of consequences in it.

Thus, in chap. ii. 20, the tense is the perfect, ' *they are dead,*' or ' *they have died.*' The aorist would have been, ' they died,' pointing to the occurrence of death.

The aorist tense is very prominent in Matthew, and denotes simply and graphically what *has taken place*. Compare the following examples of it with the A.V. rendering.

Chap. i. 24: ' Joseph *arose* from his sleep.' Chap. ii. 2: ' We *saw* his star.' Chap. ii. 15: ' Out of Egypt *did I call* My son,' referring to a past historic fact (Hosea xi. 1). Chap. iv. 16: ' Light *did spring* up.' Chap. v. 1: ' When He *had sat down.*' Chaps. v. 17; ix. 13; x. 34, 35 (*et al.*): ' I *came,*' not ' I am come.' Chap. v. 31, 38, 43: ' It *was said.*' Chap. vii. 22: ' *Did we not prophesy* . . . and *cast out* demons? ' Chap. x. 8: ' Freely *ye received.*' Chap. xi. 17: ' *We piped* unto you, and *ye did not dance*; *we wailed*, and *ye did not lament.*' Chap. xi. 25: ' *Thou didst hide* . . . and *didst reveal.*' Chap. xiii. 17: ' Many prophets and righteous (men) *desired* to see (those things) which ye see, and *did not see* (them); and to hear (those things) which ye hear, and *did not hear* (them).' Chap. xiii. 19, 20, 22, 23: ' He that *was sown.*' Chap. xiii. 44: ' A man *found* and *hid.*' Chap. xv. 13: ' Which my heavenly Father *planted* not.'

These examples only indicate what a wealth of instruction a proper translation of this tense offers.

(iv) More Faithful Rendering

For the most part, the R.V. is to be preferred for its more faithful and consistent rendering of certain words, some of which are in the margin, being preferred by the American revisers.

' Possessed with demons,' becomes ' demoniacs ' (iv. 24; viii. 16, 28, *et al.*). ' Devils,' becomes 'demons ' (viii. 31; ix. 34, *et al.*), and in places ' devil ' is translated ' demon ' (ix. 32; xi. 18; xv. 22; xvii. 18). ' Holy Ghost,' becomes ' Holy Spirit' (i. 18, 20; iii. 11; xii. 31, *et al.*). ' Hell ' becomes ' Gehenna ' (v. 22, 29; x. 28, *et al.*), or ' Hades ' (xi. 23; xvi. 18).

Distinction is drawn between the Temple with its courts (*hieron*, xxvi. 55), and the Sanctuary, the dwelling-place of God (*naos*, xxvii. 5).

(v) Clearing Up of Obscurities

'Take no thought,' which suggests indifference, becomes
'be not anxious,' which is an exhortation not to worry (vi. 25).
'Scrip' is exchanged for the better understood 'wallet' (x.
10). 'Usury' becomes 'interest' (xxv. 27). We use the word
'prevent' in the sense of 'hinder,' but it once meant 'to anticipate.' In chap. xvii. 25, for 'Jesus prevented him' (A.V.), the
R.V. has, 'Jesus spake first to him' (cf. 1 Thess. iv. 15). 'Pres-
ently' becomes 'immediately' (xxi. 19), and 'even now'
(xxvi. 53). 'Tribute' money, which was not a civil but a religious
tax, becomes 'the half shekel' (xvii. 24). 'Testament' becomes
'covenant' (xxvi. 28). 'Offend' becomes 'causeth to stumble'
(v. 29, 30), and 'offence' becomes 'stumbling-block' (xv. 23).
'Strawed' becomes 'spread' (xxi. 8), and 'hast not strawed'
becomes 'didst not scatter' (xxv. 24, 26). 'By and by he is
offended' becomes 'straightway he stumbleth' (xiii. 21).
'Coasts' becomes 'borders' (ii. 16). 'Goodman of the house'
becomes 'householder' (*oikodespotēs*, xxiv. 43, and should be
so in xx. 11).

(vi) Correction of Errors

Simon was not of Cana, nor was he a Canaanite, of heathen
stock, but he was a Cananæan, which is the Aramaic form of
the Greek *Zēlōtēs*, 'Zealot' (x. 4, cf. Luke vi. 15; Acts i. 13).
'Between the *temple* and the altar' is 'between the *sanctuary* and
the altar' (xxiii. 35; see under iv). 'Sat' is 'reclined,' for the
Jews did not sit at table as we do (ix. 10; xiv. 19, and always).
'Presented' becomes 'offered' (ii. 11), the word which is used
of religious offerings in the worship of God. 'The end of the
world' becomes 'the consummation of the age' (xxiv. 3).

(vii) An Illustration of Comparative Study

The above examples show the importance of comparing our
two great Versions, but a specific illustration of comparative
study should further convince us of its importance.

PARABLE OF THE SOWER
(Chapter xiii. 3-9, 18-23)

VERSE	A.V.	R.V.
3	A Sower	*The* sower
4	When he sowed	*As* he sowed
	The fowls	The *birds*
	Devoured them up	Devoured them (*up* omitted)
5	Some fell upon stony places	*Others* fell upon *the rocky* places
	Forthwith they sprung up	*Straightway* they *sprang* up
6	When the sun was up	When the sun was *risen*
7	And some fell among thorns	And *others* fell *upon the* thorns
	The thorns sprung up	The thorns *grew* up
8	But other fell into good ground	*And others* fell *upon the* good ground
	And brought forth fruit	And *yielded* fruit
	Some an hundredfold	Some *a* hundredfold
	Some sixtyfold	Some *sixty*
	Some thirtyfold	Some *thirty*
9	Who hath ears to hear	*He that* hath ears (*to hear* omitted)
18	Hear ye therefore	Hear *then* ye
19	The wicked one	The *evil* (one)
	And catcheth away	And *snatcheth* away
	That which was sown	That which *hath been* sown
	This is he which received seed	This is he *that was sown*
20	But he that received **the** seed into stony places	*And* he that *was sown upon* the *rocky* places
	The same is he	*This* is he
	And anon	And *straightway*
21	Dureth for a while	*Endureth* for a while
	For when	*And* when
	By and by he is offended	*Straightway* he *stumbleth*
22	He also that received seed among	*And he* that *was sown* among
	The care of this world	The care of *the* world (age)
23	But he that received seed into the good ground	*And* he that *was sown upon* the good ground
	Is he	*This* is he
	Which also	*Who verily*
	An hundredfold	*A* hundredfold

3 ' The,' probably some actual sower was in view.
4 ' As,' points to the very process of sowing.
5 ' Upon the rocky places.' This shows that what is referred to is not a field covered with loose stones, such as would help to retain its moisture, but to a rocky bed covered over with a thin sprinkling of earth.
7 ' Upon the thorns,' which were lurking in the ground, but were not yet flourishing.
19 ' Hath been sown,' shows that while the sowing was completed the seed still lay undisturbed in the heart of the wayside hearer.
   ' He that was sown.' The seed is identified with the person receiving it (20. 22).

In the reading syllabus at the beginning of the study of each Gospel it is recommended that, as a preparation for the studies following, the whole Gospel be read first in the A.V., and then in the R.V., and also in a modern translation. For the first two readings a Parallel, a Two Version, or an Interlinear Bible will be best, that the student may see the differences between the Versions as he reads.

QUESTIONS

1 What need and occasion were there for a Revised Version of the New Testament?
2 In St. Matthew's Gospel name three passages in which the A.V. introduces the definite article where it should not be; and six passages in which it omits it where it should be.
3 Name, with their meanings, the seventeen Greek prepositions.
4 What is the difference in meaning between *apo* and *ek*? Give two passages in Matthew in which *apo* occurs, and two in which *ek* occurs, bringing out their meanings.
5 Translate Matthew xxi. 19, giving the prepositions their proper force.
6 How is the meaning of the preposition *para* reflected in a word in John xiv. 16, and one in Heb. ix. 9?
7 What, respectively, do the *present, imperfect, perfect,* and *aorist* tenses denote? Give an illustration of each in the first Gospel.
8 Give examples, in Matthew, of the more accurate rendering of the Revised Version.
9 Illustrate, also from Matthew, the way in which the R.V. clears up obscurities.
10 Study carefully, side by side, the two Versions of Matt. xiii. 3-9, 18-23.

LITERATURE

' The Expository Value of the Revised Version ' G. Milligan
'Some Lessons of the Revised Version of the
        New Testament '   -   -   -   -   Bp. Westcott
Authorized or Revised?'   -   -   -   Dean Vaughan
'Addresses on the Revised Version of Holy
        Scripture '.   -   -   -   -   -   S.P.C.K.
    Classical Revision of the New Testament ' W. M. Nicolson
' Remarks on the Revised Version of the New
        Testament '   -   -   -   -   B. W. Newton
'Holy Bible ' (Two Version Edition)   -   (Pickering and Inglis)
    Revised Standard Version of the New Testament ' (1946, Nelson)
    The New Testament Newly Translated '   -   Ronald A. Knox
    8

YEAR		NAME OF MONTH		FESTIVALS	SEASON
SACRED	CIVIL	JEWISH	ENGLISH		
I	7	**Nisan** or **Abib** Exod. xii. 2; xiii. 4 Ezra vii. 9 Neh. ii. 1 Esth. iii. 7	March-April	14th **Passover.** Exod. xii. 1-51 15th-21st. Days of Unleavened Bread (Lev. xxiii. 6) 16th First-fruits of Barley Harvest presented (Lev. xxiii. 10-14; Deut. xvi. 9; 2 Kings iv. 42)	Latter or Spring rains (Joel ii. 23; Deut. xi. 14) Streams in flood (Josh. iii. 15, cf., 1 Chron. xii. 15; Jer. xii. 5) (Ezra x. 9; John xviii. 18) Barley, wheat, figs (Zech. x. 1; Mark xi. 13; Matt. xxi. 19) Apricots ripening
II	8	**Zif,** later **Iyyar** 1 Kings vi. 1, 37 2 Chr. xxx. 15	April-May	14th Second, or Little Passover for those who could not keep the first (Num. ix. 10, 11)	Principal harvest month in lower districts (Ruth i. 22) Wheat begins to ripen
III	9	**Sivan** Esth. viii. 9	May-June	6th **Pentecost,** or Feast of Weeks, or of Harvest, Loaves of first-fruits of Wheat harvest presented (Exod. xxiii. 19; Lev. xxiii. 17, 20; Deut. xvi. 9, 10; xxvi. 2, 10; Esth. viii. 9)	Summer begins. No rain until October. Heavy dews (Psa. cxxxiii. 3; Hos. xiv. 5; Job xxix. 19; 1 Sam. xii. 17; Prov. xxvi. 1; Hos. vi. 4; xiii. 3)
IV	10	**Tammuz** Zech. viii. 19	June-July		Hot. Country parched and dry Grapes begin to ripen
V	11	**Ab** Ezra vii. 9	July-August		Intense heat. Principal fruit month: Grapes, figs, olive, walnut
VI	12	**Elul** Neh. vi. 15	Aug.-Sept.		Intense heat. General grape harvest (2 Kings iv. 18-20; Psa. cxxi. 6; Isa. xlix. 10; Rev vii. 16)

VII	1	**Tishri**, or **Ethanim** 1 Kings viii. 2 2 Chr. v. 3	Sept.-Oct.	1st **Feast of Trumpets** (Lev. xxiii. 24, 25) **New Year's Day** (Num. xxix. 1) 10th **Day of Atonement** (Lev. xvi. 29, 30; xxiii. 27, 28) 'The Fast' (Acts xxvii. 9) the only one enjoined by the law 15th-21st **Feast of Tabernacles**, or ingathering. Living in tents (Lev. xxiii. 34). First-fruits of Wine and Oil (Deut. xvi. 13). The Harvest Home, and greatest national festival. A final thanksgiving for the year's crops. Commemoration of the Wanderings (Lev. xxiii. 39, 43) 22nd 'The Great Day' (Num. xxix. 35; John vii. 37)	Former or earlier autumnal rains begin (Joel ii. 23; Deut. xi. 14) Planting begins. Nights frosty (Gen. xxxi. 40) Ploughing and Sowing begin (Prov. xx. 4; Eccles. xi. 4) Hot days. Cold nights Ploughing and Sowing begin, in whatever weather, as time runs short (Prov. xx. 4; Eccles. xi. 4)
VIII	2	**Bul**, or **Cheshvan** 1 Kings vi. 38	Oct.-Nov.		Wheat and Barley sown. Continued rain. Gathering of latter grapes; also olives
IX	3	**Chisleu**, or **Kislev** Neh. i. 1 Zech. vii. 1	Nov.-Dec.	25th **Feast of Dedication** for 8 days; commemoratory of the purification of the Temple (defiled by Antiochus Epiphanes, Dan. xi. 31) by Judas Maccabeus (1 Macc. iv. 52-59), or (from the general illumination made) Feast of Lights. The anniversary of the erection of David's altar on Araunah's threshing floor	Winter begins (John x. 22) Snow on highlands
X	4	**Tebeth** Esth. ii. 16	Dec.-Jan.		Mid-winter. Coldest month Rain, hail, snow (Josh. x. 11) on higher hills. Groves, pastures of the Jordan valley scarlet with anemones and poppies. Oranges ripening. Lower districts becoming green with corn
XI	5	**Shebat** Zech. i. 7	Jan.-Feb.		Weather becoming warmer. In sheltered localities almond and peach trees begin to blossom. Winter figs on leafless trees. Oranges ripe
XII	6	**Adar** Esth. iii. 7; ix. 21-28	Feb.-Mar.	14th-15th **Feast of Purim**, or Lots, in commemoration of the deliverance recorded in Esther, which is read in the Synagogues	The latter rains begin on which, plenty or famine, the crops and pastures depend Almond trees in blossom Oranges and lemons in the lowlands

The Twelve Apostles

THE word *apostolos* is worth considering. It is *apo-stolos*, and is derived from *apo-stellō*. *Stollos* means an expedition, a voyage, a journey, and *stellō* means to despatch on an expedition, to set out on a journey; and *apo* means away from; so that *apostellō* means to send forth, or away, usually on some mission; and the *apostolos* is the one so sent.

Both the verb and the noun occur very often in the New Testament, the verb usually being translated *send*, and the noun, *apostle*. The verb occurs 97 times, and the noun 9 times in the Gospels.

The title *apostoloi* was given in a special sense to the Twelve, but was not confined to them. Paul, Barnabas, and James the Lord's brother, are called apostles, and the use of the word was even wider (cf. Rom. xvi. 7), and it is once applied to Christ (Heb. iii. 1).

(i) LISTS OF THE APOSTLES

Of these there are four, as follows:

MARK iii. 16-19	MATTHEW x. 2-4	LUKE vi. 14-16	ACTS i. 13 (26)
1 S I M	O N	P E T E	R
2 James	Andrew	Andrew	James
3 John	James	James	John
4 Andrew	John	John	Andrew
5	P H I	L I P	
6 Bartholomew	Bartholomew	Bartholomew	Thomas
7 Matthew	Thomas	Matthew	Bartholomew
8 Thomas	Matthew	Thomas	Matthew
9 J A	M E S	(o f A l p h	a c u s)
10 Thaddæus	Thaddæus	Simon the Zealot	Simon the Zealot
11 Simon the Cananæan	Simon the Cananæan	Judas (of James)	Judas (of James)
12 Judas Iscariot	Judas Iscariot	Judas Iscariot	—

Observe that the Twelve are divided into three groups of four Apostles each, in all four lists.

In all the lists Peter heads the first group, Philip, the second group, and James (of Alphæus) the third group.

In all the lists each group has the same persons, but after the first name there is variety in the order. In group 1, Mark and Acts agree, in the A.V., but in the R.V. John comes before James; and Matthew and Luke agree. In group 2, Mark and Luke agree; and Matthew and Acts agree in putting Matthew last. In group 3, Mark and Matthew agree; and Luke and Acts agree, except that in Acts the name of Judas Iscariot is dropped out because of his death, and Matthias takes his place (i. 26). In the three Synoptic lists, Peter is at the top, and Judas Iscariot at the bottom.

There is no list of the Twelve in the Fourth Gospel, their having existed being assumed (vi. 67, 70; xx. 24).

(ii) SURNAMES OR APPELLATIONS OF THE APOSTLES

SIMON is called Peter, and Cephas, both words meaning rock (Mark iii. 16; John i. 42).

JAMES and JOHN are called Boanerges, meaning 'sons of thunder,' probably because they were of a fiery temper (Mark iii. 17; ix. 38; Luke ix. 54).

THOMAS is called Didymus, which is Greek for a 'twin' (John xi. 16; xx. 24; xxi. 2). As in all three Synoptics he is coupled with Matthew, quite possibly they were twins. Plummer says: 'The coincidence between the name and his twin-mindedness (James i. 8; iv. 8) is remarkable'; and Trench says: 'In him the twins, unbelief and faith, were contending with one another for mastery, as Esau and Jacob in Rebecca's womb.'

JAMES is called the Less (Mark xv. 40), which has been supposed to distinguish him from the other James, John's brother, but as the word is *mikros*, it probably refers to his having been *little* of stature.

LEVI (Luke v. 27) is called Matthew, which means 'the gift of God,' a name which seems to have been adopted by him after his call (Matt. ix. 9; x. 3; Mark ii. 14).

JUDAS (of James, Luke vi. 16; Acts i. 13) is called Thaddæus in Matt. x. 3; Mark iii. 18; and Lebbæus in Matt. x. 3, A.V

Lebbæus is only a marginal explanation of Thaddæus. Dr.
A. T. Robertson says that both appellations are terms of endear-
ment, but Dean Alford says it is impossible to say what they
mean.

SIMON is called the Cananæan (Matt. x. 4; Mark iii. 18), and
the Zealot (Luke vi. 15; Acts i. 13). Cananæan does not mean
' Canaanite,' nor ' man of Cana,' but is the Greek form of the
Aramaic *Kanan*, which means Zealot. The fierce party of the
Zealots acknowledged no king save God. This Apostle, before
his call, may have belonged to this sect of fanatics, who thought
any deed of violence justifiable for the recovery of national
freedom.

JUDAS is called Iscariot, which probably means ' man of
Kerioth,' a place ten miles from Hebron, in the southern border
of Judah. If this is the meaning of Iscariot, Judas was the only
non-Galilean among the Apostles.

(iii) PARENTS OF THE APOSTLES

SIMON PETER, and ANDREW, were the sons of Jonas (or John,
R.V.; John i. 42; xxi. 15).

JAMES and JOHN were the sons of Zebedee and Salome (Matt.
xx. 20; xxvii. 56: Mark xv. 40; xvi. 1).

MATTHEW, or Levi, was the son of Alphæus (Mark ii. 14).

JAMES, the Less, and JUDE, were the sons of Alphæus and Mary.
This Alphæus is not the same as the father of Matthew. In
John xix. 25, it would seem that Mary, the wife of Clopas (not
Cleopas, Luke xxiv. 18, a sister of our Lord's mother) is the
mother of James the Less, and Jude, so that Clopas was Alphæus.

JUDAS was the son of Simon (John vi. 71; xiii. 26). In both
these references the word ' Iscariot ' is attached to Simon and
not to Judas, which means that father and son had the same
name because they were from Kerioth, in Judæa (see under (ii),
Judas).

(iv) HOMES OF THE APOSTLES

Peter, Andrew, James, John, and Philip lived at Bethsaida
(Mark i. 16-20; John i. 44; xii. 21).

Peter, Andrew, James, and John later on lived at Capernaum (Mark i. 21, 29).

John later still lived at Jerusalem (Acts iii. 1; xv. 6; Gal. ii. 1, 9), and finally at Ephesus. Dr. Plummer says: 'That St. John did work at Ephesus during the latter part of his life may be accepted as certain, unless the whole history of the sub-apostolic age is to be pronounced doubtful.'

Matthew also lived at Capernaum (Mark ii. 1, 14).

Bartholomew, i.e. Nathanael, lived at Cana of Galilee (John xxi. 2).

Thomas, James the Less, Jude, and Simon the Zealot, all lived in Galilee, so that Judas Iscariot was the only Judæan among the Apostles.

(v) Occupations of the Apostles

Peter, Andrew, James, and John were fishermen (Mark i. 16, 19).

Before his conversion Matthew was a Tax Collector (Matt. ix. 9).

(vi) Relations of the Apostles

It would appear that many of the Apostles were related to one another and to Christ. Simon and Andrew were brothers, James and John were brothers. James the Less and Jude were brothers. Philip and Bartholomew (Nathanael) may have been brothers. As Andrew went to find his brother, it is likely that Philip went to find his (John i. 40, 41, 43-45).

Thomas and Matthew may have been brothers (see under (ii)).

If Salome, the wife of Zebedee, was the sister of the Virgin (John xix. 25; see under (iii)), James and John were the cousins of Jesus, and He may have had other relations among His Apostles. (See p. 62).

(vii) Writings of the Apostles

Of the Twelve Apostles three have written Holy Scripture. Matthew, a Gospel; Peter, two Epistles, in addition to his being responsible for Mark's Gospel; John, a Gospel, three Epistles, and the Revelation. Thus nine of the twenty-seven books of the New Testament, or one third of the whole, are the work of Apostles.

(viii) MINISTRY AND END OF THE APOSTLES

For these particulars we are dependent largely upon tradition, and cannot attain to certainty.

SIMON PETER was the first leader of the Christian Church (Acts i-xv., Gal. ii. 9); and it is supposed that he was crucified upside down, at Rome (cf. John xxi. 18, 19).

JAMES (of Zebedee) preached in Judæa. Was beheaded by Herod Antipas, about A.D. 44 (Acts xii. 1, 2).

JOHN (of Zebedee). Laboured in Jerusalem, and from Ephesus among the Churches of Asia Minor. Was banished to Patmos in the reign of Nero, or of Domitian; was liberated, and died a natural death at Ephesus (cf. John xxi. 20-23).

ANDREW, originally a disciple of John the Baptist. Preached in Scythia, Greece, and Asia Minor. Was crucified on a St. Andrew's Cross.

PHILIP, preached in Phrygia, and died a martyr at Hierapolis.

BARTHOLOMEW, a missionary in Armenia. Was flayed to death.

THOMAS, laboured in Parthia, Persia, and India. Suffered martyrdom near Madras, at Mount St. Thomas.

MATTHEW, ministered in Ethiopia. Was martyred.

JAMES the Less, preached in Palestine and Egypt, in which latter country he was crucified.

JUDE, preached in Assyria and Persia, in which latter country he was martyred.

SIMON the Zealot. Was crucified.

JUDAS Iscariot, served nowhere, and hanged himself (Matt. xxvi. 14-16; xxvii. 3-5; Acts i. 16-20).

If these traditions have any truth in them, only one of the Apostles died a natural death; one committed suicide; and ten suffered martyrdom, four of them by crucifixion.

QUESTIONS

1 In what months respectively, Jewish and English, were the Feasts of Passover, Pentecost, and Tabernacles celebrated?
2 Name the Twelve Apostles.
3 How often, and where, is the list of the Apostles recorded?
4 How are the lists of the Twelve divided?
5 Name some features of these lists.
6 Who were the parents of Peter, John, and Matthew?
7 Who, of the Apostles, have written Holy Scripture, and what?
8 Write a brief account of Peter and John.
9 What were the occupations of the Apostles so far as is known?
10 Was Nathanæl one of the Twelve?
11 Were any of the Apostles related to one another, or to Jesus?
12 Was Judas Iscariot a converted man? If not, why was he an Apostle?

LITERATURE

'The Glorious Company of the Apostles' -   - J. D. Jones
'Bible Characters' -   -   -   -   -   - Alexander Whyte
'Pastor Pastorum' -   -   -   -   -   - H. Latham
'The Training of the Twelve' -   -   -   - A. B. Bruce
For both the 'Jewish Calendar,' and the 'Apostles,'
    see Hastings' Bible Dictionary, and Dictionary
    of Christ and the Gospels .
Smith's Bible Dictionary -   -   -   -   - ———
The New Schaff-Herzog Encyclopædia of Religious
    Knowledge
Encyclopædia of Religion and Ethics -   -   - ———
The Standard Lives of Christ -   ·.   ·.   -   ———·

The Herodian Family

ELEVEN members of the Herodian family are mentioned in the New Testament, in the Gospels and Acts, and it is important that their relation to one another be understood, and that the several Herods be distinguished.

The following names are not inclusive, some having been omitted because they are not relevant to our present purpose.

(a) DIAGRAM

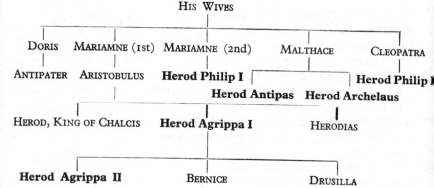

Herod the Great

HIS WIVES

DORIS	MARIAMNE (1st)	MARIAMNE (2nd)	MALTHACE	CLEOPATRA
ANTIPATER	ARISTOBULUS	**Herod Philip I**		**Herod Philip II**
		Herod Antipas **Herod Archelaus**		

HEROD, KING OF CHALCIS   **Herod Agrippa I**   HERODIAS

Herod Agrippa II   BERNICE   DRUSILLA

The names in black type are of importance for the Gospels and Acts.

(b) REFERENCES

Herod the Great	-	Matt. ii. 1-3, 7, 9, 12-19, 22; Luke i. 5
Herod Philip I	-	Matt. xiv. 3; Mark vi. 17; Luke iii. 19
Herod Antipas	-	Matt. xiv. 1, 3, 6, 9; Mark vi. 14, 16-22, 25-27; Luke iii. 1-19; viii. 3; ix. 7, 9; xxiii. 7-12, 15; Acts iv. 27; xiii. 1
Herod Archelaus	-	Matt. ii. 22; Luke xix. 12-27
Herod Philip II	-	Luke iii. 1
Salome - -	-	Matt. xiv. 6 ff; Mark vi. 22 ff
Herod Agrippa I	-	Acts xii
Herodias	-	Matt. xiv. 3, 6 ff.; Mark vi. 17, 19, 22 ff.
Herod Agrippa II	-	Acts xxv. 13 ff.; xxvi. 1
Bernice	-	Acts xxv. 13, 23; xxvi. 30
Drusilla	-	Acts xxiv. 24

(c) NOTES

Herod the Great - made King by the Romans, B.C. 40. Sole King of Judæa, B.C. 37. Died B.C. 4. Christ was born in his reign.

Aristobulus - married Bernice, the daughter of Salome, and sister of Herod the Great. He was the son of the first Mariamne, and was put to death by his father in B.C. 6.

Herod Philip I - The son of the second Mariamne. He married Herodias, and Salome was his daughter.

Herod Antipas - The Tetrarch of Galilee. He married the daughter of Aretas, the King of Arabia, and later, Herodias, the wife of Herod Philip I. He was the son of Malthace. He beheaded John the Baptist. Jesus appeared before him in the Passion Week. He was banished in A.D. 40.

Archelaus - Son of Malthace. Ethnarch of Judæa, Idumæa, and Samaria, B.C. 4. Was deposed and banished in A.D. 6.

Herod Philip II - Son of Cleopatra. Tetrarch of Iuræa and Trachonitis. He married Salome, the daughter of Philip I and Herodias. Died A.D. 34.

Herod Agrippa I - Son of Aristobulus, and grandson of Herod the Great by the first Mariamne. He succeeded to the Tetrarchy of Philip II, in A.D. 37, and of Herod Antipas, in A.D. 40. Judæa and Samaria were added in A.D. 41. He killed James, the brother of John, and was eaten of worms in A.D. 44.

Herodias - The daughter of Aristobulus and the first Mariamne. She married Philip I, whom she left for Herod Antipas. Salome was her daughter.

Herod Agrippa II - Son of Agrippa I, A.D. 48-53. Succeeded to Tetrarchy of Philip II, A.D. 53-70. Was the last Herodian Prince. He heard Paul's defence. After the fall of Jerusalem, in A.D. 70, he retired to Rome, and died in A.D. 100.

Bernice - Daughter of Herod Agrippa I, and sister of Agrippa II. She married Herod, King of Chalcis, the son of Aristobulus and the first Mariamne.

Drusilla - Daughter of Herod Agrippa I; sister of Agrippa II, and of Bernice. She married Felix, Governor of Judæa, before whom Paul made his defence.

"*After visiting Palestine, Renan found it to reflect so thoroughly the life and lessons of Jesus, that to him it appeared like a fifth Gospel. The teaching of Jesus in Galilee and Judæa respectively has a flavour of the soil. This feature is one of the numberless traces of reality that mark the life of Christ as delineated in the four Gospels, and that justify the remark that it were far more wonderful that the life should have been a myth, than that it should have been a reality.*"

DR. BLAIKIE,
'Witness of Palestine to the Bible.'

THE GOSPELS
VIEWED SYNTHETICALLY

PART II—PARTICULAR

Division A

THE GOSPELS VIEWED SYNTHETICALLY

Part II—PARTICULAR

I

KEY PLAN OF READING

TWELVE STUDIES

2

THE WRITINGS

WHEN we turn to the first four Books in the New Testament we see that the headings are, ' The Gospel according to Saint Matthew,' Mark, Luke, John, by which is meant that these men wrote them. In the first, are 28 chapters; in the second, 16; in the third, 24; and in the fourth, 21; 89 chapters altogether. The first three are called the *Synoptic* Gospels (Greek: *sun* and *opsis*, conspectus, seeing together) because they present the same general view of the several events, because they go over the same ground in the story they tell, whereas the author of the Fourth Gospel follows lines of his own. For this reason the writers of the first three Records are called the *Synoptists*. These Gospels which, as to size, are mere pamphlets, are the most precious Writings in all the world. But for what we are told in them there would have been no preceding Old Testament, and no following Acts, Epistles, and Revelation. They are the heart of Divine revelation, because they are the record of the manifestation of God on earth, in the Person of His Son, for the purpose of redemption.

3

DESIGNATION

The term *The Gospels*, was used in a technical sense, first of all by Justin Martyr in the second century, and by it he meant the Four Gospels which we have. By *gospel* is meant *good news*, and by *Gospels*, the presentation of that news by the writers of these records. The *Good News* of these records is the message of salvation, so that, in reality, there is but one Gospel. The term is found in this sense in *Matthew* (iv. 23; ix. 35; xxiv. 14; xxvi. 13), and in *Mark* (i. 1, 14, 15; viii. 35; *et al.*). The verb *to preach good tidings* occurs ten times in *Luke's* Gospel (i. 19; ii. 10; iii. 18; iv. 18, 43; vii. 22; viii. 1; ix. 6; xvi. 16; xx. 1), but the substantive does not occur.

The verb, *euaggelizo*, meaning *to preach the gospel*, to bring or declare good tidings, occurs in the New Testament 54 times, of which 10 are in the Gospels. The substantive *euaggelion*, meaning *gospel*, from *eu*, good, and *aggelia*, message, occurs in the New Testament 77 times, of which 12 are in the Gospels. The word, *euaggelistēs*, meaning *evangelist*, occurs 3 times in the New Testament, but not in the Gospels. From this we get our words evangel, evangelic, evangelical, evangelicalism, evangelically, evangelism, evangelistic, evangelize, evangelist, and evangelization.

Each of the Gospels has its own character. From the time of Irenæus (end of 2nd century) they were likened to the Cherubim of Ezekiel's vision, and there are traces of this in Christian art, as far back as the fifth century. Every possible allocation of the figures has been made, but that which seems best to agree with the character of the Gospels is the Lion to Matthew, the Ox to Mark, the Man to Luke, and the Eagle to John; because Matthew presents the King; Mark, the servant; Luke, the Son of Man; and John, the Son of God. Early Christian writers compared these Gospels to the river which flowed out of Eden to water the Garden of God, and which was parted into four (Gen. ii. 10-14), and truly ' the gold of that land is good.'

Matthew's Gospel is for the Jews; Mark's is for the Romans; Luke's is for the Greeks; and John's is for the Christian Church. Matthew's is the Gospel of the Past; Mark's, of the Present; Luke's, of the Future; and John's is the Gospel of Eternity. Matthew's Gospel is Didactic; Mark's is Anecdotal; Luke's is Historical; and John's is Spiritual. These generalizations are sufficiently distinctive to be worthy of note. (See 'Diagrammatic View of the Gospels,' p. 95).

4

CHARACTER

These Gospels cannot, in any sense, be called Lives of Christ, because of their evident fragmentariness. Assuming that they were written independently, the omissions in Matthew, Mark, and Luke plainly show that it was not the intention of the authors of them to write the full story of Jesus as they knew it first-hand (Matthew), or second-hand (Mark, Luke). In illustration of this, observe that Matthew says nothing about Christ's ascension,

9

although he was a witness of it; and none of these writers says anything about, what, probably, was the greatest act of Jesus, alike in itself and its consequences, the raising of Lazarus. Observe, also, that many miracles which Jesus performed are barely referred to (Matt. iv. 23, 24; xii. 15; xv. 30, 31: John ii. 23 ; xix. 2), and John speaks of 'many signs which are not written ' (xx. 30; xxi. 25). The fragmentariness of these Gospels is best seen in the fact that, with the exception of the Infant narratives, and the story of Jesus' first Passover, they have nothing to say (except in two verses, Luke ii. 40, 51, 52) about thirty-two of Christ's thirty-five years of life on earth.

On the other hand, these Records are more than *notes* on the words and deeds of Jesus. Justin Martyr frequently quotes from the ' Memoirs of the Apostles, which are called Gospels,' and perhaps the word *memoirs* best describes them.

5

AUTHORSHIP

Reference has been made to the words at the head of each of these Books, *The Gospel according to*. By *according to* (Greek: *kata*) is not meant (*a*) that the writer is the originator of his Gospel; nor (*b*) that an unnamed person is reporting some one else; but (*c*) that the good news of salvation is told by these four men, Matthew, Mark, Luke, and John, or whoever is supposed to have written them.

Assuming that the Gospels were written by the men whose names they bear, observe that three of them were Jews, and one a Gentile. Observe, also, that two of them, Matthew and John, were Apostles; that one of them, Mark, was the companion of an Apostle (Peter); and that the other, Luke, was not related in any way to the Twelve.

But the question of authorship, especially of the First and Fourth Gospels, is one of considerable controversy, and the whole matter should be thoroughly explored, as in no case is the title of a Book of the New Testament part of the original document.

St. Matthew

Dr. Plummer has said that the authorship of the First Gospel
' is a complicated problem not yet adequately solved.'

We have said that the word ' according to ' does not affirm
or deny that the person named in the title is the writer of the
Gospel, but implies ' conformity to a type.' Whether or not
Matthew the Apostle wrote the Gospel which bears his name
must be determined on more substantial ground than that of the
title attached to the Writing.

Modern Biblical scholarship is almost unanimous in its opinion
that this Gospel was not written by Matthew the Apostle, but
antiquity is unanimous in the belief that the Apostle was the
writer of it. This belief is borne witness to by Papias, Irenæus,
Origen, Eusebius, and a number of other writers from the end
of the second century onwards. (For these names see ' Church
Fathers,' Div. A, Part I, Sec. 3, iii, p. 38).

The earliest tradition is a brief statement which Eusebius
quotes from Papias, Bishop of Hierapolis, not long after A.D.
110, to the effect:

> ' So then, Matthew, indeed, in the Hebrew language put
> together the Logia in writing; but as to their interpretation,
> each man dealt with it as he was able.'

Take special note of this statement, as it is of vital importance,
and will be used again. It has been the cause of endless controversy, because it is not certain what is meant by the *Logia*,
or Doctrines (literally, Words); but the independent witness
of Origen leaves no room for doubt as to what was the unanimous
belief from the end of the second century. He says: ' As I have
learned by tradition concerning the Four Gospels, which alone
are received without dispute by the Church of God under heaven:
the first was written by St. Matthew, once a tax-gatherer, afterwards an Apostle of Jesus Christ, who published it for the benefit
of the Jewish converts, composed in the Hebrew language.'

This statement may seem to settle the question, but there are
difficulties which cannot be overlooked, two of which must
be mentioned.

Firstly: It can be regarded as certain that our canonical Gospel was not written in Hebrew (Aramaic), but in Greek, which fact contradicts the testimony of Origen, and of Papias, if by the *Logia* he meant the Gospel which we have.

Secondly: We find in Matthew the substance of 606 out of the 661 verses of Mark's Gospel, or to put it another way, of the 1068 verses of Matthew (in the R.V.) all but 462 are dependent on Mark; that is, the whole of Mark is traceable in Matthew, with the exception of 55 verses. (See pp. 86, 186, 253).

But it is objected, an Apostle who had known the Lord so directly and intimately, and for so long, would not be likely to take over so much material from the record of one who was not an Apostle at all.

The question is, can these conflicting facts and ideas be harmonized?

To take the second objection first : Papias, quoted above, said of Mark that he ' became Peter's interpreter, and wrote accurately as many things as he remembered of the things said or done by Christ' (p. 134); and Origen, speaking of the Gospels, says: 'The second is that according to Mark, who prepared it as Peter guided him.'

Similar witness is borne by Justin Martyr, Tertullian, Irenæus, Jerome, and Eusebius. Matthew, therefore, by using Mark, was really using the material supplied by the discourses of Peter, which discourses Mark heard, and, in all likelihood, made notes of, which notes are the substance of the second Gospel. The report of Peter's sermon at Cæsarea (Acts x. 34-43), is remarkably like the general outline of Mark's Gospel. (See pp. 183, 188).

Matthew, therefore, by quoting Mark, would be using the Memoirs of another Apostle, of an Apostle who was called before he was. Dr. W. C. Allen, however, goes so far as to say: ' It is indeed not impossible, but it is very improbable, that an Apostle should rely upon the work of another for the entire framework of his narrative '; and he asserts that in ascribing this Gospel to the Apostle ' tradition has gone astray.'

As to the first objection: everything turns upon whether or not our canonical Gospel is to be identified with the *Logia* of which

Papias speaks, and which, he declares, was written by Matthew.

If these two Writings are one and the same, we are confronted with an insoluble problem, which briefly is this: Papias declares that Matthew wrote in Hebrew, but it is certain that our canonical Matthew was not translated from Hebrew into Greek, but was written in Greek.

It is not necessary, however, to assume the identity of Papias' *Logia* and our St. Matthew, although it seems clear that Matthew wrote something in Hebrew for Hebrews, as both Papias, Irenæus, and Origen affirm, and there are the best of reasons for supposing that it was a preliminary Collection of the Saviour's Sayings, which he afterwards incorporated, in part at least, in the canonical Gospel, which he wrote in Greek.

This simple assumption harmonizes the seeming contradictions, and has in support of its possibility the fact that Josephus wrote his History first in Hebrew, and then in Greek, for universal circulation.

In any case, the value of this Gospel is not dependent on who wrote it, but upon its contents. Nevertheless, in the absence of absolute proof to the contrary, it does not show a want of intelligence to believe that it is of Apostolic authority.

Though a majority of scholars attribute the Gospel to an unknown evangelist, whom they call the 'compiler,' we accept the verdict of Origen, already quoted (except that Matthew wrote in Hebrew: pp. 131, 250), and of Dr. Morison, when he says: 'There is, indeed, no evidence that, within the circle of the early Christian Church, it was ever doubted that *Matthew's Gospel* was really Matthew's. There is still no more reason to doubt it, than there is to doubt that Virgil's *Aeneid* was written by Virgil, or that Bunyan's *Pilgrim's Progress* was composed by the tinker of Elstow.' (See Div. B, Matthew's Gospel, Sec. 8, 'Sources,' p. 251).

St. Mark

It may be accepted as sufficiently attested that Mark wrote the Second (really the First) Gospel, and that for his material he was largely dependent upon the preaching of Peter. This is the verdict of the Church Fathers from the second century.

Papias puts on record, what he must have received on good authority, that:

> 'Mark, having become Peter's interpreter, wrote accurately, though not in order, all that he remembered of the things which were either said or done by Christ. For he was neither a hearer of the Lord nor a follower of Him, but afterwards, as I said (followed) Peter, who used to adapt his instructions to the needs (of his hearers), but without making a connected report of the Lord's sayings. So that Mark committed no error when he wrote down some things just as he remembered them; for of one thing he made a purpose from the first, not to omit any one of the things which he heard, or state anything falsely among them.'

Dr. Plummer says of this statement that it 'is evidence of the highest importance. Papias can hardly have got this information much later than A.D. 100, and he got it from one who was contemporary with Apostles and the earliest Christian tradition.'

It has been supposed that by 'the interpreter of Peter' is meant that Peter, though no doubt he was bi-lingual, speaking both Aramaic and Greek, did not know the latter language well enough to preach in it, and that Mark translated Peter's Aramaic into Greek for those whom he addressed in Rome, who would not understand Aramaic.

Irenæus, Tertullian, Clement of Alexandria, Origen, Jerome, and Eusebius, all affirm, in substance, what Papias had said, and present-day scholarship is in harmony with this witness. (For these names, see 'Church Fathers,' p. 38).

St. Luke

Since Sir William Ramsay wrote his epoch-making books on Paul and his world, increasingly fewer critics have called into question the Lucan authorship of the Third Gospel. Adolph Harnack, who at first was opposed to it, became one of the most powerful advocates of it.

Witness is borne to Luke's authorship of this Writing by Irenæus, Tertullian, Clement, Origen, Gregory of Nazianzus, Jerome, and Eusebius. Indeed, as Dr. Plummer says, 'the voice of the first eight centuries pronounces strongly for him and for no one else' as the author of the Third Gospel and the Acts. No unprejudiced reader can doubt that the same man wrote this Gospel and the Acts.   In both are the same general vocabulary and style; in both it is evident that the author is a man of considerable culture; in both there is reason to believe that the author is a medical doctor, and both make reference to a man named Theophilus (Luke i. 1; Acts i. 1).   Luke alone of anyone known answers to the requirements of these two books.   (See under ' Luke and Paul,' p. 360).

St. John

In approaching the study of the Fourth Gospel two problems confront us, the problems of authorship and historicity.   From the beginning of the 19th century the Apostolic authorship of this Gospel has been called into question by a number of acute scholars, and by a number of equally acute scholars the Apostolic authorship has been defended.

We think that this controversy has been overdone.   The Gospel does not say who its author was, and if it could be finally proved that the Apostle John did not write it, that fact would not invalidate the Gospel, for the truth of a message does not stand or fall with some particular theory as to authorship, but is determined by the intrinsic qualities of the message itself.

It is well, however, that the Bible student should know, in a general way at least, the main lines of the controversy.

To the question, Who was the author of this Gospel? three answers have been given:

(a) that the author was John the Apostle, who describes himself as ' the disciple whom Jesus loved ':

(b) that the author was not the Apostle John, but another John known as ' the Presbyter,' who is described in the Gospel as ' the disciple whom Jesus loved ':

(c) that the author was a disciple of the Apostle John, who, by personal intercourse, derived his information from the Apostle, much as Mark derived his from Peter, so that the Gospel is really a dual product.

These views are known as the *conservative*, the *mediating*, and the *partition* theories.   Theory (b) is based upon the references in 2 John 1, and 3 John 1, to ' the Elder ' (lit., ' the Presbyter '), and a brief reference made by Papias, a writer of the first half of the second century, to the effect that he gathered information from the presbyters, among whom he names John, whom he distinguishes from the Apostle of that name. No writer for a hundred years after Papias supported the view that there were two Johns to be reckoned with, relative to the authorship of the Fourth Gospel, and the existence of such a person, as distinct from the Apostle, cannot be proved.

Theory (c) is a compromise between (a) and (b), and is without proof or value. Mark, behind whom was Peter, is well known, but the supposed person behind John the Apostle is unknown to history; and, in any case, it is much more reasonable to conclude that the Apostle wrote what he knew, than that he got someone else to write it.

Theory (a) has overwhelming support from both external and internal evidence.

(i) EXTERNAL EVIDENCE

It is an undeniable fact that about the last quarter of the second century this Gospel was accepted as authoritative, and assigned to the Apostle John, there being no trace of a contrary opinion, except what was said by Papias. Irenæus, Clement of Alexandria, Tertullian, and Eusebius who had access to many works which are now lost, all affirm that John the Apostle wrote this Gospel.

(ii) INTERNAL EVIDENCE

The traditional argument proves, in gradually contracting circles: (a) that the author of the Gospel was a Jew; (b) that he was a Jew of Palestine; (c) that he was an eye-witness of what he describes; (d) that he was an Apostle; and (e) that he was the Apostle John. These points have been fully wrought out by Meyer, Luthardt, Lange, Godet, Lightfoot, Ezra Abbott, Sanday, and Westcott. The argument of Westcott is massive and conclusive, and a summary of it is here given.

(1) Indirect Internal Evidence

(a) *The Author was a Jew*

' He is familiar with Jewish opinions and customs, his composition is impressed with Jewish characteristics, he is penetrated with the spirit of the Jewish dispensation. The vocabulary, the structure of the sentences, the symmetry and numerical symbolism of the compósition, the expression and the arrangement of the thoughts, are essentially Hebrew. The Old Testament is the source of the religious life of the writer. His Jewish opinions and hopes are taken up into and transfigured by his Christian faith, but the Jewish foundation underlies his whole narrative.' The Evangelist vindicates the Law as of Divine authority.

(b) *The Author was a Jew of Palestine*

This is proved by his local knowledge. He speaks of places with an unaffected precision, as familiar in every case with the scene which he wishes to recall; he moves about in a country which he knows (i. 28; ii. 1, 11; iii. 23; iv. 46; xi. 18, 54; xxi. 1, 2). The writer of the Fourth Gospel is evidently at home in Jerusalem as it was before its fall in A.D. 70 (v. 2; ix. 7; xviii. 1; xix. 13, 17, 20, 41). He has an accurate knowledge of the Temple and its ritual (ii. 14-16, 20; viii. 20; x. 22; esp. chaps. vii. viii). The author's quotations from the Old Testament show that he was not dependent on the Septuagint (LXX), but was acquainted with the original Hebrew.

(c) *The Author was an Eye-witness of what he Describes*

His narrative is marked by minute details of persons, and time, and number, and place, and manner, which cannot but have come from a direct experience.

PERSONS -	-	vi. 5, 7; xii. 21; xiv. 5, 8, 22; xiii. 25; iii. 1; vii. 50; xix. 39; xi. 1 ff; xii. 1 ff; vi. 71; xii. 4; xiii. 2, 26; xviii. 10, 13, 26
TIME	-	ii. 13, 23; v. 1; vi. 4; vii. 2; x. 22; also i. 29, 35, 43; ii. 1; xii. 1, 12; xiii. 1; xix. 31; xx. 1, 26; iv. 6, 52; xix. 14; xiii. 30; xviii. 28; xx. 1; xxi. 4; vi. 16; xx. 19; iii. 2
NUMBER -	-	i. 35; ii. 6; vi. 9, 19; xix. 23; xxi. 8, 11; also, iv. 18; v. 5; xii. 5; xix. 39
PLACE	-	i. 28; iii. 23; iv. 46; v. 14; vi. 59; viii. 20; x. 40; xi. 30, 54, 56; xviii. 1
MANNER -	-	i. 35-51; xiii. 1-20; xviii. 15-27; xxi. 1-14
OTHER DETAILS		vi. 9; xi. 32; xii. 3, 13; xiii. 30; xviii. 3; xix. 23; xx. 7; xxi. 17; also, xiii. 24; xviii. 6; xix. 5; xxi. 20

(d) *The Author was an Apostle*

This follows almost necessarily from the character of the scenes which he describes. He exhibits intimate acquaintance with the feelings of ' the disciples.' He knows their thoughts at critical moments (ii. 11, 17, 22; iv. 27; vi. 19, 60; xii. 16; xiii. 22, 28; xxi. 12). He had an intimate knowledge of Jesus (xi. 33; xiii. 21; ii. 24; iv. 1; v. 6; vi. 15; vii. 1; xvi. 19; vi. 6, 61, 64; xiii. 1, 3, 11; xviii. 4; xix. 28).

(e) *The Author was the Apostle John*

As the writer is exact in defining the names in his Gospel (i. 42; xi. 16; xx. 24; xxi. 2; vi. 71; xii. 4; xiii. 2, 26; xiv. 22) it is presumed that the unnamed person of xiii. 23; xix. 26; xx. 2; xxi. 7, 20, is himself. If someone else had written this Gospel it is unthinkable that he would not have mentioned by name so distinguished an Apostle as John.

(2) Direct Internal Evidence

Bishop Westcott selects and expounds three important passages: i. 14; xix. 35; xxi. 24; each bearing directly on the authorship of the Gospel. His verdict on these passages is: ' The Fourth Gospel claims to be written by an eye-witness, and this claim is attested by those who put the work in circulation.'

Considering it proved that John the Apostle wrote this Gospel, it will be well for us to learn what we may of him personally. (See Div. B, St. John: Sec. 2, p. 398).

6

DATE AND PLACE OF WRITING

It used to be fashionable to assign late dates to the Evangelic Records, but more recent scholarship has moved steadily back in this regard. It appears certain that the chronological order of these Records is, Mark, Matthew, Luke, John; and confidently it can be said that the last of these belongs to the last decade of the first century, probably about 95 A.D. In all likelihood Luke's Gospel was written during the two years of Paul's captivity at Cæsarea (Acts xxiv. 27), that is, between 58 and

60 A.D. We know it was written before the Acts (i. 1), a Book which must be placed not later than 63 A.D. It is practically certain that Matthew's Gospel was written before the destruction of Jerusalem in 70 A.D., criticism to the contrary notwithstanding; and if it preceded Luke's Gospel, as would seem to be the case, it may well have been written between 56 and 58 A.D. As Mark's Gospel is the earliest of the four it may be assumed that it was written before 56 A.D., and, in all likelihood, nearer 50 A.D.

These dates are not matters for dogmatism, but it is not unscholarly to assume, in the light of all the evidence at present available, that the first three Gospels were written before 70 A.D., a fact which has a bearing on the interpretation of them.

Absolute certainty is not reached as to the places of writing, but it is supposed that Mark wrote in Rome; Matthew, in Jerusalem; Luke, in Cæsarea; and John, in Ephesus.

Set out these particulars in tabular form for ready reference

7

ORIGIN

The origin of the Synoptic Records may be considered along two distinct lines, one dealing with their *sources*, and the other, with their *design*. Both these lines of investigation are important, and a true view cannot be obtained by pursuing either of them without the other. Criticism has concentrated on the former almost exclusively, and exposition largely on the latter; to the impoverishment of both.

The question of the *sources* of these Gospels, which is called ' The Synoptic Problem,' is not yet settled, and probably never will be. (See 'The Synoptic Problem,' Div. A, Pt. I, 8, p. 83). In the consideration of it two opposite perils, let it be repeated, should be avoided: (*a*) indifference to what can be known of the composition and construction of these Gospels, and (*b*) such occupation with the pursuit of this inquiry that one's appreciation of and subjection to what is written is endangered.

Here we must keep to broad lines, and leave students of the Gospels to pursue in detail, as inclination may direct, the numerous lines of Synoptic research.

The following points are largely agreed upon, and should be noted:

(i)   That the chronological order of these Records is, Mark, Matthew, Luke.

(ii) That Matthew and Luke drew largely from Mark. Of Matthew's 1068 verses (R.V.), about 500 are from Mark's 661 verses; and of Luke's 1149 verses (R.V.) about 320 are from Mark. Only from 50-55 verses of Mark are not to be found in either Matthew or Luke. (See pp. 86, 132, 181, 186, 253).

(iii) That Matthew and Luke had a source which consisted chiefly of Sayings and Discourses of Christ, which was a written Greek document, and was prior to Mark, the earliest of the Synoptics. The evidence of this is that about 250 verses in both Matthew and Luke show close parallelism and similarity, and are distinct from all other material in these Gospels. This document is called Q, from the German *Quelle*, meaning *Source*. It does not exist, and is somewhat hypothetical.

(iv) That in addition to what Matthew and Luke have drawn from Q and Mark, there are in Matthew about 300 verses, and in Luke about 580 verses, from other sources (p. 86).

(v)   That beneath and behind all other source material is the *Oral* Gospel which was proclaimed by the early evangelists. In these messages, which were delivered in many quarters, there must have been a common deposit of evangelic fact and truth.

(vi) That, in addition to all this, there is in Matthew and Luke a considerable amount which is peculiar to each of these Evangelists.

These facts are of more than academic interest and importance, and every student of the Gospels should have some knowledge of them.

That the Gospels are so composed need occasion no surprise, because the use of sources is characteristic of the Scriptures. (See Div. A: Pt. I, 8, p. 84).

For what reason the selections of material were made in the Gospels will become more evident when we consider, in Sec. 10, why there are *four* Gospels; but what is now clear, as to the origin of these Records, is that they were produced independently, at different times, in different places; that they are compilations, and that, though they have their own characteristics of outlook and expression, yet they perfectly harmonize in their witness to Jesus the Messiah.

8

INSPIRATION

What has just been said may lead some, to whom these particulars may be new, to ask: 'But what about inspiration?' The question suggests an idea of inspiration which may not be valid. Let it be said, with reference to the Gospels, and all the Scriptures, that no doctrine of inspiration should be *imposed upon* the Sacred Writings, but *drawn from* them. It is fatal to frame a theory of inspiration, and then attempt to explain the Scriptures in the light of it. The right method is to let a doctrine of inspiration arise out of the facts. Examine the Evangelic Records in the light of this principle.

A fact to be observed is that *the individuality of the writers is preserved*. Each of the Four has his style of writing, mode of expression, and arrangement of material. This fact is destructive of the mechanical dictation theory of inspiration.

Another fact is that in the material common to two or more of the writers *there is great variety of report*. Take, for instance, the title over the Cross, in Matt. xxvii. 37, Mark xv. 26, Luke xxiii. 38, and John xix. 19. If by *verbal* inspiration is meant that each Evangelist has recorded the exact words of the inscription, the theory does not fit the facts, for no two of them say the same thing. This, however, does not mean that they are in error, or contradictory.

Still another fact is that *the writers were not supernaturally informed of particulars which they could obtain by inquiry*. Sufficient proof of this is much of Luke's Gospel. In his preface (i. 1-4) are two important statements; (*a*) that 'many had taken in hand to draw up a narrative' of Jesus' life and work, and to some of these records no doubt Luke had access; and (*b*) that his own method was to 'trace the course of all things accurately from the first'; that is, he obtained information from many quarters, and he was under the necessity to do so as he was not an apostle, and had no first-hand knowledge of the things about which he wrote.

Inspiration, therefore, must be understood in a way which will make room for these facts.

The inspiration of the Gospels is not to be looked for in fulness and uniformity of record, but in the quality of what is recorded. No one can read these Writings, and the Apocryphal Gospels, without discerning the vast difference between them.   The latter were never recognized as of Apostolic authority, but the reception of the former was immediate and universal.

It is important to notice, says Dr. Orr, that ' inspiration belongs primarily to the *person*, and to the *book* only as it is the product of the inspired person.' With this in view we can easily see that the person would be and was guided by the Spirit of God, both to apprehend truth and select material, and when four persons did this with the same subject, we should expect the variety which necessarily characterises different points of view.

9

GENUINENESS

It may be thought unnecessary to speak of this matter, because if a writing is Divinely inspired, it must be genuine. Yet, the considerations are distinct. Those who question the plenary (full) inspiration of the Gospels are bound to face the evidence of their genuineness, that is, that they are true Apostolic productions. The dates already given may be challenged, but that these Records are products of the first century cannot be doubted, because the evidence is too strong. In keeping with the aim of this book, to promote thought and research, this evidence is presented briefly.

It is an indisputable fact that long before the close of the second century the Gospels were widely circulated and well known. Tertullian (200 A.D.) says: ' Of the Apostles, John and Matthew instil faith into us, whilst of Apostolic men, Luke and Mark afterwards renew it.' Clement of Alexandria (190 A.D.) repeatedly alludes to the Four Records which we have. Irenæus (180 A.D.) names the four Evangelists, and likens their Gospels to the Cherubim. The Muratorian Canon (160 A.D.), which is a celebrated and valuable fragment, mutilated at the beginning, and at the end, speaks of Luke's Gospel, and of John's, in such a way as to make it practically certain that the missing parts spoke of Matthew's and Mark's Gospels also.

A Harmony of the Gospels, called ' Diatessaron ' (Greek: *dia tessaron*, by four), was written by Tatian about the middle of the second century. In the Apologies of Justin Martyr (150 A.D.), frequent reference is made to the Memoirs, or Memorabilia of the Apostles, by which, undoubtedly, he meant the Gospels which we have. Paley says that almost a complete Life of Christ might be extracted from Justin's works.

Lastly, Papias (120 A.D.) who, it is believed, was a disciple of the Apostle John, makes reference to Mark's Gospel, and Matthew's, in a way that proves that they were known at that early date.

We see, then, that throughout the whole of the second century there is abundant evidence that the Four Gospels which we have were written in the first century, were written by those whose names they bear (see under 'Authorship,' Sec. 5, p. 130), were genuine records of the life of Christ, and were reverenced as Sacred Books.

10

NUMBER

It is simply a fact that from the beginning, the Christian Church never recognized more than Four Gospels, and these were the Four which we have. No other Gospels were admitted among the Sacred Books of the early Christians; neither in the writings of the Fathers, nor in the manuscripts of the New Testament, are any other Gospels mentioned as having received the authority and sanction of the Church.

Other Gospels were written and disseminated, chiefly in the second century, yet, long before the end of that century, our Four, and these only, were received by the Church as of any authority. The fact that in 160 A.D. Tatian made a Harmony of these Four is evidence enough of this. Irenæus (180 A.D.) mentions four, and these Four, naming Matthew, Mark, Luke, and John as the authors.

But why are there *Four* Gospels? Why not one, or five, or more? Tatian combined the Four into One, and so may be said to be the father of Gospel Harmonies; but Harnack tells us that, although this work obtained a wide circulation in the East, it did not find acceptance in the Church, because it was regarded as essential to safeguard the apostolic tradition embodied in the separate Records.

When all is said that can be said on the subject of the *sources* to which these Records are indebted, the question, Why are there Four? remains to be answered; and it can be answered only by a thorough examination of the *design* of each (cf. p. 139).

Irenæus says: ' Since there are four regions of the world in which we live, and four principal winds, and since the Church is spread over all the world, and the Gospel is the pillar and ground of the Church, it is fitting that the Church should have four pillars breathing out immortality, and imparting life to men.' He also likened the Gospels to the Cherubim of Ezekiel; Matthew to the man; Mark to the eagle; Luke to the ox; and John to the lion. These symbols are given in different orders by Athanasius, Augustine, Jerome, and other Fathers; but, though there may be an analogy between these symbols and the Gospels, the fact of there being four only cannot be accounted for in this way.

The Problem of the Synoptic Gospels has been handled in at least four different ways. (1) Harmonists, like Tatian, have tried to get over the difficulties by combining the Four Records in one. (2) Allegorists, like Irenæus, have adopted an arbitrary and fanciful method of explaining why there are four. (3) Rationalists, like Strauss and Renan, have discredited the Records by denying their historicity. (4) Historians, like Neander, and theologians, like Westcott, have followed the line of sound historical criticism, and have done much to solve the problem of design.

Three great historic races, the Hebrew, the Greek, and the Roman, helped to prepare the world for the Advent of the Messiah; the Hebrew, on the side of religion; the Greek, on the side of literature and art; and the Roman, on the side of law and politics. These ideologies may be spoken of, respectively, as Judaism, Hellenism, and Imperialism. These peoples and phases of thought are representative for all time, and in the light of this fact the Gospels must be viewed.

Christ came to fulfil and to transcend the noblest ideals of men. He was not only a man, but also Man, and His life and work were the perfect answer to the needs and longings of these great representative peoples. As the Gospel was preached to them it was adapted to them, and the result is seen in the Synoptic Records. Matthew is adapted to the Jews; Mark, to the Romans; and Luke, to the Greeks; and the Fourth Gospel is adapted to the need of the Christian Church, which is composed of people of all nations ' who have washed their robes, and made them white in the blood of the Lamb.'

This account of the matter is a satisfactory answer to the question, Why Four Gospels? for it explains, as no other theory does, their agreements, differences, and peculiarities.

That the Synoptics were written for peoples of different race was believed from an early date. Irenæus says: ' The Gospel of St. Matthew was written for the Jews, who specially desired that it should be shown that the Christ was the seed of David; and St. Matthew endeavours to satisfy this desire, and therefore commences his Gospel with the genealogy of Christ.'

Eusebius, the historian, endorses the widespread tradition that Mark wrote his Gospel under the direction of Peter, at the request of the brethren at Rome, and with a special view to circulation in Italy, and among the Romans generally.

Both Origen and Gregory Nazianzen affirm that Luke wrote his Gospel for the sake of those Greeks who turned to the faith.

These two factors, then, *sources* and *design*, meet in the finished product of the Synoptic Gospels. In the midst of much that is uncertain, three facts can be relied upon, viz.:

(a) that the Gospels are compilations, some of their sources being clearly traceable;

(b) that each of them has a specific end in view; and

(c) that the writers were guided in the selection of their material to that end, by the Holy Spirit.

II

RELATIONS

The Gospels sustain a fourfold relation: to the Old Testament; to the Apostolic Writings; the Three to the Fourth; and the Three to each other.

10

(i) THE RELATION OF THE GOSPELS TO THE OLD TESTAMENT

No one can read any of them without realizing that their story has its beginning somewhere else. The first verse in Matthew speaks of David and Abraham. The second and third verses in Mark refer to ' the prophets,' and quote from Malachi and Isaiah. The fifth verse in Luke mentions Abia and Aaron. The seventeenth verse in John speaks of Moses, and the twenty-first verse of Elijah. Evidently, then, something has gone before, to which these Gospels are related, and without some knowledge of which they cannot be understood.

As we proceed to read, we find in these Gospels numerous citations from and allusions to the Old Testament. The figures are: in Matthew, 128; in Mark, 63; in Luke, 96; and in John, 43; the grand total being 330 citations and allusions (p. 96); and these are from at least twenty-four of the thirty-nine Books of the Old Testament. Absolute accuracy in the matter of citations and allusions is not possible, because many of the references are so fused that separation is difficult. (For the details see p. 97, and Div. B; under each Gospel, 'Old Testament References').

When these references are examined, it will be found that most of them relate to the Messiah, and affirm, first, that He is predicted in the Old Testament Scriptures, and, second, that these prophecies are fulfilled in Jesus of Nazareth.

The Gospels, therefore, are organically related to the Bible which was in existence at the beginning of our era. As you read them, put O.T. in the margin beside every citation or allusion, and then construct the story of the Messiah from these references: His Virgin Birth; descent from Abraham, through David; place of birth; forerunner; His mission, ill-treatment, death, burial, resurrection, ascension; together with His offices and titles.

1 Isa. vii. 14	6 Isa. lxi. 1	11 Psa. lxviii. 18
2 Gen. xii. 7	7 Isa. l. 6	12 Psa. ii. 7
3 2 Sam. vii. 12, 13	8 Psa. xxii. 16	13 Isa. xlii. 1
4 Mic. v. 2	9 Isa. liii. 9	14 Num. xxiv. 17
5 Isa. xl. 3	10 Psa. xvi. 10	15 Deut. xviii. 18

(See DIV. C, Section 3, ' Prophecies of the Messiah,' p. 479).

(ii) THE RELATION OF THE GOSPELS TO THE APOSTOLIC WRITINGS

The latter are related to the former as the former are related to the Old Testament, for the Apostolic Writings are rooted in, and grow out of the facts which the Evangelists record.

But for the Gospels, the Acts, Epistles, and Revelation would have no meaning. They would be a lock without a key; a superstructure without a foundation; an end without a beginning.

All the preachers and writers of the Apostolic period assume and declare that Jesus of Nazareth was the Son of God and the Redeemer of the world. Their mutual testimony is that ' there is none other name under heaven given among men, whereby we must be saved '; and the final vision is of ' a Lamb, as it had been slain.' If some one who had never heard of the Bible were given only the Apostolic Writings to read, would he not say, I want the first part of the story?

We see, then, that the Gospels rest on the Old Testament, and that the Acts, Epistles, and Revelation rest on the Gospels. The Bible is, therefore, an organism; every part of it is related to every other part, the subject of the whole being Christ the Redeemer. This revelation, consequently, is in three stages:

In the Old Testament, the *Preparation* for Christ.
In the Evangelic Records, the *Manifestation* of Christ.
In the Apostolic Writings, the *Realization* of Christ.

(iii) THE RELATION OF THE SYNOPTIC GOSPELS TO THE FOURTH

The first Three Gospels and the Fourth differ in many ways, of which the following should be specially noted:

1 In the Three, the scene of Christ's ministry is laid chiefly in Galilee, but in the Fourth, it is chiefly in Judæa.
2 In the Three, the ministry would appear to have lasted little more than a year, but in the Fourth, three Passovers are recorded, so that the ministry must have extended over several years.
3 The events narrated in the Three differ from those in the Fourth. Excluding the Passion Week, all four Gospels have only three incidents in common: the miraculous feeding of the five thousand, the walking on the Sea of Galilee, and the anointing by Mary, the sister of Lazarus. John omits the miraculous birth, the baptism, the temptation, the transfiguration, the institution of

the Supper, and the agony in Gethsemane. On the other hand, six of the eight miracles which John records are omitted in the Synoptics and so are the call of the first five disciples, the first cleansing of the temple, the interviews with Nicodemus and the Samaritan woman, the discourses on the Bread of Life, the Light of the World, Spiritual Freedom, the Good Shepherd, and the farewell discourses in the upper room, and on the way to Gethsemane.

4 What is reported of Christ's teaching differs in these Records. In the Three it is given chiefly in parables, but in the Fourth there are no parables (unless the Vine, and the Good Shepherd are regarded as such); but instead are discourses, ' for the most part of a subjective and mystical character, relating to the deep things of God.'

5 The Three present the outward and earthly aspect of our Lord's life; the Fourth, the inward, and the heavenly.

6 The Three record His deeds; the Fourth, His words.

7 The Three reflect specially His humanity; the Fourth, specially His Divinity.

Mark carefully these seven points of difference as you read these Gospels. (See ' Diagrammatic View of the Gospels,' p. 95).

(iv) The Relation of the Synoptic Gospels to Each Other

Notwithstanding exhaustive investigation by experts, it can confidently be said that the Synoptic Problem—how the first Three Gospels were compiled—remains unsolved (p. 83); but our inability to explain should not prevent our observing carefully these finished products, comparing and contrasting them with one another. In this exercise we should examine their general harmony, their detailed agreement, passages peculiar to each, and their main points of difference.

(a) General Harmony

The Synoptic Gospels agree in locating our Lord's ministry in Galilee until the period of His Passion. References to the earlier Judæan ministry are only indirect and inferential. The great events of our Lord's life and work are common to all Three: His Forerunner, His baptism, temptation, discourses, and miracles; His selection of the Twelve ; His transfiguration, the announcement of His coming sufferings, His last journey to

SAMARIA

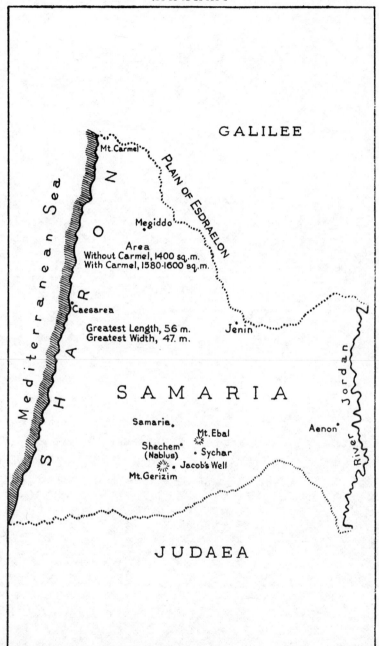

GALILEE

Mt. Carmel

PLAIN OF ESDRAELON

S H A R O N

Mediterranean Sea

Megiddo

Area
Without Carmel, 1400 sq. m.
With Carmel, 1580-1600 sq. m.

Caesarea

Greatest Length, 56 m.
Greatest Width, 47 m.

Jenin

SAMARIA

Samaria.

Mt. Ebal

Shechem
(Nablus)

Sychar

Jacob's Well

Mt. Gerizim

Aenon

River Jordan

JUDAEA

Jerusalem, His betrayal, passion, crucifixion, burial, and resurrection.

It is important to see that, notwithstanding their many differences, a harmonious whole is presented to us by the combined narrative of the Gospels.

(b) *Detailed Agreement*

This harmony is, however, not only general, but particular also, extending to the narration of many incidents, and to close identity of language. Many of these incidents are recorded by all three Evangelists, and many of them by two of them only, in various combinations: Mark and Matthew, Mark and Luke, and Matthew and Luke. Any good Harmony of the Gospels will make these combinations clear.

Mark, Matthew, and Luke

Taking Mark as the basis for reference, the following are found in all three Records:

i. 2-8	-	Ministry of the Baptist.
i. 9-11	-	Baptism of Jesus.
i. 12, 13	-	Temptation of Jesus.
i. 14-20	-	Call of Four Disciples.
i. 29-34	-	Cure of Peter's Mother-in-law.
i. 40-45	-	Cleansing of a Leper.
ii. 1-12	-	Healing of a Paralytic Man.
ii. 13-17	-	Call of Matthew, and his Feast.
ii. 18-22	-	On Feasting and Fasting.
ii. 23-28	-	Discourse on the Sabbath.
iii. 1-6	-	Cure of a Man with a Withered Hand.
iii. 31-35	-	The True Kindred of Christ.
iv. 1-20	-	Parable of the Sower.
iv. 30-34	-	Parable of the Mustard Seed.
iv. 35-41	-	Stilling of the Tempest.
v. 1-20	-	Cure of a Gerasene Demoniac.
v. 21-43	-	Healing of a Woman, and the Raising of Jairus' Daughter.
vi. 6-13	-	The Twelve Sent Forth.
vi. 7-13	-	Mission of the Twelve.
vi. 14-16	-	Herod's Guilty Fears.
vi. 30-44	-	Feeding of the Five Thousand.
viii. 27-30	-	Peter's Confession of Jesus' Messiahship.
viii. 31-ix. 1	-	On Saving and Losing Life.
ix. 2-8	-	The Transfiguration of Jesus.

Mark and Matthew

Still taking Mark as the basis for reference, the following are found in it and Matthew only:

ix. 9-13	-	Question about Elijah.
ix. 42-50	-	On Causing to Stumble.
x. 1-12	-	Concerning Divorce.
x. 35-45	-	Petition of the Sons of Zebedee.
xi. 12-14	-	Withering of the Fig Tree.
xi. 20-25	-	The Withered Fig Tree.
xii. 28-34	-	The First Commandment.
xiv. 3-9	-	The Anointing of Jesus before His Passion.
xiv. 55-64	-	Trial of Jesus
xv. 16-19	-	Soldiers mock Jesus.
xv. 34, 35	-	An Utterance of Jesus on the Cross.
xvi. 1 -	-	Women Visit the Tomb.
xvi. 15-18	-	Jesus Appears to over Five Hundred Disciples.

Mark and Luke

Incidents found in these two Gospels, but not in Matthew; Mark still being the basis of reference:

i. 21-28	-	The Casting Out of an Unclean Spirit.
i. 35-38	-	Declaration on Preaching the Gospel.
iv. 21-25	-	Giving Heed to the Light.
v. 18-20	-	Jesus and the Gerasene.
ix. 38-40	-	The Apostles and a Man who was Casting Out Demons.
xii. 41-44	-	The Widow and her Mite.
xvi. 12, 13	-	Jesus on the way to Emmaus.
xvi. 14 -	-	The Appearance to Ten Disciples.
xvi. 19, 20	-	The Ascension.

Matthew and Luke

The following are found in these two Gospels, but not in Mark. Matthew is the basis of reference:

iii. 7-10	-	The Baptist's address to the Scribes and Pharisees.
iii. 13-19	-	Choosing Twelve Apostles.
iv. 1-11	-	The Threefold Temptation of Jesus.
v. 1, 2, 3-12, 21-48		The Sermon on the Mount.
vii. 1-6, 7-12, 13-viii. 1	-	The Sermon on the Mount.
viii. 19-22	-	Address to would-be Disciples.
x. 24-33	-	Exhortations to the Disciples.
xi. 2-19	-	Mission of the Baptist's Disciples to Christ.
xi. 20-24	-	Woe on the Cities of Galilee.
xi. 25-27	-	The Gospel and the Worldly-wise.
xii. 33-37	-	The Good and the Evil.
xii. 38-45	-	Jesus and the Request for a Sign from Heaven.
xiii. 33	-	Parable of the Leaven.
xviii. 12-14	-	Parable of the Lost Sheep.
xxiv. 45-51	-	The Faithful and Unfaithful Stewards.

(c) *Passages Peculiar*

A feature of the Synoptic Gospels, not less impressive and important than the foregoing, is the appearance in each of incidents and discourses which are not found in the other two.   There must be a reason for this.   The fact is part of the problem of the *sources* of these Gospels, but it belongs much more to the problem of their *design* (cf. Secs. 7 and 10, pp. 139, 143).   It has been estimated that Matthew has 410 verses peculiar to himself; Mark, at least 30; and Luke, 634; and these peculiarities are in the narrative portions, which, in Matthew, occupy about one fourth; in Mark, one half; and in Luke, one third.   (See pp. 189, 260, 350).   It may safely be claimed that the selection of the material in each Gospel, under the guidance of the Holy Spirit, had for its end the adaptation of each to the people for whom it was written (cf. Sec. 10, p. 143).

Matthew

The appeal here is to the Jews, and so here only are the following:

The Genealogy of Jesus traced from Abraham ...	i. 1-17
The Annunciation to Joseph	i. 18-25
The Sermon on the Mount (as a whole: cf. p. 293) ...	v-vii
The Original Mission of the Twelve	x
Woes against the Scribes and Pharisees	xxiii
Parables condemnatory of the Jews: the Unmerciful Servant; the Labourers in the Vineyard; the Two Sons; the Marriage of the King's Son; the Ten Virgins; and the Talents	xviii; xx; xxi; xxii; xxv; xxv

There is a Genealogy in Luke's Gospel, but it is different; and in Luke are scattered parts of the Sermon on the Mount (p. 156).

In this Gospel are many other additions which point to its adaptation to the Jews, among which are the following:

Jesus is called ' Emmanuel.'

He is ' born King of the Jews.'

The expression, ' the Kingdom of Heaven ' (Heavens) occurs here only, and 33 times (A.V., p. 276).

Jerusalem is the ' Holy City,' the ' Holy Place,' and the ' City of the great King.'

Our Lord is the ' Son of David.'

The term, ' that it might be fulfilled,' or its equivalent, occurs not fewer than 15 times, and links this Gospel with the Old Testament, which is introduced by citations and allusions 129 times. (See pp. 267-270).

There are other peculiarities, which should be searched out with the help of a Harmony, and a Concordance.

Mark

Four passages are peculiar to this Gospel, the rest being found in Matthew or Luke (cf. Sec. 7, p. 140). These passages are:

The seed growing secretly	iv. 26-29
Healing of the deaf and dumb man	vii. 32-37
Healing of the blind man near Bethsaida	viii. 22-26
The young man who fled, leaving his garment behind	xiv. 51, 52

About thirty of Mark's 661 verses are peculiar to him, but estimates vary from fifty to eighty. (See Div. B, Mark; Sec. 13, p. 189).

It may be difficult to see what special application these selections have, but there is distinct evidence that Mark wrote for Gentile readers, and specially for Romans. This is shown (a) by the interpretation of Aramaic translations, such as *Boanerges* (iii. 17), *Bartimaeus* (x. 46), *Abba* (xiv. 36) *Eloi, Eloi, Lama Sabachthani* (xv. 34), and *Gehenna* (ix. 43); (b) by the interpretation of Jewish customs (which never occurs in Matthew), as in vii. 22 ff, xii. 42, xv. 42; (c) by the absence of mention of the Jewish law; (d) by the geographical description of the Mount of Olives, which no Jew would need (xiii. 3). (See p. 169, and Index IV).

Other evidence that the writer of this Gospel had Roman readers specially in mind, is the use of several Latin words, in Greek form, which are not found in the other Gospels: *soldier-of-the-guard* (vi. 27), *pots* (vii. 4), *farthing* (xii. 42), *centurion* (xv. 39, 44, 45); as well as of Latin words which occur elsewhere: *bed* (ii. 4), *Praetorium* (xv. 16), *census* (xii. 14 *tribute*), and *scourged* (xv. 15). (See Index IV).

Further evidence of the adaptation of Mark to the Roman, the man of action rather than of reflection, is the occurrence forty-one times of the word *eutheōs*, translated ' straightway,' 'anon,' 'immediately,' and 'forthwith,' and of *euthus*, six times more; the omission of long discourses, such as are found in Matthew; the omission of parables of Jewish significance; the use of the Roman division of night into four watches (xiii. 35); and the general graphic character of the whole narrative, a feature which would commend it to the Roman people, especially of the middle classes, engaged in practical business, legal affairs, commercial enterprises, and military campaigns, and migrating in frequent journeys from place to place. (See Division B, Mark; Section 16, p. 193).

Luke

That this Gospel was written for Gentiles, and specially adapted to Greek readers, is borne witness to in many ways. Luke himself was of Greek origin, and his Gospel is addressed to a certain Theophilus, in all probability a Greek Christian of some position and influence.

There is a lot of material in this Gospel which is peculiar to it, of which the following are the principal portions:

The birth and childhood of the Baptist, and of Jesus	i., ii.
Jesus' genealogy in the line of Mary	iii. 23-28
The first rejection at Nazareth	iv. 16-31
The call of followers to full discipleship	v. 1-11
Raising of the widow's son at Nain	vii. 11-17
Anointing of Jesus' feet by a sinful woman in the house of a Pharisee, and the parable of the Two Debtors	vii. 36-50
The second tour of Galilee	viii. 1-3
Jesus goes privately to Jerusalem through Samaria	ix. 51-56
The mission of the Seventy, and their return	x. 1-24
A lawyer's question answered, and the parable of the Good Samaritan	x. 25-37
Jesus the Guest of Martha and Mary	x. 38-42
The disciples are encouraged to pray, and the parable of the Importunate Friend	xi. 1-13
Blasphemous accusation of league with Beelzebub	xi. 14-36
The Pharisees and lawyers are denounced in a Pharisee's house	xi. 37-54
A discourse on various subjects, and the parables of the Rich Fool, the Waiting Servants, and the Wise Steward	xii.

In THE GREAT INTERPOLATION (x. 1-xviii. 14) there is much that reflects the Gentile aim of the Gospel, as, for example, the parables of the Good Samaritan, the Marriage Feast, the Prodigal Son, and the Ten Lepers.

It has been calculated that if the total contents of the several Gospels be represented by 100, in Matthew the coincidences are 58 and the peculiarities 42; in Mark, coincidences 93 and peculiarities 7; in Luke, coincidences 41 and peculiarities 59; and, to add the Fourth Gospel, coincidences 8 and peculiarities 92. (See page 189).

(d) *Points of Difference*

That there are differences in the narration of incidents by any two or all three Evangelists, must be obvious to every careful reader. These differences are not discrepancies, but reflect the freedom and adaptation of the first gospel tradition, and they are seen in variations of several kinds, of which the following are examples.

(1) DIFFERENCES IN THE MATTER OF CONTENT
The preceding section on Passages Peculiar is ample illustration of this.

(2) DIFFERENCES IN THE RECORDING OF EVENTS
In Matthew, the royal descent of Jesus through David and Joseph is given, whereas, in Luke, His natural descent through Nathan and Mary is given. Matthew mentions the visit of the wise men; Luke relates the visit of the shepherds.

(3) DIFFERENCES IN THE ORDER OF THE MATERIAL WHICH THEY HAVE IN COMMON
In Matthew, the Sermon on the Mount is given as one connected discourse, but in Luke much of it is found in about twenty different places (pp. 152, 293).

MATTHEW	LUKE	MATTHEW	LUKE
v. 3-12	vi. 20-23	vi. 24	xvi. 13
v. 13	xiv. 34, 35	vi. 25-34	xii. 22-31
v. 15	xi. 33	vii. 1-5	vi. 37-42
v. 18	xvi. 17	vii. 7-11	xi. 9-13
v. 25, 26	xii. 57-59	vii. 12	vi. 31
v. 31, 32	xvi. 18	vii. 13, 14	xiii. 23, 24
v. 38-48	vi. 27-30, 32-36	vii. 15-20	vi. 43-45
vi. 9-15	xi. 1-4	vii. 23	xiii. 27
vi. 19-21	xii. 33, 34	vii. 24-27	vi. 47-49
vi. 22, 23	xi. 34-36		

Matthew and Mark say that the blind man was cured as Jesus was leaving Jericho (xx. 29; x. 46); Luke says it was as Jesus entered Jericho (xviii. 35).

We have every reason to believe that where there is a difference of order in the presentation of events in the Gospels, it is because moral and spiritual considerations are given precedence over the chronological.

(4) DIFFERENCES IN THE AMOUNT OF MATERIAL WHICH THEY HAVE IN COMMON
In Matthew there are nine beatitudes (v. 3-11), but in Luke there are only four (vi. 20-22). In Mark, only the fact of Jesus' Temptation is mentioned (i. 12, 13), but in Matthew and Luke a detailed account is given (iv. 1-11; iv. 1-13).

(5) DIFFERENCES WHICH ARE VERBAL

For 'good things' in Matthew (vii. 11), Luke has 'the Holy Spirit' (xi. 13). For 'the Spirit of God' in Matthew (xii. 28), Luke has the 'finger of God' (xi. 20). For 'this mountain' in Matthew (xvii. 20), Luke has 'this sycamine tree' (xvii. 6). For 'the holy city' in Matthew (iv. 5), Luke has 'Jerusalem' (iv. 9). For 'led up' and 'led' in Matthew and Luke (iv. 1; iv. 1), Mark has 'driveth' (i. 12).

Only by the use of a Harmony of the Gospels can all these significant differences be seen, and only by seeing them can one appreciate the Divinely guided design of these Records.

QUESTIONS

SECTION 2

1 What is the significance of the names Matthew, Mark, Luke, and John, at the head of the four Gospels?
2 How many chapters are there in each Gospel?
3 In what way are the Old Testament and the Apostolic Writings dependent for their existence upon the Gospels?
4 In what three ways may the Gospels be approached, and what is meant by the terms used to designate these ways?
5 Why is the constant reading of the text of the Gospels so important?

SECTION 3

6 By whom, and when, was the term 'The Gospels,' first used, referring to our Four?
7 What does the word 'gospel' mean?
8 What is the distinction between the gospel and the Gospels?
9 Name one verse in Matthew, and one in Mark, in which the word 'gospel' occurs, and two references in Luke to 'preaching the gospel.'

SECTION 4

10 How does Justin Martyr designate the Gospels, and what is implied by his designation?
11 Give four illustrations of the fragmentary character of the Gospels.
12 Excepting the Infant narratives, what do the Evangelists tell us of the more than thirty years of Jesus' life in Nazareth?

SECTION 5

13 What is meant by 'according to,' at the head of each Gospel?
14 Were all the Evangelists Jews and Apostles?
15 What is the testimony of the second century on the matter of the authorship of the Gospels?

SECTION 6

16 What is the chronological order of the Gospels?

17 When was the Fourth Gospel written?

18 What are the years within which, probably, Mark, Matthew, and Luke, respectively, were written?

19 What is the event in Jewish history beyond which it is unlikely that any of the first three Gospels was written?

SECTION 7

20 What two matters of importance are included in the consideration of the origin of the Gospels?

21 What two perils are to be avoided in endeavouring to trace the sources of the Gospels?

22 How much of Mark is incorporated in Matthew and Luke?

23 On what ground is it supposed that Matthew and Luke use a lost document?

24 What Scripture warrant is there for the belief that the Evangelists used sources of information?

SECTION 8

25 What is to be avoided with reference to the subject of Biblical inspiration?

26 On what principle should a true doctrine of inspiration be reached?

27 Name three facts for which a true doctrine of inspiration will allow.

28 In what does the inspiration of the Four Gospels consist, and how can it be illustrated from outside of them?

29 Is it the writer or the writing that is inspired, or both?

30 What bearing has the idea of an inspired writer upon the fact of variety in the Gospels?

SECTION 9

31 What is meant by 'genuineness' when claimed for the Gospels?

32 Can the ideas of 'genuineness' and 'inspiration' be separated?

33 What evidence is there that the Gospels are products of the first century of our era?

34 How early, and by whom in the second century, are the Gospels referred to as of Apostolic authority?

SECTION 10

35 What evidence is supplied in the second century that the Four Gospels, and these only, were accepted as of Apostolic authority?

36 What reason did Irenæus give for there being Four Gospels, and did any other notable Fathers share his view?

37 In what ways has the problem of Four Gospels been treated? Associate with each the name of a representative advocate of the view.

38 Which were the three great representative peoples of old, and in what way did each help to prepare the way for the Advent of the Messiah?

39 What evidence is supplied by the early Church Fathers that the Gospels are related to these representative peoples?

SECTION 11   (a)

40 What four relations do the Gospels sustain?

41 Give illustrations of the relation of the Gospels to the Old Testament.

42 How many Old Testament citations and allusions are there in the Four Gospels, and what are the figures for each of the Gospels?

43 Name a dozen Messianic predictions in the Old Testament.

44 What is the relation of the Apostolic Writings to the Gospels?

45 What are the stages of the Christ-revelation in the Old Testament, Gospels, and Apostolic Writings respectively?

(b)

46 What is the meaning of the word ' Synoptic,' and of what is it used in our study?

47 Name seven respects in which the Synoptic Gospels and the Fourth Gospel differ.

48 What are the only three incidents which all the Gospels have in common?

49 Name six outstanding events in Jesus' life which John omits.

50 What six miracles does John record which are omitted by the Synoptists?

51 Name four great discourses in the Fourth Gospel which are omitted by the Synoptists.

52 What parables are there in the Fourth Gospel?

(c)

53 To what four lines of study do the Synoptic Gospels invite?

54 Name seven main events in the life of our Lord which are recorded by all the Synoptists.

55 Name ten things which are recorded by Mark, Matthew, and Luke.

56 Name five things which are recorded by Mark and Matthew only.

57 Name two incidents which are recorded by Mark and Luke only.

58 Name seven particulars which are recorded by Matthew and Luke only.

(d)

59 Name four things which are peculiar to Matthew's Gospel.

60 What evidence is there in Matthew's Gospel that it was written for Jews?

61 What four passages are peculiar to Mark's Gospel?

62 What evidence is there in Mark's Gospel that it was written for Gentiles, and especially for Romans?

160 A GUIDE TO THE GOSPELS

63 What great section in Luke's Gospel occurs nowhere else?

64 Name four other portions of Luke's Gospel which are peculiar to it.

65 What evidence is there in Luke's Gospel that it was written for Gentiles, and especially for Greeks?

66 Name five kinds of ' differences ' to be found in the Synoptic Gospels, and illustrate each.

LITERATURE

' A Harmony of the Gospels for Historical Study '	Stevens and Burton
' A Harmony of the Gospels for Students of the Life of Christ '	A. T. Robertson
' The Bible Handbook '	Angus and Green
' Introduction to the Synoptic Gospels '	Paton J. Gloag
' The New Testament and its Writers ' (chaps. i-vi)	J. A. McClymont
' Introduction to the Study of the Gospels '	Bishop Westcott
' Why Four Gospels? '	Daniel S. Gregory
' Differences of the Four Gospels '	Andrew Jukes
' The Christ of the Logia '	A. T. Robertson
' The Students' Introduction to the Synoptic Gospels '	E. Basil Redlich
' The Origin of the New Testament '	A. Harnack
Articles on the Gospels in Hastings' Dictionary of the Bible, and Dictionary of Christ and the Gospels	———
The International Standard Bible Encyclopædia	
' Some Notes on the Gospels '	D. M. McIntyre (I.V.F.)
' Are the New Testament Documents Reliable? '	F. F. Bruce (I.V.F.)
' How to Understand the Gospels '	Anthony C. Deane
' Leading Ideas of the Gospels '	Bishop Alexander
' The Common Traditions of the Synoptic Gospels '	Abbot and Rushbrooke
' The Traditional Text of the Holy Gospels '	Burgon and Miller
' Horæ Evangelicæ '	T. R., and H. A. Birks
' Love Incarnate'	The Earl of Lytton
' The Life, Teaching, and Works of the Lord Jesus Christ, arranged as a Continuous Narrative of the Four Gospels according to the Revised Version'	(Pickering & Inglis)
'The New Bible Handbook'	(I.V.F., 1947)
'The Fascination of the Book'	E. W. Work
'The Work and Words of Jesus'	A. M. Hunter

THE GOSPELS
VIEWED ANALYTICALLY

ST. MARK

St. Mark

OUTLINE OF STUDY

ST. MARK'S GOSPEL

BEFORE beginning to study this Gospel read it through three times, each time, if possible, at a sitting (about 2 hours):

First time, in Weymouth's *New Testament in Modern Speech*; or in *The Twentieth Century New Testament*; or in Moffatt's Translation.

Second time, in the Authorized Version.

Third time, in the Revised Version, or The Revised Standard Version (1946).

In these three readings use no books, but only the text of the Gospel. Having done this, do the reading prescribed in the following Studies. The system is that in each Study a part of the Guide be read, and a portion of the Gospel. Where possible the reading is related to the part of the Guide assigned for reading, as, for example, in the Parables, and Miracles; but this cannot always be done, as for example, in the parts relating to sources, date, and other subjects; but read carefully the part of the Guide which is appointed, and the portion of the Gospel which is attached to it, whether these are related or not.

The object is twofold: first, to familiarize oneself with the text of the Gospel by repeated reading; and secondly, to follow the various Studies which constitute the Guide.

KEY PLAN OF READING

FIFTY FOUR STUDIES

2

THE AUTHOR

IN this Gospel there is no reference to its author, and yet there is no matter less disputed among New Testament scholars than that it was written by one whose name was Mark.

This name occurs eight times in the New Testament, sometimes simply Mark, or Marcus, sometimes John, and sometimes 'John, whose surname was Mark,' or, 'John who was called Mark' (Acts xii. 12, 25; xiii. 5, 13; xv. 37-39; 1 Peter v. 13; Phile. 23, 24; Col. iv. 10; 2 Tim. iv. 11).

JOHN was his Jewish, and MARK his Roman name.

1 The first mention of him is in Acts xii. 12, from which passage we learn that he was the son of one Mary, a woman of some means, who lived in Jerusalem, and whose home was the rendezvous of many of the early Christians.

2 When Paul and Barnabas returned from Jerusalem to Antioch, Mark went with them (Acts xii. 25).

3 When these Apostles set out on their first missionary journey, they took Mark with them as 'minister,' or attendant (Acts xiii. 5).

4 When they reached Perga, in Pamphilia, Mark left them and returned to Jerusalem (Acts xiii. 13).

5 Over this defection Paul and Barnabas parted company when a second missionary tour was proposed, and Barnabas took Mark with him to Cyprus (Acts xv. 37-39).

6 Some years later he was with Peter at Babylon, which, no doubt, means Rome (1 Peter v. 13).

7 Several years later again, he was with Paul at Rome (Col. iv. 10; Phile. 23, 24).

8 Finally, Paul, during his last Roman imprisonment, asks Timothy to come to him, and to bring Mark also (2 Tim. iv. 11).

We learn, incidentally, from these passages that Mark was cousin to Barnabas (Col. iv. 10), and that Peter was his spiritual father (1 Peter v. 13), unless this reference means simply that Mark was as a son to the Apostle.

Tradition says that Mark was with Peter in Rome; that he was sent by Peter on a mission to Egypt; that he founded the Church in Alexandria, and became its first Bishop; and that he was martyred there in A.D. 68. There is a further tradition that some merchants removed his remains to Venice, where a great church is built in his honour.

We may safely assume that the John Mark of the Acts, the Mark of the Pauline Epistles, and the traditional author of the Second Gospel are one and the same person.

Swete tells us that Hippolytus, a Church writer of the beginning of the third century, who lived at Rome, has a story that Mark had the nickname of ' stump-fingered ' (*kolobodaktulos*), or ' Mark of the short finger.' The ordinary preface to the Vulgate Version, states that after his conversion to Christianity the Evangelist amputated one of his fingers in order to disqualify himself for the Jewish priesthood, but the preface to another version of the Vulgate asserts that he was born with one short finger. The defect may have been congenital, or due to accident. The tradition, in all likelihood, is based on fact, and Swete says that ' such a defect, to whatever cause it was due, may have helped to mould the course of John Mark's life; by closing against him a more ambitious career, it may have turned his thoughts to those secondary ministries by which he has rendered enduring service to the Church.'

3

FOR WHOM WRITTEN

WE may regard it as certain that Mark wrote for GENTILE readers in general, and for ROMAN readers in particular. This view is supported not only by external testimony, such as that of Irenæus, Clement of Alexandria, Jerome, and others, but also by much internal evidence.

The GENTILE destination of the Gospel appears from its having fewer Old Testament quotations and allusions than have Matthew and Luke, about 63, as against about 128 in Matthew, and between 90 and 100 in Luke (see under section, 'The Old Testament in the Gospels,' pp. 96, 146); from the interpretation of Aramaic words, such as *Boanerges* (?) (iii. 17), *Talitha cumi* (v. 41), *Ephphatha* (vii. 34), *Gehenna* (ix. 43), *Bartimaeus* (x. 46), *Abba* (xiv. 36), *Golgotha* (xv. 22), *Eloi, Eloi*,

Lama Sabachthani (xv. 34), and from the explanation of Jewish customs (e.g. vii. 2 ff.); from the explanation of the value of 'two mites,' xii. 42; from the absence of mention of the Jewish law; and from the geographical description of the Mount of Olives, of which no Jew would have need (xiii. 3). He explains, also, what *Corban* is (vii. 11), and that the Jews do not eat until they have ' diligently ' washed (vii. 3); he also explains when the Passover was killed (xiv. 12), when the ' preparation ' was (xv. 42), and that the Jordan is a river (i. 5). (See p. 153, and Aramaic Words, Index IV).

That ROMAN readers are in view is supported on the ground, somewhat slender perhaps, that Mark alone mentions that Simon the Cyrenian was the father of Alexander and Rufus (xv. 21; cf. Rom. xvi. 13); and also because of his use of several Latin words which are not found in the other Gospels: ' soldier-of-the-guard,' *speculator* (*spekoulatōr*, vi. 27); 'pots,' *sextarius* (*xestēs*, vii. 4, 8); 'farthing,' *quadrans* (*kodrantēs*, xii. 42); *centurio* (*kenturiōn*, xv. 39, 44, 45). Other Latin words, which occur in the other Records also, are, ' bed,' *grabbatus* (*krabbatos*, ii. 4, 9, 11, 12); *Praetorium* (*praitōrion*, xv. 16); *census* (*kēnsos*, xii. 14); *flagellare* (*phragelloō*, xv. 15). See pp. 153, 184, and Latin Words, Index IV).

To these somewhat precarious indications we must add the general tone of this Gospel, which would be calculated to appeal especially to the Roman mind, as Matthew's does to the Hebrew, and Luke's to the Greek. At any rate, in Rome it ' had a powerful environment in which to take root.'

The Old Testament Scriptures and prophecy, which meant so much to the Jew, would count for nothing with the Roman, who was ignorant of both. Reason and philosophy, so convincing to the Greek would mean little to the Roman, who was a man of action rather than of contemplation. ' The Gospel for him must present the character and career of Jesus from the Roman side, or point of view, as answering to the idea of Divine power, work, law, conquest, and universal sway. To the Roman these are the credentials of Jesus, no less essential than prophecy to the Jew, and philosophy to the Greek.'

Mark, adapting his Gospel to the need of the Roman, omits much which Matthew and Luke record, and records some things which they omit. For example, the discourses which make up so large a part of Matthew are not found in Mark, and he omits also the parables which have a special Jewish significance; for example: the Unmerciful Servant (xviii), the Labourers in the Vineyard (xx), the Two Sons (xxi), and the Marriage of the King's Son (xxii). Dr. Lindsay says: ' Many of Mark's Greek words and phrases are expressly forbidden by the grammarians, but would naturally "find place in the mongrel Greek of the slaves and freedmen who formed the first congregations of the Church at Rome." '

4

DATE OF WRITING

IN attempting to fix the date of this Gospel the critics range from A.D. 44 to A.D. 75. Recent criticism is decidedly in favour of a date prior to the destruction of Jerusalem, in A.D. 70. The question is part of the 'Synoptic Problem' (Div. A, p. 83).

After a hundred years of discussion, says Canon Streeter, there is now almost universal agreement that Mark is the earliest of the Gospels, so that, if we can fix approximately the date of Luke we shall be able to place Mark within narrow limits.

It is reasonable to assume, as Harnack does, that as at the end of the Acts there is no reference made by Luke to the issue of Paul's last trial, that event, therefore, had not yet taken place. If that be so, and if, as is commonly thought, the end of Acts brings us to A.D. 63, and Paul's release from his first Roman imprisonment, and seeing that Luke's Gospel was written before the Acts (i. 1), probably at Cæsarea, about A.D. 58-60, the former of these dates, A.D. 58, will fix at one end the date limit of Mark. It seems certain, therefore, that this Gospel was written between A.D. 46 and A.D. 56, and, as Allen, Nolloth, and Robertson think, the evidence as a whole points to A.D. 50 as the most probable date. If this be so, then Mark is the earliest

of the New Testament Writings, with the possible exception
of the Epistle of James.

There is a tradition that Mark wrote his Gospel after Peter's
death. This is based on the statement of Irenæus, in his ' Work
Against Heresies,' that ' after the departure (*exodus*) of Peter
and Paul, Mark, the disciple and interpreter of Peter, even he,
delivered to us in writing the things which were preached by
Peter.' If ' departure ' here means death, and if, as is commonly
believed, Peter suffered martyrdom in A.D. 68, then the date
of Mark would be between A.D. 68 and A.D. 70. Internal evidence,
however, is in favour of the early date.

5

PLACE OF WRITING

CHRYSOSTOM observes that ' Mark is said to have composed his Gospel in EGYPT at the solicitation of his disciples
there.' If that be true, the place would be Alexandria, as tradition connects Mark with that city.

Storr argues for ANTIOCH in Syria, and Birks, for Cæsarea,
but, says Salmond, ' ancient testimony, so far as it bears on the
question, is almost wholly on the side of ROME.'

The testimony referred to reaches from Irenæus of Lyons,
in the latter half of the second century (Div. A, ' Church Fathers ,'
p. 39), and it is held by most scholars to-day. This view finds
warrant and confirmation in 1 Peter v. 13, if so be, as is generally
believed, ' Babylon ' stands for Rome.

6

GENUINENESS AND AUTHENTICITY

IN the study of any of the Biblical Writings, the matters of
its genuineness and its authenticity are of great importance,
so it will be well for us to understand the meaning of these
terms, and the difference between them.

Writers on these subjects differ in their interpretation of them,
but the sense in which we use them here is as follows:

GENUINENESS. This relates to whether we have in the Gospels

a trustworthy representation of the original text, and whether
what is recorded is true to fact, and is authoritative.

AUTHENTICITY.   This relates to whether the Books were
written by the persons whose names they bear.

A book may be genuine which is not authentic, and a book
may be authentic which is not genuine. A book may be neither
genuine nor authentic, and a book may be both.

For example: If it can be shown that Mark's Gospel relates
matters of fact as they really happened, but that the record was
not written by Mark, the Gospel would be genuine, but not
authentic.

If it can be shown that this Gospel was written by Mark,
but that what is written is not trustworthy, it would be authentic,
but not genuine.

If it can be shown that the contents of this Gospel are not
true to fact, and that it was not written by Mark, the record
is neither genuine nor authentic.

If it can be shown that the contents are true and trustworthy,
and that the Gospel was written by Mark, it is both genuine
and authentic.

The present questions, therefore, are:

(1) Is this Gospel true and authoritative?
(2) Was this Gospel written by John Mark?

(1) **Genuineness**

Is this Gospel true and authoritative?

The answer to the question is applicable to all the Gospels,
and is, in a word, that very early, and without dissent, witness
was borne to the genuineness of all Four Gospels. Dr. Salmond
says: ' It may be regarded as proved that towards the end of
the second century our Four Gospels were universally accepted
in the Catholic Church as the peculiarly trustworthy records
of the Saviour's life '; and Prof. Norton says: ' About the end
of the second century the Gospels were reverenced as sacred
books by a community dispersed over the whole world, composed of men of different nations and languages. There were,
to say the least, sixty thousand copies in existence. They were
read in the assemblies of Christians; they were continually

quoted and appealed to, as of the highest authority; their reputation was as well established among believers from one end of the Roman Empire to the other, as it is among Christians at the present day. The general reception of the Gospels as books of the highest authority at the end of the second century, necessarily implies their celebrity at a much earlier period, and the long operation of causes sufficient to produce so remarkable a phenomenon.'

(a) TESTIMONIES FROM THE END TO THE MIDDLE OF THE SECOND CENTURY

TERTULLIAN (A.D. 200). (Div. A, 'Church Fathers,' p. 38). 'Of the Apostles, John and Matthew instil faith into us, whilst of apostolic men, Luke and Mark afterwards renew it.'

CLEMENT OF ALEXANDRIA (A.D. 190). Speaking of the Gospels, he says: 'Those that contained the genealogies were first written'; that Mark wrote his Gospel from matter preached by Peter; and that John 'last of all . . . wrote a spiritual Gospel.'

Referring to a passage taken from an apocryphal gospel, he says: 'We do not find this statement in the Four Gospels which have been handed down to us.'

IRENAEUS (A.D. 180). 'Matthew issued a written Gospel among the Hebrews in their own dialect, while Peter and Paul were preaching at Rome, and laying the foundation of the Church. After their departure, Mark, the disciple and interpreter of Peter, did also hand down to us in writing what had been preached by Peter. Luke, also, the companion of Paul, recorded in a book the gospel preached by him. Afterwards, John, the disciple of the Lord, who also had leaned upon His breast, did himself publish a Gospel during his residence at Ephesus in Asia.'

Whether Irenæus refers to our canonical Gospel by Matthew, or to another production, and whether or not he is correct in saying that Mark wrote after Peter's death, does not invalidate this testimony, and so need not be considered here.

TATIAN (A.D. 160). This Assyrian, becoming a Christian, wrote a Harmony of the Gospels, which he named *Diatessaron*, signifying *by means of four*. The four are our canonical Gospels. There is no trace of any non-canonical Gospel, and so Tatian's 'is a work of unique evidential value,' a great buttress of the genuineness of our Four Gospels.

JUSTIN MARTYR (A.D. 150). In this writer's two *Apologies* he speaks frequently of the *Memoirs of the Apostles*, and although the Gospels are not named it is clear from his quotations from or references to them that these are what he means by *Memoirs*. Paley says that from Justin's works might be extracted almost a complete Life of Christ.

(b) TESTIMONIES FROM THE MIDDLE OF THE SECOND CENTURY TO THE APOSTOLIC AGE

ARISTIDES (A.D. 140-145). This Athenian philosopher addressed an *Apology* to the Emperor Antoninus, in which, criticizing both pagan idolatry and Jewish worship, he extolled the gospel. In this appreciation he has a résumé of the principal facts of the gospel history, which, almost certainly, indicates that his reference is to our canonical Four Gospels.

BASILIDES (A.D. 125-130). This Gnostic heretic taught in the reign of Hadrian. In his writings are quotations from or references to the Gospels of Matthew, Luke, and John, as there are in the writings of Valentinus, another Gnostic heretic who taught in Rome about A.D. 140-150.

PAPIAS (A.D. 120-125). He is believed to have been a disciple of the Apostle John. Certain fragments which we have of his writings are of great interest and evidential value, especially his references to Matthew's and Mark's Gospels. He says that ' Matthew wrote the Oracles in Hebrew,' and also that ' Mark, having become the interpreter of Peter, wrote accurately all that he remembered of the things that were either said or done by Christ.'

For the correctness or otherwise of what he and Irenæus say about Matthew having written in Hebrew, see what is said in our study of that Gospel and elsewhere (pages 91, 92, 250).

IGNATIUS (A.D. 107-115). In his famous *Letters*, he not only speaks of the *gospel* in the abstract, in the sense of gospel teaching, but he makes numerous quotations from Matthew, Luke, and John. Mark is not quoted for the reason, probably, that so much of his Gospel is contained in Matthew and Luke.

CLEMENT OF ROME (A.D. 96). In his *Letter* to the Church of Corinth, he makes use of Matthew's and Luke's Gospels on the Sermon on the Mount.

BARNABAS (A.D. 70-90). The companion of Paul of this name has been credited with having written the *Epistle of Barnabas*, which is universally admitted to be of great antiquity. Clement of Rome says he was one of the Seventy. Whether these conjectures be true or not, the *Epistle* is of interest because of a reference which it has to Matthew's Gospel; and if this was known to him, in all likelihood Mark and Luke were also.

THE TEACHING (DIDACHÉ) OF THE TWELVE APOSTLES (A.D. 80-100). The author of this Writing, towards the end of the first century, ' possessed, as well as the Churches whom he addressed, a Gospel collection containing Matthew and Luke certainly, and probably also John.' Mark is not referred to, probably because it was regarded as included in Matthew and Luke.

Such is the evidence for *the genuineness* of the Gospels as a whole. Dr. Gloag says that ' no classical writing of the ancients has the same amount of testimony. When we consider the universal acceptance of these Gospels towards the close of the second century, the reverence shown to them as sacred books, their wide distribution throughout all the provinces of the Roman Empire, the explicit testimony of Justin Martyr to them in the middle of that century, their translation into the Latin and Syriac languages, we cannot fail to be convinced that they are the genuine records of the life of Christ.'

(2) **Authenticity**

Was this Gospel written by John Mark?

Much of the evidence produced under *Genuineness* answers this question also, but there are other testimonies, or fuller. The most ancient direct testimony that Mark wrote this Gospel, is that of Papias, quoted by Eusebius:

> ' Mark, the interpreter of Peter, wrote carefully down all that he recollected, but not according to the order of Christ's speaking or working. For, as I think, he neither had heard Christ, nor was a direct follower of Him. But with Peter, as already said, he was afterward intimate, who used to preach the gospel for the profit of his hearers, and not in order to construct a history of the sayings of the Lord. Hence Mark made no mistake, since he so wrote some things as he was accustomed to repeat them from memory, and since he continually sought this one thing— neither to omit anything of those things which he had heard, nor to add anything false to them.'

The only question which arises as to Mark's authorship relates to chap. xvi. 9-20. It may be said that this section presents the chief textual problem in the New Testament. The Manuscripts show three endings to the Gospel, which may be called the *Short Ending*, an *Intermediate Ending*, and the *Long Ending*. The first of these makes the Gospel end at verse eight, which, Prof. Farmer thinks, is just possible, though abrupt.

The *Intermediate Ending* is not regarded as genuine, and the view of most modern scholars is that the *Long Ending*, our Mark xvi. 9-20, is not from the pen of Mark, but from one, Aristion, a disciple of the Apostle John. If this conclusion be correct, the paragraph does not, on that account, lose its value. Dr. Salmond says: ' Though it may not have belonged to the original form of the Gospel, it must have been added to it at a very early date, by the original hand, or by some other competent witness—some informed companion or disciple of Mark '; and he adds, ' The paragraph remains an independent and historically credible account of the events of the Forty Days, of very ancient date, and of primitive authority.'

In none of the Gospels is it said who wrote it, but if Luke wrote the Acts (and it is certain that he did), we may assume, from Acts i. 1, that he is the author of the Gospel which bears his name. Equally sure may we be, because of the most ancient testimonies, that Mark wrote the Gospel which bears his name. The authorship of both Matthew and John has been vigorously challenged and debated, and many scholars still believe that these are not the writings of Apostles, but of Matthew, an Evangelist, and of John, a Presbyter. We advocate the correctness of the traditional view. (See pp. 130-138).

7

MARK AND PETER

THE evidence for the connection between Mark and Peter is twofold, external and internal, and both are replete.

(a) EXTERNAL EVIDENCE

Mark and Peter are connected with one another both in Scripture and in tradition. Peter calls Mark his ' son,' and implies that Mark is at Rome with him (1 Peter v. 13). Dr. Swete says that ' one of the oldest and most trustworthy of Christian traditions represents Mark as St. Peter's interpreter, and as the author of a collection of memoirs which gave the substance of Peter's teaching.' (Page 176).

This tradition, as we have seen, goes back to Papias, and is continued by Justin Martyr, Irenæus, Clement of Alexandria, Hippolytus, Tertullian, Origen, Eusebius, Epiphanius, Jerome, and others (see under ' Genuineness and Authenticity,' p. 171).

No reasonable motive can be assigned for this long and uniform testimony, except the conviction that these statements were founded on fact, and that the facts presented in the Gospel correspond very fairly with it.

(b) INTERNAL EVIDENCE

The Gospel begins at the point when Peter attached himself to the Lord. Not a word is said concerning the early years, or

12

of that part of Jesus' earthly life which preceded His public appearance.

Throughout this Gospel special attention is paid to the ministry in Galilee (i. 14-ix. 50), and particularly to Christ's activities in the neighbourhood of Capernaum, which was Peter's place of residence. The general character of the Gospel points to an eye-witness as directly or indirectly its author, and there are touches which indicate such first-hand knowledge as Peter would have.

We are told about Peter's home, and his mother-in-law, the disciples are described as ' Simon, and they that were with him ' (i. 36), and Mark alone tells us that they and Peter followed after Jesus when He withdrew to a solitary place at the beginning of His ministry (i. 36).

Mark says that it was Peter who called the Lord's attention to the withered fig tree (xi. 21). He also tells us that it was Peter and his brother who asked Jesus on the Mount of Olives about the destruction of the Temple (xiii. 3); and that the angel at the tomb specified that Peter be told of the resurrection (xvi. 7).

The whole of chap. i. 29-37 is full of touches peculiar to this Gospel which imply that they are Peter's. Compare this passage with its parallels in Matthew and Luke.

In the record of the healing of the paralytic (ii. 1-12), are similar details such as imply an eye-witness, and others are found in i. 43; iii. 5; vi. 39; viii. 12; ix. 33, 34; x. 14, 33, 50; xi. 13, 21.

It is worthy of notice that details favourable to Peter are omitted in this Gospel, while others, not favourable, are recorded (cf. viii. 27-33, with Matt. xvi. 13-23). Compare, also, Mark's and Matthew's accounts of Peter's denials of his Lord.

Mark does not mention the incident of Peter walking on the sea (Matt. xiv. 28, 29), nor the capture of the fish in which was found the Roman coin (Matt. xvii. 24-27), nor his mission along with John to prepare the Passover (Luke xxii. 8), nor the fact that he accompanied John to the sepulchre (John xx. 2-6).

It has been well said of this Gospel, 'the hand that transcribed the story may be that of St. Mark, but the voice that speaks is unquestionably that of St. Peter, who was on the spot.'

8

MARK'S GOSPEL AND THE OTHER SYNOPTICS

THE first three Gospels are called *Synoptic* (*sun*, together, and *opsis*, view), because they look at the life of Jesus from a common point of view, and a matter of great importance is the relation in which they stand to one another.

In answer to the question, Which is the original Gospel? each of the three has been claimed by scholars to be such, but on grounds which are arbitrary and unscientific. To-day the issue is narrowed down to the following alternatives:

(*a*) Whether the three made use of an original written Gospel, now lost.

(*b*) Whether the three made use of a common Oral Gospel.

(*c*) Whether Matthew or (and) Luke borrowed from Mark.

(*d*) Whether Mark borrowed from Matthew or (and) Luke.

The truth, it would seem, is to be found in the following assumptions:

(1) That Matthew and Luke used an Oral Gospel, 'in which a cycle of representative facts about Jesus were described in language which had become stereotyped by usage.'

(2) That Matthew and Luke, and perhaps Mark also, used documentary sources.

(3) That Mark is the earliest of the Synoptic Records, and most nearly represents the Oral Gospel of early apostolic preaching.

(4) That both Matthew and Luke made large use of Mark.

(5) That, therefore, Mark is not an abridgment of Matthew and Luke, but the latter are enlargements and re-arrangements of Mark, to which in each Gospel is added a large amount of material from other sources.

To Mark, therefore, must be accorded first place in historical value, because it ranks first in order of time, and is incorporated almost bodily in Matthew and Luke. (See Div. A, 'The Synoptic Problem,' p. 83—; and Div. B, pp. 261, 356).

9

MARK'S GOSPEL IN THE EARLY CHURCH

BY the middle of the second century our Four canonical Gospels were recognized as being genuine and having unique authority (see under ' Genuineness,' p. 142), and this is true of these Four only.

Yet, the fact remains that Mark's Gospel, though the first of the Four to be written (see previous section), and though its genuineness was never disputed (see under ' Genuineness,' p. 172), it did not appeal in any special manner to the interests of the ancient Church, and it received comparatively little attention from the early theologians. Indeed, says Dr. Plummer, ' it was in danger of being lost as completely as that other document, which was used by both Matthew and Luke, side by side with Mark, the document which is now called Q.'

Evidence of this fact is ample.

(a) References to Mark in Sub-Apostolic Writings are few. For example, the references of Tertullian (A.D. 200) to Mark are only about one-tenth of his references to either Matthew or Luke.

(b) The place of Mark in the ancient Catalogues and Manuscripts reflects the judgment of the early Church as to its relative importance. In none of these was it ever put first, though it was the first to be written, but in some of them it was put last of the Four.

(c) Irenæus and other writers made the four Cherubim in Ezekiel i., and the four Living Creatures in Rev. iv. symbols of the Four Gospels, but they differ a lot in their assignment. Three times Matthew is likened to a Man, Luke to a Calf, and John to an Eagle; but Mark only is likened to all four, Eagle, Lion, Man, and Calf, which reflects the difficulty the early Church had in forming a definite judgment as to the place and office of this Gospel.

How, then, is this fact to be accounted for? Certain things which are widely agreed upon among scholars to-day will help to explain it. It can safely be assumed:

(1) that the Synoptic Records were all written before the destruction of Jerusalem in A.D. 70;

(2) that Mark was the first of the three to be written, and must have been written early;

(3) that almost the whole of Mark is to be found in Matthew and Luke.

It is easy to see from these facts that Matthew especially would tend to throw Mark into the background, for in it readers had not only the most of Mark—all indeed, with the exception of about 55 verses (see pp. 86, 132, 186, 253), but also all the rich material of Matthew which is not in Mark. It was natural that the greater should supplant the less.

Moreover, it was early believed that Mark was an abridgment of Matthew, a view which received the weighty sanction of Augustine, whose opinion was followed by most theologians for fourteen centuries. We now know that this view was a mistake, but the idea would naturally make Mark of comparatively little importance, for readers would prefer the full text to an abridgment.

The neglect of Mark was further promoted by the appearance of Luke's Gospel, which, though not as popular as Matthew, ' at once became far more popular than Mark.'

To-day, however, the situation is changed. Largely due to the criticism which arose at the end of the eighteenth century, three things may be said to be established; viz:

(i) That Mark's is the earliest of the canonical Gospels;

(ii) That it comes nearest to the Oral Gospel of early apostolic preaching ;

(iii) That the other Gospels, Matthew and Luke, are enlargements and rearrangements of this earlier vivid picture of our Lord and His work. (See under ' Mark and the Other Synoptics,' p. 179).

From this survey we see that ' it remained,' as Dr. Swete says, ' for a later age to realize and appreciate to the full the freshness and exactness of the first-hand report which has descended to us from the senior Apostle through the ministry of John Mark.'

The study of the Gospels should, therefore, begin with Mark, which may have been written as early as A.D. 50 (see under

'Date of Writing,' p. 170), and be followed by Matthew (about
A.D. 58); then Luke (about A.D. 58-60), and finally by John
(about A.D. 95).   (See Div. A, Pt. II, Sec. 6, p. 138).

10

MARK'S SOURCES

SEEING that Mark was not one of the Twelve, from whence
did he get his information? Luke was not of the Apostolate,
but he tells us why and how he came to write his Gospel (i. 1-4),
but we have no such information in Mark.   There is, however,
a wealth of external testimony which can leave us in no doubt
as to the main origin of this Gospel, and the internal testimony
is in harmony with it.

(i). No one now disputes that Mark's main source was the
preaching of Peter.   This was the belief of the post-apostolic
Church, and it was this fact, no doubt, which saved this Gospel
from exclusion from the Canon, and, perhaps, from oblivion.
' If we had no information as to the authorship of the second
Gospel, or the connection of Mark with Peter, we should never
have had any reason for supposing that Mark might have written
it ' (Plummer).

The belief that behind Mark's record is Peter's knowledge,
can be traced through three hundred years, from the beginning
of the second century to the end of the fourth.   For this evidence
in detail see sections ' Genuineness and Authenticity,' and
' Mark and Peter ' (pp. 171-177).   The evidence of Peter's
influence in this Gospel is quite clear. whether Mark wrote it
during the Apostle's life, or after his death, as Irenæus supposes,
and irrespective of where he wrote it.

It is not without significance that Peter's name occurs in this
Gospel almost as often as in Matthew and in Luke, notwithstanding that Mark is so much shorter than either of these.   Simon,
Peter, or Simon Peter is mentioned in Matthew twenty-eight
times, in Luke twenty-seven times, and in Mark twenty-five
times.   Of Mark's references to the name in separate contexts,
four are peculiar to him (i. 36; xi. 21; xiii. 3; xvi. 7).

Dr. Swete says the tradition that Mark is indebted to Peter is at once too early and too widespread to be abandoned, unless the evidence of the Gospel itself renders its acceptance impossible, which it does not.

The ground covered by Mark is an expansion of the report of Peter's sermon at Cæsarea (Acts x. 34-43), beginning with the Baptism of John, and ending with the Ascension (cf. Acts i. 21, 22). Mark may even have been one of the ' six ' with Peter on this occasion (Acts x. 23; xi. 12), and may have made fragmentary notes of this and of other discourses by Peter (p. 132).

We must not conclude, however, that Mark was simply a reporter of Peter, for the freedom of his own personality is clearly evident in his style, and in the selection of his material, in what he uses, and what he omits. The eyes are Peter's but the pen is Mark's (see under ' Mark and Peter,' p. 177).

(ii). Peter, however, was not Mark's only source. Dr. Plummer says: ' Even some things which Peter might have told him may have been derived by Mark from others, for when he wrote other eye-witnesses still survived, and there was abundance of oral tradition.'

(iii). Then, there is the matter of Q (*Quelle*, source). This is a lost document from which, it is believed, Matthew and Luke drew. It is sometimes called the *Logia* of Jesus, of which Papias speaks, and it consisted mainly of Sayings of Jesus. It is practically certain that Q preceded Mark; Dr. Streeter thinks, by as much even, as twenty years. Prof. Ramsay and Dr. Salmond suggest that it was written during the ministry of Jesus, probably by Matthew, the tax-gatherer. The question is—Did Mark know of, and use Q? Dr. Streeter and Dr. Sanday think that there are traces of this document in Mark, but perhaps it is best to take Dr. Plummer's view that no sure answer can be given to the question. One difficulty in the way of supposing that Mark did use Q, is in the fact that, in that event, Matthew and Luke, by incorporating so much of Mark, would have worked over the Q material twice.

(iv). But there are some things in this Gospel which, in all probability, are Mark's own, for there were things which he himself could remember, as, for example, events in the Passion

Week which he may well have witnessed, and could never forget. This becomes certain if the young man of the episode in chap. xiv. 51, 52, was Mark himself.

This, in substance and summary, is probably all that can be said about the Sources of Mark's Gospel.

II

MARK'S DESIGN

BOTH the third and fourth Gospels declare the object with which they were written (Luke i. 1-4; John xx. 31), but the second Gospel does not explain its design.

It has been thought that this is what is called a ' tendency-writing '; that it was undertaken with a definite dogmatic or ecclesiastical object. The view is that the writer's materials were carefully selected with the idea of reconciling ' two sharply contrasted parties in the Church, one holding by Peter and the more Jewish conception of Christianity, and the other adhering to Paul and the freer Gentile ideas.'

This is a highly unnatural view to take of so simple and straightforward a narrative, though we must believe that in giving a plain, reliable account of the deeds and words of the Lord Jesus, and the events of His life, as he had received them, in the main, from Peter, the writer was guided to the selection of his materials with *some* object in view, an object which external and internal evidence should disclose.

Not only is there the tradition which associates Peter and Mark with Rome, but in the Gospel itself there is much which leads to the view that *Mark wrote for Roman Christians*, such, for instance, as the frequent use of Latin words, the explanation of Jewish customs, and the use of the Roman division of the watches (xiii. 35) instead of the Jewish division, which the other Evangelists retain (cf. Luke xii. 38). (For details, see under, 'For Whom Written,' p. 168).

Matthew is adapted to the Jewish outlook, and Luke to the Greek, but Mark is adapted to the Roman. All three outlooks were governed by the idea of *power*, but whereas in Matthew, what dominates is the *power of purpose*, and in Luke, the *power of thought*, in Mark it is the *power of will*. These three powers answer to the outlooks respectively of the Jew, the Greek, and the Roman.

The Romans were people of action rather than of thought, and in addressing them more especially, Mark presents Christ as the mighty Worker rather than as the profound Thinker, the Man who conquers by doing. Hence this vivid and rapid record, with little of discourse, and much of movement and accomplishment.

Dr. Wordsworth says that the features of this Gospel would 'commend it to the acceptance of a great body of the Roman people, especially of the middle classes, engaged in practical business, legal affairs, commercial enterprises, and military campaigns, and migrating in frequent journeys from place to place. Such an Evangelical Manual as this would be particularly appropriate and serviceable to them.'

Clement of Alexandria, who flourished in the latter part of the second century (see under 'Church Fathers,' Div. A, p. 38), made a statement in the sixth book of his Institutions (not now extant, but quoted by Eusebius) bearing on this subject, which is of considerable value. It is to the effect that when the gospel was preached to the Romans, 'such a light of piety shone into the minds of those who heard Peter that they were not satisfied with once hearing, nor with the unwritten doctrine that was delivered, but earnestly besought Mark (whose Gospel is now spread abroad) that he would leave in writing for them the doctrine which they had received by preaching; nor did they cease until they had persuaded him, and so given occasion for the Gospel to be written which is now called after Mark.'

We may assume, then, that guided by the Spirit of God, Mark presented the Redeemer to the Romans in a manner in keeping with their mode of thought and life, and calculated to win them over to Christianity. He is here seen as the wonder-working Son of God (i. 1. See p. 170).

OMISSIONS IN MARK'S GOSPEL

IT is obvious that Mark's Gospel is the shortest of the Four, having but 16 chapters as against 28 in Matthew, 24 in Luke, and 21 in John; but only by a comparison of the Four can we realize how unspeakable our loss would have been had only Mark's Gospel been given to us. Of the Four, it is this Gospel we could best dispense with, that is, with the least loss, as the whole of it, with the exception of 50-55 verses, is incorporated in Matthew and Luke (see pp. 86, 132, 140, 253, 261). But looking the other way there are priceless riches in Matthew, Luke, and John, of which Mark gives no account at all.

Supposing we had Mark's Gospel only, what would we have lost? The answer to this question is in the tabulation of what he omits, as follows:

> The whole of the more than thirty years of Jesus' preparation for His ministry; that is—the two genealogies; the annunciations to Zacharias, Mary, and Joseph; Mary's visit to Elisabeth; the births of John and Jesus; the angels and the shepherds; the circumcision of Jesus, and His presentation in the temple; the visit of the Wise Men from the East; the flight into Egypt, and return to Nazareth; the childhood at Nazareth; Jesus' first Passover; and the long, silent years at Nazareth.

At this point Mark runs parallel with Matthew and Luke in relating the beginnings of the gospel; but, as do Matthew and Luke, he omits the contents of John's first four chapters, which record:

> The Baptist's confession before the priests and Levites, and his witness to the Messiah, the Lamb of God; the first five followers of Jesus; the first miracle; the first cleansing of the temple; the discourse with Nicodemus; John's testimony to Christ at Aenon; the discourse with the woman of Samaria; the gospel in Sychar; and the healing of the nobleman's son.

Passing over the first rejection of Jesus at Nazareth, which Luke records, Mark at this point runs parallel with Matthew and Luke for a considerable time, to the choosing of the Twelve, but from this event he omits:

> The Sermon on the Mount; the healing of the centurion's servant; the raising of the widow's son; the Baptist's last message; and the anointing in Simon's house.

From this point, Mark, in chapters iii. 20-ix. 50, runs parallel with Matthew, or Luke, or both, for nearly eighteen months, omitting, however, the healing of two blind men and a dumb demoniac; and the discourse on the Bread of Life.

After this there is a long break in Mark's record, wherein are omitted:

> Christ at the Feast of Tabernacles; the woman taken in adultery; the discourse on the Light of the World, and the one on Spiritual Freedom; the healing of the man born blind; the talk on the Good Shepherd; Christ at the Feast of Dedication; the raising of Lazarus; and the withdrawal to Ephraim, all in John's Gospel.

And of Luke's record he omits:

> The mission of the Seventy; the Good Samaritan; the visit to Martha and Mary; a discourse on prayer; discourses against the Pharisees; teaching concerning trust in God, and coming judgment; the Galileans slain by Pilate; the woman healed on a Sabbath; the question whether few are saved; reply to the warning against Herod; discourse at a Pharisee's table; parables of the great supper, on counting the cost of discipleship, the lost coin, the prodigal son and elder brother, the unjust steward, the rich man and Lazarus; concerning forgiveness and faith; healing of the ten lepers; discourse on the coming of the Kingdom; parable of the unjust judge; the story of the Pharisee and Publican; the conversion of Zacchæus; and the parable of the ten pounds.

After some more parallel accounts, Mark omits the story of the coming of the Greeks to Jesus, and the following discourse; and the Jews' rejection of Christ. A few more parallels, and Mark omits the Upper Room discourses, and Christ's intercessory prayer.

The day of the Crucifixion, and from then on to the Ascension, Mark runs parallel with the other Evangelists, omitting only the report of the watch; the appearance of Jesus to Thomas and the Ten, and the appearance to the Seven by the Sea of Galilee.

Read these items again and again, and you will feel deeply what we owe to Matthew, Luke, and John. The following is a tabular reference-statement of Mark's omissions, in chronological order as far as this can be determined.

We readily see that preaching, record, and teaching are distinguishable, though they may all be handling the same subject. Mark's Gospel is preaching, Luke's is record, John's is teaching, and Matthew's combines all three. Preaching, as to substance and length, must be popular in a sense and degree which does not apply to teaching, and which record does not aim at, and this fact accounts for the content and scope of Mark's Gospel, and also for what is omitted. Teaching is for a select audience, but preaching is for the people, *hoi polloi*, and so the substance of the Fourth Gospel could never be popularized, and the substance of Mark's Gospel made and makes no select appeal. The early preaching took the line of narrative rather than of discourse, and was directed to the imagination and emotions rather than to the intellect.

If this be true we must see that the Fourth Gospel, even if it had been written within forty years of Christ's ascension, would not have been suitable for oral use by the evangelists; but it was eminently suitable for the instruction of the Christian Church after two generations of Christian reflection.

When Peter went to a gathering of Romans at Cæsarea, we may assume that in addressing them he presented to them in substance the oral Gospel which the evangelists were everywhere proclaiming, and what that was we see in Acts x. 34-43. Summarily Peter spoke about two things only, the ministry (37, 38), and the sacrifice and triumph (39-41) of Jesus Christ, beginning from 'the baptism which John preached,' and ending with the appearance of the risen Lord to His Apostles.

Now this is exactly the ground covered by Mark's Gospel which, for the most part, is Peter's record. Chapter x. 45 divides the record into the two parts of ministry and sacrifice, and the Gospel begins at the point of the baptism, and ends with the manifestation of the risen Christ. We may say then that Mark's Gospel is the detailed record of the summarized Gospel preached in the house of Cornelius. To have added the extra which Matthew, Luke, and John supply would largely have destroyed the object which the first evangelists had in view. (See pages 85, 87-89).

From this Table it will be seen that in the Revised Version Matthew has 442 verses, Luke 723 verses, and John 748 verses, which verses Mark omits, a total of 1913 verses. This is 845 verses more than all the verses in Matthew, 764 verses more than all the verses in Luke, and 1047 verses more than all the verses in John. (See pp. 193, 216, 225-234). If Mark's Gospel represents substantially the first Oral Tradition, we see how very much was excluded from it.

Matthew	Luke	John
		i ... 1-18
	i ... 1-4	
i ... 1-17	iii ... 23-38	
i. 18-.ii 23	i. 5-ii. 52	
iii ... 7-10	iii ... 7-14	
		i. 19-iv. 54
	iv ... 16-30	
iv ... 13-16	iv ... 31, 32	
		v ... 1-47
v. 1-viii. 1 viii ... 5-13	vi ... 17-49 vii ... 1-10 vii ... 11-17	
xi ... 2-19	vii ... 18-35	
xi ... 20-30		
	vii ... 36-viii. 3	
xii ... 38-45 xiii ... 24-30 xiii ... 33-53 ix ... 27-34		
		vi ... 22-71
xvii ... 24-27 xviii ... 15-35 viii ... 19-22	ix ... 57-62	
		vii ... 2-9
	ix ... 51-56	vii ... 10
		vii. 10-x. 21
	x. 1-xiii. 21	
		x ... 22-42
	xiii. 22-xvii. 10	
		xi ... 1-54
	xvii. 11-xviii. 14	

MATTHEW	LUKE	JOHN
xx ... 1-16		
	xix ... 1-28	
		xi. 55-xii. 1, 9-11
	xix ... 39-44	
xxi ... 10-16		
		xii ... 20-50
xxi ... 28-32 xxii ... 1-14 xxiii ... 1-39 xxiv. 26-28, 37-41, 43-51 xxv ... 1-46		
	xxii ... 14-16, 24-30 xxij ... 17, 18	
		xiii ... 1-20
xxvi ... 25		xiii ... 23-30
		xiii ... 31-35
	xxii ... 35-38	
		xiv-xviii. 12-14, 19-23
xxvii ... 3-10		
	xxiii ... 6-12	
xxviii ... 2-4		
	xxiv ... 9-12	xx ... 1-10
	xxiv ... 13-32	
xxviii ... 9-15		
	xxiv ... 33-35	
		xx ... 26-xxi. 25
	xxiv ... 44-49	

MATERIAL PECULIAR TO MARK'S GOSPEL

LARGE parts of Matthew, Luke, and John are peculiar to these Gospels respectively, but comparatively little is peculiar to Mark, because all but 50-55 verses of it is incorporated in the other Synoptics (p. 253), and John's Gospel supplements all three.

Bishop Westcott says that if the total contents of the several Gospels be represented by 100, the following result is obtained:

Gospel	Peculiarities	Coincidences
Mark	7	93
Matthew	42	58
Luke	59	41
John	92	8

From this it will be seen that the peculiarities and the coincidences are in the inverse order, fewest peculiarities in Mark, and most in John; most coincidences in Mark, and fewest in John.

Not including passages in Mark which give in greater detail what may be found in Matthew, or Luke, or both, it may be said that Mark has some 65 verses in whole or in part which are peculiar to his record, although Dr. Swete claims that 'as a result of the characteristic fulness of Mark, some eighty verses in his Gospel find no direct parallel in the other Synoptists,' and Sir John Hawkins reckons the number to be fifty verses.

(a) The 65 verses referred to, peculiar to Mark, are: i. 1; ii. 27; iii. 8-12, 19b-21; iv. 26-29; v. 4, 5; vi. 19-21, 31, 52; vii. 2-4, 32-37; viii. 22-26; ix. 21-27, 30, 48-50; xi. 16; xii. 32-34; xiii. 33-37; xiv. 51, 52; xv. 7b, 8, 25, 44, 45b; xvi. 16-18.

After the opening verse of the Gospel, these pieces record among others, the dictum concerning the Sabbath; the fear of Jesus' relatives lest He become mentally deranged; the parable of the seed growing secretly; healing of the Gerasene; the hatred of Herodias; healing of a demon-possessed boy; the inquiring Scribe; the healing of a deaf mute; the healing of a blind man in Bethsaida; the parable of the porter; the young man who fled, and a commission from the risen Lord.

All these items are in keeping with the practical character of the Gospel.

In some way mark in your Bible these 'peculiar' passages.

(b) In addition to these passages a list should be made of items which, although having a parallel in Matthew, or Luke, or both, are given in such detail as to be themselves peculiarities. These are in Dr. Swete's figure of eighty verses.

To the foregoing 65 verses should be added the following: i. 2, 33; iii. 17b; iv. 36b; vi. 37b; vii. 24b; viii. 14b, 18; ix. 15, 20; x. 10, 32b (not 32c); xii. 29; xiv. 18, 56b, 59; xv. 21b; xvi. 8b. These references represent substantially all that is peculiar to this Gospel.

14

THE OLD TESTAMENT IN MARK'S GOSPEL

IT is impressive that Mark, the earliest of the Four Gospels, has so much of the Old Testament in it, especially when we remember that it was not written for Jews, but for Gentiles. The number of references is variously estimated, ranging from twenty-three (Lindsay) to sixty-eight (Swete). It is safe to say that there are, at any rate, sixty-three references, by which is meant quotations and allusions (pp. 96, 146). The following list should be carefully checked and studied.

	GOSPEL	PARALLEL	OLD TESTAMENT
1	* i. 2	—	Mal. iii. 1
2	* i. 3	M. L.	Isa. xl. 3
3	i. 15	—	Old Testament prophecy implied
4	i. 44	M. L.	Lev. xiii. 49
5	ii. 24	M.	Exod. xx. 9-11
6	ii. 25, 26	M. L.	1 Sam. xxi. 6
7	* iv. 12	M. L.	Isa. vi. 9 f.
8	iv. 29	—	Joel iii. 13
9	iv. 32	M. L.	Ezek. xvii. 23; Dan. iv. 12, 21
10	vi. 15	M.	Mal. iv. 5; Deut. xviii. 15
11	vi. 18	M.	Lev. xviii. 16; xx. 21
12	vi. 34	M.	1 Kings xxii. 17; Num. xxvii. 17 Ezek. xxxiv. 5
13	* vii. 6	M.	Isa. xxix. 13
14	* vii. 10a	M.	Exod. xx. 12; xxi. 17; Deut. v. 16
15	* vii. 10b	M.	Exod. xxi. 17

	GOSPEL	PARALLEL	OLD TESTAMENT
16	*viii. 18	—	Jer. v. 21; Ezek. xii. 2
17	viii. 28	M.	cf. refs. to Mark vi. 15
18	ix. 4	M. L.	Moses; Elijah
19	ix. 11, 12a, 13	M.	Mal. iv. 5
20	ix. 12b	M.	Psa. xxii. 6, 7; Isa. liii. 2, 3; Zech. xiii. 7
21	* ix. 48	—	Isa. lxvi. 24
22	x. 3, 4	M.	Deut. xxiv. 1-4
23	* x. 6	M.	Gen. i. 27
24	* x. 7	M.	Gen. ii. 24
25	* x. 19	M. L.	Exod. xx. 12-17; Deut. v. 16-20
26	x. 27	M. L.	Gen. xviii. 14; Zech. viii. 6
27	* xi. 9	M.	Psa. cxviii. 25, 26
28	* xi. 17a	M. L.	Isa. lvi. 7
29	* xi. 17b	M. L.	Jer. vii. 11
30	xii. 1	M. L.	Isa. v. 1 f.
31	* xii. 10, 11	M. L.	Psa. cxviii. 22 f.
32	* xii. 19	M. L.	Deut. xxv. 5: Gen. xxxviii. 8
33	xii. 24	M.	Old Testament
34	* xii. 26	M. L.	Exod. iii. 6
35	* xii. 29	—	Deut. vi. 4
36	* xii. 30	M	Deut. vi. 5
37	* xii. 31	M. L.	Lev. xix. 18
38	* xii. 32a	—	Deut. vi. 4
39	* xii. 32b	—	Deut. iv. 35
40	* xii. 33a	M. L.	Deut. vi. 5
41	* xii. 33b	M. L.	Lev. xix. 18
42	* xii. 33c	—	1 Sam. xv. 22
43	* xii. 36	M. L.	Psa. cx. 1
44	*xiii. 8	M. L.	Isa. xix. 2
45	*xiii. 12	M. L.	Mic. vii. 6
46	*xiii. 14	M.	Dan. ix. 27; xi. 31; xii. 11
47	*xiii. 19	M.	Dan. xii. 1
48	*xiii. 22	M.	Deut. xiii. 1
49	*xiii. 24, 25a	M.	Isa. xiii. 10
50	*xiii. 25b	M.	Isa. xxxiv. 4
51	*xiii. 26	M. L.	Dan. vii. 13
52	xiii. 27	M.	Deut. xxx. 4
53	xiv. 12	M. L.	Exod. xii
54	xiv. 18	—	Psa. xli. 9
55	xiv. 24	M.	Exod. xxiv. 8; Zech. ix. 11
56	xiv. 26	M.	From Psalm cxiv-cxviii
57	*xiv. 27	M.	Zech. xiii. 7
58	xiv. 49	M.	Scriptures
59	xiv. 62	M.	Psa. cx. 1ff.; Dan. vii. 13
60	xv. 24	M. L.	Psa. xxii. 18
—	xv. 28 (A.V.)	L.	Isa. liii. 12
61	xv. 29	M.	Psa. xxii. 7; cix. 25
62	* xv. 34	M.	Psa. xxii. 1
63	xv. 36	M.	Psa. lxix. 21

In this list observe:

  1 That there are 63 references (xv. 28 is omitted in the R.V.).
  2 That 23 of them have parallels in M=Matthew, and L=Luke.
  3 That 30 of them have parallels in M=Matthew only.

4 That there is one parallel in L=Luke only (A.V.).

5 That 10 of them are peculiar to Mark; *italicised*.

6 That of these 63 references 36 are quotations, verbal, or nearly so, and the remainder are allusions. The quotations are indicated by an asterisk.

7 That of the 36 quotations only 4 relate to Christ personally (xii. 36; xiii. 26; xiv. 27; xv. 34); 2 to John the Baptist (i. 2, 3); and practically all the others are related to conduct (except ix. 48; xii. 26; xiii. 8, 14, 19, 22, 24, 25).

8 That 16 of the 39 Books of the Old Testament are drawn upon, and of these chiefly (and in this order) Deuteronomy, Psalms, Exodus, and Daniel.

9 That of these 63 references all but 18 are uttered by the Lord. Trace these eighteen.

10 That of the 661 verses in Mark's Gospel (R.V.) 61, or nearly one-tenth, contain Old Testament references.

To get the most benefit from these facts they should be placed in your copy of this Gospel, and frequently referred to.

15
CHRIST'S WORDS IN MARK'S GOSPEL

IN the A.V. of this Gospel there are 678 verses, and of these, 285 in whole, or in part, record words of our Lord. In the R.V. there are 661 verses (vii. 16; ix. 44, 46; xi. 26; xv. 28; xvi. 9-20, being omitted), and of these 277 record His words. The following are the number of verses in the various chapters which have Jesus' words (A.V.). (See pp. 272, 366, 418).

Chs.		Vers.	Chs.		Vers.	Chs.		Vers.	Chs.		Vers.
i.	...	6	v	...	8	ix.	...	25	xiii	...	34
ii.	...	15	vi.	...	7	x.	...	32	xiv.	...	26
iii.	...	13	vii.	...	20	xi.	...	12	xv.	...	2
iv.	...	32	viii.	...	19	xii.	...	30	xvi.	...	4

From these the R.V. omits eight (vii. 16; ix. 44, 46; xi. 26), and the two oldest Greek manuscripts omit xvi. 15-18.

In each of seven of the sixteen chapters are twenty or more verses which report Christ's words. In some way mark, in your Bible, these 285 passages for ready reference. They constitute approximately three-sevenths of the whole Gospel. In Matthew, Christ's words are about three-fifths of the whole; in Luke,

nearly one half; and in John, not quite one half. The following
should be studied:

GOSPEL	VERSES (A.V.)	VERSES (R.V.)	VERSES OF CHRIST'S WORDS	PROPORTION OF GOSPEL
Matthew -	1071	1068	644	Three-fifths
Mark -	678	661	285	Three-sevenths
Luke -	1151	1149	586	Nearly half
John -	879	866	419	Not quite half
	3779	3744	1934	

From this it will be seen that in the Gospels are 3779 verses
(A.V.), and of these, 1934, more than half, record words uttered
by our Lord. These 1934 verses contain more wisdom than
can be found in all the literatures of the world, because the
utterances are divine and authoritative. (See pp. 272, 366, 418).

16

MARK'S STYLE AND DICTION

THE inspiration of the Scriptures does not destroy the individuality of the writers. The personality of each is stamped on
what he has written; each has his style and diction, and it is this
fact which makes comparative study of the Gospels so fascinating.
No one can read these Records without observing, and being
impressed by, their differences, although they so largely travel
over the same ground of subject matter.

Matthew is methodical and massive. Luke is artistic and
graceful. John is abstract and profound. And Mark, in contrast
to these, is conversational, colloquial, graphic, concise, abrupt,
vigorous, forceful, realistic.

Not the sayings, but the doings of Jesus dominate this Gospel,
and an aim of the writer is to impress his readers with the rapid,
ceaseless energy of the Saviour.

(1) There are many words for which Mark shows a preference,

and which are characteristic of his style.   (The figures in brackets are the number of occurrences):

> *Go out,* or *go forth* (11): *go in,* or *enter* (8): *ask* (25): *again* (30): *rule over* (27): *depart* (15): *unclean spirit* (11): *gospel* (8): *bring* (15): *straightway,* immediately, forthwith, anon (41): and the adverb *euthus,* six times more: *crowd,* or multitude (38): *to reason* (7): *to look up* (7): *to look upon* (4): *amazed* (4): *power,* authority (10): *take* (6): *rebuke* (9): *pass by* (4): *look round about* (6): *go before* (5): *call unto* (9): *to question with* (6): *go away* (15).

(2). Mark is specially fond of accumulating negatives: *mē* occurs not fewer than 53 times, and *ŏu* not fewer than 90 times; both words mean *not.*   Instances of a double *mē* are:

> "See thou speak *nothing* to *no one*" (i. 44): "*no longer* any room, *not even* at the door" (ii. 2): "let *no one* eat fruit of thee *no more* for ever" (xi. 14).

Instances of a double *ŏu* are:

> "*No one* is able, *not one*" (iii. 27): "*no one* was able to bind him, *not even* with chains" (v. 3): "He did *not* suffer *not one* to accompany him" (v. 37): "He was *not* able there *not any* work of power to do" (vi. 5): "Ye suffer him *no longer nothing* to do . . . " (vii. 12): "*no longer* they saw *not one*" (ix. 8): "*no one no more* dared to question him" (xii. 34).

All such instances are clear in the Greek, though not always obvious in the English, because a literal translation would not be a good one.

(3)   For illustration of Mark's colloquialism see:

> i. 10, *Parting-asunder*: i. 16, *casting-around*: ii. 21, *sews on*: v. 23, *at-the-last-extremity*: xiii. 11, *be-not-careful-beforehand*: xiv. 19, *one by one*: xiv. 41, *it is enough*: xiv. 72, *having-thought-thereon*.

(4)   Another characteristic of Mark's style is the brief and startling way in which he reports events and sayings, *e.g.*;

> "The Spirit driveth him forth"; "I came not to call the righteous"; "the Sabbath was made for man"; "Guilty of an eternal sin"; "He marvelled because of their unbelief"; "He could not be hid," and many such like.

(5)   Yet, over against this striking brevity we find, in places, a somewhat superfluous fulness of expression, which we are not

so surprised to find in the other Synoptics. For examples of this see:

> i. 16, 32, 42: ii. 20, 23, 25: iii. 26, 27: iv. 2, 39: v. 15: vi. 4, 25: vii. 13, 20, 21, 23: viii. 17, 28: ix. 2, 3: x. 22, 30: xi. 4: xii. 14, 44: xiii. 19, 20, 29, 34: xiv. 15, 43, 58, 61, 68: xv. 1, 26: xvi. 2.

(6) Noticeable also is Mark's use of double words and phrases:

> i. 12, 13, *"into the wilderness. And He was in the wilderness"*; i. 45, he began *to publish it much*, and to *spread abroad* the matter"; v. 3-5, "he had his dwelling *in the tombs* . . . day and night *in the tombs,*" and other instances.

(7) Particularly noticeable as characterizing this Gospel is the writer's use of his tenses, especially the *historic present*, and the *imperfect*. The historic present represents an action as going on, and not yet finished. The imperfect represents an action as going on in past time. Mark habitually uses the former, where the action is finished: and the latter, where a tense telling of completed action would have been correct.

For the purpose of comparison let it be said that the *aorist* tense simply indicates that a certain thing happened or occurred once for all, in the past (pp. 108-110).

Now compare Mark's use of these tenses with the parallel passages in Matthew and Luke.

(a) HISTORIC PRESENT

In the following passages Mark uses the *historic present* of what was *past*; "says" (*legei*), not "said": ii. 5, 8, 17, 25: iii. 4, 34: viii. 29: ix. 5, 19: x. 23, 27, 42. In the parallel passages Matthew and Luke use the *aorist* tense, the past of what was past, "said" (*eipen*), not "says."

Mark	Historic Present	ii. 5	ii. 8	ii. 17	ii. 25	iii. 4	iii. 34
Matthew	Aorist	ix. 2	ix. 4	ix. 12	xii. 3	xii. 11	xii. 49
Luke	Aorist	v. 24	v. 22	v. 31	vi. 3	vi. 8	viii. 21

Mark	Historic Present	viii. 29	ix. 5	ix. 19	x. 23	x. 27	x. 42
Matthew	Aorist	xvi. 16	xvii. 4	xvii. 17	xix. 23	xix. 26	xx. 25
Luke	Aorist	ix. 20	ix. 33	ix. 41	xviii. 24	xviii. 27	—

It is estimated that there are 151 of these *historic presents* in Mark: 93 in Matthew: 9 or 11 in Luke, and 162 in John.

In explanation of the few *historic presents* in Luke, and the many in John and Mark, Dr. A. T. Robertson says, Luke "is the scientific historian, while Mark and John are the dramatists," and, that Mark would use the tense 'as a man of the people who heard it in daily use around him, while Luke would have Greek education enough to know that it was not common in the cultured speech of his time.' Dr. Robertson says also, 'Modern literary English abhors this "idiom," but it ought to be preserved in translating the Gospels in order to give the same element of vividness to the narrative.'

It will be profitable to take a passage and write the narrative in the *past tenses* to which it belongs, and put by the side of it Mark's narrative in the *historic presents*, for in this way it will be seen how much more graphic and impressive is Mark's narrative.

Mark ii. 3-10

3	They *came* to Him and *brought* a paralytic, *being borne* by four.	They *come* to Him (pres. ind.) *bringing* (pres. part. act.) a paralytic *being borne* (pres. part. pass.) by four.
4	And not *having been able* to come near to Him.	And not *being able* (pres. part.) to come near to him.
5	Jesus *said* to the paralytic.	Jesus *says* (pres. ind.) to the paralytic.
6	There were some of the Scribes who sat there, and *reasoned* in their hearts.	There were some of the Scribes *sitting* (pres. part.) there, and *reasoning* (pres. part.) in their hearts.
8	Jesus knowing in His spirit that thus they *reasoned* with themselves.	Jesus thoroughly knew (2 aor. part.) in His spirit that they *are reasoning* (pres. ind. mid.) with themselves.
9	He *said* to the paralytic.	He *says* (pres. ind.) to the paralytic.

(b) IMPERFECT

In the following passages Mark, by using the *imperfect tense* instead of the *aorist*, "conveys the impression of an eyewitness describing events which passed under his own eye":

> v. 18, "He besought"; vii. 17, "He asked"; xii. 41, "He saw," and, "were casting"; xiv. 55, "sought," and "did find."

Other graphic tense touches, selected from the first four chapters only, are:

> "He saw the heavens *opening*" (i. 10); "the angels *continued to minister* unto Him" (i. 13); "they *went on bringing* unto Him all that were diseased" (i. 32); "*continued in prayer*" (i. 35); "there *cometh* a leper" (i. 40); "they *continued* to *come* to Him" (i. 45); "*He was speaking* the word unto them" (ii. 2); "wherein the sick of the palsy *was lying*" (ii. 4); "*He is blaspheming*" (ii. 7); "*continued glorifying* God" (ii. 12); "*He gave Himself to teaching them*" (ii. 13); "publicans and sinners *were sitting* also together with Jesus", and "they *were following* Him" (ii. 15); "*He was eating*" (ii. 16); "*were fasting*" (ii. 18); "*He was going through* the cornfields" (ii. 23); "they *kept watching* Him" (iii. 2); "how is Satan able *to go on casting* out Satan?" (iii. 23); "a multitude *was sitting* about Him" (iii. 32); "*He went on teaching* them" (iv. 2); "*springing up and increasing*" (iv. 8); "*should go on sleeping* and rising . . .*"; "*should be springing* and *growing up*" (iv. 27); "without a parable He *was not in the habit of speaking* unto them," . . . "*His practice was to expound* all things" (iv. 34); "they *take* Him, even as He was" (iv. 36); "the waves *kept beating* into the ship, so that it *was already beginning to be filled*" (iv. 37); "carest thou not that we *are perishing*?" (iv. 38).

Those who know New Testament Greek will best be able to trace and appreciate the use Mark makes of the tenses, but those who do not know Greek will get most help in this matter by reading the *Twentieth Century New Testament*.

(8) Excepting proper names in Mark, of which there are 60, of the 1270 words of his vocabulary there are at least 80 which are peculiar to his Gospel. This is not a large number compared with Luke, for instance, who has 250 such words, but they are interesting nevertheless, and some of them especially so. They are as follows:

1	i. 16	Casting-about
2	i. 27; x. 24, 32	Amazed; Astonished (Pass.)
3	i. 35	Great-while-before-day
4	i. 36	Followed-after
5	i. 38	Elsewhere
6	i. 38	Towns, city-like village
7	ii. 4	Come-nigh-unto
8	ii. 4	Uncovered
9	ii. 21	Seweth-on
10	iii. 5	Being-grieved
11	iii. 17	Boanerges
12	iv. 27	Grow-up (be lengthened, *mēkunō*)
13	iv. 38	Pillow (cushion, *proskephalaion*)
14	v. 3	Dwelling
15	v. 5	Cutting
16	v. 13	Two-thousand
17	v. 23; vii. 25	Little—Young-daughter
18	v. 23	Lieth-at-the-point-of-death
19	v. 24, 31	Thronged; Thronging
20	v. 41	Talitha
21	v. 41	Cumi
22	vi. 27	Executioner (guardsman, *spekoulatōr*)
23	vi. 39	By-companies, a table-party
24	vi. 40	In-Ranks
25	vi. 53	Drew-to-the-shore
26	vi. 55	Ran-through
27	vii. 3	(Oft)=Diligently (R.V. Gr.)
28	vii. 4, 8	Pots
29	vii. 4	Brasen-vessels
30	vii. 8, 13	Like-things
31	vii. 11	Corban
32	vii. 22	Pride
33	vii. 26	Syrophoenician
34	vii. 32	Had-an-impediment-in-his-speech
35	vii. 34	Ephphatha
36	vii. 37	Beyond-measure
37	vii. 37; ix. 17, 25	Dumb
38	viii. 12	Sighed-deeply
39	viii. 25	Clearly
40	ix. 3	Shining (glistering, *stilbō*)
41	ix. 3	Fuller
42	ix. 8	Suddenly
43	ix. 12	Set-at-nought
44	ix. 15; xiv. 33; xvi. 5, 6	Greatly-amazed; sore-amazed; Affrighted
45	ix. 18, 20	Foameth
46	ix. 18	Gnasheth
47	ix. 20	Wallowed
48	ix. 21	Of-a-child
49	ix. 25	Came-running-together

50	ix. 36: x. 16	Had-taken-in-his-arms / Took-up-in-His-arms
51	ix. 48	Worm (44, 46, not in R.V.)
52	ix. 50	Saltless
53	x. 16	Blessed
54	x. 24	Hard, Difficult
55	x. 25	Eye
56	x. 35	Come-unto
57	x. 50	Rose (sprang up, *anapēdaō*)
58	xi. 4	A-place-where-two-ways-met
59	xi. 8	Branches
60	xii. 1	Wine-fat
61	xii. 4	Wounded-him-in-the-head
62	xii. 13	Catch
63	xii. 17	Marvelled
64	xii. 34	Discreetly
65	xiii. 11	Take-thought-beforehand
66	xiii. 34	Taking-a-far-journey
67	xiii. 35	Cock-crowing
68	xiv. 8	Anoint
69	xiv. 31	Vehemently
70	xiv. 40	Were-heavy (weighed down, *katabarunō*)
71	xiv. 44	A token agreed upon
72	xiv. 68	Porch
73	xv. 7	Insurrection
74	xv. 23	Mingled-with-myrrh
75	xv. 29	Ah
76	xv. 39, 44, 45	Centurion
77	xv. 42	The-day-before-the-Sabbath
78	xv. 46	Wrapped-in
79	xvi. 4	Rolled-away (*anakuliō*)
80	xvi. 18	Deadly

A few remarks on some of these, and other words, will illustrate the vividness of Mark's language.

(1) i 16 *Casting about (amphi-ballontas), amphiballō,* casting on both sides, now on one side, now on the other.

(2) i 35 *Very early, while yet night.* The last watch of the night, from 3.0 to 6.0 a.m., but early in this watch, while it was still quite dark.

(3) i 36 *Followed after Him*; hunted Him out (Moffatt), tracked Him to His retreat, pursued Him (*kata-diōkō*).

(4) iii 5 *He looked round on them with anger, being grieved at the hardness of their hearts.* The eyes of Jesus swept the room all round. The verb "with anger," is in the

aorist participle, indicating the momentariness of this emotion, whereas, *being-grieved*, is in the *present participle*, indicating Jesus' *continuous state of grief.*

(5) v 5 *Cutting-up* himself (*katakoptō*), hacking himself to pieces.

(6) vi 40 In *ranks* (*prasiai-prasiai*). The word *prasia* means a garden bed, a plot of ground. The idea in the text is that these fifties and hundreds formed separate plots as in a garden, and, in all likelihood, their many-coloured clothes made these plots look like beds of gorgeous flowers.

(7) vii 3 *Oft* (*pugmē*) *with the fist.* "The word is used in late Greek for the length of the arm between the fist and the elbow" (SWETE), and so, *diligently* (R.V.).

(8) vii 22 *Pride*; a compound word (*huper-ēphania*) meaning *appearance-over*, and so, stuck up, superior, setting all others at nought.

(9) vii 26 A Greek, a Syro-Phoenician. "A Greek in religion, a Syrian in tongue, a Phoenician in race" (A. B. BRUCE).

(10) vii 32 *Had-an-impediment-in-his-speech.* This is one compound word in the Greek (*mogilalos, mogis*, with difficulty, and *laleō*, to speak) meaning to speak with difficulty, a stammerer.

(11) viii 12 *Sighed-deeply* (*anastenazō*). The simple verb is found in vii. 34, but the compound verb, here only, *ana-stenaxas*, means that the Lord sighed from the bottom of His heart, that His spirit was stirred to its depths.

(12) viii 25 *Clearly*; *tēlaugōs*, from *tēle*, afar, and *augeō*, to shine, and so, brilliantly, or clearly.

(13) ix 18 *Taketh* him; a word used by ancient doctors for fits. It is our word catalepsy (*katalabē*).

(14) x 50 *Rose.* The word is a compound, *ana*, up, and *pēdaō*, to leap, and so, to spring or leap up.

(15) xii 13 *Catch*; *agreuō*, to entrap or catch; related to *agra* in Luke, v. 4, 9, a haul.

(16) xii 34 *Discreetly* (*nounechōs*); literally, intelligently, from *nous*, intellect, and *echō*, to have.

(17) xiii 11 *Take-(no)-thought-beforehand.* The verb here is from a word which means to-be-drawn-in-opposite-directions, to-be-distracted, hence anxiety, worry, against which we are warned (*pro-merimnaō*). The verb without the prepositional prefix (*pro*) is used throughout Matt. vi. 25-34.

Of the 80 words peculiar to Mark in the New Testament, about half of them are found in the LXX, the Greek Old Testament.

(9) Nowhere is Mark more fascinating than in his references to the familiar things of life. Dr. Swete has called attention to a number of these. The following should be looked up and marked:

(1) CLOTHING.—Girdle, i. 6; Shoe, i. 7; Thong (latchet), i. 7; Garment, ii. 21; Sandal, vi. 9; Tunic (coat), vi. 9; Border of garment, vi. 56; Robes, xii. 38; Linen Cloth, xiv. 51, 52; Purple, xv. 17, 20.

(2) FOOD.—Honey, i. 6; Wine, ii. 22; Bread, iii. 20; Herb, iv. 32; Fragment, vi. 43; Meat, vii. 19; Small Fish, viii. 7; Leaven, viii. 15; Vinegar, xv. 36.

(3) HOUSE, AND ITS PARTS.—House, i. 29; xi. 17 (different words, Greek, *oikia, oikos*); Door, ii. 2; Roof, ii. 4; Housetop, xiii. 15; Guest-chamber, xiv. 14; Upper-room, xiv. 15; Porch, xiv. 68 (*Mark only*); Hall, Palace, xiv. 54; xv. 16 (same word).

(4) UTENSILS AND TOOLS.—Bottle, ii. 22; Bed, iv. 21; vi. 55 (two words, Greek, *klinē, krabbatos*); Bushel, iv. 21; Candle, iv. 21; Candlestick, iv. 21; Scrip, vi. 8; Charger, vi. 25, 28; Basket, vi. 43; viii. 8 (two words, Greek, *kophinos, spuris*); Pot, vii. 4, 8 (*Mark only*); Cup, ix. 41; Mill-stone, ix. 42; Alabaster-box, xiv. 3; Pitcher, xiv. 13; Dish, xiv. 20; Sword, xiv. 43.

(5) COINS.—Money, vi. 8; xiv. 11 (two words, Greek, *chalkos, argurion*); Money-changer, xi. 15; Penny, xii. 15; Farthing, xii. 42; Mite, xii. 42.

(6) DIVISIONS OF TIME.—Eventide (lit. late the hour), xi. 11 (*Mark only*); Hour, xiii. 11; Cock-crowing, xiii. 35 (*Mark only*); Early-in-the-morning, xiii. 35; xvi. 2 *et al*; Even, xiii. 35; Midnight, xiii. 35; Evening, xiv. 17; Third time, xiv. 41; Sixth, xv. 33.

(7) RELIGIOUS PRACTICES.—Synagogue, i. 21; Cleansing, i. 44; Sabbath, ii. 27, 28; Bless, vi. 41; Tradition, vii. 3, 5; Washing, vii. 4; Corban, vii. 11; Give-thanks, viii. 6; Fasting, ix. 29; Sacrifice, ix. 49; Temple, xi. 15; Whole-burnt-offering, xii. 33; Treasury, xii. 41; Council, xiii. 9; Sing-a-hymn, xiv. 26; Feast, xv. 6; Day-before-the-Sabbath, xv. 42 (*Mark only*); Preparation, xv. 42.

(8) MARRIAGE.—Wife's-mother, i. 30; Bridechamber, ii. 19; Bridegroom, ii. 19; Wife, vi. 17; Marry, vi. 17; xii. 25; Bill of divorcement, x. 4.

(9) SERVICE.—Hired-servant, i. 20; Minister, x. 43; Servant, x. 44; xiv. 54 (two words, Greek, *doulos*, *hupēretēs*,=*hupo* and *eretēs*, a rower); Porter, xiii. 34; Maid, xiv. 66, 69.

(10) PUNISHMENT.—Torment, v. 7; Behead, vi. 16; Prison, vi. 17, 27; Beat, xii. 3, 5; Prisoner, xv. 6; Cross, xv. 21.

(11) AGRICULTURE AND OTHER RURAL PURSUITS.—Corn-fields, ii. 23; Harvest, iv. 29; Sickle, iv. 29; In Ranks, vi. 40 (*Mark only*); Hedge, xii. 1; Tower, xii. 1; Wine-fat, xii. 1 (*Mark only*); Husbandman, xii. 1, 2; Vineyard, xii. 9.

(12) TRADE.—Exchange, viii. 37; Ransom, x. 45; Let-out, xii. 1.

(13) MILITARY MATTERS.—Legion, v. 9, 15; High-Captain, vi. 21; Executioner, vi. 27 (*Mark only*); Band, xv. 16; Centurion, xv. 39, 44, 45 (*Mark only*).

(14) BOATING AND FISHING.—Cast-around, i. 16 (*Mark only*); Fisher i. 16, 17; Net, i. 18; Ship, i. 19, 20; Little-ship, iii. 9; iv. 36; Hinder-part-of-the-ship, iv. 38; Pillow, iv. 38 (*Mark only*); Draw-to-the-shore, vi. 53 (*Mark only*).

(15) ANIMALS.—Camel, i. 6; x. 25; Dove, i. 10; Wild-beast, i. 13; Fowl, iv. 4, 32; Swine, v. 11-14; Dog, vii. 27, 28; Colt, xi. 2, 4, 5, 7.

(16) DISEASE.—Rend, i. 26; ix. 26; Fever, i. 31; Leprosy, i. 42; Possessed-with-a-demon, v. 15, 16; Deaf, vii. 32, 37; With-one-eye, ix. 47.

(17) TREATMENT OF THE DEAD.—Ointment, xiv. 3, 4; Burying, xiv. 8; Wrap-in, xv. 46 (*Mark only*); Sweet-spices, xvi. 1.

It will be observed that thirteen of the above words occur in Mark only, and three of them reflect the craft of Peter, from whom, probably, Mark got them (i. 16; iv. 38; vi. 53).

17

MIRACLES IN MARK'S GOSPEL

OF the 35 miracles recorded in the Gospels, 20 are in Matthew, 20 in Luke, 7 in John, and 18 in Mark. These numbers do not include summaries of miracles, which are numerous.

Of the 18 miracles in Mark, 2 only are not recorded elsewhere, 4 are recorded in one other Gospel, 11 in two other Gospels, and 1 in three other Gospels (see pp. 551-553).

The numbers preceding these miracles represent the order in which they appear in Mark's Gospel.

1 **In Mark Only** (2)
   13 Deaf and Dumb Man Healed   -   -   - Mark vii. 31-37
   15 Blind Man Healed at Bethsaida -   -   - Mark viii. 22-26

2 **In Mark and One Other Gospel** (4)
   1 Demoniac in the Synagogue at Capernaum - Mark i. 23-28
                                                Luke iv. 31-36
   12 Daughter of a Syrophœnician Woman Healed Mark vii. 24-30
                                                Matt. xv. 21-28
   14 Four Thousand Fed -   Mark viii. 1-9; Matt. xv. 32-39
   18 Cursing of the Fig Tree   Mark xi. 12-14; Matt. xxi. 18, 19

3 **In Mark and Two Gospels** (11)
   2 Peter's Mother-in-law Cured   -   -   - Mark i. 29-31;
                                 Matt. viii. 14-17; Luke iv. 38, 39
   3 Healing of a Leper -   -   -   -   - Mark i. 40-45;
                                 Matt. viii. 2-4; Luke v. 12-16
   4 Healing of a Paralytic   -   -   -   - Mark ii. 3-12;
                                 Matt. ix. 2-8; Luke v. 18-26
   5 Healing of a Withered Hand   -   -   - Mark iii. 1-5;
                                 Matt. xii. 9-14; Luke vi. 6-11
   6 Stilling a Storm -   -   -   -   -   - Mark iv. 35-41;
                                 Matt. viii. 18, 23-27; Luke viii. 22-25
   7 Gergasene Demoniac Cured   -   -   - Mark v. 1-20;
                                 Matt. viii. 28-34; Luke viii. 26-39
   8 Raising of Jairus' Daughter   -   Mark v. 22-24, 35-43;
                           Matt. ix. 18, 19, 23-29; Luke viii. 41, 42, 49-56
   9 Healing of a Woman with an Issue of Blood   Mark v. 25-34;
                                 Matt. ix. 20-22; Luke viii. 43-48
   11 Walking on the Sea -   -   -   -   - Mark vi. 45-52;
                                 Matt. xiv. 24-33; John vi. 16-21
   16 Lunatic Boy Cured -   -   -   -   - Mark ix. 14-29;
                                 Matt. xvii. 14-18; Luke ix. 38-43
   17 Blind Bartimæus and Another Man Restored   Mark x. 46-52;
                                 Matt. xx. 29-34; Luke xviii. 35-43

4 **In Mark and Three Gospels** (1)
   10 Five Thousand Fed -   -   -   -   - Mark vi. 35-44;
                           Matt. xiv. 14-21; Luke ix. 12-17; John vi. 4-13

In addition to these 18 specific miracles, reference is made ten times to miracles not specified in detail (i. 32-34; i. 39; iii. 9-12; iii. 22; vi. 2; vi. 5; vi. 7; vi. 13; vi. 14; vi. 53-56; see xvi. 17).

Four Greek words are employed in the Gospels to describe the works of Jesus, and three of them are used by Mark.

Teras, wonder (xiii. 22); *Dunamis*, power (vi. 2, 5, 14; ix. 39); *Sēmeion*, sign (viii. 11, 12; xvi. 17, 20); *Ergon*, miraculous deed (John vii. 3, 21).   (See p. 419.)

What is common to these words is that they are all used to characterize the supernatural works wrought by Christ in the days of His flesh. Wherein they differ is indicated by Trench in his *Synonyms*. He says:

TERAS (' wonder '), tells of ' that which for its extraordinary character is wont to be observed and kept in the memory.' It is always rendered 'wonder' in our Version.

SĒMEION (' sign '). Among all the names which the miracles bear, their *ethical end and purpose* comes out in *sēmeion* with the most distinctness, as in *teras*, with the least. It is involved and declared in the very word that the prime object and end of the miracle is to lead us to something out of and beyond itself; that, so to speak, it is a kind of finger-post of God . . . valuable, not so much for what it is, as for what it indicates of the grace and power of the doer, or of his immediate connection with a higher spiritual world (Mark xvi. 20).'

DUNAMIS (' power '). ' But the miracles are also *"powers,"* outcomings of that mighty *power* of God, which was inherent in Christ, Himself that *"great Power* of God" ' (Acts viii. 10). This word points to ' new and higher forces, *"Powers of the world to come"* (Heb. vi. 5), which have entered and are working in this lower world of ours.'

Thus, while all these words tell of supernatural works, *teras* speaks of a wonderful act; *sēmeion*, of a sign symbolizing heavenly truths; and *dunamis*, of a putting forth of Divine power. The first three words occur in Acts ii. 22.

' Jesus the Nazarene, a man set forth by God to you by works of power (*dunamesin*), and wonders (*terasin*), and signs (*sēmeiois*), which God wrought by Him in your midst.'

The following words should also be noted: "great things" (*megaleios*, Luke i. 49); "glorious things" (*endoxos*, Luke xiii. 17); "strange things" (*paradoxos*, Luke v. 26); and "wonderful things" (*thaumasios*, Matt. xxi. 15).

Bishop Westcott and others have classified these supernatural acts as (1) miracles on nature; (2) miracles on man; and (3) miracles on the spirit-world.

Of the 18 in Mark's Gospel, 5 are miracles on nature (Nos. 10, 14, 6, 11, 18, see preceding list); 9 are miracles on man (2, 3, 4, 5, 8, 9, 17, 13, 15); and 4 are miracles on the spirit-world (1, 7, 12, 16).

The miracles had a twofold value, a physical and a spiritual, a temporal and an eternal; people's bodies were healed, and that healing pointed to another and a greater, making the soul well. The *expulsion of demons* tells of Christ's power over the spirit-world of evil (1, 7, 12, 16). *The healing of Peter's mother-in-law* tells of the stilling of the restless energy of the flesh, of the feverishness of mortal life. *The healing of the leper* tells of the removal of sin's loathsome defilement. *The healing of the paralytic* tells of the removal of sin's helplessness and disability. The *healing of the withered hand* tells of the enablement Christ gives to men to work for Him. *The stilling of the storm* tells of Christ's power over the upheavals of life. *The healing of the issue of blood* tells of the removal of the weakness and waste caused by sin. *The giving sight to the blind* tells of the illumination which the Gospel brings to the darkened soul. *The healing of the deaf and dumb* tells of the awakening of man to witness for Christ. *The cursing of the fig tree* tells of the fate of the persistently unfruitful. *The walking on the sea* declares that Divine law dominates natural law. *The feeding of the multitudes* tells of the satisfaction which Christ brings to hungry souls. *The raising of the dead* tells of Christ's conquest of death, and of His gift of life to those who are ' dead in trespasses and sins.' (See pp. 290, 555).

The 18 miracles in Mark (on p. 203) do not include the two greatest miracles of all, the Resurrection, and Christ Himself. The miraculous element in the Gospel story cannot be got rid of without invalidating the whole. ' The key to miracles,' says Dr. Sanday, ' lies in the personality of God.' Men who deny the possibility or actuality of miracles, e.g., Pfleiderer, Schmiedel, Weinel, Bousset, Haeckel, Matthew Arnold, Huxley, Hume, Thompson, and in part, Harnack, are unscientific and out of date, judged by the verdict of Divine revelation, and even by human experience. Man in our time has accomplished things which a hundred years ago would have been declared impossible. Hundreds of thousands of 'planes have navigated the air, but the law of gravity has not been suspended. The Christian has no need to apologize for his belief in miracles.

Mark in your Bible the two miracles which are recorded in this Gospel only, and mark by the side of the other sixteen the references to the parallel records.

The miracles which Mark does not record (18, but see pp. 286, 554) are:

Two Blind Men Healed	The Ear of Malchus Healed
A Dumb Demon Exorcised	Water Made into Wine
Tribute Money Provided	A Nobleman's Son Healed
First Draught of Fishes	An Impotent Man at Bethesda Healed
A Widow's Son Raised	
A Woman's Infirmity Cured	Healing of a Man Born Blind
A Man with Dropsy Healed	Lazarus Raised from the Dead
Ten Lepers Healed	Second Draught of Fishes
A Blind and Dumb Man Healed	A Centurion's Servant Healed

Another Dumb Demoniac Healed

18

PARABLES IN MARK'S GOSPEL

SOME reputable writers have said that there are only four parables in this Gospel, but this is obviously incorrect. No one can affirm how many there are until it has been clearly defined what a parable is. Taking it to mean a *comparison*, there would seem to be eighteen parables in Mark.

Figures of speech are manifold, and each form is worthy of careful consideration.

FABLE - - is a fictitious narrative intended to illustrate some maxim or truth (Judges ix. 8-15; 2 Kings xiv. 9).

METAPHOR - distinctly affirms that one thing *is* another thing, from two Greek words meaning *to carry over* (Isa. xl. 6; Psa. lxxxiv. 11).

SIMILE - means *like* or *resembling* (Psa. i. 3, 4). It differs from metaphor in that it merely states resemblance, while metaphor boldly transfers the representation (cf. 1 Peter i. 24, and Isa. xl. 6).

ALLEGORY - is any statement of supposed facts which admits of a literal interpretation, and yet requires or justly admits a moral or figurative one (Gal. iv. 22-31, 24.

PROVERB   -   is a wayside saying, a trite expression, an adage
                  (the Book of Proverbs).

TYPE -   -   means *stamp* or *impress*, and has the force of *copy*
                  or *pattern* (1 Cor. x. 1-10, 11, ' ensamples,' margin
                  ' types ').

PARABLE   -   from *para*, beside, and *ballein*, to throw or cast,
                  is generally taken to mean *one thing beside another*
                  for the purpose of comparison, but the figure cannot
                  be confined to this definition.

The fable is grotesque and contrary to nature (Judges ix.
8-15), but the parable is always in harmony with nature, is
always true to the laws of the person or the thing used for the
story.

The parable is distinguishable from the proverb, though
related to it. The same Hebrew word means both parable and
proverb (*māh-shāhl*, Ps. xlix. 4; Prov. i. 6). Some proverbs are
called parables (Matt. xv. 14, 15; Luke iv. 23), and in John x.
6; xvi. 25-29, the word 'proverb' (Greek) is rendered 'parable'
(R.V. marg.).

Trench says: ' A proverb is often a concentrated parable.'
A parable may also be regarded as a continued simile, but,
strictly speaking, a parable is neither an allegory, nor a metaphor.

With these distinctions in mind we turn to Mark's Gospel.
The word ' parable ' occurs twelve times (iii. 23; iv. 2, 10, 11,
13, 33, 34; vii. 17; xii. 1, 12; xiii. 28), and, we may say, there are
eighteen parables.

1 Fishers of Men - - - -	i. 16, 17 (M. & L.)
2 The Sick and the Physician - -	ii. 17 (M. & L.)
3 The Bridegroom - - - -	ii. 19, 20 (M. & L.)
4 The New Cloth and the Old Garment	ii. 21 (M. & L.)
5 The New Wine and the Old Wine Skins - - - - -	ii. 22 (M. & L.)
6 The Divided Kingdom - -	iii. 23 (plur.), 24 (M.)
7 The Divided House - - -	iii. 23 (plur.), 25 (M.)
8 The Overcoming of the Strong Man	iii. 23 (plur.), 27 (M. & L.)
9 The Sower - - - - - -	iv. 2-8 (M. & L.)
10 The Lamp - - - - -	iv. 21, 22 (L.)

11	*The Seed Growing Secretly*	-	-	iv. 26-29
12	The Grain of Mustard Seed	-	-	iv. 30-32 (M.)
13	Inward Defilement	-	-	vii. 14-23 (M.)
14	The Offending Members	-	-	ix. 43, 45, 47 (M.)
15	The Wicked Husbandmen	-	-	xii. 1-9 (M. & L.)
16	The Rejected Stone	-	-	xii. 10, 11 (M. & L.)
17	The Fig Tree	-	-	xiii. 28, 29 (M. & L.)
18	*The Porter*	-	-	xiii. 34-37

Of these eighteen, eight are called 'parables' (Nos. 2 (Luke iv. 23, Gr.) 6, 7, 8, 11, 12, 15, 16), and two are peculiar to this Gospel (11, 18). Excluding Nos. 11 and 18, ten are found in Matthew and Luke; five more in Matthew only, and one other in Luke only. This is indicated by the letters M. and L., in the above list.

Christ's miracles are parables in deeds, and His parables are miracles in words. The parables set forth great spiritual truths in figurative forms, and this is done partly to obscure these truths from the merely curious, and partly to stimulate the inquiry of the really concerned (Matt. xiii. 10-17).

(1) FISHERS OF MEN (i. 16, 17). This tells us that in the spiritual world there are counterparts to all that is legitimate in the natural world.

(2) THE SICK AND THE PHYSICIAN (ii. 17). Jesus does not teach that there are any who are not sick, but that the great Physician can do nothing for those who think they are not.

(3) THE BRIDEGROOM (ii. 19, 20). This indicates a relationship of Christ to His people, and teaches that His presence brings joy, and His absence, sorrow; that there is a time to feast, and a time to fast.

(4) THE NEW CLOTH AND THE OLD GARMENT (ii. 21).

(5) THE NEW WINE AND THE OLD WINE SKINS (ii. 22). These are two aspects of one truth, the first being the outward, and the second the inward aspect. They announce the cleavage between Jewish ceremonialism and the gospel, and teach, first, that Christianity is not a patched-up Judaism; and second, that the new wine of the former is too strong for the old skins of the latter, that the gospel is entirely new, and cannot be adapted

to old forms. These three parables (ii. 19-22) teach that incongruous things ought not to be combined, and they enforce the law of congruity.

(6) THE DIVIDED KINGDOM (iii. 24):

(7) THE DIVIDED HOUSE (iii. 25). In defending Himself against the charge that by the Devil He was working against the Devil, Jesus uses two 'parables' (iii. 23), the Kingdom (24), and the House (25), to teach that strength and permanence can be secured only by solidarity of purpose and effort, and that where these conditions are wanting there is bound to be disintegration.

(8) THE OVERCOMING OF THE STRONG MAN (iii. 27). The Lord uses a third parable to teach that, not only are His activities not satanically wrought, but that He has conquered Satan in order to perform them.

(9) THE SOWER (iv. 2-8). This is declared to be the key to all the parabolic teaching (iv. 13). We should learn from this parable that Christ is the Master-Sower of the seeds of truth; that all His servants are under-sowers; that the seed will eventuate in harvest; that not all the seed sown is fruitful, because every kind of soil does not receive it; and that even where it is received there are degrees of fruitfulness. For other thoughts consult the parallel in the Matthew section (p. 298).

(10) THE LAMP (iv. 21, 22). This follows on that of the Sower, and is related to it. It teaches at least two things: first, that the light of Divine truth is given, not to be obscured by our commercial ('bushel'), or domestic ('bed') affairs, but to be manifested; and second, that the primary obscuration, in the parabolic form of teaching, was gradually to give way to full illumination.

Verse 22 should read: 'There is nothing hid save that it should be manifested.' This principle of the Divine operation is as true in grace as in nature and providence.

(11) THE SEED GROWING SECRETLY (iv. 26-29). This is peculiar to Mark's Gospel. It is a very encouraging parable, Dr. Swete summarizes the teaching thus: 'The functions of the sower end with the sowing; those of the reaper begin with the

harvest; all that lies between is left to the mysterious laws of growth co-operating with the soil, the sunshine and the rain.'

This is not intended to encourage the vices of indolence, indifference, and thoughtless security, but to teach the Christian labourer that there are forces at work over which he has no control, which are in God's care, and he must patiently wait for the result of their operation.

(12) THE GRAIN OF MUSTARD SEED (iv. 30-32). This parable is interpreted in two opposite ways. One interpretation is that it represents the fertility and extension of the Church, starting from a small beginning, and spreading itself over all the world.

The other interpretation is that it represents an abnormal and worse than unfortunate development, the development of the Church in the Christendom which gives shelter to ' fowls of the air,' which our Lord, in a preceding parable, has spoken of as belonging to the order of Satan (iv. 4, 15, 32). See the exposition given in the Matthew section (pp. 298-302).

(13) INWARD DEFILEMENT (vii. 14-23). This parable is clearly explained. The track of evil is not from without inward, but from within outward.

(14) THE OFFENDING MEMBERS (ix. 43, 45, 47). It is here taught that, at any cost, sin is to be shunned. In Matthew v. 29, 30, the foot is not mentioned, but, stronger than in Mark, the *right* eye and the *right* hand are specified.

The eye *sees*, the foot *goes*, and the hand *does*, and all, in the interests of what is right, must be subject to moral surgery.

(15) THE WICKED HUSBANDMEN (xii. 1-9). This is an indictment of the Sanhedrin. The ' vineyard ' is Israel; the owner of it is Jehovah; the ' husbandmen ' are the religious leaders of the Jews; the ' servants ' who were sent are the prophets; the ' one son ' is Christ Himself. It is announced that Israel's privileges would be transferred to others (xii. 12).

(16) THE REJECTED STONE (xii. 10, 11). This quotation from the Old Testament is made in connection with the parable of the Wicked Husbandmen, but is in reality a parable in itself, and teaches that the Christ whom men reject, God has highly exalted (Phil. ii. 9-11).

(17) THE FIG TREE (xiii. 28, 29).   This teaches that as the budding of this tree intimates the approach of summer, so the presence of the conditions of which Christ was speaking was the sure sign of His predicted coming again.

(18) THE PORTER (xiii. 34-37).   This is peculiar to Mark's Gospel.   It is intended to promote watchfulness on the part of Christ's people during His absence.

Get a thorough grasp of these parables and their meanings. Of the some 70 parables and parabolic illustrations in the Four Gospels (pp. 547-549), Mark does not record the following 52:

The Wheat and the Tares
The Hidden Treasure
The Pearl of Great Price
The Fish Net
The Householder Scribe
The Unmerciful Servant
The Labourers in the Vineyard
The Two Sons Called to Work
The Marriage of the King's Son
The Ten Virgins
The Talents
The Two Debtors
The Good Samaritan
The Friend at Midnight
The Rich Fool
The Waiting and Watching Servants
The Barren Fig Tree
The Great Supper
The Unfinished Tower
The Unwaged War
The Lost Bit of Silver
The Prodigal Son, and Elder Brother
The Unrighteous Steward
The Rich Man and Lazarus
The Unprofitable Servant
The Importunate Widow
The Pharisee and the Publican

The Pounds
The Door of the Sheep (pp. 447, 448, 550)
The Good Shepherd (pp. 447, 448, 550)
The Vine and the Branches (pp. 447, 448, 550)
The Two Houses
The Unclean Spirit that Returned
The Leaven in the Meal
The Master and the Thief
The Faithful and Evil Servants
The Lost Sheep
The Salt of the Earth
The Light of the World
The Adversary
Dogs and Swine
Doomed Plants
The Strait Gate and the Shut Door
The Mote and the Beam
The Broad and Narrow Ways
Good and Bad Fruit Trees
Good and Bad Treasures
The Blind Guiding the Blind
The Chief Seats at Feasts
Birds and Flowers
The Harvest Field
The Grain of Wheat

19

DISCOURSES IN MARK'S GOSPEL

THE object of this Gospel sufficiently accounts for the almost entire absence of discourses (see under ' Mark's Design,' p. 184).   While Christ is often called ' Teacher ' (twelve times),

translated 'Master' (iv. 38; v. 35; ix. 17, 38; x. 17, 20, 35;
xii. 14, 19, 32; xiii. 1; xiv. 14), the object of the Evangelist is
not to show Him in that capacity, but as the great Worker, and
this object answers to the readers he has in view, the Romans,
whose temperament was eminently practical, rather than
reflective (see under 'For Whom Written,' p. 168).

Mark, therefore, having in view the Latin race, presents that
aspect of Christ which was best calculated to impress them.

The Jew was impressed by spiritual power; the Greek, by
intellectual and æsthetic power; and the Roman, by practical
power. The Roman believed in the logic of deeds, and so he
became the mighty worker of the world, casting up highways
across empires, and conquering by force of arms.

We can see, then, that the discourses of the other Gospels
would not have impressed the Romans as they impressed those
for whom those Gospels were written; but the rapid and effective
activities of Christ were eminently calculated to impress the
practical Roman race.

In Mark's Gospel there are 661 verses (R.V.), and of these
277, in whole or part, record the words of Jesus (see under
'Christ's Words in Mark's Gospel,' p. 192).

These 277 verses contain only one major discourse (xiii),
reported in 37 verses, which is between one-seventh and one-
eighth of all Christ's words in this Gospel.

What other of His utterances there are might rightly be called
talks on various subjects: Ceremonial Washings (vii. 1-23);
Cross-bearing (viii. 34-ix. 1); Humility, Tolerance, and Offences
(ix. 33-50); Divorce (x. 5-12); Riches, Self-sacrifice, and Reward
(x. 23-31); False Ambition, or True Greatness (x. 38-45); Faith
and Prayer (xi. 23-26).

These are in no sense comparable with the discourses recorded
by Matthew (v-vii; x; xiii; xviii; xxiii; xxiv-xxv), and Mark's
one discourse of any length (xiii), which is the parallel of Matt.
xxiv, has, as we have said, but 37 verses, whereas in the whole of
Matthew's discourse there are 97 verses.

Of course Christ teaches by His parables, but as these have
been noticed separately, we do not class them as discourses.

JUDAEA

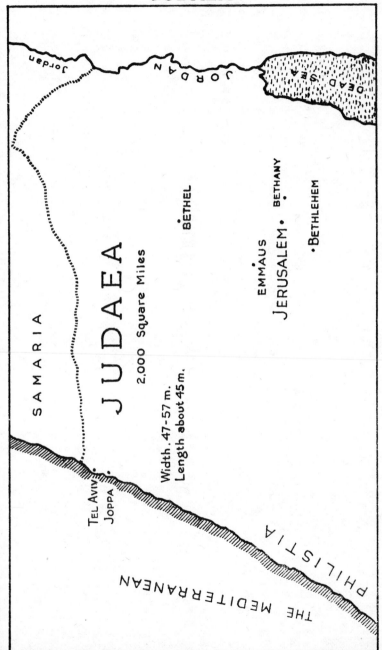

Observe, then, the fact that in this Gospel teaching other than parabolic is very limited, and understand the reason for this.

As Mark is the first of the Gospels, and as it is so largely incorporated into Matthew and Luke, and as the Olivet Discourse is recorded by all the Synoptists, the student should carefully compare this first record with the other two. Where the three records are parallel, Mark supplies details which are noteworthy, and his omissions should be carefully considered. For such an examination a *Harmony of the Gospels* will be necessary, and those who can, should consult the Greek text.

Seeing that Peter was one of the four who interrogated Jesus, a detail given by Mark only (xiii. 3), in all likelihood Mark got much of his information of what Jesus said, if not all, from Peter.

A point which must not be overlooked, when this Discourse is studied, is that Jesus said on other occasions many of the things which are here reported, and that, probably, these references to coming trouble, His coming again, and exhortations to watchfulness were in the Oral Gospel which preceded all written accounts (see Div. A, ' Synoptic Problem,' p. 83).

Compare Mark xiii. 9, 10 and Matt. x. 17, 18; also Mark xiii. 11-13, Matt. x. 19-22, and Luke xii. 11, 12; also Mark xiii. 21, Matt. xxiv. 23-27, and Luke xvii. 22-24; also, Matt. xxiv. 37-39 and Luke xvii. 26, 27; also Matt. xxiv. 16-18, Mark xiii. 14b-16, and Luke xvii. 31; also Matt. xxiv. 40, 41 and Luke xvii. 34, 35, 36; also Matt. xxiv. 28 and Luke xvii. 37; also Matt. xxiv. 43-51 and Luke xii. 39-46; also Matt. viii. 12; xiii. 42, 50; xxii. 13b; xxiv. 51; xxv. 30, and Luke xiii. 28; also Mark xiii. 12, 13, and Matt. x. 21, 22.

These references suffice to show that Jesus repeated Himself frequently, and also, that at times He wove into a single discourse many sayings He had uttered at other times, and in other places and connections (e.g. Matt. v-vii; xiii). See pp. 293, 294).

For an understanding of the Olivet Eschatological (Last Things) Discourse a large area of prophecy must be taken in, especially parts of Daniel, and of Revelation.

As the prophetic unfolding of dispensations and other periods of time is not recognized by the vast majority of commentators, what we regard to be reliable guidance on these matters need not be looked for in the commentaries, though they should be consulted for help in other ways.

Matthew's report of the Olivet Discourse is the fullest, and will be commented on in the study of that Gospel, but it will be well now to see that the Discourse arose out of two questions which some of the disciples asked:

(a) 'When shall these things be?' i.e. the destruction of the Temple buildings.

(b) 'What shall be the sign of Thy coming (*parousia*, presence), and of the end (*sunteleia*, consummation) of the world (*aiōn*, age)?'

There are really two questions in the second of these enquiries (Matt. xxiv. 3).

Observe carefully the introduction to the Discourse given by the Synoptists, marking agreements and differences (Mark xiii. 1-4; Matt. xxiv. 1-3; Luke xxi. 5-7).

(1) Jesus' attention is called by His 'disciples' to the glory of Herod's Temple, as He and they are departing from it (Matt.); 'some' (Luke); 'one of His disciples' (Mark), who probably was Peter, as he is the chief source of this Gospel.

(2) In reply Jesus predicts the destruction of the Temple.

(3) Later, on the Mount of Olives, it is reported by all the Synoptists, ' disciples,' Mark names them, asked Jesus (a) when these things would be, and (b) what would be the sign of approaching accomplishment, but in Matthew much greater definiteness is given to the second part of the inquiry respecting the ' sign.' He reports that they asked: 'What shall be the sign of *Thy coming*, and of the *consummation of the age*?' And so, in these records, we may look for the answers to three inquiries:

(a) When will the Temple be destroyed?

(b) What sign will herald Christ's coming again?

(c) What intimation will there be of the approaching end of the age?

It is most important to observe how much of Jesus' answers to these inquiries is given by each of the Evangelists.

One of the difficulties in understanding this Discourse is in the fact that two prophetic events are spoken of, and it is not at once obvious, in places, which of them is referred to. These events are, *the not distant destruction of Jerusalem*, including the Temple, of course, and *Christ's distant second advent, and the end of the age.*

If we can discover what part of the Discourse refers to the first of these events, the remainder will be much clearer (see p. 307).

It is of the utmost importance to understand that the stand-point of the disciples is Jewish. A little before this Discourse, Christ had told them in the Upper Room (John xiv-xvi) that He would leave them, and also that He would return, and now they ask *when* He will return and usher in the Days of the Messiah. The disciples knew nothing whatever of this Christian age, but expected the Messiah to release their nation from Roman domination, and to establish a visible theocracy. They expected these events to come soon. In instructing them Christ speaks:

> Of the overthrow of Jerusalem, which took place in A.D. 70;
>
> Of the long period which has reached from then until now;
>
> Of a period of great tribulation, yet to come, affecting the Jews chiefly;
>
> Of His return to the earth, and His resumption of dealings with the Jews;
>
> Of the Judgment of the living nations, and the establishment of His Kingdom.

These events are not dealt with in this order, nor are they all reported in all three Gospels. The Matthew account will be explained in the section dealing with that Book, and also Luke's account, in its place (pp. 306, 357).

Our present object is to see how much of the above unfolding is reported in Mark. This, the following plan shows:

THE OLIVET DISCOURSE	MARK	MATTHEW	LUKE
1 The Disciples call Jesus' attention to the Temple -	xiii. 1	xxiv. 1	xxi. 5
2 Jesus Predicts the Destruction of the Temple -	xiii. 2	xxiv. 2	xxi. 6
3 The disciples ask certain Questions - - -	xiii. 3, 4	xxiv. 3	xxi. 7
4 Jesus Outlines the Course of this Age (Mark and Luke supply details omitted by Matthew) - - -	xiii. 5-13	xxiv. 4-14	xxi. 8-19
5 The Destruction of Jerusalem Predicted. (Fulfilled in A.D. 70, by Titus) -	—	—	xxi. 20, 22, 24
6 The Great Tribulation -	xiii. 14-23	xxiv. 15-25	—
7 The Swiftness and Visibility of Christ's Return -	—	xxiv. 26-28	—
8 At the End of the Tribulation the Son of Man is Manifested, and Israel is Regathered - - -	xiii. 24-27	xxiv. 29-31	xxi. 25-28
9 The Suddenness of these events. The Fig Tree Parable - - -	xiii. 28-31	xxiv. 32-35	xxi. 29-33
10 The Time of the Advent known only to the Father	xiii. 32	xxiv. 36	—
11 The Surprise and Effect of the Advent illustrated by ancient history - -	—	xxiv. 37-41	—
12 Exhortation to Watchfulness - - - -	xiii. 33	xxiv. 42	xxi. 34-36
13 Watchfulness urged by the Parable of the Porter -	xiii. 34-37	—	—
14 Watchfulness urged by the Parables of: The Master of the House (43-44); The Faithful and the Unfaithful Servants (45-51) - -	—	xxiv. 43-51	—
15 Parable of the Virgins -	—	xxv. 1-13	—
16 Parable of the Talents -	—	xxv. 14-30	—
17 The Judgment of Living Nations - - - -	—	xxv. 31-46	—

In this unfolding, observe what items are omitted by Mark (5, 7, 11, 14-17); what items he records with Matthew only (6, 10); that he records no items with Luke only; and what item he alone records (13).

Specially noticeable is it that only Luke records the destruction of Jerusalem, which took place under Titus, in A.D. 70: that neither Mark nor Luke, Gospels addressed to Gentiles, records the ancient history illustration (but see Luke xvii. 26-30); that Mark and Luke omit the whole parabolic part of the Discourse given in Matt. xxiv. 45-xxv. 30, which refers to the Christian Church (see p. 309); and omit, also, what Jesus said about the Judgment of Living Nations (Matt. xxv. 31-46).

20

MARK'S PLAN

THE Plan of this Gospel is very simple, and chap. x. 45, may be regarded as the key to it:

'The Son of Man came
(a) not to be ministered unto, but to minister - i. 14-ix. 50
(b) and to give His life a ransom for many' - xi. 1-xv. 47

With these two main parts are three shorter ones, these being respectively at the beginning, in the middle, and at the end, so that the briefest outline is:

(1) The Preparation   -   -   -   -   - i. 1-13
(2) The MINISTRY IN GALILEE   -   -   - i. 14-ix. 50
(3) The Journey to Jerusalem -   -   -   - x. 1-52
(4) The PASSION WEEK   -   -   -   - xi. 1-xv. 47
(5) The Consummation   -   -   -   - xvi. 1-20

In the main, though not consistently, the order is chronological, but Mark's purpose was not to write a complete biography, far less a history, but to show the successive stages through which the ministry of Jesus passed.

There is, first, the evangelization of the lake-side towns and country, both in the tetrarchy of Antipas and in that of Philip (i. 14-vi. 30). Then the extension of this work to the rest of Galilee during intervals of enforced withdrawal from the lake-district (vi. 30-viii. 26). And then the instruction and disciplining of the men who ultimately were to carry the preaching of the Divine Kingdom to the ends of the earth (viii. 27-ix. 50).

There follows the last journey to Jerusalem (chap. x.), and finally, the events of the Passion Week, and the triumph through the grave (xi-xvi).

It will be observed that the narrative of the Passion Week is on a scale out of all proportion to that on which the Ministry is drawn. This is true of all the Gospels, but chiefly of Mark's, having regard to the brevity of his narrative. The figures are:

Matthew, xxi-xxviii, eight chapters; Luke, xix. 28-xxiv, five and a half chapters; John, xii-xxi, ten chapters; Mark, xi-xvi, six chapters; that is, Matthew gives to the Passion Week two-sevenths of his Gospel; Luke, nearly a quarter; John, nearly a half, and Mark, three-eights. The reason for this is, of course, because the redeeming act is not Christ's life and teaching, but His death and resurrection.

21

MARK'S GEOGRAPHY

TWO sections of Palestine make up the field of Mark's history, GALILEE and JUDÆA, and two cities stand prominently forward as the centres of the movement, CAPERNAUM and JERUSALEM.

The geography of Mark's Gospel falls, then, into two main parts:

   i. 4- ix. 50 ... GALILEE, ... Centre, CAPERNAUM;
   x. 32-xvi. 8 ... JUDÆA ... Centre, JERUSALEM;

and these two parts are linked together by x. 1-31, the ministry of which falls mainly in PERÆA. (See Maps III, V, VII).

Having regard to our Lord's itinerations, Mark's geographical references are singularly meagre. The places actually specified are as follows:

Bethany -	- xi. 1, 11; xiv. 3	Decapolis -	- v. 20; vii. 31
Bethphage	- xi. 1	Gadarenes,	
Bethsaida -	- vi. 45, viii. 22	Country of	- v. 1
Cæsarea Philippi	viii. 27	Galilee -	- i. 28, 39; iii. 7;
Capernaum	- i. 21; ii. 1; ix. 33		ix. 30; xiv. 28;
Dalmanutha	- viii. 10		xv. 41; xvi. 7

Galilee, Sea of -	ii. 13; iii. 7; iv. 1; v. 1, 13, 21; vi. 48, 49; vii. 31	Judæa - -	iii. 7; xiii. 14
		Coasts of -	x. 1
		Land of -	i. 5
Idumæa - -	iii. 8	Wilderness of	i. 4, 12, 13; viii. 4
Jericho - -	x. 46		
Jerusalem	i. 5; xi. 11	Nazareth - -	i. 9; xvi. 6
Jordan, at -	i. 5, 9	Olives, Mount of	xi. 1; xiii. 3; xiv. 26
„ beyond -	iii. 8; x. 1		
		Tyre and Sidon	iii. 8; vii. 31

In addition to these there are some indefinite references, such as, ' a mountain,' ix. 2, which almost certainly was one of the spurs of Mount Hermon; ' next towns ' (i. 38); ' throughout all Galilee ' (i. 28, 39. There were 240 towns and villages in Galilee.)

The more exact locality of events is frequently described by Mark as—in a house, on the road, by the seaside, among the hills, and similar expressions.

The geography of x. 32-xvi. 8 is located in Judæa, with Jerusalem as centre, but in i. 4-ix. 50, northern Palestine is the field of ministry, so that the following particulars should be carefully noticed.

Mark i. 4–ix. 50

Jordan - - - -	i. 4-11
Wilderness of Judæa - -	i. 12, 13. Probably Mons Quarantania
Capernaum and neighbourhood	i. 14-38; ii. 1-iii. 12; iii. 20-iv. 34; v. 21-43; vi. 53-vii. 23; ix. 33-50
Journey through Galilee -	i. 39-45; ix. 30-32
A Mountain - - -	iii. 13-19. Not known
Sea of Galilee - - -	iv. 35-41; vi. 48-52; viii. 13-21
Eastern Shore - - -	v. 1-20; vi. 30-47; vii. 31-viii. 9; viii. 22-26. Bethsaida
Nazareth and neighbourhood	vi. 1-13
Machærus - - - -	vi. 14-29. East of the Jordan
Coasts of Tyre and Sidon -	vii. 24-30. Phœnicia
Dalmanutha - - - -	viii. 10-12. Magadan: Matt. xv. 39
Cæsarea Philippi - -	viii. 27-38
A Mountain - - -	ix. 1-29. Mount Hermon

In the above, observe the place which Capernaum occupies in this large division of the Gospel; also, the Eastern Shore; and also the Sea of Galilee. These three dominate the whole narrative.

It is essential that these details be studied with a good map, and, if possible, with Dr. George Adam Smith's *Historical Geography of the Holy Land.*

22

FEATURES OF MARK'S GOSPEL

WHAT is said under ' Style and Diction ' is equally appropriate here, so read the former again, carefully (p. 193). Regarding the Gospel broadly, features of it are—its non-Jewish complexion; its emphasis on what Jesus *did* rather than on what He *said*; its broad chronological sequence; and the space it devotes to the events of the Passion Week. In recording three and a half years of ministry, Mark devotes about three-eighths of his whole account to the happenings of a single week (see under ' Mark's Plan,' p. 217).

The following are some of the more detailed characteristics of this Gospel.

(i) THE LOOKS OF JESUS. Six times it is said that '*He-looked-round-about*' (iii. 5, 34; v. 32; ix. 8; x. 23; xi. 11). The word (*periblepō*, fr. *peri*, around, and *blepō*, to look) means a slow, searching gaze, and occurs again in the New Testament only in Luke vi. 10.

(ii) THE GESTURES OF JESUS. vii. 33, 34. '*Having-taken*-(him)-*away* (2 aor. part. mid), from the crowd apart, *He put* (2 aor. ind. act.), His fingers to his ears, and *having-spit* (1 aor. part. act.) *He touched* (1 aor. ind. mid) his tongue and *having-looked-up* (2 aor. part. mid) to heaven, *He groaned* (1 aor. ind. act.), and *says* (pres. ind. act.) to him, "Ephphatha," that is *be-opened* (1 aor. imperat. pass.).' Observe the tenses of these eight words. VIII. 33. '*He turning* and seeing His disciples— '; a compound verb, *epi-strephō*, to turn about upon. IX. 35, 36. ' And *sitting-down* He called the twelve.' x. 16. '*Having-taken* a little child He set it in the midst, and *having-taken* (it)-*in-His-arms*—.' x. 32. '*Having-taken* (to Him)-*again* the Twelve.' The three verbs in ix. 35, 36; x. 32, are different. The first is simply ' to take '; the second is, ' to take into or embrace in one's arms '; and the third is ' to take to one's side,' or ' to receive to one's self' (*lambanō*; *en-agkalizomai*, ix. 36; x. 16 only; *para-lambanō*).

(iii) THE EMOTIONS OF JESUS. His grief, and anger, His love, and pity, His wonder, and sighs (iii. 5; vi. 6, 34; vii. 34; viii. 12; x. 14, 21). Also, His infirmities, such as hunger and weariness (iv. 38; vi. 31; xi. 12).

Especially noticeable are Mark's references to Jesus' anger, or displeasure. He uses at least four words to express this emotion as exhibited by Christ.

'He *looked-round-about* on them with *anger*' (iii. 5). The word here (*orgē*) means wrath, indignation, vengeance: cf. Matt. iii. 7; Rom iii. 5; Rev. xiv. 10.

'Jesus was *much-displeased*' (A.V.); was 'moved with indignation' (R.V.) (x. 14). The word here (*aganakteō*) signifies irritation, annoyance.

'He *straitly-charged* him' (A.V.); 'strictly-charged' (R.V.); 'sternly-charged' (R.V. marg.) (i. 43). The word here (*embrimaomai*) means open and vehement anger.

'Jesus *rebuked* the unclean spirit' (ix. 25). The word here (*epitimaō*) means 'to mete out due measure,' to censure, vehemently to reproach.

These references to Jesus' wrathful emotions are of the greatest significance, and give us a glimpse far into the Divine character. The expressions of these emotions are but the exhibitions of a permanent moral state, due to the existence of evil.

(iv) Mark also describes the impression which Jesus made upon the bystanders (i. 22, 27; ii. 12; iv. 41; vi. 2, 51; x. 24, 26); and how the needy thronged Him (i. 32; ii. 2; iii. 10, 20; iv. 1; v. 31; vi. 31, 56; viii. 2).

(v) Observe how Mark records *names* and describes *persons* with minuteness (i. 29, 36; ii. 14; iii. 6, 22; x. 46; xi. 11; xiii. 3; xiv. 33; xv. 21, 40).

(vi) He also gives details of *time*, such as, ' a great while before day,' ' when the Sabbath was come,' ' it was eventide,' ' the third hour,' ' very early on the first day of the week ' (i. 35; ii. 1; iv. 35; vi. 2; xi. 11, 19; xv. 25; xvi. 2).

(vii) There are also particulars of *place* which no one else gives, such as ' by the seaside,' ' in the Decapolis,' ' sitting on the right side ' (ii. 13; iii. 7, 8; iv. 1; v. 20; vii. 31; xii. 41; xiii. 3; xiv. 68; xv. 39; xvi. 5).

(viii) Worthy of notice also are Mark's references to *numbers*; 'about two thousand,' ' two and two,' ' by hundreds and by fifties ' (v. 13; vi. 7, 40; xiv. 30).

(ix) Mark shows a fondness of diminutives: ' little daughter,' ' damsel,' ' little dog,' ' little maid,' 'small fish,' ' crumb,' or morsel, ' little ear,' 'little child' (v. 23, 41, 42; vi. 22, 28; vii. 25, 27, 28; viii. 7; x. 4, 14, 15; xiv. 47, 66, 69).

(x) The Evangelist's descriptions are full of minute details, such as: ' with the wild beasts ' (i. 13); ' no, not even about the door ' (ii. 2); ' digging a hole in the roof ' (ii. 4); ' plucking the ears of

222 A GUIDE TO THE GOSPELS

corn' (ii. 23); 'even as He was' (iv. 36); 'on the cushion' (iv. 38); 'rent asunder,' 'fetters in pieces' (v. 4); 'green grass,' 'in ranks by hundreds and by fifties' (vi. 39, 40); 'glistering, exceeding white, so as no fuller on earth can whiten them' (ix. 3), and many others (pp. 264, 265).

(xi) The incidents and circumstances recorded by Mark only are many and very interesting, such as: 'not worthy *to stoop down and unloose* the latchet' (i. 7); '*hired servants*' (i. 20); '*Simon and Andrew, with James and John*' (i. 29); '*all the city was gathered about the door*' (i. 33); '*a great while before day*' (i.35); '*not so much as about the door*' (ii. 2); 'the palsied man was carried by *four* persons' (ii. 3); 'the bearers *uncovered the roof and broke it up*' (ii. 4); 'Levi was the *son of Alphaeus*' (ii. 14); 'the disciples *made a* path by plucking the ears of corn' (ii. 23); 'the Pharisees took counsel *with the Herodians*' (iii. 6); '*could not so much as eat bread*' (iii. 20); '*because they said, He hath an unclean spirit*' (iii. 30); '*when even was come*' (iv. 35); '*the steersman's cushion in the stern*' (iv. 38); '*carest Thou not that we perish?*' (iv. 38); '*the carpenter*' (vi. 3); '*anointed the sick with oil*' (vi. 13); '*lords, high captains, and chief estates*' (vi. 21); 'Salome *went out of the room to her mother*' (vi. 24); '*because there were so many coming and going that there was not leisure even to eat*' (vi. 31); 'the people *laid the sick in the streets*' (vi. 56); '*laid upon the bed*' (vii. 30); '*only one loaf in the boat*' (viii. 14); '*the Scribes were disputing with the disciples*'; 'the crowd *ran to greet* Jesus'; '*were amazed*' (ix. 15); 'the demoniac boy was *dumb, he gnashed his teeth, he pined away, he fell down and rolled about foaming*' (ix. 17, 18).

(xii) Special notice is taken in this Gospel of Jesus' *retirements*: after the first deeds of healing (i. 35); after the cleansing of the leper (i. 45); after the restoration of the man with the withered hand (iii. 7-13); after His rejection at Nazareth (vi. 6); after the murder of the Baptist (vi. 30-32); after the opposition of the Pharisees (vii. 24); after giving a blind man sight (viii. 27); after the first open announcement of His coming Passion (ix. 2); after His triumphal entry into Jerusalem (xi. 11); and after the purging of the Temple (xi. 19).

To these features should be added references made already to Aramaic and Latin words in Mark, and the explanation of Jewish customs and places. (See under 'For Whom Written,' p. 168).

23

ANALYSIS OF MARK'S GOSPEL

AS Mark's Gospel was the first of the Four to be written, and is almost completely incorporated in MATTHEW and

LUKE, a detailed analysis of it is given, divided into 105 sections, to aid in reading, and for ready reference.

It is presented as a Day of Service, and the several divisions of a day—dawn, morning, forenoon, midday, afternoon, evening, and night—lend themselves to the unfolding of the Divine Story.

That which characterizes these parts of the Day respectively, are *Acclamation*, a glad welcome; *Opposition*, petty criticism; *Separation* from the crowd, of a few souls who would be the school of the new teaching and the bearers of the new message; *Consummation* of the ministry, Jesus' noontide of service; *Instruction* of the inner circle as to the on-coming Passion of the Messiah; *Condemnation* by Jews and Gentiles, followed by the *Crucifixion*.

These seven parts of the Day fall into three pairs, with the Consummation as centre and crown, as follows:

Introduction. i. 1-13. The Day Before

THE DAY OF MINISTRY
- (*a*) Acclamation. i. 14-45. Dawn
- (*b*) Opposition. ii. 1-iii. 6. Morning
- (*c*) Separation. iii. 7-vi. 6. Forenoon
- (*d*) CONSUMMATION. vi. 7-viii. 26. Midday
- (*c*) Instruction. viii. 27-x. 52. Afternoon
- (*b*) Condemnation. xi. 1-xiii. 37. Evening
- (*a*) Crucifixion. xiv. 1-xv. 47. Night

Conclusion. xvi. 1-20. The Day After

On either side of the *Consummation* are the *Separation* and *Instruction* of the Apostles.   Outside of that is the *Opposition* which led to the *Condemnation*.   Enfolding all is the tragic contradiction of *Acclamation* which ended in *Crucifixion*.

On the one side of this programme is *The Day Before*, one of *Preparation for Earth's Service*; and on the other side is *The Day After*, one of *Exaltation to Heaven's Service*.

These nine lines of outline should be thoroughly mastered.

When we have apprehended the design of the author we shall realize that what he omits is significant, as well as what he records, and so the analysis will show these omissions, supplied by the other Gospels.   *The paragraphs with a vertical line on their left are what Mark omits.*   The parallels to Mark in the other Gospels are shown, and, as nearly as can be said, the years of the main parts of the story. (See pp. 186-188, and Chart).

23. ANALYSIS OF MARK'S GOSPEL

JESUS THE CHRIST AT WORK

I	II	III	IV
THE OPENING EVENTS	THE GALILEAN MINISTRY	THE PERÆAN MINISTRY	THE CLOSING EVENTS
i. 1-13 A.D. 27	i. 14-ix. 50 A.D. 28-29	x. 1-52 A.D. 30	xi. 1-xvi. 20 A.D. 30
Introduction (1)	**FIRST PERIOD** i. 14-iii. 12 A.D. 28	Discourse on Divorce (1-12)	SUNDAY to WEDNESDAY (xi.-xiv. 11)
John the Baptist and his Ministry (2-8)	First Words (i. 14, 15)	Jesus Blesses Little Children (13-16)	Claims
The Baptism and Dedication of Jesus (9-11)	Fellow Workers (i. 16-20)	The Rich Young Ruler (17-31)	Conflict
The Temptation of Jesus (12, 13)	Gracious Works (i. 21-iii. 12)	Jesus Foretells His Death (32-34)	Prophecy
	SECOND PERIOD iii. 13-vii. 23 A.D. 28-29	The Request of James and John (35-45)	Treachery
	Apostles Chosen (iii. 13-19a)	The Healing of Bartimaeus (46-52) (Jericho)	THURSDAY (xiv. 12-52)
	Challenge Rebutted (iii. 19b-35)		Passover
	Parabolic Teaching (iv. 1-34)		Gethsemane
	Works of Pity and Power (iv. 35-vi. 6)		Betrayal
	Great Events (vi. 7-vii. 23)		Arrest
	THIRD PERIOD vii. 24-ix. 50 A.D. 29	**KEY: Ch. x. 45** Minister - i. 1-x. 31 Ransom - x. 32-xvi. 20 (See p. 217).	FRIDAY and SATURDAY (xiv. 53-xv. 47)
	More Miracles (vii. 24-viii. 13)		Trials
	Instruction of the Apostles (viii. 14-ix. 50)		Crucifixion
			Burial
			SUNDAY (xvi. 1-8)
			Resurrection
			THE FORTY DAYS (xvi. 9-20)
			Appearances
			Ascension

23

ANALYSIS OF MARK'S GOSPEL

THE DIVINE SERVANT AND HIS DAY OF SERVICE

Key Text, x. 45

THE THIRTY YEARS OF PREPARATION

B.C. 5 TO A.D. 26   (OMITTED BY MARK)

Luke i. 1-4 -	Luke's Method of Research.
John i. 1-18	Christ Pre-Existent and Incarnate.
Matt. i. 1-17; Luke iii. 23-38	The Two Genealogies.
Luke i. 5-ii. 52; Matt. i. 18-ii. 23	Birth, and Childhood of the Baptist, and of Jesus.

I. THE OPENING EVENTS OF CHRIST'S MINISTRY
i. 1-13. A.D. 27

1 Introduction - - - - - - - -   1
    Luke iii. 1, 2
2 John the Baptist and his Ministry - - - -   2-8
    Matt. iii. 1-6, 11, 12; Luke iii. 3-6, 15-20

Matt. iii. 7-10 -	A Sample of the Baptist's Preaching.
Luke iii. 7-14 -	A Sample of the Baptist's Preaching.

3 The Baptism and Dedication of Jesus - - -   9-11
    Matt. iii. 13-17; Luke iii. 21-23
4 The Temptation of Jesus given in detail (Matt. iv. 1-11;
    Luke iv. 1-13) - - - - - -   12, 13

The Early Judæan and Widespread Ministry
A.D. 27

AT BETHANY BEYOND JORDAN

John i. 19-28 -	The Testimony to Jesus of John the Baptist.
John i. 29-34 -	John's Identification of Jesus as the Messiah.
John i. 35-51 -	The First Disciples of Jesus.

AT CANA IN GALILEE

John ii. 1-11	Jesus at a Wedding Feast. His First Miracle.
John ii. 12 -	Jesus at Capernaum.

AT JERUSALEM

John ii. 13-22	The First Cleansing of the Temple.
John ii. 23-iii. 21	The Interview of Nicodemus with Jesus.
John iii. 22-iv. 3	John's Loyalty to Jesus. The Departure from Judæa.

IN SAMARIA

John iv 4-42	Jesus' Interview with a Samaritan Woman at Jacob's Well.

IN GALILEE

John iv. 43-45	Jesus is Welcomed by the Galileans.

15   225

II. THE GALILEAN MINISTRY

i. 14-ix. 50.   A.D. 28-29

First Period, i. 14-iii. 12.   A.D. 28

Dawn and Acclamation (i. 14-45)

5 First Words -   -   -   -   -   -   •   •   **14, 15**
Matt. iv. 12, 17; Luke iv. 14, 15.

John iv. 46-54   Healing of a Nobleman's Son at Cana.
Luke iv. 16-30   The First Rejection at Nazareth.
Matt. iv. 13-16   The New Home in Capernaum.
Luke iv. 31, 32

6 Fellow Workers -   -   -   -   •   •   •   **16-20**
Matt. iv. 18-22; Luke v. 1-11.

7 Gracious Works -   -   -   -   •   •   •   **21-45**
(i) The Cure of a Demoniac **21-28**
Luke iv. 31-37
(ii) The Healing of Simon's Mother-in-law **29-31**
Matt. viii. 14-17; Luke iv. 38-41
(iii) Ministry After Sunset **32-34**
(iv) Prayer, Interruption, and Renewed Service   ...   **35-39**
Luke iv. 42-44; Matt. iv. 23-25
(v) The Cleansing of a Leper **40-45**
Matt. viii. 2-4; Luke v. 12-16

Morning and Opposition (ii. 1-iii. 12)

8 A Paralytic Healed and Forgiven -   •   •   -   **ii. 1-12**
Matt. ix. 1-8; Luke v. 17-26.

9 The Call of Levi, and His Feast -   •   •   -   **ii. 13-17**
Matt. ix. 9-13; Luke v. 27-32.

10 The Question Concerning Fasting -   -   •   -   **ii. 18-22**
Matt. ix. 14-17; Luke v. 33-39.

John v. 1-47 -   Healing of a Man at the Pool of Bethesda, and
Jesus' Discourse of Defence.

11 The Cornfield Incident -   -   -   -   •   -   **ii. 23-28**
Matt. xii. 1-8; Luke vi. 1-5.

12 The Withered Hand Incident -   •   •   -   **iii. 1-6**
Matt. xii. 9-14; Luke vi. 6-11.

13 Interrupted Retirement -   -   •   •   •   -   **iii. 7-12**
Matt. xii. 15-21.

Second Period (iii. 13-vii. 23)

Forenoon and Separation (iii. 13-vi. 6)

APOSTLES (iii. 13-19*a*)

14 The Choice of the Twelve Apostles   -   -   iii. 13-19*a*
  Luke vi. 12-16; Matt. x. 2-4.

Matt. v-viii. 1; }
Luke vi. 17-49 } The Sermon on the Mount.

Matt. viii. 5-13;}
Luke vii. 1-10 } Healing of a Centurion's Servant.

Luke vii. 11-17 Raising of a Widow's Son at Nain.

Matt. xi. 2-19; } John the Baptist's Inquiry, and Jesus' Eulogy
Luke vii. 18-35 } of him.

Matt. xi. 20-24 Woes on the Cities of Opportunity

Matt. xi. 25-30 Jesus' Prayer, and His Claims for Himself.

Luke vii. 36-50 Anointing of Christ's Feet by a Sinful Woman
     in the House of Simon, and the Parable of
     the Two Debtors.

Luke viii. 1-3 The Second Tour of Galilee.

PRINCIPLES (iii. 19*b*-35)

15 Christ's Sanity - - - - - - iii. 19*b*-21
16 Christ's Authority - - - - - - iii. 22-30
  Matt. xii. 22-37.
| Matt. xii. 38-45 Scribes and Pharisees Demand a Sign.
17 The Old and New Relationships - - - iii. 31-35
  Matt. xii. 46-50; Luke viii. 19-21.

PARABLES (iv. 1-34)

18 Parable of the Sower - - - • • iv. 1-9
  Matt. xiii. 1-9; Luke viii. 4-8.
19 The Interpretation - - - • • iv. 10-20
  Matt. xiii. 10-23; Luke viii. 9-15.
20 Parabolic Warnings - - - - • • iv. 21-25
  Luke viii. 16-18.
21 Parable of the Seed Growing Secretly - - iv. 26-29
| Matt. xiii. 24-30 Parable of the Tares.
22 Parable of the Mustard Seed - - - iv. 30-32
  Matt. xiii. 31, 32; Luke xiii. 18, 19.
23 The Parabolic Method - - - - - iv. 33, 34
| Matt. xiii. 33-35 Parable of the Leaven in the Meal.
| Matt. xiii. 36-53 Parables Delivered in a House to the Disciples.

MIRACLES (iv. 35-vi. 6)

24 Stilling the Storm - - - - • • iv. 35-41
  Matt. viii. 18, 23-27; Luke viii. 22-25.
25 A Gerasene Demoniac Delivered - - • v. 1-20
  Matt. viii. 28-34; Luke viii. 26-39.

The Later Judæan Ministry (A.D. 29)

IN JERUSALEM

IN JUDÆA

Parable of the Wise Steward (41-48).

Words on Divisions, Signs, and Reconciliation (49-59).

Luke xiii. 1-9   Repent or Perish. Parable of the Barren Fig Tree.

Luke xiii. 10-21 Healing of a Cripple Woman (10-17).

Parables of the Mustard Seed, and the Leaven (18-21).

John x. 22-39   Jesus at the Feast of Dedication.

III. THE PERÆAN MINISTRY (x. 1-52. A.D. 30)

John x. 40-42   Jesus Withdraws to Bethany beyond Jordan.

Luke xiii. 22-30 Teaching in Peræa on the way to Jerusalem.

Luke xiii. 31-35 Jesus Warned against Herod Antipas.

Luke xiv. 1-24   Healing of a Dropsical Man, and Three Parables (1-6).

The Chief Seats at Feasts (7-11).

Who to Invite to a Feast (12-14).

Invitation to a Great Supper (15-24).

Luke xiv. 25-35   The Cost of Discipleship, and Two Parables (25-27).

The Unfinished Tower (28-30).

The Unwaged War (31, 32).

Luke xv. 1-32   Three Parables on Finding the Lost:

The Shepherd and the Sheep (1-7).

The Woman and the Silver (8-10).

The Father and the Sons (11-32).

Luke xvi. 1   A Discourse on Various Subjects, xvi. 14-18,

-xvii. 10   and Three Parables:

The Unjust Steward (xvi. 1-13).

The Rich Man and Lazarus (xvi. 19-31).

The Unprofitable Servants (xvii. 7-10).

John xi. 1-44   Jesus Raises Lazarus from the Dead.

John xi. 45-54   The Effect of the Raising of Lazarus.

Luke xvii. 11-37 Jesus in Samaria and Galilee.

The Healing of Ten Lepers (11-19).

The Coming of the Kingdom (20-21).

The Advent of the Son of Man (22-37).

Luke xviii. 1-14 Two Parables on Prayer:

The Importunate Widow (1-8).

The Pharisee and the Publican (9-14).

52 Jesus Travels Towards Judæa by Peræa   -   -   - x. 1

53 A Question Concerning Divorce   -   -   -   - x. 2-12

Matt. xix. 1-12.

54 Jesus Blesses Little Children   -   -   -   - x. 13-16

Matt. xix. 13-15; Luke xviii. 15-17.

55 The Young Man who Lacked but One Thing -   - x. 17-22

Matt. xix. 16-21; Luke xviii. 18-23.

IV. THE CLOSING EVENTS OF CHRIST'S MINISTRY
(xi. 1-xv. 47. A.D. 30)
JERUSALEM
Evening and Condemnation (xi. 1-xiii. 37)
SUNDAY—THE DAY OF MANIFESTATION

MONDAY—THE DAY OF AUTHORITY

TUESDAY—THE DAY OF CONTROVERSY

| Matt. xxii. 1-14   The Parable of the King's Marriage Feast.

69 The Tribute Question. Pharisees and Herodians   - xii. 13-17
   Matt. xxii. 15-22; Luke xx. 20-26.

70 The Resurrection Question. Sadducees -   -   - xii. 18-27
   Matt. xxii. 23-33; Luke xx. 27-40.

71 The Great Commandment Question. A Scribe   - xii. 28-34
   Matt. xxii. 34-40.

72 The Messiah Question. Jesus   -   ▪   ▪   - xii. 35-37
   Matt. xxii. 41-46; Luke xx. 41-44.

73 Denunciation of the Scribes   -   -   ▪   ▪   - xii. 38-40
   Luke xx. 45-47.

| Matt. xxiii. 1-36 Lengthy Denunciation of the Scribes and
| Pharisees.
| Matt. xxiii. 37-39 Jesus' Indictment and Abandonment of Jerusalem.

74 The Widow's Farthing   -   -   -   -   -   - xii. 41-44
   Luke xxi. 1-4.

75 The Olivet Prophecy   -   -   -   -   -   - xiii. 1-37
   Matt. xxiv. 1-42; Luke xxi. 5-36. (See p. 216).
| Matt. xxiv. 37-41 What will happen when Christ Returns.
| Matt. xxiv. 43-45a Parable of the Master of the House.
| Matt. xxiv. 45b-51 Parable of the Faithful and Evil Servants.
| Matt. xxv. 1-13   Parable of the Ten Virgins.
| Matt. xxv. 14-30   Parable of the Talents.
| Matt. xxv. 31-46   Teaching on the Judgment of Nations.

Night and Crucifixion (xiv. 1-xv. 47)

TUESDAY still, or WEDNESDAY

76 Conspiracy of the Priests and Scribes   -   -   - xiv. 1, 2
   Luke xxii. 1, 2
| Matt. xxvi. 1-5   Jesus Predicts His Crucifixion.

77 The Devotion, Criticism, and Defence of Mary   - xiv. 3-9
   Matt. xxvi. 6-13; John xii. 2-8.
   (This may have taken place after Mark x. 52).

78 The Treachery of Judas -   -   -   -   - xiv. 10, 11
   Matt. xxvi. 14-16; Luke xxii. 3-6.

THURSDAY—THE DAY OF FAREWELL

79 Preparation for the Pascal Meal   -   -   - xiv. 12-17
   Matt. xxvi. 17-20; Luke xxii. 7-13.
| Luke xxii. 14-16, Contention among the Disciples about who should
| 24-30   be the Greatest.
| John xiii. 1-20   Jesus Washes His Disciples' Feet.

80 Jesus Speaks of His Approaching Betrayal   -   xiv. 18-21
   Matt. xxvi. 21-24; Luke xxii. 21-23; John xiii. 21, 22
| Matt. xxvi. 25; ⎫
| John xiii. 23-30 ⎬ Jesus Points out Judas as the Betrayer.
| John xiii. 31-35   Jesus Intimates His Coming Departure.

81 Jesus Institutes the Eucharist   -   -   -   xiv. 22-26
      Matt. xxvi. 26-29; Luke xxii. 17, 18, 19, 20.
82 The Disciples, especially Peter, protest their
        Loyalty to Jesus   -   -   -   -   -   xiv. 27-31
      Matt. xxvi. 31-35; Luke xxii. 31-34; John xiii. 36-38.
| Luke xxii. 35-38 Jesus Warns the Disciples of Trouble Ahead.
| John xiv.   -   Jesus' Farewell Discourse in the Upper Room.
| John xv.-xvi.   -   The Discourse on the Way to Gethsemane.
| John xvii.   -   Christ's Intercessory Prayer.
83 Jesus' Suffering in Gethsemane -   -   -   -   xiv. 32-42
      Matt. xxvi. 30, 36-46; Luke xxii. 39-46; John xviii. 1.
84 Jesus Betrayed, Arrested, and Forsaken   -   -   xiv. 43-50
      Matt. xxvi. 47-56; Luke xxii. 47-53; John xviii. 2-11.
85 Story of the Young Man who Fled -   -   -   xiv. 51, 52

FRIDAY—THE DAY OF REDEMPTION

| John xviii. 12-14,⎫ Jesus Examined before Annas, the Ex-High
| 19-23   ⎭   Priest.
86 Jesus Tried and Condemned by Caiaphas and the
        Sanhedrin, who mock and buffet Him   -   - xiv. 53, 55-65
      Matt. xxvi. 57, 59-68; Luke xxii. 54, 63-65; John xviii. 24.
87 Peter's Denials of his Master   -   -   -   - xiv. 54, 66-72
      Matt. xxvi. 58, 69-75; Luke xxii. 54-62; John xviii. 15-18, 25-27.
88 After Dawn, Jesus is Formally Condemned by the
        Sanhedrin   -   -   -   -   -   -   -   xv. 1
      Matt. xxvii. 1; Luke xxii. 66-71.
| Matt. xxvii. 3-10 Remorse and Suicide of Judas (Acts i. 18, 19).
89 Jesus Before Pilate the First Time   -   -   -   - xv. 1-5
      Matt. xxvii. 2, 11-14; Luke xxiii. 1-5; John xviii. 28-38.
| Luke xxiii. 6-12   Jesus Before Herod Antipas.
90 Jesus Before Pilate the Second Time -   -   -   xv. 6-15
      Matt. xxvii. 15-26; Luke xxiii. 13-25; John xviii. 39-xix. 16.
91 The Roman Soldiers Mock Jesus   -   -   -   xv. 16-19
      Matt. xxvii. 27-30.
92 Jesus on the Way to Golgotha -   -   -   -   xv. 20-23
      Matt. xxvii. 31-34; Luke xxiii. 26-33; John xix. 16, 17.
93 The First Three Hours on the Cross -   -   -   xv. 24-32
      Matt. xxvii. 35-44; Luke xxiii. 33-43; John xix. 18-27.
94 The Last Three Hours on the Cross -   -   -   xv. 33-37
      Matt. xxvii. 45-50; Luke xxiii. 44-46; John xix. 28-30.
95 Events Accompanying Jesus' Death   -   -   -   xv. 38-41
      Matt. xxvii. 51-56; Luke xxiii. 45, 47-49.
96 The Burial of Jesus' Body -   -   -   -   -   xv. 42-46
      Matt. xxvii. 57-60; Luke xxiii. 50-54; John xix. 31-42.
97 The Watch of the Women by the Tomb   -   xv. 47
      Matt. xxvii. 61-66; Luke xxiii. 55, 56.

234   A GUIDE TO THE GOSPELS

V. THE NEW DAY (xvi. 1-20)

SUNDAY—THE DAY OF TRIUMPH

The Resurrection of Jesus (xvi. 1-8)

98 Women Visit the Tomb about Sunrise on Sunday,
      and find the Stone rolled away   -   -   -   - xvi. 1-4
    Matt. xxviii. 1.
  | Matt. xxviii. 2-4 The Earthquake, and the Stone Rolled Away.
99 The Angel's Information and Command   -   -   xvi. 5-8
    Luke xxiv. 1-8; Matt. xxviii. 5-8.

  | Luke xxiv. 9-12; ⎫ Mary Magdalene and Other Women Report to
  | John xx. 1-10   ⎬ the Apostles, especially to Peter and John,
                      ⎭ who go to the Tomb to see.

The Appearances of Jesus

100 Appearance to Mary Magdalene -   -   •   •   xvi. 9-11
    John xx. 11-18.
  | Matt. xxviii. 9, 10 To Other Women.
  | Matt. xxviii. 11-15 Some of the Guard Report to the Jewish Rulers.
101 Appearance to Two Disciples on the Way to Emmaus   xvi. 12, 13
  | Luke xxiv. 13-32.
  | Luke xxiv. 33-35 The Report of the Two Disciples, and the News
                         of Jesus' Appearance to Peter.
102 Appearance to the Apostles -   -   -   -   -   - xvi. 14
    Luke xxiv. 36-43; John xx. 19-25.
  | John xx. 26-31   Appearance to the Apostles again, Thomas being
                         present, and was convinced.
  | John xxi -   -   Appearance to Seven Disciples by the Sea of
                         Galilee; The Miraculous Draught of Fishes.
103 The Evangelical Commission   -   -   -   - xvi. 15-18
    Matt. xxviii. 16-20.
  | Luke xxiv. 44-49 Appearance to the Disciples again, and another
                         Commission (Acts i. 3-8).

Exaltation to Heaven's Service (xvi. 19, 20)

104 The Ascension of Jesus   -   -   -   •   •   xvi. 19
    Luke xxiv. 50-51. (Acts i. 9-12).
105 The Progress of the Church   •   •   •   •   - xvi. 20
    Luke xxiv. 52, 53.

QUESTIONS

1 What does the New Testament tell us about Mark? Give four references.

2 What does tradition say about Mark?

3 What internal evidence is there that Mark wrote for Gentile Christians?

4 Within which decade of the first century is it likely that Mark was written? Give reasons for your answer.

5 What three places have been claimed for the writing of this Gospel, and which of them is likely to be the right one?

6 What is the difference between ' genuineness ' and ' authenticity '? Show, by illustration, that they are not the same.

7 How, by the end of the second century, were the Four Gospels regarded?

8 Name five men who, between A.D. 150 and A.D. 200, bear witness to the genuineness of the Gospels.

9 Name four testimonies to the genuineness of the Gospels between A.D. 100 and A.D. 150.

10 What, in summary, is the testimony of Papias to the Marcan authorship of this Gospel?

11 Is there any part of this Gospel of which the Marcan authorship is challenged, and if so, on what grounds?

12 Is there any traditional testimony to the idea that behind this Gospel is the preaching of Peter?

13 What internal evidence is there that Peter's influence dominates this Gospel? Support your answer by three illustrations.

14 Why are the the first three Gospels called ' Synoptic '?

15 In determining which is the first of the Synoptic Gospels, what four questions arise?

16 Is there any reason for believing that Mark was written before Matthew and Luke?

17 Is there any argument against the idea that Mark is an abridgment of Matthew or (and) Luke?

18 What evidence is there that Mark's Gospel was largely neglected by the early Church?

19 How is the evidence of this early neglect of Mark's Gospel to be accounted for?

20 With regard to this Gospel, what three things may now be considered as established, and how do these affect our view of the importance of Mark?

21 What reason is there for believing that Peter was the chief source of this Gospel?

22 Is it likely that Mark had other sources than Peter, and if so, what probably were they?

23 What do you understand by a ' tendency-writing,' and is it likely that Mark is such?

24 Is there any internal evidence of Mark's design in writing this Gospel?

25 Is there any external tradition which bears on Mark's design in writing this Gospel?

26 What is meant by passages ' peculiar ' to a Gospel?

27 How does Bishop Westcott tabulate the peculiarities and coincidences of the Four Gospels?

28 How many verses can be claimed as peculiar to Mark?   Name four passages.

29 Are there any other passages which, in a sense, are peculiar to Mark? If so, in what sense?   Name a few of them.

30 Approximately, how many references are there in Mark to the Old Testament, and how many of these are quotations, or nearly so?   Name some of them.

31 What Old Testament quotations are peculiar to this Gospel?

32 How many of the Old Testament Books are referred to in Mark, and which four are drawn upon chiefly?

33 How many verses are there in this Gospel (R.V.), and how many of them contain Old Testament references?

34 What verses in Mark are omitted in the R.V.?

35 How many verses in this Gospel (R.V.) contain words of our Lord, and what proportion of the whole Gospel are these verses?

36 How many verses are there in the Four Gospels, and how many of them contain words of our Lord?

37 Does Divine inspiration nullify human personality?   Justify your answer.

38 How may the human characteristics of each of the Gospels be described?

39 Name eight words which Mark uses ten times or more.

40 Give a few instances of Mark's use of double negatives.

41 Illustrate Mark's use of double words or phrases.

42 Is there anything outstanding in the way in which Mark uses his tenses?

43 What do you understand by the ' historic present ' tense?   Illustrate Mark's use of it.

44 Say what the force is of the ' imperfect ' tense, and illustrate Mark's use of it.

45 How many words are there peculiar to this Gospel?   Name a dozen of them.

46 How would you explain, iii. 5; vi. 40; vii. 26; ix. 18; xiii. 11?

47 Give two references in Mark to each of the following: clothing, food, house or parts, utensils or tools, coins, divisions of time, religious practices, marriage, service, punishment, military matters, boating and fishing, animals, and disease.

48 How many miracles are recorded in Mark, apart from groups, and which of them are peculiar to this Gospel?

49 Name six miracles recorded by Mark, other than those which are peculiar.

50 What three words are used for miracles by Mark, and what do they signify respectively?
51 How does Bishop Westcott classify the miracles? Name two in Mark of each classification.
52 What two values did the miracles have? Illustrate the value that is permanent.
53 What is the greatest of all the miracles, and why?
54 What is a parable? How often does the word ' parable,' occur in this Gospel; and how many parables does Mark record?
55 Name eight of the parables recorded by Mark.
56 How may Christ's miracles and parables be compared?
57 Explain briefly the parables recorded in ii. 21, 22; iv. 21, 22; iv. 26-29; xii. 1-11.
58 What two interpretations are given to the parable recorded in iv. 30-32; and viii. 14-21? Give reasons for your own view.
59 What reason can be given for there being so little record in this Gospel of Jesus' discourses?
60 Name three of the shorter records of His teaching.
61 Which of Jesus' discourses does Mark give at length, and where?
62 From whence, do you suppose, did Mark get his knowledge of the great Discourse?
63 What gave rise to the great Discourse, and in it what questions are answered?
64 What two outstanding events are predicted in this Discourse, and how are they related in time?
65 Name some things in Matthew's record of this Discourse which Mark omits.
66 What does Mark record which Matthew and Luke omit, in this Discourse?
67 What verse in this Gospel summarizes its contents, and what parts of the Gospel answer to this summary?
68 Summarize the plan of Mark's Gospel in five items, with references.
69 Is there anything noteworthy in Mark's record of the Passion Week?
70 Give the names of ten places mentioned by Mark.
71 Which two cities in Palestine are the centres of Mark's narrative, and where are they situated?
72 Name four characteristics of this Gospel, and illustrate them.
73 Give six instances of Mark's detail in description.
74 Name a dozen details which are found only in Mark.
75 Name, by one word, each of the seven parts into which we have divided this Gospel.
76 Which large parts of Jesus' ministry does Mark entirely omit?
77 Characterize the days of the Passion Week, Sunday to Friday.
78 What Resurrection appearances does Mark record?
79 How many times, and when, did Jesus foretell His coming Passion to His disciples?
80 Name the Twelve Apostles.

LITERATURE

'Gospel According to St. Mark.' For students
of Greek - - - - - - H. B. Swete
'St. Mark.' Cambridge Greek Testament - Alford Plummer
*'St. Mark.' The Century Bible - - - S. D. F. Salmond
'Studies in Mark's Gospel' - - - - A. T. Robertson
*'St. Mark's Gospel.' Handbooks for Bible
Classes - - - - - - T. M. Lindsay
'St. Mark. A Practical Commentary' - James Morison
'Footprints of the Son of Man as Traced by St.
Mark' - - - - - - H. M. Luckock
Articles on Mark, Mark's Gospel, Synoptic
Problem, Chronology, and related subjects
in Hastings' Dictionary of the Bible, and
Dictionary of Christ and the Gospels. Inter-
national Standard Bible Encyclopædia. The
Commentaries - - - - - - ———
'The Gospel of Mark.' Expositor's Bible - C. A. Chadwick
'Commentary on St. Mark' (4 vols.). Devotional
Library - - - - - - - J. D. Jones
'Making Good in the Ministry: A Sketch of John
Mark' - - - - - - - A. T. Robertson
'St. Mark.' International Critical Commentary E. P. Gould
'Gnomon of the New Testament.' Vol. I J. A. Bengel
'The Greek Testament.' Vol. I - - - H. Alford
'Critical and Exegetical Handbook on the Gospels
of Mark and Luke' - - - - - H. A. W. Meyer
Commentary for English Readers. Edited by
Bishop Ellicott. Vol. VI
'The Speaker's Bible' (2 vols.)
'The Expositor's Greek Testament.' Vol. I - A. B. Bruce
'Word Pictures in the New Testament.' Vol. I A. T. Robertson
'Word Studies in the New Testament.' Vol. I M. Vincent
'The Gospel of Mark' - - - - - C. R. Erdman
'Expository Dictionary of New Testament Words' W. E. Vine
'The Beginning of the Gospel' (1950) - T. W. Manson
'A New Translation of Mark's Gospel' - T. W. Manson
'The Gospel according to St. Mark' - Vincent Taylor

Add to this list books on the ' Synoptics,' and on the ' Fourth Gospel,'
in Division A.

*The most useful small volumes for general use.

THE GOSPELS
VIEWED ANALYTICALLY

ST. MATTHEW

St. Matthew

OUTLINE OF STUDY

St. Matthew's Gospel

BEFORE beginning to study this Gospel read it through three times, each time, if possible, at a sitting (about 3½ hours):

First time, in Weymouth's *New Testament in Modern Speech*; or in *The Twentieth Century New Testament*; or in Moffatt's Translation.

Second time, in the Authorized Version.

Third time, in the Revised Version, or The Revised Standard Version (1946).

In these three readings use no books, but only the text of the Gospel. Having done this, do the reading prescribed in the following Studies. The system is that in each Study a part of the Guide be read, and a portion of the Gospel. Where possible the reading is related to the part of the Guide assigned for reading, as, for example, in the Parables and Miracles; but this cannot always be done, as, for example, in the parts relating to sources, date, and other subjects; but read carefully the part of the Guide which is appointed, and the portion of the Gospel which is attached to it, whether these are related or not.

The object is twofold: first, to familiarize oneself with the text of the Gospel by repeated reading; and secondly, to follow the various Studies which constitute the Guide.

1

KEY PLAN OF READING

FIFTY-TWO STUDIES

2

THE AUTHOR

WE begin the study of this Gospel by making two observations:

(a) The value of this, or of any other Scripture, is not dependent upon our knowing who the human author was, but upon its contents.

(b) Who the writer of this Gospel was, or of any other Scripture, must be determined by all the available evidence, and not by the heading in the Bible, which has no authority in itself.

A recognition of these two facts will be of considerable value to us as we approach this Writing. (For the problem of the authorship of this Gospel see Div. A, Part II, Sec. 5, p. 131).

Assuming that Matthew the Apostle wrote this Gospel, as all tradition affirms, what are we told about him?

Before his call to the apostolic office his name was Levi. The identity of Matthew and Levi is practically beyond doubt, though it has been questioned. An examination of the three Records, relative to this man's call, will show that it is Mark and Luke who call him Levi, but he speaks of himself as Matthew. They used his old name, being unwilling after thirty years to identify him with Matthew the Apostle, but he makes the identification to show that, by the grace of God, Levi, a ' publican,' became Matthew, an Apostle (Mark ii. 13-17; Luke v. 27-32; Matt. ix. 9-13).

Matthew was a Customs officer in the territory of Herod Antipas. As a farmer of Roman taxes he must have had some education, and must have been acquainted with the Aramaic and Greek languages.

It was while he was sitting at the toll office, near Capernaum, on the Great West Road from Damascus to the Mediterranean, that Jesus called him, and it is likely that the name Levi was changed to Matthew after his call. Probably Levi was his Jewish name, and Matthew his Christian name. As, after his call to discipleship, Simon was named Peter, so Levi would, in the same circumstances, be called Matthew, which is the Greek equivalent of Theodore, and means, Gift of Jehovah.

Shortly after he became an Apostle he entertained Jesus at a feast, to which he invited other tax-gatherers, and some persons who were regarded as ' sinners ' (ix. 9-13). This event led Jesus to utter ever-memorable words on self-righteousness, on fasting and feasting, and on the old and the new dispensations (Mark ii. 14-28; Matt. ix. 10-17).

It is certain that Matthew's occupation involved familiarity with the art of writing, and with other forms of literary activity, so that it is easy to believe, what Papias affirms (p. 131), that he prepared a manual of the Sayings of Jesus, the *Logia*, or, as it is called by scholars Q, for the instruction of catechumens, and others. (See ' Synoptic Problem,' p. 83).

It is also thought that traces of his former occupation are to be seen in his use of the word ' tribute ' (*kēnsos*), for money, instead of ' penny' (*dēnarion*; cf. Matt. xxii. 19, with Mark xii. 15), and in his recording the miracle of the ' *Statēr* ' (xvii. 22-27).

There is more frequent mention of money in this Gospel than in any of the others, and more and rarer coins are introduced. Mark refers to three coins only, and these the poorest, the ' mite,' the ' farthing,' and the ' penny.' Luke refers to the ' mite,' and the ' farthing,' and also to ' pounds '; but Matthew, who was in the habit of handling money, refers to coins of the highest value at the time; to the ' talent,' for example, which was worth about sixty times as much as the 'pound.' (See p. 275).

Again, whereas, in the instructions given to the Apostles, Mark speaks of ' brass ' (vi. 8), and Luke, of ' silver ' (ix. 3), Matthew speaks of 'gold,' 'silver,' and 'brass' (x. 9). (See under 'Style and Diction' (*a*), pp. 274, 275).

Perhaps, also, we may see in the methodical arrangement of this Gospel, and in the Evangelist's use of numerals, evidences of clerical precision, and of his office methods. (See under ' Features,' p. 311).

These undersigned coincidences strongly associate with the writing of this Gospel one who had sat at the ' receipt of custom.'

3

FOR WHOM WRITTEN

Tradition is unanimous that Matthew wrote his Gospel for Jews. Irenæus says: ' Matthew issued a written Gospel among the Hebrews,' and ' The Gospel of St. Matthew was written for the Jews.' Origen says: ' St. Matthew wrote for the Hebrew.' Eusebius says: ' Matthew . . . delivered his Gospel to his countrymen.' The complexion and content of the Gospel abundantly confirm this view.

Though Matthew was not the first to be written of the canonical Gospels, it is placed first because of its relation to the Old Testament. More than any other of the Gospels, Matthew's is allied with the Hebrew Scriptures in theme and tone; their subjects are its subjects, the Messiah, Israel, the Law, the Kingdom, and Prophecy. Jewish ideas and terms characterize the whole record. Its witness would not have impressed either the Roman, for whom Mark wrote, or the Greek, for whom Luke wrote, but to Jews its significance would be inescapable.

4

DATE OF WRITING

It is agreed that this Gospel was written either shortly before, or soon after, the destruction of Jerusalem, in A.D. 70, and the evidence seems to favour the earlier date. Prof. T. W. Manson argues for 'a date round about A.D. 70.'

References to 'the City of the great King' (v. 35), 'the Temple' (xxiv. 1, 2), 'the Holy Place' (xxiv. 15), impending trouble (xxiv. 16, 20), and to 'the Holy City' (xxvii. 53), do not favour a date after Jerusalem had fallen.

The expression ' until this day ' (xxvii. 8; xxviii. 15) indicates a period of years from the time of the events referred to, but a term of some twenty years would satisfy these passages.

We may assume that the chronological order of the Synoptic Gospels is Mark, Matthew, and Luke. Mark may well have been written as early as A.D. 50-55; in spite of Dr. C. J. Cadoux's statement that 'nearly all scholars agree that the earliest of our extant Gospels, that of Mark, was written a few years before or after A.D. 70.' Matthew's Record was written probably about A.D. 58, shortly before Luke's; and almost certainly Luke wrote his Gospel at Cæsarea, in A.D. 58-60. (p. 170).

Dr. C. C. Torrey has said that there is not a word in the Synoptic Gospels which might not have been written within twenty years after the death of Jesus; that is, between A.D. 30 and A.D. 50, and although A.D. 50 is too early for Luke and Matthew, the admission indicates that the trend of scholarship has been from late to early dates for the Gospels.

5

PLACE OF WRITING

Those who believe that Matthew was written after the destruction of Jerusalem in A.D. 70, think that Antioch in Syria was the place of its composition, and those who date the Gospel before A.D. 70 regard it as having been written in Palestine, in some part of Judæa, and most likely in Jerusalem. The balance of evidence is in favour of the latter view.

6

CANONICITY

The word ' canon ' means a straight rod, a rule, or measure, and long ago the term came to be applied, not only to that which measures, but also to that which is measured, and so we speak of the canons of art, of taste, and so forth.

Applied to any Biblical writing it means that that writing is of Divine authority, and is not apocryphal, or unauthentic, that it is part of Holy Scripture, and not of doubtful inspiration.

By the canonicity of Matthew's Gospel is meant that it is of apostolic origin, and has canonical rank. This value was put upon it without question by the early Church.

At the beginning of the third century, Origen spoke of ' the Four Gospels, which alone are received without dispute by the Church of God under heaven.' The unhesitating acceptance of Matthew is decisively shown by the testimonies to it, and the use made of it in the works of Clement of Rome (A.D. 96),

Barnabas (A.D. 106), Ignatius (A.D. 115), Polycarp (A.D. 116), Papias (A.D. 120-130), Justin Martyr (A.D. 145), Irenæus (A.D. 175), Tertullian (A.D. 190), and Clement of Alexandria (A.D. 195), and by its inclusion in the Diatessaron of Tatian (A.D. 150). (For these names, see Div. A, Part I, ' Church Fathers,' p. 38).

There are over twenty witnesses before the end of the second century, to the existence and use of Matthew, and these come from all parts of the Church, so that, beyond all question, this Gospel is of canonical authority.

The canonicity of the Gospel implies its *authenticity*, that is, that it is the work of the author whose name it bears; its *genuineness*, that is, that what it says is true, and not false or fictitious; and its *integrity*, that is, that its genuineness is complete and not partial (see pp. 171, 172).

Between the years A.D. 200 and A.D. 400, sixteen catalogues of the New Testament books were published, and the Four Gospels were in them all.

7

LANGUAGE IN WHICH WRITTEN

A library has grown up on this subject, and various views have been influentially contended for.

The matter is part of the Synoptic Problem, and the section on this should be consulted. (See Div. A, Part I, Section 8, p. 83).

What is relevant at this point are the following facts:

(a) There is no evidence that our canonical Gospel was ever seen in the Hebrew (Aramaic) tongue. The Gospel which Jerome said he had seen and translated into Greek and Latin, was not Matthew's, but an apocryphal Nazarene Gospel.

(b) Matthew's Gospel was known to the early Church only in Greek.

(c) It is certain that the Greek Gospel was an original, and not a translation from a Hebrew text.

(d) All the early writers who quote this Gospel, refer only to Matthew in Greek.

This subject is of more than merely academic interest, for it helps us to understand certain references in the record, such as the translation of Hebrew words (i. 23; xxvii. 33, 46), which would have been unnecessary in a Gospel written in Hebrew; and also the explanation of customs (xxii. 23; xxvii. 8, 15), which Palestinian Jews would not need.

A Hebrew collection of *Logia*, and our Greek Gospel, serve to show that at the time of Christ two languages were spoken by Jews. Aramaic was the language of the common people, and Greek was the literary language, so that those who spoke Aramaic could read Greek.

Both Christ and Paul spoke these languages. In converse with Pilate our Lord would speak Greek, but on the Cross He spoke Aramaic. Paul, addressing Romans, spoke in Greek, but on receiving permission to address the Jews, he spoke in Hebrew (Acts xxi. 37; xxii. 2). It was quite natural, therefore, for Matthew to write in a tongue which would best be understood by Jews everywhere.

When Papias says that Matthew wrote the Divine Oracles in the Hebrew dialect, and when Irenæus says that he put forth his written Gospel amongst the Hebrews in their own dialect, they are either referring to an earlier work written in Aramaic by Matthew, and known as the *Logia* or Sayings of Jesus, or they are confusing our Gospel with some such work as the apocryphal ' Gospel according to the Hebrews.'

> NOTE.—*The Gospel according to the Hebrews* is a somewhat shadowy document. It seems to have been well known in the second century, and references are made to it by Clement, Origen, Irenæus, Eusebius, and Jerome (see p. 38). It appears to have been of early origin, probably towards the end of the first century, by an unknown author. It has been identified with the *Logia* of which Papias speaks (see p. 91, *et al*), and so attributed to Matthew; but it can be assumed that this is a mistake. On this subject consult *Hastings' Dictionary of the Bible* (Vol. 5, pp. 338-343; and *Hastings' Dictionary of Christ and the Gospels* Vol. 1, pp. 675-6).

8

MATTHEW'S SOURCES

Every student of Matthew's Gospel must admit that it is a compilation, and it is a matter of interest and importance to discover, if possible, the sources which have been drawn upon.

Assuming that Matthew's Record has a background, we should endeavour to know what it is, and we shall find the effort rewarding. Our search may proceed by way of certain statements which can be regarded as certain, or, at any rate, which may fairly be assumed.

(i) Shorthand is an ancient art, and almost certainly it was used in some form or another by the Apostles and Evangelists.

The papyri reveal that the ancients of the first century were great letter-writers, that they made notes of all sorts, and that they used shorthand. It is known that Cicero employed shorthand in the trial of Catiline.

It is likely enough that Matthew the tax-gatherer would use an abbreviated script in the customs booth at Capernaum.

It is natural and necessary, then, to suppose that the Apostles and Evangelists would make notes of the tremendous things they were hearing from day to day.

(ii) There is good reason for believing that Matthew made a collection of the Sayings of Jesus, and that these circulated in the Church from very early days.

We may assume that this collection is what Papias refers to when he says that ' Matthew compiled the *Logia* in Hebrew.'

If by *Logia* is meant the *teaching* of Jesus, rather than *narrative* material, it is easy to see that Matthew had a special interest in this, that he would make notes of Jesus' discourses, and that he would use these notes when he came to write his Gospel.

This, at any rate, is what we find, for of the Synoptics Matthew's is the Gospel of the Discourses, of which six are of considerable length, and constitute about three-fifths of the entire Record (Chaps. v-vii; x; xiii; xviii; xxiii; xxiv-xxv). (See under ' Discourses,' p. 291).

Five of these six discourses end with the formula, ' When Jesus had finished ' (vii. 28; xi. 1; xiii. 53; xix. 1; xxvi. 1), and the remaining one has a conclusion which is the equivalent of this formula (xxiii. 39).

This teaching of Christ would seem to have been the substance of Matthew's *Logia*, and so one of the sources of his Gospel.

This *Logia* document is commonly called Q, from the German *Quelle*, which means 'source.'

(iii) It is also more than likely that at an early date after the Ascension, a collection of passages from the Old Testament was made, which was designed to show that Jesus was the fulfilment of Messianic prophecy. This Manual was known as the *Testimonies*, and was widely used by Christian teachers in the second and third centuries (pp. 89, 426).

It would seem that Matthew used such a Manual, and that this accounts for at least ten or twelve passages in his Gospel which begin with the formula, 'that it might be fulfilled,' or 'then was fulfilled that which was spoken by the prophet' (i. 22; ii. 5, 15, 17, 23; iv. 14-16; viii. 17; xii. 17-21; xiii. 35; xxi. 4; xxvi. 56; xxvii. 9, 10, 35). These proof-texts in Manual form would be of great apologetic value to converts. (See 'Style and Diction' (*b*), p. 275).

This, then, may be regarded as a second source which Matthew used.

(iv) It is now beyond dispute that Mark's Gospel was the first of the Four to be written, and that Matthew and Luke made large use of it.

We have already said that of the 1068 (R.V.) verses in Matthew about 500 contain material which is found in Mark. The only passages in Mark of any length which are omitted by Matthew are: i. 23-28; i. 35-38; iv. 21-25; iv. 26-29; v. 18-20; vii. 31-37; viii. 22-26; ix. 38-41; xii. 41-44; 43 verses which, with some single verses, amount to 55 in all (pp. 186, 259).

Matthew does not take over the Mark material verbally, or completely, but he does use it as the basis of his own record. This, then, is his main source.

It is estimated that 96% of the substance of Mark, and five-sixths of its actual language are to be found in Matthew.

(v) In addition to the foregoing, there is important material which is peculiar to this Gospel as, for example, the Infancy passages at the beginning (chap. i-ii), and the Resurrection references at the end (xxvii. 51-66; xxviii. 11-15), and these, in all likelihood, Matthew derived from oral tradition, or from other written sources.

Luke speaks of records which have been lost (i. 1), and it is quite possible that Matthew saw, and, perhaps, made use of some of these.

(vi) Then, we must remember that Matthew was with Christ for about two years, and would have a lively recollection of His sayings and doings, and so would add to what he used of Peter's Memoirs recorded by Mark.

To sum up: We may safely say that in our canonical Matthew, five or six sources have been drawn upon, viz.:

> A collection of the Sayings of Jesus. commonly known as the *Logia*, or Q.
> A Manual of Messianic Prophecy.
> Mark's Gospel.
> Oral tradition.
> Sundry records which are lost (Luke i. 1).
> The Evangelist's own recollections.

His use of these sources has resulted in a Gospel which from the beginning was cherished by the Christian Church.

As Mark was Matthew's chief source it is important to know just to what extent he was indebted to him. (For this, see under ' Mark in Matthew,' p. 261).

9

MATTHEW'S DESIGN

Each of the Evangelists, under the guidance of the Holy Spirit, had an object in writing his Gospel, and plainly Matthew's object was to convince Jews everywhere that Jesus of Nazareth was the promised Messiah.

This design accounts for the Jewish complexion of the whole Record.

Make a note of the references to ' the Holy City,' and ' the Holy Place ' (iv. 5; xxiv. 15; xxvii. 53); to the ' Son of David ' (i. 1, 20; ix. 27; xii. 23; xv. 22; xx. 30, 31; xxi. 9, 15; xxii. 42, 45); to the fulfilment of prophecy (i. 22; ii. 5, 15, 17, 23; iv. 14; viii. 17; xii. 17; xiii. 35; xxi. 4, 42; xxvi. 31, 54, 56; xxvii. 9, 10); to the ' Kingdom of Heaven ' (32 times R.V.; 33 A.V.); to Jewish customs (xv. 1, 2; xxvii. 62); to the Mosaic Law (v. 17-19, 21, 27, 31, 33, 38, 43; vii. 12; xi. 13; xii. 5; xv. 6; xxii. 36, 40; xxiii. 23); to the prophets (39 references). Unless you look up all these references you are learning nothing. Read them carefully, and mark them in your Bible.

Questions which Jews would ask are answered in this Gospel, such as: Was Jesus of the lineage of David? Did He uphold the Law? Had He come to establish the Kingdom?

Messiah (Hebrew), and Christ (Greek), mean Anointed, and it was expected that the Messiah would unite in Himself the three important offices into which men were inducted by the ceremony of unction, or pouring of oil, namely, the regal, the sacerdotal, and the prophetic (1 Sam. x. 1; Exod. xl. 15; 1 Kings xix. 16).

Matthew's Gospel shows that these hopes were fulfilled in Jesus. The genealogy (chap. i) shows His royal descent; the Magi were looking for a King (ii. 1, 2). The discourses, so prominent in this Gospel, embody His prophetic ministry; and His atoning death reveals Him to be both the Priest and the Sacrifice.

Many of these references would have been pointless in a Gospel written for Romans (Mark's), or for Greeks (Luke's); and they were unnecessary by the time that John wrote, the Church having then been established.

10

MATTHEW'S PLAN

That this Gospel conforms to a certain plan which distinguishes it from the others is obvious, and the reason for such a plan should be understood.

Generally speaking, Mark's record of Christ's ministry is chronological, but although Matthew uses so much of Mark, he does not follow the chronological order of events, but assembles these in a series of groupings.

Between the Infancy narratives at the beginning (chaps. i-ii), and the Passion narratives at the end (chaps. xxvi-xxviii), there are six parts, each consisting of narrative followed by discourse, and each ending with the same formula. These parts are:

1 Chs. iii-vii -	(see vii. 28)	4 Chs. xiv-xviii	(see xix. 1)
2 Chs. viii-x -	(see xi. 1)	5 Chs. xix-xxiii	(see xxiii. 39)
3 Chs. xi-xiii -	(see xiii. 53)	6 Chs. xxiv-xxv	(see xxvi. 1)

The narrative part in each of these leads up to the discourse. (See under 'Discourses,' p. 291). The Discourses are:

1 The Sermon on the Mount - - - -	v-vii
2 The Charge to the Twelve - - - -	x. 5-42
3 The Parables of the Kingdom - - - -	xiii
4 Teaching on Greatness, and Forgiveness - -	xviii
5 Denunciation of the Pharisees - - - -	xxiii
6 The Great Apocalypse - - - - -	xxiv-xxv

An examination of some of these discourses will lead to the conclusion that they are a mosaic of teaching which Jesus gave at different times, and in different places, and are arranged in this way to produce a cumulative impression.

For example, the substance of the Sermon on the Mount is scattered throughout the whole of Luke's Gospel. (For details, see under 'Discourses,' pp. 293, 294).

MATTHEW	LUKE	MATTHEW	LUKE
v. 3-12	vi. 20-23	vi. 24	xvi. 13
v. 13	xiv. 34, 35	vi. 25-34	xii. 22-31
v. 15	xi. 33	vii. 1-5	vi. 37-42
v. 18	xvi. 17	vii. 7-11	xi. 9-13
v. 25, 26	xii. 57-59	vii. 12	vi. 31
v. 31, 32	xvi. 18	vii. 13, 14	xiii. 23, 24
v. 38-48	vi. 27-30, 32-36	vii. 15-20	vi. 43-45
vi. 9-15	xi. 1-4	vii. 23	xiii. 27
vi. 19-21	xii. 33, 34	vii. 24-27	vi. 47-49
vi. 22, 23	xi. 34-36		

Methods of instruction in Jesus' time were unlike our modern sermonic forms, and must not be judged by the latter. The teacher spoke in an aphoristic way, in brief, striking utterances on many subjects, in figurative, symbolic, and parabolic language.

The Sermon on the Mount is a good illustration of this. Here is instruction on blessedness, law-keeping, anger, adultery, divorce, oaths, retaliation, love and hate, hypocrisy, alms-giving, prayer, forgiveness, fasting, treasure-gathering, light and darkness, serving a master, trusting God, judging people, choosing a road, bearing fruit, and building a character.

It cannot be affirmed that Jesus never said all these things on the occasion referred to, but it can be affirmed that He said many of them at different times, as the foregoing table shows. (For further reference to this, see under ' Discourses,' p. 291).

In keeping with this plan of grouping, nine miracles are assembled in chaps. viii-ix (pp. 288, 289, 312), and many are referred to which are not specified (ix. 35). Of course, these miracles were not performed one after the other, and in this order, but are grouped together here, regardless of chronological sequence, in order to demonstrate the power and authority of the Messiah. (See p. 289).

This grouping plan of Matthew is full of interest. His Gospel would be used for the instruction of Jewish converts who, no doubt, would gather in study-circles. It was eminently desirable, therefore, that the instruction should be so arranged as to be easily remembered, and this Evangelist's method was well adapted to that end.

' The training and development of the memory formed an essential part of Jewish education, and in early ages, before the invention of printing made reliance on it needless, verbal memory was much stronger than it is among civilized nations to-day.' It is easy to see how useful was Matthew's mnemonic method for the end in view, and any of us now will find it easier to remember the contents of this Gospel than that of the others, a fact which is due to method.

Moving about as Christ did, from place to place, and having a constantly changing audience, He would not deliver long discourses, but would teach, as we have said, by brief, pithy utterances on many subjects, and would frequently repeat such instruction.

What He did and taught would rapidly produce a standardized form of tradition, which would be used orally by catechists, first in Palestine, and then in the great world-centres—Antioch,

17

Ephesus, Rome—and finally in every province of the Empire.

Classes for catechumens would naturally be formed, where the fullest instruction would be given orally in the most impressive manner, and in the briefest possible time.

Later on, this instruction would be committed to writing, and thus the evangelical tradition was preserved and disseminated.

It would appear that Theophilus had undergone such instruction, for Luke says: ' That thou mightest know the certainty concerning the things which thou wast taught by word of mouth ' (i. 3, 4), and ' taught,' here, is our word ' catechize,' to instruct by question and answer (*katēcheō*). For such instruction Matthew's Gospel was and is eminently adapted.

II

OMISSIONS IN MATTHEW'S GOSPEL

It is well that we should see at a glance what each of the Evangelists, respectively, omits of what the others have, so that we may realize how great would have been our loss had we but one of the Four Gospels, and also that we may see how the omissions, as well as the inclusions, contribute to the end which each Evangelist has in view. A conspectus of the whole field will be found in the Harmonistic Reading Syllabus (pp. 68-81), but it is useful to see the facts in each separate Gospel.

If, of the Four Gospels, we had had Matthew's only, we would have lost the following:

John's incomparable Prologue, Luke's Preface, and the second genealogy. The annunciation to Zacharias, and to Mary, and Mary's visit to Elisabeth. The details of the birth of John the Baptist. The coming of the angels and the shepherds at the time of Jesus' birth. The circumcision of Jesus, and His presentation in the Temple. Jesus' first Passover. John's testimony before the priests and Levites, and his recognition and acknowledgment of Jesus as the Messiah. The coming of the first five disciples. The first miracle, turning water into wine. The first cleansing of the Temple. The discourse with Nicodemus. John's testimony to Christ at Aenon. The interview of Jesus with the woman of Samaria. The Gospel in Sychar. The healing of the nobleman's son. The first rejection at Nazareth. The healing of a man at the pool of Bethesda. The raising of a widow's son at Nain. The anointing of Jesus in the house of Simon the Pharisee. The discourse on the Bread of Life. The healing of a blind man near Bethsaida. Jesus at the Feast of Tabernacles. The woman taken in adultery. Discourse on the Light of the World, and on Spiritual Freedom. The mission of the Seventy. Parable of the Good Samaritan. Jesus' visit to Martha and Mary. The healing of a man born blind. Discourse on the Good Shepherd. Jesus at the Feast of Dedication. Discourse on prayer, and the parable of the Three Friends. Teaching concerning trust in God, and coming judgment (Luke xii). The Galileans slain by Pilate. The healing of a woman with a spirit of infirmity. The word on whether few or many are saved. Jesus' message to Herod. The meal in a chief Pharisee's house, and the parables of the Chief Seats, and the Great Supper. Discourse on Counting the Cost of Discipleship, with the parables of the Unfinished Tower, and the Unwaged War. The parables of (the Lost Sheep), the Lost Piece of Silver, the Prodigal and Elder Brother, the Unfaithful Steward, and the Rich Man and Lazarus. Discourse concerning forgiveness and faith. The raising of Lazarus, and the withdrawal of Jesus to Ephraim. The healing of ten lepers. Discourse on the Coming of the Kingdom (Luke xvii. 50-xviii. 8). Parable of the Pharisee and the Publican. The conversion of Zacchæus. Parable of the Pounds. The widow's two mites. The coming of Greeks to Jesus, and what He said. The Jews' rejection of Jesus (John xii. 37-50). Most of what was done and said in the upper room at the time of the Last Supper (John xiii-xvi), and Christ's intercessory prayer (John xvii). The incomparable story of Jesus' walk and talk with two disciples on the way to Emmaus. The appearance of the risen Lord to His apostles in Jerusalem, Thomas being absent; and the appearance later, when Thomas was present. The appearance to seven apostles by the Sea of Galilee, Christ's final appearance, and His ascension.

Almost the entire substance of Mark's Gospel is to be found in Matthew's, the only omissions of any length being Mark i. 23-28, 35-39; iv. 21-29; v. 18-20; vii. 31-37; viii. 22-26; ix. 38-41; xii. 41-44; that is, 43 verses; but a good deal which Matthew takes over from Mark he abbreviates, as Sir John Hawkins and others have shown; and this is true also of passages which he has in common with Luke. For instance, in Matthew's record of the leper healed (viii. 1-4), there are 61 words, whereas there are 97 in Mark, and 98 in Luke. In the paralytic healed (ix. 1-9) there are 126 words; but 196 in Mark, and 212 in Luke. In the healing of the Gadarene demoniac (viii. 28-34), there are 136 words; but 325 in Mark, and 293 in Luke. In the healing of the issue of blood, and the raising of Jairus' daughter (ix. 18-26), there are 135 words; but 374 in Mark, and 289 in Luke. (See Matthew's Use of Mark, p. 263).

All this shows how much we owe to the other three Gospels for what each supplies of what Matthew omits; and, of course, we should recognize how much we owe to Matthew for what he records which the other Evangelists omit.

12

MATERIAL PECULIAR TO MATTHEW'S GOSPEL

The main passages at least, which are peculiar to this Gospel, should be marked in some way in your Bible, so that at a glance, when turning over the pages, you can see where and what these are.

A coloured line down the margin of your Bible by these passages may be the simplest device.

The following references are substantially correct.

Chaps. i-ii; iii. 14, 15; iv. 13-16, 23-25; v. 1, 2, 4, 5, 7-10, 13a, 14, 16, 17, 19-24, 27, 28, 31-39a, 41, 43; vi. 1-8, 10b, 13b, 16-18, 34; vii. 6, 12b, 15, 19, 28a; viii. 1, 5a, 17; ix. 13a, 26-36; x. 2a, 5b-8, 16b, 23, 25b, 36, 41; xi. 1, 14, 20, 28-30; xii. 5-7, 11, 12a (cf. Luke xiv. 5), 17-23, 36, 37, 45c; xiii. 14, 15, 18, 24-30, 35-53; xiv. 28-31; xv. 12, 13, 23-25, 30, 31; xvi. 2b, 3, 11b, 12, 17-19, 22b; xvii. 6, 7, 13, 24-27; xviii. 3, 4, 10, 14, 16-20, 23-35; xix. 1a. 9-12, 28a; xx. 1-16; xxi. 4, 5, 10, 11, 14, 15b, 16, 28-32 (cf. Luke vii. 29, 30), 43; xxii. 1-14, 33, 34, 40; xxiii. 1-3, 5, 7b-10, 15-22, 24, 28, 32, 33; xxiv. 11, 12, 14, 20, 26-28, 30a, 37-41, 43, 44; xxv. 1-46; xxvi. 1, 25, 44, 50, 52-54; xxvii. 3-10, 19, 24, 25, 36, 43, 51b-53, 62-66; xxviii. 2-4, 9-20.

This shows that of the 1068 verses in this Gospel, 387 whole verses are peculiar to it, and parts of 23 other verses, 410 in all, or more than a third of the whole Gospel.

For absolute accuracy students of the Greek should consult Rushbrooke's *Synopticon*.

The Sermon on the Mount material should be considered in the light of Luke's references. (See under ' Discourses,' Chart, p. 293).

A note should be made of the fact that of these 1068 verses, 599, and parts of 45 other verses, record our Lord's words, that is, about three-fifths of the whole Gospel. (See pp. 193, 272, 291).

If what is peculiar to Matthew had never been written, or had been lost, how greatly impoverished we would have been.

Matthew alone traces Christ's genealogy through David to Abraham; he alone tells us of the coming of the Magi; of the slaughter of the innocents; of the flight into, and return from Egypt; he alone gives us an extended report of the Sermon on the Mount; he alone tells of Peter's walking on the sea; he alone reports Christ's reply to Peter's confession; he alone records Christ's 'Woes' against the Pharisees; he alone records the Judgment of the Nations; he alone tells of Christ's betrayal by Judas for thirty pieces of silver, and of the betrayer's remorse and suicide; he alone tells of the watch at the sepulchre, of the bribing of the soldiers, and of the opening of the graves; he alone records the parables of the Tares, the Hid Treasure, the Goodly Pearl, the Fish Net, the Unmerciful Servant, the Labourers in the Vineyard, the Two Sons, the Marriage of the King's Son, the Ten Virgins, and the Talents; he alone tells of the coin in the fish's mouth; he alone preserves for us these incomparable words: 'Come unto Me, all ye that labour, and are heavy laden, and I will give you rest. Take My yoke upon you, and learn of Me; for I am meek and lowly in heart: and ye shall find rest unto your souls. For My yoke is easy, and My burden is light.'

13
MARK IN MATTHEW

That, of the Four Gospels, Mark was written first, must be regarded as a settled fact.

In the Authorized Version, Mark has 678 verses, but the last twelve verses of chap. xvi are disputed, and vii. 16; ix. 44, 46; xi. 26; xv. 28, are omitted in the Revised Version, so that in Mark there are 661 undisputed verses.

In Matthew's Gospel the substance of 606 of Mark's 661 verses is found, and as there are 1068 verses in Matthew (R.V.) we see that more than half of his Gospel is derived from Mark. As, however, not all the 606 verses are included in their entirety, it may be said with confidence that in Matthew there are about 500 verses from Mark, nearly half of Matthew's Gospel (see pp. 86, 132, 140, 186, 253).

Mark's Gospel is, therefore, Matthew's chief source, and supplies him with the narrative part of his record. Examination of this material will show that Matthew does not follow Mark's order, but uses his material in what we have seen is a grouping plan. (See under 'Sources,' and 'Plan,' pp. 253, 257).

The following table shows to what extent Mark is found in Matthew:

No.	MARK	MATTHEW	No.	MARK	MATTHEW
1	i. 1	—	57	38-41	—
2	2-8	iii. 1-12	58	41-50	xviii. 6-9
3	9-11	13-17	59	x. 1	xix. 1, 2
4	12, 13	iv. 1-11	60	2-12	3-12
5	14, 15	12-17	61	13-16	13-15
6	16-22	18-22	62	17-22	16-22
7	23-28	—	63	23-27	23-26
8	29-31	viii. 14, 15	64	28-31	27-30
9	32-34	16, 17	65	32-34	xx. 17-19
10	35-38	—	66	35-45	20-28
11	39-45	viii. 2-4	67	46-52	29-34
12	ii. 1-12	ix. 1-8	68	xi. 1-11	xxi. 1-9, 17
13	13, 14	9	69	12-14	18, 19
14	15-17	10-13	70	15-19	12-17
15	18-22	14-17	71	20-25	20-22
16	23-28	xii. 1-8	72	27-33	23-27
17	iii. 1-6	9-14	73	xii. 1-12	33-46
18	7-12	15, 16 ?	74	13-17	xxii. 15-22
19	13-19a	x. 2-4	75	18-27	23-33
20	19b-30	xii. 22-32	76	28-34	34-40
21	31-35	46-50	77	xii. 35-37	xxii. 41-46
22	iv. 1-9	xiii. 1-9	78	38-40	xxiii. 1-7
23	10-12	10-13	79	41-44	—
24	13-20	18-23	80	xiii. 1, 2	xxiv. 1, 2
25	21-25	—	81	3-13	3-14
26	26-29	—	82	14-23	15-25
27	30-32	xiii. 31, 32	83	24-27	29-31
28	33, 34	34	84	28, 29	32, 33
29	35-41	viii. 23-27	85	30-32	34-36
30	v. 1-13	28-32	86	33-37	42
31	14-17	33, 34	87	xiv. 1, 2,	xxvi. 1-5
32	18-20	—	88	3-9	6-13
33	21-34	ix. 18-22	89	10, 11	14-16
34	35-43	23-26	90	12-16	17-19
35	vi. 1-6a	xiii. 52-58	91	17-21	20-25
36	6b-13	ix. 35-x. 1	92	22-25	26-29
	—	x. 5-xi. 1	93	27-31	31-35
37	14-16	xiv. 1, 2	94	26, 32-	30, 36-
38	17-29	3-12		42	46
39	vi. 30-44	xiv. 13-21	95	xiv. 43-50	xxvi. 47-56
40	45-52	22-33	96	51, 52	—
41	53-56	34-36	97	53, 55-	xxvi. 57, 59-
42	vii. 1-23	xv. 1-20		65	68
43	24-30	21-28	98	54, 66-72	58, 69-75
44	31-37	—	99	xv. 1-5	xxvii. 2, 11-
45	viii. 1-10	29-39			14
46	11-13	xvi. 1-4		6-15	15-18,
47	14-21	5-12			20-23,
48	22-26	—	100		26
49	27-30	xvi. 13-20	101	16-19	27-30
50	31-33	21-23	102	20-23	31-34
51	34-ix. 1	24-28	103	24-32	35-44
52	ix. 2-8	xvii. 1-8	104	33-37	45-50
53	9-13	9-13	105	38-41	51-56
54	14-29	14-20	106	42-47	57-61
55	30-32	22, 23	107	xvi. 1-8	xxviii. 1, 5-8
56	33-37	xviii. 1-5			

Of the 107 Sections into which Mark is here divided, eleven are not in Matthew (1, 7, 10, 25, 26, 32, 44, 48, 57, 79, 96); some of them are abbreviated in Matthew (e.g. 30, 33, 34, 38, 54, 58, 76, 86), and some of them are extended (e.g. 4, 36, 40, 46, 49, 60, 73, 87, 95, 106).

Observe, also, that Mark's order, which is broadly chronological, is not followed by Matthew. Run your eye down the Matthew columns (p. 262) and see how irregular the chapters are (xii; x; xii; xiii; viii; ix; xiii; ix: see 'Matthew's Plan,' p. 255).

Observe, also, that large parts of Matthew are entirely wanting in Mark (e.g. chaps. i-ii; v-vii; x; xi; xxv). This means that Mark was not Matthew's only source. (See under ' Sources,' pp. 253, 254).

Except chaps. i-ii, the passages omitted by Mark are discourses, and these, in all likelihood, are derived from the *Logia* of Matthew of which Papias speaks. (See under ' Authorship,' and ' Sources,' pp. 131, 252).

14

MATTHEW'S USE OF MARK

It is profoundly interesting to observe how Matthew uses Mark's Gospel. The following is a summary of the main facts.

(i) Mark's Gospel is the basis of Matthew's, and he absorbs almost the whole of it (see pp. 140, 261).

The chief omissions are:

Healing of a Demoniac	Mark i. 23-28
Prayer before Preaching in Galilee	Mark i. 35-38
On Witnessing and Hearing	Mark iv. 21-25
Seed Growing Secretly	Mark iv. 26-29
The Request of a Healed Demoniac	Mark v. 18-20
Healing of a Deaf Stammerer	Mark vii. 31-37
Healing of a Blind Man	Mark viii. 22-26
The Uncommissioned Exorcist	Mark ix. 38-41
The Widow's Mites	Mark xii. 41-44

(See under ' Sources,' and ' Mark in Matthew,' pp. 253, 262).

(ii) Matthew does not follow the order of Mark's narrative, because, as we have seen, he employs the method of grouping his material, for example, the nine miracles of chaps. viii-ix (pp. 288, 289). Unlike Luke, he does not concern himself with chronological sequence, but aims at making an intensive impression. (See under 'Plan,' p. 255).

(iii) Matthew frequently abbreviates Mark's record. In the following illustrations the words in brackets are those of Mark which Matthew omits.

Mark i. 15; - Matt. iv. 17 -	'(The time is fulfilled, and) the Kingdom (of God) of heaven is at hand; repent ye (and believe in the Gospel).'
Mark i. 32 -	'At even (when the sun did set).'
Matt. viii. 16 -	'When even was come.'
Mark i. 42 -	'And straightway the leprosy (departed from him, and he) was made clean.'
Matt. viii. 3 -	'And straightway his leprosy was cleansed.'
Mark iv. 39 -	'And He awoke, and rebuked the wind, and (said unto) the sea ("Peace, be still," and the wind ceased), and there was a great calm.'
Matt. viii. 26 -	'Then He arose, and rebuked the winds, and the sea, and there was a great calm.'
Mark vi. 4; - Matt. xiii. 57 -	'A prophet is not without honour, save in his own country (and among his own kin), and in his own house.'

Trace other examples of this.

Many details which give vividness to Mark's Gospel are omitted by Matthew (pp. 221, 222), as, for example:

'He was with the wild beasts '	Mk. i. 13.	Matt. iv. 2
'With the hired servants ' -	Mk. i. 20.	Matt. iv. 22
'With James and John ' -	Mk. i. 29	Matt. viii. 14
'In the days of Abiathar the high priest ' - -	Mk. ii. 26.	Matt. xii. 4
'Upon the cushion ' -	Mk. iv. 38	Matt. viii. 24, 25
'About two thousand ' -	Mk. v. 13.	Matt. viii. 32
'Two hundred pennyworth '	Mk. vi. 37.	Matt. xiv. 16
'By companies . . . green . . . in ranks, by hundreds, and by fifties ' - -	Mk. vi. 39, 40.	Matt. xiv. 19

' So as no fuller on earth can whiten them ' -	Mk. ix. 3.	Matt. xvii. 2
' Three hundred pence ' -	Mk. xiv. 5.	Matt. xxvi. 8, 9
' The young man who fled naked ' - - -	Mk. xiv. 50, 51.	Matt. xxvi. 56
' The father of Alexander and Rufus ' - -	Mk. xv. 21.	Matt. xxvii. 32

But abbreviation is seen on a bigger scale than this. For example:

Mk. iii. 7-12 is given in two verses in Matt. xii. 15, 16

Mk. v. 1-20 is given in seven verses in Matt. viii. 28-34

Mk. v. 21-43 is given in nine verses in Matt. ix. 18-26

Mk. vi. 14-29 is given in twelve verses in Matt. xiv. 1-12

Mk. ix. 14-29 is given in seven verses in Matt. xvii. 14-20

(iv) On the other hand, Matthew often amplifies Mark's report. For example:

The preaching of the Baptist, which is summed up in two verses in Mark (i. 7, 8), is given six verses in Matthew (iii. 7-12). The refutation of the charge of diabolical agency, which Mark gives in nine verses (iii. 22-30), has twenty-two verses in Matthew (xii. 24-45).

The Charge of the Twelve, which Mark compresses into five verses (vi. 7-11), Matthew takes forty-two verses to report (x. 1-42).

The denunciation of the Scribes and Pharisees, which has three verses in Mark (xii. 38-40), has thirty-nine verses in Matthew (xxiii).

Jesus' great prophetic discourse, which in Mark is given a chapter of thirty-seven verses (xiii), is extended in Matthew to ninety-seven verses (xxiv, xxv).

These contractions and expansions must find their explanation in the aim which each Evangelist has in view, and the readers for whom he writes. What is distinctively Jewish is given at length in Matthew, but Mark contracts or expands to impress Gentile readers.

(v) The way in which Matthew and Mark refer to the person and character of Christ should be carefully studied. Both present Him as truly human and truly Divine, but in Mark the human aspect is emphasized, and in Matthew, the Divine.

(*a*) Matthew omits many references in Mark to Christ's emotions.

'When He had looked round about on them with anger, being grieved at the hardening of their heart' (Mark iii. 5; cf. Matt. xii. 13). 'He sighed deeply in His spirit' (Mark viii. 12; cf. Matt. xvi. 4). 'He was moved with indignation' (Mark x. 14; cf. Matt. xix. 14). 'Looking upon him loved him' (Mark x. 21; cf. Matt. xix. 21). 'Began to be greatly amazed,' in Mark (xiv. 33), becomes 'began to be sorrowful,' in Matthew (xxvi. 37).

(*b*) Matthew omits questions in Mark which might seem to imply ignorance on the part of Christ.

'What is thy name?' (Mark v. 9; cf. Matt. viii. 29, 30). 'Who touched My garments?' (Mark v. 30; cf. Matt. ix. 21). 'How many loaves have ye?' (Mark vi. 38; cf. Matt. xiv. 17). 'Why doth this generation seek a sign?' (Mark viii. 12; cf. Matt. xv. 4). 'Seest thou aught?' (Mark viii. 23; Matt. no record). 'What question ye with them?' (Mark ix. 16; cf. Matt. xvii. 14). 'What were ye reasoning in the way?' (Mark ix. 33; cf. Matt. xviii. 1, 2). 'Where is my guest-chamber?' (Mark xiv. 14; cf. Matt. xxvi. 18).

(*c*) Matthew's record in places, compared with Mark's, emphasizes the greatness of Christ's work.

Where Mark says, 'They brought to Him *all*, and He healed *many*,' Matthew says, 'They brought to Him *many*, and He healed *all*' (Mark i. 32, 33; Matt. viii. 16, 17).

On three occasions, by adding 'from that hour,' Matthew calls attention to the immediacy of the effect of the miracle, a detail which Mark omits (Matt. ix. 22; cf. Mark v. 34; Matt. xv. 28; cf. Mark vii. 30; Matt. xvii. 18; cf. Mark ix. 25).

Matthew omits the two miracles in which Christ used spittle as a means of healing (Mark vii. 31; viii. 22).

Matthew shows that Christ fed more people than Mark's record would lead us to think, by adding, 'besides women and children' (Matt. xiv. 21; cf. Mark vi. 44).

(vi) It is noticeable that Matthew omits much of what seems to be unfavourable to the Apostles in Mark's record.

In the place of a rebuke in Mark iv. 13, is a blessing in Matt. xiii. 16, 17. Mark's 'For they understood not concerning the loaves, but their heart was hardened' (vi. 51, 52), is omitted by Matthew (xiv. 32, 33).

Of Peter, on the Mount of Transfiguration, Mark says, ' he wist not what to answer, for they became sore afraid ' (ix. 6), but Matthew omits that (xvii. 4, 5).

Matthew also omits the remark, ' questioning among themselves what the rising again from the dead should mean ' (Mark ix. 9, 10; Matt. xvii. 9, 10).

For Mark's, ' they understood not the saying, and were afraid to ask Him ' (ix. 32), Matthew has, ' they were exceeding sorry ' (xvii. 23).

Matthew omits, ' they had disputed one with another in the way, who was the greatest' (Matt. xviii. 1; cf. Mark ix. 34). Of the scene in the garden, Matthew omits Mark's statement, ' they wist not what to answer Him ' (Matt. xxvi. 44; Mark xiv. 40).

Matthew omits, also, two references in Mark, to the disciples' amazement (Mark x. 24; Matt. xix. 23; Mark x. 32; Matt. xx. 17).

These illustrations show the fascination and importance of *comparative* study. The Gospel records are not contradictory, but complementary.

15

THE OLD TESTAMENT IN MATTHEW'S GOSPEL

MATTHEW'S Gospel is saturated with the Old Testament. The reason for this is that, as it was the writer's design to prove the Messiahship of Jesus, he had to draw his proofs from the Jews' Bible.

Absolute accuracy is not claimed for the following figures, because of the difficulty of tracing with precision all the references to the Old Testament, but these figures must be nearly inclusive.

References to the Old Testament may be divided into two classes, *citations* and *allusions*, citations being quotations, and allusions being more or less direct references. The total number of both classes is about one hundred and thirty. Those marked with an asterisk (*) are references made by our Lord; the remainder are in the Evangelist's narrative.

(a) CITATIONS

	MATTHEW	OLD TESTAMENT
1	i. 22, 23	Isa. vii. 14
2	ii. 5, 6	Micah v. 1, 2
3	ii. 15	Hos. xi. 1
4	ii. 17, 18	Jer. xxxi. 15
5	ii. 23	Isa. xi. 1; Jer. xxiii. 5; xxxiii. 15; Zech. iii. 8; vi. 12
6	iii. 3	Isa. xl. 3
7	*iv. 4	Deut. viii. 3
8	iv. 6	Psa. xci. 11, 12
9	*iv. 7	Deut. vi. 16
10	*iv. 10	Deut. vi. 13
11	iv. 14-16	Isa. ix. 1, 2
12	*v. 5	Psa. xxxvii. 11
13	*v. 21	Exod. xx. 13; Deut. v. 17
14	*v. 27	Exod. xx. 14; Deut. v. 18
15	*v. 31	Deut. xxiv. 1
16	*v. 33-37	Exod. xx. 7; Num. xxx. 2; Lev. xix. 12; Deut. v. 11; xxiii. 21; Isa. lxvi. 1; Psa. xlviii. 2
17	*v. 38	Exod. xxi. 24; Lev. xxiv. 20; Deut. xix. 21
18	*v. 43a	Lev. xix. 18; Deut. xxiii. 6; xxv. 19
19	*vii. 23	Psa. vi. 8
20	viii. 17	Isa. liii. 4
21	*ix. 13	Hos. vi. 6
22	*x. 35	Mic. vii. 6
23	*xi. 10	Mal. iii. 1
24	*xii. 7	Hos. vi. 6
25	xii. 18-21	Isa. xlii. 1-4
26	*xiii. 13-15	Isa. vi. 9, 10
27	xiii. 35	Psa. lxxviii. 2
28	*xv. 4-6	Exod. xx. 12; xxi. 17; Lev. xx. 9
29	*xv. 7-9	Isa. xxix. 13
30	*xviii. 16	Deut. xix. 15
31	*xix. 4	Gen. i. 27; v. 2
32	*xix. 5	Gen. ii. 24
33	*xix. 18	Exod. xx. 13-16; xxi. 17; Deut. v. 17-20
34	*xix. 19a	Deut. v. 16; Exod. xx. 12
35	*xix. 19b	Lev. xix. 18
36	xxi. 4, 5	Zech. ix. 9; Isa. lxii. 11
37	xxi. 9	Psa. cxviii. 26
38	*xxi. 13a	Isa. lvi. 7
39	*xxi. 13b	Jer. vii. 11
40	*xxi. 16	Psa. viii. 2
41	*xxi. 42	Psa. cxviii. 22, 23
42	*xxii. 31, 32	Exod. iii. 6, 15
43	*xxii. 37	Deut. vi. 5
44	*xxii. 39	Lev. xix. 18
45	*xxii. 44	Psa. xc. 1
46	*xxiii. 38, 39	Psa. cxviii. 26; Jer. xii. 7; xxii. 5
47	*xxvi. 31	Zech. xiii. 7
48	xxvii. 9, 10	Zech. xi. 13; Jer. xviii. 2; xix. 2; xxxii. 6
49	xxvii. 34, 48	Psa. lxix. 21
50	xxvii. 35	Psa. xxii. 18
51	xxvii. 39	Psa. xxii. 7; cix. 25
52	xxvii. 43	Psa. xxii. 8; lxxi. 11
53	*xxvii. 46	Psa. xxii. 1, 2

(b) ALLUSIONS

	MATTHEW	OLD TESTAMENT
1	i. 1-17	Many references
2	iii. 9	Gen. xii.
3	iii. 17	Psa. ii. 7
4	*v. 4	Isa. lxi. 2
5	*v. 7	Psa. xviii. 25
6	*v. 8	Psa. xxiv. 3-5
7	*v. 12	Various
8	*v. 34	Isa. lxvi. 1
9	*v. 35	Psa. xlviii. 2
10	*v. 43b	Deut. xxiii. 6; xxv. 19
11	*vii. 12	Old Testament
12	*viii. 4	Lev. xiv. 3
13	*viii. 11	Isa. xlix. 12
14	ix. 36	Num. xxvii. 17
15	*x. 15	Gen. xix.
16	*xi. 5	Isa. ii. 18, 19; xxxv. 5, 6; lxi. 1
17	*xi. 13	Old Testament
18	*xi. 14	Mal. iv. 5
19	*xi. 21, 22	Ezek. xxviii. 20-22; xxvi-xxvii
20	*xi. 23a	Isa. xiv. 13-15
21	*xi. 23b, 24	Gen. xix. 24
22	*xi. 29	Jer. vi. 16
23	xii. 2	Exod. xx. 10; Deut. v. 14; xxiii. 25
24	*xii. 3, 4	Lev. xxiv. 9; 1 Sam. xxi. 1-6
25	*xii. 5	Num. xxviii. 9, 10
26	*xii. 10-12	Deut. xxii. 4, et al.
27	xii. 23	Psa. cx.
28	*xii. 39-40	Jonah i. 17; ii. 1, 2; iii. 5; iv. 3
29	*xii. 41	Jonah i. 2
30	*xii. 42	1 Kings x. 1, f.; 2 Chron. ix. 1, f.
31	*xiii. 32	Dan. iv. 12, 21
32	*xiii. 43	Dan. xii. 3
33	*xiv. 4	Lev. xviii. 16; xx. 21
34	xv. 22	Psa. cx.
35	*xvi. 4	Jonah iii. 4
36	xvi. 14	Deut. xviii. 18
37	*xvi. 27	Psa. lxii. 12; Prov. xxiv. 12
38	xvii. 3, 4	Many references
39	xvii. 5	Deut. xviii. 5; Psa. ii. 7; Isa. xlii. 1
40	*xvii. 11, 12	1 Kings xix. 2, 10; Mal. iv. 5, 6
41	*xix. 7, 8	Deut. xxiv. 1
42	*xix. 26	Gen. xviii. 14; Job xlii. 2
43	xx. 30	Psa. cx.
44	xxi. 9a	Psa. cxviii. 26
45	xxi. 15	Psa. cxxxii. 11
46	*xxi. 33	Isa. v. 1, f.
47	*xxi. 44	Isa. viii. 14
48	xxii. 24	Deut. xxv. 5
49	*xxii. 29	Various
50	*xxiii. 2	Deut. xxxiii. 3; Ezra vii. 6; Neh. viii. 4
51	*xxiii. 23	Lev. xxvii. 30; Mic. vi. 8
52	*xxiii. 35	Gen. iv. 8; 2 Chron. xxiv. 20, 21
53	*xxiii. 38	Psa. cxviii. 26; Jer. xii. 7; xxii. 5
54	*xxiv. 7	Isa. xix. 2

	MATTHEW	OLD TESTAMENT
55	*xxiv. 15	Dan. ix. 27; xi. 31; xii. 11
56	*xxiv. 21	Dan. xii. 1
57	*xxiv. 23, 24	Deut. xiii. 1-3
58	*xxiv. 28	Job xxxix. 30
59	*xxiv. 29	Dan. viii. 10; Joel ii. 10, 31; iii. 15, 16
60	*xxiv. 30a	Zech. xii. 12
61	*xxiv. 30b	Dan. vii. 13; Isa. xiii. 9, 10; Ezek. xxxii. 7, 8; Amos viii. 9; Zeph. i. 14-16
62	*xxiv. 37-39	Gen. vi. 11-13; vii. 7, 21-23
63	*xxv. 31	Zech. xiv. 5
64	*xxv. 46	Dan. xii. 2
65	xxvi. 15	Zech. xi. 12, 13
66	*xxvi. 28	Exod. xxiv. 8; Lev. iv. 18-20; Jer. xxxi. 31; Zech. ix. 11
67	xxvi. 30	Psa. cxv.-cxviii.
68	*xxvi. 54	Various
69	*xxvi. 56	Various
70	*xxvi. 64	Psa. cx. 1; Dan. vii. 13
71	xxvi. 65, 66	Lev. xxiv. 16
72	xxvi. 67	Isa. l. 6
73	xxvii. 6	Deut. xxiii. 18
74	xxvii. 7	Zech. xi. 13
75	xxvii. 31	Isa. liii. 7
76	xxvii. 60	Isa. liii. 9

An examination of these tables will result in some interesting information.

(i) There are 129 Old Testament references: 53 of them are citations, and 76 are allusions.

(ii) These references are taken from 25 of the 39 books of the Old Testament, and represent every part of these Scriptures, ' the Law, the Prophets, and the Psalms ' (Luke xxiv. 44).

(iii) The books referred to are: the Pentateuch, 1 Samuel, 1 Kings, 2 Chronicles, Ezra, Nehemiah, Job, Psalms, Proverbs, Isaiah, Jeremiah, Ezekiel, Daniel, Hosea, Joel, Amos, Jonah, Micah, Zephaniah, Zechariah, and Malachi.

(iv) Make a note that there are more references to the Psalms 29, Deuteronomy, 27, and Isaiah, 26, than to any other of the books. Then come 13 to Jeremiah, 13 to Leviticus, 12 to Exodus, 10 each to Genesis and Zechariah, 9 to Daniel, and 3 each to Numbers, Ezekiel, Micah, and Malachi.

(v) The books not referred to are: Joshua, Judges, Ruth, 2 Samuel, 2 Kings, 1 Chronicles, Esther, Ecclesiastes, Song of Solomon, Lamentations, Obadiah, Nahum, Habakkuk, and Haggai; 14 in all, and 9 of these are of minor importance.

(vi) Of these 129 references (see pp. 268-270), 89 are made by our Lord, 35 citations, and 54 allusions, so that only 18 citations, and 22 allusions are in the narrative part of the Gospel. (See Sec. (i): 53 minus 35=18; and 76 minus 54=22).

Without going into matters which are of an academic character, the student of these quotations should know that some of them are taken from the Hebrew, but the majority of them are taken from the Septuagint.

> The Septuagint, or LXX (seventy), is the Greek Version of the Old Testament Hebrew Scriptures. It was made in Egypt by Alexandrian Jews. The translation began to be made in the time of Ptolemy Philadelphus, by whom it was originated about B.C. 285. The work was gradually accomplished, but the time of its completion is not known.
>
> In the time of our Lord, Hebrew was a dead language, and was not understood by ordinary Jews. Probably the Scriptures in Hebrew were used in the Synagogues, but for their private reading the Jews would use the Septuagint.

For the way in which these Old Testament references are introduced or spoken of, see under (*b*) 'Words and Phrases characteristic of Matthew's Gospel,' paragraphs (i) and (ii), (pp. 275, 276).

Four of the quotations in this Gospel are somewhat obscure in meaning, namely, ii. 15; ii. 17, 18; ii. 23; xxvii. 9, 10. The last of these was not spoken by Jeremiah, but by Zechariah (xi. 13). (For a discussion of these passages see Gloag's 'Introduction to the Synoptic Gospels,' James Morison's commentary on this Gospel, and references to these verses in any good Commentary).

The use which is made of the Old Testament in this Gospel (and elsewhere) shows that not a little of these Writings is predictive in character, and Messianic in substance. In Jewish history are to be found many types and foreshadowings of Him who was to come, the Son of God, and Son of Man, the Redeemer of the world.

Prophecy often has a double meaning, a twofold application, receiving a primary but partial fulfilment in some person or event in Jewish history, and a second and more complete fulfilment in the Messiah.

The reference in chapter ii. 15 illustrates this. The quotation is from Hosea xi. 1, which goes back to Exod. iv. 22, 23, which is the only passage where Israel is called God's 'son.' The primary reference, therefore, is to the deliverance of the Israelites from Egyptian bondage, and in Matthew that event is made to typify and predict the emergence of Jesus from Egypt after the death of Herod.

In this way examine each passage where it is said that some Old Testament passage has its fulfilment in Christ.

16

CHRIST'S WORDS IN MATTHEW'S GOSPEL

The following table shows, in each chapter, how many verses contain words of Christ.

CHAPS.	VERS.	CHAPS.	VERS.	CHAPS.	VERS.	CHAPS.	VERS.
I	—	VIII	11	XV	21	XXII	29
II	—	IX	17	XVI	19	XXIII	38
III	1	X	38	XVII	12	XXIV	49
IV	5	XI	26	XVIII	32	XXV	46
V	46	XII	32	XIX	18	XXVI	32
VI	34	XIII	47	XX	26	XXVII	2
VII	27	XIV	5	XXI	26	XXVIII	5

Of the 1068 verses (R.V.) in this Gospel (1071 in A.V.), 644 contain words of our Lord, or more than three-fifths of the whole (p. 291). By a coloured line, or some other device, these verses should be marked in your copy of the Gospel. They are as follows:

iii. 15. iv. 4, 7, 10, 17, 19. v. 3-vii. 27. viii. 3, 4, 7, 10-13, 20, 22, 26, 32. ix. 2, 4-6, 9, 12, 13, 15-17, 22, 24, 28, 29, 30, 37, 38. x. 5-42. xi. 4-19, 21-30. xii. 3-8, 11-13, 25-37, 39-45, 48-50. xiii. 3-9, 11-33, 37-52, 57. xiv. 16, 18, 27, 29, 31. xv. 3-11, 13, 14, 16-20, 24, 26, 28, 32, 34. xvi. 2-4, 6, 8-11, 13, 15, 17-19, 23-28. xvii. 7, 9, 11, 12, 17, 20-23, 25-27. xviii. 3-20, 22-35. xix. 4-6, 8, 9, 11, 12, 14, 17-19, 21, 23, 24, 26, 28-30. xx. 1-16, 18, 19, 21-23, 25-28, 32. xxi. 2, 3, 13, 16, 19, 21, 22, 24, 25, 27-40, 42-44. xxii. 2-14, 18-21, 29-32, 37-40, 42-45. xxiii. 2-39. xxiv. 2, 4-xxv. 46. xxvi. 2, 10-13, 18, 21, 23, 24, 25, 26, 27, 28, 29, 31, 32, 34, 36, 38-42, 45, 46, 50, 52-56, 64. xxvii. 11, 46. xxviii. 9, 10, 18-20.

The eight which are underlined are the longest of the utterances. These are the main discourses in Matthew, the Five *Logia* (see pp. 256, 292), and chapter xxiii; but there are briefer utterances which should be carefully studied:

(xi; xii. 3-8, 11, 12, 25-37, 39-45; xv. 1-20; xvi. 13-19, 23-28; xix; xx; xxi. 28-44; xxii. 1-14).

A comparison of the number of verses, in the respective Gospels, which contain words of Christ, shows that Matthew has the most, 644; then comes Luke with 586; John with 419, and Mark with 285. (See pp. 192, 193, 366, 418).

17

MATTHEW'S STYLE AND DICTION

It is important to study the vocabulary of each of the Evangelists, because each uses many words which are not found in the others, and these words often throw light upon the author, or on the object of the Record.

In Matthew's Gospel there are not fewer than 115 words which are found nowhere else in the New Testament.

It would be well to underline these in your Bible in such a way as to enable you to see at a glance what and where they are.

(a) WORDS FOUND IN MATTHEW'S GOSPEL ONLY

WORD	REF.	WORD	REF.
Carry-away, brought	i. 11, 12, 17	Smite, smote -	v. 39; xxvi. 67
Dream - -	i. 20; ii. 12, 13 19, 22; xxvii. 19	Mile - - -	v. 41
		Gentile - -	v. 47; vi. 7; xviii. 17
Emmanuel - -	i. 23	Use-vain-repetitions	vi. 7
Not, no wise - -	ii. 6	Much-speaking -	vi. 7
Inquired-diligently	ii. 7, 16	Secret - -	vi. 18 (twice)
Death, End - -	ii. 15	Consider - -	vi. 28
Wroth - - -	ii. 16	Wide - - -	vii. 13
Two-years-old -	ii. 16	Broad - - -	vii. 13
Lamentation - -	ii. 18	Rain - - -	vii. 25, 27
Forbad - -	iii. 14	Outer - -	viii. 12; xxii. 13; xx. 30; xxv. 30
Upon-the-sea-coast	iv. 13		
Disease - -	iv. 23; ix. 35; x. 1		
		Meet - - -	viii. 34
Lunatic - -	iv. 24; xvii. 15	Diseased-with-issue of-blood -	ix. 20
Peacemakers - -	v. 9		
Jot - - -	v. 18	Set-at-variance -	x. 35
Raca - -	v. 22	Household -	x. 25, 36
Be-reconciled -	v. 24	Violent - -	xi. 12
Agree - -	v. 25	Fellows, friend -	xi. 16; xx. 13; xxii. 12; xxvi. 50
Forswear -	v. 33		

WORD	REF.	WORD	REF.
Meek - - -	xi. 29	Eye - - -	xix, 24
Blameless, guiltless	xii. 5, 7	Hire - - -	xx. 1, 7
Chosen - -	xii. 18	Commanded, ap-	
Strive - -	xii. 19	pointed - -	xxi. 6; xxvi. 19;
Smoking - -	xii. 20		xxvii. 10
Whale - - -	xii. 40	To set upon -	xxi. 7
Sowed-upon -	xiii. 25	Wonderful-things -	xxi. 15
Tares - - -	xiii. 25, 27, 29,	Fatling - -	xxii. 4
	30, 36, 38, 40	Merchandise -	xxii. 5
Grow-together -	xiii. 30	Burned-up -	xxii. 7
Reapers - -	xiii. 30, 39	Highways -	xxii. 9
Bundles - -	xiii. 30	Entangle - -	xxii. 15
Utter - - -	xiii. 35	Tribute-money -	xxii. 19
Declare, expound,	xiii. 36; xv. 15;	Marry - - -	xxii. 24
narrate, told -	xviii. 31	Phylacteries -	xxiii. 5
Shine-forth -	xiii. 43	Master, leader -	xxiii. (8), 10
Net - - -	xiii. 47	Anise - - -	xxiii. 23
Drew-up - -	xiii. 48	Cummin - -	xxiii. 23
Vessels - -	xiii. 48; xxv. 4	Strain-at, filter-out	xxiii. 24
Departed - -	xiii. 53; xix. 1	Gnat - - -	xxiii. 24
Sink, drowned -	xiv. 30; xviii. 6	Platter - -	xxiii. 25, 26
Doubt - - -	xiv. 31; xxviii.	Like-unto -	xxiii. 27
	17	Wax-cold -	xxiv. 12
Planted - -	xv. 13	Mill - - -	xxiv. 41
Yet - - -	xv. 16	Household -	xxiv. 45
False-witness -	xv. 19; xxvi. 59	Exchangers -	xxv. 27
Canaanitish -	xv. 22	Goats - - -	xxv. 33
Fair-weather -	xvi. 2	Very-precious -	xxvi. 7
Red - - -	xvi. 2, 3	Such a man (one)	xxvi. 18
Bar, Son - -	xvi. 17	Adjure - - -	xxvi. 63
Little-faith -	xvii. 20	Curse - - -	xxvi. 74
Tribute - -	xvii. 24	Innocent - -	xxvii. 4, 24
Prevented, spake first	xvii. 25	Hanged - -	xxvii. 5
Hook - - -	xvii. 27	Bury (burying-	
Piece-of-money -	xvii. 27	ground) - -	xxvii. 7
Seventy-times -	xviii. 22	As - - -	xxvii. 10
Take-account,	xviii. 23, 24;	Washed - -	xxvii. 24
reckon -	xxv. 19	Robe - - -	xxvii. 28, 31
Talents - -	xviii. 24; xxv.	Eli - - -	xxvii. 46
	15, 16, 20, 22,	Resurrection -	xxvii. 53
	24, 25, 28	Named - -	xxvii. 57
Debt - - -	xviii. 27	Watch - - -	xxvii. 65, 66
Tell - - -	xviii. 31		xxviii. 11
Tormentors - -	xviii. 34	Countenance -	xxviii. 3
Made-eunuchs -	xix. 12		

Some of these words are of special interest when we remember that Matthew had been a tax-gatherer. A man's calling may well be reflected in what he says and writes, and here is a good illustration of the fact.

Matthew uses three *money* words which occur nowhere else: ' TRIBUTE ' (*didrachmon*, xvii. 24); ' PIECE-OF-MONEY ' (*statēr* xvii. 27), and ' TALENT ' (*talanton*, xviii. 24; xxv. 15, *et al.*).

He also uses GOLD (*chrusos*); SILVER (*arguros*); and BRASS (*chalkos*, x. 9), which do not occur in Mark, Luke, or John, but elsewhere in the New Testament, as well as words which are used by one or other of the Evangelists: FARTHING (*kodrantēs*, v. 26; Mark xii. 42), PENNY (*dēnarion*, xviii. 28; Mark xii. 15, *et al.*), SILVER-PIECE (*argurion*, xxv. 18; Mark xiv. 11, *et al.*), and TRIBUTE (*kēnsos*, xvii. 25; Mark xii. 14).

The two parables of the *talents* are recorded by Matthew only, who alone of the Evangelists would have handled large money. A *talent* was worth some sixty times as much as the *pound*, of which Luke speaks, and above eight thousand times as much as the *penny* of which Mark speaks. (See p. 247).

Such references are natural in the writing of one who had been a tax-collector. There are also references to DEBT (*opheilē*), to ACCOUNT-TAKING, or RECKONING (*sunairō*, with *logos*), and to MONEY-CHANGERS (*trapezitēs*), which do not occur elsewhere (except 'debt'), but which a 'publican' would naturally make (xviii. 23, 24, 27; xxv. 19, 27). Examine all these references, and make a note of them in your Bible; and tell someone else about them. (See under 'The Author,' p. 247).

(b) Words and Phrases Characteristic of Matthew's Gospel

In these studies some things, in different connections, are repeated. Such repetition is necessary and valuable, for we cannot know the facts too well. Turn up all references, and learn.

(i) Matthew shows that events in Jesus' life and ministry were the fulfilment of Messianic prophecy, and he introduces such passages with some such phrase as, 'that it might be fulfilled.' This expression occurs ten times (i. 22; ii. 15; ii. 23; iv. 14; viii. 17; xii. 17; xiii. 35; xxi. 4; xxvi. 56; xxvii. 35), and its equivalents are found in ii. 5, 17; v. 17, 18; xxvi. 54; xxvii. 9. (See under 'Sources,' iii, p. 253).

(ii) In the same connection the expression, 'which was spoken,' and its equivalents, is also characteristic of this Gospel, occurring not fewer than fourteen times (i. 22;

ii. 15, 17, 23; iii. 3; iv. 14; viii. 17; xii. 17; xiii. 35; xxi.
4; xxii. 31; xxiv. 15; xxvii. 9, 35); 'was said,' referring
to the Old Testament, occurs six times (v. 21, 27, 31, 33,
38, 43); and the words 'this was done, that,' occur
three times (i. 22; xxi. 4; xxvi. 56).

Thus, not fewer than thirty-three references occur in the
application of Old Testament Scriptures to the appearance and
work of Christ. Make a list of what these references are about.
Mark these in your Bible, connecting them with their Old
Testament sources.

(iii) The phrase, 'the end (consummation) of the age'
(*sunteleia tou aiōnos*), occurs five times in Matthew, and
nowhere else except in Heb. ix. 26 (xiii. 39, 40, 49;
xxiv. 3; xxviii. 20). 'The Kingdom of Heaven' (of the
heavens: *hē Basileia tōn ouranōn*), occurs thirty-two
times (33 in A.V.), and nowhere else. 'The Kingdom
of God,' which occurs in Mark fifteen times, and in
Luke thirty-three times, occurs in Matthew only five
times (vi. 33, A.V.; xii. 28; xix. 24; xxi. 31, 43).

Various interpretations are given to the phrase, 'the Kingdom
of Heaven,' and, without dogmatism, we suggest that it means
the state of the Kingdom while the King is in Heaven. In this
view the parables of chap. xiii. become luminous. (See under
'Discourses,' pp. 297-302).

(iv) The word 'Father,' used of God, occurs in Matthew
forty-six times; by itself twenty-six times; with the
words, 'in heaven,' fifteen times; and with 'heavenly,'
five times (v. 16, 45, 48; vi. 1, 9; vii. 11, 21; x. 32, 33;
xii. 50; xvi. 17; xviii. 10, 14, 19; xxiii. 9, and vi. 14, 26,
32; xv. 13; xviii. 35).

Use a concordance for the other twenty-six references, and
underline all these occurrences in your Bible.

Make a note of the fact that 'Father,' spoken of God, occurs
in Mark only five times, and in Luke, seventeen times.

(v) 'Son of David,' relative to the Messiah, occurs eight
times, and three times each in Mark and Luke.

(vi) Jerusalem is called 'the Holy City,' and 'the Holy Place' (iv. 5; xxiv. 15; xxvii. 53).

(vii) The word for 'to retire' (*anachōreō*), occurs ten times; once only in Mark, and not at all in Luke. (ii. 12, 13, 14, 22; iv. 12; ix. 24; xii. 15; xiv. 13; xv. 21; xxvii. 5).

(viii) 'To teach,' 'to instruct' (*mathēteuō*), occurs three times (xiii. 52; xxvii. 57; xxviii. 19), and only in Acts xiv. 21 besides.

(ix) 'That' (*hopōs*), as a conjunction, occurs eighteen times (ii. 8, 23; v. 16, 45; vi. 2, 4, *et al.*).

(x) 'Worship' (*proskuneō*), occurs thirteen times (ii. 2, 8, 11, *et al.*).

(xi) 'To bring to,' 'to offer,' (*prospherō*), occurs fifteen times.

(xii) 'Crowd,' 'people,' 'multitude' (*ochlos*), occurs fifty times.

(xiii) The verb 'to gather,' or 'to gather together' (*sunagō*), occurs twenty-four times; in Mark only five times, and in Luke only seven times.

(xiv) The verb 'to come to,' occurs fifty-seven times, and 'to go away,' or 'to depart' (*proserchomai*), thirty times.

(xv) 'Greatly,' or 'exceeding' (*sphodra*), occurs seven times, and once only in Mark and in Luke.

(xvi) 'Sepulchre,' or 'tomb,' (*taphos*), occurs six times, and never in Mark or Luke.

(xvii) 'Behold' (*idou*), occurs sixty-two times.

(xviii) 'For this' (*houtos-gar*), is peculiar to Matthew (iii. 3; vii. 12; xi. 10), and so is 'for thus' (*houtōs-gar*, ii. 5; iii. 15; v. 12).

(xix) The particle of transition, 'then' (*tote*), which occurs in Mark only six times, and in Luke fourteen times, occurs in Matthew ninety times.

(xx) 'Is called' (*legomenos*), is a favourite expression of this Evangelist in announcing the names of persons, or places, or surnames, occurring twelve times, as compared with once in Mark, and twice in Luke (i. 16; ii. 23; iv. 18; x. 2; xiii. 55; xxvi. 3, 14, 36; xxvii. 16, 17, 22, 33).

(xxi) The expressions 'until this day' (*mechri tēs sēmeron*), and 'to this day' (*heōs tēs sēmeron*), occur in Matthew only (xi. 23; xxvii. 8; xxviii. 15).

(xxii) The noun 'governor' (*hēgemōn*), occurs eleven times, and but once in Mark, and twice in Luke.

(xxiii) The adverb 'afterwards' (*husteron*: translated also, 'last of all,' and 'at the last'), occurs seven times, and but once in Mark, and twice in Luke.

These examples of Matthew's diction show that his Gospel has a distinctiveness which is arresting.

Make a record of these words and their occurrences, in your Bible if possible.

18

PARABLES IN MATTHEW'S GOSPEL

FOR the parables considered generally and synthetically, read carefully Div. C, Sec. II. 12, pp. 548-553.

We have in view now only the parables and parabolic material in Matthew's Gospel. Of such, giving 'parable' its widest meaning, there are not fewer than forty in this Gospel, of which thirteen are peculiar to it (p. 280), and the first thing to do is to read these parabolic passages, omitting all other material.

In the list on page 550, The Inward Light is given as a parable occurring in two Gospels, and so may be added here.

THE MATERIAL

1	v.	13	14	xii.	24-28	28	xvi.	1-4
2	v.	14-16	15	xii.	29	29	xviii.	12-14
3	v.	25, 26	16	xii.	33-37	30	xviii.	23-35
4	v.	29, 30	17	xii.	43-45	31	xx.	1-16
5	vii.	1-5	18	xiii.	3-9, 18-23	32	xxi.	28-32
6	vii.	6	19	xiii.	24-30, 36-43	33	xxi.	33-41
7	vii.	13, 14	20	xiii.	31, 32	34	xxi.	42-44
8	vii.	15-20	21	xiii.	33	35	xxii.	1-14
9	vii.	24-27	22	xiii.	44	36	xxiv.	32-35
10	ix.	12, 13	23	xiii.	45, 46	37	xxiv.	43, 44
11	ix.	14, 15	24	xiii.	47-50	38	xxiv.	45-51
12	ix.	16	25	xiii.	51, 52	39	xxv.	1-13
13	ix.	17	26	xv.	10, 11, 15-20	40	xxv.	14-30
			27	xv.	14			

Having read the passages, let us now designate these parables. The above references are in Matthew's Gospel, and those below are the parallels in Mark and Luke. Those in CAPITALS are peculiar to Matthew.

THE SUBJECTS

No.	PARABLE	REFERENCE
1	The Salt of the Earth - -	Mark ix. 50. Luke xiv. 34, 35
2	The Light of the World - -	Mark iv. 21
3	The Adversary (?) - -	Luke xii. 58, 59
4	The Offending Members -	Ch. xviii. 7-9. Mark ix. 43-48
5	The Mote and the Beam - -	Luke vi. 41, 42
6	Dogs and Swine - -	Ch. vii. 6
7	The Broad and the Narrow Ways	Luke xiii. 24
8	Good and Bad Fruit Trees -	Ch. xii. 33. Luke vi. 43-45
9	The Wise and Foolish Builders	Luke vi. 46-49
10	The Physician and the Sick	Mark ii. 17. Luke v. 31
11	The Bride and the Bridegroom -	Mark ii. 19, 20. Luke v. 34, 35
12	New Cloth on an Old Garment -	Mark ii. 21. Luke v. 36
13	New Wine in Old Wine Skins -	Mark ii. 22. Luke v. 37-39
14	Parables about Satan's Kingdom	Mark iii. 22-26. Luke xi. 14-20
15	The Strong Man - - -	Mark iii. 27.
16	Good and Bad Treasures - -	Luke vi. 43-45
17	The Unclean Spirit that Returned	Luke xi. 24-26
18	The Sower and the Soils - -	Mark iv. 1-9. Luke viii. 4-8
19	THE WHEAT AND THE TARES -	Ch. xiii. 24-30, 36-43
20	The Mustard Seed - - -	Mark iv. 30-32. Luke xiii. 18, 19
21	The Leaven in the Meal - -	Luke xiii. 20, 21
22	THE HIDDEN TREASURE - -	Ch. xiii. 44
23	THE PEARL OF GREAT PRICE -	Ch. xiii. 45, 46
24	THE FISH NET - - - -	Ch. xiii. 47-50
25	THE HOUSEHOLDER AND HIS TREAS- URES - - - - -	Ch. xiii. 51, 52
26	The Source of Defilement - -	Mark vii. 14-23
27	The Blind Leading the Blind -	Luke vi. 39
28	Red Skies - - - -	Ch. xvi. 1-4
29	The Lost Sheep - - -	Luke xv. 3-7
30	THE UNMERCIFUL SERVANT -	Ch. xviii. 23-35
31	THE LABOURERS IN THE VINEYARD	Ch. xx. 1-16
32	THE TWO SONS CALLED TO WORK	Ch. xxi. 28-32
33	The Wicked Husbandmen - -	Mark xii. 1-9. Luke xx. 9-16
34	The Rejected Stone - -	Mark xii. 10-11. Luke xx. 17-19
35	THE MARRIAGE OF THE KING'S SON	Ch. xxii. 1-14
36	The Sprouting Fig Tree - -	Mark xiii. 28-31. Luke xxi. 29-33
37	The Householder and the Thief	Luke xii. 39, 40
38	The Faithful and Evil Servants	Luke xii. 42-46
39	THE TEN VIRGINS - - -	Ch. xxv. 1-13
40	THE TALENTS - - - -	Ch. xxv. 14-30

If you put a 'P' in the margin of the copy of Matthew which you may be using, you will be able quickly to refer to these Parables, and will readily see how they are distributed throughout the Gospel. (See pp. 549-551, and App. D, p. 664).

The parables which are peculiar to Matthew, numbers 19,
22, 23, 24, 25, 30, 31, 32, 35, 39, 40, are obviously in harmony
with the design of the Gospel, having a Messianic complexion,
and being especially condemnatory of the Jews; note specially
numbers 30, 31, 35, 39, 40. (See under ' Design,' p. 254).

It is commonly said that there are ten parables peculiar to
Matthew, but chap. xiii. 52 is clearly one, though it is not
stated to be such. The Householder and His Treasures is the
octave parable in this series, and it embraces all the others. As
in musical harmony the octave is the complement of the first
note of the scale, this eighth parable answers to the first. The
Sower tells of the *reception* of what is good (8), and the Householder tells of the *impartation* of the good which has been
received; the one presents the *divine* aspect, from God to man,
and the other presents the *human* aspect, from man to man.
The Sower illustrates the work of the evangelist, and the Householder, the work of the teacher. (For fuller treatment of chapter
xiii, see under 'Discourses,' pp. 297-302).

Of the remaining parables, 27 have parallels in Mark or Luke,
or in both. Examine these parallels carefully. The other two
(numbers 6 and 28) are also peculiar to Matthew, so that this
Evangelist has, in fact, 13 parables which are not recorded
elsewhere.

The teaching of each of these parables should be prayerfully
considered. The following may serve as a guide.

1, 2 SALT AND LIGHT   ...   .   v. 13-16
Christian witness and influence. Salt arresting corruption.
Light dispelling darkness. That both are needed is a revelation
of the moral and spiritual state of the world.

3 THE ADVERSARY   ...   .   v. 25, 26
First lesson: Beware of persisting in conduct which must
expose you to the action of Him who is at once Prosecutor,
Witness, Judge, and the Executor of the Judgment.
Second lesson: One cannot be too speedy in putting an end
to bad feeling.

4 THE OFFENDING MEMBERS   ...   v. 29, 30; cf. xviii. 7-9
No sacrifice is too great if it is the only means of securing a
right moral condition.

5 THE MOTE AND THE BEAM ...   .   vii. 1-5
We should criticize ourselves rather than others.   Criticism
provokes criticism similar to itself.   The censorious spirit is
unchristian.

6 DOGS AND SWINE   ...   .   vii. 6
Economy must be exercised in the communication of religious
truth.   The ' swine,' and the ' dogs,' represent alien and heathen
men.   For ' dogs,' cf. Phil. iii. 2; Rev. xxii. 15.   The ' pearls '
represent religious truth; cf. xiii. 46.   It is useless to offer that
which is precious to those who are incapable of receiving it.

7 THE BROAD AND NARROW WAYS   ...   ...   vii. 13, 14
There are only two moral courses, and the issue of each is
congruous with it.   One leads to destruction, and the other
to life.   Everyone must choose.

8 THE GOOD AND BAD FRUIT TREES ...   ...   vii. 15-20
We must beware of untrustworthy guides.   They are often
difficult to detect, but sooner or later their conduct will betray
them.

9 THE WISE AND FOOLISH BUILDERS   ...   vii. 24-27
Each of us is building a character.   That which is not built on
Christ must face ultimate ruin.   The Lord divides mankind
into two classes only; those on the Broad, and those on the
Narrow Way; those who are as a Good, and those who are as a
Bad Fruit Tree; those who are building character wisely, and
those who are building it foolishly (vii. 13-27).

10 THE PHYSICIAN AND THE SICK   ...   ...   ix. 12, 13
Sin is a malady which only Christ can cure.   Those who do
not feel their need (11) remain sick.   Connect verses 12, 13
with Hosea, v. 13, vi. 1, 6.   This parable was acted in miracle
(viii. 1-17, *et al.*).

11 THE BRIDE AND THE BRIDEGROOM ...   ...   ix. 14, 15
Christ's presence means a feast; His absence means a fast
(cf. xxv. 5, 6; John ii. 1-11; iii. 29).   Feasting tells of joy;
fasting, of sorrow.

12 NEW CLOTH ON AN OLD GARMENT   ...   ix. 16

13 NEW WINE IN OLD WINE SKINS   ...   .   ix. 17
These parables, like numbers 1 and 2, are a pair, presenting
a truth in its outward and inward aspects.   As in the context
are John the Baptist and Jesus (14), these parables represent
two dispensations.   John represents the Old, and Jesus, the
New.   To mix the two economies would be fatal.   Judaism
cannot be repaired with Christianity, for the latter would
completely rend the former.
    The wine skins of the old dispensation cannot hold the new
wine of the new dispensation; it would burst them.   A new
spirit in religion requires a new form.

14 PARABLES ABOUT SATAN'S KINGDOM   ...   xii. 24-28
Disunion means disruption, whether in a ' kingdom,' a ' city,'
or a ' house.' Observe the gradation. Division in an individual
is a contradiction in terms. Christ is not working against
Himself, but against Satan.

15 THE STRONG MAN   ...   .   xii. 29
Not only is Satan not an ally of Christ, but is an enemy; mighty,
but not almighty, and his vanquishment has begun (cf. Isa.
xlix. 24-26). Here, as in No. 10, mark the connection between
miracle and parable (verse 22, and verse 29).

16 GOOD AND BAD TREASURES ...   .   xii. 33-37
For verse 33 see chap. vii. 17-19. In verse 35 is another
parable on the same subject. It is what is within that comes
out. Every man's heart is a store-house, and his words show
what he keeps there. Justification, or condemnation, is determined by the facts (cf. No. 27).

17 THE UNCLEAN SPIRIT THAT RETURNED   ...   xii. 43-45
This illustrates the impossibility of being morally neutral.
Goodness cannot be merely negative; it must be positive. To
be free of evil we must be full of good.
    (For parables 18-25, see under 'Discourses,' pp. 297-302).

26 THE SOURCE OF DEFILEMENT   ...   xv. 10, 11, 15-20
This teaches the same lesson as No. 17, but whereas that
parable teaches that it is what is within that comes out, be it
good or bad, this one teaches that what is bad does not proceed
from without to within, but from within outward.

27 THE BLIND LEADING THE BLIND ...   .   xv. 14
This, like the preceding parable, refers to the Pharisees. That
one refers to their teaching, and this one to themselves. False
teachers are blind guides. Great is their responsibility, and
terrible their end.

28 RED SKIES   ...   .   xvi. 1-4
What the Pharisees and Sadducees wanted from Jesus was
miraculous proof of His Messiahship. In reply, He discredits
them by showing that, whereas they could read weather signs,
whether it would be fine or foul, by the look of the sky, they
could not discern the meaning of historical and spiritual signs.
Christ's character, teaching, and doings, were evidence enough
of His Messiahship, but the people were too blind to see it
(cf. xv. 14).

29 THE LOST SHEEP   ...   .   xviii. 12-14
God's love and search for those who are spiritually astray
should determine *our* attitude towards them (10, 15). Read
Ezek. xxxiv; Luke xv. 1-7. For the ' ninety and nine ' see
Matt. ix. 12, 13; Luke xv. 25-32; xviii. 11, 12).

30 THE UNMERCIFUL SERVANT ... ... xviii. 23-35

This parable teaches the hatefulness of an unforgiving spirit; the relation to one another of Divine and human forgiveness; and that the magnitude of God's mercy is the measure of His wrath.

31 THE LABOURERS IN THE VINEYARD ... xx. 1-16

The interpretation of this parable must be in keeping with its setting in chap. xix. 16-30, especially verses 25-30. It illustrates the supreme importance in God's sight of motive as a measure of value. God attaches importance, not so much to the amount of work done, as to the spirit in which it is done (cf. xix. 27 with xx. 11, 12). God keeps His promises to those who serve Him, and He only can judge of what is just.

32 THE TWO SONS CALLED TO WORK ... xxi. 28-32

The context (24-27) will help us to interpret this parable. It discloses the insincerity and inconsistency of the ' chief priests and the elders ' (23), relative to John the Baptist and his ministry. By saying, ' I go, sir ' (30), they agreed with John's general aim. By not going (30), they disapproved of his moral earnestness, and so declined to follow him. On the other hand, many tax-collectors and harlots, who at first had no regard for John, eventually repented and entered the kingdom. Promise, if right, should be fulfilled, and if wrong, it should be repudiated.

33 THE WICKED HUSBANDMEN ... ... xxi. 33-41

Verses 45, 46 supply the key. In the preceding parable the sin of the religious leaders is exposed relative to the *past*; they had promised, but had not performed. In this parable their sin in relation to the present and the future is exposed; it is their intention to kill Jesus (37-39). They did not miss the significance of what He said (40, 41, 45, 46).

The ' Householder ' is God; the ' Vineyard ' is Israel; the ' Husbandmen ' are the Jews, and especially their religious leaders; the ' Servants ' are the prophets, and the ' Son ' is Christ.

34 THE REJECTED STONE ... ... xxi. 42-44

The men who have just been compared to vine-dressers, now become builders, and the heir, cast out of the vineyard and murdered, is now a stone thrown aside as useless. The quotation is from Psalm cxviii. 22, 23. Christ applies this Scripture to Himself, and so carries the prediction of the former parable a little further.

There, the last that is seen of the ' son ' is his death (39), but here it is declared that that Son, now represented as a ' Stone,' is to triumph, is to become ' the head of the corner.'

The figure of the ' stone,' relative to Christ, is threefold: (*a*) He is the Stone over Whom many will fall, but not to final ruin (44*a*); (*b*) He is the Stone to Whom God has given the place of honour and power (42); and (*c*) He is the Stone who, at last will fall in judgment on all who reject Him, and will destroy them (44*b*).

35 THE MARRIAGE OF THE KING'S SON   ...   xxii. 1-14

Here are two parables, not one; and verse 1 prepares us for this. The first is the Wedding Feast (1-9), and the second is the Wedding Garment (10-14). The first tells of those who despise and reject the King's invitation, that is, the religious leaders. The second tells of those who accept the invitation but do not comply with the conditions. The Gentile who dares to come before the King, while still defiled with all his pagan godlessness, is condemned as decisively as the Jew who persistently and violently refuses to come at all. There are those who are willing to come to the Feast who do not want the robe, but the King's benefits are based on His conditions.

The Great Supper of Luke xiv. 16-24, is a different story. The two should be carefully compared.

36 THE SPROUTING FIG TREE ...   .   xxiv. 32-36

This is one of the most difficult of the parables to interpret. The difficulty is twofold: first, to know what it is that ' is nigh ' (33), and second, to know what is meant by ' all these things ' (34).

All that can be said is that two things are being dealt with in this discourse, namely, the approaching destruction of Jerusalem, which took place in A.D. 70, and Christ's advent at the end of the age (1-3). These ideas are so intertwined that it is difficult to separate them and to say what refers to the near prophecy, and what, to the distant; the former seems to be referred to in verse 34, and the latter in verse 36. (See p. 307).

37 THE HOUSEHOLDER AND THE THIEF   ...   xxiv. 43, 44

38 THE FAITHFUL AND EVIL SERVANTS   ...   xxiv. 45-51

These two parables are on the need of watchfulness. The first relates to the night, and the second, to the day. The first is a house-owner, and the second, an employee. The first is exhorted to watch, because of a possible, but not a certain event, namely, the coming of a thief; and the second, because of a certain event, the time of the occurrence of which is unknown.

39 THE TEN VIRGINS   ...   .   xxv. 1-13

40 THE TALENTS ...   .   xxv. 14-30

Both these parables further illustrate the need for watchfulness (13, cf. xxiv. 37-51), and they are related to the epithets in xxiv. 45; the Virgins parable showing the need of *wisdom*, and the Talents parable, the need of *fidelity*. The first tells us what we *should not do*; and the second, what we *should do*.

In both, the judgment falls on those who have done nothing. The first is a warning against *folly*, and the second, against *faithlessness*. The first is a domestic parable, and the second a commercial one.

Some regard the Sheep and the Goats to be a parable (xxv. 31-46), but in two verses only is this figure used (32, 33), and thereafter it is a plain statement of a Judgment which is yet to come.

There are in Matthew at least seven parables of Judgment: The Unmerciful Servant (xviii. 23-35); the Labourers in the Vineyard (xx. 1-16); the Wicked Husbandmen (xxi. 33-41); the Guest without the Wedding Garment (xxii. 10-14); the Faithful and Unfaithful Servants (xxiv. 45-51); the Wise and Foolish Virgins (xxv. 1-13), and the Talents (xxv. 14-30).

But what in these is intimated in parabolic language, is here (xxv. 31-46) revealed with singular plainness and completeness.

It will be seen from all the foregoing that our Lord frequently spoke double parables, in order to present two aspects of one truth. There are at least seven such pairs in this Gospel.

1 The Salt, and the Light.
2 The Old Garment, and the Old Wine Skins.
3 The Sower and the Soils, and the Wheat and the Tares.
4 The Mustard Seed, and the Leaven in the Meal.
5 The Hidden Treasure, and the Costly Pearl.
6 The Householder and the Thief, and the Faithful and Evil Servants.
7 The Virgins, and the Talents.

Five of these (excepting 3 and 6) present the inward and outward aspects of a truth.

Observe the figures which are employed in the parables of this Gospel (the numbers in brackets refer to the preceding list, p. 279).

Salt (1), Light (2), Limbs (4), Wood (5), Dogs (6), Swine (6), Roads (7), Fruit (8, 36), Houses (9), Medicine (10), Clothes (12), Wine (13), Treasures (16, 22), Seed (18, 19, 20), Soils (18), Meal (21), Leaven (21), Pearls (6, 23), Fish (24), Net (24), Sky (28), Vineyard (31, 32, 33), Sheep (29), Stone (34), Marriage (35), Lamp (39), Oil (39), Talents (40), Food (38), Trading (40).

These figures are drawn from many spheres, the natural, physical, social, commercial, domestic, industrial, professional, criminal, agricultural, conjugal, moral, religious, and spiritual.

This is pre-eminently the Gospel of the Kingdom, and in it Jesus is presented as the Messianic King. In keeping with this dominating thought are the principal parables.

Six of the eight in chapter xiii are introduced as parables of
' the Kingdom of Heaven,' and as the eighth (51, 52) includes all
the others, it also refers to the Kingdom.

The Two Sons, recorded by Matthew only, shows how the
historical children of the Kingdom excluded themselves from it
(xxi. 28-32). The Marriage of the King's Son, also peculiar
to Matthew, has a royal complexion, and is introduced by the
words ' the Kingdom of Heaven is like unto ' (xxii. 1-14).

In the same way are introduced the parables of the Labourers,
the Virgins, and the Talents (xviii. 23; xx. 1; xxv. 1, 14).

19

MIRACLES IN MATTHEW'S GOSPEL

NO one can say how many miracles Christ performed, because
most of them are referred to collectively, and these are
greatly in excess of the number recorded in detail.

Mark in your Bible the following twelve group references:

iv. 23, 24 viii. 16   ix. 35   x. 1, 8   xi. 4, 5   xi. 20-24
xii. 15   xiv. 14   xiv. 36   xv. 30   xix. 2   xxi. 14

In addition to these twelve miracle summaries there are
recorded in this Gospel 20 specific miracles (of the 35 in the
Evangelic Records. See pp. 553, 554), and of these 20, three
are recorded by Matthew only (four, if xii. 22 is not the same as
Luke xi. 14). (See pp. 206, 554).

(a) THE TWENTY MIRACLES WHICH MATTHEW RECORDS

1 Cleansing of a Leper - - - -	viii. 1-4	
2 Healing of a Centurion's Servant - -	viii. 5-13	
3 Restoring of Peter's Mother-in-law -	viii. 14, 15	
4 Stilling of the Tempest - - -	viii. 23-27	
5 Deliverance of a Gadarene Demoniac -	viii. 28-34	
6 Healing of a Paralytic - - - -	ix. 1-8	
7 Healing of a Woman with an Issue of Blood - - - - - -	ix. 20-22	
8 Raising of the Daughter of Jairus -	ix. 18, 19, 23-26	
9 *Healing of Two Blind Men* - - -	ix. 27-31	
10 *Deliverance of a Dumb Demoniac* - -	ix. 32, 33	
11 Restoration of a Man with a Withered Hand	xii. 10-13	
12 Deliverance of a Blind and Dumb Demoniac	xii. 22	
13 Feeding of the Five Thousand - -	xiv. 15-21	
14 Walking upon the Sea - - - -	xiv. 25-33	

15 Deliverance of the Syrophœnician's Daughter	- - - -	- xv. 21-28
16 Feeding of the Four Thousand	-	- xv. 32-38
17 Deliverance of a Lunatic Boy	-	- xvii. 14-18
18 *Finding of the Stater*	- - -	- xvii. 24-27
19 Healing of a Blind Man near Jericho	-	- xx. 29-34
20 Withering of the Fig Tree	- -	- xxi. 18-22

It would help you readily to find these miracles if you put an ' M ' in the margin of your Matthew, and an ' Mg.' by the references to groups of miracles (p. 286).

By the above wording of the miracles an effort is made to distinguish different classes, e.g. *deliverance* is the word used for the five demoniacal cases.

(b) THE FIFTEEN MIRACLES WHICH MATTHEW OMITS

1 Cure of a Demoniac in a Synagogue	Mark i. 23; Luke iv. 33
2 Healing of a Deaf Mute	- - - - Mark vii. 31
3 Healing of the Blind Man at Bethsaida	- Mark viii. 22
4 First Draught of Fishes	- - - - Luke v. 1
5 Raising the Widow's Son	- - - Luke vii. 11
6 Healing the Woman with an Infirmity	- Luke xiii. 11
7 Healing of a Dropsical Man	- - - Luke xiv. 1
8 Cleansing of Ten Lepers	- - - - Luke xvii. 11
9 Healing the Ear of Malchus	- - - Luke xxii. 50
10 Turning the Water into Wine	- - - John ii. 10
11 Healing a Nobleman's Son at Cana	- - John iv. 46
12 Healing of an Impotent Man at Bethesda	- John v. 1
13 Opening the Eyes of One Born Blind	- John ix. 1
14 Raising of Lazarus	- - - - - John xi. 43
15 Second Draught of Fishes	- - - John xxi. 1

(c) THE THREE MIRACLES WHICH ONLY MATTHEW RECORDS

9 Healing of Two Blind Men	- - - ix. 27-31
10 Deliverance of a Dumb Demoniac	- - ix. 32, 33
18 Finding of the Stater	- - - xvii. 24-27

(But see No. 12; ch. xii. 22, and note on pp. 286, 553, 554).

(d) THE SEVENTEEN MIRACLES WHICH MATTHEW AND OTHERS RECORD

(i) *In Matthew and Mark—Three*:

1 Deliverance of the Syrophœnician's Daughter: No. 15, and Mark vii. 24.

2 Feeding of the Four Thousand: No. 16, and Mark viii. 1.

3 Withering of the Fig Tree: No. 20, and Mark xi. 12.

    (ii) *In Matthew and Luke—Two*:

        4 Healing of the Centurion's Servant, No. 2, and Luke vii. 1.

        5 Deliverance of a Blind and Dumb Demoniac, No. 12, and Luke xi. 14. (See pp. 286, 553, 554).

    (iii) *In Matthew, Mark, and Luke—Ten*:

        6 Stilling of the Tempest, No. 4, and Mark iv. 37; Luke viii. 22.

        7 Deliverance of the Gadarene Demoniac, No. 5, and Mark v. 1; Luke viii. 27.

        8 Raising of the Daughter of Jairus, No. 8, and Mark v. 38; Luke viii. 49.

        9 Healing of the Woman with an Issue of Blood, No. 7, and Mark v. 25; Luke viii. 43.

      10 Healing of the Paralytic, No. 6, and Mark ii. 3; Luke v. 18.

      11 Cleansing of a Leper, No. 1, and Mark i. 40; Luke v. 12.

      12 Restoring of Peter's Mother-in-law, No. 3, and Mark i. 30; Luke iv. 38.

      13 Restoration of a Man with a Withered Hand, No. 11, and Mark iii. 1; Luke vi. 6.

      14 Deliverance of a Lunatic Boy, No. 17, and Mark ix. 17; Luke ix. 38.

      15 Healing of Two Blind Men near Jericho, No. 19, and Mark x. 46; Luke xviii. 35.

    (iv) *In Matthew, Mark, and John—One*:

      16 Walking upon the Sea, No. 14, and Mark vi. 48; John vi. 19.

    (v) *In Matthew, Mark, Luke, and John—One*:

      17 Feeding of the Five Thousand, No. 13, and Mark vi. 35; Luke ix. 12; John vi. 5.

Observe that, in keeping with Matthew's method of grouping his material (see under 'Plan,' pp. 255-258), half of the 20 miracles which he records are found in chapters viii-ix, following three chapters of discourse.

> Paul says that Christ is the *power* of God, and the *wisdom* of God (1 Cor. i. 24), and Matthew illustrates the fact. The *wisdom* of God is revealed in Christ's *words* (v-vii), and His *power* is displayed in Christ's *works* (viii-ix).

In chapters v-vii is the *proclamation* of the King, and in chapters viii-ix are His *credentials*: in the one we have His *teaching*, and in the other His *touch*.

If the Healing of the Woman with an Issue of Blood, and the Raising of the Daughter of Jairus can be regarded as one act of miracle, the former always being enfolded in the latter (ix.

18-26; Mark v. 21-43; Luke viii. 40-56), then, in these two chapters Matthew records three series of triplets, which, it would seem, are intended to be typical of all Messiah's miracles. (See pp. 257, 264, 312).

FIRST SERIES:
1 Healing of a Leper.
2 Healing of a Centurion's Servant.
3 Restoring of Peter's Mother-in-law.

SECOND SERIES:
4 Stilling of the Tempest.
5 Deliverance of a Gadarene Demoniac.
6 Healing of a Paralytic.

THIRD SERIES:
7 Healing of the Woman with an Issue of Blood, and Raising of the Daughter of Jairus.
8 Healing of Two Blind Men.
9 Deliverance of a Dumb Demoniac.

Of these nine, the last two are recorded by Matthew only.

In the First Series are illustrations of Christ's power over typical diseases—leprosy, paralysis, and fever.

In the Second Series Christ is shown to be all powerful over the realm of nature, the spiritual world, and the power of sin.

In the Third Series He is seen to be the conqueror of death, as well as the restorer of disordered and defective faculties.

The remaining 10 miracles all belong to one or other of the above classifications.

The Restoring of the Withered Hand, and the Healing of Two Blind Men, are, like miracle 8 (ix. 27-31), the recovery of defective faculties.

The Deliverance of a Blind and Dumb Demoniac, of a Lunatic Boy, and of the Syrophœnician Girl, are, like miracles 5 and 9, a triumph over demons in the spiritual world.

The Walking upon the Sea, the Feeding of the Five Thousand, and of the Four Thousand, the Finding of the Stater in the Fish's Mouth, and the Withering of the Fig Tree, are works, like miracle 4, wrought in the realm of nature.

19

These 20 miracles allow of the following classification:

1 MIRACLES IN THE HUMAN REALM—EIGHT

(1) Healing of a Leper; (2) Healing of a Centurion's Servant; (3) Healing of Peter's Mother-in-law; (4) Healing of the Woman with an Issue of Blood; (5) Healing of Two Blind Men; (6) Healing of a Withered Hand; (7) Healing of a Paralytic; (8) Healing of Blind Bartimæus and another.

2 MIRACLES IN THE COSMIC REALM—SIX

(1) Stilling of the Tempest; (2) Walking on the Sea; (3) Feeding of the Five Thousand; (4) and of the Four Thousand; (5) Finding of the Stater in the Fish's Mouth; (6) Withering of the Fig Tree.

3 MIRACLES IN THE SPIRIT REALM—SIX

(1) Deliverance of a Gadarene Demoniac; (2) of the Blind and Dumb Demoniac; (3) of a Lunatic Boy; (4) of the Syrophœnician Girl; (5) of a Dumb Demoniac; (6) and of the Raising of the Daughter of Jairus.

Over human disorders, physical, nervous, and mental; over cosmic forces, on land and sea, organic and inorganic; and over the spirit realm, represented by demons and death, Christ is shown, by His miracles, to be triumphant.

These miracles, therefore, are not merely illustrations of divine revelation, but are themselves revelations. They disclose, not only that Christ is Divine, but also that He is a Saviour. To the palsied man He said, not only: ' Arise and walk,' but also, ' thy sins be forgiven thee.'

The miracles are not only evidential, but also redemptive. The various maladies on which Christ's power was brought to bear represent some aspect of the ruin which sin has wrought in man.

Leprosy represents its defiling and corrupting power in man; *blindness* tells of man's ignorance of God through sin; *deafness*, of his inability and lack of desire to hear God's voice; *dumbness* tells of man who, having no experience of God, has no testimony to bear; *palsy* speaks of the moral and spiritual enfeeblement of man, due to sin: *fever* illustrates the restlessness which sin begets in man; the *withered hand* tells of the sinner's inability to work for God; *the issue of blood* speaks of the waste of life for which sin is responsible; *demoniacal possession* proclaims the thraldom which sin imposes on man, and *death* tells of sin's ultimate penalty. (See p. 205).

We have been considering the miracles of Christ, but Christ Himself is the greatest miracle. There is the miracle of His incarnation and the manner of it; the miracle of His sinlessness; the miracle of His human subjection; the miracle of His veiled glory; the miracle of His miracles; the miracle of His teaching; the miracle of His example; the miracle of His unused power; the miracle of His voluntary and atoning death; the miracle of His resurrection; the miracle of His ascension; the miracle of His presence with and in the Christian and the Church, and the miracle of His forgiving grace and saving power.

Make a note of these words by Prof. A. B. Bruce:

> ' If a sinless Christ were taken from us on the plea that the moral order of the world knows only of imperfect men, all would be lost. Nothing less than a sinless, infallible, incomparably original man is demanded by the titles and functions ascribed to Christ. The Son of God must be holy, as God is holy. The Redeemer of sinners cannot Himself be a sinner. The Light of the world can have no share in the world's darkness. The Inaugurator of the new era of grace cannot be a commonplace man, the creature of His time, in all His thoughts a mere echo of current opinion. We could not believe such a man to be the Messiah—officially great, personally insignificant.' (' The Miraculous Element in the Gospels,' p. 320).

20

DISCOURSES IN MATTHEW'S GOSPEL

A LARGE proportion of Matthew's Record is devoted to discourses, in contrast to Mark's, and for this reason it has been called ' The Didactic Gospel.' It is said that ' Jesus went about all Galilee, teaching in their synagogues, and preaching the Gospel of the Kingdom ' (iv. 23), but Matthew says little about the ' preaching,' and much about the ' teaching.'

The words of the Messiah occupy about three-fifths of the Record, about 644 of its 1068 verses. In this respect the first Gospel is like the Fourth. Mark and Luke have less teaching and more narrative. (See under ' Christ's Words in this Gospel,' p. 272).

It is not unlikely that Matthew who, as a tax-gatherer would employ an abbreviated script in the Customs booth at Capernaum, made extensive notes of the teaching of Jesus.

Papias (A.D. 120), in a passage preserved by Eusebius, says: ' Matthew wrote the Oracles in the Hebrew dialect, but everyone translated them as he was able' (pp. 91, 92).

Some think that by the ' Oracles,' or *Logia*, Papias meant our canonical Gospel, but as there is abundant reason for believing that this Gospel was written, not in Aramaic, but in Greek, Papias must have referred to a Collection of Discourses of Jesus, which Matthew had made, and which, it would seem, he used when subsequently he wrote his Gospel. (See under ' Language in Which Written,' and under ' Sources,' pp. 250, 251).

If what there is of Mark in Matthew's Gospel is subtracted, (see under ' Mark in Matthew,' p. 261), the remainder consists almost wholly of discourses, from which we may infer that it was this Evangelist's design to give prominence to the Sayings of Christ, as Mark had done to His Doings. This is made evident by such remarks as:

> ' From that time began Jesus to preach.' ' He opened His mouth and taught them.' ' He departed thence to teach and to preach.'
>
> ' He taught them in their synagogues.' ' Jesus went about all the cities and the villages, teaching in their synagogues, and preaching the Gospel of the Kingdom ' (iv. 17; v. 2; ix. 35; xi. 1; xiii. 54).

Without doubt much of Christ's teaching was in the form of short, pregnant sentences, such as Mark has preserved; but He must also have delivered discourses of considerable length, such as Matthew and John preserve.

In this Gospel there are six such discourses, five of which are closed with the same formula: ' It came to pass when Jesus had finished ' (vii. 28; xi. 1; xiii. 53; xix. 1; xxvi. 1); and the other one has a formal ending, though not the usual formula (xxiii. 37-39. (See under 'Plan,' pp. 255, 256).

These discourses may be described as follows:

(1) Chs. v-vii   - The Sermon on the Mount.
(2) Ch.   x   - The Charge to the Twelve.
(3) Ch.   xiii   - The Parables of the Kingdom.
(4) Ch.   xviii   - Teaching on Greatness, and Forgiveness.
(5) Ch.   xxiii   - Denunciation of the Pharisees.
(6) Chs. xxiv-xxv   The Great Apocalypse.

We have seen that Matthew wrote his Gospel on a grouping plan, not on a chronological; (see under ' Plan,' p. 257); for example, chapters viii-ix, in which are three series of miracles, nine (or ten) in number (see under ' Miracles,' p. 289); it is, therefore, most likely that in some of these discourses he has brought together instruction on various subjects which Jesus gave at different times.

The Sermon on the Mount is recorded in Matthew as one connected discourse, whereas the Sayings contained in it are scattered throughout Luke's Gospel, and are to be found in at least ten different places. (See also under 'Matthew's Plan,' p. 256. Carefully examine the following:

MATT.	LUKE	MATT.	LUKE
v. 3-12	vi. 20-23	vi. 24	xvi. 13
v. 13	xiv. 34, 35	vi. 25-34	xii. 22-31
v. 15	xi. 33	vii. 1-5	vi. 37-42
v. 18	xvi. 17	vii. 7-11	xi. 9-13
v. 25, 26	xii. 57-59	vii. 12	vi. 31
v. 31, 32	xvi. 18	vii. 13, 14	xiii. 23, 24
v. 38-48	vi. 27-30, 32-36	vii. 15-20	vi. 43-45
vi. 9-15	xi. 1-4	vii. 23	xiii. 27
vi. 19-21	xii. 33, 34	vii. 24-27	vi. 47-49
vi. 22, 23	xi. 34-36	—	—

It is possible that Matthew has assembled in a single discourse our Lord's teaching on such subjects as: alms-giving, prayer, anxiety, criticism, etc., on which, it would appear, He often spoke; and it is equally possible that Christ Himself gathered up these subjects in a single discourse, in which case Luke records the scattered teaching, while Matthew records the full discourse.

What has been said of the Sermon on the Mount may be said also of the Charge to the Twelve (x). The report in Mark of what Jesus said, occupies only five verses (vi. 7-11), three of which are narrative (7-9), and two of which are quotation (10, 11); but in Matthew the report occupies 38 verses (x. 5-42).

It is observable, also, that a good deal of this Charge to the Twelve is the same as Christ's Charge to the Seventy, in Luke x, so that clearly these instructions were spoken on more than one occasion.

For Matt. x. 9-15, cf. Mark vi. 8-11; Luke ix. 3-5; x. 4-12.
For Matt. x. 19-22, cf. Mark xiii. 11-13; Luke xxi. 12-17.
For Matt. x. 26-33, cf. Luke xii. 2-9.
For Matt. x. 34, 35, cf. Luke xii. 51-53.

The same thing is observable in the Parables of the Kingdom (xiii), three of which were spoken at different times. The Sower (1-23), cf. Mark iv. 1-20; Luke viii. 4-15. The Mustard Seed (31, 32), cf. Mark iv. 30-32; Luke xiii. 18, 19. The Leaven (33), cf. Luke xiii. 20, 21.

Also parts of the Teaching on Greatness, and Forgiveness (xviii), were given at different times.

All of Matthew's six discourses have numerous parallels, chiefly in Luke. In the latter, Matt. chs. v-vii have some 38 parallels; ch. x has 54; ch. xiii has 20; ch. xviii has 17; chs. xii and xxiii have 44; and chs. xxiv-xxv have 26. And what is true of these discourses is true also of practically all our Lord's Sayings in Matthew's Gospel, fully 50 parallels being found in Luke, in addition to the foregoing; and to these must be added the parallels in Mark. (See Stevens' & Burton's 'Harmony of the Gospels,' pp. 262-277).

This comparative study is valuable as showing our Lord's method of instruction, and the themes He expounded.

Whether the discourses in Matthew are groupings of Jesus' .eaching in general, or are reports of discourses which He delivered as such, in no way affects their genuineness, authority, and value. How the Evangelist has recorded what Jesus said is of little importance in comparison with *what* He said, though it is interesting to know, as far as we may, how He taught.

Matthew tells us that Jesus' mission was threefold (iv. 23), teaching, preaching, and healing, and he gives us samples of all three, laying special emphasis on the first.

The ' teaching ' expounds the Master's message; the ' preaching ' applies it, and the ' healing ' illustrates it.

While special attention should be given to the long discourses, the sententious sayings of Jesus should be studied and memorized. Much of the Master's instruction was in crisp, pointed, and often in antithetic sentences, which readily stick in the memory.

Of course, such sentences are found in abundance in the discourses, as well as in the more casual utterances.

Make a list of these, and carry them about with you, such as:

The Beatitudes	v. 3-12
'Where your treasure is, there will your heart be also'	vi. 21
' No man can serve two masters . . . ye cannot serve God and mammon '	vi. 24
' Seek ye first the Kingdom of God and His righteousness, and all these things shall be added unto you '	vi. 33
' Judge not that ye be not judged '	vii. 1
' Ask, and it shall be given unto you; seek, and ye shall find; knock, and it shall be opened unto you '	vii. 7
' All things whatsoever ye would that men should do unto you, even so do ye also unto them '	vii. 12
' By their fruits ye shall know them '	vii. 20
' He that findeth his life shall lose it; and he that loseth his life for my sake, shall find it '	x. 39
' Wisdom is justified of her children '	xi. 19
' Come unto Me, all ye that labour and are heavy laden, and I will give you rest '	xi. 28
' Take my yoke upon you, and learn of Me, for I am meek and lowly in heart, and ye shall find rest unto your souls; for my yoke is easy, and ' my burden is light '	xi. 29, 30
' He that is not with Me is against Me; and he that gathereth not with Me, scattereth '	xii. 30
' By thy words thou shalt be justified, and by thy words thou shalt be condemned '	xii. 37

The Jewish complexion of the teaching which Matthew records is pronounced. To be impressed by this, one has only to read the Sermon on the Mount (v-vii), and then, the Upper Room Talk (John xiv-xvi). The former relates to the Law: the latter, to the Gospel; the one looks back: the other looks forward; the one presents an ethical standard: the other reveals a spiritual relation and power.

(1) THE SERMON ON THE MOUNT (v-vii)

This is the presentation of fundamental principles, or is an ethical directory, for the guidance of Christ's disciples in their conduct; it presents a rule of life for Christ's followers. There are various ways of summarizing its contents, of which the following are examples:—

THE KING'S SERVANTS:

1 The Character and Blessedness of the King's Servants	v. 1-16
2 The King's Servants and the Moral Law	v. 17-48

(2) The Charge to the Twelve (x)

The Sermon on the Mount refers to disciples in their private capacity. This Charge refers to them as representing Christ to the world.

> 'The original basis of the Commission was addressed to men called to give their whole time to this work, but as the chapter stands it applies to all believers in their capacity of witness for Christ. The ministerial function of preaching, committed to men selected for it, is only an accentuation of one of the duties expected from all Christ's followers.'

Whether the discourse was delivered as it stands here, or whether it summarizes instructions which Christ gave to His disciples at various times, the Commission, as such, remains, and it is Christ's word to His messengers.

This Discourse, like the preceding one, may be variously analysed. The following may be found useful.

The Missionary Charter:

1 *The Immediate Occasion* - - - - ix. 35-x. 15
    The Widespread Need (ix. 35-38)
    The Chosen Messengers (x. 1-4)
    The Field of Labour (x. 5, 6)
    The Appointed Task (x. 7, 8)
    The Worker's Equipment (x. 9, 10)
    The Missionary's Approach (x. 11-15)

2 *The Future Outlook* - - - - x. 16-42
    The Sufferings Involved (x. 16-23)
    The Master's Encouragement (x. 24-33)
    The Sacrifice Demanded (x. 34-39)
    The Promised Reward (x. 40-42)

With this Charge to the Twelve, compare that given to the Seventy, in Luke's Gospel (x. 1-16). The latter Commission has a much more Gentile aspect than the one given to the Twelve (Matt. x. 5), and it is in keeping with the design of Matthew that he omits it.

(3) The Parables of the Kingdom (xiii)

This Discourse is second to none of all that our Lord delivered, and the construction of it leads to the conviction that it was preached as here outlined, so that this chapter is not merely a collection of parables which Jesus spoke at different times, as chapters viii-ix, are a collection of miracles which He wrought at different times.

In no discourse so much as in this one is unity of idea and plan so evident, and it is only as it is viewed as a whole that its scope and significance can be apprehended.

The context of the Discourse (chapter xii) tells of the Jews' rejection of the Messiah, and of His rejection of them, and it was on that ' same day ' that this Discourse was delivered (xiii).

The general frame of the *narrative* is as follows:

' They went into a house ' Mark iii. 19, 31-35; cf. Matt. xii. 46-50
   He ' went out of the house ' -   -   -   -   Matt. xiii. 1
   He ' went into the house '   -   -   -   -   xiii. 36
   ' He departed thence '   -   -   -   -   -   xiii. 53

The general frame of the *Discourse* is as follows:

       (i) In Public. Four Parables (1-35)
         1 The Sower (1-23)
         2 The Wheat and the Tares (24-30)
         3 The Mustard Seed (31, 32)
         4 The Leaven in the Meal (33)

      (ii) In Private. Four Parables (36-53)
         5 The Hid Treasure (44)
         6 The Goodly Pearl (45, 46)
         7 The Fish Net (47-50)
         8 The Householder (52)

The parable of the Sower introduces all, and that of the Householder concludes all. Between these there are six parables. The first three are introduced with the word 'another' (24, 31, 33), and the last three, with the word 'again' (44, 45, 47).

The first four were delivered to the *multitude* (1-3), and the second four to the *disciples* (36, 51).

The subject of the eight parables is *The Kingdom of Heaven*. The first four treat of the External Facts of the Kingdom, as seen by all; and the second four treat of the Internal Truth of the Kingdom, as revealed to some.

The eight parables are related to one another on the plan of an introverted parallelism, as follows:

(a) The Sower. Key. Introducing. Anticipative

    (b) The Tares

      (c) { The Mustard Seed / The Leaven

      (c) { The Hid Treasure / The Goodly Pearl

    (b) The Fish Net

(a) The Householder. Key. Concluding. Reflective

This reveals that the (a's) and the (b's) are pairs, and that the (c's) are double pairs.

Read the parables of the Tares and the Fish Net together, and mark their common features; the good and the bad in both, and the destiny of each.

The 2nd, 3rd, and 4th parables are arranged as $1+2$; and the 5th, 6th, and 7th are arranged as $2+1$. Mark the inversion of the order. This may seem very artificial to our methods of thought and discourse, but it was not so to the Jews. . . . Compare the mnemonic devices of Psalm cxix, and of Lamentations.

The double pairs (c) are characterized by common features, principally in that each pair presents the inward and outward aspects of the subject treated, but in the inverse order, as follows:

(a) The Mustard Seed - - - - Outward
    (b) The Leaven - - - - Inward
    (b) The Hid Treasure - - - Inward
(a) The Goodly Pearl - - - - Outward

These features of the Discourse are of considerable importance for an understanding of its meaning.

What, then, is the meaning of what our Lord said? On this subject there never will be universal agreement. Differences of opinion are met with on the threshold as to the meaning of the *Kingdom of Heaven*. The expression occurs only in Matthew, and 32 times (33 in A.V.), but in some places at any rate, it is the equivalent of the *Kingdom of God*.

        cf. Matt. xi. 11, with Luke vii. 28.
        cf. Matt. iv. 17, with Mark i. 15.

It would appear that Matthew retains the expression ' The Kingdom of Heaven,' because the thought was familiar to the

Jews (cf. Dan. iv. 34, 37; iv. 26; vi. 26; vii. 14). Our Lord, Who spoke in Aramaic, would always use this phrase, and when writing in Greek, Matthew, in keeping with the special scope and character of his Gospel, retained it, whereas, in the other Gospels the figure was translated as being what it also, though not exclusively, meant, the Kingdom of God.

It seems clear, then, that the expressions are largely synonymous (cf. Matt. xviii. 3; Mark x. 15; Luke xviii. 7. Also Matt. xix. 23, 24; Mark x. 23-25; Luke xviii. 24, 25. Also Matt. xix. 14; Mark x. 14; Luke xviii. 16. Also Matt. v. 3; Luke vi. 20).

This means that the Kingdom of Heaven, or the Kingdom of God, is not synonymous with the Christian Church. The former is vaster than the latter; the latter is included in the former. The Royal Family is not the British Empire, but the Family is included in the Empire.

It cannot, then, be true to say that the parables of this chapter (xiii) are parables of the Church; nor can it be true to say that these parables are in no way related to the Church. They are parables of the Kingdom of Heaven, and the Church is in that Kingdom.

We may, therefore, take the expression to mean, *the state of the Kingdom in the present age*, and in this chapter that state is unfolded progressively. It began with Christ's First Advent, and it will end with His Second Advent.

These parables have been interpreted in three ways:

- (*a*) As being exclusively Jewish.
- (*b*) As representations of the condition of Christendom; that is, of the whole sphere of Christian profession between Christ's Ascension and His Second Advent.
- (*c*) As teaching great moral and spiritual lessons such as all men need always.

No one of these alone is adequate as an interpretation, and it is more than probable that there is truth in all of them. Some interpret all these parables of the period between the two Advents, and some interpret the first four only of this period, and the last three of the time beyond the Advent. Some regard the first four as referring to the professing Church, and the last three, to Israel, or the Remnant.

Some regard the parables of the Mustard Seed, and the Leaven in the Meal, as referring to the outward and inward progress of Christianity; and some regard them as predicting the progress of evil within the sphere of Christian profession.

As an aid towards a solution it may be laid down as a principle of interpretation that figures of speech are used consistently in discourse.

In the first parable the 'fowls' are evil (4, 19), and must be regarded as such in verse 32.

Everywhere in Scripture, 'leaven,' used figuratively, refers to what is evil (Exod. xii. 15; Lev. ii. 11; vi. 17; x. 12; Matt. xvi. 6; Mark viii. 15; 1 Cor. v. 6, 8; Gal. v. 9), and it would be strange if it were not so in this passage (33).

Some consider that the parables of the Hid Treasure, and the Goodly Pearl represent Christ, and some regard the seeker in both to be the Lord.

The former of these views is inconsistent with the rest of the Discourse, and with the Christian gospel, which tells, not of men seeking God, but of God seeking men.

The view taken here is that which regards the Discourse to be a prophetic unfolding of the course of this age, that is, of the period while the King is in Heaven. This period began when the Messiah entered upon His ministry—He, in the first place was the Sower—and it will finish when He comes again to end this age, and to inaugurate another.

The Discourse is an outline of the Kingdom in mystery form. The first four parables, spoken to the multitude outside, present the *external*, or *World Aspect* of the Kingdom; and the last three, spoken to the disciples inside, present the *internal*, or *Church Aspect*.

Some think that the last three parables refer, not to the Church, but to Israel, and others think that the Hid Treasure only points to Israel, or the Remnant, and that only the Goodly Pearl refers to the Church.

Whichever view we hold, it should be with respect for the views of others, and without offensive dogmatism.

Of course, these parables teach great moral and spiritual

lessons, and we should regard them in that way; but such a use of them is *application*, and not *interpretation*.

The following outline is our own angle of approach:

1 THE SOWER AND THE SOILS
    Large rejection of the Divine Word
2 THE WHEAT AND THE TARES
    Opposition to the Divine Work
3 THE MUSTARD SEED
    Perversion of the Divine Design
4 THE LEAVEN IN THE MEAL
    Corruption of the Divine Agency
5 THE HID TREASURE
    Believers viewed *individually*; ' bought with a price '
6 THE GOODLY PEARL
    Believers viewed *collectively*: ' bought with a price '
7 THE FISH NET
    Believers viewed *ultimately*: separated from all that is evil

Thus, four reveal the outward facts:

    Rejection. Opposition. Perversion. Corruption:
and three reveal the inward truth:

    Secured. Possessed. Gathered.
The eighth parable (52) includes them all.

(4) TEACHING ON GREATNESS, AND FORGIVENESS (xviii)

This Discourse is lacking in the unity which characterizes the former one (xiii), and it would seem that Matthew here brings together sayings of our Lord on various subjects which were uttered at different times.   Compare the following:

MATTHEW (xviii)	ELSEWHERE	
1-5	Mark ix. 33-37.	Luke ix. 46-48
6	Mark ix. 42	Luke xvii. 2
8, 9	Ch. v. 29, 30.	Mark ix. 43, 45, 47
12-14	Luke xv. 4-7	
15	Luke xvii. 3	John xx. 23
18	Ch. xvi. 19	
21, 22	Luke xvii. 4	

It is difficult, therefore, to present an outline of the Discourse as it is here recorded, but the following may serve as a guide.

This instruction—and that which follows in chapters xix, xx—
was given to the Apostles. Recent events had disclosed the moral
weakness of these men—disloyalty, vain ambition, jealousy,

party spirit; and in view of the coming crisis of Christ's death, resurrection, and departure, He withdrew from preaching to the world that He might teach and train men who would have to carry on after He was gone. That teaching is as applicable to us as it was to them.

(5) DENUNCIATION OF THE PHARISEES (xxiii)

' This,' says Prof. A. B. Bruce, ' is one of the great discourses peculiar to the first Gospel. . . . A weighty, deliberate, full and final statement, in the form of a dying testimony, was to be expected from One who had so often criticised the prevailing religious system in an occasional manner in His Galilean ministry . . . a summing up in the headquarters of scribism of past prophetic censures uttered in the provinces. In such a final protest repetitions might be looked for.'

For the ' repetitions ' referred to, compare the following:

MATTHEW	LUKE	MATTHEW	LUKE
4	xi. 46	25, 26	xi. 39-41
6-7a	xi. 43; xx. 46	27, 28	xi. 44
12	xiv. 11; xviii. 14	29-31	xi. 47, 48
13	xi. 52	34-36	xi. 49-51
23	xi. 42	37-39	xiii. 34, 35

The Discourse falls naturally into three parts:

    (i) Warnings to the Multitude and to the Disciples (1-12)
    (ii) Woes Pronounced on the Scribes and Pharisees (13-36)
    (iii) Wail of the Messiah over the Holy City (37-39)

(i.) *Warnings to the Multitude and to the Disciples* (1-12)

The Lord's most bitter denunciations were addressed to the men whose outward lives were respectable, and whose religious professions were the loudest, that is, against the Scribes and Pharisees.

What He here condemns are, their hypocrisy, ' they say and do not' (2-4); their ostentation, 'all their works they do to be seen of men ' (5); and their pride and love of prominence (6, 7). Against all this the disciples are warned, are reminded of their relation to the Father, and to Christ who is speaking to them, and are told again that the humblest are the greatest (8-12).

(ii.) *Woes Pronounced on the Scribes and Pharisees* (13-36)

The Revised Version omits verse 14, as it is found wanting in some ancient MSS., in some copies of the Vulgate, and in some Versions. It is, however, in other MSS., and undoubtedly was spoken by Christ (Mark xii. 40), so we may assume that there are here eight woes, and not seven only.

As Christ inaugurated His public teaching by pronouncing *eight benedictions* (v. 3-12), so here He closes His ministry by imprecating *eight woes* on the obstinate and unbelieving religious leaders of His day.

> The First is against their Perverse Obstructiveness (13)
> The Second is against their Cruel Rapacity (14)
> The Third is against their Factious Zeal (15)
> The Fourth is against their Moral Stupidity (16-22)
> The Fifth is against their Frivolous Scrupulosity (23, 24)
> The Sixth is against their Superficial Piety (25, 26)
> The Seventh is against their Religious Hypocrisy (27, 28)
> The Eighth is against their Feigned Reverence (29-36)

No more terrible words ever fell from the lips of Jesus. He was great enough to be angry with evil. There is such a thing as 'the wrath of the Little Lamb.'

(iii.) *The Wail of the Messiah over the Holy City* (37-39)

Jesus had spoken these words before (Luke xiii. 34, 35), and they are amongst the most pathetic He ever uttered.

Jerusalem, by a figure of speech, is put for its inhabitants. The points to note are: the Charge against them (37*a*); Messiah's Disappointed Purpose (37*b*); Pronouncement of Judgment (38, 39*a*); and the final Word of Hope (39*b*).

It should be observed that this Discourse has not the formula attached to it which is found in the other five (vii. 28; xi. 1; xiii. 53; xix. 1; xxvi. 1), and so we have not numbered it. The reason for this omission, probably, is that this Discourse was

20

not in the Source which incorporated the other five, presumably the *Logia* of Matthew, referred to by Papias. (See under ' Plan,' and under ' Sources,' pp. 251, 255).

(6) THE GREAT APOCALYPSE (xxiv-xxv)

(i) *Outreach of the Discourse*

This long Discourse is called (*a*) *apocalyptical*, from a Greek word which means to uncover, to unveil, to reveal; (*b*) *eschatological*, from Greek words which mean the doctrine of the last things, and (*c*) *prophetical*, in the sense, not of forth-telling, but of fore-telling, prediction.

Our Lord's first Discourse, the Sermon on the Mount, *looked back*, and this one, His last, *looks on*. Christ is the fulfiller of the past, and the unveiler of the future.

This Discourse forms a whole, divisible into certain parts which are closely related to each other.

Portions of it are recorded in Mark and in Luke, and it is of great importance to observe what they omit or add to what is in Matthew. The following will indicate this in a general way, but there are other variations in detail.

No.	MATTHEW	MARK	LUKE
1	xxiv. 1-3	xiii. 1-4	xxi. 5-7
2	,, 4-14	,, 5-13	,, 8-19
3	,, 15	,, 14*a*	—
4	—	—	xxi. 20
5	xxiv. 16-18	xiii. 14*b*-16	,, 21
6	—	—	,, 22
7	xxiv. 19	xiii. 17	,, 23*a*
8	,, 20-22	,, 18-20	—
9	—	—	xxi. 23*b*, 24
10	xxiv. 23-25	xiii. 21-23	—
11	,, 26-28	—	—
12	,, 29-31	xiii. 24-27	xxi. 25-27
13	—	—	,, 28
14	xxiv. 32-36	xiii. 28-32	,, 29-33
15	,, 37-41	—	—
16	—	xiii. 33, 34	—
17	—	—	xxi. 34, 35
18	xxiv. 42	xiii. 35*a*	,, 36*a*
19	—	,, 35*b*-37	—
20	—	—	xxi. 36*b*
21	xxiv. 43, 44	—	xii. 39, 40
22	,, 45-xxv. 46	—	—

From this it will be seen that seven of these portions are in all the Synoptics (1, 2, 5, 7, 12, 14, 18); that two are peculiar to Mark (16, 19); that six are peculiar to Luke (4, 6, 9, 13, 17, 20); that three are omitted by Luke (3, 8, 10); that one is omitted by Mark (21); that three are peculiar to Matthew (11, 15, 22), and the last of these embraces 53 of the 97 verses of the whole Discourse. (See under 'Discourses in Mark,' p. 216).

Only Matthew records the three parables, the Faithful and Evil Servants, the Virgins, the Talents, and also the Judgment of the Nations (which we have not classed as a parable, see p. 285). Read these 22 parallel passages in the order given if you would get a full impression of this wonderful Discourse.

To give anything like an adequate interpretation of the Discourse would be to traverse the entire field of prophetic truth, of which it furnishes the great salient features.

What Jesus said to His disciples on Olivet is related to all prediction, both in the Old Testament, in the Epistles, and in the Revelation, and these Scriptures severally throw light upon one another.

It would be natural to expect that Christ, in His one Prophetic Discourse, would be comprehensive; that He would confirm past predictions, and would anticipate predictions yet to be made, and that is what we find in this Apocalypse.

In the study of the Discourse, and the parallel passages in Mark and Luke, it is of the utmost importance to get a true perspective. To do this, it must be recognized that here are predictions which relate to near at hand and also to distant events. It is not easy to disentangle these, but we are not left without guidance. (See p. 215).

In the prophetic programme the following *periods* should be distinguished:

The Present Age; Daniel's Seventy Weeks of Years; The Abomination of Desolation; The Great Tribulation, and The Millennium.

And the following *events* should be in view:

The Destruction of Jerusalem by the Romans in A.D. 70; The Manifestation of the Antichrist; The Preaching of the Gospel

of the Kingdom; The Lord's Return to the Earth; The
Judgment of the Nations; The Binding of Satan; The Great
White Throne; The New Heavens and the New Earth.

Of these periods and events the following seven appear in
this Discourse, or in its parallels in Mark and Luke:

1 THE DESTRUCTION OF JERUSALEM BY THE
  ROMANS IN A.D. 70   -   -   -   -   Luke xxi. 20-24
  In this chapter, verses 20, 24 do not occur
  in Matt. xxiv. The armies of verse 20 must
  be those of Titus. Since then the Jews
  have been scattered throughout all nations.
  Jerusalem since then has been ' trodden
  down of Gentiles.'

2 THE PRESENT AGE   -   -   -   -   Matt. xxiv. 4-14
             Mark xiii. 5-13; Luke xxi. 8-19

3 THE PREACHING OF THE KINGDOM GOSPEL   Matt. xxiv. 14;
                     Mark xiii. 10

4 THE ABOMINATION OF DESOLATION
            Matt. xxiv. 15; Mark xiii. 14

5 THE GREAT TRIBULATION   Matt. xxiv. 15-26; Mark xiii. 14-23

6 THE LORD'S RETURN IN GLORY   -   -   Matt. xxiv. 27-31;
            Mark xiii. 24-27; Luke xxi. 25-28

7 THE JUDGMENT OF THE NATIONS   -   -   Matt. xxv. 31-46

(ii) *Occasion of the Discourse*

The Messiah bade farewell to Jerusalem (xxiii. 37-39), and
as He departed He predicted the destruction of the Temple
(xxiv. 1, 2). He and the disciples walked silently to Mount
Olivet and sat down. The disciples then asked Him to explain
what He had said, but they enlarged the subject. On three
matters they wanted instruction:

1 When would the Temple be Destroyed?
2 What would be the Sign of Messiah's Coming?
3 What would be the Sign of the End of the Age?

This Discourse is the answer to these inquiries.

(iii) *Outline of the Discourse*

The main subject is the Return of the Messiah, and it consists
of three parts:

1 The Jews and Christ's Return   -   -   xxiv. 4-44
2 The Church and Christ's Return   -   xxiv. 45-xxv. 03
3 The Gentiles and Christ's Return -   xxv. 31-46

These parts answer to Paul's classification in 1 Cor. x. 32.

In part one, Christ is the *Son of Man* (the designation occurs six times). In part two, He is the *Lord* (the title occurs 15 times, and *Son of Man* not once; xxv. 13*b* is not authentic; see R.V.). In part three, the *Son of Man* (xxv. 31), and the *Lord* (xxv. 37, 44) is the *King* (xxv. 34, 40).

(iv) *Outlook of the Discourse*

(1) xxiv. 4-14. The disciples had inquired about ' the end of the age ' (3), and the Lord takes up this matter (see ' end,' in verses 6, 14). He says that much must happen before the age ends, before He comes (3). These verses (4-14) describe the present age, the period of Christ's absence, and also they tell of the condition of things at the end of the age (14).

(2) xxiv. 15-28. This section is commonly taken to refer to the destruction of Jerusalem by the Romans under Titus, in A.D. 70, but that event is recorded by Luke only (xxi. 20-24). (See the 'Harmony,' on p. 216, item 5). The meaning of this passage, and its parallel in Mark xiii. 14-23, is determined by the reference to 'the abomination of desolation, spoken of by Daniel the prophet.' This reference is to the supremely important prediction in Daniel ix. 24-27. The 'Sevens' in that passage are years (cf. Gen. xxix. 27, 28), so that a period of 490 years (70×7) is in view.

This period is divided into three parts:

' Seven Sevens,' or 49 years (25);
' Sixty-two Sevens,' or 434 years (25);
' One Seven,' or 7 years (27).

It is plainly said what would happen at the close of the first two parts, that is, at the end of 483 years (26). It has been proved that our Lord rode into Jerusalem exactly

483 years, to a day, from the going forth of the decree to rebuild Jerusalem (25), and in that week the Messiah was 'cut off.' (See p. 328: Anderson).

From the crucifixion, Gabriel passes over to the end of this age, omitting the whole of it, and predicts the rise of the Antichrist, 'the Prince that shall come' (26). This Prince will make a 'Covenant' with the Jews for 'one seven,' i.e., for seven years, the last of the 'seventy' (24); but 'in the midst of seven years,' i.e. after 3½ years, he will break the covenant (27) and will introduce 'the abomination' referred to in Matt. xxiv. 15.

The latter half of this 'seven years' is 'the tribulation' (21, 29) of this and other prophetic Scriptures (Psa. ii. 5; Rev. vii. 14).

This section, then (15-28), portrays the latter half of Daniel's seventieth seven of years, 'The Great Tribulation,' the 'Day of Jacob's Trouble.' (See G. H. Pember and Sir Robert Anderson, p. 328).

(3) xxiv. 29-31. It is intimated that at the end of that sad period the Son of Man will come (27), 'immediately after the tribulation of those days' (29), and will come 'with power and great glory' (30).

(4) xxiv. 32-36. These verses tell of the certainty of the event and the uncertainty of the time. This lesson is introduced by the parable of the Fig Tree (32, 33).

(5) xxiv. 37-44. Now follow exhortations to watchfulness, enforced by the history of Noah and the Flood (37-39), and by the parable of the Householder and the Thief (43, 44). This ends the division which relates mainly to the Jews (4-44).

(6) xxiv. 45-51. This section speaks of the responsibility of the Lord's servants during His absence (the designation, Son of Man, is now dropped), and it is applicable to Christians throughout the present age, and may even reach on to the period of the Tribulation.

(7) xxv. 1-30. The reference here, as in chapter xiii, is to the whole sphere of Christian profession in this age, and in its two main aspects of character and service.

The parable of the Virgins (1-13) refers to the former, and that of the Talents (14-30), to the latter. (See under 'Parables,' p. 284).

(8) xxv. 31-46. This, the third of the main divisions of the Discourse, predicts the Judgment of the Gentile Nations. The three classes introduced are, ' sheep,' ' goats,' both of ' all nations ' (32, 33), and the King's ' brethren.'

The time of the Judgment is when Christ returns in glory (31), and the scene of it is the earth.

This Judgment is distinct from the ' Judgment Seat of Christ ' (2 Cor. v. 10; 1 Cor. iii. 12-15), which is for Christians only, and is distinct also from the Judgment of the Great White Throne (Rev. xx. 11-15), which is for individual sinners only.

21

FEATURES OF MATTHEW'S GOSPEL

(i) *Numerical Groups*

' It is often pointed out,' says Dr. Plummer, ' that in this Gospel incidents and sayings are frequently arranged in numerical groups of three, five, or seven.' ' There is nothing fanciful or mystical in these numerical arrangements. Groups of three and of seven are frequent in the Old Testament, and were in use before its earliest books were written.'

' Three is the smallest number which has beginning, middle, and end, and it is composed of the first odd number added to the first even number.'

Certain numbers are employed in the interest of orderly arrangement, and also as an aid to memory.

Jewish-Christian catechists would use them in their catechumen classes, and in this way much narrative and teaching could be held in the mind. Undoubtedly, on this account, Matthew's Gospel can more easily be remembered than any of the others.

The following are instances of the use of certain numbers.

Two.—The Evangelist shows a special fondness of arranging his sub-jects in pairs. This has been noticed already in the Parables of the Kingdom. (See under ' Discourses ' on chapter xiii, p. 299).

The Sower and Soils, and the Wheat and Tares; the Mustard Seed, and the Leaven; the Hid Treasure, and the Goodly Pearl; the Separation of the Wheat from the Tares, and of the Good Fish from the Bad.   •

Other instances are: Two Gadarene Demoniacs (viii. 28); Two Blind Men at Jericho (xx. 29, 30); Two Other Blind Men (ix. 27); Two Feedings of a Multitude (xiv., xv; Luke omits one of these); the mention of an ' ass ' as well as a ' colt ' (xxi. 7); and the Two Cries on the Cross (xxvii. 46, 50).

Three.—There are Three divisions in the Genealogy (i. 17). Each Hebrew letter denoted a number. The purpose of this Genealogy is to show our Lord's descent from David, and so ' David ' is the key name. There are three letters in the Hebrew word ' David,' and the sum of the figures of which they are the equivalents is *fourteen*: D V D. D=4, V=6, D=4: i.e. 4+6+4=14. Accordingly the table is artificially divided into three groups of *fourteen* each.

Three Angel messages to Joseph in dreams (i. 20; ii. 13; ii. 19). Three incidents of the childhood of Jesus: the visit of Magi; the flight into Egypt; and the return (ii). Three Temptations (iv. 1-11). A Triple description of the Messiah's Mission (iv. 23). A Triple illustration (v. 22). In the Beatitudes the word ' blessed ' occurs nine times, so making a treble triplet.

' Your,' occurs three times in chapter v. 16.

Three examples of righteousness: alms, prayer, fasting (vi. 1-18).

Three prohibitions: hoard not, judge not, give not (vi. 19-vii. 6).

Three degrees of prayer earnestness (vii. 7).

Three commands: ask, enter, beware (vii. 7-20).

Three pairs of contrasts (vii. 13, 17, 24-27): broad and narrow ways; good and bad trees; wise and foolish builders.

Threefold ' in Thy name ' (vii. 22). Three miracles of healing: leprosy, palsy, fever (viii. 1-15). Three miracles of power: storm, demoniacs, sin (viii. 23-ix. 8). Three miracles of restoration: health, life, sight (ix. 8-34). (See pp. 257, 264, 288, 289).

Threefold ' fear not ' (x. 26, 28, 31); Threefold ' is not worthy of Me ' (x. 37, 38); Threefold ' what went ye for to see ' (xi. 7-9); Three cities indicted: Chorazin, Bethsaida, Capernaum (xi. 20-23).

Three times' at that season ' (xi. 25; xii. 1; xiv. 1).

Threefold description of state of the Jews: empty, swept, garnished (xii. 44).   Threefold ' verily ' (xviii. 3, 13, 18).

Three classes of eunuchs (xix. 12).   Three parables of warning (xxi. 28-xxiv. 14).   Three questioners: Pharisees, Sadducees, Lawyer (xxii. 15, 23, 35).   Three faculties with which God should be loved: heart, soul, mind (xxii. 37).

The triplet, ' Scribes, Pharisees, hypocrites,' is peculiar to Matthew. It is an interpolation in Luke xi. 44 (A.V.).

In chapter xxiii are numerous triplets: teacher, father, master (8-10); temple and gold, altar and gift, heaven and throne (16-22); mint, dill, cummin, contrasted with judgment, mercy, faith (23); prophets, wise men, scribes (34); and other instances. ' Blood ' occurs three times in chapter xxiii. 35.

Three parables against negligence: the Faithful and Unfaithful Servants; the Virgins; the Talents (xxiv. 45-xxv. 30).

Three men entrusted with Talents (xxv. 15).   Three denials of Peter (xxvi. 69-75).   Three questions of Pilate (xxvii. 17, 21, 22 23).   Three mockeries of the crucified One (xxvii. 39, 41, 44).

Three signs to attest the Messiahship of the crucified One: rending of the veil; earthquake; resurrection of saints (xxvii. 51, 52).

Three women specially mentioned at the Cross (xxvii. 56).   Threefold commission to the Apostles: make disciples, baptize, teach (xxviii. 19, 20).

Look for other instances.

Five.—Matthew has five discourses, each of which is closed with the same formula (vii. 28; xi. 1; xiii. 53, xix. 1; xxvi. 1).

The Sermon on the Mount contains five corrections of inadequate conceptions of the Law, each of them introduced with the words: ' But I say unto you ' (v. 22, 28, 34, 39, 44).

There are two parables in which the number five is prominent: the Five Wise and the Five Foolish Virgins, and the Five Talents which gained other five (xxv. 2, 20).

In chapters xxi, xxii, there are five questions about authority, tribute, resurrection, commandments, and the Son of David.   There are five references to the 'Kingdom of God' (vi. 33; xii. 28; xix. 24; xxi. 31, 43).

Look for other instances.

Seven.—This number is neither as frequent nor as clear as is the number three, but it occurs.

Mark the triad of double sevens in chapter i. 1-16. The seven loaves and seven baskets (xv. 34, 37). Seven times forgiveness (xviii. 21, 22), and seventy times seven.

If chapter xiii. 52 is not admitted as a parable, there are seven in this discourse (but see p. 298).

The R.V. omits verse 14 in chapter xxiii, thus making seven woes (but see p. 305).

There are seven petitions in the Lord's Prayer, and these are divided, as seven so often is, into 3 and 4, 3 being a heavenly, and 4 an earthly number. Thus:

Heavenward { 1 Hallowed be Thy Name } in earth as it is
{ 2 Thy Kingdom come } in heaven
{ 3 Thy will be done }

Earthward - { 1 Give us this day our daily bread.
{ 2 Forgive us our debts, as we for-
{   give our debtors.
{ 3 Lead us not into temptation, but
{ 4 Deliver us from the evil one (vi. 9-13)

The doxology is not in the R.V., but let us keep it in our hearts.

In chapter xii. 45 are seven demons; and in chapter xxii. 25 are seven brethren. Some of the discourses in this Gospel easily fall into seven parts, but this is a matter which cannot be pressed. (See pp. 302, 308).

It is quite clear, therefore, that Matthew deliberately employs certain numbers for certain purposes in composing his Gospel, and this device should enable us the more easily to master its contents.

(ii) *The Limited and Universal Scope of this Gospel*

The significance of Matthew's Gospel will be missed if we fail to see that in tone and outlook it is both particular or Jewish, and Catholic or universal.

The particularistic element is unmistakable. It is evident in references to Jerusalem, to David, and to the Law; it is clear in many of the parables, and in the numerous references to the Old Testament. This element is to be seen also in such expressions as:

'Go not into the way of the Gentiles, and into any
city of the Samaritans enter ye not; but go rather
to the lost sheep of the house of Israel '-   -   -   x. 5, 6
'Ye shall not have gone over the cities of Israel, till
the Son of Man be come'   -   -   -   -   x. 23
'I am not sent but to the lost sheep of the house of
Israel'   -   -   -   -   -   -   -   -   xv. 24
'Ye shall sit upon twelve thrones, judging the twelve
tribes of Israel'   -   -   -   -   -   -   xix. 28
'The Scribes and Pharisees sit in Moses' seat; all
therefore, whatsoever they bid you observe, observe
and do'   -   -   -   -   -   -   -   xxiii. 2, 3

Christ's genealogy is traced through David to Abraham (i. 1),
and this descent is emphasized (xii. 23; xxi. 9, 15; xxii. 42).
Jesus is the Messianic King (ii. 2; xxi. 5; xxvii. 11, 29, 37, 42).
Palestine is 'the land of Israel' (ii. 20, 21); its people is Israel
(viii. 10; x. 6; xv. 34); its towns are 'the cities of Israel' (x. 23),
and God is 'the God of Israel' (xv. 31).

The catholic element is also unmistakable. Matthew records
the coming of the Magi (ii), and the coming to Jesus of the
Roman officer (viii. 5). He also reports what Jesus said about
Tyre, and Sidon, and Sodom, and Nineveh, and favourably
of these in contrast to Chorazin, Capernaum, and Jerusalem
(xi. 20-24; xii. 41).

Mark also the world-wide references in such passages as
viii. 11; xii. 21; xxii. 9; xxiv. 14; xxviii. 19. A world outlook
is evident also in passages which tell of the rejection of the
chosen race (viii. 12; xxi. 41, 43; xxii. 7; xxiii. 38).

Thus the book which opens within the narrow limits of Jewish
thought, ends with the great commission, 'Go ye, and make
disciples of all the nations.'

(iii) *Contrasts*

The dualism which characterizes the whole Bible, that is,
the presence of good and evil, with no third classification, is
prominent in this Gospel.

There are beatitudes and woes (v, xxiii); love and hate; blessing
and cursing; good and evil; the just and the unjust (v. 44, 45);
sincerity and hypocrisy (vi. 1-5, 16-18); God and mammon

(vi. 24); faith and anxiety (vi. 25-34); the broad way and the narrow, good and bad fruit; wise and foolish builders (vii. 13-27); the healthy and the sick; the righteous and sinners (ix. 12, 13); good and bad soil; wheat and tares; good and bad fish (xiii); the humble and the proud (xviii. 1-4); the faithful and the negligent servant (xxiv. 45-51); the wise and the foolish virgins; the diligent and the indolent servants; the sheep and the goats (xxv).

Of course, these contrasts are not peculiar to this Gospel, but they are emphatic in it, and reveal the fundamental facts of revelation and experience which make the Bible necessary.

(iv) *Angles and Aspects*

Matthew's Gospel can be viewed from many angles, each of which presents an aspect of its value.

It is the *Didactic Gospel*, preserving precious discourses of our Lord. It is *the Gospel of the Past Fulfilled*, showing Christ to be the realization and embodiment of the institutions, types, and prophecies of the old dispensation. It is *the Gospel of the True Judaism*, making it clear that the new age preserves all that was vital in the old, while shedding its forms and ceremonies. It is the *Gospel of Sacrifice*, revealing that Christ came, not only to teach, but to die; not only to reign, but to suffer. It is the *Gospel of Judgment*, discriminating character, separating the good from the bad, and condemning the evil. It is also the *Gospel of the Future*. Matthew is the only Evangelist who speaks definitely of the Church (xvi. 18; xviii. 17). The reference in xviii. 17, while applicable to the Christian community, almost certainly meant, at that time, the Jewish Assembly, the Elders and Congregation of the Synagogue; but about the reference in xvi. 18, there can be no doubt.

Peter, divinely illumined, confesses that Jesus is the Messiah, and the Son of God. Christ accepts the verdict, and says that, on that revealed truth (not on Peter) He would build His Church, the Church of the Ephesian and Colossian Epistles (Eph. ii. 20-22; 1 Peter ii. 4, 5), the Church that came into being on the Day of Pentecost.

JESUS THE MESSIAH

I	II	III	IV
The Coming of the Messiah, and His Preparation for Ministry	The Ministry of the Messiah in Word and Deed	The Messiah's Instruction of His Apostles, in View of the Cross	The Final Events of the Messiah's Earthly Ministry
I. I-IV. II B.C. 5-A.D. 27	IV. 12-XVII. 21 A.D. 27-29	XVII. 22-XX. 34 A.D. 29-30	XXI. I-XXVIII. 20 A.D. 30
			THE REJECTION OF HIS CLAIMS xxi. I-xxiii. 39
	ENUNCIATION OF PRINCIPLES iv. 12-vii. 29		The Public Messianic Acts of Jesus - - xxi. I-17
	DEMONSTRATION OF AUTHORITY viii. I-ix. 34		The Final Conflict of the Nation with Jesus - xxi. 18-xxii. 46
HIS ANCESTRY - - i. I-17	PROMULGATION OF MESSAGE ix. 35-xi. 30	While Still in Galilee THEIR RELATION TO HEAVENLY THINGS - xvii. 22-xviii. 35	The Great Indictment and Farewell of Jesus xxiii. I-39
HIS ADVENT - - i. 18-ii. 23	OPPOSITION TO CLAIMS xii. I-xvi. 12		THE CONSUMMATION OF HIS WORK xxiv-xxviii
HIS AMBASSADOR - iii. I-12	REVELATION OF PERSON xvi. 13-20	On the Way to Jerusalem THEIR RELATION TO EARTHLY THINGS xix. I-xx. 34	Christ's Vision of the End - xxiv-xxv
HIS ADVANCE - iii. 13-iv. 11	DECLARATION OF PLAN xvi. 21-28		Christ's Passion for the World xxvi-xxvii
	MANIFESTATION OF GLORY xvii. 1-21		Christ's Victory through the Grave - - xxviii

General Summary

Detailed Outline

(c) The Cross and the Tomb (xxvii. 27-66)
    In the Common Hall (27-31)
    On the Road (31, 32)
    At Golgotha (33-50)
      The First Three Hours:
        9-12 a.m. (33-44)
      The Second Three Hours:
        12-3 p.m. (45-50)
    Phenomenal Happenings (51-56)
    Jesus Buried by Joseph (57-61)
    The Sanhedrin and the Tomb (62-66)
(iii) *Christ's Victory through the Grave* ... xxviii. 1-20
    The Empty Tomb (1-8)
    The Appearance to Certain Women (9, 10)
    The Bribing of the Guard (11-15)
    The Appearance to the Eleven (16, 17)
    The Final Word (18-20)
      A Claim (18)
      A Charge (19, 20a)
      A Promise (20b)

QUESTIONS

Read these carefully once, putting a mark beside those you can answer immediately; then, write the answers to these, and check them by the Studies.

For those which you cannot thus answer refer back to the Studies where the information is, and put the answer down in your own words. This might be done in groups of five, or of ten, to prevent mental indigestion. Do this test well enough to be able to answer orally 75% of the questions.

When you have reached this stage you will want to teach someone else.

1 What was the unanimous belief of the early Church as to the authorship of this Gospel?
2 Who was Papias, when did he live, and what did he say about a Writing by Matthew?
3 Does the testimony of Papias raise a problem, and if so, what is it?
4 What is the supposed relation of Matthew's Gospel to Mark's?
5 What would you say to the objection that the Apostle Matthew would not use material supplied by the non-Apostolic Mark?
6 Has Matthew's supposed use of Mark any bearing on the question of the language in which the Apostle wrote his Gospel?
7 If Matthew wrote his Gospel in Greek, how is the testimony of Papias to be explained?
8 What do you know about the Evangelist Matthew?
9 Is there any evidence in this Gospel that the author was familiar with money values, and has this any bearing on who the author was?
10 At about what date was this Gospel written? Give reasons for your answer.
11 Where, in all likelihood, was this Gospel written?

12 For whom was this Gospel written? Support your answer with evidence.

13 What does the word 'canon' mean, and what do you understand by the claim that Matthew's Gospel is canonical?

14 Who, of the early Church Fathers, affirm the canonicity of this Gospel?

15 What three things does the canonicity of a writing imply?

16 What evidence is there that this Gospel is a compilation?

17 Is there any historical evidence that behind Matthew's and Luke's Gospels there was a document, or documents, of which they knew, and which they used?

18 Is there anything in Matthew's Gospel that supports the theory of a non-canonical source, or sources?

19 What evidence is there that Mark was written before Matthew, and before Luke?

20 Is there any likelihood that in this Gospel is material from other than written sources?

21 Can you name five possible sources which meet in this Gospel?

22 What was the object of this Evangelist in writing a Gospel?

23 Cite evidence that this Gospel is distinctively Jewish in character.

24 Is there any evidence that this Gospel is Messianic in complexion, as none of the others is?

25 On what plan has Matthew constructed his Gospel, and how does it compare with Mark's and Luke's plans?

26 Can any reason be given for Matthew's having adopted the plan which he follows?

27 How would a plan like Matthew's affect the spread of the good news?

28 Approximately, how many words does Matthew use which are not found elsewhere in the New Testament? Name twenty-five such, with references.

29 Say what references Matthew makes to money, and say how these compare with those made by Mark and Luke.

30 How often does the phrase, 'that it might be fulfilled' occur in this Gospel, and what is its significance?

31 What other phrase or phrases occur in Matthew which connect it with the Old Testament?

32 How often does 'the kingdom of heaven' occur in Matthew, and what do you think it means?

33 What is the difference between the 'kingdom of heaven' and 'the kingdom of God'?

34 Name half-a-dozen other words or phrases which are characteristic of this Gospel.

35 How do the Beatitudes of Matt. v, and the Lord's Prayer of chapter vi compare with Luke's record in his chapters vi and xi?

36 If it is true that Matthew absorbs almost the whole of Mark's Gospel, why does he not follow Mark's chronological order?

37 Give instances of how Matthew abbreviates Mark's Record.

38 Give instances of how Matthew amplifies Mark's Record.

39 Name some differences between Matthew's and Mark's way of referring to Christ, also to what He said and did.

40 What difference is discernible between Matthew's and Mark's way of referring to the disciples?

41 Approximately, how many citations from the Old Testament are there in this Gospel, and how many allusions?

42 Name a dozen citations, and a dozen allusions.

43 What do you understand by the ' Septuagint,' or ' LXX '?

44 What, in the main, do these references to the Old Testament in Matthew affirm, and what light is thrown upon the Old Testament by Matthew's use of it?

45 Approximately, how many parables, longer and shorter, are there in this Gospel?

46 How many parables are peculiar to Matthew, and what are they?

47 What do you suppose the lesson is of:
    The Mote and the Beam. The Physician and the Sick. The New Cloth on the Old Garment. The New Wine in the Old Wine-skins. The Unclean Spirit that Returned. The Labourers in the Vineyard. The Mustard Tree. The Leaven in the Meal. The Talents?

48 Name three of our Lord's double parables.

49 Name a dozen figures which are employed in the parables in Matthew.

50 Are any of Matthew's parables distinctively Messianic, and if so, which?

51 Approximately, how many groups of miracles does Matthew refer to?

52 How many specified miracles are there in this Gospel, and which of them are recorded by Matthew only?

53 Which are the miracle chapters in this Gospel, and how many miracles are recorded in them?

54 How may the miracles in the miracle chapters be classified?

55 How may all the miracles recorded by Matthew be classified?

56 What outstanding truth is taught by the miracles?

57 In what ways do the maladies in the miracles represent sin?

58 What proportion, approximately, of this Gospel is devoted to discourses as distinct from narrative?

59 How many major discourses are there in Matthew, and by what formula are they distinguished? Name them.

60 How, is it supposed, was Matthew able to embody these discourses in his Gospel?

61 Is it likely that any of these discourses have been given shape to by Matthew's grouping method? If so, illustrate.

62 Name a dozen striking sentences in the discourses of Jesus.

63 Write down an outline of the Sermon on the Mount.

64 What is the construction of the discourse in Matthew xiii?

65 How many parables are there in chapter xiii; how are they divided, and how may they be related to one another?

66 In what ways have the parables in chapter xiii been interpreted?

67 What is the teaching of Jesus on the subject of Greatness?

68 What is His teaching on Forgiveness, and how does He illustrate it?

69 What is the outstanding feature of the discourse in chapter xxiii?

70 Characterize the woes which Jesus uttered against the Pharisees.

71 Where, elsewhere, is the substance of chapter xxiv to be found?

72 What do you understand by the words ' apocalyptical,' and ' eschato-logical,' and to which of Christ's discourses are these words applicable?

73 What was the occasion of Christ's last discourse?

74 What seven prophetic events are discernible in chapters xxiv, xxv?

75 What are the three main divisions of this last discourse?

76 What do you understand chapter xxiv. 15 to mean?

77 How is Daniel ix. 24-27 related to Matthew xxiv. 15-28?

78 What will take place at the end of the ' Tribulation,' and how are men exhorted to relate themselves to it?

79 To what period does xxiv. 45-xxv. 30 belong?   Give reason for your reply.

80 How are the parables of the Virgins and the Talents related to one another?

81 Who do the Foolish Virgins, and the Unfaithful Servant represent?

82 How do you understand chapter xxv. 31-46, and what other Judgments must be distinguished from this one?

83 Name some of the minor discourses in this Gospel.

84 Do you see anything noteworthy in the Genealogy in chapter i. 1-17?

85 Give eighteen illustrations of Matthew's fondness for triplets.

86 Illustrate this Evangelist's use of fives and sevens.

87 Show from this Gospel that Christ's mission was both limited and universal, was both Jewish and Gentile.

88 Name some of the sharp contrasts which appear in this Record.

89 About what proportion of this Gospel is found nowhere else?

90 Name half-a-dozen of the major passages peculiar to Matthew.

91 Mention half-a-dozen narrative incidents which are found in this Gospel only.

92 In what ways may this Gospel, as a whole, be characterized?

93 How would you distinguish between and explain the discourses in this and in the Fourth Gospel?

94 Why is this Gospel placed first, seeing that it was not the first to be written?

LITERATURE

Bible Dictionaries
    Articles on: Matthew. Gospel of Matthew. Gospels.
        Miracle. Parable. Christ's Teaching.
    Hastings' Bible Dictionary - - - - ——
    Dictionary of Christ and the Gospels - - ——
    International Standard Bible Encyclopædia - ——
'Exegetical Commentary on the Gospel According to
    St. Matthew.' Most valuable - - - Alfred Plummer
'Introduction to the Synoptic Gospels.' Scholarly
    and conservative - - - - - - P. J. Gloag
'A Practical Commentary on the Gospel According to
    St. Matthew.' Full and suggestive - - - James Morison
'St. Matthew's Gospel.' Handbooks for Bible Classes.
    Good - - - - - - - E. E. Anderson
'The Gospel of Matthew.' Very useful   Charles R. Erdman
'St. Matthew.' The Century Bible. Much in little
    compass - - - - - - - W. F. Slater
'St. Matthew.' Cambridge Greek Testament. For
    students of Greek. Very good - - - A. Carr
'The Companion Bible' (Part V) - - E. W. Bullinger
'Parables of the Kingdom' - - G. Campbell Morgan
Commentaries:
    The Speaker's; Ellicott's; Matthew Henry's; Pulpit Commentary;
    Expositor's Greek Testament, on Matthew, by A. B. Bruce (for
    students of Greek); the Speaker's Bible (3 vols.), a mine of homi-
    letical material; H. A. W. Meyer's Commentary
'The Bible Handbook' - - - - Angus and Green
'The Great Prophecies of the Centuries Concerning
    Israel and the Gentiles' - - - - G. H. Pember
'The Great Prophecies of the Centuries Concerning
    the Church' - - - - - - G. H. Pember
'The Coming Prince' - - - Sir Robert Anderson
'Daniel in the Critic's Den' - - - Sir Robert Anderson
'Gnomon of the New Testament.' Vol. I - J. A. Bengel
'The Greek Testament.' Vol. I - - - H. Alford
'The Gospel of St. Matthew.' The Expositor's
    Bible - - - - - - - M. Gibson
'Word Pictures in the New Testament.' Vol. I - A. T. Robertson
'Word Studies in the New Testament.' Vol. I - M. Vincent
'St. Matthew.' International Critical Commentary W. C. Allen
'Jesus in the First Gospel' - - - - J. A. Findlay
'Expository Dictionary of New Testament Words' W. E. Vine
'The Origins of the Gospel According to St.
    Matthew' - - - - - - G. D. Kilpatrick
                              (1947)
'The New Bible Handbook' - - - - (I.V.F., 1947)

THE GOSPELS
VIEWED ANALYTICALLY

ST. LUKE

St. Luke

OUTLINE OF STUDY

St. Luke's Gospel

BEFORE beginning to study this Gospel read it through three times, each time, if possible, at a sitting (about 3 hours):

First time, in Weymouth's *New Testament in Modern Speech*; or in *The Twentieth Century New Testament*; or in Moffatt's Translation.

Second time, in the Authorized Version.

Third time, in the Revised Version, or The Revised Standard Version (1946).

In these three readings use no books, but only the text of the Gospel. Having done this, do the reading prescribed in the following Studies. The system is that in each Study a part of the Guide be read, and a portion of the Gospel. Where possible the reading is related to the part of the Guide assigned for reading, as, for example, in the Parables and Miracles; but this cannot always be done, as, for example, in the parts relating to sources, date, and other subjects; but read carefully the part of the Guide which is appointed, and the portion of the Gospel which is attached to it, whether these are related or not.

The object is twofold: first, to familiarize oneself with the text of the Gospel by repeated reading; and secondly, to follow the various Studies which constitute the Guide.

I

KEY PLAN OF READING

FORTY-TWO STUDIES

2

THE AUTHOR

ASSUMING that Luke wrote the Gospel with which his name is associated (see Div. A, Part II, Sec. 5, 'Authorship,' p. 134) we should learn what we may about him.

(i) References

He is referred to by name three times only (Col. iv. 14: Phile. 24; 2 Tim. iv. 11), and these references tell us that he was a 'physician,' that he was one of Paul's 'fellow labourers,' and that he was with Paul during his last imprisonment.

In addition to these three references we may learn much indirectly about Luke from the Acts. The writer of this Book is the author of the Gospel (Acts i. 1; Luke i. 1-4), and he is included in what are called the 'we' sections in the Acts (xvi. 10-17; xx. 4-15; xxi. 1-18; xxvii. 1-xxviii. 16), and being the Apostle's fellow-traveller and physician he was a witness of and a sharer in the events recorded in these sections.

(ii) Nationality

It is practically certain that Luke was a Gentile. In Col. iv. 10-14, six persons send greetings, and they are divided into three and three. The first three, Aristarchus, Marcus, and Justus are, Paul says, 'of the circumcision' (11). The second three are mentioned separately, and almost all critics are agreed that the implication is that Luke was not a Jew. The affirmation in Scofield's Bible that he was a Jew is not accompanied by any proof, and indications, other than this reference, are against it.

Furthermore, it would seem that Luke was a Greek, and not a Roman, for in Acts xxviii. 2, 4, he speaks of the inhabitants of Malta as 'barbarians,' and his companion, Paul, distinguishes such from 'Greeks' in Rom. i. 14.

Being a Greek, Luke cannot be identified with Lucius, a kinsman of Paul, and therefore a Jew (Rom. xvi. 21); nor can he be identified with 'Lucius of Cyrene,' of Acts xiii. 1, for the author of the Acts would not so describe himself.

(iii) Birthplace

It cannot be said for certain where Luke was born, but what

evidence there is, points to Antioch in Syria. An ancient reading (Codex Bezæ) of Acts xi. 27, 28, says; 'When we were gathered together one of them stood up and said,' which implies that Luke was associated with Antioch during the stay of Barnabas and Saul there. Eusebius speaks of 'Luke being by birth of those from Antioch.' Jerome plainly speaks of 'Luke the physician of Antioch.' The Acts seems to confirm this view. The only deacon whose locality is named, is 'Nicolas, a proselyte of Antioch,' whom Luke would know (vi. 5), and from a number of passages it is evident that the author of the Acts was well acquainted with that city (xi. 19-27; xiii. 1; xiv. 19, 21, 26; xv. 22, 23, 30, 35; xviii. 22).

(iv) Conversion

Certainty cannot be reached as to when, where, or through whom Luke was brought to a saving knowledge of Christ, but it is not improbable that Paul was his spiritual father. Prof. Ramsay's idea that Luke and Paul never met before the incident at Troas is very unlikely, even if it could be proved that the 'man' of the vision was Luke (Acts xvi. 8-10).

(v) Education

The author of this Gospel and of the Acts was a man of genuine culture, as his use of his materials shows. For his medical studies he would go to Alexandria, Athens, or Tarsus, and most probably to Tarsus. At that city was a school of philosophy and literature unequalled at that time, and there Luke would receive a good classical education, and would study medicine. Without doubt Paul attended the university there (Acts ix. 11; xi. 25), and it is quite likely that he and Luke were contemporary students, and that then and there began their life-long friendship.

(vi) Profession

Luke was a medical doctor. This is proved, as we shall see, by his use of medical terms in both his Writings, as well as by the declaration of Paul, in Col. iv. 14. It seems clear that he practised medicine in Malta. In Acts xxviii. 8, we are told that Paul 'cured' the father of Publius miraculously, and in verse 9 we read that others 'who had infirmities . . . came and were

healed.' The word ' healed ' is not the same as ' cured,' in verse
8, and Prof. Ramsay says it means ' received medical treatment,'
whether cured or not (cf. *iaomai* (8) and *therapeuō* (9), whence
therapeutics). When Paul speaks of him as a 'beloved physician'
he certainly implies that he knew him in that capacity. Probably
he saved Paul's life in the frequent attacks of malaria which the
Apostle had.

(vii) Paul's Companion

When Luke first met Paul we do not know, but we do know
that he travelled with him. The ' we ' sections of the Acts,
already referred to, prove this (p. 334). During the second
missionary journey he accompanied the Apostle from Troas to
Philippi (A.D. 51, 52). During the third missionary journey
(A.D. 58) he was again at Philippi with Paul, and went with him
to Jerusalem, and it is clear that he was with him during the
voyage and shipwreck until the arrival in Rome (A.D. 60-61).
(Acts xvi. 10-17: xx. 4-15; xxi. 1-18: xxvii. 1-xxviii. 16: Col.
iv. 14: Phile. 23, 24: 2 Tim. iv. 11).

(viii) Versatility

Dr. Plummer characterizes Luke as ' the most versatile of all
the New Testament writers,' and Dr. .W N. Simcox, says that
of all these writers, ' his mind, if not the greatest, was the most
many-sided.' Notwithstanding that so little is said of him, we
are made aware of a man who was at once a historian, a medical
doctor, a psychologist, an artist, a poet, a mystic, a traveller,
a missionary, a devoted friend, and a great Christian.

We can understand Renan speaking of his Gospel as ' the
most literary of the Gospels,' and ' the most beautiful book in
the world.'

(ix) Conjectures

Certain theories concerning Luke are here mentioned as of
passing interest, and while possibility can be claimed for some
of them, others are contradicted by what is recorded in his
Gospel, or the Acts. It has been supposed that he was a personal
disciple of Jesus, that he was one of the Seventy, that he was one
of the two to whom our Lord spoke on the Emmaus Road, that
he wrote the Epistle to the Hebrews, that he was one of the Greeks

who desired to see Jesus (John xii), that he was the ' man '
whom Paul saw in a vision at Troas (Acts xvi), that he had been
a slave in the household of Theophilus, a wealthy Government
official in Antioch, that Theophilus had trained him as a physician,
that he got converted and told his master, who became interested,
and at last was himself converted; that the first thing Theophilus
did as a Christian was to give Luke his freedom, and that this
accounts for the introduction of Theophilus in both the Gospel
and the Acts (i. 1; i. 3); that he (Luke) is 'the brother' whose
praise in the gospel was spread through all the Churches, and
that Titus, also a Greek (Gal. ii. 3), was his brother (2 Cor.
viii. 18; xii. 18, where ' the brother ' has the force of ' his
brother ').

A tradition, traceable from the 6th century, says that Luke
was a painter, and in the 13th century he appears as the patron
saint of painters. There is no evidence that he painted with a
brush, but he certainly has done so with his pen, and has exercised
a profound influence upon Christian art by his life-like por-
trayals of character in his Gospel and the Acts. Dr. W. N.
Simcox says that, "'Christian painters have mainly derived their
inspiration ' from Luke; that ' he is the Father of Christian art,
from the Good Shepherd wrought on chalices, or in the cata-
combs of the second and third centuries, through the Madonnas
and Holy Families of the Middle Ages, down to Michael Angelo's
' Conversion of St. Paul,' and Raphael's ' Deliverance of St.
Peter.'"

3

FOR WHOM WRITTEN

INTERNAL evidence shows that Luke the Greek wrote his
Gospel for Gentiles in general, and for Greeks in particular.
(See under 'Nationality,' and 'Design,' pp. 134, 334, 344).
Explanations of Jewish customs and localities are given, which
Jews would not have needed, such as, ' Capernaum, *a city of
Galilee*' (iv. 31); ' the country of the Gadarenes, *which is over
against Galilee*' (viii. 26); ' the Mount *that is called the Mount
of Olives*' (xxi. 37); ' the feast of unleavened bread—*which is*

called the Passover' (xxii. 1); ' Arimathæa, *a city of the Jews*' (xxiii. 51); ' Emmaus, *which was from Jerusalem about three score furlongs*' (xxiv. 13).

The genealogy of Jesus is traced to Adam, the father of the human race, and not, as in Matthew, to Abraham only, the father of the Hebrews (Matt. i. 1; Luke iii. 38). The reigns of Roman Emperors are employed for marking the date of Jesus' birth, and of John's preaching (ii. 1; iii. 1). The Mosaic Law is not much appealed to as of interest to his readers. Luke has no parallels to Matt. v. 17, 19, 20, 21, 27, 31, 33; xii. 5-7, 17-20; xv. 1-20. References to the Old Testament are only about thirty fewer than in Matthew, but the difference lies in the character and purpose of the references. (See under 'The Old Testament in Luke,' p. 363). Little is said about the fulfilment of prophecy, a subject which would not greatly interest Gentile readers.

Other evidences of the Gentile complexion of this Gospel are found in Luke's use of ' Master,' or ' Teacher,' for ' Rabbi '; of ' lawyer ' for ' Scribe '; of ' verily,' or ' of a truth,' for ' amen ' (which occurs only 8 times in this Gospel, but 32 times in Matthew, cf. Luke iv. 25; ix. 27; xii. 44; xxii. 59); of ' lake ' for ' sea ' of Galilee.

His fondness for the word ' people ' (*laos*), where the other Synoptists use 'multitude' (*ochlos*). The figures are: '*people*,' in Mark, 3 times; in Matt., 15 times; in Luke (Gospel), 36 times, and in Acts, 48 times: '*multitude*,' in Mark, 38 times; in Matt., 50 times; in Luke (Gospel), 41 times, and in Acts, 22 times: i.e ' people ' occurs in Luke twice as often as in Matt. and Mark together; and ' multitude,' twice as often in Matt. and Mark together as in Luke.

His fondness, also, for some indefinite expression like ' many,' a word which he uses in the singular 18 times in the Gospel, and 22 times in the Acts, and in the plural, 30 times in the Gospel, and 27 times in the Acts.

To like purpose are such expressions as, ' a light to lighten *the Gentiles*'; He shall bring peace on '*the earth* good will to *men*,' and that ' repentance and remission of sins shall be preached in His name among *all nations* ' (ii. 32; ii. 14; xxiv. 47);

and also the fact that Luke substitutes Greek for Hebrew names such as ' Zealot ' for ' Canaanite ' (vi. 15; Acts i. 13; cf. Matt. x. 4), and ' skull ' for ' Golgotha ' (xxiii. 33; cf. Matt. xxvii. 33).

It is worthy of note, also, that Luke characterizes demons as ' unclean,' or ' wicked ' (iv. 33; viii. 2), because Gentiles believed in good demons, whereas, to Jews, all demons were evil.

In Matt. vii. 23, the word ' lawlessness ' (*anomia*) is used which represents the Jewish point of view, but in the parallel passage in Luke xiii. 27, the word 'injustice' (*adikia*) is used, which represents the Greek point of view.

Another evidence that Luke wrote for Gentiles is the noticeable absence of many Hebrew or Aramaic words which are found in the other Gospels, as, for example, *Abba*, *Boanerges*, *Gabbatha*, *Hebrew*, *Emmanuel*, *Ephphatha*, *Corban*, *Messiah*, and *Hosanna* (Index IV).

Full honour is done in this Gospel to the Mosaic Law as binding on Jews (ii. 21, 27, 39; v. 14; x. 26; xvi. 17, 29-31; xvii. 14; xviii. 20), yet only 33 verses are given to the Sermon on the Mount as against 111 verses in Matthew.

Luke says little about the fulfilment of prophecy, which would not greatly interest Gentile readers (iii. 4; iv. 21; xxi. 22; xxii. 37; xxiv. 44).

Having regard to the general character of this Gospel, we may assume that the Theophilus to whom it is dedicated was a Gentile, and probably a Greek, though the name, Dr. Plummer says, ' was common among Jews,' and if tradition can be trusted, he was not a native or inhabitant of Palestine.

4

DATE AND PLACE OF WRITING

THE dates claimed for the writing of Luke's Gospel range from A.D. 58 to A.D. 135. There are three main theories which circle round the dates, respectively, A.D. 100, A.D. 80, and A.D. 60. The late date, A.D. 95-105, is claimed on the assumption that Luke made use of the *Antiquities* of Josephus, which was written in A.D. 94. Of this, however, there is no proof, and this theory must be abandoned. The intermediate date, A.D. 75-80, is influentially supported, but there are strong considerations against it, of which the following are the main;

> The Acts was written after the Gospel (Acts i. 1), and the history of the Acts does not take us beyond A.D. 63, when Paul was a prisoner in ' his own hired house ' in Rome (xxviii. 30). Between A.D. 63 and A.D. 75 great events occurred: for example, the burning of Rome in A.D. 64, the martyrdom of Paul, about A.D. 68, and the destruction of Jerusalem in A.D. 70. If Luke did not write his Gospel before A.D. 70, why did he say nothing about these events? So far from doing so his report of Christ's prediction, in Luke xxi. 24, more than implies that Jerusalem was still standing.

The simplest explanation of Luke's silence in the Acts about all these events, is that he finished the Book in A.D. 63, before they took place. That being so, his Gospel must have been written before this date (Acts i. 1), and probably a year or two earlier, sometime between A.D. 58 and A.D. 62.

This result throws light on the *place of writing*. Luke was with Paul during the latter's captivity in Cæsarea, A.D. 58-60, for the ' we,' ' us,' and ' our,' in Acts xxvii, following on the Cæsarean trial of xxiii. 33-xxvi, as also in xxi. 8, include the writer of the Book, who was Luke, who also was with Paul at Rome in A.D. 61-63 (Acts xxviii. 16). The Gospel, then, could have been written either at Cæsarea or at Rome, or commenced at Cæsarea and finished at Rome between A.D. 58 and A.D. 63.

Other cities regarded as possibly the places in which this Gospel was written are Alexandria, Ephesus, and Corinth, but the fact is, we have not sufficient data upon which finally to decide between these various theories.

<h1 style="text-align:center">5</h1>

<h2 style="text-align:center">CANONICITY</h2>

MARCION, a heretic who flourished in the middle of the second century, wrote a gospel which, it is now generally admitted, was but a mutilated edition of Luke's Gospel. It is valuable as a witness to the circulation of the third Gospel at that time. Justin Martyr also knew and used this Gospel early in the second century. Irenæus declares that ' Luke, the companion of Paul, put down in a book the gospel preached by him (Paul).' Tatian's *Diatessaron*, Harmony of the Gospels, included Luke (A.D. 140). The Muratorian Fragment (A.D. 170-200), a catalogue of the New Testament books, begins with Luke, as the ' third Gospel,' implying the other two. Its statement is: ' The third book of the Gospel is that according to Luke. Luke, the well-known physician, wrote it in his own name according to (the general) belief, after the ascension of Christ, when Paul had associated him as one zealous for correctness (i.e. one who took pains to find out the facts).' (See chap. i. 1-4).

Tertullian, and Clement of Alexandria, make many references to this Gospel, assigning it to Luke. Origen affirms that this Gospel was written for the sake of those Greeks who turned to the faith.

Gregory Nazianzen says that, 'Luke, the companion of Paul, wrote the wonderful works (in his Gospel) for Greeks.' Jerome says that, ' The third (Gospel) is that of Luke, the physician, a native of Antioch in Syria.'

There are in all some sixteen witnesses, distributed all over the Church, who, before the end of the second century, testify either directly or indirectly to the existence and use of Luke in the Church as authoritative Scripture, in addition to the witnesses of the third and fourth centuries. The evidence, therefore, of the canonicity, that is, of the genuineness and authenticity of this Gospel is incontrovertible. (See pp. 142, 171, 172).

6

LUKE'S SOURCES

THE matter of sources of the Gospels of Matthew and Luke is of great interest, and although all questions which can be asked may not be answered, internal evidence will carry us some way towards finding an answer to them.

A careful reading of Luke's Gospel will reveal certain facts:

(*a*) There is much material common to him and Mark, not found in Matthew.

(*b*) There is material common to him and Matthew, not found in Mark.

(c) There is material common to him, and Matthew, and Mark.

(d) There is material which is not found in Matthew, or Mark.

(e) There is material which is of a definitely Hebrew complexion, notably chaps. i-ii, in contrast to the prevailing tone of the Gospel.

These facts constitute a problem which, perhaps, will never be fully solved, but about them some things can be said with a large degree of certainty or probability.

(1) Luke himself tells us that he had at his disposal ' many ' narratives relating to Jesus' life and ministry (i. 1-4). He does not specify these sources, and probably they have all been lost, unless Mark be excepted.

(2) It is certain that Luke used Mark's Gospel, nearly, if not altogether, in the form in which we have it. It is estimated that about 320 of Mark's 661 verses (R.V.) are found in Luke, that is, nearly half of Mark (Harnack says three-fourths). (See under 'Mark in Luke,' p. 356).

(3) Some material common to Luke and Matthew, other than what is derived from Mark, leads to the conclusion that they both used another source, which is known as Q (German, *Quelle*, source), or the *Logia* of Matthew, referred to by Papias.

Q contained some narrative, but chiefly, it would seem, discourses of our Lord. (See under 'Synoptic Problem,' p. 83). Of this hypothetical document there must have been more than one form, because the material common to Matthew and Luke is used very differently by the Evangelists.

(4) Luke i-ii, and iii. 23-38, must have been derived from a distinct source, and perhaps a written source, as the conclusions in i. 80; ii. 40; ii. 52, would seem to indicate; and such memoirs or memoranda may well have existed in certain families, or assemblies.

The Bethlehem Narrative must have come from those whose story it is, and probably from Mary, Jesus' mother, as Prof. Ramsay argues.

(5) There is another, and probably an oral source, which may be referred to as Herodian. Luke displays a special knowledge of matters relating to the Court of the Herods (iii. 1, 19; viii. 3; ix. 7-9; xiii. 31; xxiii. 7-12; Acts xiii. 1). ' Here,' says Dr. Sanday, ' we have a glimpse of a circle from which St. Luke

probably got his account of the quarrel and reconciliation between Pilate and Herod, as well as of the circumstances of the death of Herod Agrippa I, and of the facts relating to Agrippa II ' (xxiii. 7-12; Acts xii. 20-23; xxv. 13).

(6) In the two Lucan ' Interpolations,' the ' Lesser,' vi. 20-viii. 3; and the ' Greater,' ix. 51-xviii. 14, are passages from Mark and from Q, but there are also passages which do not seem to have been derived from any of the foregoing sources; e.g. the Widow's Son at Nain; the Ministering Women; the Seventy; the Good Samaritan; Mary and Martha; the Rich Fool; the Slaughtered Galileans; the Dropsical Man Healed; the Lost Coin; the Two Brothers; the Rich Man and Lazarus; the Samaritan Leper; the Unrighteous Judge; the Pharisee and the Publican, and other bits; and there is the large section, xxii. 14-xxiv. 17. It is natural to ask from whence Luke got this information.

Luke's association with Paul brought him into touch with many who could tell him much. We have referred to Mark, and to Mary, but Luke probably met some of the Twelve, and Jesus' brethren, and while he was with Paul at Cæsarea, in A.D. 58-60, he would be sure to meet Philip the Evangelist and his daughters (Acts xxi. 8-19; most probably another source), and, perhaps, Zacharias, Elisabeth, Martha, and Mary, and others of that circle who would be able to give him information more or less at first hand.

In his Preface (i. 1-4) Luke speaks, not only of drawn-up narratives, but also of ' eye-witnesses and ministers of the Word,' who orally delivered what they knew. It is not at all improbable that the material so far unaccounted for in this Gospel was derived from those with whom Luke was in contact while he was in Palestine.

It is likely, then, that Luke had six or seven sources: (1) the ' many ' narratives referred to in his Preface; (2) Mark's Gospel; (3) Q, or the *Logia* of Matthew; (4) Mary, the mother of Jesus, and her immediate circle; (5) information derived from the Court of Herod; (6) what he learned from many important people he must have met in Palestine by virtue of his association with Paul, and probably (7) Philip of Cæsarea and his daughters.

At all events, we may be assured from what we know of Luke that he had authentic sources of information open to him, and that he used them with the utmost care. He went about his work systematically, under the guidance of the Holy Spirit, and the result reveals a man of culture, an accurate historian, and a devoted Christian.

7

LUKE'S DESIGN

THE design of Luke in writing this Gospel may be regarded as twofold, *immediate* and *ultimate*. He tells us in his Preface that his *immediate* design was that Theophilus might know the certainty of the things concerning which he was instructed (i. 4); but his *ultimate* design was to convey these truths to those who had no instruction, and that those he had in view were Greeks is demonstrated by the contents and form of the Gospel. (See under 'For Whom Written,' p. 337).

If it be true that Matthew wrote for Jews, Mark for Romans, and Luke for Greeks, we must look for the proof, first in the character and need of these peoples respectively, and then in the adaptation of the Gospels to the respective requirements of these peoples.

The Jew was characterized by deep religious feeling, the Roman by strength of will for action, and the Greek by great intellectual power. To the Greek people belong Homer, and Plato, and Aristotle, and Demosthenes. They were the representatives of universal humanity, and the great ideal towards which they worked was the perfect man. But by making their gods in their own image, they deified vice as well as virtue, and so their religion was unspiritual and debasing, and their hearts were restless and despairing (Acts xvii. 16, 21, 23).

The presentation of Christ in Luke's Gospel has in view these characteristics and needs. The human perfection which they sought is here manifested, their intellectual hunger could here be satisfied, and their religious aspirations may now be purified and realized. The presentation of Christ in Matthew, and in Mark, would not answer to the Greek need, but in Luke the answer is given in the Perfect Man.

8

LUKE'S PLAN

LUKE'S plan is plainly stated in his Introduction (i. 1-4), every word of which is important for a right understanding of his task. Mark carefully these fifteen particulars.

(1) Before Luke wrote his Gospel others had made attempts to rehearse in orderly fashion, ' *to draw up a narrative,*' of various ' *matters* ' about Christ.

(2) ' *Many* ' had undertaken so to do.

(3) These efforts did not include the apocryphal gospels, which did not appear until later.

(4) The subject of these narratives was ' *matters* ' connected with Christ's life which had been brought to a close.

Instead of ' *which are most surely believed,*' read ' *which have been carried through to the end,*' i.e. ' *fulfilled.*'

(5) The details of these narratives had been handed down, ' *delivered,*' by persons who had been ' *eye-witnesses* ' of them, and who orally proclaimed them, ' *having been attendants of the word.*' The writers of these narratives were not, therefore, themselves Apostles.

(6) Luke himself had not been an eye-witness of the things narrated, but had heard this oral witness, for, he says, ' they delivered them to *us.*'

(7) The testimony of these eye-witnesses began with the ministry of Jesus, for this is what is meant by the words, '*all the time . . . beginning from*' (Acts i. 21, 22).

(8) As Luke had fuller knowledge, in consequence of wide research of these things, than they had who drew up the first narratives, and than they had who first proclaimed the ' matters,' he felt justified in recording his researches. He says, ' *it seemed good also to me to write.*'

(9) For the writing of such a Record, Luke made careful preparation. With the aid of the ' many ' narratives, the tradition of the ' eye-witnesses,' and the testimony of the ' ministers of the Word,' he mentally followed along by the side of these events, or, as he says, ' *I have gone carefully over them all myself from the very beginning* '—(Moffatt).

(10) This examination and investigation he made ' *accurately* ' (*akribōs*), that is, in great detail.

(11) This ' accurate ' investigation he made ' *from the first,*' that is, from the commencement of the Sacred Story in the annunciations and births of John and Jesus, and not, as in the ' many narratives ' from the commencement of Jesus' ministry only.

(12) Luke's narrative is with ' *method* ' (*kathexēs*), that is, it is in chronological sequence for the most part.

(13) The record was made for one addressed as 'excellent Theophilus,' lover of God, probably a Gentile holding a high office.

(14) This Theophilus had been orally '*instructed*' (*katēcheō*), in these things about Christ, that is, he had been, as the word means, a *catechumen*.

(15) Luke writes his narrative in order that Theophilus might '*fully know*' (*epiginōskō*), how true were the things which he had been taught; that he might know 'the certainty of the words,' that is, might know that the faith which he had embraced had 'an impregnable historical foundation.'

This compact Introduction is written in the purest literary style of the Greeks, and awakens our highest expectations. No other of the Evangelists has a historical introduction. While it is certain that Luke had Mark's Gospel beside him when he wrote, or, at any rate, before the Gospel assumed its present form, it is most unlikely that he refers to it among the 'many' of verse one. So well did Luke do his work that these other narratives were altogether supplemented, and perished.

9

LUKE'S STYLE AND DICTION

DR. PLUMMER says that Luke 'is the most versatile of all the New Testament writers.' This verdict is based partly on the fact of Luke's two styles, Greek and Hebrew. His Preface (i. 1-4) is in remarkably elegant and idiomatic Greek, and this suddenly changes to the intensely Hebraistic Greek of chaps. i-ii, and, thereafter, he returns to the Greek style, less pure than that of the Preface, and not without Hebrew elements. But this is a matter for the scholar, rather than for the general reader of the Gospel, though it is worth noting in passing.

What is of general interest and should be carefully considered is the richness of Luke's vocabulary. In the Grimm-Thayer Lexicon it is shown that 312 words are found in this Gospel only in all the New Testament, but as 52 of these are doubtful, and 11 occur in the Old Testament references from the LXX, we can say that 249 are definitely peculiar to Luke. There are another 61 words which occur in this Gospel and the Acts only, and these together make a total of 310 words which are Luke's alone. Sir John Hawkins, in his *Horae Synopticae*, makes the number of words peculiar to the Gospel only 251, and to the Gospel and Acts only 58, a total for Luke of 319. Dr. S. Davidson lists more than 420 words which are used by Luke, and not by the other Evangelists.

The following examples of the richness of Luke's vocabulary are given in order to create interest and promote research.

Those who know Greek will naturally have an advantage here, but others who know how to use a Greek Lexicon will be able to gain much.

(I)

i 42 ' Spake-out (*anaphōneō*), from *ana*, up, and *phōneō*, to utter a sound or cry, to speak up; followed by ' with loud voice,' *phōnē*, sound, and *megas*, intense, great.

ii 8 ' Lodging-in-the-fields ' (*agrauleō*), from *agros*, field, and *aulē*, court. The shepherds were making the field their court.

ii 38 ' Gave thanks ' (*anthomologeomai*), from *homologeō*, to speak the same thing, with *anti*, over against, which means that Anna *kept repeating* her thanksgiving.

vi 30; xii. 20. ' Ask again,' ' Require ' (*apaiteō*), from *aiteō*, to ask, and *apo*, from; hence, to ask back, to reclaim, to exact something that is due as the soul entrusted to a man by God for a time. In the first passage the goods were ' taken-away,' and so were due to him from whom they were taken.

vi 35 'Hoping for nothing again ' (*mēden apelpizō*), from *mēden*, nothing, or no one, and *apo*, from, and *elpizō*, to hope. The A.V. reads, ' hoping for nothing again,' which means that the lender expects nothing back; but the R.V. reads, ' never despairing,' and in the margin, ' despairing of no man,' which means that we are not to give up hope of getting the money back.

vii 41; xvi 5. ' Debtors ' (*chreōpheiletēs*), from *chreos*, a debt; *opheiletēs* one who owes, from *opheilō*, to owe: hence, one who owes a debt.

ix 51 ' Receiving (him) up ' (*analēpsis*), from *ana*, up, and *lēpsis*, a receiving; derived from *analambanō*, used of the Ascension in Acts i. 2, 11, 22; 1 Tim. iii. 16.

x 31, 32. 'Pass by on the other side ' (*antiparerchomai*), from *anti*, opposite, over against, *para*, by, and *erchomai*, to come, or go, and so, to pass by on the opposite side; a double compound.

xi 8 ' Importunity ' (*anaideia*), from *aidōs*, a sense of shame, but with the negative *a*(n), i.e. shamelessness, impudence, effrontery, and so here, of one persisting in his entreaty.

xi 53 ' To make (him) speak ' (*apostomatizō*), from *apo*, from, and *stoma*, the mouth. In this passage it means that the Scribes and Pharisees enticed Jesus to speak by questioning Him.

xiii 7 'Dresser of one's vineyard' (*ampelourgos*), from *ampelos*, a vine, and *ergazomai*, to work.

xiv 10 'Go-up' (*prosanabainō*), from *pros*, suggesting 'motion to' a place, *ana*, up, and *bainō*, to go, or to come, and so the meaning in this setting is 'come, move up.'

xiv 12 'Bid again' (*antikaleō*), from *kaleō*, to call, summon, invite, with *anti*, over against, in turn, i.e. to invite again, a return invitation.

xiv 13, 21. 'Maimed' (*anapēros*), from *ana*, up, and *pēros*, lame, i.e. lame all the way up. (W.H., *anapeiros*).

xvii 18 'Stranger' (*allogenēs*), from *allos*, another, and *genos*, a race, sprung from another race: spoken of a Samaritan: to Jews, an alien (cf. John iv. 9).

xix 15 'Had gained by trading' (*diapragmateuomai*). In verse 13, the verb *pragmateuomai* occurs, meaning to transact business, to trade, and in verse 15, *dia* is prefixed, meaning thoroughly, or earnestly, and so, to undertake a business for the sake of gain.

xxi 34 'Surfeiting' (*kraipalē*), from *kras*, the head, and *pallō*, to toss about, and so giddiness and headache caused by drinking wine to excess (see Trench's Synonyms).

xxii 31 'May sift' (*siniazō*), to winnow; *sinion* means a sieve. In this passage it has the significance of 'by inward agitation to try one's faith to the verge of overthrow.'

xxiv 17 'That ye have' (*antiballō*), from *ballō*, to throw, with *anti*, over against and so meaning 'to throw in turn, back and forth like a ball, from one to another: a beautiful picture of conversation as a game of words'; to exchange.

(2)

From these examples it will be seen how picturesque is Luke's language. The following are a few more examples of the more than 300 words used by Luke only.

Declaration (i. 1): *eye-witness* (i. 2): *beckon* (i. 22): *to trouble* (i. 29): *old age* (i. 36): *make signs to* (i. 62): *commune, or noise abroad* (i. 65: vi. 11): *custom* (ii. 27): *do violence to,* or *put in fear* (iii. 14): *keep* (iv. 10): *feast* (v. 29: xiv. 13): *continue all night* (vi. 12): *laugh* (vi. 21, 25): *cease* (vii. 45): *fall asleep* (viii. 23): *to glister* (ix. 29): *be awake* (ix. 32): *depart* (ix. 33): *foaming* (ix. 39): *plough* (ix. 62): *bag,* or *purse* (x. 4: xii. 33: xxii. 35, 36): *wipe off* (x. 11): *pour in* (x. 34): *be gathered thick together* (xi. 29): *cast into* (xii. 5): *division* (xii. 51): *shut* (xiii. 25): *cost* (xiv. 28): *finish* (xiv. 29, 30): *murmur* (xv. 2: xix. 7): *riotous* (xv. 13): *ring* (xv. 22): *accuse* (xvi. 1): *deride* (xvi. 14: xxiii. 35): *full of sores* (xvi. 20): *lighten,* or *shine* (xvii. 24: xxiv. 4): *chief among the publicans* (xix. 2): *austere* (xix. 21, 22): *lay even with the ground* (xix. 44): *be very attentive,* or *hang on* (xix. 48): *spy* (xx. 20): *depart out* (**xxi.** 21): *perplexity* (xxi. 25): *men's hearts failing them* (xxi. 26): *without, in the absence of* (xxii. 6, 35): *to desire* (xxii. 31): *cast* (xxii. 41): *be the more fierce* (xxiii. 5): *give sentence* (xxiii. 24): *meat* (xxiv. 41).

Without a knowledge of what words are peculiar to Luke, anyone with any literary taste can appreciate what Renan has said is 'the most beautiful book that has ever been written.'

10

MATERIAL PECULIAR TO LUKE'S GOSPEL

THE material peculiar to Luke's Gospel is a phenomenon which is difficult to account for, and much ingenuity has been at work in an attempt to explain the facts.

First of all take your copy of Luke and mark the following passages in some way which will enable you to see at a glance what parts of the Gospel are peculiar to its author.

(1)

1	i.	I-iii. 2, 10-15, 18-20, 23-38
2	iv.	1a, 13b, 14a, 15-30
3	v.	1-11, 17, 29, 39
4	vi.	11a, 12b, 17a, 24-26, 33, 34, 37b, 38a
5	vii.	3-5, 7a, 10-17, 20, 21, 29, 30, 36-50
6	viii.	1-3, 12b
7	ix.	9b, 18a, 28b, 29a, 31-33, 43, 44a, 51-56, 61, 62
8	x.	1, 8b, 17-20, 25, 26, 28-42
9	xi.	5-8, 12, 27, 28, 37, 38, 40, 41, 44, 45, 46a, 53, 54
10	xii.	1, 2, 13-21, 29b, 32, 33a, 35-38, 41, 47-50, 52, 54, 57
11	xiii.	1-17, 22, 23, 25-27, 31-33
12	xiv.	1-14, 15-25, 28-33
13	xv.	3, 6-32
14	xvi.	1-12, 14, 15, 19-31
15	xvii.	3-5, 7-19, 20-22, 28-30, 32, 37a
16	xviii.	1-14, 31b, 34, 43b
17	xix.	1-28, 37, 39-44
18	xx.	16b, 20b, 26a, 35a, 36b, 38b, 39
19	xxi.	12a, 18, 19, 21b, 22, 23b, 24, 25b, 26a, 28, 34-38
20	xxii.	3a, 15, 16, 19b, 20, 27-32, 35-38, 40, 43-45a, 48b, 49, 51, 53b, 61a, 65-68
21	xxiii.	2, 4-15, 22b, 23, 27-31, 34a, 39-43, 45a, 46, 48, 51a, 53b, 56
22	xxiv.	4a, 5b, 7, 8a, 11-53

These references may be divided into three classes, (*a*) where only part of a verse is peculiar; of these there are 46; (*b*) where single verses are peculiar; of these there are 58; (c) where two verses or more in a group are peculiar; of these there are 44 groups, representing 527 verses. The result is 46 + 58 + 527 = 631 verses in Luke which contain matter which is peculiar to his Gospel. Other results have been arrived at by those who have investigated the matter, and absolute accuracy is difficult to reach, but for our purpose it is not necessary so long as we are aware of the main facts. In Luke there are 1149 verses (R.V.), so that the matter which is peculiar amounts to half the Gospel plus 56 verses.

(2)

An examination of the above passages will show that Luke alone has preserved for us some of the most beautiful treasures which we possess. He alone records the Infancy narratives, in two long chapters; the Call of Simon to Apostleship; the Anointing of Jesus by the Sinner; the Mission of the Seventy; the Story of Martha and Mary; the Signs of the Times; the Conditions of Discipleship; the Conversion of Zacchæus; the Two Robbers; the Walk to Emmaus; the Farewell Instructions and Departure.

Luke alone records seven occasions on which Jesus prayed (iii. 21; v. 16; vi. 12; ix. 18; ix. 29; xi. 1; xxiii. 34, 46). He alone records the questions put by the people to John the Baptist, and his answers (iii. 10-14); Jesus' weeping over Jerusalem (xix. 39-44); the bloody sweat (xxii. 44); the fact of Jesus being sent to Herod (xxiii. 7-12); and Jesus' words to the women who followed Him to the Cross (xxiii. 27-31).

Luke also supplies numerous details not recorded by Mark or Matthew. For example: the sixfold date (iii. 1); illuminating additions to what Mark and Matthew tell us (e.g. iii. 15, 21; iv. 13, 15, 40, 42; v. 1, 12, 15, 16; vi. 12; viii. 47); Jesus' supplication for Peter (xxii. 31, 32): 'Pray that ye enter not into temptation' (xxii. 40, 46); and phrases such as 'praising God,' 'blessing God,' 'give praise,' and 'God's servant.' (Pages 371, 372).

(3)

In addition to these, six of the twenty *Miracles* which Luke records are in this Gospel only (but see pp. 286, 287, 553, 554, App. A).

1 Miraculous Draught of Fishes	v. 1-11
2 Raising of the Widow's Son	vii. 11-17
3 Healing of a Woman who had a Spirit of Infirmity	xiii. 10-17
4 Healing of a Man with Dropsy	xiv. 1-6
5 Cleansing of Ten Lepers	xvii. 11-19
6 Healing of Malchus' Ear	xxii. 49-51

The other fourteen Miracles recorded by Luke, which are found in one or more of the other Gospels, are as follows:

7 Cure of a Man with an Unclean Spirit ... iv. 33-37
(Mark i)

8 Healing of Simon's Mother-in-law ... ... iv. 38, 39
(Mark i; Matt. viii)

9 Healing of a Leper ... ... v. 12-16
(Mark i; Matt. viii)

10 Healing of a Paralytic ... ... v. 18-26
(Mark ii; Matt. ix)

11 Healing of a Man with a Withered Hand ... vi. 6-11
(Mark iii; Matt. xii)

12 Healing of the Servant of a Centurion ... vii. 1-10
(Matt. viii)

13 Stilling the Storm ... ... viii. 22-25
(Mark iv; Matt. viii)

14 Cure of a Gadarene Demoniac ... ... viii. 26-39
(Mark v; Matt. viii)

15 Healing of the Daughter of Jairus ... viii. 41, 42, 49-56
(Mark v; Matt. ix)

16 Healing of an Afflicted Woman ... ... viii. 43-48
(Mark v; Matt. ix)

17 Feeding of the Five Thousand ... ... ix. 12-17
(Mark vi; Matt. xiv; John vi)

18 Cure of a Demoniac Boy ... ... ix. 38-43
(Mark ix; Matt. xvii)

19 Cure of a Deaf and Dumb Demoniac ... xi. 14
(See pp. 553, 554) (Matt. xii)

20 Healing of Blind Men near Jericho ... ... xviii. 35-43
(Mark x; Matt. xx)

(4)

Of the thirty-five *Parables* in this Gospel, nineteen are here only:

1 The Two Debtors	vii. 41-43
2 The Good Samaritan	x. 30-37
3 The Friend at Midnight	xi. 5-8
4 The Rich Fool	xii. 13-21

The other sixteen Parables recorded by Luke, which are found in one or more of the other Gospels, are as follows:

These Miracles and Parables should be named and numbered in your Bible. If your margin is narrow, you could mark M.1 and P.1, and so on, and for those which are peculiar to this Gospel I suggest M.1. p., P.1. p, and so on. (App. A, B, C).

The Resurrection Appearances are not here included as miracles, but without doubt, they are such.

It is observable that these ' peculiar passages ' in Luke complete the Synoptic history at the beginning, middle, and end of the life of our Lord.

II

OMISSIONS IN LUKE'S GOSPEL

WHETHER at the beginning, when Luke began to write his Gospel, or later, when he had made the first draft of it, he came into possession of Mark's Gospel, and made much use of it, it is clear that some 368 of his 1149 verses are Marcan. (See under 'Luke's Use of Mark,' p. 359). Matthew also had Mark's Gospel, and he made a larger use of it than Luke did. The question, therefore, arises: Why did Luke omit so much of Mark? That he did omit much is the more remarkable because his Gospel is more comprehensive than any of the others: he begins the story earlier, and carries it on further than any of the others, if Mark xvi 9-20 (the disputed conclusion) (see under 'Authenticity,' p. 176) be excluded: yet, this notwithstanding, for some reason or another, he passes over much of the Mark material which he had at his disposal.

First of all, observe what of Mark he does omit. We see, under ' Mark in Luke,' p. 356, that of the 121 sections into which Mark's Gospel is divided, Luke omits 41. What are these 41 about?

1	Mk. i. 1-20 -	An examination of the details of these verses, with the parallels in Luke, can lead to the conclusion that Luke, while following Mark's order here, has another and a fuller source, Q, no doubt.
2	Mk. iii. 19b-30	Christ is accused of being in league with Beelzebub. For iii. 22-27, cf. Luke xi. 14, 15, 17, 18, 21, 22.
	Mk. iv. 26-29	Parable of the Seed Growing Secretly.

23

4 Mk. iv. 30-32   Parable of the Mustard Seed. This occurs in Luke xiii. 18, 19; but in quite a different connection, and seems to show that Christ used this parable on various occasions, though, of course, it may be an instance of postponed reference to Mark.

5 Mk. iv. 33, 34   Parable of the Leaven in the Meal. This appears in Luke xiii. 20, 21; and what is said of the Mustard Seed parable applies here also.

6 Mk. vi. 1-6 -   Jesus' last visit to Nazareth. The visit of Luke iv. 16-30, was His first visit of the ministry.

7 Mk. vi 17-29   The Story of Herod, Herodias, and John the Baptist.

8-17 Mk. vi. 45-viii. 26. This is what is called the Great Omission. The subject matter of it is: Jesus walking on the sea; His ministry in the Plain of Gennesaret; the question of ceremonial washings, and the teaching based upon it; the healing of a Syrophœnician's daughter; ministry in Decapolis; the healing of a deaf mute; feeding of the four thousand; an encounter with Pharisees near Dalmanutha; the leaven of the Pharisees, and of Herod; a blind man healed at Bethsaida.

The events of vi. 45-viii. 26 represent 74 verses in Mark, omitting vii. 16 (R.V.), almost exactly one-ninth part of his 661 verses (R.V.). Attempts have been made to account for this omission, and the most feasible is that given by Sir John Hawkins. Summarily it is this: that Luke was under the necessity to economize in his use of the much material at his disposal on account of his limited space, and in his selection his method was to avoid, as far as possible, sayings and incidents which were the same or similar to such as he already had in what he had written before he came across Mark. For instance, Luke had the miracle of the Feeding of the Five Thousand, and so omits Mark's miracle of the Feeding of the Four Thousand. Again, Luke had the record of one storm on the Lake (viii. 22-25), and did not see the necessity for recording another storm (Mark vi. 45-52). And again, Luke had in his narrative a general account of miracles worked on the Plain of Gennesaret (vi. 17-19), and so omitted another similar group of miracles recorded in Mark (vi. 53-56).

You will observe that these three incidents occur in the section of Mark which Luke omits (vi. 45-viii. 26), and in a similar way

Sir John Hawkins accounts for the omission of the other incidents in this section.

But the question will arise: What need was there to economize space? Dr. Sanday points out that 'the Gospels were written each on a separate roll of papyrus. These rolls were, roughly speaking, of the same average length. The blank rolls of papyri were cut into convenient lengths, ranging within certain accepted limits.'

This fact is in the word *tomē*, which does not mean a ponderous book, but a section or part of a book (Gr. *tomos*), from the Greek *temnō*, to cut, and so, a length of papyrus. Sir F. Kenyon has calculated that the Gospel of Mark would take up about 19 feet of an average-sized roll; Matthew, about 30 feet; John, about $23\frac{1}{2}$ feet, and Luke, from 31 to 32 feet, so that without this Marcan section (vi. 45-viii. 26) Luke's is the longest of the Gospels. Dr. Sanday says: ' I have little doubt that St. Luke was conscious of being pressed for space, and that he felt obliged to economize his materials. (See p. 444).

18	Mk. viii. 31-33	Jesus' Rebuke of Peter.
19	Mk. ix. 9-13	Descent from the Mount of Transfiguration.
20	Mk. ix. 41-50	The Matter of Offences (cf. Luke xiv. 34; xvii. 2).
21	Mk. x. 1	Jesus' Departure from Galilee.
22	Mk. x. 2-12	The Matter of Divorce.
23	Mk. x. 35-45	The Ambitious Request of the Sons of Zebedee.
24	Mk. xi. 12-14	The Barren Fig Tree.
25	Mk. xi. 19-26	The Withering of the Fig Tree.
26	Mk. xii. 28-34	The Question of a Scribe (cf. Luke x. 25-27).
27	Mk. xiii. 18-23	The Tribulation, and False Christs.
28	Mk. xiii. 33-37	The Parable of the Porter.
29	Mk. xiv. 3-9	The Anointing at Bethany (cf. Luke vii. 36-38).
30	Mk. xiv. 27, 28	' I will smite the shepherd.'
31	Mk. xiv. 51, 52	Incident of the Young Man.
32	Mk. xiv. 55-64	The Trial before the High Priest.
33	Mk. xv. 3-5	The Silence of Jesus before His Accusers.
34	Mk. xv. 6-11	Jesus or Barabbas.
35	Mk. xv. 16-20	The Mockery of the Soldiers.
36	Mk. xv. 23	Jesus Offered Wine Mingled with Myrrh.
37	Mk. xv. 24b, 25	Distribution of Garments, and Hour of Crucifixion.
38	Mk. xv. 27-30	The Two Crucified Robbers.
39	Mk. xv. 34b-36	Jesus' Cry at the Ninth Hour.
40	Mk. xv. 44, 45	Pilate Gives Jesus' Body to Joseph.
41	Mk. xvi. 1	Two Marys Bring Spices to the Tomb.

These 41 omissions of Mark in Luke represent 252 verses, (253 in A.V., but vii. 16; ix. 44, 46; xi. 26, and xv. 28 are not in the R.V.), or nearly two-fifths of Mark's Gospel. Most of the passages omitted by Luke are used by Matthew. The remarks under Mark vi. 45-viii. 26, above, explain also the omissions by Luke of most of the 41 passages (p. 354).

If we had had Luke's Gospel only, how much we would have lost! The Annunciation to Joseph; Visit of the Magi; Flight into Egypt; Christ's Early Judæan Ministry recorded in John i. 19-iv. 42; the Nobleman's Son; the Infirm Man at the Pool of Bethesda; the Unpardonable Sin; Two Blind Men Healed; a Dumb Demoniac Cured; Jesus' Rejection at Nazareth; Jesus Walking on the Water; Discourse on the Bread of Life; Eating with Unwashen Hands; the Syrophœnician's Daughter; Feeding the Four Thousand; Demand of Pharisees and Sadducees for a Sign; the Blind Man near Bethsaida Healed; the Coin in the Fish's Mouth; Discourses recorded in John vii-viii; the events of John ix-xi; Request of James and John; the Anointing by Mary of Bethany; Cursing of the Fig Tree; the Events of John xii; the Upper Room Events—the Passover, Conversations and Prayer; the Young Man with the Linen Garment; the Protest of the Twelve that they would never leave Jesus, and their subsequent desertion; the Threefold Repetition of the Slumber of the Three Disciples in Gethsemane; the Bribing of the Roman Guard; the Appearances of Jesus to Thomas, to Seven Disciples by the Sea of Galilee, and to the Apostles on a Mountain in Galilee.

On the other hand, if we had not had Luke's Gospel, how much we would have lost. (See under 'Material Peculiar to Luke,' p. 349).

12

MARK IN LUKE

THAT, of the Four Gospels, Mark was written first must be regarded as a settled fact. In the A.V. of Mark's Gospel there are 678 verses, but the last twelve of chapter xvi are disputed, and vii. 16, ix. 44, 46, xi. 26, xv. 28, are omitted in the R.V., so that there are only 661 undisputed verses. Not fewer

than 368 of these (see under 'Luke's Use of Mark,' p. 358), and
perhaps as many as 395, are found with little or no change in
Luke, that is, nearly the half of Mark, and the proportion of the
actual words of Mark in Luke is 53 per cent., a larger percentage
than in Matthew.

The following Table shows where Mark is, and is not, found
in Luke:

	Mark	Luke		Mark	Luke
1	i. 1-20	—	45	viii. 27-30	ix. 18-21
2	i. 21-28	iv. 31-37	46	viii. 31-33	—
3	i. 29-31	iv. 38, 39	47	viii. 34-ix. 1	ix. 23-27
4	i. 32-34	iv. 40, 41	48	ix. 2-8	ix. 28-36a
5	i. 35-39	iv. 42-44	49	ix. 9-13	—
6	i. 40-45	v. 12-16	50	ix. 14-29	ix. 37-43a
7	ii. 1-12	v. 17-26	51	ix. 30-32	ix. 43b-45
8	ii. 13, 14	v. 27, 28	52	ix. 33-37	ix. 46-48
9	ii. 15-17	v. 29-32	53	ix. 38-40	ix. 49, 50
10	ii. 18-22	v. 33-39	54	ix. 41-50	—
11	ii. 23-28	vi. 1-5	55	x. 1	—
12	iii. 1-6	vi. 6-11	56	x. 2-12	—
13	iii. 7-12	vi. 17-19	57	x. 13-16	xviii. 15-17
14	iii. 13-19a	vi. 12-16	58	x. 17-22	xviii. 18-23
15	iii. 19b-30	—	59	x. 23-27	xviii. 24-27
16	iii. 31-35	viii. 19-21	60	x. 28-31	xviii. 28-30
17	iv. 1-9	viii. 4-8	61	x. 32-34	xviii. 31-34
18	iv. 10-12	viii. 9, 10	62	x. 35-45	—
19	iv. 13-20	viii. 11-15	63	x. 46-52	xviii. 35-43
20	iv. 21-25	viii. 16-18	64	xi. 1-11	xix. 28-38
21	iv. 26-29	—	65	xi. 12-14	—
22	iv. 30-32	—	66	xi. 15-18	xix. 45-48
23	iv. 33, 34	—	67	xi. 19-26	—
24	iv. 35-41	viii. 22-25	68	xi. 27-33	xx. 1-8
25	v. 1-13	viii. 26-33	69	xii. 1-12	xx. 9-19
26	v. 14-17	viii. 34-37	70	xii. 13-17	xx. 20-26
27	v. 18-20	viii. 38, 39	71	xii. 18-27	xx. 27-38
28	v. 21-34	viii. 40-48	72	xii. 28-34	—
29	v. 35-43	viii. 49-56	73	xii. 35-37a	xx. 41-44
30	vi. 1-6	—	74	xii. 37b-40	xx. 45-47
31	vi. 7-13	ix. 1-6	75	xii. 41-44	xxi. 1-4
32	vi. 14-16	ix. 7-9	76	xiii. 1, 2	xxi. 5, 6
33	vi. 17-29	—	77	xiii. 3-13	xxi. 7-19
34	vi. 30-44	ix. 10-17	78	xiii. 14-17	xxi. 20-23
35	vi. 45-52	—	79	xiii. 18-23	—
36	vi. 53-56	—	80	xiii. 24-27	xxi. 25-27
37	vii. 1-13	—	81	xiii. 28-32	xxi. 29-33
38	vii. 14-23	—	82	xiii. 33-37	—
39	vii. 24-30	—	83	xiv. 1, 2	xxii. 1, 2
40	vii. 31-37	—	84	xiv. 3-9	—
41	viii. 1-10	—	85	xiv. 10, 11	xxii. 3-6
42	viii. 11-13	—	86	xiv. 12-16	xxii. 7-13
43	viii. 14-21	—	87	xiv. 17	xxii. 14
44	viii. 22-26	—	88	xiv. 18-20	xxii. 21-23

	Mark	Luke		Mark	Luke
89	xiv. 22-25	xxii. 19, 20	106	xv. 23	—
90	xiv. 27, 28	—	107	xv. 24a	xxiii. 33b
91	xiv. 29-31	xxii. 33-34	108	xv. 24b, 25	—
92	xiv. 26, 32-42	xxii. 39-42, 45, 46	109	xv. 26	xxiii. 38
			110	xv. 27-30	—
93	xiv. 43-50	xxii. 47-53	111	xv. 31, 32	xxiii. 35-37
94	xiv. 51, 52	—	112	xv. 33, 34a	xxiii. 44
95	xiv. 53, 54	xxii. 54	113	xv. 34b-36	—
96	xiv. 55-64	—	114	xv. 37	xxiii. 46
97	xiv. 65-72	xxii. 63-65, 55-60	115	xv. 38-41	xxiii. 45b, 47-49
98	xv. 1	xxiii. 1	116	xv. 42, 43	xxiii. 50-52
99	xv. 2	xxiii. 3	117	xv. 44, 45	—
100	xv. 3-5	—	118	xv. 46	xxiii. 53
101	xv. 6-11	—	119	xv. 47	xxiii. 55
102	xv. 12-15	xxiii. 20-25	120	xvi. 1	—
103	xv. 16-20	—	121	xvi. 2-8	xxiv. 1-8
104	xv. 21	xxiii. 26			
105	xv. 22	xxiii. 33a			

Of the 121 sections into which Mark is here divided, 41 are not in Luke, and specially noticeable is the Great Omission of Mark vi. 45-viii. 26, 74 or 75 verses. (See under 'Omissions of Luke,' pp. 353-355).

It should also be observed that in what Luke has of Mark, the latter's order of events is largely followed, which is not the case in Matthew.

Attention should be paid, also, to what is Non-Marcan in Luke. (See next page).

13

LUKE'S USE OF MARK

A COMPARISON of the Gospels of Luke and Mark will show that the latter was not the former's primary source, as it was Matthew's. Dr. Streeter has pointed out that if one eliminates from Luke all the Marcan passages, *what remains is a unity*, and that this residuum is the first sketch of Luke, or what he calls *Proto-Luke*.

The theory is that Luke's special material and Q constituted the first stage or draft of his Gospel, and that coming across Mark he took into his record what served his purpose, with the result that much less of Mark is found in Luke than in Matthew, and the blocks of the Non-Marcan and the Marcan material alternate.

Scholars differ as to precisely how much of Mark there is in Luke, but the following table may be regarded as substantially correct, and it illustrates how Luke used Mark.

NON-MARCAN			MARCAN	
VERSES	PASSAGES	TOTAL	PASSAGES	VERSES
200	i. 1-iv. 30	200	—	—
—	—	14	iv. 31-44	14
11	v. 1-11	11	—	—
—	—	44	v. 12-vi. 16	44
86	vi. 17-viii. 3	86	—	—
—	—	103	viii. 4-ix. 50	103
350	ix. 51-xviii. 14 (omit xvii. 36, R.V.)	350	—	—
—	—	29	xviii. 15-43	29
27	xix. 1-27	27	—	—
—	—	11	xix. 28-38	11
6	xix. 39-44	6	—	—
—	—	102	xix. 45-xxii. 13	102
7	xxii. 14-20	7	—	—
—	—	3	xxii. 21-23	3
9	xxii. 24-32	9	—	—
—	—	2	xxii. 33-34	2
4	xxii. 35-38	4	—	—
—	—	27	xxii. 39-65	27
24	xxii. 66-xxiii. 19 (omit xxiii. 17, R.V.)	24	—	—
—	—	7	xxiii. 20-26	7
7	xxiii. 27-33	7	—	—
—	—	5	xxiii. 34-38	5
5	xxiii. 39-43	5	—	—
—	—	21	xxiii. 44-xxiv. 1-8	21
45	xxiv. 9-53	45	—	—
781		1149		368

This diagram shows that there are in Luke 1149 verses (R.V.), and of these 781 are Non-Marcan, and 368 are Marcan, that is, less than one third of Luke represents Mark.

An unsolved problem is why Luke omits Mark vi. 45-viii. 26, seventy-four verses (vii. 16 not in R.V.). Of the several ways of explaining the omission, the most likely to be correct is that Luke, being under the necessity to economize space (see p. 354), deliberately passed over the section ' because its contents seemed to him unsuitable for his Gospel, or at least not so suitable for it as other materials which he had ready for use' (Hawkins), and at that we must leave it.

In considering Luke's use of Mark three things should be observed:

(a) that Luke does not always follow Mark's order of events:
(b) that Luke does not always reproduce Mark's words and phrases, even where it is evident that Mark is before him:
(c) that here and there in the Marcan portions, Non-Marcan bits occur, and in the Non-Marcan portions, Marcan bits occur.

14

LUKE AND PAUL

(1)

FOR a long time Luke was the most intimate companion of Paul, and this cannot but have had an influence upon the thought and outlook of the Evangelist, and this influence is abundantly evident in his Gospel, which exhibits the liberal and spiritual nature which characterized Paul's preaching and teaching.

Luke, like Paul, emphasizes *faith*, and *repentance*, and *mercy*, and *forgiveness*. Tertullian, who says that Mark was the ' interpreter' of Peter, says that Paul was the 'illuminator' of Luke; that is, he enlightened him as to the essential character of the gospel. And Irenæus writes: 'Luke, the companion of Paul, put down in a book the gospel preached by him' (Paul), and in another place: ' That Luke was inseparable from Paul and his fellow-labourers in the gospel is shown by himself '; and Origen says that Luke's is ' the Gospel commended by Paul.' To like purpose are statements by Jerome, Eusebius, and others.

In Luke's Gospel, as in Paul's Epistles, are emphasized the universality of salvation, and the boundlessness of Divine grace.

' It is tolerably certain,' says Dr. Maurice Jones, ' that it was from St. Paul that St. Luke learnt the true significance of the Cross of Christ '; and Dr. Samuel Davidson says that ' the mind of the Evangelist was impregnated with the views and phraseology of Paul '; and that Luke's Gospel ' presents remarkable coincidences with Paul's Epistles in language and ideas, which could not have been accidental. The writer must have known and used Pauline literature.'

The word 'grace' occurs about 146 times in the New Testament, and only 21 of these are outside of Paul's and Luke's Writings. The word 'faith' is found in about 243 places, and only 53 times outside of Paul's and Luke's Writings.

Sections of Luke which are in peculiar accordance with Paul's 'gospel' are, iv. 16-30; vii. 36-50; xv. 1-32; xix. 1-10; xxiii. 39-43; but there are also more detailed correspondences. Many scores of words are common to the Lucan and Pauline literature, and many passages are parallel.

Sir John Hawkins shows that 32 words are found in Matthew and Paul only; 22 in Mark and Paul only; 21 in John and Paul only; but 103 in Luke and Paul only (in each case with or without Acts also); that is, words found in Luke and Paul only are as many as are found in the other three Gospels together, plus 28.

(2)

The following references illustrate the similarity between Paul's thought and language and Luke's. These references should be carefully examined.

LUKE	PAUL	LIKENESS
iv. 22	Eph. iv. 29; Col. iv. 6	Gracious words. Speech with grace
iv. 32	1 Cor. ii. 4	Word, power. Speech, power
vi. 36	Rom. xii. 1; 2 Cor. i. 3	Mercies of God. Father of mercies
vi. 39	Rom. ii. 19	Blind, lead. Guide, blind
vi. 48	1 Cor. iii. 10	Laid the foundation
viii. 12	Rom. i. 16; 1 Cor. i. 21	Belief and Salvation
viii. 13	1 Thess. i. 6	Receive the Word
viii. 15	Col. i. 10, 11	Fruitfulness with patience
ix. 56	2 Cor. x. 8	Not to destroy
x. 7	1 Tim. v. 18	Labourer worthy of his reward
x. 8	1 Cor. x. 27	Eat what is set before you
x. 20	Phil. iv. 3	Names in heaven. In Book of Life
x. 21	1 Cor. i. 19, 27	The wise and the prudent
xi. 7	Gal. vi. 17	Trouble me not. Let no man trouble me
xi. 41	Tit. i. 15	Things clean. Things pure.
xi. 49	1 Thess. ii. 15	Persecuting the prophets
xii. 35	Eph. vi. 14	Having loins girded
xii. 42	1 Cor. iv. 2	A faithful steward
xviii. 1	2 Thess. i. 11; Col. iv. 12	Praying always
xxi. 34	1 Thess. v. 3-8	Soberness; sudden destruction

Such parallels could easily be multiplied, and the student should seek out others. The full force of the comparisons can be felt only by those who examine the passages in the original, observing the general style and structure of sentences, as well as the terms and ideas peculiar to both; but without a knowledge of Greek, much treasure can be found.

(3)

The following are some of the more than a 100 words which are used by Paul and Luke only:

Adēlos - -	'Which appears not'; 'uncertain' (Luke xi. 44; 1 Cor. xiv. 8).
Aichmalōtizō	'Lead away captive'; 'bring into captivity' (Luke xxi. 24; 2 Cor. x. 5).
Anathema -	'Curse'; 'accursed'; 'anathema' (Acts xxiii. 14; Rom. ix. 3; 1 Cor. xvi. 22).
Analiskō -	'Consume' (Luke ix. 54; Gal. v. 15; 2 Thess. ii. 8).
Analuō - -	'Return'; 'depart' (Luke xii. 36; Phil. i. 23).
Anoētos -	'Fool'; 'unwise'; 'foolish' (Luke xxiv. 25; Rom. i. 14; Gal. iii. 1, 3).
Biōtikos -	'Of this life'; 'pertaining to this life' (Luke xxi. 34; 1 Cor. vi. 4).
Diaireō -	'Divide' (Luke xv. 12; 1 Cor. xii. 11).
Endoxos -	'Glorious'; 'honourable' (Luke xiii. 17; Eph. v. 27; 1 Cor. iv. 10).
Exousiazō -	'Exercise authority upon'; 'have power of' (Luke xxii. 25; 1 Cor. vii. 4).
Zōgreō -	'Catch'; 'take captive' (Luke v. 10; 2 Tim. ii. 26, 'take alive').
Kateuthunō -	'Guide'; 'direct' (Luke i. 79; 1 Thess. iii. 11).
Krataioō	'Wax strong'; 'be strong' (Luke i. 80; 1 Cor. xvi. 13).
Methē - -	'Drunkenness' (Luke xxi. 34; Gal. v. 21).
Metadidōmi	'Impart'; 'give' (Luke iii. 11; Rom. xii. 8).
Hosiotēs -	'Holiness' (Luke i. 75; Eph. iv. 24).
Pagis - -	'Snare' (Luke xxi. 35; Rom. xi. 9).
Panoplia -	'All armour'; 'whole armour' (Luke xi. 22; Eph. vi. 11, 13).
Plērophoreō -	'Things which are most surely believed'; 'make full proof of' 'be fully known' (Luke i. 1; 2 Tim. iv. 5, 17).
Presbutēs -	'Old man'; 'aged' (Luke i. 18; Philem. 9).
Spoudaiōs -	'Instantly'; 'diligently' (Luke vii. 4; Tit. iii. 13).

Hupōpiazō	-	'Weary'; 'keep under' (Luke xviii. 5; I Cor. ix. 27).
Philarguros	-	'Covetous' (Luke xvi. 14; 2 Tim. iii. 2).
Phronēsis	-	'Wisdom'; 'prudence' (Luke i. 17; Eph. i. 8).
Charitoō	-	'Highly favoured'; 'make accepted' (Luke i. 28; Eph. i. 6).

These words will give some idea of the suggestiveness of the phrases and words which are peculiar to Paul and Luke, the theologian and the scientist, the divine and the historian. What Peter was to Mark, Paul was to Luke, only Paul had a much abler medium to work upon, and Paul himself was much abler than Peter. Paul and Luke made a great combination.

15

THE OLD TESTAMENT IN LUKE'S GOSPEL

IT is commonly affirmed that there are comparatively few references in Luke to the Old Testament, in contrast, for instance, with the number of such references in Matthew's Gospel; but this is not correct. There are about 130 references, i.e. quotations and allusions, in Matthew; and between 90 and 100 in Luke (p. 338).

The difference between Luke's and Matthew's references lies in their character and purpose. Matthew, being the Gospel for the Jews, builds heavily on the Old Testament, and often such expressions occur as, 'that it might be fulfilled,' 'which was spoken,' 'was said,' 'this was done that' (see Matthew, under 'Sources,' 'Style and Diction,' pp. 253, 275), but in Luke little is said about the fulfilment of prophecy, because that would not greatly interest Gentile readers (iii. 4; iv. 21; xxi. 22; xxii. 37; xxiv. 44), and all but the first of these references occur in sayings of Christ addressed to Jews.

In Matthew it is not difficult to distinguish between citations and allusions, but in Luke it is not so easy, because many of the Old Testament references are mere reproductions, more or less conscious, of the words of Scripture.

The Old Testament references in Luke may be classified as (a) direct citations; (b) direct references, but not citations; and (c) echoes of Old Testament passages.

(a) Direct Citations

Of these there are about two dozen, and of these about a score are in utterances of Jesus.

	LUKE	O. T.		LUKE	O. T
1	i. 17	Mal. iv. 5, 6	13	viii. 9, 10	Isa. vi. 9, 10
2	i. 37	Gen. xviii. 14 (lxx)	14	x. 26, 27	Deut. vi. 5
			15	x. 27	Lev. xix. 18
3	ii. 23	Exod. xiii. 2, 12	16	xiii. 27	Psa. vi. 8
4	ii. 24	Lev. xii. 8	17	xviii. 20	Exod. xx. 12-14
5	iii. 4-6	Isa. xl. 3-5	18	xix. 46a	Isa. lvi. 7
6	iv. 4	Deut. viii. 3	19	xix. 46b	Jer. vii. 11
7	iv. 8a	Deut. vi. 13	20	xx. 17	Psa. cxviii. 22, 23
8	iv. 8b	Deut. x. 20; 1 Sam. vii. 3	21	xx. 28	Deut. xxv. 5
9	iv. 10, 11	Psa. xci. 11, 12	22	xx. 41-44	Psa. cx. 1
10	iv. 12	Deut. vi. 16	23	xxii. 37	Isa. liii. 12
11	iv. 18, 19, 21	Isa. lxi. 1, 2	24	xxiii. 34b	Psa. xxii. 18
12	vii. 27	Mal. iii. 1	25	xxiii. 46	Psa. xxxi. 5

(b) Direct References, but Not Citations

	LUKE	O. T.		LUKE	O. T.
1	i. 8-10	Lev. xvi. 17	25	xiv. 11	Prov. xxix. 23; Ezek. xxi. 26
2	i. 15	Num. vi. 3	26	xvii. 14	Lev. xiii. 2
3	i. 32	Psa. cxxxii. 11; Isa. ix. 7	27	xvii. 26	Gen. vii.
4	ii. 21	Gen. xvii. 12; Lev. xii. 3	28	xvii. 27, 29, 32	Gen. xix. 23-26
5	ii. 22	Lev. xii. 6	29	xix. 10	Ezek. xxxiv. 11, 16
6	ii. 23	Exod. xiii. 2	30	xix. 44	Psa. cxxxvii. 9; Hos. xiii. 16
7	ii. 24	Lev. v. 11; xii. 8			
8	ii. 34	Isa. viii. 14	31	xx. 18a	Isa. viii. 14, 15
9	ii. 52	1 Sam. ii. 26	32	xx. 18b	Dan. ii. 34, 35, 44, 45
10	iv. 25, 26	1 Kings xvii. 1, 9			
11	iv. 27	2 Kings v. 14			
12	v. 14	Lev. xiii. 49	33	xx. 37	Exod. iii. 1-6, 15
13	vi. 3, 4	1 Sam. xxi. 6	34	xxi. 10, 11	2 Chron. xv. 6; Isa. xix. 2, 17
14	ix. 30, 33	Exodus; 1 Kgs.			
15	ix. 54	2 Kings i. 10, 12	35	xxi. 22	Isa. xxxiv. 8; lxiii. 14; Hos. ix. 7
16	x. 4	2 Kings iv. 29			
17	xi. 29, 30	Jonah i. 17			
18	xi. 31	1 Kings x. 1	36	xxii. 20	Exod. xxiv. 8; Zech. ix. 11
19	xi. 32	Jonah i. 2			
20	xi. 51	Gen. iv. 8; 2 Ch. xxiv. 20, 21	37	xxii. 69	Dan. vii. 13
			38	xxiii. 30	Isa. ii. 19; Hosea x. 8
21	xii. 53	Micah vii. 6	39	xxiii. 34a	Isa. liii. 12
22	xiii. 28	Genesis, et al.	40	xxiii. 35a	Psa. xxii. 7, 17
23	xiii. 29	Mal. i. 11; Isa. lix. 19	41	xxiii. 35b	Isa. xlii. 1
24	xiv. 10	Prov. xxv. 6, 7	42	xxiii. 36	Psa. lxix. 21

THE RIVER JORDAN

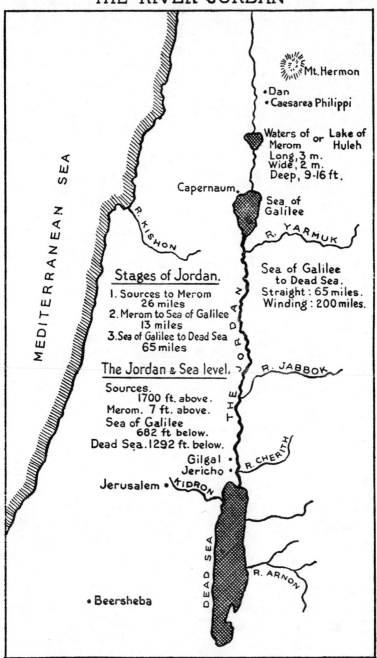

MEDITERRANEAN SEA

Mt. Hermon

• Dan
• Caesarea Philippi

Waters of or Lake of
Merom   Huleh
Long, 3 m.
Wide, 2 m.
Deep, 9-16 ft.

Capernaum •

Sea of
Galilee

R. KISHON

R. YARMUK

Sea of Galilee
to Dead Sea.
Straight : 65 miles.
Winding : 200 miles.

Stages of Jordan.
1. Sources to Merom
   26 miles
2. Merom to Sea of Galilee
   13 miles
3. Sea of Galilee to Dead Sea
   65 miles

The Jordan & Sea level.
Sources.
   1700 ft. above.
Merom. 7 ft. above.
Sea of Galilee
   682 ft. below.
Dead Sea. 1292 ft. below.

THE JORDAN

R. JABBOK

R. CHERITH

Gilgal •
Jericho •

Jerusalem • KIDRON

DEAD SEA

R. ARNON

• Beersheba

(c) Echoes of Old Testament Passages

	LUKE	O. T.		LUKE	O. T.
1	i. 46-55	1 Sam. i. 11; ii. 1-8; Psa. cxi. 9; Psa. lxxxix 16; Job v. 11; Job xii. 19; Psa. cvii. 9; Isa. xli. 8; Gen. xvii. 19	11	xiii. 27	Psa. vi. 8
			12	xiii. 34	Scattered
			13	xvi. 17	Deuteronomy
			14	xvi. 18	Deut. xxiv. 1-4; Jer. iii. 1
			15	xvii. 3	Lev. xix. 17
			16	xx. 9	Isa. v. 1, 2
			17	xxi. 24	Deut. xxviii. 64;
2	i. 68-79	Psa. xli. 13; cvi. 48; 2 Sam. ii. 10; Psa. cvi. 10; Psa. cxxxii. 17; cv. 8, 9; Gen. xii. 3			Psa. lxxix. 1; Isa. lxiii. 18; Dan. viii. 13 Zech. xii. 3
			18	xxi. 25	Isa. xiii. 10; xxiv. 23; Ezek.
3	ii. 30-32	Isa. xl. 5; xlii. 6; xlv. 25; xlvi. 13; xlix. 6; lii. 10; lx. 3; xxv. 7; Psa. xcviii. 2			xxxii. 7; Joel ii. 10,31; iii. 15
			19	xxi. 26	Isa. xxxiv. 4
			20	xxi. 27	Dan. vii. 13
			21	xxi. 35	Eccles. ix. 12
			22	xxii. 1	Exod. xii
4	vi. 24	Amos. vi. 1	23	xxiii. 31	Ezek. xx. 47
5	vi. 25	Isa. lxv. 13, 14	24	xxiii. 49	Psa. xxxviii. 11;
6	vii. 22	Isa. xxxv. 5, 6			lxxxviii. 8
7	x. 15	Isa. xiv. 13-15	25	xxiv. 5	Isa. viii. 19
8	x. 19	Psa. xci. 13	26	xxiv. 27, 32	All O. T.
9	x. 28	Lev. xviii. 5	27	xxiv. 44, 45	All O. T.
10	xiii. 19	Dan. iv. 12, 21	28	xxiv. 46	Isa. liii. 3, 5

It is interesting to observe that the majority of these Old Testament references of all classes are in the Non-Marcan parts of this Gospel (see diagram under 'Luke's Use of Mark,' p. 359), and that many of them are in Luke's special source for chapters i-ii. (See under 'Luke's Sources,' p. 342).

With the exception of vii. 27, all the citations are from the LXX (Greek Version of the Old Testament), a natural thing for a Greek to do who was writing for Greeks.

Absolute accuracy in the number of references to the Old Testament is not possible as, in places, many are so fused that separation is difficult; e.g. in i. 46-55, and in i. 68-79; but the above references must be almost complete.

16

CHRIST'S WORDS IN LUKE'S GOSPEL

IN Luke's Gospel there are 1151 verses in the A.V., and 1149 in the R.V. Of these, 586 verses contain words of Christ, that is, more than half the Gospel.

CHS.	VERS.	CHS.	VERS.	CHS.	VERS.	CHS.	VERS.
i	—	vii	25	xiii	26	xix	26
ii	1	viii	24	xiv	28	xx	27
iii	—	ix	23	xv	29	xxi	32
iv	13	x	34	xvi	30	xxii	36
v	16	xi	44	xvii	31	xxiii	8
vi	36	xii	57	xviii	27	xxiv	13

It will be seen at once that with the exception of chaps. i, ii, iii, iv, v, xxiii, and xxiv, each chapter in the Gospel has over 20 verses which record words of Christ, the principal chapters, as to the number of the words, being the vi, x, xi, xii, xvi, xvii, xxi, xxii.

Study these sayings one by one, and compare them with the sayings in the other Gospels (pp. 192, 272, 418).

17
FEATURES OF LUKE'S GOSPEL

EACH of the Gospels has its characteristics because each was written for a specific purpose, and bears the impress of the writer's individuality. The following are some of the features of the Third Gospel.

(i) Comprehensiveness

Mark's Gospel begins with the ministry of the Baptist, and ends with the Lord's ascension and the going forth of the preachers. Matthew's Gospel begins with the genealogy and birth of Jesus, and ends with the great commission of the Apostles. John's Gospel begins with a declaration that the Eternal Word became incarnate, passes on immediately to the ministry of the Baptist, and ends with Jesus and some disciples in conversation on the shore of the Galilean Lake.

But Luke's Gospel goes behind Mark's and Matthew's, and begins with the annunciations of John and Jesus; it then relates the story of their infancy, and ends with the ascension of Jesus, and the joy of the Apostles, so that this Gospel is more comprehensive, that is, it comprehends more than any of the others, beginning earlier (except for John's Prologue), and ending later, if so be Mark xvi. 9-20, the disputed ending, was not part of the original Mark. (See p. 176).

(ii) **Universalism**

In Luke there is no narrow nationalism, but a broad outlook upon the world. Men are seen as men, of whatever nation or clime, and Jesus is presented as the Redeemer of them all. This Gospel contains the word ' *sinners* ' more often than all the other records together: in Matthew, 5 times; in Mark, 5 times; in John, 4 times; but in Luke 16 times.

The writer is fond of the words *grace, salvation, evangelize,* and *Saviour*. Here the Gentiles are seen in the light of redemption. The gospel of Christ is for the whole world. The angels, at the beginning, proclaim good will to all men (ii. 14). Simeon foretells the infant Saviour as ' a light to lighten the Gentiles ' (ii. 32). ' All flesh ' are to see the salvation of God (iii. 6).

The other Evangelists record the mission of the *Twelve*, but Luke alone tells of the mission of the *Seventy*, as representing the nations of the world (chap. x, cf. Gen. x). No preference is given to the Jews over the Samaritans; on the contrary, the disciples are rebuked for wishing to call down fire on the latter (ix. 54), it is a Samaritan who has compassion on a needy man (x. 33), and the one leper of the ten, who returned to give thanks, was a Samaritan (xvii. 16).

Christ came to seek and to save that which was lost ' (xix. 10). Repentance and remission of sins is to be preached unto all nations (xxiv. 47).

In all this Luke's outlook is that of his dear friend, Paul, and his Gospel illustrates the Pauline doctrine of justification for all by faith. Luke's Gospel gives Christianity a universal significance. Study, i. 53; ii. 7, 8, 24, 32; iii. 6, 12, 13, 38; iv. 18, 25-27; v. 27-32; vi. 20, 21; vii. 9, 22, 37-50; ix. 51-56; x. 1, 30-37; xiii. 29; xiv. 13, 21; xv. 1, 2, 11-32; xvi. 20, 23; xvii. 11-19; xviii. 9-14; xix. 2-10; xxi. 24; xxiii. 43; xxiv. 47.

(iii) **The Individual**

Because it is universal in its scope this is the Gospel of *the individual.* Salvation is not of nations, or of families, but of individuals. Luke presents Christ, not as a Christianizer of peoples, but as the Saviour of people.

A study of the parables which Luke selects makes this plain. Matthew's are parables of the Kingdom, but Luke's are parables of men and women, and proclaim the message of salvation to each of them. Observe this in the 19 parables which are peculiar to this Gospel (see under 'Material Peculiar to Luke,' pp. 351, 352); for example, the Good Samaritan, the Friend at Midnight, the Great Supper, the Lost Coin, and the Prodigal Son.

In the narrative parts of this Gospel Christ's regard for the individual is equally evident. The individual dominates the Record from beginning to end. Its portraits are incomparable.

Zacharias, Elisabeth, Mary, Simeon, Anna, Martha and her sister, Simon, Levi, the Centurion, the Widow of Nain, the Baptist, the Gadarene, Jairus, the Woman with an Infirmity, the Would-be Disciples, Zacchæus, the Magdalene, Cleopas and his Companion, Simon the Cyrenian, Joseph of Arimathæa. No greater condemnation is there of the exaltation of the State at the expense of the individual than Luke's Gospel. Here, in flaming letters is emphasized the unspeakable value of the individual soul.

(iv) **Sympathy**

This is the Gospel of sympathy especially for the outcast; sympathy, not with sin, but with the sinner. The R.V. margin of chapter vi. 35, reads, ' despairing of no man,' an exhortation which is characteristic of the attitude of Jesus throughout this Record. Jesus has pity for all who are in need, and Luke illustrates this by recording that the boy of Nain was the *only* son of his mother (vii. 12); that the ' little maid ' of Jairus was his *only* daughter (viii. 42): and that the lunatic boy was the father's *only* son (ix. 38).

In this Gospel Jesus is the Good Shepherd seeking lost sheep, and the Good Samaritan caring for wayside victims. He did not reject the immoral woman of chap. vii. 36-50; nor hesitate to befriend the unethical Zacchæus of chap. xix. 5; nor to forgive the repentant robber of chap. xxiii. 42, 43. He pardons a helpless debtor (vii. 42); aids a needy friend (xi. 5-8); entertains outcasts (xiv. 21), and listens to the cry of widows (xviii. 1-8).

'In this Gospel the harlot and the criminal, the prodigal and the social pariah, of whatever class or condition, are freely offered the society and the service of the purest and the best.'

The Christ of Luke is the Friend of sinners. It is no marvel that this Gospel, more than all the others, may be said to have given birth and inspiration to all the great reformatory movements—the care for the poor, the deaf, the dumb, the insane, the maimed, the widowed, and orphaned, the aged, even the criminal—which distinguish modern Christendom. It is, in a peculiar sense, the Gospel for those for whom, in all ages, this world has had no gospel.

Christ's sympathy, however, is discriminating. It is not incompatible with severity towards the self-sufficient, the self-righteous, the thoughtless, and the frivolous (xii. 19; xiii. 1, 11; xvi. 19-31). To Christ 'the emotion of penitent faith is more sincere and more precious than a life of prudent orthodoxy; undissembling wickedness is less hateful than disguised insincerity.' It was so, and it is so.

(v) **Forgiveness**

This is also pre-eminently the Gospel of *forgiveness*. The idea of forgiving is represented by three words in the Greek New Testament, and Luke employs them all. Together, they mean to acquit graciously and set at liberty (*aphiēmi, charizomai, apoluō*).

To the man taken with a palsy Jesus said, ' thy sins are forgiven thee,' and by saying so He claimed to be Divine (v. 18-26). In the parable of the Two Debtors both were frankly forgiven, and the sinful woman who was represented by one of them, heard the quickening word, ' thy sins are forgiven ' (vii. 36-50).

Christ exhorts us to forgive if we would be forgiven, and bids us pray for forgiveness (vi. 37; xi. 4). He tells us what can, and what cannot be forgiven (xii. 10). He also bids us forgive as

24

often as a trespasser shows repentance (xvii. 3, 4), and He Himself on the Cross prayed, ' Father, forgive them, for they know not what they do ' (xxiii. 34).

But forgiveness is shown in this Gospel where the word does not occur. Conscience-stricken Peter (v. 8-10), the Returning Prodigal (xv), the Praying Publican (xviii), the Repentant Zacchæus (xix), and the Dying Thief (xxiii), are all forgiven; and Christ declares that 'repentance and remission of sins should be preached in His name among all nations' (xxiv. 47). All who are conscious of the grace of forgiveness will love this Gospel.

(Read 'The Christian Experience of Forgiveness,' H. R. Mackintosh).

(vi) Prayer

The place which Luke gives to the subject of *prayer* is noticeable. In nine passages he tells of prayers which Jesus offered in the crises of His life, and seven of these he alone records:

At His Baptism; after a day of miracles; before choosing the Apostles ; before the first prediction of His Passion ; at His Transfiguration ; before teaching the Apostles how to pray ; when the Seventy returned and made their report ; in Gethsemane; and on the Cross (iii. 21; v. 15, 16; vi. 12; ix. 18; ix. 29; x. 17, 21; xi. 1; xxii. 39-46; xxiii. 34, 46).

Insistence on the duty of prayer is the subject of two parables which no other Evangelist has preserved (xi. 5-13; xviii. 1-8). Luke alone relates the declaration of Jesus that He had made supplication for Peter (xxii. 31, 32), and also His charge to the Twelve (xxii. 40, 46).

Prayer is a human necessity and a natural function of man, and we can understand its being given prominence in the Gospel which specially emphasizes the manhood of Jesus, whose habit it was to pray (iv. 42; v. 16; ix. 10; xi. 1; xxi. 37).

Trace Christ's exhortations to pray, recorded by Luke (vi. 28; x. 2; xi. 9-13; xviii. 1; xxii. 40, 46), and note that he alone records the parable of the Pharisee and the Publican, which teaches how, and how not, to pray.

The prayer-lessons in the Gospel are taught by exhortation, illustration, and demonstration.

(*a*) EXHORTATION

Prayer and Enemies ... ... vi. 28
(cf. xxiii. 34; Acts vii. 59, 60)
Prayer and Service ... ... x. 2
Prayer and Need ... ... xi. 9-13
Prayer and Faith ... ... xviii. 1
Prayer and Temptation ... ... xxii. 40, 46

(*b*) ILLUSTRATION

The Friend at Midnight ... ... xi. 5-8
Prayer is never out of season.
The Unrighteous Judge ... ... xviii. 1-8
Prayer will be answered, but the answer may be
delayed.
The Pharisee and the Publican ... ... xviii. 9-14*a*
Real and unreal prayer.

(*c*) DEMONSTRATION

Prayer was a habit of Christ's life ... ... iv. 42; v. 16;
ix. 10; xi. 1; xxi. 37; xxii. 31, 32
Christ prayed in all the crises of His life (see par. on p. 370, and refs.)
Further, we may learn from this Gospel something about
(1) Prayer for Oneself ... ... xviii. 13
(2) Prayer for Others ... ... xi. 5-13
(3) Prayer that Persists ... ... xviii. 1-8; xi. 9, 10
(4) Prayer that was answered before it was offered xv. 18, 19, 21
(5) Prayer that should not have been offered ... xv. 12
(6) Prayer that was not a Prayer ... ... xviii. 11, 12
(7) Prayer that was too late ... ... xvi. 22-31
cf. Matt. xxv. 10-12

(vii) **Songfulness**

Another feature of this Gospel is its *songfulness*. It begins
and ends with songs, and there is rejoicing all the way along.
Luke is the first great Christian hymnologist, not as a creator,
but as a preserver of sacred songs.

He alone records the *Ave Maria* (i. 28-31), the *Magnificat*
(i. 46-55), the *Benedictus* (i. 68-79), the *Gloria in Excelsis* (ii.
14), and the *Nunc Dimittis* (ii. 29-32). These are the last of
the Hebrew Psalms, and the first of the Christian hymns.

More often in this Gospel than in any other are references
to '*glorifying God*' (ii. 20; v. 25 f.; vii. 16; xiii. 13; xvii. 15;
xviii. 43); to '*praising God*' (ii. 13, 20; xix. 37); and to '*blessing
God*' (i. 64; ii. 28; xxiv. 53).

The words *rejoice* and *joy* occur nineteen times here, as against
twenty-six in Mark and Matthew together. Here, too, we have

exult, and *exultation* (i. 14, 44, 47; x. 21), *leap for joy* (vi. 23), *laughter* (vi. 21), and *merriment* (xv. 23, 32).

Zacchæus received the Lord '*joyfully*'; the shepherd brought home the lost sheep '*rejoicing*,' and would have all his friends and neighbours '*rejoice*' with him; there is '*joy*' in the presence of the angels of God over every sinner that repents; the father bids the household '*make merry*,' because the prodigal had come back; and the Gospel ends with 'they returned to Jerusalem with *great joy*, and were continually in the temple *praising and blessing* God' (xxiv. 52, 53).

(viii) Social Life

Luke's references to *social life* must not be overlooked. In this Gospel we see more of Christ in His social intercourse with man than in any of the other Records. Luke alone records our Lord's entertainment in the house of Simon the Pharisee (vii. 36-50), of another, where He denounced the Pharisees (xi. 37-44), and of a third, where, on a Sabbath day, He healed a dropsical man (xiv. 1-4).

With artless simplicity he draws pictures of the social intercourse of Jesus, in the home at Bethany, in the house of Zacchæus, and on the way to and during the supper at Emmaus (x. 38-42; xix. 1-10; xxiv. 13-32).

Many of the parables of this Gospel are marked by sympathy with the details of ordinary home life, such as patching old clothes, supplying a belated traveller with refreshment, a steward attending to the needs of his master, a woman sweeping her house in search of a lost coin, the home-joy upon a prodigal's return, a farmer's employee, a woman making bread, tending a wounded man, and the master of a house rising and shutting the door.

In relating the parable of the mustard seed, Matthew says that it is sown, '*on the earth*,' Mark makes a man sow it '*in his field*,' but Luke tells us that a man sowed it '*in his own garden*' (xiii. 19). Dr. Plummer regards this as due to Luke's love of homely scenes.

Luke, more than any other of the Evangelists preserves what

is homely and familiar, ourselves in our manifold relations and circumstances, and he shows how Christ is related to it all (v. 36; x. 30-37; xi. 5-8; xii. 42-48; xiii. 20, 21, 25; xv. 8-10, 11-32; xvii. 7-10.

(ix) Poverty and Wealth

The attention which Luke gives to the matters of *poverty and wealth* is very marked. This is seen in his selection of parables, seven or eight of which refer to this matter, and also in his selection of the sayings of Jesus (iv. 18; vi. 20, 24; xii. 33; xiv. 13). (Consult the list under 'Material Peculiar to Luke,' Parables, pp. 351, 352).

The teaching is not that poverty is good, and that wealth is bad, but that while poverty is not a spiritual handicap, wealth may be.

This has been called the Gospel of the Ebionites (a word derived from the Hebrew *ev-yōkn*, the poor), because it delights to record the Saviour's mercy towards the poor, the humble, and the despised (ii. 24; vi. 20-25, 30; viii. 2, 3; xii. 16-21, 33; xiv. 12-15; xvi. 13, 19-25, *et al.*).

Luke narrates the visit of Gabriel to a lowly maiden at Nazareth, and to humble shepherds. He also records the story of *Dives and Lazarus*, and of the *Rich Fool*. He tells of the exaltation of the humble who choose the lowest seats, and records the counsel to the disciples to 'sell what they have,' and to the Pharisees to 'give alms.'

The dangers of money and the compensations of poverty are emphasized by Luke, the story of the *Rich Ruler* illustrating the one (xviii. 18-25), and that of the *Great Supper* illustrating the other (xiv. 16-24). Bishop Alexander has shown that 'selfishness, feverishness, restlessness, is drawn in deathless and terrible lines by our Lord in an awful parable peculiar to this Gospel (xii. 13-21). The rich man, just before a death of violence, held that dreadful dialogue in his own heart. *Seven futures*, in rapid succession, to show that such satisfaction as riches can give is always in the distance; then, *six presents*, and all selfish. 'So is he that layeth up treasure for *himself*, and is not rich towards God.'

The *futures* are; What shall I do? Where shall I lay up my
fruits? This will I do. I will take away. I will build. I will
lay up. I will say.

The *presents* are: Thou hast. Laid up. Take thy rest.
Eat. Drink. Be merry.

It is Luke that records our Lord's sermon at Nazareth, with
its key-note, ' to preach good tidings to the poor ' (iv. 17-21).
It is Luke that records the *Magnificat* which says,

> ' He hath put down princes from their thrones,
>   And hath exalted them of low degree.
>   The hungry He hath filled with good things,
>   And the rich He hath sent empty away.'

Yet, it is this writer who relates that women of means ministered
to Jesus with their substance, and who records the story of
Zacchæus by whom Jesus was entertained.

The first of the Beatitudes relates to the ' poor,' and the first
of the Woes, to the ' rich ' (vi. 20, 24), yet no one is blessed
because he is poor, nor cursed *because* he is rich. What is condemned is ' the mammon of unrighteousness ' (xvi. 9).

(x) Women

Another characteristic of Luke's Record is his portraits of
womanhood. Study the incomparable portraits of Elisabeth,
and the Virgin (i-ii), of Anna (ii), of Martha and Mary (x), and
his references to Mary called Magdalene, to Joanna, to Susanna
(viii. 2, 13). There are also his graphic pictures of the widow
of Nain, of the woman who was a sinner, of the woman who was
'bowed together,' and of the women who ministered to Jesus of
their substance (vii, xiii, viii).

In addition to these Luke introduces an interrupting woman
(xi. 27), a woman sweeping in a house (xv. 8 ff.), a persistent
widow (xviii. 1 ff), women who ' bewailed and lamented ' Jesus
(xxiii. 27), women who witnessed the crucifixion (xxiii. 49)
and women in the resurrection story (xxiv).

The word ' woman ' occurs in Matthew 30 times, in Mark,
19 times, in John, 19 times, but in Luke, 43 times; and it is

worthy of note that the Gospels have no record of any woman who actually opposed Jesus Himself during His ministry.

Not without reason has this been called 'the Gospel of womanhood become Christian, or on its way to Christ.' It is impressive that these notices of women are given in the Gospel for the Gentiles, for among them especially woman was degraded, and all of them who came into contact with the Saviour could have said, 'Christ first taught us that we were women.' The Rabbis in their liturgy thanked God that they were not born women, but Christ has enfranchized them socially and spiritually, and has given them a place of great honour in history.

It is true that a woman dragged the race down to sin, and it is also true that a woman brought the Redeemer into the world. Women were the last at the Cross, and the first at the Tomb.

For a good illustration of the prominence given to women in this Gospel, and also of its having been written for Gentile readers, compare chap. xi. 31, 32 with Matt. xii. 41, 42, and note that in the latter passage the ' men ' are mentioned first, but in Luke, ' the queen.' Note, also, that Matthew says, ' the men of Nineveh shall rise in judgment with this generation ' (xii. 41), but Luke says, ' a queen of the south shall rise up in the judgment with the men of this generation ' (xi. 31). Every woman, and especially women in the East, should thank God for this Gospel.

(xi) **Children**

This is also the Gospel of *infancy and childhood*. Luke alone tells us about the birth, infancy, and childhood of John the Baptist. He adds to what Matthew says about the birth and infancy of Jesus, and alone gives us the incomparable story of Jesus' first Passover (ii. 41-50).

Luke alone says that parents brought to Jesus their ' babes ' (xviii. 15), records the story of the widow's ' only son ' (vii. 11-15), and notes that the epileptic boy was the father's ' only ' child (ix. 38).

He alone tells of the circumcision, the presentation in the Temple, and the growth of Jesus at Nazareth. He alludes to the human existence of our Lord before birth (i. 41), as a babe

(ii. 16), as a little child (ii. 27), as a boy (ii. 40), and as a man (iii. 22).

'Certain chapters of the Third Gospel will always be the chapters we shall most delight to read to the children, and the chapters which the children will be most delighted to hear. They will always love best the Gospel with the story of the Shepherds and the Angels, the Gospel which tells how Jesus allowed the mothers to bring their babies to Him, the Gospel written by the 'beloved physician' who loved the little folks, and so thought it worth while to write a part of his story for them.'

(xii) Characters

In this Gospel we have the most wonderful delineations of human character as revealed by the presence of Christ. The Gospel of the *physician* is also the Gospel of the *psychologist*. Luke exhibits insight into human nature, and knows the ways of God's Spirit with man. He draws pictures of persons by a few artistic touches. Study the portraits of Zacharias, Elisabeth, the Virgin, Simeon, Anna, Martha, Mary, Zacchæus, Cleopas and his companion, the widow of Nain, the ten lepers, the demoniac in the Synagogue, the paralytic, the man with the withered hand, the man of Gergesa, Jairus, the woman bowed down, the afflicted boy, the man deaf and dumb, the blind man near Jericho, the rich ruler, and others.

In addition to these living persons our Lord's parabolic characters should receive careful attention: the Two Debtors; the Sower; the Good Samaritan; the Two Friends who met at midnight; the Rich Fool; the Tower Builder who failed; the King who did not fight; the Pharisees who were clambering for Chief Seats; the Shepherd looking for a Lost Sheep; the Woman sweeping a house to find a coin; the Prodigal Son; the Elder Brother; Lazarus the beggar; Dives the selfish man of wealth; the Dishonest Steward; the Importunate Widow; the Praying Pharisee and Publican; the Wicked Husbandmen; and the Men who received each a Pound.

If the miracles are parables in deeds, the parables are miracles in words. The parable of the Leaven in the Meal is told in 15 words; the Two Debtors, in 28 words; the Mustard Seed, in

28 words; the Foolish King, in 39 words; the Foolish Builder, in 44 words; the Two Houses in 65 words, and so on. These portraits and pictures have become part of the common stock of thought in Christendom, and many of the descriptive phrases have become part of our language currency.

But the greatest portrait of all, in Luke, is that of Christ. Matthew presents Him as King; Mark, as Servant; John, as God; and Luke, as Man. In this Gospel 'the divinity of Jesus is shaded and toned, and at the same time beautified by His rare humanity.' In Luke He is the noble Teacher, Friend, and Helper of mankind, the Physician for the hurt of sin.

(xiii) Medical Terms

Paul speaks of Luke as ' the beloved physician ' (Col. iv. 14), and the evidence of his profession is abundant in his Gospel and the Acts. It has been shown by Hobart, Harnack, and others, that Luke's Writings are full of medical terms and of medical interest. Harnack holds that medical points determine Luke's narrative, that preference is shown for stories of healing, that his language is coloured by technical medical terms, that traces of medical diagnosis occur, and that medical phraseology appears, apart from cases of healing, and that where Luke is speaking as an eye-witness the medical element is specially clearly visible.

Mark the following evidence of this medical complexion in the Gospel. In chap. viii. 43, Luke modifies Mark's caustic comment that the woman with the issue of blood ' *had suffered many things of many physicians, and had spent all that she had, and was nothing bettered, but rather grew worse* ' (Mark v. 26). In Luke (viii. 43) this statement is softened to ' *she was not able to be healed by any*,' implying that it was a chronic case for which physicians were not to blame.

In the account of the demoniac in the synagogue (iv. 35), Luke says that the evil spirit came out of him ' *having done him no hurt*.' In the story of Simon's mother-in-law he notes that she ' *was holden with a great fever*,' and that Jesus '*stood over her*,' as if in careful contemplation of the symptoms of the patient, by way of diagnosis (iv. 38, 39). Of the leper, Luke says that he was ' *a man full of leprosy*,' a bad case (v. 12). In chap. xvii.

11-19, he speaks simply of 'lepers,' and Hobart thinks that Luke, by the use of these two ways of describing the disease, which had three forms, means to draw a distinction in accord with the diagnosis of Hippocrates, a medical writer, B.C. 460-357.

Luke notes that it was the '*right hand*,' of a certain man, that was withered (vi. 6), and the '*right ear*' of Malchus that was lost (xxii. 50), evidence of the medical habit of specification.

This Evangelist alone observes that the Gadarene '*for a long time had worn no clothes*' (viii. 27), which, to a physician, would be a symptom that the man was insane.

Luke alone, in the story of Jairus' daughter, says that Jesus 'commanded that *something be given her to eat*' (viii. 55), revealing a physician's interest in a little child's welfare. In chap. xviii. 25, Luke does not use the word for the ordinary needle (*rhaphis*) employed by Mark and Matthew, but says, *dia trēmatos belonēs*, both medical terms, and used by Luke only: *trēma* was the great medical word for a perforation of any kind, and *belonē* was the surgical needle, a word used by Galen, a Greek physician, A.D. 130-200.

In addition to such particulars as these Luke exhibits a professional interest in medical matters in the portions of the Gospel which are his only (e.g. ix. 2; x. 9, 17). He quotes the passage in Isaiah (lxi. 1 f.) which refers to Jesus' healing mission (iv. 18, 19). Of the six miracles which are peculiar to Luke, five are miracles of healing. (See under 'Material Peculiar to Luke,' p. 351). In the story of the Good Samaritan, a story which only Luke gives, the expressions '*half dead*,' '*bound up his wounds*,' '*pouring on them oil and wine*,' and '*took care of him*,' indicate a professional man's interest (x. 25-37), as do also, in another story (xvi. 19-28), '*full of sores*,' '*cool*,' and '*in anguish*,' which two latter expressions are common in medical writers, the second for pain, and the first for alleviation.

Luke records that Jesus sent forth His missionaries both to preach and to heal (ix. 2; x. 9); and he alone preserves Christ's proverb, '*physician heal thyself*' (iv. 23).

This Evangelist tells us that the son of the widow '*sat up*' on the bier, like a patient in bed (vii. 15), and the word, with this meaning, was used, we are told, by medical writers. Luke makes it clear that the woman with the spirit of infirmity was suffering from curvature of the spine, and he uses technical language when he says that ' *she was bowed together*, and *could in no wise lift herself up*,' and, ' immediately *she was made straight* ' (xiii. 10-17). Medical writers employ this latter word for '*to straighten*', to put into natural position abnormal or dislocated parts of the body (Hobart).

The evidence that Luke in his Gospel betrays the habits of mind of a physician is cumulative and conclusive, and the Acts bears the same testimony.

(xiv) Contrasts

Luke's Gospel is distinguished for its number of striking *contrasts*, which are as lights and shadows throughout the wonderful story. There are the doubting Zacharias, and the believing Virgin; the anxious Martha, and the devout Mary; the proud Pharisee and the humble Publican; the indulgent Dives, and the mendicant Lazarus; the callous Priest and Levite, and the compassionate Samaritan; the unthankful nine lepers, and the grateful one; the Prodigal Son, and the Elder Brother; the self-righteous Simon, and the penitent woman; the repentant malefactor, and the blaspheming one; Barabbas, and Jesus. There are the contrasts also between the angels and the shepherds; between the loquaciousness of the shepherds and the majestic silence of Mary; between Heaven and Bethlehem.

And in the parables we have the New Cloth and the Old Garment; the New Wine and the Old Wine Skins; the House on the Rock and the one on the Sand; the Faithful and the Unfaithful Steward; the Lost Sheep and the Ninety-nine; the One Coin and the Nine Pieces.

There is also the portrait of the Son of Man, sublime in noble wrath as well as in noble tenderness, Who uttered the parable of the Rich Man and Lazarus, as well as those of the Shepherd and his Sheep, and the Prodigal and his Father.

And, finally, there is the striking contrast between the beginning and the end of this Gospel; between a helpless babe coming into this world, and an omnipotent Saviour leaving it.

(xv) **Angels**

Our most complete revelations, whether of the functions of the holy angels towards the Saviour during His life on earth, or of their relation to us, are to be found in Luke. The word *angel*, or *angels*, of celestial beings, occurs 23 times in this Gospel.

An Angel appeared to Zacharias in the Temple, and to Mary at Nazareth (i). An Angel came upon the shepherds near Bethlehem, and a multitude of them sang to the shepherds the *Gloria in Excelsis*, and then returned to heaven (ii). The devil misapplied an Old Testament passage about angels, when tempting Jesus in the wilderness (iv. 10). Our Lord announced that when He comes again He will be accompanied by angels (ix. 26). Also, He declared that in a coming judgment He will confess or deny men ' before the angels of God,' according to whether men have owned or denied Him (xii. 8, 9). It is revealed that when sinners repent there is ' joy in the presence of the angels of God ' (xv. 10). Lazarus was carried by angels to Abraham's bosom (xvi. 22). Our Lord revealed that in the life to come the redeemed shall be ' equal unto the angels ' (xx. 35, 36). An angel appeared to Jesus in Gethsemane, and strengthened Him (xxii. 43). Certain women saw a vision of angels at the sepulchre after Jesus had risen (xxiv. 23: cf. verses 4, 5).

There are more glimpses of the unseen world in this than in any other Gospel. It resounds with angel songs, and with the music of their wings.

(xvi) **Doublets**

There are in Matthew and Luke a number of instances of repetitions of the same or closely similar sentences. In Matthew there are at least 22 of these, and at least 14 in Luke. For the latter, examine carefully the following passages:

(1) viii. 16, and xi. 33; (2) viii. 17, and xii. 2; (3) viii. 18, and xix. 26; (4) ix. 3, and x. 4; (5) ix. 23, and xiv. 27; (6) ix. 24, and xvii. 33; (7) ix. 26, and xii. 9; (8) ix. 46, and xxii. 24; (9) x. 25, and xviii. 18; (10) xi. 43, and xx. 46; (11) xii. 11, 12, and xxi. 14, 15; (12) xiv. 11, and xviii. 14; (13) xix. 44, and xxi. 6; (14) xxi. 23, and xxiii. 29. These doublets are of more than ·

passing interest and importance. While it is true that Luke's space was limited, and that that fact may account for his omitting Mark vi. 45-viii. 26 (see under ' Omissions of Luke,' p. 354), because he had in his own record similar incidents to those which Mark records in that section, it is also true that he duplicates not a little.

There are two songs in chap. i. Both Simeon and Anna welcome the infant Christ in the Temple (ii. 28, 38). He records the conversion of two publicans, Levi, and Zacchæus (v; xix). The mission of the Twelve is followed by the mission of the Seventy (ix; x). True disciples are equal to Christ's relations, and to His mother (viii. 21; xi. 28). Twice there is a dispute as to who is the greatest (ix. 46; xxii. 24). Two persons are raised from the dead (vii. 14; viii. 54), and no other Evangelist gives more than one example. There are two instances of cleansing lepers (v. 13; xvii. 14); two of forgiving sins (v. 20; vii. 48); three healings on the Sabbath (vi. 6; xiii. 10; xiv. 1); and four castings out of demons (iv. 35; viii. 29; ix. 42; xi. 14). The Rash Builder is followed by the Rash King (xiv. 28-32). There are the Lost Sheep, and the Lost Coin (xv. 1-10). These doublets show that similar sayings were spoken by our Lord more than once, on different occasions, and in different places. And why not? The minister who never repeats himself can easily be a bad teacher.

Summarizing the Third Gospel Dean Farrar says:

> ' Such, then, is the Gospel of St. Luke;—the Gospel of the Greek and of the future; of catholicity of mind; the Gospel of hymns and of prayers; the Gospel of the Saviour; the Gospel of the universality and gratuitousness of salvation; the Gospel of holy toleration; the Gospel of those whom the religious world regards as heretics; the Gospel of the publican, and the outcast, and the humble poor, and the weeping Magdalene, and the crucified malefactor; the Gospel of the lost piece of money, and of the lost sheep; the Gospel of the Good Samaritan, and of the Prodigal Son; the Gospel of the saintly life, of pity, of forgiveness obtained by faith, of pardon for all the world; the Gospel of grace and of the glad tidings of free salvation; the Gospel of Him who was, as we all are, the Son of Adam, and Who died that we all might be the sons of God. Such are its lessons. Have not some of us very much misread and mistaken them? Has the best Christian among us all done more than just begun to spell out their meaning.'

18. ANALYSIS OF LUKE'S GOSPEL

THE MAN CHRIST JESUS

I	II	III	IV
ADVENT OF THE SON OF MAN	**PREPARATION** OF THE SON OF MAN	**MINISTRY** OF THE SON OF MAN	**TRIUMPH** OF THE SON OF MAN
I. 5-II. 52 B.C. 5-A.D. 8	III. I-IV. 13 A.D. 26-27	IV. 14-XIX 27 A.D. 27-30	XIX. 28-XXIV. 53 A.D. 30
Preface (i. 1-4)		**Part One**	
		SERVICE IN THE LIGHT OF THE CROSS	THE GREAT CONFLICT (xix. 28-xxiii. 56)
THE ANNUNCIATIONS - i. 5-56	THE FORERUNNER OF JESUS (iii. 1-20)	*Galilean.* *Chiefly Jewish* (iv. 14-ix. 50)	The Approach (xix. 28-xxii. 38)
Of John (i. 5-25)			The Struggle (xxii. 39-xxiii. 43)
Of Jesus (i. 26-56)	THE BAPTISM OF JESUS (iii. 21, 22)	Commencement - iv. 14-44	The Issue (xxiii. 44-56)
		Course - v. I-vi. II	
		Consummation - vi. 12-viii. 56	
JOHN THE PROPHET - i. 57-80	THE GENEALOGY OF JESUS (iii. 23-38)	Conclusion - ix. I-50	THE GRAND CONQUEST (xxiv)
		Part Two	The Opened Grave (1-12)
JESUS THE SAVIOUR - ii. 1-52	THE TEMPTATION OF JESUS (iv. 1-13)	SERVICE ON THE WAY TO THE CROSS	The Opened Scriptures (13-32)
His Birth (1-38)			The Opened Understanding (33-49)
His Infancy (39, 40)		*Judaean and Peraean* *Chiefly Gentile* (ix. 51-xix. 27)	The Opened Heaven (50-53)
His First Passover (41-50)		Principles of the Kingdom Defined ix. 51-xiii. 21	
His Growth to Manhood (51, 52)		Subjects of the Kingdom Described xiii. 22-xvii. 10	
		Coming of the Kingdom Declared xvii. 11-xix.27	

General Summary

18

ANALYSIS OF LUKE'S GOSPEL.

PREFACE (i. 1-4)

I. THE ADVENT OF THE SON OF MAN ... ... i. 5-ii. 52
1 THE ANNUNCIATIONS (i. 5-56)
2 JOHN THE PROPHET (i. 57-80)
3 JESUS THE SAVIOUR (ii. 1-52)

II. THE PREPARATION OF THE SON OF MAN   iii. 1-iv. 13
1 THE FORERUNNER OF JESUS (iii. 1-20)
2 THE BAPTISM OF JESUS (iii. 21, 22)
3 THE GENEALOGY OF JESUS (iii. 23-38)
4 THE TEMPTATION OF JESUS (iv. 1-13)

III. THE MINISTRY OF THE SON OF MAN ... iv. 14-xix. 27
Part One
SERVICE IN THE LIGHT OF THE CROSS
(iv. 14-ix. 50)

Galilean.   *Chiefly Jewish*

1 COMMENCEMENT OF THE MINISTRY (iv. 14-44)
2 COURSE OF THE MINISTRY (v. 1-vi. 11)
3 CONSUMMATION OF THE MINISTRY (vi. 12-viii. 56)
4 CONCLUSION OF THE MINISTRY (ix. 1-50)

Part Two
SERVICE ON THE WAY TO THE CROSS
(ix. 51-xix. 27)

Judæan and Peræan.   *Chiefly Gentile*

1 JESUS DEFINES THE PRINCIPLES OF HIS KINGDOM (ix. 51-xiii. 21)
2 JESUS DESCRIBES THE SUBJECTS OF HIS KINGDOM (xiii. 22-xvii. 10)
3 JESUS DECLARES THE COMING OF HIS KINGDOM (xvii. 11-xix. 27)

IV. THE TRIUMPH OF THE SON OF MAN ... xix. 28-xxiv. 53
1 THE GREAT CONFLICT (xix. 28-xxiii. 56)
2 THE GRAND CONQUEST (xxiv. 1-53)

Detailed Outline

PREFACE (i. 1-4)

I. THE ADVENT OF THE SON OF MAN ... ... i. 5-ii. 52
1 The Annunciations ... ... i. 5-56
(i) Announcement of the Birth of John the Baptist (i. 5-25)
   (*a*) Zacharias and Elisabeth (i. 5-7)
   (*b*) The Promise of a Son (i. 8-23)
   (*c*) A Hope Justified (i. 24, 25)

III. **THE MINISTRY OF THE SON OF MAN** ... iv. 14-xix. 27
Part One
SERVICE IN THE LIGHT OF THE CROSS
(iv. 14-ix. 50)
Galilean. *Chiefly Jewish*

1 **The Commencement of the Ministry** ... ... iv. 14-44
The Claim of Jesus to be the Christ

   (i) AT NAZARETH ... ... iv. 14-30
     (a) The Opening of the Ministry in Galilee (iv. 14, 15)
     (b) The Reception in the Synagogue at Nazareth (iv. 16-30)
       (1) The Reading (iv. 16-19)
       (2) The Address (iv. 20-22)
       (3) The Charge (iv. 23-27); (23, 24; 25, 26; 27)
       (4) The Result (iv. 28-30)

   (ii) AT CAPERNAUM ... ... iv. 31-44
     (a) Christ's Authoritative Word (iv. 31, 32)
     (b) Christ's Authenticating Work (iv. 33-44)
       (1) A Man Healed (iv. 33-37)
       (2) A Woman Healed (iv. 38, 39)
       (3) Many Healed (iv. 40, 41)
       (4) Widespread Preaching (iv. 42-44)

2 **The Course of the Ministry** ... ... v. 1-vi. 11
The Claim of Jesus Challenged

   (i) The Call of Four Disciples (v. 1-11)
   (ii) The Cleansing of a Leper (v. 12-16)
   (iii) The Healing of a Paralytic (v. 17-26)
   (iv) The Call and Feast of Levi (v. 27-29)
   (v) Discourse on Fasting (v. 30-39)
   (vi) Controversy over the Plucking of Corn Ears on the Sabbath (vi. 1-5)
   (vii) Controversy over the Healing of a Man on the Sabbath (vi. 6-11)

3 **The Consummation of the Ministry** ... vi. 12-viii. 56
The Claim of Jesus Considered

   (i) The Call of the Twelve Apostles (vi. 12-16)
   (ii) The Sermon on the Plain (vi. 17-49)
     (a) The Human Material for the Kingdom (vi. 17-19)
     (b) Qualifications for Admission to the Kingdom (vi. 20-26)
       (1) Condition of Happiness (vi. 20-23)
       (2) Causes of Misery (vi. 24-26)
     (c) Obligations of those that Enter the Kingdom (vi. 27-45)
       (1) ON LOVE ... ... vi. 27-36
         (a) Its Manifestations (vi. 27-31)
           Active (vi. 27, 28)
           Passive (vi. 29, 30)
           The Principle (vi. 31)
         (b) Its Disinterestedness (vi. 32-36)
           Heavenly and Earthly Love Compared (vi. 32-34)
           Divine Love is the Standard (vi. 35, 36)
       (2) ON CRITICISM ... ... vi. 37-45
         (a) The Principle Stated (vi. 37, 38)
         (b) The Principle Illustrated (vi. 39-45)
           Leaders and Led (vi. 39)
           Teachers and Taught (vi. 40)
           Reformers and Reformed (vi. 41, 42)
           Effecive and Ineffective (vi. 43-45)

The chronology of this part of the narrative—The Triumph of the Son of Man—follows tradition as it is expressed, for instance, in Gospel Harmonies, but tradition is open to challenge, and in this instance, I submit, is in error. (See Div. C, Sec. 14, p. 569). The traditional view is followed in the Analysis only for the sake of convenience, and in order not to divert the thought of the reader by introducing a critical question. What is affected, in any case, is not the order of events, but only when they occurred.

QUESTIONS

1 Of what nationality was Luke, and what was his profession?
2 Where was Luke likely to have been educated?
3 Where is Luke named in the New Testament, and in what connections?
4 Read with caution the conjectures relative to Luke.
5 With whom was Luke intimately associated, and for what purpose or purposes?
6 What external and what internal evidence is there that Luke wrote the Gospel which bears his name?
7 About what date is it likely that this Gospel was written? Support your answer.
8 At what place or places could Luke have written his Gospel?
9 What evidence is there that this Gospel was written for Gentiles?
10 What evidence is there that this Gospel was written for Greeks?
11 State as fully as you can what Luke says in his Introduction (i. 1-4), about his purposes and method in writing this Gospel.
12 What Sources had Luke at his disposal for writing?
13 How are the details in chaps i-ii best accounted for?
14 Approximately how much of Mark's Gospel does Luke use?
15 Say in what way Luke's Gospel is more complete than any of the others.
16 What large section of Mark does Luke omit, and can the omission be explained?
17 What two large parts of this Gospel are Luke's alone?
18 Can the larger of these two parts be accounted for?
19 Name some other parts which are peculiar to Luke.
20 What was Luke's design in writing?
21 Approximately how many words does Luke employ which are not found elsewhere in the New Testament?
22 Give a few instances of Luke's picturesque language.
23 Name ten events which Luke alone records.
24 Name ten events in Mark's Gospel which Luke omits, in addition to the large section of Mark referred to in question 16.
25 How many parables does Luke record, and how many of these does he alone record?
26 Name six parables peculiar to Luke, and six others.
27 How many miracles does Luke record, and how many of these does he alone record?
28 Name the miracles which are recorded by Luke only.
29 Name ten features of this Gospel.
30 What evidence is there in this Gospel that Luke was a physician? Give references.
31 Which of Luke's parables relate to poverty and wealth?
32 What is the teaching in this Gospel on forgiveness?
33 Illustrate by references Luke's emphasis on the subject of prayer.
34 Classify Luke's references to prayer.

35 What prominence is given to women in this Gospel, and can it be explained?

36 What women are mentioned in this Gospel?

37 Justify the statement that this is the Gospel for children.

38 What is said in this Gospel about angels?

39 Where is it recorded that Jesus was entertained in people's houses?

40 Name the Songs recorded by Luke, say where they are, and show by references that this is the Gospel of joy.

41 What evidence does this Gospel furnish of Jesus' pity for sinners?

42 Name ten living characters and ten parabolic characters in this Gospel.

43 Name some striking character contrasts in this Gospel.

44 Show that this Gospel presents Christ as the Saviour of all men.

45 Illustrate the influence of Paul upon Luke's thinking and writing.

46 Give six instances of Luke's use of doublets.

47 Is there anything impressive about the arrangement of the Marcan and Non-Marcan parts of Luke?

48 Are the Sermon on the Plain, and the Parable of the Pounds, varied versions of the Sermon on the Mount, and the Parable of the Talents which are given by Matthew? Justify your answer.

49 How do you account for the difference between Matthew's and Luke's Genealogies of Jesus?

50 What references are there in Luke to Jesus' childhood and early life?

51 How many Old Testament references are there in this Gospel, and how may they be classified?

52 What is the difference between Matthew's and Luke's references to the Old Testament?

53 About how many words are peculiar to Paul and Luke only? Name some of them.

54 Give evidence that this is pre-eminently the Gospel of the individual.

55 Name, with references, the four main divisions of Luke given in the Analysis.

56 Is it reasonable to believe that Jesus performed miracles?

57 Which is the greatest of all the miracles?

58 Name some points in the Olivet Discourse, as it is recorded by Mark or Matthew, which Luke omits.

59 Name some things which happened on each day of the Passion Week, Sunday to Sunday.

60 What are the four ' opened ' things in chapter xxiv?

61 Is there any reason for supposing that what Luke wrote influenced John in the selection of his material?

62 Show that the writer of this Gospel is the author of the Acts.

LITERATURE

'Luke, the Historian, in the Light of Research' A. T. Robertson
'St. Luke.' I.C.C. (For Advanced Students) - A. Plummer
'Commentary on St. Luke's Gospel ' (2 vols.) - F. Godet
'St. Luke's Gospel.' Handbooks for Bible Classes T. M. Lindsay
'St. Luke.' Devotional Commentary (3 vols.) - J. M. E. Ross
'Luke, the Physician ' - - - - - A. Harnack
'Luke, the Physician ' - - - • - Sir W. M. Ramsay
'The Medical Language of St. Luke' • - W. K. Hobart
'St. Luke.' The New Century Bible - - W. F. Adeney
'St. Luke.' Cambridge Greek Testament for
  Schools and Colleges - - - - - F. W. Farrar
'The Most Beautiful Book in the World ' - Hayes
'Introduction to the Synoptic Gospels ' - - P. J. Gloag
  Articles on Luke, and on his Gospel, in the Bible
  Dictionaries - - - - - - ——
'The Special Characteristics of the Four Gospels ' H. M. Luckock
'Introduction to the Study of the Gospels ' - Bishop Westcott
'The Four Gospels ' - - - - - Maurice Jones
'The Gospels ' - - - - - - Vincent Taylor
'Some New Testament Problems ' - - - Arthur Wright
'Critical and Exegetical Handbook on the Gospels
  of Mark and Luke ' (2 vols.) - - - H. A. W. Meyer
'Gnomon of the New Testament.' Vol. II - J. A. Bengel
'The Greek Testament.' Vol. I - - - H. Alford
'Commentary for English Readers' (Ellicott).
  Vol. VI - - - - - - - ——
'Notes on the Greek Testament.' St. Luke A. Carr
'The Expositor's Greek Testament.' Vol. I - A. B. Bruce
'The Speaker's Bible ' (4 vols.) - - ——
'The Gospel of St. Luke.' The Expositor's Bible H. Burton
'Recent Discoveries in St. Luke's Writings ' - G. Mackinlay
'The Gospel of an Artist and Physician ' - - C. Bickersteth
'St. Luke, Evangelist and Historian ' - - H. McLachlan
'Word Pictures in the New Testament.' Vol. II - A. T. Robertson
'Word Studies in the New Testament.' Vol. I - M. Vincent
'The Gospel of Luke ' - - - - - C. R. Erdman
  Expository Dictionary of New Testament Words' W. E. Vine
'Commentary on the Gospel of Luke' (1950) N. Geldenhuys

THE GOSPELS
VIEWED ANALYTICALLY

ST. JOHN

St. John

OUTLINE OF STUDY

St. John's Gospel

BEFORE beginning to study this Gospel read it through three times, each time, if possible, at a sitting (about $2\frac{1}{2}$ hours):

First time, in Weymouth's *New Testament in Modern Speech*; or in *The Twentieth Century New Testament*; or in Moffatt's Translation.

Second time, in the Authorized Version.

Third time, in the Revised Version, or The Revised Standard Version (1946).

In these three readings use no books, but only the text of the Gospel. Having done this, do the reading prescribed in the following Studies. The system is that in each Study a part of the Guide be read, and a portion of the Gospel. Where possible the reading is related to the part of the Guide assigned for reading, as, for example, in the Discourses and Miracles; but this cannot always be done, as, for example, in the parts relating to sources, date, and other subjects; but read carefully the part of the Guide which is appointed, and the portion of the Gospel which is attached to it, whether these are related or not.

The object is twofold: first, to familiarize oneself with the text of the Gospel by repeated reading; and secondly, to follow the various Studies which constitute the Guide.

I

KEY PLAN OF READING

FIFTY STUDIES

2

JOHN THE APOSTLE

ASSUMING that John the Apostle is the author of this Gospel (See Div. A, Part II, Sec. 5, St. John, pp. 135-138), let us learn what may be known about him.

The particulars may be classified and summarized under six heads: the home and occupation of John; his discipleship and service-life; references to him in the history of the Church; the portrait of him derived from tradition; his character as reflected in his writings; and his place in the apostolic age.

(i) THE HOME AND OCCUPATION OF JOHN

His home town was Bethsaida (i. 44; Luke v. 10), and there was a family of four, the father and mother, Zebedee, and Salome, and two sons, James and John (Mark i. 19, 20; xv. 40; Matt. xxvii. 56). The father and sons were fishermen (Matt. iv. 21); Salome, the mother, was ambitious for her boys (Matt. xx. 20, 21; Mark x. 35-37). There is clear evidence that the family was prosperous, for they had hired servants, they ministered of their substance, and they were influential in official quarters (Mark i. 20; Matt. xxvii. 56; Luke viii. 3; John xviii. 15, 16; xix. 27).

(ii) THE DISCIPLESHIP AND SERVICE-LIFE OF JOHN

He was first a follower of John the Baptist (i. 35, 40), and he left him to follow Christ. There appear to have been three stages in his fellowship with Christ: *attachment* (i. 40); *discipleship* (Matt. iv. 21, 22); and *apostleship* (Luke vi. 13, 14). John's relation to Jesus was unique. If, as is conjectured, Salome was the sister of Jesus' mother, John would be Jesus' cousin. (See Div. A, Pt. I, 6, p. 62, Salome). He was one of the first two disciples to be called (i. 35-40); one of the first Apostles named (Matt. iv. 18-22); one of the three privileged Apostles (Mark v. 37; Matt. xvii. 1; xxvi 37); one of the four who drew forth our Lord's great prophetic discourse (Mark xiii. 3); and one of the two sent to prepare the Passover (Luke xxii. 8). He was 'the disciple whom Jesus loved' (xiii. 23; xix. 26; xx. 2; xxi. 7, 20), and to whom He committed the care of His mother (xix. 25-27).

(iii) REFERENCES TO JOHN IN THE HISTORY OF THE CHURCH

John appears three times in the Acts: in the Temple (iii. 1); before the Council (iv. 13); and at Samaria (viii. 14). After the general reference to him in Acts xv. 2, 22, 23, our next contact with him is about eighteen years later (A.D. 69), in the Book of the Revelation (i. 1, 4, 9), and about twenty-six years later still (A.D. 95), in his Gospel, and the Epistles which bear his name.

(iv) THE PORTRAIT OF JOHN DERIVED FROM TRADITION

Tradition tells us that John left Jerusalem and went to Asia. That, perhaps on account of the deaths of Paul, Peter, Timothy, and Titus, which would leave the Asian Churches without a leader, John settled at Ephesus, and afterwards became bishop there. That at Ephesus he spent a great part of his life, died, and was buried there, tradition affirms.

It was probably about A.D. 69 that the Apostle was banished to Patmos, where he received and recorded the visions of the Revelation. (See p. 459). Jerome places his death about A.D. 98.

Many stories are told of the aged Apostle, and there is no reason to believe that they are spurious. That there is a basis in fact for each of them is the more likely, seeing that they reflect his character as that is portrayed in the New Testament. The story of 'John and the Robber' reflects his tender love; 'John and Cerinthus,' reflects his devotion to truth; and 'John and the Partridge' reflects his calm and meditative disposition. (These stories are related in Dean Farrar's ' Early Days of Christianity,' and elsewhere, and should be read).

(v) THE CHARACTER OF JOHN AS REFLECTED IN HIS WRITINGS

He was retiring and reticent in disposition. When he and Peter are named together the latter is named first, though John became a disciple before Peter. When the Apostle refers to himself he always suppresses his name (xiii. 23; xix. 26; xx. 2; xxi. 7, 20). He was contemplative and mystical rather than

practical and executive. Yet he was capable of fiery zeal, and is
called a 'son of thunder' (Mark iii. 17; Luke ix. 49, 50, 54-56;
1 John ii. 22; iii. 8, 15; iv. 20).

(vi) THE PLACE OF JOHN IN THE APOSTOLIC AGE

Here is Godet's fine estimate:

> 'The hour for work had sounded in the first place for Peter.
> He had founded the Church in Israel, and planted the standard
> of the New Covenant on the ruins of the theocracy. Paul had
> followed. His task had been to liberate the Church from the
> restrictions of an expiring Judaism, and to open the door of the
> Kingdom of God to Gentiles.
>
> John succeeded them, he who was first to come, and whom his
> Master reserved to the last. He completed the fusion of these
> heterogeneous elements of which the Church had been formed,
> and he raised Christendom to the relative perfection of which it
> was then capable. It may be said, then, that Peter *formed* the
> primitive Church, Paul *emancipated* it, and John *established* it.'

In his Gospel, John shows that the Man of Galilee was God;
his Epistles show that it was God Who became Man; and the
Revelation shows that ultimate universal victory over all the forces
of evil will be through and for the God-Man.

3

FOR WHOM WRITTEN

THE character of each Gospel determines for whom it was
written. Obviously Matthew was written for Jews, as witness
its references to *prophecy* fulfilled, to the 'city of the great king,'
to David, and so on. Mark and Luke as obviously were written
for Gentiles; Mark especially for Romans, and Luke for Greeks,
Mark emphasizing the ideal of *power*, and Luke, the ideal of
perfection.

As the Hebrews, the Romans, and the Greeks were the three
great representative peoples of the world, we may well ask for
whom John could write. The answer to this inquiry is found
in a consideration together of the author, the date, and the
complexion of the Fourth Gospel.

If, as we believe, John had the Synoptics before him (see under
' Relation to the Synoptics ' p. 430), he, in the light of the situation at the close of the first century, would wish to put on record

—and his followers would wish him to do so—those more spiritual aspects of Christ's ministry which had not been recorded by the Synoptists, and for which the Jews, the Romans, and the Greeks were not then ready. All early tradition confirms this view. Clement of Alexandria, quoted by Eusebius, says, 'Last of all, John, observing that in the other Gospels those things were related that concerned the body (of Christ), and being persuaded by his friends, and also moved by the Spirit of God, wrote a spiritual Gospel.' The witness of Papias, Irenæus, Jerome, Gregory Nazianzen, and Augustine, is to the same effect. (For these names see Div. A, 'Church Fathers,' p. 38).

By the close of the first century, more than two generations after Christ's ascension, the number of Christians in the world must have been very great, and, in the light of apostolic teaching, there was created the need for fuller knowledge concerning Christ than that which the Synoptists had given. This need was felt, not by Jews, or Romans, or Greeks, as such, but by the Christian Church, and in God's good providence, he who had known Christ most intimately, who had leaned on His breast, was spared to write in such a way as to supply the need.

John, therefore, wrote for the Christian Church as a whole, and for the world at large, and has presented the profounder aspects of the Gospel for which previous training had filled the universal Church with an intense longing.

4

DATE AND PLACE OF WRITING

THE concurrence of testimony converges on the close of the first century as the time when this Gospel was written, and we may regard the reasons for this belief as conclusive.

(1) There is entire absence of any reference to the destruction of Jerusalem in A.D. 70, either anticipatively or reflectively, and this points to a date either long before or long after that event, and all the evidence is against its being before.

(2) It is certain that this Gospel was written after the other three, and that the writer was acquainted with the Synoptics. He takes for granted that his readers had already, through some

source or other, become acquainted with the principal facts of the gospel history. For illustration of this, note the following:

In chap. i. 40 it is assumed that Simon Peter was known. In chap. iii. 24, it is taken for granted that his readers knew that the Baptist was imprisoned, and the Evangelist would have them know that the events which he is relating took place before the imprisonment. In chap. vi. 70, R.V., he assumes it is known that *twelve* Apostles had been appointed. In chap. i. 32, the baptism of Jesus is not expressly mentioned, but it is implied. The ascension of Jesus is not related, but it is referred to three times (iii. 13; vi. 62; xx. 17).

(3) The Evangelist omits much which the Synoptists record, and records much which they omit. In addition to this, he is full where they are concise, and concise where they are full. These facts give the impression that he intended to supplement the other Gospels. (See under 'Relation to the Synoptics,' p. 430).

John is silent about the birth and baptism of Jesus, and also about the institution of the Lord's Supper, but these events are implied in his record: the birth, in i. 45; vii. 41, 52; the baptism, in iii. 5; and the Lord's Supper, in vi. 47-58.

(4) The teaching of this Gospel betrays 'a maturity of the Christian consciousness which would have been impossible at an earlier stage of the Church.' It is true that this mature teaching was given by Christ (see 'Discourses,' p. 421), but evidently it formed no part of the Oral Tradition, nor of the first written sources of the Synoptics. (See Div. A, 'Synoptic Problem,' p. 83). In God's wise providence the record of these profound utterances was reserved for a time when the beliefs of the Church had received doctrinal formulation, especially by the Epistles of Paul.

It is safe, then, to assume that this Gospel was written in the last decade of the first century, and probably about A.D. 95. The verdict of Bishop Westcott is that 'it was written after the other three, in Asia, at the request of the Christian Churches there, as a summary of the oral teaching of St. John upon the Life of Christ, to meet a want which had grown up in the Church at the close of the Apostolic age.'

As to the *place of writing*, it is practically certain that John, who resided in Ephesus, wrote his Gospel there. Irenæus expressly states that this was so, Jerome agrees, and early tradition generally, is unanimous on the point.

5

CANONICITY

BY *canonicity* is meant the right of any work to be regarded as Holy Scripture, and, for the New Testament, this right depended on apostolicity; and this being established, there was no longer any question as to recognition. The apostolic authorship of the Fourth Gospel secured for it a place in the New Testament canonical books, so that what has been said under ' Authorship ' is relevant here. (See Div. A, Pt. II, p. 135).

To that, however, must be added the evidence supplied by the Fathers that the Fourth Gospel was recognized. From the middle of the second century this Gospel was generally known and received as of apostolic origin and weight.

POLYCARP, of Smyrna (martyred about A.D. 155, according to Lightfoot), the disciple of John, quotes from his First Epistle (iii. 8; iv. 3), when he writes; ' Everyone who does not confess that Jesus Christ has come in the flesh is Anti-Christ; and whosoever does not confess the testimony of the Cross is of the devil.' The evidence for the Epistle is, at the same time, evidence for the Gospel.

In IGNATIUS, of Antioch (martyred not later than about A.D. 116), we read; ' I desire the bread of God, the heavenly bread, the bread of life which is the flesh of Jesus Christ, the Son of God, . . . and I desire the drink of God, namely, His blood, which is incorruptible love and eternal life ' (cf. John iv. 14: vi 32, 33, 54, ff.).

PAPIAS, of Hierapolis (between A.D. 110 and 140), a fellow-student of Polycarp, and who may himself have heard John, according to Eusebius quoted testimonies from John's First Epistle.

TATIAN, a disciple of Justin (A.D. 160-170) quotes clearly from John i. 3, 5, and iv. 24.

JUSTIN MARTYR (martyred A.D. 165) says: 'And he (the Baptist) cried to them, I am not the Christ, but the voice of one crying; for He that is stronger than I shall come' (cf. John i. 23, 27). And again, 'For Christ also said, Except ye be born again, ye shall not enter into the kingdom of heaven. Now that it is impossible for those who have once been born to enter into their mothers' wombs is manifest to all' (cf. John iii. 3-5).

Like evidence is borne also by THEOPHILUS, of Antioch (A.D. 170-180), IRENÆUS (A.D. 120-200), CLEMENT OF ALEXANDRIA (A.D. 155-220), and TERTULLIAN (A.D. 160-222), so that it can confidently be said that before the close of the second century the proof of the existence of the Fourth Gospel, and of the uniform belief that John was the author, is irrefragable. (See Div. A, ' Church Fathers,' p. 38).

<h1 style="text-align:center">6</h1>

JOHN'S SOURCES

WE have seen that Mark had a source in Peter, and to some extent, Streeter thinks, in Q; that Matthew had Mark, Q, his first-hand knowledge, and possibly a Manual of Prophecy; and that Luke had Mark, Q, a Herodian source, information from interviews, and probably other sources. (See pp. 182, 251, 341).

But when we come to the Fourth Gospel we find that this problem does not arise, for, while John had the Synoptics before him, so far from making use of them, he seems to avoid them, and draws upon his own knowledge and experience. It is true that in this Gospel there are some passages, not many, which show agreements in language with Mark and Luke: xii. 1-8 with Mark xiv. 3-9; xii. 3, with Luke vii. 38; and xiii. 38, with Luke xxii. 34; but if John in such passages draws upon Mark and Luke, it is not as sources of information, but because these passages were relevant to his purpose, and gave him the opportunity to cast more light on the incidents related. What he says in his Epistle is peculiarly applicable to his Gospel: 'That which we have heard, that which we have seen with our eyes, that which we beheld, and our hands handled concerning the Word of Life, that which we have seen and heard declare we unto you ' (1 John i. 1-3).

With these words read in the Gospel xix. 35; xxi. 24. John had no need, like Luke, to find sources of information, for he knew first-hand what he wanted to say, or rather, what the Holy Spirit wanted him to say.

Bishop Westcott has said that if the Gospels' material be represented by 100, in John's Gospel 92 are peculiar, and only 8 coincident with the Synoptics. (See p. 436).

7

JOHN'S DESIGN

THE Apostle has been credited with various intentions in writing his Gospel, and most of them contain an element of truth. There is clearly discernible in the record a *supplemental* aim. Dr. Salmon says: 'Whether it be intended or not, the fact is certain that the Fourth Gospel is supplemental to the other three'; and Bishop Westcott says: 'As a matter of fact the Fourth Gospel does supplement the other three, which it presupposes.' Much the larger part of this Gospel is a record of that which the Synoptists omit.

It is true, also, that within certain limits a *polemical* aim is here; that is, that the writer has in mind certain errors which characterized his time, and which are combated by what he writes.

Dr. Vincent Taylor speaks of John's 'reaction against *Docetic tendencies* which viewed the humanity of Jesus as one of "appearance," separated God from contact with matter, and taught a doctrine of intermediaries. It is probably for this reason that he avoids nouns like "knowledge," "wisdom," and "faith," beloved in Gnostic circles, and uses the corresponding verbal forms.' In harmony with opposition to this heresy is John's emphasis on Christ's humanity (cf. i. 14; iv. 6; xi. 33, 38; xix. 28, 34). It cannot be said that it was John's object to refute the errors of his time, but this Gospel in fact does so, because the exhibition of the Truth was necessarily their refutation.

Then, there is here a *doctrinal* aim; that is, the Evangelist intends to set forth the teaching of Jesus more fully and profoundly than is done in the Synoptics. A reference to the discourses in this Gospel will show how wonderfully this aim has been achieved. (See ' Discourses,' p. 421).

But these aims must be regarded as quite secondary in the light of John's own explicit declaration of design. He says:

> ' Many other signs therefore did Jesus in the presence of the disciples, which are not written in this book: but these are written, that ye may believe that Jesus is the Christ, the Son of God; and that believing ye may have life in His name ' (xx. 30, 31, R.V.).

These two verses must be thoroughly understood if we would rightly appraise and appreciate this Gospel. Mark carefully the following points:

(1) From abundance of material John made a careful selection. He had a knowledge of 'signs' about which he 'did not write' in his Gospel.

(2) John intentionally omitted much which had already appeared in other Writings. ' Which are not written in *this* book,' clearly implies *other* books, and these others are the Synoptic records.

(3) John's selection of material was made with a twofold object in view, namely (*a*) to create a particular conviction; and (*b*) to precipitate a particular experience. This is expressed by the word, 'in order that' (*hina*).

(4) The particular conviction which John would create is *intellectual* (though not exclusively so); 'that ye may believe'; and the particular experience which he would precipitate is *moral*, namely, 'that ye may have life in His name.'

(5) The *intellectual conviction* which John would create is twofold, corresponding to two parties:

(*a*) he would convict the *chosen people* that the historical Jesus is 'the Christ,' the Messiah in Whom all types and prophecies are fulfilled: and

(*b*) he would convict *all mankind* that this same Jesus is 'the Son of God,' and therefore stands in a certain relation to all men.

(6) John would have the *moral experience* wrought in Jew and Gentile alike, by bringing them, through faith, into the possession of 'life,' in this Lord Jesus Christ's 'name.'

(7) The object of this Gospel is, therefore, to show the Christhood and Godhead of Jesus, by presenting irrefutable evidence, in order to create faith in the hearts of men, with a clear view to their having eternal life.

These doctrinal and experimental objects must be seen together, for they are related to one another as root to fruit.

8

JOHN'S PLAN

THE plan of this Gospel is in keeping with its object. 'This is,' says Westcott, 'to express as briefly as possible the parallel development of faith and unbelief through the historical presence of Christ. The Evangelist is guided in the selection, in the arrangement, and in the treatment of his materials by his desire to fulfil this purpose.'

There are few more perfect literary structures.

The relation to one another of three ideas constitutes the plan. These ideas may be summarized in the words *revelation, rejection, reception,* and all three appear in every part of the Gospel. First, there is a divine *revelation,* and then it is shown that this revelation must have one or other of two issues in the hearts of men: either they *reject* it, or they *receive* it; either they disbelieve, or they believe; unbelief or faith must result from the revelation made known.

John selects no material which does not serve to exhibit this truth. He strikes these notes in his Prologue (i. 1-18), and they are heard right through to the end. In the Prologue the *revelation* is in verses 1-5; the issue of *rejection,* in verses 6-11; and the issue of *reception,* in verses 12-18. For the complete thought read verses 1-5, 11, 12.

Following the Prologue are five parts, each exhibiting the design of the writer.

In Part I, we are shown *The First Manifestations of the Word, and the Beginnings of Faith and Unbelief* (i. 19-iv. 54).

In Part II, one of the two issues is taken, and we are shown *The Development of Unbelief in Israel* (v-xii).

In Part III, the other issue is taken, and we are shown *The Development of Faith in the Disciples* (xiii-xvii).

In Part IV, we are shown *The Consummation of Unbelief in Israel* (xviii, xix).

In Part V, we are shown *The Consummation of Faith in the Disciples* (xx).

Then, in the Epilogue (xxi), though not so clearly, the three ideas of the Prologue meet again, the *manifestation* of the Lord for the correction of *unbelief*, and the confirmation of *faith*.

This Plan shows the unity of the Fourth Gospel. It is not a collection of miscellanies relative to the life and ministry of Jesus, neither is it a biography of Him, but it is a selection of materials wrought into a spiritual pattern, presenting Jesus as the God-Man, for the acceptance of men unto the saving of their souls. (See 'Features,' No. (iii), p. 448).

9

CHRONOLOGY OF JOHN'S GOSPEL

JOHN'S Gospel is the basis of our chronology of Jesus' life. The Evangelist likes to tell of things in historical sequence. Illustration of this is seen in his report of the opening week of Jesus' public ministry, where he distinguishes five distinct days on which something happened (i. 28, 29, 35, 39, 43); and other such notes of time are: 'the third day' (ii. 1); 'after this' (ii. 12); 'after the two days' (iv. 43); 'on the morrow' (vi. 22); 'two days' (xi. 6); 'four days' (xi. 17); 'six days' (xii. 1); 'on the morrow' (xii. 12); 'after eight days' (xx. 26). To these references must be added occurrences of 'after this,' 'after these things,' and 'afterward' (ii. 12; v. 14; xi. 7, 11; xix. 28, 38).

From the Synoptic narratives the ministry of Jesus would appear to have lasted for one year only, but from John's, a duration of three years, or more, is assigned. By this Gospel, and by it alone, can we establish the dates and reconstruct the external framework of Jesus' ministry.

John is careful to record the visits of Jesus to Jerusalem for the national feasts. The following are his references: First Feast of Passover (ii. 12, 13); 'A Feast,' almost certainly of Purim (v. 1); Second Feast of Passover (vi. 4), to which Jesus did not go; Feast of Tabernacles (vii. 2); Feast of Dedication (x. 22); Third Feast of Passover (xii. 1). 'Such a series of dates,' says Godet, 'traced with a firm hand, with natural intervals, forms a sufficient guide to us as to the course and duration of the Lord's Ministry, and enables us to draw up a rational plan of it.'

TABLE I

Period	Reference	Event	Duration
1	i. 19-ii. 12	From the Baptism of Jesus, Jan. A.D. 27, to the First Passover, Apr. 11-18, A.D. 27	3 months
2	ii. 13-iv. 42	From the First Passover, Apr. 11-18, A.D. 27, to the Departure for Galilee, Dec., A.D. 27.	8 months
3	iv. 43-v. 47	From the Departure for Galilee, Dec., A.D. 27, to May, A.D. 28 *about*	5 months
4	vi. 1-71	From May, A.D. 28, to the Withdrawal to Northern Galilee, May, A.D. 29 *about*	12 months
5	vii. 1-viii. 59	From May, A.D. 29, to the Final Departure from Galilee, Nov., A.D. 29 *about*	6 months
6	ix. 1-xii. 11	From Nov., A.D. 29, to the Entry into Jerusalem, Sunday, Apr. 2, A.D. 30 *about*	5 months
7	xii. 12-xix. 42	From Sunday, Apr. 2, A.D. 30, to the Resurrection Sunday, Apr. 9, A.D. 30	8 days
8	xx. 1-xxi. 25	From Sunday, Apr. 9, A.D. 30, to the Ascension, Thursday, May 18, A.D. 30	40 days

TABLE II

Period	Reference	Year	Month	Day
1	i. 19-51	A.D. 27	Feb.	—
	ii. 1-12	,,	Mar.	—
2	ii. 13-iii. 21	,,	Apr.	—
	iii. 22-24	,,	May	—
	iii. 25-36	,,	Aug.	—
	iv. 1-3	,,	Nov.	—
	iv. 4-42	,,	Dec.	—
3	iv. 43-45	,,	Dec.	—
	iv. 46-54	A.D. 28	Jan.	—
	v. 1-47	,,	Mar.	—
4	vi. 1-15	A.D. 29	Mar.	—
	vi. 16-71	,,	Apr.	—

PERIOD	REFERENCE	YEAR	MONTH	DAY
5	vii. 1-viii. 11	A.D. 29	Sept.	—
	viii. 12-59	,,	Oct.	—
6	ix. 1-41	,,	Oct.	—
	x. 1-42	,,	Nov.	—
	xi. 1-54	A.D. 30	Jan.	—
	xi. 55-xii. 11	,,	Apr.	—
7	xii. 12-19	,,	Apr. 2	Sunday
	xii. 20-50	,,	Apr. 4	Tuesday
	xiii. 1-xviii. 12	,,	Apr. 6	Thursday
	xviii. 13-xix. 42	,,	Apr. 7	Friday
8	xx. 1-25	,,	Apr. 9	Sunday
	xx. 26-xxi. 25	—	Apr. 9-May 18	—

From Table I it will be seen that Christ's ministry lasted for about three years and five months. Absolute exactness as to time is not possible, but the dates given are approximate. By the two Tables it should be observed that there are considerable gaps in John's narrative, but these can be filled in by the Synoptics. These eight periods should be marked off in your Bible.

For another view of the chronology of The Last Week see the article on 'The Day of the Crucifixion' (pp. 569-577).

10
GEOGRAPHY OF JOHN'S GOSPEL
CHAPTERS I. 1-IV. 54

Galilee		(2) i. 43-ii. 12			(5) iv. 43-54
Samaria				(4) iv. 1-42	
Judæa	(1) i. 1-42		(3) ii. 13-iii. 36		

This represents the year A.D. 27 of Jesus' Ministry.

CHAPTERS IV. 54-XI. 16

Galilee	(5) iv. 43-54		(7) vi. 1-vii. 9		(9) x, between 21 and 22		
Peræa							(11) x. 40-xi. 1[
Judæa		(6) v. 1-47		(8) vii. 10-x. 21		(10) x. 22-39	

This represents the years A.D. 28 and 29 of Jesus' ministry.

CHAPTERS XI. 16-XXI. 25

Galilee ...			(13) xxi
Peræa ...	(11) x. 40-xi. 16		
Judæa ...		(12) xi. 17-xx. 31	

This represents the year A.D. 30 of Jesus' Ministry.

Study these geographical movements with Tables I and II of the 'Chronology' (p. 409). It will be observed that Jesus had six periods of ministry in Judæa, five in Galilee, one in Samaria, and one in Peræa; and as the Galilean ministry included excursions into Phœnicia, Ituræa, and the Decapolis, the whole Land was visited, from Judæa to Syria, on both sides of the Jordan. (See Maps).

II

JOHN'S STYLE AND DICTION

NONE of the Evangelists has so limited a vocabulary as the Apostle John, but none of them makes better use of what he has. His style is unique in many respects; a thing to be felt rather than to be defined. Dr. Plummer says: 'The most illiterate reader is conscious of this quality; and the ablest critic cannot analyse it satisfactorily.' The language is Greek, but the thought is Hebrew.

(i) John's sentences usually stand by themselves, so that while there is continuity of thought, there is little in form of expression. For illustration of this examine chap. i. 1-5 (R.V.). There are here ten statements, and the only connecting link is a six times repeated 'and' (*kai*).

> 'In the beginning was the Word, *and* the Word was with God, *and* the Word was God. The same was in the beginning with God. All things were made by Him, *and* without Him was not anything made that hath been made. In Him was life, *and* the life was the light of men; *and* the light shineth in the darkness, *and* the darkness apprehended it not.' (Memorize and master these five verses, in the Greek, if you can). (See p. 454).

Yet these ten sentences are vitally related, pervaded by the same thought, which the writer develops as he proceeds.

The Gospel is chiefly written in short sentences, and, says Prof. Luthardt, 'the shorter they are, the weightier, as a rule.' Illustrations of this impressive brevity are:

> 'I that speak unto thee am He' (iv. 26). 'I am the bread of life' (vi. 35). 'Did not Moses give you the law? And yet none of you keepeth the law. Why go ye about to kill Me?' (vii. 19). 'I am the light of the world' (viii. 12). 'Whosoever committeth sin is the servant of sin' (viii. 34). 'Before Abraham was, I am' (viii. 58). 'I and My Father are one' (x. 30). 'Thy brother shall rise again' (xi. 23). 'I am the resurrection and the life' (xi. 25). 'Where have ye laid Him? Come and see. Jesus wept' (xi. 34, 35). 'And it was night' (xiii. 30). 'Let not your heart be troubled' (xiv. 1). 'Whom seek ye? . . . I am He' (xviii. 4, 5): 'Now Barabbas was a robber' (xviii. 40).

These are the brief phrases of a lofty style, and bear in their simple brevity the stamp of grandeur.

(ii) Another peculiarity of John's style is that he expresses an idea both negatively and positively. (See p. 455).

> 'All things were made by Him, and without Him was not anything made that hath been made' (i. 3, R.V.).
>
> 'He was not that light, but was sent to bear witness of that light' (i. 8).
>
> 'He confessed, and denied not' (i. 20).
>
> 'God sent not His Son into the world to condemn the world; but that the world through Him might be saved' (iii. 17).
>
> (cf. iii. 15, 16, 18, 20, 36; iv. 42; v. 23, 24; viii. 23, 35, 47; ix. 39; x. 28; xv. 5, 6).

(iii) Note also, the frequent appearance of short statements which break up the surrounding sentences: 'it was the tenth hour'; 'the same day was the Sabbath'; 'now Jesus loved Martha and her sister' (i. 40; v. 9; xi. 5; xi. 35; xiii. 30; xviii. 40, *et al.*).

(iv) John's two most characteristic particles are 'that' (*hina*), and 'then' (*oun*). The first points to the belief that nothing happens without a purpose; and the second, to the belief that nothing happens without a cause. In these senses 'that' occurs over 60 times, and 'then' over 190 times. Examples of 'that' are seen in i. 7, 22, 31; iii. 17, 21; v. 23, 34, 40; vi. 5, 28, 30, 40, 50; ix. 3, 36, 39. Examples of 'then' are seen in ii. 22; iii. 25, 29; iv. 1, 6, 46; vi. 5; vii. 25; viii. 12, 21; x. 7; xii. 1, 3, 9, 17, 21.

Another phrase characteristic of the Gospel is 'after this'

(*meta touto,* or *meta tauta*), which is used as a form of transition from one part of the narrative to another. It is found in ii. 12; iii. 22; v. 1; vi. 1; vii. 1; and then it disappears, except for xi. 7; and its place is taken by *oun*, ' then,' ' therefore,' or *de*, ' and.' For *oun* see, xi. 3, 6, 12, 14, 16, 17, 20, 21, 31, 32, 33, 36, 38, 41, 45, 47, 54; xii. 1, 9, 17; xviii. 3, 4, 6, 7, 10, 11, 12, 17, 19, 28; xix. 1, 16, 23, 31, *et. al.* For *de* see vi. 10, 51; viii. 17; ix. 14; xi. 2; xv. 27, *et. al.* (Trace other occurrences in Young's ' Analytical,' or Strong's 'Exhaustive' Concordance).

(v) Another feature of John's style is the repetition of a word or sentence, which serves to underline the thought he would communicate. (See p. 455).

> 'In the beginning was the *Word*, and the *Word* was with God, and the *Word* was God' (i. 1).
> 'He was in the *world*, and the *world* was made by Him, and the *world* knew Him not' (i. 10).
> 'If I bear *witness* of myself, my *witness* is not true. There is another that beareth *witness* of Me, and I know that the *witness* which he *witnesseth* of Me is true' (v. 31, 32).
> 'I am the *Good Shepherd*; the *Good Shepherd* giveth His life for the sheep' (x. 11).
> (Cf. v. 46, 47; xi. 33; xv. 4, 5, 13, 14; xvii. 14-19; xviii. 18, 25).

(vi) Hebrew form is characterized by parallelism, and John, full of the spirit of Hebrew poetry, frequently employs this form.

> 'A servant is not greater than his lord;
> neither one that is sent, greater than he that sent him' (xiii. 16).

> 'Peace I leave with you,
> My peace I give unto you.
> Let not your heart be troubled,
> Neither let it be afraid' (xiv. 27).

The use of a word serves as the keynote of a discourse, and in one or two instances, of the whole Gospel. At the beginning two sentences are used which are returned to again and again. 'In Him was life' (i. 4), runs through the whole Gospel (iii. 15, 16, 36; iv. 14; v. 24, 26; vi. 35, 40, 47, 48, 51, 54, 57; xi. 25; xiv. 6). 'The life was the light of men' (i. 4, 5, 7, 8, 9; iii. 19; viii. 12; ix. 5; xii. 35, 46). These are like notes which, when once struck, continue to vibrate in the ear and in the soul.

To these illustrations may be added references to the reception

of Jesus by men. Again and again are references to men believing
or not believing on Him. For 'believing,' see ii. 11, 22; iv. 39,
41, 53; vii. 31; viii. 30; x. 42; xi. 45; xii. 11, 42; and for 'not
believing,' see i. 10, 11; iii. 32; v. 16, 18; vii. 1, 19, 30, 32, 44;
viii. 20, 40, 59; x. 31, 39; xi. 8, 53, 57; xii. 37.

In like manner are repeated acknowledgments of Jesus (iv.
29, 42; vi. 14, 69; ix. 17; xi. 27; xvi. 30); and accusations against
Him (vii. 20; viii. 48, 49, 52; x. 20, 21).

Sometimes the parallelism is antithetic, the second clause
being the opposite of the first.

> 'He confessed, and denied not' (i. 20).
> 'I give unto them eternal life,
>   and they shall never perish' (x. 28).

(Cf. iii. 11; v. 37; vi. 35, 55, 56; xv. 20; xvi. 20).

(vii) It has been said that there is nothing analogous to John's
language in the whole of sacred or profane literature. He uses
fewer words than any of the Synoptists, but while these are poor
in number, they are profound in meaning.

A list should be made of John's dominating words, and these
should be carefully studied. The number attached to the following words is that of their occurrence. (See p. 456).

Know (ginōskō, 56; oida, 86: total 142). Father (Patēr, 118).
Believe (pisteuō, 100). World (kosmos, 78). See (eidon, 36; blepō,
15; horaō, 30; theōreō, 19; theaomai, 5: total 105). Verily (amēn,
50 in 25 pairs). Love (agapē, 9; agapaō, 36). Witness, bear
witness, testify, bear record (martureō, 33). Witness, testimony,
record (marturia, 14). Life (zōē, 19); to live (zaō, 18); quicken
(zōopoieō, 3). Bios for life does not occur in John's Gospel. Abide,
dwell, remain, continue, endure, tarry, be present (menō, 40).
Glory (doxa, 41). Judge (krinō, 19; krisis, 11). For ever, never
(aiōn, 12); Everlasting, with life (8); Eternal, with life (9), (aiōnios).
Ask (aiteō, 11); ask, desire, pray, beseech (erōtaō, 29). Send
(apostellō, 28); he that is sent (apostolos, 1). Works, signs (ergazomai,
8; ergon, 23; deed, 4). Truth (alētheia, 25); true, truly (alēthēs,
15); true (alēthinos, 9); of a truth, verily, surely, indeed (alēthōs,
10). Sin (hamartanō, 4; hamartia, 17); sinner (hamartōlos, 4).
Name (onoma, 25). Light (phōs, 23; phōtizō, 1). Miracle (sēmeion,
17). Behold (ide, 18). Hour (hōra, 26). Heaven (ouranos, 19).
Come, several hundred times, representing about sixteen words
in the Greek (see erchomai). Receive (lambanō, 45; with para,
3; with kata, 4). Then (115), so (8); now (4); therefore (64);
truly (1); and (2); but (2), all oun.

Note the great words which enter into the texture of the Prologue:

Word, Life, Light, Darkness, Witness, Believe, World, Received, Glory, Grace, Truth, Fulness, Father, Came, and *Became.*

(viii) It is characteristic of John to express himself in sharp antitheses, so brought forward as to suggest a concrete existence: light and darkness; life and death; truth and falsehood; love and hate; faith and unbelief; Christ and the world. Thought thus expressed is easily remembered, and truth thus communicated has upon it the impress of finality.

'If the author has only a few terms in his vocabulary,' says Godet, 'these terms may be compared to the pieces of gold with which great lords make payment.'

(ix) The number of words peculiar to John's Gospel is small, compared, for instance, with Luke's. The latter has over 300, but John has 82 for certain, and about a dozen doubtfuls, apart from peculiar phrases. These words are as follows:

i. 41	Messiah (iv. 25)		ix. 6	Spittle
ii. 6	Firkins		ix. 6	To-(and) on-(the)-ground
ii. 6, 7	Water-pots (iv. 28)			(xviii. 6)
ii. 8, 9	Draw (iv. 7, 15)		ix. 6, 11	Anointed
ii. 8, 9	Ruler-of-the-feast		ix. 31	Worshipper-of-God
ii. 14	Changers-of-money		x. 1	*Some-other-way*
ii. 15	Money		x. 22	Feast-of-the-Dedication
ii. 15	Scourge		xi. 11	*Awake-out-of-sleep*
ii. 16	Merchandise		xi. 13	Taking-rest
iii. 4	Old		xi. 16	Didymus (xx. 24: xxi. 2)
iv. 9	Have-dealings		xi. 16	Fellow-disciple
iv. 11	To-draw-with		xi. 35	Wept
iv. 12	Cattle		xi. 39	Stinketh
iv. 23	*Worshipper*		xi. 39	Four-days
iv. 35	*Four-months*		xi. 44	Grave-clothes
v. 2	Sheep-gate		xi. 44	Bound-about
v. 2, 4, 7	Pool (ix. 7, 11)		xii. 3	Pound (xix. 39)
v. 3	Moving		xii. 6	Bag (xiii. 29)
v. 13	Had-conveyed-himself-		xii. 13	Branches
	away		xii. 14	Young-ass
vi. 9, 11	Fish (xxi. 9, 10, 13)		xiii. 4, 5	Gird (xxi. 7)
vi. 9, 13	Barley		xiii. 4, 5	Towel
vi. 13	Had-eaten		xiii. 5	Basin
vi. 22	Went-with (xviii. 15)		xiii. 18	*Heel*
vii. 2	Tabernacles		xiii. 26	Sop
vii. 14	About-the-midst-of		27, 30	
vii. 17	*Whether*		xiii. 38,	Verily, verily (50 times,
vii. 23	*Are-ye-angry*		*et al*	in 25 doubles)
vii. 38	*Shall-flow*		xiv. 2, 23	Mansions, *abode*
viii. 4	In-the-very-act		xiv. 27	*Let-it-be-afraid*
viii. 7	*Without-sin*		xv. 2, 4,	*Branch*
ix. 1	Birth		5, 6	

xvi. 2	Out-of-the-Synagogue (ix. 22; xii. 42)		xix. 23	Without-seam, Woven
xviii. 1	Brook		xix. 31, 32	Legs
xviii. 3	Lanterns		33	
xviii. 11	*Sheath*		xix. 34	Spear
xviii. 13	Father-in-law		xix. 34	Pierce
xviii. 18	Fire-of-coals (xxi. 9)		xix. 39	Aloes
xviii. 37	Then		xx. 15	Gardener
xix. 13	Gabbatha		xx. 22	Breathe-on
xix. 13	Pavement		xx. 25	Nails
xix. 19, 20	Title		xxi. 3	A-fishing
xix. 20	Latin		xxi. 5	*Meat*
xix. 23	Woven		xxi. 7	Fisher's-coat, upper garment

The fourteen words in *italic* occur in utterances of our Lord.
It should be observed that there are some words which the
Evangelist does not use, which occur in the Synoptics; e.g.,
the age, power, rebuke, gospel, parable, command or declare,
faith, wise, wisdom; and John nowhere notices Scribes, publicans,
lepers, or demoniacs.

(x) Among notable phrases in this Gospel are:

'Cometh into the world' (i. 9; iii. 19; vi. 14; ix. 39); 'came into
His own' (i. 11); 'born of God'; 'born again'; 'born of the
Spirit' (i. 13; iii. 3, 5-8); 'taketh away the sin of the world' (i.
29); 'descending from heaven' (i. 32); 'came down from heaven'
(iii. 13; vi. 33, 38, 41, 42, 50, 51, 58); 'resurrection of life . . .
of condemnation' (v. 29; xi. 25); 'giveth life unto the world'
(vi. 33); 'the last day' (vi. 39, 40, 44, 54; vii. 37; xi. 24; xii. 48);
'walk in darkness'; 'walk in the night' (viii. 12; xi. 10; xii. 35);
'abide in'—Christ, the word *menō*, (viii. 31; xiv. 10; xv. 4-7, 9,
10); 'came from God' (viii. 42); 'walk in the day' (xi. 9); 'the
prince of this world' (xii. 31; xiv. 30; xvi. 11); 'was come from
God' (xiii. 3); 'love one another'; 'love me' (xiii. 34; xiv. 15,
21, 23, 24, 28, 31; xv. 12, 17; xxi. 15, 16); 'came out from God';
'camest forth from God'; 'came forth from the Father' (xvi. 27,
30, 28); 'came out from Thee' (xvii. 8); 'answered and said'
(34 times).

(xi) A certain uniformity in John's style is very noticeable.
An outstanding illustration of this is his habit of putting the
verb first in his sentences (in the Greek). In chap. i, every one
of the verses, 40-52 (except 44), commences in this way; and the
same is true in the following passages: ii. 17-20; iii. 3-5, 9, 10;
iv. 3-7, 9-11, 13, 15-17, 19, 21, 23, 25, 26, 28, 30, 33, 34, 46,
48-50, 52, 53; vi. 7-11; xi. 23-25, 27, 39, 40, 41, 47, 56, 57;
xiii. 36-38; xiv. 5-11; xviii. 5, 11, 14, 15, 17, 18, 20, 23, 24-26,
28-31, 33-40, *et al.*

Another illustration is the repetition of such expressions as:

> 'Bare record, and cried, saying' (i. 15); 'they asked Him, and said unto Him' (i. 25); 'answered, saying' (i. 26); 'bare record, saying' (i. 32); 'He answered and said' (i. 49, 50, 51; iii. 3, 9, 10, 27; iv. 10, 13, 17; v. 19; vi. 29, 43; vii. 16; viii. 48; ix. 20, 30; xii. 30; xiii. 7, *et. al.*); 'cried . . . as He taught, saying' (vii. 28); 'spake, saying' (viii. 12), etc.

(xii) Another characteristic of the Gospel is the frequent occurrence of intermediate sentences. Illustrations of this are:

> 'It was about the tenth hour' (i. 39); 'now Philip was from Bethsaida' (i. 44); 'it was about the sixth hour' (iv. 6); 'and on the same day was the Sabbath' (v. 9); 'now the Passover, the feast of the Jews, was at hand' (vi. 4); 'now there was much grass' (vi. 10); 'howbeit there came other boats' (vi. 23); 'now it was the Sabbath' (ix. 14); 'and it was the feast of the dedication at Jerusalem' (x. 22); 'now Jesus loved Martha' (xi. 5); 'and it was early' (xviii. 28); 'now it was the Preparation of the Passover; it was about the sixth hour' (xix. 14).

To these must be added the use of explanatory sentences such as:

> 'But He spake of the temple of His body' (ii. 21); 'this He said to prove him' (vi. 6); 'for Jesus knew from the beginning who they were that believed not' (vi. 64); 'but this He spake of the Spirit' (vii. 39); 'this they said, tempting Him, that they might have (whereof) to accuse Him' (viii. 6); 'they perceived not that He spake to them of the Father' (viii. 27); 'these things said his parents, because they feared the Jews' (ix. 22); 'they thought that He spake of taking rest in sleep' (xi. 13); 'now this he said, not because he cared for the poor, but because he was a thief, and having the bag took away what was put therein' (xii. 6, R.V.); 'this He said, signifying by what manner of death He should die' (xii. 33; xxi. 19); 'these things said Isaiah, because he saw His glory; and he spake of Him' (xii. 41).

Also, it is the Evangelist's habit to explain Hebrew words:

> 'Rabbi (which is to say, being interpreted, Master)' (i. 38); 'the Messiah (which is, being interpreted, Christ)' (i. 41); 'Cephas (which is by interpretation, Peter)' (i. 42); 'Messiah cometh (who is called Christ)' (iv. 25); 'which is called in Hebrew, Bethesda' (v. 2); 'the pool of Siloam (which is by interpretation, Sent)' (ix. 7); 'the Pavement, but in Hebrew, Gabbatha' (xix. 13); 'the place of a skull, which is called in Hebrew, Golgotha' (xix. 17); 'Rabboni, which is to say, Master' (xx. 16).

John's style as a whole may be said to be contemplative, not controversial; calm, not militant; simple, yet profound; direct rather than oblique; transparent and yet deep. It is essentially

27

the spiritual Gospel rather than the historical. The word 'heaven' occurs 19 times, in the singular only, and always with the article, 'the heaven,' for this is the heavenly or, as Clement of Alexandria said, the 'spiritual Gospel.'

12
CHRIST'S WORDS IN JOHN'S GOSPEL

IN John's Gospel there are 879 verses (A.V.), or 866 (R.V., see p. 193), and 419 of these contain words of our Lord, nearly half the Gospel. The number of verses in whole, or part, in the various chapters, which record His words, are as follows:

CHS.	VERS.	CHS.	VERS.	CHS.	VERS.	CHS.	VERS.	CHS.	VERS.
i	8	v	33	ix	8	xiii	22	xvii	26
ii	5	vi	37	x	29	xiv	28	xviii	11
iii	17	vii	17	xi	17	xv	27	xix-xx	5 / 10
iv	20	viii	40	xii	20	xvi	29	xxi	10

For ready reference these verses should be marked, in some way, in your Bible (see pp. 192, 272, 366). (For fuller references see 'Discourses,' pp. 421-425).

13
MIRACLES IN JOHN'S GOSPEL

OF the 35 miracles recorded by the Evangelists (but see pp. 286, 287, 553, 554), 8 are in this Gospel, 7 of them being wrought before Christ's death, and 1 after His resurrection. Of these eight, six are peculiar to this Gospel, and two are found elsewhere. The six which John alone records are:

Turning Water into Wine - - - - - ii. 1-11
Healing a Nobleman's Son - - - - iv. 46-54
Healing an Impotent Man at Bethesda - - v. 1-9
Giving Sight to a Man Born Blind - - ix. 1-7
The Raising of Lazarus from the Dead - xi. 17-44
The Draught of Fishes - - - - xxi. 1-14

The two miracles recorded elsewhere are:

Feeding the Five Thousand - - - - vi. 1-14
                              Mark vi; Matt. xiv; Luke ix
Walking on the Sea - - - - vi. 16-21
                              Mark vi; Matt. xiv

In the Gospels miracles are designated 'mighty works' (lit. powers: Matt. xi. 20, 21, 23, *et al.*); 'wonders' (John iv. 48; Matt. xxiv. 24; Mark xiii. 22); 'works,' referring to miracles, 18 times in John's Gospel (cf. v. 20, 36; vii. 3; ix. 3, 4); and 'signs,' occurring 17 times in John's Gospel (cf. ii. 18; iv. 48; vi. 30; xx. 30, translated 'sign'; and ii. 11, 23; iii. 2; iv. 54; *et al.*, translated 'miracle.')

'Mighty Works,' means *a putting forth of Divine power.* It does not occur in this Gospel. 'Wonders,' means *a wonderful act,* and it occurs once in this Gospel. 'Works,' which signifies *deeds designed to arrest attention,* and 'signs,' which points to *deeds which symbolize spiritual truths,* are the two words which John uses for miracles. Miracles as 'works' were part of 'the work' which Christ came to do (xvii. 4). They were designed to arrest attention, create wonder, and promote faith (cf. v. 20). (See Mark's Gospel, 'Miracles,' pp. 203, 204).

Miracles, as 'signs,' were intended to 'make men feel the mysteries which underlie the visible order' (Westcott).

The eight miracles in this Gospel, relative to their spiritual significance, may be classified as follows:

1 The Fundamental Character of the Christian Gospel.

LIFE BY FAITH.		COMMENCEMENT
(i) *Water Turned into Wine* - - - - ii. 1-11		
The Nature of the Blessing: *Newness of Life*		
(ii) *The Boy Restored* - - - - - iv. 46-54		
The Condition of the Blessing: *Faith*		

2 The Manifold Provision in Christ for all who Believe and Live.

LIFE UNFOLDING.		COURSE
(iii) *The Paralytic Healed* • • • v. 1-9		
Energy Given.		
(iv) *The Multitude Fed* - • • • vi. 1-14		
Sustenance Provided		
(v) *Walking on the Sea* - • • • vi. 16-21		
Guidance Vouchsafed.		
(vi) *Sight Restored* - - • • • ix. 1-7		
Enlightenment Granted.		
(vii) *Lazarus Raised* - • • • xi. 17-44		
Victory over Death.		

3 Satisfaction in the Morning, when the Night of Toil is Over.

LIFE PERFECTED.   CONSUMMATION

(viii) *The Draught of Fishes*   -   ·   -   -   xxi. 1-14
Fulness and Fellowship.

In this way Christ's 'works' were 'signs.'

Make a careful study of these miracles, and observe that, as not in the Synoptics, they are frequently made the text of discourses. Compare ii. 23-25, with iii. 1-15; v. 1-9, with v. 10-47; vi. 1-14, with vi. 26-59, specially verses 35, 41, 48, 51; chap. ix, with chap. x. The performing of the miracles always had behind it a spiritual motive and meaning.

In his *Introduction to the Study of the Gospels*, Bishop Westcott says: 'It is not, I believe, fanciful to see a significance even in the number of these miracles. *Seven* are included in the record of Christ's ministry, and an *eighth* completes the typical representation of His work after His resurrection. *Seven*, according to the early belief, was the figure of a completed creation; *eight*, the figure of the resurrection, or new birth.' It should be noticed that the miracles in this Gospel are presented as manifestations of Christ's glory, rather than, as in the Synoptics, expressions of His compassion (cf. ii. 11). No instance of demon expulsion is mentioned in John.

This Evangelist records at length the Raising of Lazarus from the dead, an event which produced a tremendous effect, but which, nevertheless, the Synoptists do not record. Also, John alone names the man who drew the sword at the gate of Gethsemane (xviii. 10; cf. Mark xiv. 47; Matt. xxvi. 51; Luke xxii. 50). The reason for the omission of these facts by the Synoptists was, no doubt, as Godet suggests, out of consideration for the safety of the persons concerned (cf. John xii. 10); but when John wrote (A.D. 95), there was no longer any need for such precaution, for, presumably, Peter and Lazarus were dead.

Many unspecified miracles are referred to by John in ii. 23; iii. 2; vi. 2; vii. 31; xi. 47; and xii. 37.

14

DISCOURSES IN JOHN'S GOSPEL

NO one can read the Gospels carefully without noticing how different are the discourses in the Fourth Gospel from those in the Synoptics; a difference, not of expression merely, but of substance. In the Synoptics the discourses are, as Dr. Plummer says, 'simple, direct, and easily intelligible, inculcating, for the most part, high moral principles which are enforced and illustrated by numerous parables and proverbs; whereas the discourses in the Fourth Gospel are many and intricate, inculcating, for the most part, deep mystical truths which are enforced by a ceaseless reiteration tending to obscure the exact line of the argument, and illustrated by not a single parable, properly so-called.'

This difference has led some scholars to affirm that Jesus never spoke the words which here are attributed to Him, any more than Socrates spoke the words which Plato attributed to him, but that these discourses are the utterances of a Christian mystic of a late date.

Against this view we put the saying of Matthew Arnold, that 'the doctrine and discourses of Jesus (in the Fourth Gospel) cannot in the main be the writer's, because in the main they are clearly out of his reach'; that is to say, no man could have conceived the ideas which are here recorded; they can have come only from Him who spake as never man spake (vii. 46). And Dr. James Orr says: 'The supreme guaranty of their (the Gospels) trustworthiness, is found in the narratives themselves; for who in that (or any) account could imagine a figure so unique and perfect as that of Jesus, or invent the incomparable sayings and parables that proceeded from His lips! Much of Christ's teaching is high as heaven above the minds of men still.' When, therefore, writers say that the Evangelist 'put words into the mouth of Jesus,' and this is frequently said, let us remember that they are giving some man credit for something of which no man has ever been capable. Dr. Reynolds has well said: 'It is inconceivable that the author of the Gospel invented, rather than recited, marvellous utterances of the Christ; that he appealed to his imagination, rather than to his memory, for the significant portraiture of Him who was pre-eminently 'Grace and Truth,' 'the Truth,' ' the Life,' and ' the Light of the World.''

There is no ground for supposing that He who spoke according to the records of the Synoptists could not have spoken according to the record of the Fourth Gospel. That there are striking differences between these records is obvious, but differences are not necessarily contradictions, or incompatibilities, and they have been at times exaggerated. Godet says: 'We find at least twenty-seven sayings of Jesus occurring in John which appear almost identically the same in the Synoptics'; a fact which points both to a common origin, and to a deep harmony of teaching. For illustration compare:

JOHN	MATTHEW	JOHN	MATTHEW
ii. 19	xxvi. 61	xiii. 3	xi. 27
iv. 44	xiii. 57	xiii. 16	x. 24
vi. 35	v. 6	xiii. 20	x. 40
vi. 37	xi. 28, 29	xiv. 18	xxviii. 20
vi. 46; i. 18	xi. 27	xv. 20	x. 25
xii. 25	x. 39	xvi. 32	xxvi. 31

But it is natural to wonder how John, who wrote in the last decade of the first century, could have remembered for sixty-five years what his Master had said. Four considerations should satisfy this wonderment. First: it is evident that these discourses are not verbatim, but are summaries. Second: it is more than likely that John, having heard Jesus speak, would almost immediately make notes of what he had heard. Third: the Jews were blessed with very retentive memories, and were accustomed to store in their minds the words of their most honoured teachers. Fourth: Jesus had promised divine help in this matter: 'The Holy Spirit, whom the Father will send in

My name, He shall . . . bring to your remembrance all that I said unto you' (xiv. 26).

It is true that in John's report of Christ's teaching 'there is an element, impossible to separate now, which comes from himself. (See 'Features; Comments,' p. 453). His report is sometimes a literal translation of the very words used, sometimes the substance of what was said put into his own words: but he gives us no means of distinguishing where the one shades off into the other.'

That the discourses in this Gospel present a problem should not be denied. Their similarity of thought and expression with John's First Epistle is obvious; but it may be said that the beloved disciple had for so long contemplated the teaching of his Master that his own thought and expression were moulded to that model.

Coming now to the discourses themselves, we may say that there are fourteen, as follows:

1	The New Birth	iii. 1-21
2	The Water of Life	iv. 4-26
3	The Source of Life, and the Witnesses	v. 19-47
4	The Sustainer of Life	vi. 26-59
5	The Fountain of Truth	vii. 14-29
6	The Light of the World	viii. 12-20
7	The True Object of Faith	viii. 21-30
8	Spiritual Freedom and Descent	viii. 31-59
9	The Shepherd of the Flock	x. 1-21
10	The Oneness of Christ with the Father	x. 22-38
11	The Redeemer of the World	xii. 20-36
12	The Coming Separation and Related Problems	xiii. 31-xiv. 31
13	The Nature and Issues of Union with Christ	xv
14	The Holy Spirit and the Future	xvi

These discourses are clearly divisible into two parts. The first is *Public Instruction* (i-xii), and here Christ presents Himself to the *World* as *The Ultimate Reality*. The second is *Private Instruction* (xii-xvi), and here Christ reveals Himself to the *Disciples* as *The Eternal Sufficiency*.

The following outlines are designed to lead to a truer appreciation of the scope, depth, and unity of these discourses.

(A) PUBLIC INSTRUCTION
(Chapters i-xii)

CHRIST REVEALS HIMSELF TO THE WORLD AS THE ULTIMATE REALITY.

I. **As Life** - - - - - - Chaps. i-vii (cf. i. 1-5
  1 LIFE, IN RELATION TO MEN.
    (i) The Way of Life (iii. 1-21; ver. 3).
    (ii) The Offer of Life (iv. 4-26; vv. 10, 14).
  2 LIFE AS REVEALED IN CHRIST.
    (iii) The Source of Life (v. 19-47; vv. 21, 26).
    (iv) The Sustainer of Life (vi. vv. 35, 41, 51).
    (v) The Fulness of Life (vii. ver. 38).

II. **As Light** - - - - - - Chaps. viii-ix (cf. i. 6-13)
  1 The Claim to be the Light (viii. 12-20; ver. 12).
  2 The Consequence of Refusing the Light (viii. 21-30; ver. 24).
  3 A Test of Belief in the Light (viii. 31-47; vv. 35, 36).
  4 A Revelation of the Eternity of the Light (viii. 48-59; vv. 51, 58).
  5 A Demonstration of the Power of the Light (ix. vv. 5-7).

III. **As Love** - - - - -Chaps. x-xii (cf. i. 14-18)
  1 The Love of the Shepherd (x. 1-21; ver. 11).
  2 The Love of the Son (x. 22-39; vv. 30, 33, 36).
  3 The Love of the Friend (xi. 1-xii. 11; xi. 5).
  4 The Love of the Saviour (xii. 12-50; ver. 32).

(B) PRIVATE INSTRUCTION
(Chapters xiii-xvi)

CHRIST PRESENTS HIMSELF TO THE DISCIPLES AS THE ETERNAL SUFFICIENCY.
Preparation (xiii. 1-30)

(a) The Feet-washing and its Lesson - - - xiii. 1-20
(b) The Exclusion of Judas Iscariot - - - xiii. 21-30

I. **Relating to the Past** - - - - xiii. 31-xiv. 31
  CONSOLATION.   Exhortation to FAITH

THE COMING SEPARATION AND RELATED PROBLEMS

  1 INTRODUCTION (xiii. 31-35)
    (i) The Glorification of the Son and the Father (xiii. 31-33).
    (ii) The Demand this Would Make on the Disciples (xiii. 34, 35).

  2 THE PROBLEMS (xiii. 36-xiv. 24)
    (i) PETER'S PROBLEM (xiii. 36-xiv. 4).
      'Why must I be separated from Thee?'
    (ii) THOMAS' PROBLEM (xiv. 5-7)
      'Not knowing the goal, how can we know the way?'
    (iii) PHILIP'S PROBLEM (xiv. 8-21).
      'Let us see the Father, and we shall be satisfied.'
    (iv) JUDAS' PROBLEM (xiv. 22-24).
      'Why is Thy Self-manifestation limited to Thy Disciples?'

3 Conclusion (xiv. 25-31).
   (i) The Promise of Further Light (xiv. 25, 26).
   (ii) The Legacy of Peace (xiv. 27).
   (iii) The Reason for the Separation (xiv. 28-31).

II. **Relating to the Present** · · · · - xv. 1-xvi. 4a
   Instruction.   Appeal to Love

THE NATURE AND RESULTS OF UNION WITH CHRIST

  1 The Nature of this Union · · · - xv. 1-10
        Illustration of the Vine, revealing:
    (i) Discipline. (1, 2).
    (ii) Dependence. (3, 4).
    (iii) Responsibility. (5, 6).
    (iv) Privilege. (7, 8).
    (v) Inspiration. (9, 10).

  2 The Results of this Union · · · xv. 11-xvi. 4a
    (i) The Disciples and one another (xv. 11-13).
       Love and Sacrifice.
    (ii) The Disciples and Christ (xv. 14-16).
       Friendship and Privilege.
    (iii) The Disciples and the World (xv. 17-xvi. 4a).
       Hatred and Persecution.

III. **Relating to the Future** · · · - xvi. 4b-33
   Prediction.   Incentives to Hope

THE HOLY SPIRIT AND THE PROSPECT

  1 The Holy Spirit · · · · · · xvi. 4b-15
    (i) Christ and the Spirit (xvi. 4b-7).
    (ii) The World and the Spirit (xvi. 8-11).
    (iii) The Disciples and the Spirit (xvi. 12-15).

  2 The Prospect - · · · · · - xvi. 16-33
    (i) Sorrow shall be turned into Joy (xvi. 16-24).
    (ii) Mystery shall be turned into Vision (xvi. 25-30).
    (iii) Trial shall be turned into Triumph (xvi. 31-33).

It is illuminating to compare the Sermon on the Mount (Matt. v-vii) with the Upper Room Talk (John xiii-xvi). The one looks back; the other looks on. The one is the consummation of the past; the other is the inauguration of the future. The one is fulfilment; the other is prophecy. The one is Jewish in complexion; the other is Christian. The one relates to the Kingdom; the other to the Church. These distinctions help us to understand the difference in the outlook and purpose of these Gospels respectively.

15

THE OLD TESTAMENT IN JOHN'S GOSPEL

DR. PLUMMER has rightly said that 'the Fourth Gospel is saturated with the thoughts, imagery, and language of the Old Testament'; and Bishop Westcott has said that 'without the basis of the Old Testament, the Gospel of St. John is an insoluble mystery.' Estimates of the number of references to the Old Testament in this Gospel vary. Dr. S. Davidson says there are 26; Westcott and Hort say 20; another says 44; but there are probably not fewer than 124 references in all, sayings and details which cannot be understood apart from the Old Testament.

Some of these references are in the utterances of Christ, and others, in the utterances of the Evangelist, John the Baptist, Andrew, Philip, Nathanael, Peter, Nicodemus, Pilate, Martha; the Jews, the People, the Pharisees, certain Samaritans, and the woman of Samaria.

References are made to Abraham, Jacob, Joseph, Moses, Elijah, David, Isaiah, Micah, Zechariah, and the Prophets. Some of these references are quotations, and some are allusions; references particular and general; direct and indirect.

The quotations, of which there are 19, are from six of the Old Testament books: Exodus, Numbers, Deuteronomy, Psalms, Isaiah, and Zechariah; and the allusions, of which there are about 105, are from twelve of the books: each book of the Pentateuch, 2 Samuel, Psalms, Proverbs, Isaiah, Jeremiah, Micah, and Zechariah; but an allusion may be traced to more than one passage or book.

Seven times reference is made to Scripture being fulfilled (xii. 38; xiii. 18; xv. 25; xvii. 12; xviii. 9; xix. 24, 28, 36). Such references in Matthew are introduced by a formula, which suggests that they are derived from a written source, and it has been thought that there existed in the Apostolic days a Jewish collection of Old Testament passages held to be predictive of Messiah, called the *Testimonies*, and it may be that John used this Manual as well as Matthew (see pp. 89, 253). In this Gospel these fulfilments always have reference to particular verses of the

Old Testament, the words of which fit the incident which the Evangelist has recorded.

All the Old Testament references in this Gospel should be carefully studied in their settings, and the subjects of them noted.

(a) QUOTATIONS

JOHN	OLD TESTAMENT	JOHN	OLD TESTAMENT
i. 23	Isa. xl. 3	xii. 14, 15	Zech. ix. 9
i. 51	Gen. xxviii. 12	xii. 27	Psa. vi. 3; xlii. 6
ii. 17	Psa. lxix. 9	xii. 38	Isa. liii. 1
vi. 31, 32	Exod. xvi. 4, 15; Psa.	xii. 39-41	Isa. vi. 9, 10
	lxxviii. 24, 25	xiii. 18	Psa. xli. 9
vi. 45	Isa. liv. 13	xv. 25	Psa. xxxv. 19; lxix. 4
viii. 17	Deut. xvii. 6; xix. 15;	xvi. 22	Isa. lxvi. 14
	Num. xxxv. 30	xix. 24	Psa. xxii. 18
x. 16	Ezek. xxxiv. 23;		
	xxxvii. 24	xix. 36	Exod. xii. 46; Num. ix.
x. 34, 35	Psa. lxxxii. 6		12
xii. 13	Psa. cxviii. 25 f.	xix. 37	Zech. xii. 10

These quotations relate to the Forerunner of Christ, to Christ's zeal, to the manna in the wilderness, to Christ the divine Teacher, to the authority of witness, to the Deity of Christ, to Christ's welcome as He entered Jerusalem in the Passion Week, to the manner of His entrance into Jerusalem, to the people's rejection of Him, and the reason for it, to the treachery of Judas, to the world's causeless hatred of Christ, to the casting of lots for His garment, to His bones not being broken, and to the people beholding Him on the Cross.

(b) ALLUSIONS

JOHN	OLD TESTAMENT	JOHN	OLD TESTAMENT
iii. 14	Num. xxi. 8, 9	viii. 5	Lev. xx. 10
iv. 20	Deut. xxvii. 4, 12	viii. 33, 39	Gen. xii.; xv.
iv. 37	Job xxxi. 8; Mic. vi. 15	viii. 39, 40	Gen. xii. (Gal. iii. 7, 9)
v. 10	Jer. xvii. 21, 22, 27	viii. 52, 53	Zech. i. 5
v. 45-47	Deut. xviii. 15	viii. 56	Gen. xxii. 14
vi. 49	Exod. xvi. 15	viii. 57	Abraham
vii. 2	Lev. xxiii. 34	viii. 58	Exod. iii. 14
vii. 22, 23	Lev. xii. 3	ix. 28, 29	Moses
vii. 37, 38	Prov. xviii. 4	ix. 31	Prov. xxviii. 9
	Isa. xii. 3; lviii. 11	xii. 34	Psa. lxxxix. 4; cx. 4;
vii. 42a	Psa. lxxxix. 3, 4;		Isa. ix. 7
	cxxxii. 11	xvii. 12	Psa. xli. 9; cix. 8, 17
vii. 42b	Mic. v. 2	xix. 28, 29	Psa. lxix. 21
vii. 41, 52	Isa. ix. 1, 2 (Matt. iv.		
	15, 16)		

These are a few of the many allusions, and they refer to the serpent on the pole, Mount Gerizim as a centre of worship, sowing and reaping, carrying burdens on the Sabbath, the manna in the wilderness, circumcision, the flow of living water, Bethlehem, the birth-place of Christ, stoning for adultery, God not hearing sinners, the eternity of Christ, Judas, the son of perdition, and Christ thirsting on the Cross.

Of the quotations, one is made by John the Baptist, seven by the author of the Gospel, one by a crowd, and ten by Jesus. Of the allusions, one is by the woman of Samaria, seven by Jews, two by persons in a crowd, one by a healed man, one by a number of people, two by the Evangelist, and eleven by Jesus.

These references to the Old Testament call attention to two things, namely, to the spiritual interpretation of Old Testament events, and to the fact that all prophecy should be brought into connection with Christ. The history and experiences of the Israelites were typical and prophetical; so John the Baptist was the herald of Christ (i. 23); Jacob's dream pointed to the Incarnation (i. 51); the manna told of Christ, the Bread from Heaven, the only true sustenance of men (chap. vi); the Passover foreshadowed the death of Christ (xix. 36); the serpent on the pole typified the saving efficacy of Christ's death, where faith is exercised (iii. 14); Moses predicted Christ as Prophet (v. 46, 47); the Feast of Tabernacles anticipated Christ, and the coming of the Holy Spirit (vi. 35; vii. 2, 37-39; Exod. xvii. 6; Num. xx. 11); the 'seed of David' was Christ (vii. 42); Abraham looked for Christ (viii. 56; Heb. xi. 13); psalmists and prophets announced the permanence of Christ (xii. 34); and David predicted Christ's thirst on the Cross (xix. 28, 29).

The special place of Israel in the history of redemption, furnishing the medium out of which the new dispensation should spring, is illustrated by chapters i. 11; iv. 22; and Bishop Westcott points out that the only three Old Testament saints who are mentioned by the Lord, or by the Evangelist, in connection with the Messiah, Abraham, Moses, and Isaiah, ' cover and represent the three successive periods of the training of the people . . . the patriarchal, the theocratic, and the monarchical.' No one but a Jew could have handled the Old Testament Scriptures in this way.

It is very important to observe this interpretation of the Old Testament in the Gospel, because it shows that Judaism was a preparation for Christianity, and that the Messianic types and prophecies were fulfilled in Christ. 'The Christian theology of the Evangelist is based upon the theology of the Old Testament' (i. 45; iv. 22; v. 46; viii. 56).

Look again at the references to the brazen serpent, the manna, the paschal lamb, the water from the rock, the pillar of fire (viii. 12), the shepherd, and the vine.

The Fourth Gospel is saturated with the thoughts, imagery, and language of the Old Testament, and one of the objects of the writer is to show that the people who possessed these Scriptures, and studied them most diligently, failed to recognize the Christ, and refused to believe in Him (v. 39, 40, R.V.).

JOHN AND ISAIAH

Prof. Luthardt has pointed out that 'there is a striking agreement between the Fourth Gospel and the second part of Isaiah' (xl-lxvi). This is a fruitful suggestion, and should be followed out. In illustration of the fact are the following parallels.

SUBJECT	ISAIAH	JOHN
The Shepherd who gathers, feeds, and carries His Lambs	xl. 11	x.
Water for the thirsty in the Desert ...	xli. 18; xliv. 3; xlviii. 21; xlix. 10; lv. 1	iv. 13, 14; vi. 35; vii. 37
Hunger Satisfied	xlix. 10	vi. 35
Guidance	xlii. 16; xlviii. 17	xiv. 6
Light for the Blind	xlii. 7; xlix. 6, 9; lx. 1	viii. 12; ix. 1, ff.
Liberty for the Bound	xlix. 9; lviii. 6	viii. 36
Divine Instruction	l. 4, 5	v. 30

Subject	Isaiah	John
The Elimination of Fear	xli. 10; li. 7	xiv. 1
The Divine Comforter	li. 12	xiv. 16
The Bringer of Peace and Judgment ...	lii. 7; lvii. 19; xlviii. 22; lvii. 12	xiv. 27; xvi. 11 xii. 31
Universal Salvation	xliii. 19; xlv. 22; xlix. 12, 20-22; lvi. 7, 8; lx. 3, 5; lxvi. 1; liv. 5	iv. 21-24; x. 16; iii. 16
The Gift of the Spirit	lix. 21	xiv. 26; xv. 26; xvi. 13

These parallels, though not all that may be traced, are sufficient to show how much the roots of this Gospel are in the Old Testament, and especially in the Book of the Evangelical Prophet.

16

JOHN'S RELATION TO THE SYNOPTIC GOSPELS

THE relation of the Fourth Gospel to the Synoptics will best be seen by an examination of three things—parallels, omissions, and material peculiar.

(1) **Parallels**

There are numerous points in which John's Gospel coincides with the Synoptic narratives.

(i) They agree that Jesus was born at Bethlehem (vii. 42: cf. Matt. ii; Luke ii); that His early home was at Nazareth (i. 46; cf. Matt. ii. 23; Luke ii. 51); that later He resided at Capernaum (ii. 12; vi. 17, 24: cf. Matt. iv. 13; Mark ii. 1; Luke vii. 1); and that John the Baptist was His forerunner (i. cf. Matt. iii; Mark i; Luke iii).

They mention Joseph, Mary, and the brethren of Jesus (i. 45; ii. 1-12; vi. 42; vii. 3, 5; xix. 25; cf. Matt. xii. 46; Mark iii. 31;

Luke iii. 23). They recognize Twelve Apostles (vi. 67; xx. 24; cf. Matt. x. 2-4; Mark iii. 14-19; Luke vi. 13-16). They record the feeding of the five thousand, and the walking on the sea (vi. 1-21; cf. Matt. xiv. 13-33; Mark vi. 32-52; Luke ix. 10-17). They tell of the anointing of the Lord at Bethany (xii. 1-8; cf. Matt. xxvi. 6-13; Mark xiv. 3-9). They describe the triumphal entry into Jerusalem (xii. 12-15; cf. Matt. xxi. 4-9; Mark xi. 7-10; Luke xix. 35-38).

Other parallels relate the trial scenes, Peter's denials, the conduct of Pilate, the title on the Cross, the presence of the women at the Cross, the manner of Jesus' death, the place of His burial, and the witnesses of His resurrection.

From this it will be seen, as Dr. Reynolds says, that 'the most impressive facts and cardinal events in this marvellous narrative are common to all four Evangelists; that John's narrative presupposes on the part of his readers a knowledge of the Synoptics, and throws in return great light upon them.'

When John selected incidents which the Synoptists had recorded, he did so, under the guidance of the Holy Spirit, because they helped the object he had in view in writing this Gospel (xx. 30, 31).

(ii) There are at least twenty-six lines of Synoptic parallel in John's Gospel.

1 Departure of Jesus from Judæa for Galilee - Mark i. 14
      Matt. iv. 12; Luke iv. 14; John iv. 3

2 The Return of the Twelve from their Mission, and Jesus' retirement with them to Bethsaida, followed by a Multitude - - - - Mark vi. 30-34
      Matt. xiv. 13, 14; Luke ix. 10, 11; John vi. 1-3

3 Feeding of the Five Thousand - - - Mark vi. 35-44
      Matt. xiv. 15-21; Luke ix. 12-17; John vi. 4-13

4 Jesus prevents the people from making Him a political King - - - - - Mark vi. 45, 46
      Matt. xiv. 22, 23; John vi. 14, 15

5 Jesus walks upon the Sea, and joins His Disciples on the Boat - - - - - Mark vi. 47-52
      Matt. xiv. 24-27, 32, 33; John vi. 16-21

6 The Feast in the house of Simon the Leper, where Mary anoints Jesus for His Burial - Mark xiv. 3-9
      Matt. xxvi. 6-13: John xii. 2-8

7 Jesus' Triumphal Entry into Jerusalem as the
  Messiah - - - - - - - Mark xi. 1-11
        Matt. xxi. 1-11, 14-17; Luke xix. 29-44; John xii. 12-19

8 At the Paschal Meal Jesus intimates that He will
  be Betrayed - - - - - - Mark xiv. 18-21
        Matt. xxvi. 21-25; Luke xxii. 21-23; John xiii. 21-30

9 Jesus Warns the Disciples against desertion,
  especially Peter. All protest their loyalty - Mark xiv. 27-31
        Matt. xxvi. 31-35; Luke xxii. 31-34; John xiii. 36-38

10 Jesus Goes to Gethsemane - - - Mark xiv. 26, 32
        Matt. xxvi. 30, 36; Luke xxii. 39, 40; John xviii. 1

11 Jesus is Betrayed, Arrested, and Forsaken - Mark xiv. 43-47
        Matt. xxvi. 47-52; Luke xxii. 47-51; John xviii. 2-12

12 Jesus before Caiaphas - - - Mark xiv. 53
        Matt. xxvi. 57; Luke xxii. 54; John xviii. 24

13 Peter thrice denies his Lord - - - Mark xiv. 54, 66-72
  Matt. xxvi. 58, 69-75; Luke xxii. 54-62; John xviii. 15-18, 25-27

14 Jesus before Pilate the first time - - Mark xv. 1
        Matt. xxvii. 1, 2; Luke xxiii. 1; John xviii. 28

15 Pilate asks Jesus if He is a King - - Mark xv. 2
        Matt. xxvii. 11; Luke xxiii. 3; John xviii. 33, 34

16 Pilate finds no fault in Jesus - Luke xxiii. 4: John xviii. 38b

17 The offer to release Jesus or Barabbas - Mark xv. 9-11
      Matt. xxvii. 17, 18, 20, 21; Luke xxiii. 18, 19; John xviii. 39, 40

18 Pilate's vain attempt to release Jesus - - Mark xv. 12-15
        Matt. xxvii. 22-26; Luke xxiii. 20-25; John xix. 5b-7

19 On the Way to Golgotha - - - Mark xv. 20-23
        Matt. xxvii. 31-34; Luke xxiii. 33; John xix. 16, 17

20 Jesus on the Cross. The Two Robbers.
  Jesus' Garments. The Superscription. The
  Mocking - - - - - - - Mark xv. 24-32
        Matt. xxvii. 35-44; Luke xxiii. 33-38; John xix. 18-24

21 Jesus Dies - - - - - Mark xv. 36, 37
        Matt. xxvii. 48-50; Luke xxiii. 46; John xix. 28-30

22 The Burial. Joseph of Arimathea - - Mark xv. 42-46
        Matt. xxvii. 57-60; Luke xxiii. 50-54; John xix. 38-42

23 Women visit the Tomb - - - Mark xvi. 2-4
        Luke xxiv. 1, 2; John xx. 1

24 The report of the women. Peter and John
  visit the Tomb - - - - - Luke xxiv. 9-12
        John xx. 2-10

25 The appearance to Mary Magdalene, and the
  message to the Apostles - Mark xvi. 9, 10: John xx. 11-18

26 Jesus shows the Apostles His hands and His
  feet - - - - - - - Mark xvi. 14
        Luke xxiv. 36-40; John xx. 19, 20

In this list of 26 items, the actual parallels to the Synoptics in John's Gospel have been registered as nearly as possible, but it will be found that in the ground covered John elaborates certain events, supplying what the Synoptists omitted.

(iii) In item 8, there is only one verse in the Synoptics, which tells us that Jesus pointed out the betrayer (Matt. xxvi. 25), but in John there are eight verses (xiii. 23-30).

In item 9, John records five verses of introduction which the Synoptists omit (xiii. 31-35).

In item 11, narrating the coming of Judas to arrest Jesus, John has eight verses for one in each of the Synoptics (xviii. 2-9).

In item 13, for one verse in each of the Synoptics which tells of Peter's entrance into the Court of the High Priest, John has four verses of detail (xviii. 15-18).

In item 14, John gives ten verses of detail which the Synoptists omit (xviii. 28-33, 35-38).

Between items 17 and 18 John supplies five verses of detail which the Synoptists omit (xix. 1-5a).

In item 18, John supplies eight verses of detail which the Synoptists omit (xix. 8-15).

In item 20, John gives the fullest details about the seamless robe (xix. 23, 24), and about the inscription on the Cross (xix. 20-22). He alone, also, tells of Jesus' committal of His mother to John (xix. 25-27).

In item 21, John alone gives the details about the breaking of the legs (xix. 31-37).

In item 22, John alone tells us that Nicodemus embalmed Jesus' body (xix. 39, 40), and that the tomb was in a garden (xix. 41).

In item 24, John alone relates that 'another disciple' accompanied Peter to the tomb, and that they both entered it (xx. 2-10). Undoubtedly the 'other disciple' was John himself.

In item 25, for two verses in Mark (xvi. 9, 10), John has eight verses of detail (xx. 11-18) of an event about which Matthew and Luke say nothing.

In item 26, John alone says why the disciples were behind
28

shut doors, and he alone narrates the story of Thomas' absence and presence at the time of Jesus' appearances to His Apostles (xx. 21-29).

All these items should be carefully read in a Harmony of the Gospels (pp. 68-81).

(2) Omissions

The omissions in this Gospel must be regarded in the light of the Evangelist's purpose (xx. 30, 31). In this Gospel there are events which, though not definitely recorded, are certainly implied, as, for instance, the choosing of the Twelve (vi. 70), but there are seven cardinal and momentous events which John does not include in his narrative. These are, the Birth, the Baptism, the Temptation, and the Transfiguration of Christ; the Institution of the Lord's Supper, the Agony in the Garden, and the Ascension.

These omissions may be accounted for in two ways: first, because the facts were widely promulgated in the Synoptic Gospels; and second, because to have repeated them would not have promoted the object which John had in mind when he wrote, namely, to show that Jesus was the Son of God, and thereby to create faith (xx. 30, 31).

1. The Birth of Christ

This is referred to (i. 14), but not described, for John goes behind it to declare the Personality, the Deity, and the Eternity of the Son, and to declare also that the Son is the power of creation, and the source of life. After the revelation of the Prologue (i. 1-18), there was no need for details of the Birth such as Matthew and Luke give.

2. The Baptism of Christ

This is implied in John's narrative (i. 32, 33; iii. 5; iv. 2) but is not described, because the Baptism was designed to reveal Christ's representative and vicarious *manhood* (Matt. iii. 13-15), and not His *Deity*.

3. The Temptation of Christ

This is not recorded, though it is implied that He was tempted (xii. 31; xvi. 11), because as the Son of God He could not be tempted.   Satan said: 'If Thou be *the Son of God*,' and Jesus replied: '*Man* shall not live by bread alone' (Matt. iv. 3, 4). For John to have recorded the Temptation would not have proved that Jesus was the Son of God (xx. 30, 31).

4. THE TRANSFIGURATION OF CHRIST

This is not recorded by John, though to have done so would have been in harmony with his purpose (xx. 30, 31; cf. Matt. xvii. 5), but instead of repeating what was well known, he saturates his Gospel with the idea which found expression in the Mount of Transfiguration, namely, the Glory of Christ (cf. i. 14, 18; ii. 11; xii. 28, 41; xvii. 5, 24), and passages which reveal Him as Light (i. 9; iii. 19-21; viii. 12; ix. 5).

5. THE INSTITUTION OF THE LORD'S SUPPER

Mark xiv. 17-21, and John xiii, are parallel, and tell of Jesus and His disciples celebrating the Passover, and it was not until after Judas had left the company that the Supper was instituted, which is recorded in Mark xiv. 22-25; Matt. xxvi. 26-29; Luke xxii. 17-20; I Cor. xi. 23-26; but not in John's Gospel, the place of it being between chapters xiii and xiv.   But why does John not record so important an event?   For answer let two things be said: (*a*) When this Evangelist wrote his Gospel (about A.D. 95), the Lord's Supper was a well-established ceremony in the Christian Church, and so there was no need for him to relate its historic origin, especially in view of the fact that this had been done by the Synoptists: (*b*) The omission does not imply that John was indifferent to the matter.   On the contrary, the *origin* of the ceremony being so well known, he devotes himself to a record of its *meaning* (chapter vi), which the Synoptists do not relate.

6. THE AGONY IN THE GARDEN

As in the case of the Supper, so in this, the facts being clearly stated by the Synoptists, John spreads the agony of Jesus over his entire Gospel, from the wilderness of Judæa to the Cross itself (iv. 34; v. 30; vi. 38; viii. 29, 38; xi. 33-35; xii. 23-33; xvii. 4).   It will be observed that the design of John is to show that the whole career of Jesus was characterized by experiences

which the Synoptists concentrate in specific events.   The
language of chapter xviii. 11 forcibly recalls that of Mark xiv.
36, Matt. xxvi. 39, Luke xxii. 42.

7. THE ASCENSION OF CHRIST

The omission of this event is not peculiar to John, for neither
Mark nor Matthew records it, if it can be shown that Mark
xvi. 9-20 does not belong to this Gospel (these verses are omitted
by the two oldest Greek MSS., and by some other authorities;
see p. 176); but the event is not overlooked in the Fourth Gospel
(iii. 13; vi. 62; xx. 17); and, on the assumption that the Apostle
John wrote the Apocalypse also, it is clear that he believed that
Jesus was seated at the right hand of God (Rev. v. 6; xv. 1-4; xix.
11-16).   (Other omissions of this Gospel are referred to under
' Features; Fragmentariness,' p. 446).

(3) **Material Peculiar to John**

Bishop Westcott has said that if the total contents of the
several Gospels be represented by 100, the following table is
obtained:

Gospel	Peculiarities	Coincidences
MARK -	7	93
MATTHEW	42	58
LUKE -	59	41
JOHN -	92	8

From this it will be seen that over 90 per cent of the material
in the Fourth Gospel is peculiar to it, and what this peculiar
material is, any Harmony will show.

(i) Practically all that is *not* peculiar in this Gospel is: iv. 3; vi.
1-21; xii. 2-8, 12-19; xiii. 21, 22, 36-38; xviii. 1, 3, 10, 11, 25-28*a*,
33, 38*b*-40; xix. 16-23*a*, 28-30, 38, 40-42; xx. 1-3, 19*b*-20.

Mark these passages in your Bible (preferably in colour) and
indicate in some way that they show material which is found
elsewhere. *All the rest is peculiar to John.*

(ii) Of this peculiar material note especially the Interview with Nicodemus (iii. 1-21); Jesus in Samaria (iv. 5-42); Healing of Man Born Blind (ix); the Raising of Lazarus (xi); the Interview with the Greeks (xii. 20-50); Six Miracles; the Discourses, and the Appendix (xxi). (See, ' Miracles,' and ' Discourses,' pp. 418, 421-425).

The material peculiar to this Gospel must be explained, as the omissions are, on two grounds: first, that it is designed to advance the writer's object (xx. 30, 31); and second, that it helps to complete the record which the Synoptists had given. Each of the Evangelists has material peculiar to his Gospel which can be accounted for by his design. Note what this material is in each case, by carefully studying the Harmony (pp. 68-81).

17

JOHN AND LUKE

(1)

IN 1911 a Dr. Gumbel issued a little book, the design of which was to show that John had Luke's Gospel before him when he wrote, and selected his material according to what he found there; that he limited himself to filling up the gaps in Luke's narrative, omitting everything which Luke had narrated, except in those cases where his own eye-witness and ear-witness enabled him to add useful interpretation or detail.

There are large tracts of Jesus' life and ministry for which Luke did not possess the material, or, if he did, did not choose to use it, and it is this material which John supplies. Throughout the Fourth Gospel there is an avoidance of incidents related by Luke, and a studious silence with regard to what had already been written, a silence so discriminating and complete as to preclude the possibility of its being accidental.

If it can be shown that these two Gospels fit into one another as the two halves of a broken jug, so that every indentation of the one corresponds to every protuberance of the other, not a little will have been done to solve some of the problems which have clung to the Fourth Gospel.

The best way to test out this theory is by an examination of the contents of these two Gospels in their relation to one another.

#	EVENT	LUKE	JOHN	CHRONOLOGY
1	The Eternal Word who became Incarnate	—	i. 1-18	—
2	Genealogy of Jesus Traced Back to Adam	iii. 23-38	—	—
3	Annunciation of the Birth of John the Baptist	i. 5-25	—	6 B.C. Sept.
4	Annunciation of the Birth of Jesus the Messiah	i. 26-38	—	5 B.C. Mar.
5	Mary's Visit to Elisabeth	i. 39-56	—	5 B.C. Ap.
6	Birth of the Baptist, and a Summary of Thirty Years	i. 57-80	—	5 B.C. Ju.
7	Birth of Jesus at Bethlehem	ii. 1-7	—	5 B.C.: Dec.
8	The Angels and the Shepherds	ii. 8-20	—	,,
9	Circumcision and Presentation of Jesus	ii. 21-38	—	4 B.C.: Jan.-Feb.
10	The Child brought from Egypt to Nazareth	ii. 39	—	5 B.C.: May (?)
11	The Childhood of Jesus	ii. 40	—	4 B.C.-A.D. 8
12	Jesus' First Passover	ii. 41-50	—	A.D. 8: Mar.
13	Summary of 18 Years of Jesus' Life at Nazareth	ii. 51, 52	—	A.D. 8-26
14	Ministry of John the Baptist	iii. 1-18	—	A.D. 26
15	Baptism of Jesus	iii. 21-23	—	A.D. 27: Jan.
16	Temptation of Jesus	iv. 1-13	—	A.D. 27: Feb.-Mar.
17	The Baptist's Testimony to the Sanhedrin's Deputation		i. 19-28	A.D. 27: Mar.
18	The Baptist's Identification of Jesus as the Messiah		i. 29-34	,,
19	The First Disciples of Jesus		i. 35-51	A.D. 27: Mar.
20	Jesus' First Miracle, at Cana		ii. 1-11	,,
21	Jesus Visits Capernaum		ii. 12	A.D. 27: Mar.-Ap.
22	Jesus Cleanses the Temple while Attending the Passover		ii. 13-22	A.D. 27: Ap.
23	Jesus' Interview with Nicodemus		ii. 23– iii. 21	A.D. 27: Ap.
24	Parallel Ministries of Jesus and the Baptist	iii. 19, 20; iv. 14	iii. 22-36	,,
25	Jesus' Reasons for Leaving Judaea		iv. 1-3	A.D. 27: Dec.
26	Jesus in Samaria		iv. 4-42	,,
27	Arrival of Jesus in Galilee	iv. 14, 15	iv. 43-45	,,
28	Healing of a Nobleman's Son at Cana	—	iv. 46-54	,,

	EVENT	LUKE	JOHN	CHRONOLOGY
57	Attempt to Proclaim Christ as King	—	vi. 14, 15	"
58	Jesus Walks Upon the Sea	—	vi. 16-21	"
59	Discourse on the Bread of Life, and its Effects ...	—	vi. 22-71	"
60	Peter's Great Confession near Cæsarea Philippi ...	ix. 18-21	—	A.D. 29: Sum.
61	Jesus Foretells His Death and Resurrection. The Cost of Discipleship	ix. 22-27	—	"
62	The Transfiguration of Jesus	ix. 28-36	—	"
63	Healing of a Demoniac Boy	ix. 37-43	—	"
64	Jesus Again Foretells His Death	ix. 43-45	—	"
65	The Twelve Contend as to who shall be the Greatest. Jesus' Teaching on Humility	ix. 46-48	—	A.D. 29 : Sept. (?)
66	Jesus Rebukes John's Mistaken Zeal ...	ix. 49, 50	—	"
67	Jesus at the Feast of Tabernacles	—	vii. 1-52	A.D. 29: Oct.
68	Story of an Adulteress	—	vii. 53– viii. 11	"
69	Discourses on the Light of the World, and Spiritual Freedom	—	viii. 12-59	A.D. 29: Oct.
70	Jesus Goes to Jerusalem through Samaria ...	ix. 51-62	—	A.D. 29: Nov.
71	Healing of a Man Born Blind	—	ix. 1-41	A.D. 29: Dec.
72	Discourse on the Good Shepherd	—	x. 1-21	"
73	Mission of the Seventy	x. 1-24	—	"
74	A Lawyer's Question. Parable of the Good Samaritan	x. 25-37	—	"
75	Jesus Visits Martha and Mary at Bethany ...	x. 38-42	—	"
76	Jesus at the Feast of Dedication	—	x. 22-39	"
77	Jesus Retires Beyond Jordan. Many follow Him and Believe	—	x. 40-42	"
78	Jesus Teaches a Model Prayer. Parable of the Three Friends	xi. 1-13	—	A.D. 30: Jan.
79	Blasphemous Accusation against Jesus ...	xi. 14-36	—	"

	EVENT	LUKE	JOHN	CHRONOLOGY
109	The Question about the Resurrection	xx. 27-40	—	A.D. 30: Mar.
110	An Unanswerable Question	xx. 41-44	—	,,
111	Scribes and Pharisees Denounced	xx. 45-47	—	,,
112	The Poor Widow and her Two Mites	xxi. 1-4	—	,,
113	The Desire of Certain Greeks to See Jesus leads Him to Speak of His Death and Coming Glory	—	xii. 20-36	,,
114	Reflection on the Unbelief of the Jews	—	xii. 37-50	,,
115	Jesus' Olivet Discourse on the Destruction of Jerusalem and the End of the Age	xxi. 5-38	—	,,
116	Approach of the Passover. Judas Bargains to Betray Jesus	xxii. 1-6	—	,,
117	Preparation for the Paschal Meal	xxii. 7-13	—	,,
118	At the Supper	xxii. 14-18	—	,,
119	The Apostles' Contention, and Jesus' Rebuke	xxii. 24-30	—	,,
120	Jesus Washes the Disciples' Feet	—	xiii. 1-20	,,
121	The Paschal Meal. Jesus Points out the Betrayer	xxii. 21-23	xiii. 21-30	,,
122	The Lord's Supper Instituted	xxii. 19, 20	—	,,
123	Jesus Addresses His Disciples	—	xiii. 31-35	,,
124	Peter Protests his Loyalty. Jesus Foretells his Denials	xxii. 31-34	xiii. 36-38	,,
125	Incident of the Two Swords	xxii. 35-38	—	,,
126	Farewell Discourse in the Upper Room	—	xiv. 1-31	,,
127	Discourse on the Way to Gethsemane	—	xv.-xvi.	,,
128	The Intercessory Prayer	—	xvii.	,,
129	Arrival at Gethsemane	xxii. 39, 40	xviii. 1	,,
130	The Agony in Gethsemane	xxii. 40-46	—	,,
131	Betrayal, Arrest, Desertion	xxii. 47-53	xviii. 2-12	,,
132	The Trial Before Annas	—	xviii. 12-14, 19-23	,,

443

Of the 163 items in this summary, 99 are in Luke only, 43 are in John only, and 21 are common to them both; that is, John omits 99 items which he could have included in his record, but did not, because Luke had recorded them; but he found that Luke had omitted 43 important items, probably because he had not room for them on his roll, and so John supplies these. (See 'Luke's Gospel,' Sec. 11, pp. 353-355).

Respecting the 21 items which are common to them both, it will be found that John adds some details which are not found in Luke, which enrich the narrative.

(II)

Writing of Luke and John, Harnack says: 'There is something to be said for the view that St. John had knowledge of the Lucan Writings, but no real evidence can be adduced in its favour. It is possible that they both are only dependent upon a common source. . . . No traces of the dependence of St. John upon the Lucan Writings can be discovered by means of the Lexicon. . . . Nevertheless, the possibility that the fourth Evangelist read the Lucan Writings must be left open.' Notwithstanding these statements, Harnack goes on to show that there is a connection between John and Luke which does not exist between John and either Matthew or Mark. He gives a list of 88 words which John has in common with Luke, which are not found in Matthew or Mark. Of these, 30 are exclusively common to Luke and John, that is, they are found only in their Writings, assuming that Luke wrote the Acts, and John, the Revelation and the Epistles which bear his name. These 30 words are:

Arm	-	Luke i. 51; John xii. 38; Acts xiii. 17
Answer	-	Luke ii. 47; xx. 26; John i. 22; xix. 9
Bosom	-	Luke vi. 38; xvi. 22, 23; John i. 18; xiii. 23; Acts xxvii. 39
Wipe	-	Luke vii. 38, 44; John xi. 2; xii. 3; xiii. 5
Dine	-	Luke xi. 37; John xxi. 12, 15
Garden	-	Luke xiii. 19; John xviii. 1, 26; xix. 41
Well, Pit	-	Luke xiv. 5; John iv. 11, 12; Rev. ix. 1, 2
Neighbour	-	Luke xiv. 12; xv. 6, 9; John ix. 8
Dip	-	Luke xvi. 24; John xiii. 26; Rev. xix. 13
Breast	-	Luke xviii. 13; xxiii. 48; John xiii. 25; xxi. 20; Rev. xv. 6

Distribute - -	Luke xviii. 22; xi. 22; John vi. 11; Rev. xvii. 13
Run before - -	Luke xix. 4; John xx. 4
Napkin - -	Luke xix. 20; John xi. 44; xx. 7; Acts xix. 12
At any time, Never	Luke xix. 30; John vi. 35; viii. 33; i. 18; v. 37; 1 John iv. 12
Covenant, Agree -	Luke xxii. 5; John ix. 22; and Acts
Linen cloth -	Luke xxiv. 12; John xix. 40; xx. 5, 6, 7
Declare, Tell -	Luke xxiv. 35; John i. 18; and Acts
Hither, Here -	Luke xxiv. 41; John iv. 15, 16; and Acts

and the following 12 words are found in John and the Acts, but not in Luke's Gospel, and without doubt John had access to the Acts:

leap, spring up; those things that please; tarry, continue, abode; draw; call, choose; gird, beckon; side; signify; porch; draw, drag, hail; small cord, rope.

These words in common with Luke definitely suggest John's acquaintance with the Writings of that Evangelist, in view of John's own very limited and distinctive vocabulary. (See ' Style and Diction,' pp. 411-416).

(III)

Further evidence of a connection between John and Luke is in the following facts:

Both speak of 'Salvation,' which does not occur in Matthew or Mark - - - -	Luke i. 69, 71, 77; Acts iv. 12; xiii. 26, 47; xvi. 17; John iv. 22
In both Jesus is the 'Saviour,' a word which does not occur in Matthew, or Mark -	Luke ii. 11; Acts v. 31; xiii. 23; John iv. 12; 1 John iv. 14
They alone mention the High Priest, Annas	Luke iii. 2; Acts iv. 6; John xviii. 13, 24
In both, Jesus passes through the midst of His foes and escapes arrest - - - -	Luke iv. 29, 30; John viii. 59; x. 39
In both, is a miraculous draught of fishes -	Luke v; John xxi
In both Jesus knows the thoughts of men -	Luke vi. 8; John ii. 24, 25
In both the goal of Jesus' earthly history is His ascension into Heaven - - -	Luke ix. 51; John xiv. 2; xvi. 7
They alone record stories of Martha and Mary	Luke x; John xi
Both quote Jesus' words, 'my friends'; and His words, 'the love of God' which do not occur in Matthew or Mark - - -	Luke xii. 4; John xv. 14-16; Luke xi. 42; John v. 42

Both speak of things which happened at Siloam	Luke xiii. 4; John ix. 7, 11
Both show an interest in Samaria, and the Samaritans - - - - - -	Luke xvii. 11;
John iv. 4, 5, 9; Luke ix. 52;	John iv. 9, 39, 40
Neither Matthew nor Mark, but both Luke and John tell that the tomb in which Jesus' body was laid had not been used before -	Luke xxiii. 53; John xix. 41

These, and other details, make it practically certain that John
paid special attention to what Luke had written.

18
FEATURES OF JOHN'S GOSPEL

MUCH that has already been said could well fall under this
heading, for it is characteristic of this Gospel: references
to the feasts; details of time; style and diction; the discourses;
the great omissions; the passages peculiar; and the geography
of the Gospel. Work over these characteristics again.

But in addition to these there are certain features which must
not be overlooked. Of such we select seven.

(i) **Fragmentariness and Unity**

That John's narrative is *fragmentary* will at once be seen by
reference to a Harmony of the Gospels. It begins in the middle
of John the Baptist's ministry. It omits the opening events of
Christ's ministry. It has almost nothing to say about the great
Galilean and Peræan ministries of Jesus. It refers to the Apostles
without having made any reference to the founding of the
apostleship (vi. 70). Judas is referred to as a person well known
(vi. 71). Without having been named it is assumed that Martha
and Mary were well known (xi. 1). Miracles which Jesus
performed, and which the Evangelist does not record, he,
nevertheless, mentions (ii. 23; iii. 2; iv. 45; vi. 2. This occurs
also in the Synoptics, p. 553).

Chapter i covers a period of about one month, March, A.D. 27;
chapters ii-iii, a period of about eight months, March-November,
A.D. 27; chapter iv, a period of about four months, December,
A.D. 27-March, A.D. 28; chapters v-vi, a period of about eighteen
months, April, A.D. 28-September, A.D. 29; chapters vii-xi, a
period of about six months, October, A.D 29-March, A.D. 30; and

chapters xii-xxi, a period of about six weeks, April-May, A.D. 30.

From this it will be seen how little John tells us of Jesus' activities during over three years of ministry. Passages which illustrate this are: iii. 22; iv. 1-3; vii. 1; x. 40-42; xi. 54; and also the references to 'signs,' which are not detailed: ii. 23; iii. 2; iv. 45; vi. 2; vii. 3, 21; x. 32; xi. 47; xii. 37; xx. 30; xxi. 25. Examine these references carefully.

Underlying this fragmentariness is an unmistakable *unity*. The design and the plan of the Gospel show this. (See these Sections, pp. 405-408).

What John omits is as significant as what he includes. Had he included what he omits his design would have been frustrated (xx. 30, 31). One idea unifies these fragments of narrative, one purpose brings them into a sublime harmony, namely, to show that in Jesus God was manifested, and that this revelation compels men to accept or to reject Him, and also to show that faith brings life; and unbelief, death.

(ii) **Imagery**

There are no parables, strictly speaking, in the Fourth Gospel, for the reason, probably, that the Synoptics, which were in circulation, had adequately illustrated Jesus' parabolic method, and because it was John's intention to repeat as little as possible what was already available, and to put on record, in keeping with his object (xx. 30, 31), what the Synoptists had omitted. Consequently, John gives more attention to the direct than to the parabolic instruction, as being best suited to the aim he had in view, and to the need of the growing Church at the close of the first century. (See pp. 211, 550).

But though there are no parables in this Gospel it is not wanting in imagery, which is a closely related form of instruction. Examples of this are, the *temple* (ii. 19), the *new birth* (iii. 3), the *wind* (iii. 8), the *bride* and the *bridegroom* (iii. 29), the great *harvest* (iv. 35), the *lamp* (v. 35), *living water* (vii. 37), *night* and *day* (ix. 4), the *shepherd* (x.), the *door*, and the *porter* (x. 7-9), the *vine* (xv. 1-7). Each of these figures is a parable in germ, and in the allegoric discourses about *bread* and *wine* the Evangelist shows how, in different ways, Jesus taught essential truths.

The word 'parable' occurs once in the A.V. (x. 6), and 'proverb' twice in the A.V.; 'dark saying,' margin 'parable,' in the R.V. (xvi. 25, 29), but in all three places the word is not *parabolē*, but *paroimia*, which means 'a wayside discourse.' This entire omission of all the Synoptic parables is noteworthy.

(iii) Symbolism

By *symbolism* let us understand the representation and impartation of moral and spiritual truth by the images or properties of natural things. Of this there is not a little in the Fourth Gospel. Dr. Plummer says: 'The whole Gospel from end to end is penetrated with the spirit of symbolical representation'; and Dr. Farrar says: 'The arrangement of the Book is throughout constructed with direct reference to the sacred numbers three and seven.' Much attention need not be given to this fact, but it should not be, as it usually is, entirely overlooked.

Both *three* and *seven* would seem to stand for completeness.

(i) The completeness of *three* is seen in the divisions of time, past, present, and future; in the three degrees of comparison, positive, comparative, and superlative; and in the sum of human capabilities, thought, word, and deed.

This Gospel begins with the greatest threefold declaration ever made (i. 1). It would seem that John's plan of record is grouped round three Passovers, at the beginning, in the middle, and at the end of Jesus' ministry (ii. 13; vi. 4; xi. 55). John records three great allegories, the *Sheep-fold*, the *Good Shepherd*, and the *Vine* (x.; xv). The Prologue is in three sections (i. 1-5, 6-11, 12-18). John's fundamental theme is threefold, *revelation*, resulting in *reception*, or *rejection*. Three ideas are in the warp and woof of the story, and are characteristic also of the First Epistle, namely, *life*, *light*, and *love*.

Three times Jesus said: 'I will raise him up at the last day' (vi. 39, 40, 44). Three of the Seven Sayings on the Cross are recorded in this Gospel (xix. 25-30; p. 578).

(ii) The Hebrew word for *seven* comes from a root which means to be full or satisfied, to have enough of. Illustrating the completeness of Christ's dealings with the Samaritan woman it is noteworthy that He spoke to her seven times (iv. 7, 10, 13-14, 16,

17-18, 21-24, 26).   It should be observed, also, that seven times Christ declared Himself to be the 'I AM' (iv. 26; viii. 28, 58; xiii. 19; xviii. 5, 6, 8; cf. Exod. iii. 14), and that by seven symbolisms He shows what HE IS, the *Bread of Life* (vi. 35, 41, 48, 51); the *Light of the World* (viii. 12; ix. 5); the *Door of the Sheep* (x. 7, 9); the *Good Shepherd* (x. 11, 14); the *Resurrection and the Life* (xi. 25); *the Way, the Truth, the Life* (xiv. 6); and the *True Vine* (xv. 1, 5).

In this Gospel a sevenfold witness to Christ is recorded: of the Father (v. 34, 37; viii. 18); of the Son Himself (viii. 14; xviii. 37); of Christ's works (x. 25; v. 36); of Scripture (v. 39-46); of the Forerunner (i. 7; v. 35); of the Disciples (xv. 27; xix. 35); and of the Holy Spirit (xv. 26; xvi. 14).

The careful reader will find other instances of the use of these numbers.   (See p. 311, Sec. 21).

In chapter vi. the phrase 'came (or cometh) down from heaven' occurs seven times as a solemn refrain (33, 38, 41, 42, 50, 51, 58); and in the Upper Room Discourse the phrase 'these things have I spoken unto you,' also occurs seven times (xiv. 25; xvi. 1, 4, 6, 25, 33; xviii. 1).

Also the arrangement of the Gospel betrays a deliberate sevenfold grouping; see the *Analysis*, with its five Divisions, with a Prologue and an Epilogue.

Dr. Bernard takes the view that 'John did not set any special value on the number seven. . . . The intentional presence of the number seven in the narrative and the structure of the Fourth Gospel is not proved. He does not deal in allegory, but in facts.'   But the student of the Gospel must judge for himself, remembering that the Book of the Revelation (John's) is heptadic throughout, the word 'seven' (*hepta*) occurring 57 times.

(iv) **Characters**

No Gospel is so rich in typical groups and in personalities as is the Fourth, and all are types of faith or unbelief, brought to light by the self-revelation of Christ.   (See p. 407).

(i) In this Gospel, 34 individuals are brought to our notice; 23 of them are named, and 11 are unnamed.   Of the 23, it may be said that 15 are of special, and 8 of secondary importance.

29

(1) PERSONS NAMED (23):
    (a) *Of Special Importance* (15)
NINE APOSTLES: John, Peter, Andrew, Philip, Thomas, Nathanael
                (Bartholomew), James of Zebedee, Judas (Lab-
                bæus), Judas Iscariot.
OTHERS: MEN: John the Baptist, Nicodemus, Pilate.
     WOMEN: Martha, Mary, the Magdalene.
    (b) *Of Secondary Importance* (8)
Lazarus, Caiaphas, Joseph of Arimathæa, Mary of Clopas, Annas, Barabbas, Simon Iscariot, Malchus.
(2) PERSONS UNNAMED (11):
The mother of Jesus, the woman of Samaria, the nobleman, the paralytic, 'a woman,' the man born blind, his parents, Jesus' aunt, two disciples.

Here is a great revelation of character, and, in some sense, these people represent all people who come into touch with Christ.

John the mystic, Peter the impulsive, Andrew the missionary, Philip the inquirer, Thomas the cautious, Nathanael the guileless, James the 'zealot,' Judas the obscure, Judas the traitor, John Baptist the austere, Nicodemus the seeker, Pilate the worldling, Martha the anxious, Mary the worshipper, Mary Magdalene the devoted, Lazarus the lowly, Caiaphas the unscrupulous, Joseph of Arimathæa the brave, Mary of Clopas, the follower, Annas the intriguer, Barabbas the robber, Mary, mother of Jesus, the 'blessed,' the woman of Samaria the insensible, the nobleman the susceptible, the paralytic the helpless, 'a woman' the fallen, the blind man the forthright, his parents the cowards, Jesus' aunt, Salome, the ambitious, Simon Iscariot the unfortunate father, Malchus the victim.

A few words, or acts, lay open the souls of the most of these in the light of Christ's presence. The vividness, the vigour, the life of these portraitures cannot be mistaken or gainsaid. Each of them should be carefully studied, not merely as people who lived long ago, but as people who are living now.

(ii) In addition to these individuals are groups of people who are sketched with vividness and precision. Of such there are at least nine, and each group has its characteristic.

The Disciples of John the Baptist: so short-
  sighted and jealous - - - - iii. 26
The Disciples of Jesus: so wanting in under-
  standing - - - - - - iv. 33; xi. 12
The Samaritans: so ready to believe iv. 42
The Brothers of Jesus: so lacking in faith - vii. 3-5
The Multitude: oscillating between belief and
  and infidelity - - - - - vii. 20, 26, 41
The Pharisees: proud and opposing - - vii. 48; ix. 40

The Jews: claiming to be Abraham's seed, yet wanting to kill the Messiah	viii. 33, 37, 40
The Chief Priests: at once claiming and denying their national independence	xi. 48; xix. 15
The Greeks: who desired to have an interview with Jesus, represent at the close of His ministry the Gentile world, as the Magi had done at the beginning of it	xii. 20-36

Truly this is a crowded canvas, and each character lived and is living.

Spend all the time you can on this feature of John's Gospel.

(v) The Messiah

A careful reading of this Gospel by the side of the Synoptics will show that whereas in them the recognition of Jesus as the Messiah is represented as coming gradually, in the Fourth Gospel it is represented as present from the beginning. In the Synoptics He is not recognized as the Messiah even by the disciples before the Confession of Peter, and not by the public before His triumphal entry into Jerusalem, but in the Fourth Gospel there is no such delay. This fact has been used against the historical reliability of this Gospel, but however it may be explained the fact remains.

> In chapter i, Jesus is twice greeted as the Messiah (41, 45); is twice described as the Son of God (34, 49); and at this early stage the Baptist points to Him as 'the Lamb of God Who taketh away the sin of the world' (29, 36).
>
> It is said that His disciples believed on Him from the first (ii. 11), and that in Jerusalem at the Passover, 'many believed on His name' (ii. 23). In chapter iii, advanced teaching is given to Nicodemus, and the Baptist is represented as using very exalted language about Him (iii. 31-36). In chapter iv, Jesus reveals Himself as the Messiah to the Samaritan woman (26), and we are told that many of the Samaritans not only believed on Him, but actually acknowledged Him as 'the Saviour of the world' (39-42). In chapter v He is accused of 'making Himself equal with God' (18). In chapter vi the people are so carried away by enthusiasm that they want to force Him to place Himself at their head (15), and once more very advanced teaching is imparted.

It is not our present task to explain this fact, but only to point it out. (See Dr. Sanday, '*The Criticism of the Fourth Gospel*,' pp. 155-160, 208-210).

(vi) **History and Dogma**

John differed widely from the Synoptists in his treatment of history. The latter were satisfied to record events simply as illustrating Christ's life and work, but John recorded those only from which he was able to deduce dogmatic truths or principles, Dr. Luckock says: 'Where they wrote history alone, he wrote history with a commentary upon it. He was, in short, "a theologian" first; an historian second.'

Of this characteristic of the Fourth Gospel there are four outstanding illustrations.

1 Chap. iv. In verses 5-12, the historical fact is recorded of Jesus' contact with the woman of Samaria, but in verses 13-26 it is shown that the value of this incident is in the spiritual use which Jesus made of it. The water in the well is made to illustrate the life in the heart of the believer, and this leads on to Jesus' revelation of Himself as the Messiah.

2 Chap. vi. In verses 1-13, John records, as do all the Synoptists, the incident of the feeding of the five thousand. There the Synoptists leave it, but John goes on to record that Jesus based on that incident His great discourse on *The Bread of Life*, which was Himself (22-58).

3 Chap. ix. In verses 1-34, the story is told of the healing of the man who was born blind, but this is only an illustration in the physical realm of what Christ had been teaching of the spiritual realm, that He was *The Light of the World*, and *The Source of Truth* (chap. viii. 12-59).

4 Chap. xi. Here is the story of Jesus' love for the family at Bethany (5), and the raising of Lazarus from the dead, but this immediately follows the discourse in chapter x, in which Christ presents Himself as Love, under the figure of the Good Shepherd giving His life for the Sheep. The work of Love, in chap. xi, cost Him His life (45-53).

In the first two of these instances the spiritual teaching follows the historical facts, and in the second two it precedes them. This dogmatic value which John records of Jesus' acts and contacts is of great importance, and goes far to justify the view of Clement of Alexandria that John 'produced a spiritual Gospel.'

(vii) **The Author's Comments**

An unmistakable feature of this Gospel is the comments of

the writer, of which there are probably not fewer than twenty-two. Let us first of all tabulate the passages:

ii. 21	vi. 61, 64	xi. 13	xviii. 32
ii. 24, 25	vi. 71	xi. 51	xx. 30, 31
iii. 16-21	vii. 5	xii. 6	xxi. 19
iii. 31-36	vii. 22	xii. 33	xxi. 23
iv. 8	vii. 39	xii. 36b-43	xxi. 25
iv. 44	viii. 27		

In chapters ii. 21; vii. 39; xii. 33, John offers an explanation of the words of Jesus. In ii. 24, 25; vi. 61, 64, he comments on the knowledge of Jesus. In vii. 22; viii. 27, he points out a misunderstanding on the part of the Jews, and in xi. 13, of the disciples. In iv. 44, he tells us what Jesus said about His rejection in His own country. In xviii. 32, he notes that certain words of the Jews correspond with what Jesus had said about His death. In xii. 6, and xii. 43, he ascribes motives to Judas, and to the rulers. In iv. 8; vi. 71, vii. 5; xi. 51, he supplies explanations. In xx. 30, 31, he declares the scope and purpose of his Gospel. In xxi. 23, he explains a misunderstood saying of Jesus, and verse 25 is almost certainly the word of the Evangelist.

The longest comments by the writer of the Gospel are in chapter iii. 16-21, 31-36, the first being a comment on Jesus' Discourse on the New Birth, and the second, a comment on Jewish unbelief as foreshadowed in prophecy. This is the view of Neander, Tholuck, Bengel, Westcott, Moulton, Bernard and others; but Hengstenberg, Meyer, Godet, Alford, Lange, Reynolds, and others, do not admit the view, and hold that verses 16-21 can quite well be the words of Jesus, and that verses 31-36 can quite well be the words of John the Baptist.

It is enough for our purpose to have pointed out these views, and to say that as there are so many comments of the Evangelist in this Gospel, these two longer passages may also be his. It is easier to believe that in iii. 31-36, we have the words of the Evangelist than the words of the Baptist.

If, however, the passages iii. 16-21, 31-36, be not admitted as comments of the writer, about the others there can be no doubt, and these constitute a feature of this Gospel.

19

THE JOHANNINE WRITINGS

IN this Guide we do not study the three Epistles which bear
John's name, nor the Book of the Revelation, but it is relevant
to our present purpose to enquire whether or not there are
correspondences in these five Writings which point to a common
authorship, and to a progressive purpose.

(i) JOHN'S GOSPEL AND THE FIRST EPISTLE

This Epistle presupposes the Gospel in some shape or other,
and it is a philosophical companion to it. That both Writings
came from the same hand may be regarded as certain, and as
John the Apostle has been shown to be the author of the Gospel
he must have been the author of the Epistle also. (See ' Authorship,' p. 135).

(*a*) The style of the Gospel is that of the Epistle. In both
are found numerous short sentences connected generally by the
particle 'and.' These sentences are complete in themselves, and
yet each prepares the way for those which follow. For example:
In John i. 1-5, R.V., there are ten statements, and eight of them,
at any rate, are complete in themselves, yet there is a continuity
of thought, which is indicated by the six occurrences of ' and.'
(See p. 411 (i)).

1 'In the beginning was the Word, *and*
2 The Word was with God, *and*
3 The Word was God.
4 The same was in the beginning with God.
5 All things were made through Him, *and*
6 Without Him was not anything made that hath been made
7 In Him was life, *and*
8 The life was the light of men. *And*
9 The light shineth in the darkness, *and*
10 The darkness apprehended (or overcame) it not.'

The same thing is observable in the Epistle. In i. 5-10, R.V.,
there are twelve statements, most of them complete in themselves,
and they are connected only by the particle 'and,' which is
repeated six times.

1 'God is Light, *and*
2 In Him is no darkness at all.
3 If we say that we have fellowship with Him and walk in the darkness, we lie, *and*
4 We do not the truth.
5 But if we walk in the light, as He is in the light, we have fellowship one with another, *and*
6 The blood of Jesus His Son cleanseth us from all sin.
7 If we say that we have no sin, we deceive ourselves, *and*
8 The truth is not in us.
9 If we confess our sins, He is faithful and righteous to forgive us our sins, *and*
10 To cleanse us from all unrighteousness.
11 If we say that we have not sinned, we make Him a liar, *and*
12 His word is not in us.'

(*b*) These two passages illustrate another characteristic of the author, namely, to express an idea both positively and negatively. (See pp. 411, 412; (ii)). For example, in the Gospel:

'All things were made through Him, and
Without Him was not anything made that hath been made' (i. 3).
'He confessed, and denied not' (i. 20).
'Shall not perish, but have everlasting life' (iii. 15, 16)

In the Epistle:

'God is light, and in Him is no darkness at all' (i. 5).
'Is true, and is no lie' (ii. 27).
'Whosoever abideth in Him sinneth not: whosoever sinneth hath not seen Him, neither knoweth Him' (iii. 6).
'He that knoweth God heareth us; he who is not of God heareth us not' (iv. 6).

(*c*) Another characteristic of both Gospel and Epistle is the author's way of emphasizing a truth by repeating a word. In the Gospel, v. 31-39, the word 'witness' occurs eleven times, and in the Epistle, v. 6-11, it occurs nine times. Notice the repetition of ' love,' in Gospel xiv. 21-24 (see p. 413 (v)), and in Epistle iv. 7-12.

(*d*) A development of this characteristic is the use in both Gospel and Epistle of certain words and phrases which are favourites with the Evangelist. Study the following table of occurrences (and see p. 414 (vii)).

WORD	GOSPEL	EPISTLE	SYNOPTICS
Witness - -	47	13	21
Love - -	45	52	37
Commandment -	11	14	19
Life - - -	37	9	27
Manifest - -	10	10	13
World - -	80	23	15
Abide - -	39	24	12
Truth - -	59	16	18

These comparisons are very impressive. In the Synoptics, Matthew, Mark, Luke, *witness* occurs only 21 times, but in John's two Writings, 60 times; *love*, 37 times against 97; *commandment*, 19 times against 25; *life*, 27 times against 46; *manifest*, 13 times against 20; *world*, 15 times against 103; *abide*, 12 times against 63; and *truth*, 18 times against 75. This shows the intimate connection between the Fourth Gospel and the First Epistle, and goes far to prove a common authorship.

(*e*) Dr. Bernard says: 'The two works proceed from the same theological environment, and (omitting the narrative portions of the Gospel) deal with the same theme. The doctrines of eternal life, of the mutual indwelling of God and man, of Christian believers as the children of God, begotten with a spiritual begetting, of the love of God and love of the brethren, of the Son of God as come in the flesh, are especially characteristic of both books.' In both, Jesus is the 'Saviour of the world,' and the 'only begotten Son of God'.

The connection between the two Prologues is unmistakable (Gospel i. 1-5, 14; Epistle i. 1-3) 'in the beginning' (*en archē*), and ' from the beginning ' (*ap 'archēs*); ' in Him was life,' and ' the Word of Life '; ' the life was the light of men,' and ' the Life was manifested unto us'; 'We beheld the glory,' and 'We have seen and heard.'

Both the Gospel and the Epistle contemplate the Parousia, or Second Coming of the Lord, but with a difference of emphasis (Gospel xiv. 3; Epistle ii. 28; iii. 2). In the Gospel it is implied that Jesus is the first Paraclete, the Spirit being 'another' (xiv. 16), but in the Epistle, and here only, He is explicitly described as such (ii. 1). In the Gospel the disciple abides in Christ, and

Christ in him (vi. 56; xv. 4 f.); but in the Epistle he who has
faith in Christ abides in God and God in him (iv. 15, 16). 'The
Gospel is Christocentric, the Epistle, Theocentric.'

(ƒ) In *The Tests of Life*, Dr. Law presents three important
lists designed to show the vital connection between the Fourth
Gospel and the First Epistle. The first cites coincidences of
verbal expression which are *peculiar* to these two Writings, of
which there are upwards of sixty. The second is a list of verbal
coincidences *not peculiar* to these two Writings, yet *characteristic*
of them, of which there are about fifty. The third is a list of
passages in which there is *coincidence in thought*, though not in
words, of which there are upwards of thirty.

In the first of these categories examine a dozen examples.

TERM	GOSPEL	EPISTLE
The Word	i. 1, 14	i. 1
Have seen and bear witness ...	i. 34; iii. 11, 32	i. 2
Darkness (metaphorically) ...	i. 5: six times	i. 5: five times
To do the truth	iii. 21	i. 6
Paraclete (Comforter)	xiv. 16	ii. 1
New Commandment	xiii. 34	ii. 7, 8
Little Children (*teknia*) ...	xiii. 33	ii. 1
Little Children (*paidia*) ...	xxi. 5	ii. 13, 18
The World Knew Him Not ...	i. 10; xvii. 25	iii. 1
Murderer	viii. 44	iii. 15
Saviour of the World	iv. 42	iv. 14
The Witness of the Spirit ...	xv. 26	v. 6

(g) Taken together these two Writings emphasize two aspects
of one great truth. The Gospel shows that 'Jesus is the Christ,
the Son of God' (xx. 31), and the Epistle insists that the Son of
God is Jesus (iv. 2, 3). The Gospel underlines Christ's divinity,
and the Epistle, His humanity. The one moves from the historical to the eternal, and the other, from the eternal to the
historical; and both exhort to such faith in Christ as shall lead
to fellowship with Him, with the Father, and with all believers.

In the Gospel, which deals with a situation which existed
more than sixty years before John wrote it, the controversies
of Judaism are prominent, but in the Epistle, which reflects the
situation when John wrote, in the last decade of the first century,
the former controversies had dropped out, and Gnosticism had
come into full view as the most formidable opponent of the
Christian religion (1 John iv. 2).

(ii) John's Gospel and the Second and Third Epistles

That the Second and Third Johannine Epistles are from the same hand no one can deny (cf. 2 John 1 with 3 John 1; and 2 John 12, 13, with 3 John 13, 14), and internal evidence shows that that hand was John's, the Apostle. This has been challenged on the ground that the writer describes himself as 'the Presbyter,' in both Epistles, but it has yet to be shown that the Presbyter was not the Apostle. If he had not been, it is extremely unlikely that these little Notes would ever have received canonical recognition.

Having seen the strength of the evidence for the apostolic authorship of the Fourth Gospel (see ' Authorship,' p. 135), it may confidently be assumed that these Second and Third Epistles, as well as the First, bearing John's name, are from the Apostle's hand (cf. 1 John i. 4, with 2 John 12; 1 John ii. 7, with 2 John 5; 1 John iii. 23, 24, with 2 John 9; 1 John iii. 22-24, with 2 John 5, 6; 1 John iv. 2, 3, with 2 John 7).

The internal evidence which shows the connection between the First and Second Epistles, shows the connection also between the Second and Third (2nd, 1, 2; 3rd, 8, 12; 2nd, 4; 3rd, 3, 4; 2nd, 3; 3rd, 6; 2nd, 5; 3rd, 5). Note, also, turns of phrase in 2 and 3 John which recall both the Gospel and First Epistle, 2 John 9, with 1 John v. 12; 3 John 12, with John xxi. 24; 3 John 12, with John xv. 27.

'We hold,' says Dr. Bernard, 'that the cumulative evidence available from the style and diction of (these) two short letters sufficiently proves that they are written by the same hand that wrote the Gospel and the First Epistle.'

The Johannine doctrines move, as in an ellipse, around the foci *Love* and *Truth*, and the following table shows the dominance of these ideas.

	Gospel	1 Epistle	2 Epistle	3 Epistle	Synoptics
LOVE -	45	46	4	2	28
TRUTH	59	16	5	7	18

In these numbers the word *love* includes the verb and the noun, but not *beloved*, which occurs 6 times in the First Epistle, 4 times in the Third Epistle, and 8 times in the Synoptics. The occurrences of *truth* include *true*, *truly*, *verily*, and *indeed*, all from the same root.

(iii) JOHN'S GOSPEL AND THE REVELATION

A person bearing the name of John is mentioned five times in the Revelation, and claims to be the writer of the Book (i. 1, 4, 9; xxi. 2; xxii. 8). This John is surely the Apostle. The external evidence for this is early, clear and conclusive, as it is for the authorship of the Fourth Gospel.

Between the Gospel and the Apocalypse there are differences of language, both in vocabulary and style, but these, says Westcott, 'answer to differences in situation, and are not inconsistent with identity of authorship.'

Influential objection has been taken to the view that the Gospel and the Revelation were from the same hand. Dr. Bernard, on the ground of their difference of style and diction, definitely affirms that they cannot be attributed to the same author, but the matter is not quite as simple as that. If the Apocalypse was written in the time of Nero, about A.D. 67-68, and the Gospel in the time of Domitian, about A.D. 95-96, the difference between the Greek of the one Writing and of the other could be accounted for, for in the course of thirty years a man's style in any language would greatly improve. Of course, this explanation does not hold for those who believe that the Apocalypse was written in the time of Domitian.

Over against the problem of style and diction is the fact that the affinities of the Gospel and First Epistle with the Apocalypse are many, and indicate a common authorship.

They all point to a supreme conflict between the powers of good and evil. In them all, Christ is the central figure. In them all, elements are separated by judgment. In them all, it is declared that Christ will come again.

But there is more detailed evidence for the common authorship of these Writings, evidence supplied by the occurrence of certain words and ideas.

The Gospel tells of the piercing of Christ's side, and of the issue therefrom of blood and water (xix. 34); the First Epistle speaks of the water and the blood (v. 6); and the Apocalypse refers to the piercing of Jesus (i. 7).

The Gospel introduces our Lord as the Word, and as being with the Father (i. 1); the First Epistle opens in the same way (i. 1, 2); and in the Apocalypse also He is the 'Word of God' (xix. 13).

The word 'witness,' which occurs in John's Gospel and Epistles 65 times, occurs 19 times in the Apocalypse.

In the Gospel Christ is the 'Lamb' (i. 29, 36, *amnos*) of the 'little lambs' (xxi. 15, *arnia*), and in the Apocalypse 28 times He is said to be the 'little Lamb' (*arnion*).

The 'blood' of Christ as virtuous is referred to 5 times in the Gospel, 4 times in the First Epistle, and 4 times in the Apocalypse.

The idea of *victory* is also found in these Writings; once in the Gospel; 7 times in the First Epistle, and 17 times in the Apocalypse.

The expressions 'keep my word,' or 'keep my sayings,' are not used by any other New Testament writer, but they are in John's Gospel seven times, in the First Epistle once, and twice in the Apocalypse.

In both Gospel and Apocalypse the figure of 'manna' is used in a spiritual sense (Gospel vi. 31-35; Apocalypse ii. 17). 'Water' also is used in both Writings in this way (Gospel vii. 37; Apocalypse xxii. 17).

Both Gospel and Apocalypse teach the pre-existence of Christ (Gospel i. 1; iii. 13; vi. 33, 38, 51, 62; xvi. 28; Apocalypse i. 8; xxii. 13). In both divine honours are ascribed to Christ (Gospel i. 23; x. 30; xvii. 5; Apocalypse vii. 10; xx. 6; xxi. 22, 23; xxii. 1). In both it is declared that atonement is made by Christ's death (Gospel x. 11, 15; xi. 51, 52; xv. 13; Apocalypse v. 9), and also in the First Epistle (ii. 2; iii. 16). In both it is affirmed that the Son will be the Judge (Gospel v. 22-29); Apocalypse xix. 11 f).

These references will suffice to show how intimately related to John's Gospel are the three Epistles and the Revelation, and they should encourage us to study these five Writings together.

They have often been compared. In the Gospel, John is seen as a historian, in the First Epistle as a pastor, in the private Letters as a friend, and in the Apocalypse as a prophet. In the Gospel Christ is in the world, in the Epistles He is in the heart, and in the Apocalypse He is in Heaven. In the Gospel we have a summary of Christian theology, in the Epistles, of Christian ethics, and in the Apocalypse, of Christian politics.

JESUS THE SON OF GOD

PROLOGUE	A	B	C	D	E	EPILOGUE
Revelation of the Word, and its Inevitable Consequences of Faith and Unbelief	First Manifestations of the Word and the Beginnings of Faith and Unbelief	Development of Unbelief in Israel	Development of Faith in the Disciples	Consummation of Unbelief in Israel	Consummation of Faith in Disciples	Manifestation of the Word for the Correction of Unbelief, and the Confirmation of Faith
I. 1-18. A.D. 27	I. 19-IV. 54. A.D. 27	V-XII. A.D. 28-30	XIII-XVII. A.D. 30	XVIII-XIX. A.D. 30	XX. A.D. 30	XXI. A.D. 30
1 REVELATION OF THE WORD (i. 1-5a)	**1.** OPENING EVENTS (i. 19-ii. 11) Testimonies of the Baptist (i. 19-37) Beginnings of Messiah's Work (i. 38-51) The First Miracle (ii. 1-11)	CONFLICT (v-xii) **1** Commenced (v-viii)	**1.** PREPARATION (xiii. 1-30) Feet-washing (xiii. 1-20) Judas Excluded (xiii. 21-30)	**1** ARREST OF CHRIST (xviii. 1-11)	**1** APOSTLES AT THE TOMB (xx. 1-10)	**1** CHRIST AND SEVEN APOSTLES (xxi. 1-14) The Fishing (1-8) The Feast (9-14)
2 REJECTION OF THE WORD (i. 5b-11).	**2.** THE UNFOLDING STORY (ii. 12-iv. 54)	**2** Continued (ix-x)	**2.** REVELATION (xiii. 31-xvi. 33) Discourses in the Upper Room (xiii. 31-xiv. 31) Discourses on the Way to the Garden (xv. 1-xvi. 33)	**2** TRIALS OF CHRIST (xviii. 12-xix. 16) Ecclesiastical (a) Jewish (xviii. 12-27) Civil (b) Roman (xviii. 28-xix. 16)	**2** APPEARANCES OF THE LORD (xx. 11-29)	**2** CHRIST AND TWO APOSTLES (xxi. 15-23) Peter (15-19) John (20-23)
3 RECEPTION OF THE WORD (i. 12-18)	Jesus in Judæa (ii. 12-iii. 36) Jesus in Samaria (iv. 1-42) Jesus in Galilee (iv. 43-54)	**3** Concluded (xi-xii)	**3.** INTERCESSION (xvii) Christ and the Father (1-5) Christ and the Apostles (6-19) Christ and the Church (20-26)	**3** DEATH OF CHRIST (xix. 17-42)	**3** CLOSE AND PURPOSE OF THE RECORD (xx. 30, 31)	**3** CONCLUSION (xxi. 24, 25) Author of the Record (24) Unrecorded Works (25)

20

ANALYSIS OF JOHN'S GOSPEL

General Summary

PROLOGUE (i. 1-18)

THE REVELATION OF THE WORD, AND ITS INEVITABLE CONSEQUENCES OF FAITH AND UNBELIEF.

DIVISION A (i. 19-iv. 54)

THE FIRST MANIFESTATIONS OF THE WORD, AND THE BEGINNINGS OF FAITH AND UNBELIEF.

DIVISION B (v-xii)

THE DEVELOPMENT OF UNBELIEF IN ISRAEL.

DIVISION C (xiii-xvii)

THE DEVELOPMENT OF FAITH IN THE DISCIPLES.

DIVISION D (xviii-xix)

THE CONSUMMATION OF UNBELIEF IN ISRAEL.

DIVISION E (xx)

THE CONSUMMATION OF FAITH IN THE DISCIPLES.

EPILOGUE (xxi)

THE MANIFESTATION OF THE LORD FOR THE CORRECTION OF UNBELIEF AND THE CONFIRMATION OF FAITH.

This Summary Outline should be carefully marked in your Bible and memorized before proceeding further.

Detailed Outline

PROLOGUE (i. 1-18)

The Revelation of the Word, and its Inevitable Consequences of Faith and Unbelief.

DIVISION A (I. 19-IV. 54)

The First Manifestations of the Word, and the Beginnings of Faith and Unbelief.

DIVISION B (V-XII)

The Development of Unbelief in Israel.

ANALYSIS OF JOHN'S GOSPEL 465

Christ Presents Himself to the Disciples as the Eternal Sufficiency.

(i) THE DISCOURSES IN THE UPPER ROOM ... xiii. 31-xiv. 31
The Coming Separation and Related Problems
CONSOLATION. EXHORTATION TO FAITH
(a) INTRODUCTION ... ... xiii. 31-35
(1) The Glorification of the Son and the Father (xiii. 31-33)
(2) The Demand this would make on the Disciples (xiii. 34, 35)
(b) THE PROBLEMS ... ... xiii. 36-xiv. 24
(1) PETER'S Problem (xiii. 36-xiv. 4)
Why must I be separated from Thee?
(2) THOMAS' Problem (xiv. 5-7)
Not knowing the goal, how can we know the way?
(3) PHILIP'S Problem (xiv. 8-21)
Let us see the Father and we shall be satisfied
(4) JUDAS' Problem (xiv. 22-24)
Why is Thy Self-manifestation limited to Thy Disciples?
(c) CONCLUSION ... ... xiv. 25-31
(1) The Promise of Further Light (xiv. 25, 26)
(2) The Legacy of Peace (xiv. 27)
(3) The Reason for the Separation (xiv. 28-31)

(ii) THE DISCOURSES ON THE WAY TO THE GARDEN xv. 1-xvi. 33
I. FIRST DISCOURSE ... ... xv. 1-xvi. 4a
The Nature and Results of Union with Christ
INSTRUCTION. APPEAL TO LOVE
(a) THE NATURE OF THIS UNION ... ... xv. 1-10
(1) Discipline (xv. 1, 2)
(2) Dependence (xv. 3, 4)
(3) Responsibility (xv. 5, 6)
(4) Privilege (xv. 7, 8)
(5) Inspiration (xv. 9, 10)
(b) THE RESULTS OF THIS UNION ... ... xv. 11-xvi. 4a
(1) The Disciples and One another (xv. 11-13)
Love and Sacrifice
(2) The Disciples and Christ (xv. 14-16)
Friendship and Privilege
(3) The Disciples and the World (xv. 17-xvi. 4a)
Hatred and Persecution

II. SECOND DISCOURSE ... ... xvi. 4b-33
The Holy Spirit and the Prospect
PREDICTION INCENTIVE TO HOPE
(a) THE HOLY SPIRIT ... ... xvi. 4b-15
(1) Christ and the Spirit (xvi. 4b-7)
(2) The World and the Spirit (xvi. 8-11)
(3) The Disciples and the Spirit (xvi. 12-15)
(b) THE PROSPECT ... ... xvi. 16-33
(1) Sorrow shall be turned into Joy (xvi. 16-24)
(2) Mystery shall be turned into Vision (xvi. 25-30)
(3) Trial shall be turned into Triumph (xvi. 31-33)

3 THE INTERCESSION xvii
(i) Christ and the Father (xvii. 1-5)
(ii) Christ and the Apostles (xvii. 6-19)
(iii) Christ and the Church (xvii. 20-26)

30

QUESTIONS

1 What three views have been held respecting the authorship of this Gospel, and how may they be designated?
2 Which of these views has the most support from external and internal evidence?
3 Touching the matter of authorship, what five points does the Gospel itself bring to light?
4 Where did the Apostle John live, and who were the other members of the family?
5 What was the family occupation, and what evidence is there that they were well-off?
6 When and how did John first get associated with Jesus?
7 What further and fuller association had he with Jesus?
8 Give evidence that John was a privileged Apostle.
9 What references are there to the Apostle John in the Acts?
10 To what place was John banished, and what happened there?
11 How and how often does John refer to himself in his Gospel?
12 How would you estimate the place of John in the Apostolic Age?
13 Give four reasons for supposing that the Fourth Gospel was written towards the close of the first century.
14 Is there anything in the quality of what John writes which points to a late date of writing?
15 What evidence is there in 'John' that there was a current Gospel tradition?
16 Where is it supposed this Gospel was written?
17 For whom did John write his Gospel? Give reasons for your answer.
18 Did John employ sources for his Gospel?
19 What witness is there to the canonicity of this Gospel?
20 Can the views be supported that John, in writing his Gospel, had a supplementary and a doctrinal aim?
21 What does the Evangelist say was his design in writing his Gospel?
22 Analyse the passage in which this design is declared.
23 What is the plan by which John's design is carried out?
24 How is the plan of this Gospel revealed in its Prologue?
25 How many verses are there in the Prologue and how many in the Epilogue?
26 What, by references, are the five parts of the plan of this Gospel, and how may each be described?
27 How many Feasts are mentioned in this Gospel, and what Feasts are they?
28 Into what eight periods may this Gospel be divided?
29 Name some other chronological data in this Gospel.
30 Outline the geographical movements of Christ's ministry in this Gospel.
31 Name several features of John's style.
32 Name eighteen of John's dominating words.

33 Name a dozen words and ten phrases which are peculiar to this Gospel.

34 How may John's style be characterized?

35 How many miracles does John record, what are they, and how many of them are not recorded elsewhere?

36 What, where, and why, was the first miracle?

37 How may the spiritual teaching of the miracles in this Gospel be described?

38 How are some of these miracles related to discourses recorded by John?

39 Why does only John record the raising of Lazarus, and the name of the man who cut off the ear of Malchus?

40 How many verses are there in this Gospel, and how many of them record Christ's words?

41 In the matter of discourses, how does this Gospel compare with the Synoptics?

42 What problem do the discourses in 'John' raise?

43 How would you answer the objection that John could not have remembered these discourses for sixty-five years?

44 Name six of the discourses in this Gospel, with references.

45 Into what two categories may the discourses be divided?

46 How may the discourses in chaps. i-xii be analysed?

47 How may the discourses in chaps. xiii-xvi be analysed?

48 What four problems are raised, and by whom, in chaps. xiii-xiv ?

49 In which chapters are found the discourses on—The New Birth; the Light of the World; the Shepherd of the Sheep; the Source of Life; Union with Christ; the Holy Spirit and the Future?

50 How may the Sermon on the Mount and the Upper Room Talk be compared?

51 How many references are there in this Gospel to the Old Testament, and how may they be classified?

52 How many books of the Old Testament are quoted from or alluded to, and which?

53 Name half a dozen Old Testament passages quoted by John.

54 Name ten allusions to the Old Testament in this Gospel.

55 By whom are the quotations and allusions made?

56 To what two great facts do these references to the Old Testament call attention?

57 What Old Testament saints does John name, and in what connection?

58 In what three respects may this Gospel be related to the Synoptics?

59 How many lines of parallel are there between this Gospel and the Synoptics? Name half a dozen of them.

60 What reason can be given for there being any parallels in 'John' to the Synoptics?

61 What seven great omissions are there in this Gospel? Comment on three of them.

62 According to Bishop Westcott, what proportion of the material in this Gospel is peculiar to it?

63 Name four of the more important passages peculiar to this Gospel.

64 Is there any reason for supposing that John selected his material in the light of what Luke had written? Support your answer.

65 Name a dozen words which occur in Luke and John only.

66 How would you illustrate the fragmentariness of this Gospel?

67 Approximately what periods are covered respectively by chapters i; ii-iii; iv; v-vi; vii-xi; xii-xxi; and in what years do they fall?

68 What proof is there that in the fragmentariness of this Gospel is a sublime unity?

69 How would you account for the fact that there are no parables in this Gospel?

70 What word here is translated 'parable,' and what does it mean?

71 What imagery akin to parables is found in this Gospel, and where?

72 Does the writer of this Gospel make special use of the numbers 'three' and 'seven'? Support your answer.

73 How many persons are brought to notice in this Gospel? How many of them are named, and how many unnamed?

74 Name ten prominent people in this Gospel, and refer to half a dozen unnamed persons.

75 How may Peter, Judas, Nicodemus, Pilate, Nathanael, and Martha, be characterized?

76 Name half a dozen groups of people referred to by John.

77 What distinguishes this Gospel from the Synoptics in its teaching concerning the Messiah?

78 In connection with what events do we find the discourses on the Bread of Life, and the Good Shepherd, the Water of Life, and the Light of the World?

79 Name a dozen passages which are comments by the author of this Gospel.

80 Name the sevenfold witness to Christ presented in this Gospel.

81 What seven things does Christ claim to be, following the words, 'I am'?

82 How may it be shown that the Gospel and the first Epistle which bears John's name are the work of the same author?

83 Name half a dozen words which occur frequently in the Gospel and the first Epistle.

84 What are the standpoints of the Gospel and the First Epistle respectively, relative to Christ?

85 What two words are prominent in John's Gospel and his three Epistles, and how, in the matter of frequency, do they compare with occurrences in the Synoptics?

86 How may it be shown that John's 2nd and 3rd Epistles are by the writer of the Gospel and First Epistle?

87 What affinities are there between this Gospel and the Apocalypse?

88 Name some important words and ideas which occur in both the Gospel and the Apocalypse, and what do these occurrences prove?

89 How is Christ seen in John's Gospel, Epistles, and Apocalypse respectively?

90 What are the three parts of the Prologue to this Gospel, and how is the first of them reflected in the First Epistle?
91 Who were Christ's first five disciples?
92 What are the three divisions of Christ's Intercessory Prayer?
93 What references are there in this Gospel and the First Epistle to Christ's Return?
94 Give six instances of belief, and four of unbelief, in this Gospel.
95 How do the Evangelist's references to John the Baptist differ from those of the Synoptics?

LITERATURE

'Gospel of John' - - - - - - Bp. Westcott
'St. John's Gospel.' Handbooks for Bible Classes
 (2 vols.) - - - - - - - G. Reith
'St. John.' Cambridge Greek Testament for Schools
 and Colleges - - - - - A. Plummer
'Commentary on St. John's Gospel' (3 vols.) - F. Godet
'St. John.' Pulpit Commentary (2 vols.) - H. R. Reynolds
'St. John.' The Century Bible - - - J. A. McClymont
'The Gospel of John.' Expositor's Bible (2 vols.) M. Dods
'St. John.' International Critical Commentary
 (2 vols.) - - - - - - - J. H. Bernard
'Introduction to the Johannine Writings' - - P. J. Gloag
'The Apostle John' - - - - - - Griffith Thomas
'The Son of Zebedee' - - - - - H. P. V. Nunn
'The Tests of Life' - - - - - - R. Law
'Helps to the Study of St. John's Gospel' - W. H. T. Gairdner
'Introduction to the Study of the Gospels' - Bp. Westcott
'Introduction to the Literature of the New Testament' J. Moffatt
'The Messages of the Books' - - - - F. W. Farrar
'The Early Days of Christianity.' Vol. II - - F. W. Farrar
'Leading Ideas of the Gospels' - - - Bp. Alexander
'Suggestive Commentary on St. John' (2 vols.) Van Doren
'The Criticism of the Fourth Gospel' - - W. Sanday
'The Central Teaching of Jesus Christ' - T. D. Bernard
'Word Pictures in the New Testament.' Vol. V - A. T. Robertson
'Word Studies in the New Testament.' Vol. II - M. Vincent
'Gnomon of the New Testament.' Vol. II - J. A. Bengel
'Critical and Exegetical Handbook on the Gospel of
 St. John' (2 vols.) - - - - - H. A. W. Meyer
'The Speaker's Bible' (2 vols.) - - - ——
'The Fourth Evangelist' - - - - - C. F. Nolloth
'The Gospel of John' - - - - - C. R. Erdman
'The Character and Authorship of the Fourth Gospel' J. Drummond
'The Transcendence of Jesus Christ' (ch. v.) - F. Cawley
Articles on the Fourth Gospel in Hastings' Dictionary of the Bible; Dictionary of Christ and the Gospels; International Standard Bible Encyclopædia
'Readings in St. John's Gospel'   William Temple

DIVISION C

THE GOSPELS
VIEWED CHRISTOLOGICALLY

THE GOSPELS VIEWED CHRISTOLOGICALLY

KEY PLAN OF READING

SEVENTY STUDIES

2

THE PREPARATION FOR CHRIST'S ADVENT

THE Gospels are the most important part of Holy Scripture because all that preceded them led up to them, and all that follows emerges from them. If the revelation of the Gospels were to be removed, the Old Testament would be an enigma, and the remainder of the New Testament would never have been written. These two parts of the Bible, comprising sixty-two of its sixty-six Books, derive their value from the four which we call the Gospels.

Christ is the focal Fact of history. All history before Him was a preparation for His First Advent, and all history since He came has been a preparation for His Second Advent. Between the *expectation* of the Old Testament, and the *experience* of the Acts, Epistles and Revelation, is the '*Exegesis*' of God, Jesus Christ, the Redeemer of man (John i. 18, Gr.; 'declared' is *exegeted*, that is, expounded).

Dionysius 'the Little,' showed great insight when he dated our era from the birth of Christ, for, as Schaff says, He is 'the centre and turning-point not only of chronology, but of all history, and the key to all its mysteries. Around Him, as the Sun of the moral universe, revolve at their several distances all nations and all important events in the religious life of the world; and all must, directly or indirectly, consciously or unconsciously, contribute to glorify His name and advance His cause. The history of mankind before His birth must be viewed as a preparation for His coming, and the history after His birth as a gradual diffusion of His spirit and progress of His kingdom.'

The process of preparation for Christ was twofold: the approach of God to man, and the approach of man to God. The first of these was in *Judaism*, and was direct and positive; the second was in *Heathenism*, and was indirect, and mainly negative.

(1) In *Judaism* the true religion was prepared for man, and in *Heathenism* man was prepared for the true religion. The history of the Chosen People is in two parts; first, the period of their isolation from all the world; and second, the period of their

dispersion throughout all the world. The first of these periods was for the revelation of the world-religion to them; and the second was for the propagation of the world-religion by them. The first of these periods reached from Abram to Jeremiah, and in it the promises, principles, and predictions of the world-religion were vouchsafed to Israel. The second of these periods began with the captivity of Judah in Babylonia, and by this means witness was borne in the heart of heathenism to the true religion, by such as Mordecai, Esther, Daniel, and Nehemiah.

Later, with the establishment everywhere of synagogues, and the translation of the Hebrew Scriptures into Greek, highways were cast up for the Advent of the Messiah.

(2) The preparation of *Heathenism* for the coming of Christ was manifold, both negative and positive. On the negative side *the Eastern Powers, Babylonia and Persia*, proved that luxury and material grandeur cannot save and satisfy mankind; and on the positive side they furnished the agencies and theatre for the Jewish dispersion, and thus, for the early dissemination of the germs of the world-religion. On the negative side *the Middle Power, Greece*, proved that the highest human culture and civilization are unable to save and satisfy mankind; and on the positive side it furnished the language, at once perfect and universal, in which the world-religion was to find its fittest expression. On the negative side *the Western Power, Rome*, proved that human power and sovereign will are not sufficient to save and satisfy mankind; and on the positive side it furnished the highways along which the world-religion was freely and rapidly carried to all mankind.

In short, the Pagan World revealed that Orientalism, Hellenism, and Imperialism, were totally unable to remove human guilt and bring peace to man's heart; and, at the same time, it furnished the Messiah, through the Jew, with a point of contact, a perfect language, and an open highway.

Thus, says Schaff, the way for Christ and Christianity was prepared on every side; positively and negatively, directly and indirectly; in theory and in practice; by truth and by error; by false belief and by unbelief; by Jewish religion, by Grecian culture, by Roman conquest; by the vainly attempted amalgamation of Jewish and heathen thought; by the exposed impotence of natural civilization, philosophy, art, and political power; by the decay of the old religions; by the universal distraction and hopeless misery of the age, and by the yearnings of all earnest and noble souls for the religion of salvation.

And so, 'when the fulness of the time was come, God sent forth His Son, made of a woman, made under the law, to redeem them that were under the law, that we might receive the adoption of sons' (Gal. iv. 4, 5).

QUESTIONS

1 How are the Scriptures before and after the Gospels related to the latter?
2 What is the place of Christ in history?
3 What was the twofold preparation-process for Christ's Advent, and how may it be designated?
4 To whom, and in what period of their history, was the world-religion revealed; and how and when was it propagated?
5 In what two ways did Heathenism unconsciously make preparation for the Advent of Christ?
6 Show in what ways the Eastern, Middle, and Western Powers made this twofold preparation.

LITERATURE

'The Preparation for Christianity' - - - R. M. Wenley
'The Environment of Early Christianity' - - S. Angus
'Background of the Gospels' - - - - W. Fairweather
'Between Malachi and Saint Matthew' - - G. M. Forde
'From Malachi to Matthew' - - - - R. W. Moss
'Between the Old and New Testaments' - - R. H. Charles
'The Gentile and the Jew.' (2 vols.) - - J. J. I. Döllinger
'Roman Ideas of Deity in the last century before
    the Christian Era' - - - - - W. W. Fowler
Conflict of Religions in the Early Roman Empire' T. R. Glover
'Personal Religion in Egypt before Christianity' - W. M. F. Petrie
'Paganism and Christianity' - - - - J. A. Farrer
Hastings' Dictionary of the Bible, and Dictionary
    of Christ and the Gospels - - - - ——
Encyclopædia of Religion and Ethics - - ——
The Church Histories of Schaff, and Neander - ——

3

PROPHECIES OF THE MESSIAH

THERE are two kinds of prophecy, preaching and prediction; forth-telling, and fore-telling, and the latter of these is as clearly evident in the Old Testament as is the former. The correspondence between what in the Old Testament is declared would be, and what in the New Testament is said to be, is so complete and minute, that one wonders how anyone with any respect for his intelligence could ever call the fact into question.

Porphyry recognized that what is supposed to be prophecy in the Book of Daniel is so accurately verified in history, that, he said, the supposed prophecies must have been written after the events; and Bolingbroke admitted that the death of Christ was so distinctly foretold in the Book of Isaiah that, this sceptic claimed, Jesus brought about His own crucifixion in order to furnish His disciples with an argument from prophecy.

Predictive prophecy has for its subjects the Israelites, the Gentiles, and the Messiah. It is with the last of these only that we are now concerned.

Messianic prophecy may be classified as direct, and indirect, or as literal, and typical, and about many passages in each classification one can speak with confidence.

(1) Indirect or Typical Prediction

The whole sacrificial system of Israel was typical of the work which Christ wrought on Calvary. This is declared in such passages as: 'Christ our Passover is sacrificed for us' (1 Cor. v. 7); 'Behold the Lamb of God, which taketh away the sin of the world' (John i. 29), and 'Every priest standeth daily ministering and offering oftentimes the same sacrifices, which can never take away sins: but this man, after He had offered one sacrifice for sins for ever, sat down on the right hand of God' (Heb. x. 11, 12; cf. ix. 28; 1 Peter i. 18, 19).

The passover ceremony of Exodus xii pointed to Christ, as did the offerings of Lev. i-vii, and the Great Day of Atonement (Lev. xvi), but long before this, Christ's redemptive sacrifice was typified in the first slaughter of animals (Gen. iii. 21), in the acceptance of Abel's offering, while Cain's was rejected (Gen. iv. 1-5), and in the incident of Abraham and Isaac on Mount Moriah (Gen. xxii).

It is clear, also, that the following are typically predictive of Christ.

(i) THINGS

The *Manna* (Exod. xvi; cf. John vi. 48-51); the *Old Corn*, telling of Christ's resurrection, as the manna told of His incarnation (Josh. v. 11, 12; cf. John xii. 24); the *Smitten Rock* (Exod. xvii. 6; cf. 1 Cor. x. 4); the *Tabernacle* and its furniture (Exod. xl; cf. John i. 14, R.V., Heb. ix. 11); the *Temple* (1 Kings v. 1-5; cf. Matt. xii. 6; John ii. 19); the *Rent Veil* (Exod. xxvi. 31-33; Lev. xvi. 2; cf. Matt. xxvii. 51; Heb. ix. 8; x. 19, 20); the *Ark* and *Mercy-Seat* (Exod. xxv. 10-22; Psa. xl. 8; cxix. 11; cf. Heb. ix. 1-5).

(ii) PERSONS

Melchisedec (Gen. xiv. 17-20; cf. Isa. ix. 6, 7; xxxii. 1; Zech. vi. 13; Heb. v. 6, 10; vii. 1-11); *Aaron* (Lev. viii; cf. Heb. v. 1-5); *Isaac* (Gen. xxii. 1-12; cf. John iii. 16; x. 17; Rom. viii. 32); *Joseph* (Gen. xxxvii-l; cf. (*a*) Gen. xxxvii. 3; Matt. iii. 17; (*b*) xxxvii. 4, 5; John xv. 25; (*c*) xxxvii. 8; Luke xix. 14; (*d*) xxxvii. 18; Matt. xxvii. 1; (*e*) xl. 2, 3, 13; xli. 9, 12; Luke xxiii. 32, 41, 43; (*f*) xl. 15; John viii. 46; (*g*) Psa. cv. 20; Acts ii. 24; (*h*) xli. 38; John v. 20; Acts x. 38; (*i*) xli. 39; Col. ii. 3; (*j*) xli. 40; Isa. ix. 6, 7; (*k*) xli. 55; John ii. 5; (*l*) xli. 57; Isa. xlix. 6; (*m*) xlii. 8; John i. 10, 11; (*n*) xlv. 1; Luke xxiv. 31; (*o*) xlv. 8; Acts ii. 23; (*p*) xlix. 22; John xv. 5; (*q*) 1 Chron. v. 2; Rom. viii. 29); *Moses* (Deut. xviii. 18; cf. Luke xxiv. 19; John i. 19-27); *David*: rejected (2 Sam. xv; cf. Luke xix. 14); re-enthroned (2 Sam. xix. 8-15; cf. Rev. i. 7; v. 5-14); *Solomon* (2 Sam. vii. 12-16; cf. Luke i. 31-33; Heb. i. 8; Rev. xi. 15).

(2) Direct or Literal Prediction

That Christ was predicted centuries before He came will not be questioned by anyone who believes that He is 'The Truth' (John xiv. 6), and that the Apostles spake by the Holy Spirit. Peter, in the house of Cornelius, said, 'To Him give all the prophets witness' (Acts x. 43). In Achaia, Paul 'mightily convinced the Jews, publicly, showing by the Scriptures that Jesus was the Christ' (Acts xviii. 27, 28); and when, before Agrippa, declaring that Jesus was the Messiah, he said that he spake 'none other things than those which the prophets and Moses did say should come,' and he appealed to the king by asking, 'Believest thou the prophets?' (Acts xxvi. 22, 27); and the last glimpse we get of him in the Acts shows him at Rome expounding and testifying the kingdom of God, 'persuading the Jews concerning Jesus, both out of the law of Moses, and out of the prophets' (Acts xxviii. 23).

That Peter's and Paul's view of the matter was Christ's is perfectly clear. Addressing the Jews He said: 'If ye believed Moses, ye would believe Me, for he wrote of Me. But if ye believe not his writings, how shall ye believe My words?' (John v. 46, 47); and to the two disciples on the Emmaus road, He said: 'O foolish men, and slow of heart to believe in all that the prophets have spoken! Behoved it not the Christ to suffer these things, and to enter into His glory? And beginning from Moses and from all the prophets, He interpreted to them in all the Scriptures the things concerning Himself' (Luke xxiv. 25-27, R.V.); and later, He said to all the Apostles at Jerusalem: 'These are My words which I spake unto you, while I was yet with you, how that all things must needs be fulfilled, which are written in the Law of Moses, and the Prophets, and the Psalms, concerning Me.' Then opened He their mind, that they might understand the Scriptures; and He said unto them, 'Thus it is written, that the Christ should suffer, and rise again from the dead the third day; and that repentance and remission of sins should be preached in His name unto all the nations, beginning from Jerusalem' (Luke xxiv. 44-47, R.V.).

These words were spoken after He was risen from the dead, and they confirmed what He had said before He died: 'Behold, we go up to Jerusalem, and all the things that are written by the prophets shall be accomplished unto the Son of Man' (Luke xviii. 31); and as He was about to enter into the agony of Gethsemane, He said: 'This which is written must be fulfilled in Me, And He was reckoned with transgressors: for that which concerneth Me hath fulfilment' (Luke xxii. 37, R.V.).

It is simply a fact that in the Old Testament there are scores of passages which predict the coming, the mission, and the person of Christ, for which exact fulfilments are found in the New Testament. These passages answer as perfectly to one another as the fingers of one hand do to the fingers of the other.

Forecast and fulfilment are set over against one another in such a way as to leave all but the wilfully blind convinced and worshipful.

The following references prove and illustrate this claim. They divide the subject into three parts which together embrace the whole field of Christology, namely, Christ's human pedigree, redemptive programme, and Divine Person.

(a) CHRIST'S HUMAN PEDIGREE

Prediction	Fulfilment
(i) To be the Woman's Seed	
Genesis iii. 15	Matthew i. 18
(ii) To be Born of a Virgin	
Isaiah vii. 14	Matthew i. 22, 23
(iii) To be of the Line of Abraham	
Genesis xii. 3, 7; xvii. 7	Galatians iii. 16; Rom. ix. 5
(iv) To be of the Tribe of Judah	
Genesis xlix. 10	Hebrews vii. 14 / Revelation v. 5
(v) To be of the House of David	
2 Samuel vii. 12, 13	Romans i. 3 / Luke i. 31-33

(b) CHRIST'S REDEMPTIVE PROGRAMME

So complete is Old Testament prediction here, that we are able to distinguish the time divisions of Christ's life on earth.

1 The Thirty Years of Preparation

Prediction	Fulfilment
(i) To be Born at Bethlehem	
Micah v. 2, 3	Matthew ii. 6 / Luke ii. 4, 15
(ii) To be Called Immanuel	
Isaiah vii. 14	Matthew i. 23

(iii) To be Worshipped by Gentiles

Isaiah lx. 3, 6, 9	Matthew ii. 11

(iv) To Be Called Out of Egypt

Hosea xi. 1	Matthew ii. 15

(v) To Have a Forerunner

Isaiah xl. 3	Matthew iii. 1-3
Malachi iii. 1	Mark i. 2, 3

II The Three Years of Ministration

Prediction	*Fulfilment*

(i) To be Filled and Anointed by the Spirit

Isaiah xi. 2, 3; lxi. 1	Luke iii. 22; iv. 18
	John iii. 34

(ii) To Come on a Saving Mission

Isaiah lxi. 1	Luke iv. 16-19

(iii) To be a Worker of Miracles

Isaiah xxxv. 5, 6	Matthew xi. 4, 5

(iv) To be a Light to the Gentiles

Isaiah xlii. 1, 6	Luke ii. 32
	Acts xiii. 47

(v) To be the Blesser of Gentiles

Isaiah xi. 10	Romans xv. 9-12

(vi) To be a Man of Sorrows

Isaiah liii. 3	Hebrews ii. 18; iv. 15

(vii) To be Rejected of Men

Psalm lxix. 8	John i. 11; vii. 5
Isaiah liii. 3	

(viii) To be Deserted

Zechariah xiii. 7	Matthew xxvi. 31

(ix) To be Scourged and Spat Upon

Isaiah l. 6	Matthew xxvi. 67; xxvii. 26

(x) To be Given Vinegar to Drink

Psalm lxix. 21	Matthew xxvii. 34, 48

(xi) To be Pierced with Nails

Psalm xxii. 16	Luke xxiii. 33 John xx. 25

(xii) To be Forsaken of God

Psalm xxii. 1	Matthew xxvii. 46

(xiii) To be Surrounded by Enemies

Psalm xxii. 7, 8; cix. 25	Matthew xxvii. 39, 40 Mark xv. 29, 30

(xiv) To be Numbered with Transgressors

Isaiah liii. 12	Mark xv. 28 Luke xxii. 37

(xv) To Agonize with Thirst

Psalm xxii. 15	John xix. 28

(xvi) To Commend His Spirit to God

Psalm xxxi. 5	Luke xxiii. 46

(xvii) His Garments to be Distributed

Psalm xxii. 18	John xix. 23, 24 Luke xxiii. 34

(xviii) No Bone of His to be Broken

Psalm xxxiv. 20 Numbers ix. 12	John xix. 33-36

(xix) To be Buried with the Rich

Isaiah liii. 9 (Heb.)	Matthew xxvii. 57-60

III The Forty Days of Confirmation

Prediction	*Fulfilment*

(i) To Rise from the Dead without Seeing Corruption

Psalm xvi. 9, 10	Acts ii. 27, 31; xiii. 33-35

(ii) To Ascend into Glory

Psalm lxviii. 18; xxiv. 7-10	Acts i. 9 Ephesians iv. 8

(c) Christ's Divine Person

Prediction	Fulfilment

(i) The Eternal Son

Psalm ii. 7, 12	Acts xiii. 33 Matthew iii. 17 Hebrews i. 5; v. 5

(ii) Incarnate by Birth

Isaiah ix. 6	Luke ii. 11

(iii) The Suffering Servant

Isaiah xlii. 1; lii. 13-15	Matthew xii. 18 Philippians ii. 7

(iv) The Rejected Corner Stone

Psalm cxviii. 22	Matthew xxi. 42 Acts iv. 11 Ephesians ii. 20

(v) The Morning Star

Numbers xxiv. 17	Revelation xxii. 16

(vi) The Greatest Prophet

Deuteronomy xviii. 18	Acts iii. 22

(vii) A Greater Priest than Aaron and Melchisedec

Exodus xxviii. 1 Numbers xvi. 40 Psalm cx. 4	Hebrews v. 4, 5 Hebrews v. 6, 10 Hebrews vii. 11-28

(viii) Seated at God's Right Hand

Psalm cx. 1	Matthew xxii. 44 Hebrews x. 12, 13

(ix) The Priest-King

Genesis xiv. 18	Hebrews vii. 1, 14-17

(x) THE SMITING SCEPTRE

Numbers xxiv. 17	Revelation xix. 15

(xi) THE RULER OF THE HEATHEN

Psalm ii. 8	Revelation ii. 27

(xii) THE UNIVERSAL KING

Zechariah xiv. 9 Psalm cx. 1-3	Acts ii. 34, 35 1 Corinthians xv. 25 Revelation xi. 15

(xiii) THE PRINCE OF PEACE

Isaiah ix. 6	Ephesians ii. 14-18

(xiv) HIS KINGDOM EVERLASTING

Daniel ii. 44; iv. 34; vii. 13, 14, 27	Luke i. 33 Hebrews xii. 28

(xv) THE BRANCH

(a) The Branch as Sovereign   ...   Jeremiah xxiii. 5, 6
MATTHEW'S GOSPEL

(b) The Branch as Servant   ...   Zechariah iii. 8
MARK'S GOSPEL

(c) The Branch as Man   ...   ...   Zechariah vi. 12
LUKE'S GOSPEL

(d) The Branch as God   ...   ...   Isaiah iv. 2
JOHN'S GOSPEL

(For a development of this subject see the author's 'Christ the Key to Scripture.' Pickering & Inglis).

Dr. A. T. Pierson has said that there are three canons by which true prophecy can be tested.

1 It must be such an unveiling of the future, that no mere human foresight or wisdom could have guessed it.
2 The prediction must deal in details sufficiently to exclude shrewd guesswork.
3 There must be such lapse of time between the prophecy and the fulfilment as precludes the agency of the prophet himself in effecting or affecting the result.

Judged by these canons the foregoing Messianic prophecies are shown to be genuine, and their value as evidence is beyond serious challenge.

QUESTIONS

1 How may the literature of Old Testament prophecy be classified?
2 How may the Messianic prophecies be classified?
3 What warrant is there for believing that there are Messianic types in the Old Testament?
4 Name four Messianic types of *things*, and four of *persons*, giving Old Testament and New Testament references.
5 Name eight respects in which Joseph is typical of Christ.
6 Give references to show that Peter and Paul believed that Christ was predicted in the Old Testament.
7 Give references to show that Christ believed that He was predicted in the Old Testament.
8 Name three predictions relative to Christ's human pedigree; and three which belong to His thirty years of preparation.
9 Name ten predictions which belong to the period of Christ's ministry.
10 Name half a dozen predicted aspects of Christ's person and work.
11 In what four aspects is Christ predicted as the Branch, and how are these related to the Four Gospels?
12 What three canons does Dr. Pierson lay down as tests of genuine prophecy?

LITERATURE

'Many Infallible Proofs' - - - -	A. T. Pierson
'Christ in all the Scriptures' - - -	A. M. Hodgkin
'The Study of the Types' - - -	A. R. Habershon
'The Witness of the Psalms to Christ and Christianity' - - - - -	Bishop Alexander
'The Divinity of Our Lord.' Lecture II -	H. P. Liddon
'Typology of Scripture' - - - -	Patrick Fairbairn
'Christology of the Old Testament' (4 vols.)	E. W. Hengstenberg
'Introduction to the Study of the Gospels.' (pp. 29, 30, 159-164) - - - -	Bishop Westcott
'Messianic Prophecy' - - - -	P. J. Gloag
'Messianic Prophecy' - - - -	E. Riehm
'The Messianic Hope' - - - -	Case
'Messianic Prophecies in Historical Succession'	F. Delitzsch
'The Messiah in Jewish History' - -	Greenhouse
'The Evolution of the Messianic Idea' •	Oesterley

4
CHRONOLOGY OF CHRIST'S LIFE

IN works treating of New Testament chronology the letters A.U.C. will frequently be found. These are the abbreviated form of *anno urbis conditae*, or *ab urbe condita*, and refer to the establishment or building of Rome.

The year of Rome corresponding to the year 1 of the Christian era was 753. To get any year of Rome before or after Christ the figure must be subtracted from or added to this basic date. For example, if Herod died 4 years before the Christian era, in B.C. 4, the year of Rome would be 753 minus 4, i.e. 749; or, if Christ died in A.D. 30, the year of Rome would be 753 plus 30, i.e. 783.

The chronology of the period covered by the life of our Lord is intricate and uncertain, and only approximation to exactness can be claimed. The four events around which all discussion gathers are:

1 The Date of the Nativity.
2 The Date of the Baptism.
3 The Duration of the Ministry.
4 The Date of the Crucifixion.

(1) THE DATE OF THE NATIVITY

This must be determined in relation to the death of Herod the Great, which, it is generally agreed, was in B.C. 4. Jesus' birth preceded this date, and, it would seem, within two years of it (Matt. ii. 16), so that, almost certainly, Jesus was born about B.C. 5, i.e., A.U.C. 748.

(2) THE DATE OF THE BAPTISM

An important reference for this is Luke iii. 1-3, 21, 23. From this, and other references (cf. John ii. 13, 19, 20), the latest date for the Baptism must be A.D. 27. The phrase, 'Jesus was beginning to be about thirty years old,' is 'an elastic one, and will cover any age from 28 to 32' (Turner). See John viii. 57 (cf. Num. iv. 2, 3).

(3) THE DURATION OF THE MINISTRY

Various periods have been argued for from one to four years. Two years, or less, would satisfy the requirements of the Synoptics, but the Fourth Gospel requires longer, and how much longer will be determined by how many Passovers this Evangelist refers to. In his Gospel there are seven notes of time between the Baptism and the Crucifixion. Three of these refer to Passovers (ii. 13, 23; vi. 4; there is another reading; xi. 55, xii. 1); one to a Feast of Tabernacles (vii. 2); one to a Feast of Dedication (x. 22); one to harvest-time (iv. 35); and one to an unnamed Feast (v. 1). This last has been regarded as Pentecost, Trumpets, Dedication, and Purim, but it may have been a Passover, and if so, John refers to four such, which would make Jesus' ministry of at least three years' duration, and we may assume that it lasted for about three and a half years.

THE FEASTS IN JOHN'S GOSPEL

Feast	Date	Ref.	Description
PASSOVER ...	A.D. 27	ii. 13, 23	"The Jews' Passover"
PURIM (?) ...	A.D. 28	v. 1	"A feast of the Jews"
PASSOVER ...	A.D. 29	vi. 4	"The Passover, a feast of the Jews was nigh"
TABERNACLES	A.D. 29	vii. 2, 8	"The Jews' feast of Tabernacles" "This feast"
DEDICATION	A.D. 29	x. 22	"The feast of the Dedication"
PASSOVER ...	A.D. 30	xi. 55; xii. 1, cf. Mark xiv. 1; Mt. xxvi. 2, 17; Lk. xxii. 1	"The Jews' Passover"

(4) THE DATE OF THE CRUCIFIXION

(See 'The Day of the Crucifixion,' p. 569).

Chronological details can be found in the Bible Dictionaries, but the following summary will serve the present purpose.

A.U.C.	B.C.	EVENTS
748	5	Birth of Jesus.
749	4	Circumcision and Presentation of Jesus. Coming of the Magi.
		Flight into Egypt. Massacre of the Innocents.
		Death of Herod the Great.
		Return of the Family to Nazareth
	A.D.	
761	8	Jesus' First Passover.
780	27	The Baptism and the Temptation of Jesus.
		First Passover of Jesus' Ministry (John ii. 13, 23)
		Cleansing of the Temple.
781	28	John the Baptist Imprisoned.
		A Passover, some think, but more probably Purim (v.i).
		Jesus Begins His Ministry in Galilee.
		The Call of Four Disciples at Capernaum.
		Jesus' First Circuit in Galilee.
		The Choice of Twelve Apostles.
		The Sermon on the Mount.
		The Parables of the Kingdom.
782	29	Commission of the Twelve.
		Death of John the Baptist.
		Feeding of the Multitude, and Discourse on the Bread of Life.
		Peter's Confession that Jesus is the Christ.
		The Transfiguration.
		Final Departure from Galilee.
		Jesus at the Feast of Tabernacles (John vii. 2).
		Commission of the Seventy.
		Jesus Attends the Feast of Dedication (John x. 22).
783	30	Ministry in Peræa.
		Lazarus Raised from the Dead.
		Jesus passes through Jericho on the way to Jerusalem.
		Public Entry into Jerusalem.
		Second Cleansing of the Temple.
		Jesus' Conflict with the Authorities.
		The Prophetic Discourses on Olivet.
		The Supper at Bethany.
		Jesus' last Passover (John xi. 55, xii. 1).
		The Upper Room Discourse.
		Gethsemane.
		The Arrest and Trials.
		The Crucifixion.
		The Resurrection.
		The Appearances.
		The Ascension.

QUESTIONS

1 In chronology what do the letters A.U.C. signify?

2 What year of Rome corresponds to the year 1 of the Christian era?

3 What are the four events around which discussion gathers in the chronology of Christ's life?

4 How are the birth of Jesus and the death of Herod the Great related in time, and does this relation indicate approximately the date of Jesus' birth?

5 What references are there in the Gospels to the time, approximately, of Christ's baptism?

6 Wherein lies the problem of the duration of Christ's ministry?

7 What references are there in the Fourth Gospel to Feasts, and what bearing have they on the duration of Christ's ministry?

8 What Feasts, is it supposed, are referred to in John's Gospel?

9 Give an event for each of eight approximate dates in Christ's life.

LITERATURE

Articles on New Testament Chronology in the standard
 Bible Dictionaries - - - - - - ——
Introduction in Commentaries on the several Gospels:
 Plummer, Westcott, Bernard, Godet, H. A. W.
 Meyer, etc.
'The Bible Student's Life of our Lord' - - S. J. Andrews
Harmonies of the Gospels (see p. 82) - - ——

5

DIAGRAM OF THE MESSIAH'S MINISTRY

THE true end of a synthetical and analytical study of the Gospels is a Christological apprehension of them. The theme of supreme value is not the Gospels themselves, as documents, but the revelation which they record and communicate.

Christ does not derive His value from the Gospels, but they derive their value from Him. No study of these Records is fruitful which does not confront the student with Christ and His claims upon us all; in other words, the end of study is not academic, but practical; not knowledge, but religion.

While it is not possible to place in chronological sequence all the contents of the Gospels, it is possible to get a broad outline of Jesus' life and ministry, and it is most important so to do.

This may be said to consist of nine main divisions, as follows.

THE LIFE AND WORK OF JESUS THE CHRIST

THE THIRTY YEARS OF PREPARATION		I
THE OPENING EVENTS		II
EARLY JUDÆAN		III
SAMARITAN		IV
FIRST PERIOD	GALILEAN	V
SECOND PERIOD		
THIRD PERIOD		
LATER JUDÆAN	THE MINISTRY	VI
PERÆAN		VII
THE CLOSING EVENTS		VIII
THE FORTY DAYS OF CONFIRMATION		IX

This diagram should be thoroughly mastered, and it will help the student to remember the Outline if it be observed that divisions I and IX answer to one another; also II and VIII; and between these is Christ's ministry in the three main provinces of Palestine, Judæa, Samaria, and Galilee. It should be observed that the Galilean ministry is central, and that it is in three periods, of which the central, or second one, is the longest and fullest of any of the ministry periods. On one side of the Galilean ministry are the Judæan and the Samaritan, and on the other side, the Judæan and the Peræan.

The early Judæan and Samaritan ministries are recorded by John only (ii. 13-iv. 42), and the fullest account of the Peræan ministry is given by Luke (xiii. 22-xix. 28).

There are not many notes of time in the Gospels, and these are chiefly in the Fourth, but there is reason for assuming that Christ's ministry lasted from three to three and a half years, from the Autumn of A.D. 26 to the Spring of A.D. 30 (pp. 489, 490).

If this be correct, the approximate periods would be:

DIVISION II	-	-	3 months.
„ III	-	-	8 months.
„ IV	-	-	A few days.
„ V			First period — 5 months.
			Second period — 12 months.
			Third period — 6 months.
„ VI		-	3 months.
„ VII	-	-	$3\frac{1}{2}$ months.
„ VIII	-	-	1 week.

Mark these in the diagram. (See pp. 68-81).

A good Harmony of the Gospels is necessary if one is to know what events, doings, and sayings, belong to each of the nine divisions. A good Life of Christ is also desirable (p. 494, and Index III).

QUESTIONS

1 In how many main divisions may the life of Christ be divided?
2 Name the first two and the last two of these divisions.
3 Which is the central division of Jesus' ministry, and how is it sub-divided?
4 Who alone records the Early Judæan and Samaritan ministries, and in what chapters?
5 Who gives the fullest account of the Peræan ministry, and in what chapters?
6 Approximately how long did Christ's ministry last, and in what years?
7 Draw from memory a diagram of Christ's life and work.

LITERATURE

'A Harmony of the Gospels for Students of the
Life of Christ' - - - - - A. T. Robertson
'A Harmony of the Gospels for Historical Study'   Stevens & Burton
'The Life of Jesus Christ.' Brief and Valuable   James Stalker
'The Bible Student's Life of Our Lord.' Should
be possessed - - - - - - S. J. Andrews
'A People's Life of Christ.' Popular   -   -   J. Paterson Smyth
'The Days of His Flesh.' Good -   -   -   David Smith
'The Life of Christ.' Very readable and inform-
ative - - - - - - - F. W. Farrar
'The Original Jesus.' Most valuable   -   -   Otto Borchert
'Jesus and the Gospel.' Lucid and scholarly -   James Denney
'The Life and Times of Jesus the Messiah.' A
standard work. (2 vols.) - - - - Alfred Edersheim
'The Crises of the Christ' - - - - G. Campbell Morgan
'The Life and Words of Christ' (2 vols.)   -   C. Geikie
'Our Lord's Life on Earth' - - - - W. Hanna
'The Life of Christ' - - - - - G. Papini
'In the Steps of the Master'   -   -   -   H. V. Morton
'Historical Geography of the Holy Land'   -   G. A. Smith
'Sinai and Palestine' - - - - - A. P. Stanley
'Historical Charts of the Life and Ministry of
Christ' - - - - - - - G. E. Croscup
'Palestine Explored'   -   -   -   -   -   J. Neil
'Sacred Sites of the Gospels'   -   -   -   W. Sanday
'Outlines of the Life of Christ'   -   -   -   W. Sanday
'The Journeys of Jesus Christ'   -   -   -   A. T. Schofield
'Handbook of Palestine and Trans-Jordan'   -   H. C. Luke and
E. Keith-Roach

In addition to these books, reference should be made, if
possible, to articles on this subject in Hastings' Bible Dictionary,
in Dictionary of Christ and the Gospels; and in the International Standard Bible Encyclopædia, and in Smith's Bible
Dictionary.

6

A SYLLABUS OF THE GOSPEL STORY

CONTENTS

In this Syllabus, as in the 'Harmonistic Reading Syllabus' (Div. A, Pt. I, pp. 68-81), the traditional view is followed of events in the Passion Week. It is only right that this should be done so long as the order of the events is a subject of controversy, but the view which this Guide follows is set forth in Sec. 14: 'The Day of the Crucifixion' (p. 569).

PART I

THE THIRTY YEARS OF PREPARATION

B.C. 5 to A.D. 26

1 John's Prologue
2 Luke's Preface
3 Annunciation to Zacharias
4 Annunciation to Mary
5 Annunciation to Joseph
6 Mary's Visit to Elisabeth
  The *Magnificat*
7 John Baptist Born
  The *Benedictus*
8 The Angels and the Shepherds
  The *Gloria in Excelsis*
9 The Circumcision of Jesus
10 The Presentation in the Temple
  Simeon
  The *Nunc Dimittis*
  Anna
11 The Two Genealogies
12 The Wise Men from the East
13 The Flight into Egypt
14 The Massacre of the Babes

THE GALILEAN MINISTRY

SECOND PERIOD

MAY TO APRIL.   A.D. 28-29

From the Choosing of the Twelve to the Withdrawal into Northern Galilee. Spring, A.D. 28-Spring, A.D. 29. About One Year.

THE GALILEAN MINISTRY

THIRD PERIOD

MAY TO OCTOBER.   A.D. 29

From the Withdrawal into Northern Galilee to the Final Departure for Jerusalem. Spring, A.D. 29-Autumn, A.D. 29. About Six Months.

PART VI

THE LATER JUDÆAN MINISTRY

OCTOBER TO DECEMBER. ABOUT THREE MONTHS.   A.D. 29

PART VII

THE PERÆAN MINISTRY

149 Jesus Rebukes the Selfish Ambition of James and John
         THE GREATNESS OF SERVICE   ...   . D
150 HEALING OF BLIND BARTIMAEUS AND ANOTHER   ...   ... M
151 The Conversion of Zacchæus
152 Parable of THE POUNDS   ...   . P

PART VIII

THE CLOSING EVENTS OF CHRIST'S MINISTRY

A.D. 30. SPRING. APRIL.

This syllabus of the Passion Week follows the traditional view, not because it is the author's view, but in order not to raise a controversial subject at this point. For the revised chronology see 'The Day of the Crucifixion,' page 569 (cf. p. 389).

Sunday
Day of Demonstration

153 Two Disciples fetch a Colt
154 Triumphal Entry into Jerusalem
155 Prediction over Jerusalem
156 Jesus in the City and the Temple
157 Retirement to Bethany

Monday
Day of Authority

158 A FIG TREE CURSED   ...   . M
159 Second Cleansing of the Temple

Tuesday
Day of Conflict

160 The Fig Tree Withered
161 UTTERANCE ON PRAYER AND FAITH   ...   . D
         Priests, Scribes, Elders
162 Christ's Authority Challenged
163 Parable of THE TWO SONS   ...   . P
164 Parable of THE WICKED HUSBANDMEN   ...   . P
165 Parable of THE REJECTED STONE   ...   . P
166 Parable of THE MARRIAGE FEAST AND WEDDING GARMENT P
         Pharisees and Herodians
167 UTTERANCE ON TRIBUTE MONEY   ...   . D
         Sadducees
168 The Resurrection Question
         A Scribe
169 The First Commandment
170 Christ's Unanswerable Question
171 DENUNCIATION OF THE SCRIBES AND PHARISEES   ...   ... D
172 Lament over Jerusalem
173 Liberality of a Poor Widow
174 Greeks Desire to See Jesus
175 Parable of a GRAIN OF WHEAT   ...   . P

Wednesday
Day of Silence

Thursday
Day of Preparation

Friday
Day of Suffering

Saturday

Day of Absence

Part IX

THE FORTY DAYS OF CONFIRMATION

A.D. 30

April—May

Sunday

Appearances of Jesus During the Following Thirty-nine Days:

229 Sixth: To the Eleven. Thomas Present
230 Seventh: To Seven Disciples by the Sea
231 SECOND MIRACULOUS DRAUGHT OF FISHES　...　...　...　M
232 Conversation of Jesus and Peter
233 Jesus on the Future of Peter and John
234 Eighth: To James, His Brother
235 Ninth: To the Eleven, and 500 Disciples in Galilee
236 Tenth: To the Eleven in Jerusalem, and on Olivet
237 The Final Commission
238 The Ascension
239 The Angels' Message
240 The Prayer Meeting at Jerusalem
241 The Election of a 12th Apostle
242 THE DAY OF PENTECOST

INDEX

Parts	Discourses	Miracles	Parables	Sections	Section-Totals
I	—	—	—	18	18
II	—	—	—	8	26
	—	1	—	—	—
III	—	—	—	4	30
	1	—	—	—	—
IV	—	—	—	3	33
	2	—	—	—	—
V	—	—	—	76	109
VI	1, 8, 7	9, 14, 7	22. 2	—	—
	—	—	—	18	127
VII	9	3	10	—	—
	—	—	—	25	152
VIII	10	—	14 (or 13)	—	—
	—	4	—	65	217
IX	9	2	11 (or 12?)	—	—
	—	—	—	25	242
	—	1	—	—	—
	Totals: 47	41	59, or 60	242	242

Any seeming discrepancy between numbers given here, and in other parts of the Guide, is due to parables being included in, or regarded as discourses, and to specific miracles and groups of miracles being listed together.

7

THE TWO GENEALOGIES

Matthew i. 1-17   Luke iii. 23-38

THE Genealogies of our Lord given by Matthew and Luke have formed the subject of endless discussion, and divers conclusions have been reached. Sceptics of all ages from Porphyry and Celsus to Strauss have declared that it is impossible to reconcile the contradictions of the two accounts, and many who are not sceptics agree that they cannot be harmonized.

Dean Alford says that reconciliation is impossible. Dr. Bacon says that nearly all writers of authority abandon the effort to reconcile them. Dr. Barnard admits two independent accounts, and says that 'they can be harmonized only by suppositions which are incapable of proof, and hardly probable.' Dr. Lindsay says that 'if we start with the fact that St. Matthew, in order to get his generations into sets of fourteen, omitted several names (a common practice among the Jewish Genealogists), the reconciliation of the two descents is very simple, and the supposed difficulties are easily explained by well-known Jewish practices.' Dr. Sweet says that 'most of the difficulties are removed at one stroke, and the known facts harmonized, by the simple supposition that Luke has given us the meeting point of the lineage, both of Joseph and Mary who are akin.'

In the light of these views one is prepared to face difficulties and to come, perhaps, to no definite conclusion.

The first thing to do is to look carefully at the Genealogies. For purpose of comparison we must reverse the order of Luke.

The spelling of the names is according to the A.V., but the R.V. also should be consulted.

Matthew	Both		Luke
—	—		1 Adam
—	—		2 Seth
—	—		3 Enos
—	—		4 Cainan
—	—		5 Maleleel
—	—		6 Jared
—	—		7 Enoch
—	—		8 Mathusala
—	—		9 Lamech
—	—		10 Noe
—	—		11 Sem
—	—		12 Arphaxad
—	—		*Cainan*
—	—		13 Sala
—	—		14 Heber
—	—		15 Phaleg
—	—		16 Ragau
—	—		17 Saruch
—	—		18 Nachor
—	—		19 Thara
—	(1) Abraham	20	—
—	(2) Isaac ...	21	—
—	(3) Jacob ...	22	—
—	(4) Juda(s) ...	23	—
—	(5) Phares ...	24	—
—	(6) Esrom ...	25	—
—	(7) Aram ...	26	—
—	(8) Aminadab ...	27	—
—	(9) Naasson ...	28	—
—	(10) Salmon ...	29	—
—	(11) Booz ...	30	—
—	(12) Obed ...	31	—
—	(13) Jesse ...	32	—
—	(14) David ...	33	—
(15) Solomon	—		34 Nathan
(16) Roboam	—		35 Mattatha
(17) Abia	—		36 Menan
(18) Asa	—		37 Melea
(19) Josaphat	—		38 Eliakim
(20) Joram	—		39 Jonan
Ahaziah	—		—
Joash	—		—
Amaziah	—		—
omitted	—		—

Matthew	Both	Luke
(21) Ozias	—	40 Joseph
(22) Joatham	—	41 Juda
(23) Achaz	—	42 Simeon
(24) Ezekias	—	43 Levi
(25) Manasses	—	44 Matthat
(26) Amon	—	45 Jorim
(27) Josias	—	46 Eliezer
Jehoahaz	—	—
Jehoiakin	—	—
omitted	—	
(28) Jechonias	—	47 Jose
(Jehoiachin)		
Zedekiah	—	—
omitted	—	—
—	—	48 Er
—	—	49 Elmodam
—	—	50 Cosam
—	—	51 Addi
—	—	52 Melchi
—	—	53 Neri
—	(29) Salathiel ... 54	—
—	(30) Zorobabel 55	—
(31) Abiud	—	*Rhesa*
(32) Eliakim	—	56 Joanna
(33) Azor	—	57 Juda
(34) Sadoc	—	58 Joseph
(35) Achim	—	59 Semei
(36) Eliud	—	60 Mattathias
(37) Eleazar	—	61 Maath
—	—	62 Nagge
—	—	63 Esli
—	—	64 Naum
—	—	65 Amos
—	—	66 Mattathias
—	—	67 Joseph
—	—	68 Janna
—	—	69 Melchi
—	—	70 Levi
(38) Matthan	(38) Mattha(n)(t) 71	71 Matthat
	Matthan and Matthat	
	may be the same	72 Heli
(39) Jacob		
	(40) Joseph ... 73	—
	(41) JESUS ... 74	

An examination of these names and numbers gives the following results:

(i) Matthew's genealogy has 41 names to and including Jesus.

(ii) Luke's genealogy has 74 names to and including Jesus.

(iii) Matthew and Luke have 19 names in common, if Matthan and Matthat are the same person; and 18 if they are not.

(iv) Besides the names common to both Evangelists, Matthew has 22 (23), and Luke 55 (56) names.

(v) Luke has 19 names before Matthew begins.

(vi) Matthew gives 14 names between David and Shealtiel, and Luke 20.

(vii) Matthew gives 8 names between Zerubbabel and Joseph (including Matthan), and Luke gives 16 (including Matthat).

(viii) *Rhesa*, between 55 and 56 in Luke's list, is not a proper name, but a Chaldee title meaning 'Prince.' Some Jewish copyists did not understand this, and so wrote 'Zerubbabel begat Rhesa,' whereas it should be 'Zerubbabel Rhesa,' i.e., Zerubbabel the Prince.

(ix) Matthew divides his genealogy into three parts of fourteen generations each (i. 17), but in order to do this, in the second part he omits three names, and in the third part he omits three names, and he counts both David and Jechonias twice.

(x) Luke's genealogy has no artificial arrangement like Matthew's and he has 33 names which Matthew has not.

(xi) In Matthew the genealogy descends from Abraham, the father of the Hebrew race, but in Luke the genealogy ascends to Adam, the father of the human race. Each of these lines is in keeping with the object and readers which the writers had in view; the one Jewish, and the other Gentile.

(xii) Matthew employs the word 'begat' throughout, but Luke says 'the son of.'

(xiii) Matthew's line is traced from David through Solomon, but Luke's is traced from David through Nathan. Both were sons of David.

(xiv) *Cainan*, between 12 and 13 in Luke's list, is undoubtedly an interpolation in certain copies of the Septuagint (LXX) towards the close of the 4th century A.D. 'The evidence against his existence is to the utmost possible degree clear, full, and positive, and not liable to any mistake or perversion. On the contrary, the evidence for his existence is inferential, obscure, or open to the suspicion of falsification.'—(Lord A. Hervey).

(xv) In Matthew's pedigree Salathiel (Shealtiel) is said to be the son of Jechonias (Jehoiachin), but in Luke, the son of Neria. No error can be demonstrated here, for there is a possible explanation.

In Jer. xxii. 24-30, it is predicted that Coniah (Jehoiachin) would be childless, therefore he could not have been the father of Salathiel, but it is possible and probable that he adopted the seven sons of Neri, the twentieth from David in the line of Nathan.

TRANSJORDAN
In Old Testament and in New Testament Times

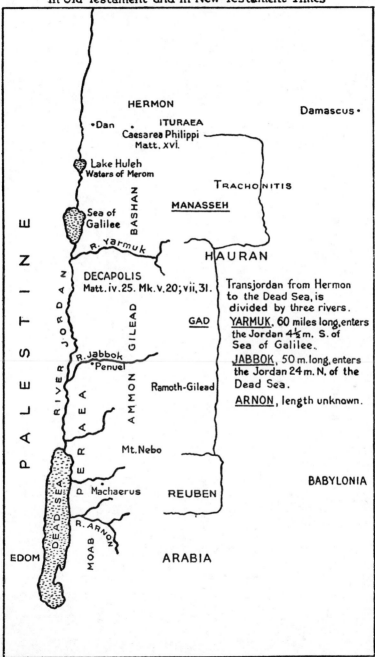

HERMON

Damascus •

•Dan · ITURAEA
Caesarea Philippi
Matt. xvi.

Lake Huleh
Waters of Merom

TRACHONITIS

BASHAN

MANASSEH

Sea of Galilee

R. Yarmuk

HAURAN

DECAPOLIS
Matt. iv. 25. Mk. v. 20; vii, 31.

GAD

GILEAD

JORDAN

RIVER JORDAN

R. Jabbok
•Penuel

Ramoth-Gilead

AMMON

PERAEA

Mt. Nebo

DEAD SEA

□ Machaerus

REUBEN

BABYLONIA

R. ARNON

MOAB

EDOM

ARABIA

PALESTINE

Transjordan from Hermon
to the Dead Sea, is
divided by three rivers.
YARMUK, 60 miles long, enters
the Jordan 4½ m. S. of
Sea of Galilee.
JABBOK, 50 m. long, enters
the Jordan 24 m. N. of the
Dead Sea.
ARNON, length unknown.

This seems to be intimated in Zech. xii. 12, where we read of 'the family of Nathan apart,' as well as 'the family of David apart.' If this were so, Salathiel would be the posterity of Jechonias by an adoption in the line of Nathan.

(xvi) In Matthew's genealogy, Joseph is said to be the son of Jacob, but in Luke, the son of Heli. Attempts to explain this may be considered unsatisfactory (see later note), but all might be clear if we had some missing information. As long as this and other seeming discrepancies in the two genealogies are capable of harmonization in natural and probable ways, by reasonable inferences, we should not conclude that they are contradictory and unreliable.

Perhaps the main difficulty is in the fact of there being two genealogies. Why should there be? Three views are held:

(1) That both genealogies give the descent of Joseph; Matthew's the *real*, and Luke's the *legal* descent.
(2) That Matthew gives Joseph's legal descent as successor to the throne of David, and that Luke gives his real parentage.
(3) That Matthew gives the real descent of Joseph, and Luke, the real descent of Mary.

The discussion of these views must not be separated from the fact of the Virgin Birth. If both genealogies are entirely Joseph's there would be no proof in them that Mary was of Davidic descent, and such proof was necessary seeing that Joseph was not Jesus' natural father, though after his marriage he became His legal father.

If it be argued that Luke's genealogy could not be that of Mary, because the genealogies of women were never given, we can point to the fact that, contrary to all custom, Matthew introduces into his genealogy the names of several women, each of them having a strange history. Dr. Barnard says: 'Proof of the Davidic descent of Mary can be obtained from the New Testament only by assuming the truth of the doctrine of the Virgin Birth.'

The Davidic descent of Jesus was never questioned; His claim to be the Messiah was never contested on the ground that His descent from David was doubtful (Matt. xii. 23; xv. 22; xx. 30, 31; xxi. 9, 15). Those who did not accept the Virgin Birth would know that Jesus' title was determined by Joseph's line, and those who did accept the Virgin Birth must have had some reason for believing that Mary was of Davidic descent. (See the quotation from Dr. Sweet on p. 505).

If Matthan, No. 38 in Matthew's genealogy, and Matthat, No. 71 in Luke's, were the same person, we see that Jacob and Heli were brothers. Luke tells us that Joseph was the son of Heli, and it is conjectured with much probability that Mary was the daughter of Jacob. If it is assumed that Jacob, having no son, adopted Joseph, his nephew and heir, we see that Mary married a relation, and that she, as well as Joseph, was descended from David, Joseph in the line of Solomon, and Mary in the line of Nathan.

Matthew's genealogy in three parts of 14 generations each has more in it than a casual or merely critical reading would apprehend. Prof. A. B. Bruce says that 'the mention of the mother (Matt. i. 16) was wholly unnecessary and unusual from a genealogical point of view,' but there are the names of four other women also—Tamar, Rahab, Ruth, and Bathsheba. This is without precedent in Jewish genealogies, and must be accounted for in some way.

One might have expected the genealogist to observe discreet silence respecting these women, seeing that three of them were stained with sin, and one of them was a foreigner. Surely the reason for naming them here is to show that He who came to 'save that which was lost,' the Friend of sinners, does not scorn such descent. This gospel in the genealogy is a revelation of the gracious character of the Christian message.

A further examination of the pedigree will show that the three periods reflect respectively different forms of government, Judges, Kings, Priests; Theocracy, Monarchy, Hierarchy, all summed up in Christ; or they may be intended to reflect Israel's fortunes, first growth, then decline, and finally ruin, making urgent the need of the redemption which Jesus brought.

Another point should not be overlooked. The object of Matthew was not to present a complete succession, but only to make sure that there was no break in the line, and that no name appeared which did not belong to the line. The all-important name was DAVID, which occurs five times. The letters of proper names had a numerical value, and in this name D—4, V—6, D—4, make a total of 14, and this fact may have led Matthew to divide his genealogy into three parts of 14 generations each.

QUESTIONS

1 How many names are there, respectively, in the genealogies recorded in Matthew's and Luke's Gospels, and how many of these occur in both Gospels?
2 Say in what way or ways these two genealogies are different.
3 Name three features which characterize the genealogy in Matthew's Gospel.
4 What three explanations are given of there being two genealogies?
5 What bearing have these genealogies on the subject of the Virgin Birth?
6 Why is there no genealogy in Mark and John?
7 Does the omission of certain royal names in Matthew's genealogy invalidate the record?
8 What women are mentioned in Matthew's genealogy? Say what you know about each of them.
9 From whence would Luke get his genealogical knowledge?
10 Was Joseph a bachelor or a widower when he married Mary?
11 Who affirm, and on what ground, that Mary had no children but Jesus?
12 Who was Rhesa?

LITERATURE

The Bible Dictionaries: Hastings', Smith's, International Standard
The Commentaries: For Various Views -   - ————
'A Harmony of the Gospels': Explanatory Note 5 -   A. T. Robertson
'The Bible Student's Life of our Lord'   -   - S. J. Andrews
'Cambridge Greek Testament: St. Matthew'   - A. Carr
'Cambridge Greek Testament: St. Luke': Excursus II. F. W. Farrar
'The Century Bible': St. Matthew   -   -   - W. F. Slater
'The Century Bible': St. Luke -   -   -   - W. F. Adeney
Lives of Christ: Edersheim, Farrar, Geikie, and others.

8

THE BIRTH OF CHRIST

TWO of the Four Gospels plainly declare that Jesus was born of a Virgin. So astonishing a statement challenges both our attention and investigation.

1 THE MEANING OF VIRGIN BIRTH

By this expression is not meant: *immaculate conception*, the Roman Catholic dogma that Mary, the mother of Jesus, was conceived and born without original sin; nor *miraculous birth*, for there is no evidence that the process of birth was in any way exceptional; nor *supernatural conception* merely, for that is true of Isaac, and of John the Baptist; but by Virgin Birth we are to understand that, contrary to the course of nature, Jesus was Divinely conceived in the womb of Mary.

2 THE VIRGIN BIRTH BELIEVED, AND DISBELIEVED

Although this claim has been scornfully attacked by un-believers, it has been accepted by the Christian Church from the beginning, and is incorporated in all the great Christian Creeds—the Apostles', the Athanasian, and the *Te Deum*.

In the early Church only the narrowest and most back-ward of Jewish-Christian sects called this tradition into question, the Gnostics denying our Lord's real humanity, and the Ebionites denying His real Divinity. But for two generations or more the tradition has been challenged within the Christian Church, and to-day, by a multitude of professing Christians, it would not be contended for.

It is well, therefore, that we should re-examine this Article of Faith with great care, in the light of all that has been said up to date about it. All that we attempt here is to summarize the main argument.

3 THE CHIEF OBJECTIONS TO THE VIRGIN BIRTH

It is urged against the acceptance of this Article that the tradition is found in two of the Gospels only; that Mark and John knew nothing of it; that the rest of the New

Testament is silent on the subject; that all the Gospels speak of Jesus as the son of Joseph and Mary; that the Virgin Birth story formed no part of the oldest Apostolic tradition (Acts i. 22), and that there is no reference to it in earliest Christian preaching.

It is further alleged that the belief and its record grew out of a mistaken application of Old Testament prophecy, or from contact with, or in imitation of, pagan myths; that it is no necessary part of the Christian Faith, and that nowhere in the New Testament is anything based upon it.

Now, if all this is true, there is nothing more to be said. But is it true?

It is noteworthy that these objections come chiefly from those who do not recognize any supernatural element in Christ's life. It is not a case of objection to this miracle only, but to all miracles.

Of course, if the humanitarian, or purely naturalistic view of Christ's Person be the true one, not only does the Virgin Birth tradition go, but all that is supernatural in the Gospels must go also, the Incarnation, the Sinless Life, the Atoning Death, and the Resurrection. This indicates the momentous importance of the subject.

4 THE GOSPEL WITNESSES TO THE VIRGIN BIRTH

It has been said that not only are Matthew and Luke the only evangelists who give the Birth Story, but that they do not agree with each other. It is simply a matter of fact, however, that though these Records are entirely independent, their points of agreement are many and minute.

Both declare that Jesus was born in the last days of Herod; that He was conceived by the Holy Spirit; that His mother was a virgin; that she was betrothed to Joseph; that Joseph was of the house and lineage of David; that Jesus was born at Bethlehem; that by divine direction He was called Jesus; that He was declared to be a Saviour; that Joseph knew beforehand of Mary's condition and its cause; and that, nevertheless, he took Mary to wife, and assumed full parental responsibility for her child; that the annunciation and birth

33

were attended by revelations and visions; that after the birth of Jesus, Joseph and Mary dwelt in Nazareth; and where the narratives appear to differ, closer investigation shows that they are not contradictory, but complementary. Now, let us clearly understand that the question before us is not one of theology, but of fact. Either our Lord was born of a virgin, or He was not. The narratives are either historically true, or they are deliberate fiction. The main sources of our information are Matthew and Luke, and each of these stands or falls as a whole. It is entirely a matter of evidence, and all the evidence goes to show that these Records are genuine documents of the Apostolic Age; that they were written by the men whose names they bear; and that the story of the Virgin Birth was in each of them from the beginning.

5 THE NARRATIVE SOURCES OF THE VIRGIN BIRTH

But the question will arise: From whence did these writers derive the idea of the Virgin Birth? The reply must be found in one or other of three alternatives.

(i) *That the Source of this Story is Jewish and Prophetical.*

It is claimed that it is derived from a misinterpretation and misapplication of Isaiah vii. 14, which reads, 'A virgin shall conceive, and bear a son, and thou shalt call his name Immanuel.'

Now, Dr. Edersheim gives a list of four hundred and fifty-six Old Testament passages which were Messianically interpreted by the Jews, but this one is not among them, and was never so interpreted. Such an idea was wholly foreign to the Jewish mind, which sacredly regarded family life.

(ii) *That the Source of this Story is Gentile and Mythological.*

It is said that if the Virgin Birth tradition be not a fact, it must be a myth, conforming to the myth-forming spirit which ascribes a superhuman origin to great men or religious heroes. Such a mythological source for this tradition has been sought in Egyptian, Grecian, Roman, and Babylonian directions.

But two considerations make such an origin incredible and impossible: first, there was no time for the growth of such a myth in the Church, for between Christ's Ascension and the latest of these Gospel Records, was a period of about thirty years only; and second, had the tradition been of mythical origin, it would have been vigorously repudiated alike by Jews and Christians; yet, we find that it was an accepted fact in the first generation of the Church's history.

These Jewish and Pagan theories mutually exclude one another, and both are untenable. We are therefore thrown back on the third alternative, namely:

(iii) *That the Source of this Story is Christian and Historical.*

The idea of the Virgin Birth could not have arisen so soon if it had not been a fact, nor have been accepted so early and universally if it had not been historical. The only two persons from whom this story could have come were Joseph and Mary themselves, and it seems clear that Joseph's account dominates Matthew's record, and that Mary's account dominates Luke's.

6 THE ALLEGED SILENCE OF THE VIRGIN BIRTH

This is much more imaginary than real, and it would not be difficult to show that this argument can prove too much.

But what are the facts? Doubt has been cast on the Virgin Birth because Mark's Record, which is known to be the earliest of the Four, says nothing about it. For the same reason, doubt might be cast upon the fact that Jesus was born at all, for Mark does not mention it.

Nor can it be regarded as certain that the Fourth Gospel makes no reference to the Virgin Birth. For instance, one cannot be perfectly sure that chapter i. 13 should not read: 'Who was born,' rather than 'Who were born.' There is some evidence for the former of these renderings, which, if valid, would be a direct reference to Jesus' supernatural origin. But accepting the text as it stands, surely it is a fair inference that if those who believe are spiritually not 'born of the will of the flesh,' Jesus, the Eternal Son, was physically not so born.

In any case, silence does not necessarily prove ignorance. But ignorance in the case of John is impossible, for he had access to the Synoptic Records, and Mary, Jesus' mother, lived with him after the crucifixion; and had he known that the tradition was not true, is it credible that he would have said nothing about it? Surely his alleged silence is rather evidence for the fact.

But further, it is argued that as Paul never refers to the Virgin Birth he therefore did not know of it, or did not believe it. It might as well be said that he did not believe in the existence of Mary, because he never once mentions her.

But is it imaginable that Paul did not know the truth about the origin of Jesus, seeing that for so long Luke, who records the story, was his close companion?

Moreover, is it true that Paul does not refer in his Writings to this fact? Is it not implied in Rom. v, where he writes of the two Heads—Adam of one order, and Christ of another? If Christ was a son of Adam by natural generation He was a continuation of the old order, and not a new beginning.

And is there not a reference to this event in 1 Cor. xv. 47, when he speaks of 'the second man from heaven'?

And is the fact not suggested by Gal. iv. 4, which says: 'God has sent forth His Son made (become) of a woman'?

Indeed, it is not too much to say that the preaching and teaching of the Apostles everywhere assume this fact, and are built upon it, although there were very good reasons why it was not given a specific place in their ministry.

They all believed and taught the resurrection. But if there was a miracle at the end of Christ's career on earth, could there not have been one at the beginning; and is the idea of Virgin Birth more wonderful than the idea of resurrection?

Again, the Apostles believed and taught the sinlessness of Jesus. But is not this fact and truth a proof that He had not a human father? Every son and daughter of sinful Adam has been a sinner; and if Jesus was sinless, surely it is evidence that He was not of that order.

And again, the Apostles believed and taught the incarnation of God. But if Jesus was God, as well as man, how could the incarnation have become a fact by the process of natural generation? We do not trace these three great truths—the Resurrection, the Sinlessness, and the Deity of Jesus—*from* the Virgin Birth, but *to* it; and, if they be granted, surely *it* becomes a necessity.

7 THE PRACTICAL VALUE OF THE VIRGIN BIRTH

The attitude of very many Christians is that, assuming this tradition to be fact, it is not vital for faith. That may be so, but it is vital for the facts on which faith rests. If Jesus was not sinless, He cannot be our Saviour; but if Joseph was His father, He was not sinless. If, then, salvation is a practical matter, surely that which makes it possible must be of vital importance. But again, if Jesus was not more than man, He cannot be our Redeemer; but if Joseph was His father, He was not more than man. If, then, redemption is a vital matter, surely that which makes it possible must also be vital.

The unique personality and saving power of Jesus Christ must be accounted for, but they cannot be accounted for on the theory that He was a product of the human race; but postulate the Virgin Birth, accept the witness that He was 'conceived by the Holy Ghost' and 'born of the Virgin Mary,' and all that follows is understandable.

We cannot over-emphasize the fact that the witness of the New Testament stands or falls *as a whole*. No body of men has ever lived that was competent to say that certain parts of the Record were true, and therefore to be accepted; and that other parts were untrue, and therefore to be rejected. To say that Jesus had human parents is to say that He was a product of the human race; but if He was 'God's only Son,' and is 'our Saviour,' He was not a product of the human race, but His *eisodos* as well as His *exodos* was, according to the Records, unique, miraculous, and Divine. In spite, therefore, of intellectual difficulties, which are inevitable, the Christian should affirm his faith in 'Jesus Christ . . . born of the Virgin Mary,' to Whom be praise and honour and glory, now and for ever.

QUESTIONS

1 What is *not* meant by Virgin Birth?
2 Who, in the early Church, called this matter in question?
3 How is the subject borne witness to in the Creeds of the Church?
4 What objections are urged against belief in the Virgin Birth?
5 What is Matthew's and Luke's witness to the Virgin Birth worth?
6 What three sources are alleged to account for the records of two Gospels that Jesus was born of a Virgin? Criticize the first two of these claims.
7 From whom are the records in the Gospels likely to have been derived?
8 Is it certain that there are no references to the Virgin Birth outside of Matthew and Luke? Support your answer.
9 Of what practical value is the fact of the Virgin Birth?

LITERATURE

'The Virgin Birth of Christ' * -   -   -   -   - J. G. Machen
'The Virgin Birth of Christ' -   -   -   -   - James Orr
'Birth and Infancy of Jesus Christ'   -   -   - L. M. Sweet
'Our Lord's Virgin Birth'   -   -   -   -   - R. J. Knowling
Works on the Apostles' Creed. Critical Commentaries
on St. Matthew, and St. Luke   -   -   -   - ——
Lives of Christ. Articles on the Virgin Birth, and Birth
of Christ, in the Standard Bible Dictionaries. The
Encyclopædia of Religion and Ethics.

* Of the late Prof. Machen's book, *The Virgin Birth of Christ,* the late Prof. H. R. Mackintosh said: "This work is genuinely learned; it displays a thorough mastery of relevant literature . . . his style of reasoning is conciliatory . . . he uses studiously moderate language . . . his book must take rank as *the* book on the strictly conservative side."

"He may justly claim to have shown that the story of the Virgin Birth has an exquisite natural fitness, and that its vogue is nearly impossible to explain save by the hypothesis of its truth."—*British Weekly.*

9

THE NAMES AND TITLES OF CHRIST

IT is an impressive fact that in the Four Gospels no fewer than forty-six Names and Titles are given to our Lord, and these alone constitute a 'whole body of divinity.' Half of them are peculiar to one or other of the Gospels, and the others occur in two or more of the Records.

The following Table should be carefully examined. The figures represent the number of occurrences of these designations.

(A) Occurring in One Gospel Only

NAME	MATT.	MARK	LUKE	JOHN
Emmanuel	I	—	—	—
My Beloved	I	—	—	—
Master (Kathēgētēs) ...	I	—	—	—
Righteous One ...	2	—	—	—
Servant (Pais)	I	—	—	—
Governor	I	—	—	—
God my Saviour ...	—	—	I	—
Saviour Christ the Lord	—	—	I	—
Dayspring	—	—	I	—
Consolation	—	—	I	—
God	—	—	—	4
Only Begotten ...	—	—	—	4
Truth	—	—	—	I
Way	—	—	—	I
Life	—	—	—	2
True Vine	—	—	—	I
Lamb	—	—	—	2
Word	—	—	—	4
Bread	—	—	—	10
Door	—	—	—	I
I am	—	—	—	I
Saviour of the World	—	—	—	I
Messiah	—	—	—	2
Resurrection	—	—	—	I
Paraclete	—	—	—	I

(B) Occurring in More Than One Gospel

NAME	MATT.	MARK	LUKE	JOHN
Son	11	3	5	17
Beloved Son	2	3	3	—
Son of God	9	3	6	9
Son of David ...	9	4	4	—
Son of Man	30	14	25	12
Jesus	142	77	84	239
Jesus Christ	6	1	—	3
Christ	9	5	11	16
King	14	6	5	14
Lord	59	10	57	48
Rabbi, Rabboni ...	2	4	—	8
Teacher (*Kurios*) ...	11	12	21 (23)	7
Didaskalos	12	12	16	7
Epistatēs	—	—	7	—
Despotēs (of God) ...	—	—	1	—
Shepherd	2	1	—	5
Light	1	—	1	19
Prophet	2	1	5	5
Head	1	1	1	—
Stone	2	1	2	—
Rock	3	—	2	—
Heir	1	1	1	—
Man	4	1	6	16
Jesus of Nazareth ...	3	4	3	4
Lord Jesus	—	1	1	—
Holy One	—	1	1	1
Bridegroom	6	3	2	3

From this it will be seen that six of the designations are peculiar to Matthew, four to Luke. fifteen to John, and none to Mark.

Observe that the name *Jesus* occurs over 542 times, and most of them in John, the Gospel of the Son. The next most frequent title is *Lord*, occurring 174 times; the third is *Son of Man*, occurring 81 times, and the fourth is *Teacher* (two words in the Greek, *Didaskalos*, *Epistatēs*), occurring 54 times, and *Despotēs*, of God, once (Luke ii. 29).

Variations of the foregoing numbers, in books which refer to them, are due to the Version used, A.V. or R.V., and to doubtful texts in some places.

All that we may know about our Lord's Person is implied by and involved in these Names and Titles.

Remember that Mark's is the first of the Four Records, and represents the earliest preaching tradition, and then observe that Christ is spoken of there as the Son, the Beloved Son, the Son of God, the Son of Man, the Christ, and Lord, so that the belief that Jesus was more than man, indeed, that He was God, was held and proclaimed from the beginning. This is a fact of great importance.

The titles which claim special attention are, The Son of Man, The Son of God, and The Christ (Messiah).

THE SON OF MAN

IN MATTHEW:

viii. 20; ix. 6; x. 23; xi. 19; xii. 8, 32, 40; xiii. 37, 41; xvi. 13, 27, 28; xvii. 9, 12, 22; (xviii. 11); xix. 28; xx. 18. 28; xxiv. 27, 30, 30, 37, 39, 44; xxv. (13), 31; xxvi. 2. 24, 24, 45, 64.

IN MARK:

ii. 10, 28; viii. 31, 38; ix. 9, 12, 31; x. 33, 45; xiii. 26 (34); xiv. 21, 21, 41, 62.

IN LUKE:

v. 24; vi. 5, 22; vii. 34; ix. 22, 26, 44 (56), 58; xi. 30; xii. 8, 10, 40; xvii. 22, 24, 26, 30; xviii. 8, 31; xix. 10; xxi. 27, 36; xxii. 22, 48, 69; xxiv. 7.

IN JOHN:

i. 51; iii. 13, 14; v. 27; vi. 27, 53, 62; viii. 28; xii. 23, 34, 34; xiii. 31.

It will be seen that this title occurs in Mark 14 times, and once more in the A.V.; in Matthew, 30 times, and twice more in the A.V.; in Luke, 25 times, and once more in the A.V.; and in John, 12 times; that is, it occurs 81 times in the Gospels in the R.V., and four more in the A.V., 85 in all (p. 535).

The title is never used of the Lord by anyone but Himself. Wherever it is used of Christ it has the article before both 'Son,' and 'Man,' with one exception (John v. 27), whereas, when used of anyone else, as often in Ezekiel, it never has the article. The only other occurrences of the title are in Acts vii. 56; Heb. ii. 6; Rev. i. 13; xiv. 14; that is 89 times in the New Testament, and only four times outside the Gospels.

The first and last occurrences present an impressive contrast:

MATT. VIII. 20 (R.V.)	REV. XIV. 14 (R.V.)
'The foxes have holes, and the birds of the heaven (have) nests (lodging-places); but the Son of Man *hath not where to lay His head.*'	'I saw, and behold, a white cloud; and on the cloud one sitting like unto the Son of Man, *having on His head a golden crown,* and in His hand a sharp sickle.'

Observe, also, the first and last occurrences of the title in each Gospel.

VIII. 20 MATTHEW XXVI. 64	
'The Son of Man hath not where to lay His head.'	'The Son of Man sitting at the right hand of power, and coming on the clouds of heaven.'

II. 10 MARK XIV. 62	
'The Son of Man hath power on earth to forgive sins.'	'The Son of Man sitting at the right hand of power, and coming with the clouds of heaven.'

V. 24 LUKE XXIV. 7	
'The Son of Man hath power on earth to forgive sins.'	'The Son of Man must be delivered up into the hands of sinful men, and be crucified, and the third day rise again.'

I. 51 JOHN XIII. 31	
'Ye shall see the heaven opened, and the angels of God ascending and descending upon the Son of Man.'	'Now is the Son of Man glorified, and God is glorified in Him.'

An examination of this title will show that almost always it relates Christ to the earth, whereas the title Son of God has a much wider significance. (Pages 535, 536).

THE SON OF GOD

IN MATTHEW:
  iv. 3, 6; viii. 29; xiv. 33; xvi. 16; xxvi. 63; xxvii. 40, 43, 54.
IN MARK:
  (i. 1); iii. 11; v. 7, "Son of the God, the Most High'; xv. 39.
IN LUKE:
  i. 35; iv. 3, 9, 41; viii. 28, 'Son of the God, the Most High'; xxii. 70.
IN JOHN:
  i. 34, 49; v. 25; (vi. 69); ix. 35; x. 36; xi. 4, 27; xix. 7; xx. 31.

It is here seen that this title occurs in Matthew 9 times; in Mark, 3 times, and once more in the A.V.; in Luke, 6 times; and in John, 9 times, and once more in the A.V.; that is, it occurs in the Gospels 27 times in the R.V., and 29 in the A.V. In the rest of the New Testament this title occurs 17 times in the R.V., and 19 times in the A.V. (Page 536).

The main distinction between the titles Son of God, and Son of Man, is in that the former expresses the relation of Christ to the Father, and the latter relates to His dominion in the earth.

To these passages must be added all those in which Christ calls God His Father, implying, of course, His Sonship. Such passages are as follows: in Matthew, 23; in Mark, 3; in Luke, 11; and in John, 116; and passages in which He is called 'The Son,' and 'The Beloved Son.' Angels are called 'sons of God' (Job i. 6; xxxviii. 7), and so are Christians (Rom. viii. 14, 19), but Christ alone is 'The Son of God,' and He distinguishes Himself as such from all others when He says, 'My Father, and your Father' (John xx. 17). When He taught His disciples to say, 'Our Father, Who art in heaven,' He did not include Himself, for the prayer does not apply to Him. Those who claim that this view of Christ is a product of the Fourth Gospel, should remember that the same claim is made in the first of the Gospels, Mark's (i. 11; ix. 7, et al.), and therefore was part of the Oral Tradition.

THE CHRIST (MESSIAH)

There are several classes of passages related to this title: (i) passages in which Jesus refers to Himself as 'The Christ'; (ii) those in which others refer to Him as such; (iii) those in which He is called 'The Son of David'; (iv) those in which He is called the King of Israel, or of the Jews; (v) and those which relate Him to the Kingdom of Old Testament prediction. The following are some of the relevant passages:

(i, ii).   Matt. i. 17; ii. 4; xi. 2; xvi. 16: Mark viii. 29; xii. 35; xiv. 61;
xv. 32: Luke ii. 26; iv. 41; xxii. 67; xxiv. 26, 46: John i. 20, 25;
i. 41; iii. 28; iv. 29; vii. 26, 27, 31, 41, 42; x. 24; xx. 31.

(iii) Matt. i. 1; ix. 27; xii. 23; xxi. 9, 15: Mark x. 48; xii. 35, 37: Luke
xviii. 38, 39; xx. 41, 44: but not in John's Gospel, which is for the
Christian Church.

(iv) Matt. v. 35; xxi. 5; xxv. 34, 40: Mark xv. 2, 9, 12, 26, 32: Luke
xix. 38; xxiii. 3, 37, 38: John xii. 13, 15; xviii. 33, 39; xix. 3, 14,
15, 19, 21.

(v) Matt. iv. 17, 23; v. 3, 10, 19, 20; vii. 21; ix. 35; xii. 28; xvi. 19,
28: Mark i. 15; iv. 11, 26, 30; x. 14, 15, 23, 24, 25: Luke iv. 43;
vi. 20; viii. 1, 10; ix. 2, 11, 27, 62; xiii. 18, 20, 28, 29.   In John's
Gospel Kingdom references are not to the Messianic Kingdom,
which is earthly, but to the Kingdom of God which is spiritual
(iii. 3, 5; xviii. 36).

QUESTIONS

1 What four names or titles of our Lord occur most frequently in the
Gospels?
2 Which Gospel has, peculiar to itself, the most names or titles?
Name some of them.
3 What titles are there in Mark's Gospel which tell of the Deity of
Jesus?
4 How many names or titles are given to Jesus in the Gospels?
5 What do these names and titles declare or imply as to Jesus' person,
character, and work?
6 How many times does the title 'The Son of Man' occur in each of
the Gospels?
7 Name three passages in each of the Gospels in which 'The Son of
God' occurs.
8 Are others besides Christ called sons of God? If so, who, and
where?
9 How and where does Christ distinguish His Sonship from that of
others?
10 Name five classes of passages in which the Messiahship of Jesus is
declared, and give a reference or two in each.
11 Why is Christ not called 'The Son of David' in the Fourth Gospel?

LITERATURE

'The Theology of the New Testament' - - G. B. Stevens
'The Kingdom of God' - - - - A. B. Bruce
'The Lord of Glory' - - - - - B. B. Warfield
'The Jewish and the Christian Messiah' - V. H. Stanton
'The Honour of His Name' - - - - Sir R. Anderson
'The Christology of Jesus' - - - - J. Stalker
'The Companion Bible': Part V. Appendix 98 - E. W. Bullinger
'The Principles of Theology': pp. 32-36 - Griffith Thomas
The Bible Dictionaries - - - - ——
The Commentaries - - - - - ——

10

THE PERSON OF CHRIST

THE true doctrine of the Person of Christ is the most momentous in the whole realm of thought, for on it everything else depends.

A wrong apprehension or a false interpretation of this doctrine, necessarily will lead to mental confusion, or fatal error.

The Biblical Christology embraces the Messianic prophecies of the Old Testament, the testimony of Christ in the Gospels, and the teaching of the Apostles in the Acts, Epistles, and Apocalypse. Of these sources of information the second is the most important, for in the Gospels we see and hear Christ Himself. What is reflected doctrinally and experimentally in the Acts and Epistles is presented historically in the Gospels, and upon the life and testimony of Christ, Christology is based.

The teaching of the Gospels does not derive its value from the doctrinal formulations in the Epistles, but, on the contrary, the historical manifestation as set forth in the Gospels determined the doctrines of the Epistles.

Christian theology, therefore, has its roots, not in the Epistles, but in the Gospels. Ever and anon we are thrown back upon these Evangelical Records for all that matters for life and faith.

Of course, there is in the Gospels no formulated doctrine of Christ's Person, but we find there all the material which has made possible a true Christology.

The problems which later on gave rise to the theological controversies in the Church for over six centuries arose out of the Writings of the New Testament, and can be solved only by them. The Four Records of Christ's life, work, and teaching are so simple, with the simplicity of profoundness, that only the theological reader can discern what problems of personality they contain; yet it is well that the average reader should know what these problems are, and how they were thrashed out in the following centuries in Councils and Creeds.

Four factors are necessary for a complete conception of Christ's Person:

1 That He was truly *human,* so that everything that can be predicated of man as man—not of man as fallen—can be predicated of Him.

2 That He was truly *Divine,* so that everything that can be predicated of God can be predicated of Him.

3 That the human and the Divine were united in *One Person*; that is, that Christ had not a double personality, but was one Self.

4 That the *two natures* in the one Person of Christ were inseparably united, and yet were not mingled, or confounded.

I. Controversies of the Church

Around these points all Christological controversies have gathered, and these necessitated and eventuated in doctrinal statements or creeds, for the guidance of the whole Christian Church throughout this dispensation.

The foregoing truths were not challenged by the great body of believers in the early centuries, but later on, by speculative theologians. These, for the most part, were good and able men, but had great intellectual difficulty in accepting the current beliefs of the Church relative to the incarnation of God.

Some denied Christ's true humanity; some, His true Divinity; some impugned the integrity of His human nature; some held that He had a twofold personality; some believed that He had but one nature; some contended that the two natures in Him were so intermingled as to be indistinguishable; and some believed that the effect of the union of the two natures was the production of a *tertium quid,* or third nature. If there is scarcely an echo of these things to-day as subjects of live controversy it is due, for the most part, to those Christian scholars who confronted these doubts with the Word of God, and gave final expression to the truths which constitute the doctrine of the Reformed Churches.

(1) THE HUMANITY OF CHRIST

(i) *Docetism*

This is from the Greek verb, *dokeō,* which means to *appear,* to *seem to be.*

The Docetæ were a sect which arose in the second century, and denied the reality of Christ's human body. This heresy was based on the assumption that matter was inherently evil.

Some Docetæ, believing that Christ was only good, were driven to the conclusion that His human body was merely phantasmal. Others admitted that He had a real body, but taught that it was formed of some ethereal or celestial substance, and was not material.

(ii) *Apollinarianism*

Apollinaris, A.D. 310-390 (?), was bishop of Laodicea in A.D. 362. The Apollinarians maintained that Christ was truly a man, but denied the integrity or completeness of His human nature. They held that He had a true body, and an animal soul, but, in place of a rational spirit, they put the *Logos*, the Eternal Son; and so, while they did not deny Christ's humanity, they mutilated it, by teaching that, while He had a true *sōma*, and an animal *psuchē*, He had not a rational *pneuma*, or *nous*. If this were true Christ's manhood would not have been complete.

(2) THE DIVINITY OF CHRIST

(iii) *Ebionism*

From a Hebrew word meaning 'poor' (*ev-yōhn*).

The Ebionites denied the reality of the Divine nature of Christ, and held Him to be merely man, whether naturally or supernaturally conceived. They taught, however, that He stood in a peculiar relation to God from the time of His Baptism.

The Cerinthian Ebionites (Cerinthus was an Alexandrian Jew, and a Gnostic heretic, who lived in the days of the Apostle John) distinguished between *Jesus* and *Christ*, and taught that the Divine Christ came upon the human Jesus at His Baptism, and left Him before He died on the Cross.

(iv) *Arianism*

Arius, A.D. 256-336, was a presbyter of the Church of Alexandria in the early part of the fourth century.

This heresy was the denial of the Deity of Christ. The Arians taught that the Son is totally and essentially distinct from the Father; that He is, in fact, only the first and noblest of those created beings whom God the Father formed out of nothing, and the instrument which the Father used in creating the material universe, and, therefore, that He was inferior to the Father both in nature and in dignity.

(3) THE UNITY OF CHRIST'S PERSONALITY

(v) *Nestorianism*

Nestorius was Bishop of Constantinople, A.D. 428-431. This sect divided the personality of Christ, teaching that He had not a single self-conscious personality, but two, one Divine, and one human, that in Him were two separate and diverse Selves.

The Nestorian error lay in not distinguishing between a *nature* and a *person*. Instead of a blending of the two natures into one Self, the Nestorian scheme placed two Selves side by side. There was God, and there was man, but there was no God-Man.

(4) THE TWO NATURES IN THE PERSON OF CHRIST

(vi) *Eutychianism*

Eutyches was an abbot of Constantinople in the fifth century. This is the opposite error to Nestorianism. It asserted the unity of self-consciousness in the person of Christ, but it denied the duality of His natures.

Eutyches taught that in the incarnation the human nature was transmuted into the Divine, so that the resultant was one person and one nature. This doctrine was known as *Mono-physite* (*monē phusis*, one only nature). It denied the integrity of Christ's two natures by confusing them, running them together, so as to make a third nature, separate and different from either the human or the Divine, and this was also called a *tertium quid*, or third nature. This controversy convulsed the Eastern Church for more than a hundred years, weakened its power, and facilitated the conquest of Mohammedanism.

(vii) *Monothelitism*
(*Monon*, one, and *thelēma*, the will)

This is the doctrine that, while Christ had two natures He had but one will. Nestorius had taught that Christ had two person-alities, and Eutyches, that He had but one nature, and then in the 7th-8th centuries, the question was raised—was the will of Christ twofold, like His nature, or one, like His person? To affirm that Christ had not a human will was to deny that He had a human nature, for will is one of the essential elements or faculties of a rational nature. This controversy lasted from A.D. 633-680.

II. Councils and Creeds

These controversies necessitated Councils and Creeds, at and in which the Church, East and West, pronounced on the matters under dispute.

Of the sixteen principal Councils which were held between A.D. 305 and A.D. 451, four stand out prominently with reference to the subject of Christology.

(1) THE COUNCIL OF NICAEA

This was called by the Emperor Constantine in A.D. 325, and was attended by 318 bishops. The Deity and Sonship of Christ was the great subject of this Council, and at it *Arianism* was condemned.

(2) THE COUNCIL OF CONSTANTINOPLE

This was called by the Emperor Theodosius I, in A.D. 381, and was attended by 150 bishops. It was concerned chiefly with the subject of the Deity and Personality of the Holy Spirit but embraced also reference to the Person of Christ, and at it, *Apollinarianism* was condemned.

On the subject of Christ's Person the Nicæno-Constantino-politan Creed says:

> '(We believe) . . . in one Lord Jesus Christ the only-begotten Son of God, begotten of the Father before all worlds. Light of Light, Very God of Very God, Begotten, not made, being of one substance with the Father; by whom all things were made, who for us men and for our salvation came down from heaven, and was incarnate by the Holy Ghost, of the Virgin Mary . . .'

(3) THE COUNCIL OF EPHESUS

This was called by the Emperor Theodosius II, in A.D. 431, and was attended by 200 bishops. The subject of the unity of Christ's personality was discussed, and *Nestorianism* was condemned.

(4) THE COUNCIL OF CHALCEDON

This was called by the Emperor Marcian, in A.D. 451, and was attended by 630 bishops. Here the subject was, in a more comprehensive way, the Person of Christ, and its findings were the condemnation of *Apollinarianism*, *Nestorianism*, and *Eutychianism*. It said:

34

(1) We then following the holy Fathers all with one consent teach men to confess one and the same Son, our Lord Jesus Christ, the same perfect in Godhead, and also perfect in manhood;

(2) True God, and at the same time truly man, of a reasonable soul and body;

(3) Consubstantial with the Father according to His Godhead, and consubstantial with us according to His manhood, in all things like unto us apart from sin;

(4) Begotten both before all worlds of the Father according to His Godhead, and also in these latter days, on account of us and our salvation, of the Virgin Mary, the Mother of God, according to His manhood;

(5) One and the same Christ, Son, Lord, only-begotten, to be acknowledged in two natures without confusion, change, division, separation;

(6) The distinction of natures being by no means taken away by the union, but rather the property of each nature being preserved and concurring in one person and one substance, not parted or divided into two persons, but one and the same Son, and only-begotten, God the Word, the Lord Jesus Christ;

(7) According as the Prophets from the beginning have spoken concerning Him, and the Lord Jesus Christ Himself has taught us, and the creed of the holy Fathers has handed down to us.

Paragraph 1 condemns Docetism, Ebionism, and Arianism; paragraph 2, Apollinarianism; paragraph 4, Nestorianism, and paragraph 5, Eutychianism.

These 'laboured and heavy-laden clauses' have done the utmost which intellect can to express what must ever remain profound mysteries, and they still state the beliefs of the Greek, Latin, and Evangelical Protestant Churches.

The truths, therefore, to which these Councils gave expression are:

(a) *A true incarnation.* That a true and whole human nature entered into abiding union with the Divine personality of the eternal *Logos*, so that they constitute, from the moment of the supernatural conception, one individual life.

(b) *The distinction between 'nature' and 'person.'* *Nature*, substance, or essence, denotes the totality of powers and qualities which constitute a being; while *Person* is the ego, the self-conscious, self-asserting and acting subject. The *Logos* assumed, not a human person—else we should have two persons, a Divine and a human —but human nature, which is common to us all.

(c) *The God-Man* (*Theanthrōpos*) as the result of the incarnation. Christ is not two persons (*Nestorianism*), nor a compound (*Apollinarianism, Monophysitism*), but one person, at once wholly Divine, and wholly human.

(*d*) *The duality of natures in Christ.* The distinction of the natures without 'confusion, change, division, separation,' is what is meant; the Divine ever remaining Divine, and the human ever human, yet the two having continually one common life.

III. Christology of the Gospels

We have glanced at the controversies of the Church of the early centuries, and at the Councils and Creeds which were their necessary products; and now we must consider on what ground the generally accepted orthodox doctrine of the Person of Christ is based.

If this doctrine originated with the Apostles, especially Paul, it will be in vain to look for it in the Gospels; but if, as is the case, the Apostolic doctrine is rooted in the Gospels, we shall find all that is distinctive in it in these Records.

Shultz says: 'Paul is the creator of the theological doctrine of the Godhead of Christ, especially of the doctrine of the Christ in distinction from the doctrine of Jesus as the Christ.'

Whether this is true or not can be determined only by a thorough examination of the Evangelical Records.

The outstanding features of the Pauline theology are the Deity and the Saviourship of Christ. He takes his stand upon two great truths, namely, that Jesus is the eternal Son of God, and that the Son became incarnate in Jesus for the redemption of the world. Did Paul originate these ideas, or were they derived from authentic sources? Are the Christologies in James, Peter, Hebrews, the Johannine Epistles, and the Apocalypse original, or are they derived? One way or the other the answer will be found in the Gospels, and any traceable sources which may have lain behind them.

The outstanding question is not—is Jesus human? but is He Divine? If His Deity can be demonstrated we may well accept the verdict of the Chalcedonian and Athanasian Creeds on the subjects of the Unity of His Person, and the Duality of His Nature.

The order of this inquiry should be: 1, John; 2, Luke; 3, Matthew; 4, Mark; 5, Q. In this order we move from the latest to the earliest records.

(1) CHRIST IN THE FOURTH GOSPEL

(a) *The Humanity of Jesus*

In this Gospel no room is left for doubt as to the true humanity of Christ; a real incarnation is plainly declared. 'The Word became flesh' (i. 14), that is, 'He entered upon a mode of existence in which the experiences that belong to human beings would also be His.' He came as a man (i. 30), confessed Himself man (viii. 40), and died as a man (xix. 15). He is referred to as man sixteen times. His human origin was well known (vii. 27). He descended to earth, and left a glory behind to which He was to return (iii. 13; xvii. 5). As man He was inferior to the Father (xiv. 28). He declared himself to be 'a man who hath told you the truth' (viii. 40). He possessed a human soul (xii. 27), and bodily parts (vi. 53; xx. 27). He was subject to physical infirmities (iv. 6; xix. 28), and to all the common human emotions (vi. 11, 23; xi. 33, 35, 38, 41; xii. 27; xiii. 21, 34; xiv. 21; xv. 11; xvi. 27; xvii. 13). He differed from other men only in that He was without sin (viii. 46; xiv. 30). The charge that in the Fourth Gospel we have an incarnation without real humanity will not stand the test of facts.

(b) *The Divinity of Jesus*

The purpose of the Fourth Gospel is clearly set forth, namely, 'that (we) might believe that Jesus is the Christ, the Son of God, and that believing (we) might have life through His name' (xx. 31). The object throughout is to show that it was 'the true God' (1 John v. 20) who was 'made flesh' (John i. 14).

This is stated profoundly, yet with the utmost clearness, in the Prologue to the Gospel (i. 1-18). Here Christ is declared to be the sum total of what is Divine. The Word, or *Logos*, 'was in the beginning,' 'was with God,' and 'was God' (1). He is the Creator of all things, and the source of life and light (3, 4). This Divine person 'came' to this world (11); He 'became flesh, and dwelt among us' (14); and He who did so was 'the only-begotten of the Father' (14); 'the only-begotten Son, Who *is* in the bosom of the Father,' and Who has 'expounded Him' (18). Nothing could be plainer or more sublime than this.

If it be objected that these are the statements of one who is

writing under the influence of Greek and Hebrew speculative
thought, it is enough to reply that Christ's witness to Himself,
as recorded in this Gospel, entirely corroborates the teaching of
the Prologue. The discourses bear witness to the Speaker's
essential Deity, and the only way to evade this fact is to deny that
Jesus ever spoke these words, a length to which the naturalistic
critics do not hesitate to go, until, according to Professor W. B.
Smith, Jesus is merely a myth.

But turning away from such rationalism, we should ponder
carefully what our Lord's own conception was of His higher
nature. He said: 'I am from above' (viii. 23); 'I am not of
this world' (xvii. 16); 'Before Abraham was, I am' (viii. 58);
'I and the Father are one' (x. 30); 'He that hath seen Me hath
seen the Father' (xiv. 9; viii. 19; xii. 45). Also He declared
His eternal pre-existence, and that He shared the Father's
glory (iii. 13; vi. 62; viii. 42; xvii. 8).

The names and titles given to Christ in this Gospel are profoundly impressive. He is called *God* (i. 1; cf. v. 18; x. 33;
xx. 28: twice with the article); *the Son*, 17 times, 14 of them
being spoken by Christ; *the Son of God*, 9 times, 4 of them
spoken by Christ; *the only-begotten Son*, 4 times, 2 of them by
Christ (i. 14, 18; iii. 16, 18); *the Son of Man*, 12 times, and
always by Christ; *Jesus*, about 240 times, which shows that He
whom the writer calls God is Jesus of Nazareth (i. 45; xviii. 5,
7; xix. 19); *Jesus Christ* (i. 17; xvii. 3); *Christ*, or *The Christ*,
or Messiah, 16 times; *King*, 14 times; *Lord*, used by Himself
5 times, and used of Him by others 43 times; *Saviour* (iv. 42);
Rabbi, Rabboni, 8 times; *Teacher*, 7 times; *Lamb of God* (i. 29,
36); *Shepherd*, 5 times; *The Word*, 4 times (i. 1, 14); *the Light*,
19 times, 13 of them by Christ Himself; *Holy One* (vi. 69, R.V.);
Prophet, 5 times; *the Life* (xi. 25; xiv. 6); *the Bread*, 10 times;
the Door (x. 7); *the Truth* (xiv. 6); *the True Vine* (xv. 1); *the
Way* (xiv. 6); *I am* (viii. 58); *the Resurrection* (xi. 25); *Paraclete*
(xiv. 16); *Bridegroom* (iii. 29). (See pp. 519, 520).

These designations, as Dr. Warfield says, 'supply a most
compelling mass of evidence—to Christ's pre-existence, and to
His superhuman dignity,' and it is simply inconceivable that

any monotheistic Jew could ever bring himself to speak of any man in these terms, or make any man to speak of himself in these terms, even if he had the intelligence to create them.

(2) CHRIST IN THE SYNOPTIC RECORDS

If the naturalistic critics, Bousset, E. F. Scott, W. B. Smith, Shailer Matthews, Von Soden, Schmidt, Schmiedel, Pfleiderer, Keim, Schenkel, Zeller, Jülicher, Harnack, Schweitzer, and such like, could eliminate the Fourth Gospel altogether, they would not get rid of their troubles, because all the Synoptic Gospels confront them with the same testimony. Dr. Bacon says: 'Either Synoptics or John,' but at bottom the two pictures are the same. Dr. A. T. Robertson says: 'The historic Jesus with His humanity is as vivid in John's Gospel as in the Synoptics, and the Christ (Messiah) is as plain in the Synoptics as in the Fourth Gospel.'

In the Synoptics and in John's Gospel we have Jesus described both as the Son of God, and the Son of Man. It is impossible to appeal from the Christology of John to that of the Synoptists. 'Those who will not have a divine Christ,' says Dr. Warfield, 'must seek their human Jesus outside the entire evangelical literature.'

The difference between the Synoptists and John is a question of degree rather than a sort of treatment. 'The Synoptists and John certainly stand on the same level in their estimate of the person of Jesus, and differ in their presentation of it only in the relative emphasis they throw on this or the other aspect of it.' The proof of this fact is in the Records themselves.

(a) The Humanity of Jesus

He identifies Himself with men (Matt. iv. 4; Luke iv. 4); receives the imputation of humanity (Matt. xi. 19; Luke vii. 34); and makes frequent reference to His body and its parts (Matt. xxvi. 12, 26; Mark xiv. 8, 22; Luke xxii. 19, 20; xxiv. 39; vii. 44-46; Mark xiv. 24). He speaks of His soul (Matt. xxvi. 38; Mark xiv. 34); and of human dread as He confronts death (Luke xii. 50); and He gives expression to His sense of desolation on the Cross (Matt. xxvii. 46; Mark xv. 34). Nothing that is human is alien to Him except sin (Matt. vii. 11; ix. 12; xii. 34, 39; Luke xi. 13, 29).

In Matthew and Luke are recorded His birth into this world, His childhood, and growth to manhood (Matt. i. 11; Luke ii), and in all the Synoptics are recorded His Baptism and Temptation (Matt. iii. iv; Mark i; Luke iv). Human emotions are attributed to Him, such as anger, grief, pity; He suffered in the flesh, and finally He died outside Jerusalem's walls.

The Docetic idea that Christ had not a real human body, that His humanity was apparent and not real, is denied on every page of the Gospels.

(b) *The Divinity of Jesus*

This great truth is not less evident in the Synoptics than in the Fourth Gospel, though there is a change of emphasis. All the Gospels set before us a Jesus Christ who is at once God and man, and one undivided person.

In Mark xiii. 32 Jesus places Himself in an ascending scale of being, above 'the angels in heaven,' and elsewhere He presents Himself as the Lord of the angels (Matt. xiii. 41, 49; xxiv. 31; xxv. 31; Mark viii. 38). God's angels are *His* angels (Luke xii. 8, 9; xv. 10); God's Kingdom is *His* Kingdom (Matt. xii. 28; xix. 24; xxi. 31, 43; Mark and Luke often); God's Elect are *His* Elect (Mark xiii. 20; Luke xviii. 7).

In Mark xiii. 32, Christ is speaking out of a Divine self-consciousness, and He designates Himself the unique Son of God, declaring, not that He *was* such, but that at the moment of speaking He *is* such.

In the Synoptics, as in John's Gospel, Christ is the Son of Man, and the Son of God.

Son of Man occurs in Matthew 32 times (A.V.; in the R.V. 30 times); in Mark 14 times, in Luke 25 times, and in John 12 times (see pp. 521, 522); that is, it occurs in Luke twice as often as in the Fourth Gospel, and in Matthew nearly three times as often. Of this designation Dr. Warfield says: 'It intimates on every occasion of its employment our Lord's consciousness of being a supramundane Being, who has entered into a sphere of earthly life on a high mission, on the accomplishment of which He is to return to His heavenly sphere, whence He shall in due season come back to earth, now, however, in His proper majesty, to gather up the fruits of His work and consummate all things. It is a designation, therefore, which implies at once a heavenly pre-existence, a present humiliation, and a future glory; and He proclaims Himself in this future glory no less than the universal King seated on the throne of judgment for quick and dead (Mark viii. 38; Matt. xxv. 31).' This title is used by Jesus of Himself, and by no one else of Him.

Son of God occurs in Matthew 9 times, in Mark 3 times, and in Luke 6 times, and in John 9 times (see pp. 520, 523, 524); thus, in Matthew it occurs as often as in John's Gospel. The occurrences of this designation forbid our regarding it as a relationship to God which is predicted of angels, and of regenerated persons (Job i. 6; Rom. viii. 14; 1 John iii. 1). On the contrary it implies and declares a relationship entirely unique, and one which is eternal. Nothing in John's Gospel goes beyond what Christ declared of Himself in Matthew xi. 27.

> 'All things have been delivered unto Me of My Father, and no one knoweth the Son, save the Father, neither doth any know the Father save the Son, and he to whomsoever the Son willeth to reveal Him' (R.V.).

This is a claim to Deity or equality with God in the Johannine sense, and this unique relation constitutes the only ground of His appeal to men to come to Him to learn of God (Matt. xi. 28-30).

To like purpose is the utterance in Matt. xxviii. 19.

> 'Go ye, therefore, and make disciples of all the nations, baptizing them into the name of the Father, and of the Son, and of the Holy Spirit, teaching them to observe all things, whatsoever I commanded you, and lo, I am with you all the days, even unto the consummation of the age' (R.V., and margin).

Here the three Persons of the Holy Trinity, *the* Father, *the* Son, *the* Spirit are distinguished, and yet they are all united under one name. Christ thus places Himself by the side of the Father and the Spirit as together with them constituting the one God, and so announces Himself to be in all respects equal to the Father and the Holy Spirit.

In addition to the designation, Son of God, He is spoken of

as the *Son* 19 times in the Synoptics, and in connection with
this, must be placed the references to God as 'the Father,' about
80 times; and as 'My Father,' about 30 times. Never did Christ
say *our* Father, including Himself with His disciples, but drew
a sharp distinction between their relation to God, and His own.

> 'I am not yet ascended to My Father; but go to My brethren, and
> say unto them, I ascend unto *My* Father, and *your* Father, and
> *My* God, and *your* God' (John xx. 17). (Pages 543, 619).

Then there is the great Confession of Peter, which Christ
accepted and confirmed.

> 'Thou (Jesus) art the Christ, the Son of the Living God' (Matt.
> xvi. 16).

By accepting this confession Jesus affirms that He is the promised
Messiah and the eternal Son of God, an affirmation which is
the truth, or is the most horrible blasphemy.

We see, then, that the Christology of the Fourth Gospel is
that also of the Synoptics, so that if these latter were all written
before A.D. 70, as is likely, in the seventh decade of this era it
was the faith of the Christian community that Jesus Christ was
a Divine Person.

(3) Christ in the Primitive Tradition

But, we are told, there were documents behind the earliest of
the canonical Gospels. Two, at least, have been postulated, a
Primitive or Ur-Mark, and a document which is known as Q
(from *Quelle*, source). Both these documents are hypothetical,
but if there was a Primitive Mark it must have been, as Abbott
and Rushbrooke suggest, in harmony with the original Oral
Tradition, which certainly would not be without a Christology,
or with one in conflict with later tradition.

It is generally accepted that behind Mark's Gospel is the
Apostle Peter (see Div. B, under ' Mark,' pp. 177-179), and if
this be so of the Gospel as we have it, we can but infer that any
earlier recension of it must have been dominated by the same
influence, and what Peter taught about Christ can be seen in his
sermon delivered in the house of Cornelius (Acts x. 34-43). In
this brief abstract four tremendous things are predicated of Christ.

(i) 'He is the Lord of all' (36)

Dr. Knowling says of this: 'The words seem to express the way in which the speaker would guard against the thought that Jesus of Nazareth was simply on a level with those who were spoken of as Apostles, as 'sent' might, perhaps, suggest to his hearers' (cf. Acts ii. 33, 34).

(ii) 'He is ordained of God to be the Judge of Quick and Dead' (42)

These words definitely ascribe to Christ divine powers, and He to whom they are given is said to be a 'man' (xvii. 31), and also, the Father's 'Son,' and the 'Son of Man' (John v. 22, 27).

(iii) 'To Him give all the Prophets witness' (43)

This is a definite recognition of the Messiahship of Jesus, for it was to the Christ that the prophets bore witness, as Christ Himself had said (Luke xxiv. 27, 44; John v. 39).

(iv) 'Through His Name whosoever believeth in Him shall receive remission of sins' (43)

No stronger witness to the Divinity of Christ's Person could be given than this. Of none other could it be said, except blasphemously, that only by faith in him can sins be forgiven.

This, then, was Peter's oral teaching about Christ, and when Mark reported Peter, as Papias tells us he did (see Div. A., Pt. II, p. 134), he had no other Christ to set before his readers, and when Matthew and Luke absorbed in their records almost the whole of Mark's Gospel, they bore witness to the same God-Man.

If the critical claim be conceded that Matthew and Luke use a document which the critics call Q (see the 'Synoptic Problem,' Div. A, Pt. 1, p. 83-93), the passages in that document which these two Evangelists make use of, show beyond any question that this earliest source had the same Christology which we find in the Synoptics and the Fourth Gospel.

The passages which Luke is supposed to have drawn from Q include:

iii. 7-9, 16, 17; iv. 3-12; vi. 20-49; vii. 6b-9, 18-23, 24-28, 31-35; ix. 57-62; x. 2-16, 21-24; xi. 9-52; xii. 1b-12, 22-59; xiii. 18-35; xiv. 26, 27, 34, 35; xvi. 13, 16-18; xvii. 1-6, 20-37.

An examination of these passages will show that a record which goes back, as Sir Wm. Ramsay believes, to the life-time of Jesus, bears as clear evidence of His real humanity and true Divinity as any following record, though not, of course, as fully.

Here is the record of the Temptation, in which the devil twice calls Jesus the 'Son of God,' and all these temptations turn on the issue of His Sonship (iv. 3-12).

Here, also, Christ claims to be the Son of Man, with all that this designation implies (vii. 34; ix. 58; xi. 30; xii. 8, 10, 40; xvii. 22-30). (See Dr. Warfield's Exposition, p. 535).

Here, also, in reply to John the Baptist's inquiry, Jesus claims to be the promised Messiah (vii. 19-23). Harnack thinks that this is the most important passage in Q concerning the personality of Jesus, because here He appeals to His works in proof of His Messiahship. Here, also, Jesus speaks only as one could who has a Divine self-consciousness, when, for example, He says that those who rejected Him were rejecting God (x. 16).

And here is the tremendous passage in which He claims a relation to and knowledge of the Father, and a power to make the Father known, which can mean nothing if it does not declare His full and proper Deity. 'Speaking in the most solemn manner,' says Dr. Warfield, 'He not only presents Himself as the Son, as the sole source of knowledge of God, and of blessedness for men, but places Himself in a position, not of equality merely, but of absolute reciprocity and interpenetration of knowledge with the Father.' He speaks 'as if the being of the Son were so immense that only God could know it thoroughly, and the knowledge of the Son so unlimited that He could know God to perfection. The peculiarly pregnant employment here of the terms 'Son,' and 'Father,' over against one another is explained to us in the other utterance, in Matt. xxviii. 19.'

Here, also, Christ claims to be the Lord of men, and our future Judge (xii. 35-48). Also He claims the devotion and loyalty of men, over all other devotions and loyalties, and promises reward 'before the angels' to all who give it (xiv. 26, 27; xii. 8, 9).

No one on earth could have invented such ideas as these between the years A.D. 27-45, that is, from the beginning of

Christ's public ministry to about fifteen years after His ascension, a period within which Q could well have been written. If Mark was written as late as A.D. 60 (it might have been ten years earlier), and if, as Dr. Streeter thinks, Q was written twenty years before Mark, it is entirely possible that Sir Wm. Ramsay and Dr. Salmon are correct in thinking that Q was written during the life-time of Jesus, which would account for the omission of the Passion Week events.

This skeleton outline of the ground on which the Chalcedonian Creedal statement rests, must be seen abundantly to warrant what there is said. The doctrine of Christ's Person is not an apostolic creation, but arose out of the facts of Christ's life and teaching, and is to be found alike in the Oral Gospel and the most primitive records of it, and so in all the canonical Gospels.

Speaking of the Chalcedonian Creed, Dr. Warfield says: 'There is nothing here but a careful statement in systematic form of the pure teaching of the Scriptures, and, therefore, this statement has stood ever since as the norm of thought and teaching as to the Person of the Lord' (see p. 530).

We may say, then, that the subject is central in, and vital to Christianity.

The heart of Christian doctrine is the Person of Christ; His *Person*, not His *Work*, for if He was not what the Gospels represent Him to be, His Work as Redeemer and Saviour is invalid. It is not His Work which gives value to His Person, but His Person which gives value to His Work.

We cannot explain Christ's Person, but we may and should accept what is declared of Him. There is one word which embodies the truth about His Person, namely, *Theanthrōpos*, which means God-Man (*Theos* and *anthrōpos*). Though His Divine and human natures, are not separable, we must examine the evidence for them separately.

(1) THE HUMANITY OF CHRIST

In the Gospels Christ's humanity is everywhere assumed and declared. Two facts constitute the truth.

(i) *His Humanity was Real and not Feigned*

He was born, was dependent on a mother, and was subject to

the authority of a home. As a child He grew in stature, knowledge, and wisdom. He was subject to human infirmities. He hungered and ate; He thirsted and drank; He tired and slept. References are made to His body, hands, feet, eyes, head, finger, legs, and side. He possessed human emotions, and shared human experiences. He rejoiced, and sorrowed; was compassionate, angry, and He loved. He was tempted and resisted. He craved for sympathy. He felt the need of prayer, and prayed for Himself. He suffered in body, in mind, and in spirit; and at last He died (John i. 14; Matt. i. 25; Luke i. 31; ii. 7, 11, 12, 21, 40, 51, 52; vii. 34; xi. 27; Matt. iv. 2; xxi. 18; John xix. 28; Matt. viii. 24; John iv. 6; Luke x. 21; Mark x. 21; iii. 5; Matt. ix. 36; John xi. 33-35; xii. 27; Mark i. 35; Luke xxiii. 46).

(ii) *His Humanity was Perfect and not Faulty*

Christ's Apostles claimed that He was sinless (Acts iii. 14; Rom. viii. 3; 2 Cor. v. 21; Heb. iv. 15; vii. 26; 1 Peter i. 19; ii. 22; 1 John iii. 5); and, of course, they referred to Him as a man. That Jesus would be sinless is implied in the announcement of Gabriel to Mary (Luke i. 35); and He Himself claimed so to be (John viii. 46; xiv. 30).

The fact of importance is not was He 'able not to sin' (*posse non peccare*), nor was He 'not able to sin (*non posse peccare*), but that He did not sin. And let us not suppose that, on that account, His humanity was not real, for real humanity is not what we are, but what God intended us to be.

This characteristic of Christ's nature is implied in the designation *Son of Man*. 'It does not merely assert His real incorporation with our kind; it exalts Him indefinitely above us all as the true representative, the ideal, the pattern Man. His is the Human Life which does justice to the idea of Humanity. He is the Archetypal Man.' (Liddon).

Reflect upon the fact that Jesus never confessed sin, and so never asked for pardon. Nowhere is there any evidence that He ever felt personal remorse. Never did He exhibit any dread of the penal future. His moral sorrows were not His own, but were a burden laid on Him by His love for others. He claimed that He always did the Father's will (John viii. 29). He did not pray with His disciples the prayer He taught them, because it includes a confession of sin.

This great fact and truth has been challenged; at least nine passages being pointed to as showing moral imperfection in Jesus. These relate to His lingering in Jerusalem after His parents had left (Luke ii. 43); His being baptized by John (Matt. iii. 13-15); His clearing the Temple Court (John ii. 13-22); His seeming callousness about a domestic duty (Luke ix. 59, 60); His answer to the Ruler (Mark x. 18); the matter of the demons and the swine (Mark v. 12, 13); His apparent harsh treatment of a woman (Mark vii. 25-28); His prayer in the Garden (Matt. xxvi. 39); and His cry on the Cross (Mark xv. 34).

For a detailed discussion of these incidents, see Godet's *Defence of the Faith*, pp. 222-231; but until you can read that, reflect upon the fact that 'the memory of these incidents brought to Jesus no tremor of regret in later hours.'

(2) THE DIVINITY OF CHRIST

Evidence of Christ's Divinity is in the warp and woof of the Gospel Records, especially in the Fourth, and it is manifold. Assuming the reliability of these Records, examine carefully all passages which assume or declare Christ's Divinity.

(i) *The Witnesses*

(a) DEMONS - - - -	Matt. viii. 28, 29; Mark i. 23, 24; Luke iv. 41
(b) ANGELS - - - -	Luke ii. 9-11
(c) ENEMIES - - -	Matt. xxvii. 54
(d) FRIENDS - - - -	John xi. 27
(e) APOSTLES - - -	Matt. xvi. 16; John i. 49; xx. 28
(f) THE FATHER - - -	John v. 31, 37; xii. 28; Matt. iii. 17; xvii. 5
(g) THE HOLY SPIRIT - -	John xv. 26; xvi. 13, 14
(h) THE SCRIPTURES - -	John v. 39, 47
(i) CHRIST'S WORKS - -	John v. 36; x. 25; xiv. 11; xv. 24
(j) CHRIST'S NAMES AND TITLES	Examine the Table of these on pages 519-524, and find references to Beloved Son, Son of God, Emmanuel, God my Saviour, Only-Begotten, I Am, and Lord Jesus.

Special attention should be given to the claims of Christ, and these are twofold:

(ii) *Christ's Claims for Himself*

'He distinctly, repeatedly, energetically preaches Himself' (Liddon). The meaning of His claims is too clear to be mistaken; His claims, for example, to be the Way, the Truth, the Life, the Light of the World, the Bread of Life, the Water of Life, the Good Shepherd, the Door, the Vine (John xiv. 6; viii. 12; vi. 35; iv. 14; x. 7, 9, 11; xv. 1).

He claims to be on terms of equality with the Father (John v. 17, 18, 21, 22, 23; x. 30, 33); to forgive sins (Matt. ix. 6; Mark ii. 7, 10); to give eternal life (John x. 27, 28). He claims to have existed before His birth (John xvii. 5; viii. 58; iii. 13; vi. 33, 62); to have come down from heaven, and declares His intention to return thither.

He claims absolute authority for His teaching (Matt. vii. 24, 26; xxviii. 20; Luke x. 16; John v. 24). He unites Himself with the Father and the Spirit as together constituting the Godhead (Matt. xxviii. 19). He declares that universal power is His (Matt. xxviii. 18). And, as already said, He always separates Himself from men in His relation to God, never including Himself with them in an 'our Father,' but distinguishing Himself by saying, 'My Father, and your Father; My God, and your God' (Matt. vi. 9; John xx. 17). (See pp. 537, 615).

He claims that His death is atoning; and that thereby all men without distinction will be drawn to Him (Mark x. 45; Luke xix. 10; John xii. 32, 33). He claims to be above all, and to be the Judge of all mankind (John iii. 31; v. 26, 27; xiii. 13; Matt. xxv. 31-46).

But in addition to all this are:

(iii) *Christ's Claims Upon Men*

He does not invite, but demands discipleship (Matt. iv. 19; viii. 22; xix. 21; Mark ii. 14). His Apostles are bidden to resent resistance to His doctrine (Matt. x. 12-15). Men are to give themselves up to Him unreservedly; no rival claims, however strong, no natural affection, however legitimate and sacred, may interpose between Himself and the soul of His follower (Matt. x. 37; Luke xiv. 26; xii. 51-53; ix. 59-62).

He claims to be the satisfier of man's deepest need, and the giver of rest to the burdened soul (John vii. 37-38; Matt. xi. 28). He claims to be not only the supreme Teacher, but also the perfect Lesson (Matt. xi. 29). He claims that to eat Him is to live (John vi. 54-57); and that he who obeys Him shall never see death (John viii. 51).

The Fourth Gospel is our chief source in evidence of the Divinity of Christ, but that evidence is unmistakably in the Synoptics also. Study carefully Matt. xi. 27, and xvi. 13-17, passages than which there are none more important in the New Testament. Find and mark all passages in which the Sonship of Christ is declared or implied (e.g., Matt. vii. 21; x. 32; xii. 50; xxi. 37; xxii. 2; Luke ii. 40-52).

Christ, then, was human and Divine, but we must not think of these as being distinct and separate in Him. Their relation must remain to us a mystery, but the evidence of each is abundant, and the necessity for both is obvious. Had He not been Man, He could not have sympathized with us; and had He not been God He could not have saved us.

THE APOSTLES' CREED

I Believe

In God the Father Almighty, Maker of heaven and earth: And in Jesus Christ His only Son our Lord; Who was conceived by the Holy Ghost, Born of the Virgin Mary; Suffered under Pontius Pilate, Was crucified, dead, and buried; He descended into hell; The third day He rose from the dead; He ascended into heaven; And sitteth on the right hand of God the Father Almighty; From thence He shall come to judge the quick and the dead.

I Believe

In the Holy Ghost;
The Holy Catholic Church;
The Communion of saints;
The Forgiveness of sins;
The Resurrection of the body;
And the Life everlasting.

QUESTIONS

1 What makes a true apprehension of the Person of Christ so important?
2 Where are we to look for the roots of a true Christology, and why?
3 What four factors are necessary for a complete conception of Christ's Person?
4 What do you understand by Docetism; Apollinarianism; and Ebionism?
5 What do you understand by Arianism; Nestorianism; Eutychianism; and Monothelitism?
6 When did Apollinaris, Arius, Nestorius, and Eutyches live?
7 Name four great Councils of the Christian Church, and give the dates of them.
8 Say what heresy, or heresies were condemned at each of these Councils.
9 Is the Pauline theology original or derived?
10 Name with references half-a-dozen passages in the Fourth Gospel which tell of Christ's humanity.
11 What names and titles are given to Christ in the Fourth Gospel?
12 Assuming that the document Q existed and was a source drawn upon by Matthew and Luke, can it be shown from this Primitive Tradition that Christ was Divine?
13 What witness is borne in the Synoptic Gospels to Christ's Divinity?
14 Illustrate from the Fourth Gospel the fact of Christ's Divinity.
15 Illustrate from the Gospels that Christ's humanity was real, and not feigned; and that it was perfect, and not faulty.
16 What witnesses are there in the Gospels to Christ's Divinity?
17 What claims did Christ make for Himself? Give references.
18 How would you answer the challenge that a man's claims for himself are not valid?
19 Give illustrations of Christ's claims upon men.
20 How do Christ's claims for Himself and His claims upon men prove His Divinity? Cite references.
21 Is there any discord between the Synoptics and the Fourth Gospel on the subject of Christ's Person?

LITERATURE

'The Person of Jesus Christ' - -	H. R. Mackintosh
'The Person of Christ in Modern Thought'	E. Digges La Touche
'Christ in Modern Theology' - - -	A. M. Fairbairn
'The Divinity of Christ' - - -	H. P. Liddon
'The Lord of Glory' - - - -	B. B. Warfield
'Jesus and the Gospel' - - - -	J. Denney
'The Transcendence of Jesus Christ' - -	F. Cawley

Expositions of the Apostles' Creed. Treatment of the Person of Christ
in works by Dorner, Hodge, Strong, Mosheim, Shedd, Neander.

Articles on the Person of Christ in the Standard Bible Dictionaries—
Smith's, Hastings', International Standard Bible Encyclopaedia.

Lives of Christ, by Edersheim, Farrar, Geikie, Hanna, Paterson Smyth,
David Smith, Stalker, and others.

For other important works see Index III. 16-18.

II

THE WORK OF CHRIST

IT is necessary that we apprehend quite clearly why Christ
came to this world, that we get the true perspective of His
advent. To this end we should observe that repeatedly Christ
spoke of His first advent as *a coming*. Only once did He say
that He was *born*, and then He immediately added, 'and for this
cause *came* I into the world' (John xviii. 37). His *coming* clearly
points, not to the Nativity, but to the Incarnation (John xvi. 28),
and so it implies pre-existence. Not in this sense has anyone
else ever *come*.

To this truth, Martha bore witness when she said to Jesus:
'Yea, Lord, I believe that Thou art the Christ, the Son of God,
who should *come* into the *world*' (John xi. 27), and the distinction
between the *birth* and the *coming* is plain in the prophecy, 'Unto
us a child is *born*; unto us a Son is *given*' (Isa. ix. 6).

Speaking of the purpose of His incarnation Christ says: 'I am
not *come* to call the righteous . . . to repentance' (Matt. ix. 13);

'The Son of Man *came*, not to be ministered unto, but to minister, and to give His life a ransom for many' (Matt. xx. 28); 'The Son of Man is *come* to seek and to save that which was lost' (Luke xix. 10); 'I *came* down from heaven, not to do mine own will, but the will of Him that sent Me' (John vi. 38); 'For this cause *came* I unto this hour' (i.e., to die, John xii. 23-33).

In the Fourth Gospel Christ always speaks of the object of His coming as a 'work' (*ergon*), and as a work which the Father gave Him to do. 'My meat is to do the will of Him that sent Me, and to finish His *work*' (iv. 34); 'My Father *worketh* hitherto, and I *work*' (v. 17); 'The *works* which the Father hath given Me to finish, the same *works* that I do, bear witness of me, that the Father hath sent Me' (v. 36); 'I must *work* the *works* of Him that sent Me' (ix. 4); 'The *works* that I do in My Father's name, they bear witness of Me (x. 25); 'Many good *works* have I showed you from My Father; for which of these *works* do ye stone Me?' (x. 32); 'If I do not *the works* of My Father, believe Me not' (x. 37, 38); 'The Father that dwelleth in Me, He doeth the *works*' (xiv. 10); 'Believe Me for the very *works*' sake' (xiv. 11); 'The *works* that I do' (xiv. 12); 'I have done the *works* which none other man did' (xv. 24); 'I have finished the *work* which Thou gavest Me to do' (xvii. 4).

Only once in the Synoptics is this word, *ergon*, used of Christ's works (Matt. xi. 2), and then it is not used by Christ Himself. The Synoptic word is *dunamis*, which means *mighty work*, a *work of power*.

These works of Christ were His miracles, but the miracles considered, not in themselves as an end, but as pointing from the physical to the spiritual, or, in other words, His many works pointed to His great work, which was ' to give His life a ransom for many.' Christ came to this world, not to live, but to die. We die because we must, but He died because He chose to. His death was the main feature of His life.

It is because of this that one-third of each of the Synoptics, and one half of the Fourth Gospel are occupied with the events of the Passion Week.

Over thirty years of Christ's life are passed over in silence, except for what is recorded in a few verses, and the Synoptists omit the first nine months of His ministry, but they all write in detail about the events which immediately led to the Cross, and of the crucifixion and resurrection.

Obviously, then, the important thing in Christ's life was not His teaching, nor His miracles, but His death and resurrection. This is *the work* which, on the Cross, Christ said was 'finished'; and this is the work to which all the first preachers bore witness. See the sermons recorded in the Acts, and the witness of the Epistles.

A gospel without the Cross is not the Christian gospel, and, indeed, is no gospel at all. Paul summarizes the true gospel when he says that 'Christ died for our sins . . . and was buried, and rose again the third day . . . and was seen . . .' (1 Cor. xv. 3-5).

12
THE METHOD OF CHRIST'S TEACHING

FOLLOWING the Father's command to men to listen to His Son (Matt. xvii. 5), study carefully these two lines of witness to Christ's teaching:

(*a*) What He claimed for His utterances. Matt. vii. 24, 26; xxiv. 35; Mark iv. 21-25; Luke viii. 15, 18, 21; John viii. 51; xii. 47-50.

(*b*) The impression made on the people by His utterances. Matt. vii. 28; Mark x. 24; xii. 37; Luke iv. 22; v. 1, 15; vi. 17; xv. 1; xxi. 38; xxiv. 19; John iii. 2; vii. 46.

'Never man spake like this Man,' is true alike of Jesus' method, style, and themes. His public work divides itself broadly into three channels: *preaching*, or the proclamation of the gospel; *teaching*, or the exposition of the gospel; and *healing*, or the illustration of the gospel (Matt. iv. 23); and, speaking generally, the appeal in *preaching* was to the multitude, and in *teaching*, to the disciples.

Jesus wrote nothing, so that all His messages were oral, delivered by the sea, on mountain slopes, along the dusty roads, and beneath the friendly roof.

The characteristics of His teaching are simplicity, concreteness, brevity, vividness, and picturesqueness.

(1) Imagery

It has been shown that His sources of imagery are many, and for the following, references should be sought out:

(i) Natural Phenomena:
   Sun, light, lightning, earthquakes, fire, clouds, storm, rain.

(ii) Animate Nature:
   (a) *Creatures.*—Camel, ox, sheep, wolf, ass, fox, swine, dog, fish, birds, serpents.
   (b) *Plants.*—The olive, sycamore, fig, mustard trees; the lily, reed, thorns, anise, mint, cummin.

(iii) *Human Life*:
   (a) *Physical.*—Flesh and blood, the eye, ear, hands, feet; hunger, thirst, sleep, sickness, laughing, weeping, death.
   (b) *Domestic.*—Houses, lamps, seats, food, cooking, bread; birth, mother, sister, brother, children, service, marriage.
   (c) *Commercial.*—Fisherman, tailor, builder, merchant, business, debts.
   (d) *Pastoral and Agricultural.*—Shepherds, sheep, husbandmen, soil, tillage, sowing, growth, harvest, vineyard, wine.
   (e) *Civil.*—Robbery, violence, judgment, punishment, taxes.
   (f) *Social.*—Marriage, hospitality, feasts, salutations, journeying.
   (g) *Religious.*—Alms, tithes, fasting, prayer, sabbath, temple.
   (h) *Historical.*—References to John the Baptist, the slaughter of the Galileans, fall of the Tower of Siloam, Herod Antipas, Herod the Tetrarch, Herod Archelaus, the Good Samaritan.

(2) **Parables**

Our Lord's chief method was to teach by parables, and in this way great moral truths were and are taught by homely illustration. In essence, many of His illustrations are parables, and so viewed, about 70 are found in the Gospels, though, in the stricter sense of narrative parables, there are fewer than that number. (On pp. 278, 279, Nos. 6 and 28 are regarded as parables).

We divide these parables into two lists; in the first those which commonly are regarded as parables, and in the second, illustrations which have a parabolic value.

(i) *Principal Parables*

(a) Recorded in One Gospel Only

1 The Wheat and the Tares	-	-	- Matt. xiii. 24-30, 36-43
2 The Hidden Treasure	-	-	- Matt. xiii. 44
3 The Pearl of Great Price	-	-	- Matt. xiii. 45, 46
4 The Fish Net	-	-	- Matt. xiii. 47-50
5 The Householder	-	-	- Matt. xiii. 51, 52
6 The Unmerciful Servant	-	-	- Matt. xviii. 23-35
7 The Labourers in the Vineyard	-	-	Matt. xx. 1-16
8 The Two Sons Called to Work	-	-	Matt. xxi. 28-32
9 The Marriage of the King's Son	-	-	Matt. xxii. 1-14

10 The Ten Virgins - - - - Matt. xxv. 1-13
11 The Talents - - - - Matt. xxv. 14-30
12 The Sheep and the Goats (p. 285) - Matt. xxv. 31-46
13 The Seed Growing Secretly - - - Mark iv. 26-29
14 The Householder and the Porter - - Mark xiii. 34-37
15 The Two Debtors - - - - Luke vii. 41-43
16 The Good Samaritan - - - Luke x. 30-37
17 The Friend at Midnight - - - Luke xi. 5-8
18 The Rich Fool - - - - Luke xii. 13-21
19 The Waiting and Watching Servants - Luke xii. 35-38
20 The Barren Fig Tree - - - Luke xiii. 6-9
21 The Great Supper - - - - Luke xiv. 16-24
22 The Unfinished Tower - - - Luke xiv. 28-30
23 The Unwaged War - - - - Luke xiv. 31, 32
24 The Lost Bit of Silver - - - Luke xv. 8-10
25 The Prodigal Son and Elder Brother - Luke xv. 11-32
26 The Unrighteous Steward - - - Luke xvi. 1-13
27 The Rich Man and Lazarus - - Luke xvi. 19-31
28 The Unprofitable Servants - - - Luke xvii. 7-10
29 The Unjust Judge - - - Luke xviii. 1-8
30 The Pharisee and the Publican - - Luke xviii. 9-14
31 The Pounds - - - - Luke xix. 11-27
32 The Door of the Sheep - - - John x. 1-10
33 The Good Shepherd - - - John x. 11-18, 25-30
34 The Vine and the Branches - - - John xv. 1-6

The passages in John's Gospel are commonly regarded as allegories, not as parables, and it is true that the Evangelist never speaks of parables.

(b) RECORDED IN TWO GOSPELS

35 The Inward Light - - Matt. vi. 22, 23; Luke xi. 34-36
36 The Two Builders - Matt. vii. 24-27; Luke vi. 46-49
37 The Unclean Spirit that Returned Matt. xii. 43-45; Luke xi. 24-26
38 The Leaven in the Meal Matt. xiii. 33; Luke xiii. 20, 21
39 The Master and the Thief Matt. xxiv. 43, 44; Luke xii. 39, 40
40 The Faithful and Evil Servants Matt. xxiv. 45-51; Luke xii. 42-46
41 The Lost Sheep - Matt. xviii. 12-14; Luke xv. 3-7

(c) RECORDED IN THREE GOSPELS

42 The Savourless Salt - - - - Matt. v. 13
Mark ix. 50; Luke xiv. 34, 35
43 The Lighted Lamp - - - - Matt. v. 15
Mark iv. 21; Luke viii. 16, 17; xi. 33
44 The Bride and the Bridegroom - - Matt. ix. 14, 15
Mark ii. 19, 20; Luke v. 34, 35
45 The New Cloth on an Old Garment - Matt. ix. 16
Mark ii. 21; Luke v. 36
46 The New Wine in Old Wine-skins - - Matt. ix. 17
Mark ii 22; Luke v. 37-39

47 The Sower and the Soils   - - - Matt. xiii. 3-9, 18-23
            Mark iv. 1-9; Luke viii. 4-8
48 The Mustard Seed   - - - Matt. xiii. 31, 32
            Mark iv. 30-32; Luke xiii. 18, 19
49 The Wicked Husbandmen - - Matt. xxi. 33-41
            Mark xii. 1-9; Luke xx. 9-16
50 The Rejected Stone - - - Matt. xx. 42-46
            Mark xii. 10, 11; Luke xx. 17-19
51 The Sprouting Fig Tree - - - Matt. xxiv. 32-35
            Mark xiii. 28-31; Luke xxi. 29-33

(ii) *Parabolic Illustrations*

1 Fishers of Men Matt. iv. 19; Mark i. 16, 17; Luke v. 10
2 The Salt of the Earth - - - Matt. v. 13
3 The Light of the World   Matt. v. 14-16; Luke xi. 34-36
4 Dogs and Swine - - - - Matt. vii. 6
5 Doomed Plants - - - - Matt. xv. 13
6 The Strait Gate and the Shut Door - Luke xiii. 23-30
7 The Mote and the Beam - - Matt. vii. 1-5; Luke vi. 41, 42
8 The Broad and Narrow Ways - - - Matt. vii. 13-14
9 Good and Bad Fruit Trees - Matt. vii. 16-20; Luke vi. 43-45
10 The Physician and the Sick - - Matt. ix. 12-13
            Mark ii. 17; Luke v. 31, 32
11 The Offending Members: Hand, Foot, or Eye
            Matt. v. 29, 30; Mark ix. 43, 45, 47
12 Birds and Flowers - Matt. vi. 25-34; Luke xii. 22-31
13 Parables about Satan's Kingdom Matt. xii. 24-28; Mark iii. 23-26
14 The Strong Man - - - - Matt. xii. 29, 30
            Mark iii. 27; Luke xi. 17-22
15 Good and Bad Treasures - - - Matt. xii. 34-37
16 The Blind Guiding the Blind Matt. xv. 14; Luke vi. 39
17 The Chief Seats at Feasts - - - Luke xiv. 7-11
18 The Harvest Field - - - - John iv. 35-38
19 The Grain of Wheat - - - - John xii. 23-26
20 Defilement -   Matt. xv. 10, 11, 15-20; Mark vii. 14-23

(iii) *The Parables in Christ's Plan of Work.*

Refer to the plan of Christ's Life and Work on pp. 492, 504, and make a note that in Parts I to IV there are no parables; in Part V, the great Galilean Ministry, there are no parables in Period 1; but there are twenty-two in Period 2; and two in Period 3. In Part VI there are ten; in Part VII, fourteen; in Part VIII, eleven, or twelve, and in Part IX, none. From this we see that in the second Galilean Period most of the parables were spoken (24), and that this beginning of Jesus' parabolic teaching continued to the end (Part IX excepted).

Why Christ employed this method as a medium of instruction

is stated in Matt. xiii. 10-17. Care should be taken in studying the parables to distinguish between *interpretation* and *application*. All the Bible is *for* us, but it is not all *about* us. Interpretation is limited by the original intent of the parable, and this intent is determined by occasion and circumstance; but application is not limited, for the way in which it can help us is its meaning for us. Interpretation is dispensational and prophetic. Application is moral and practical. The principles of interpretation can be learned from the two parables which Christ Himself has interpreted (Matt. xiii. 18-23, 36-43).

It is not only interesting but also important to discern *Christ in His parables*. Trace the following in the parable lists already given: He is a Judge, a Nobleman, a Bridegroom, a Creditor, a Master, a Merchantman, a Host, a Shepherd, a Sower, a Husbandman, a Physician, and a Builder.

Trace, also, where people are represented as: sons, servants, virgins, guests, debtors, travellers, worshippers, builders, habitations, soil, seed, sheep, goats, fish, treasure, light, and salt.

Observe that the parables are compared and contrasted, that a number of them go in pairs, which present in several cases the outward and inward aspects of the same subject, and so we have: the Pharisee and the Publican, Dives and Lazarus, the Two Sons, the Prodigal and Elder Brother, the Two Foundations, Good and Bad Trees, the Patch and the Garment, the Wine and Wine-skins, the Sheep and the Goats, the Wheat and the Tares, the Tower and the War, the Good and the Bad Soils, the Faithful and the Unfaithful Servants, the Treasure and the Pearl, the Whole and the Sick, the Watchers and the Sleepers, the Two Debtors, the Salt and the Light, the Marriage Feast and the Great Supper, and the Talents and the Pounds.

Our Lord's present absence and His coming again are prominent in some parables, together with our obligation in view of both; e.g.:

> The Sower is absent; we should bear fruit; He is coming to reap.
> A Feast is prepared; we should be assembling; the Host will enter.
> The Man has departed; we should trade with our talents; the Man is coming back.

Judgment, also, is prominent in the parables, and it is both *retributive* and *distributive*; punishment for guilt, and reward for faithfulness. For these ideas study the Wheat and the Tares, the Good and Bad Fish, the Guests with and without a Wedding Garment, Good and Evil Servants, Wise and Foolish Virgins, the Sheep and the Goats, the Diligent and the Negligent Servants.

Study, also, the *Kingdom* parables, and especially the ten or more in Matthew which begin with the words, 'The Kingdom of Heaven is like—.'

A list should be made of the practical themes of which the parables treat, such as Riches (Luke xii. 16-21; xvi. 19-31); Anxiety (Mark iv. 26-29); Joy (Luke xv. 6, 7, 9, 10, 24, 32; Matt. xiii. 44; John iv. 36-38; xv. 11); the Word of God (Matt. vii. 24, 26; xiii. 3-9, 18-23; John x. 4, 27); Service (Luke xvii. 7-10; xix. 12-27; xx. 1-16; Matt. xxv. 14-30); Watchfulness (Matt. xxiv. 42-51; xxv. 1-13; Luke xii. 35-48); Diligence (Matt. xxv. 14-30; Luke xix. 12-27); Compassion (Luke vii. 41-42; x. 30-37; Matt. xviii. 23-35); Prayer (Luke xi. 5-8; xviii. 1-8; xviii. 9-14; xv. 18, 21; xvi. 23, 24, 27, 28, 30).

(3) **Miracles**

Another means whereby Christ taught was miracles. His parables were miracles in words, and His miracles were parables in deeds. Bishop Westcott has said that the miracles and the parables 'are exactly correlative to each other; in the one we see the personality and power of the Worker, and in the other the generality and constancy of the Work; . . . in the one we are led to regard the manifoldness of Providence, and in the other to recognize the instructiveness of the Universe.'

Not all that Christ said or did is recorded, and relative to the latter, this is witnessed to by the many references to unparticularized miracles which He performed (Matt. iv. 23, 24; ix. 35; xi. 21; Mark vi. 53-56; Luke iv. 40-41; v. 15; vi. 17-19; vii. 21; John ii. 23; iii. 2; iv. 45; xx. 30; xxi. 25). (See p. 203).

The specified miracles on record are thirty-five in number—unless Matt. xii. 22, and Luke xi. 14 are regarded as separate (Nos. 12 and 28 on p. 554)—and are here classified according to the number of times they are recorded. The figures in brackets on the left-hand side indicate their chronological order.

Chronological Order   (a) RECORDED IN ONE GOSPEL ONLY (18)

(1) Water Made into Wine -   -   -   -   John ii. 1-11
(2) A Nobleman's Son Healed   -   -   -   John iv. 46-54
(3) Impotent Man at Bethesda Healed   -   John v. 1-9
(4) First Miraculous Draught of Fishes-   -   Luke v. 1-11
(11) A Widow's Son Raised   -   -   Luke vii. 11-17
(12) Blind and Dumb Man Cured   •   -   Matt. xii. 22
(17) Two Blind Men Healed   -   •   -   Matt. ix. 27-31
(18) A Dumb Demon Exorcised -   •   -   Matt. ix. 32, 33
(22) A Deaf and Dumb Man Healed   -   -   Mark vii. 31-37
(24) A Blind Man Healed   -   -   •   -   Mark viii. 22-26
(26) Tribute Money Provided   -   •   -   Matt. xvii. 24-27
(27) Healing of a Man Born Blind   •   -   John ix. 1-7
(28) A Dumb Demoniac Healed   -   •   -   Luke xi. 14
(29) A Woman's Infirmity Cured   •   -   Luke xiii. 10-17
(30) A Man with Dropsy Healed -   •   -   Luke xiv. 1-6
(31) Lazarus Raised from the Dead   •   -   John xi. 17-44
(32) Ten Lepers Healed   -   -   •   -   Luke xvii. 11-19
(35) The Ear of Malchus Healed -   -   -   Luke xxii. 49-51
(36) Second Miraculous Draught of Fishes   -   John xxi. 1-14

(Perhaps Luke xi. 14 and Matt. ix. 32, 33, or xii. 22 are the same).

(b) RECORDED IN TWO GOSPELS (5)

(5) A Demoniac Liberated   Mark i. 23-28; Luke iv. 33-37
(10) A Centurion's Servant Healed   Matt. viii. 5-13; Luke vii. 1-10
(21) A Syro-Phœnician Woman's Daughter
      Healed   -   -   Matt. xv. 21-28; Mark vii. 24-30
(23) Four Thousand Fed   Matt. xv. 32-38; Mark viii. 1-9
(34) A Fig Tree Cursed   Matt. xxi. 18-22; Mark xi. 12-14

(c) RECORDED IN THREE GOSPELS (11)

(6) Healing of Peter's Mother-in-law   -   -   Matt. viii. 14, 15
                        Mark i. 29-31;   Luke iv. 38, 39
(7) A Leper Cured   -   •   -   -   -   Matt. viii. 2-4
                        Mark i. 40-45; Luke v. 12-16
(8) A Paralytic Healed   •   -   -   -   Matt. ix. 2-8
                        Mark ii 3-12; Luke v. 18-26
(9) A Man with a Withered Hand Healed   -   Matt. xii. 10-13
                        Mark iii. 1-5; Luke vi. 6-11
(13) Stilling the Storm   •   -   -   -   Matt. viii. 23-27
                        Mark iv. 35-41; Luke viii. 22-25
(14) Two Demoniacs Liberated   -   -   -   Matt. viii. 28-34
                        Mark v. 1-20; Luke viii. 26-39
(15) A Woman's Issue of Blood Staunched   -   Matt. ix. 20-22
                        Mark v. 25-34; Luke viii. 43-48
(16) The Daughter of Jairus Raised   -   -   Matt. ix. 18, 19, 23-26
                  Mark v. 22-24, 35-43; Luke viii. 41, 42, 49-56
(20) Walking on the Sea   •   -   -   -   Matt. xiv. 25-33
                        Mark vi. 45-52; John vi. 16-21

(25) Cure of an Epileptic Boy - - - Matt. xvii. 14-18
          Mark ix. 14-29; Luke ix. 38-43
(33) Two Blind Men Healed - - - Matt. xx. 29-34
          Mark x. 46-52; Luke xviii. 35-43

(d) RECORDED IN FOUR GOSPELS (1)

(19) Five Thousand Fed - - - - Matt. xiv. 15-21
      Mark vi. 35-44; Luke ix. 12-17; John vi. 1-14

It should be observed that three of these miracles tell of the raising of the dead—of a child, a young man, and an adult; nine relate to nature; four of them to creative power; four to providential blessing; one to judgment; and twenty-three relate to healing.

The boundaries of these miracles are themselves miracles—the Virgin Birth of Jesus, and His Resurrection and Ascension.

The miracles have two great values: (a) they are a revelation of God; and (b) they are a revelation of man. The healing miracles represent the ruin caused by sin, and God's power and will to repair it.

Death tells of our state by nature; leprosy, of the defilement of sin; palsy, of the enfeebling power of sin; blindness, of the ignorance caused by sin; demoniacal possession, of the enmity stirred by sin; deafness, of the indifference engendered by sin; dumbness, of the speechlessness on spiritual matters which sin produces; fever, of the contagion and restlessness due to sin; impotence of hands and feet, of the sinner's inability to work for God, or to walk with Him (p. 205).

Christ could teach by miracles what He could teach in no other way. There was nothing miraculous in the parables; all was natural and inevitable: the seed growing, the leaven working, the light shining; but not by parables could He show how the blind might see, the dumb speak, and the deaf hear; miracles had to be performed to teach these lessons. Christ was not a conjuror, but a Teacher.

Henry Norris Bernard, in his *The Mental Characteristics of the Lord Jesus Christ*, says:

'The miracles of Christ formed part of that warfare which was ever waging between the Son of God and the power of evil which He was manifested to destroy. The rage of the elements, the roaring wind, and the surging waves ever seeking to engulf the fishers' boat; that fell sickness racking with pain man's body; the paralysis of the mental powers destroying man's intellect, and leaving him a prey to unreasoning violence, or to unclean desires; the death which shrouded him in the unknown darkness of the tomb—these things were to the Saviour's vision but objective forms of the curse of sin which it was His mission to remove. The Kingdom of God and the Kingdom of Satan were brought together in opposition. The battle between the Lord's Christ and the great Adversary was ever going on. Man's infirmities and his sicknesses, in the eyes of Christ, were the outward symbols of the sin which was their cause. So the inspired writer, in the healing of the sick, and in the casting out of devils, sees direct blows given, which, in the end, shall cause Satan's empire to totter to its fall. Every leper cleansed, every blind man restored to sight, every helpless paralytic made to walk, every distracted man brought back to the sweetness of life and light of reason, above all the dead recalled to life—each, in the salvation accorded them, furnished a proof that a greater than Satan was here, and that the Kingdom of God was being manifested upon earth.'

(4) Discourses

In addition to instruction by imagery, parable, and miracle, Christ taught by plain discourses. Some of these are recorded with considerable fulness, and others more briefly. It is impossible to exaggerate the importance of these utterances of Christ, so they should be constantly before us and studied through all our days.

The following order is not chronological, but as the discourses appear in the Gospels:

SUBJECT	REFERENCE
1 The Sermon on the Mount ..	Matt.v.2-vii.27; Luke vi.20-49
2 The Twelve Commissioned ..	Matt. x. 5-42; Mark vi. 6-13; Luke ix. 1-6
3 Witness to the Baptist	Matt. xi. 2-19; Luke vii. 18-35
4 Woes on the Cities of Opportunity	Matt. xi. 20-24
5 Coming to the Father through the Son	Matt. xi. 29, 30
6 On a Blasphemous Charge, and the Demand for a Sign ..	Matt. xii. 22-45; Mark iii. 23-29; Luke xi. 14-36
7 On the Tradition of the Elders ..	Matt. xv. 1-20; Mark vii. 1-23
8 On His Messiahship, Approaching Death, and Coming Glory	Matt. xvi. 13-28
9 On Humility, Offences, and Forgiveness	Matt. xviii; Mark ix. 38-50
10 On Divorce	Matt. xix. 1-12; Mark x. 1-12

SUBJECT	REFERENCE
11 On Entering the Kingdom of God	Matt. xix. 16-30; Mark x. 17-31; Luke xviii. 18-30
12 On False Ambition	Matt. xx. 20-28; Mark x. 35-45
13 On Faith and Prayer	Matt. xxi. 18-22; Mark xi. 20-26
14 On the Resurrection	Matt. xxii. 23-33; Mark xii. 18-27; Luke xx. 27-40
15 The Scribes and Pharisees Denounced	Matt. xxiii. 1-39; Mark xii. 38-40; Luke xx. 45-47
16 The Destruction of Jerusalem, and the Second Advent ...	Matt. xxiv., xxv. ; Mark xiii. 1-37; Luke xxi. 5-36
17 On Gaining and Losing Life ...	Mark viii. 34-38; Luke ix. 23-27
18 On Love	Mark xii. 28-34
19 On Forgiveness and Gratitude ...	Luke vii. 36-50
20 The Seventy Commissioned ...	Luke x. 1-20
21 Denunciation of the Pharisees and Lawyers	Luke xi. 37-52
22 On Hypocrisy, Fear, Confession, and Blasphemy	Luke xii. 1-12
23 On Anxiety	Luke xii. 22-34
24 On Watching	Luke xii. 35-48
25 On Christ and Divisions	Luke xii. 49-53
26 On Discernment	Luke xii. 54-59
27 On Exclusion from the Kingdom of God	Luke xiii. 22-30
28 On Offences, Forgiveness, and Faith	Luke xvii. 1-10
29 On the Last Days	Luke xvii. 22-37
30 On True Greatness	Luke xxii. 24-30
31 On the New Birth...	John iii. 1-21
32 On the Water of Life	John iv. 4-26
33 On Sowing and Reaping	John iv. 31-38
34 On the Source of Life	John v. 19-47
35 On the Bread of Life	John vi. 26-59
36 On the Fountain of Truth ...	John vii. 14-29
37 On the Light of the World ...	John viii. 12-20
38 On the True Object of Faith ...	John viii. 21-30
39 On Spiritual Freedom and Descent	John viii. 31-59
40 The Door and Shepherd of the Flock	John x. 1-21
41 Christ's Oneness with the Father	John x. 22-38
42 The Redeemer of the World ...	John xii. 20-36
43 Christ's Departure from Earth, and Problems which arise therefrom	John xiii. 31-xiv. 31
44 The Nature and Issues of Union with Christ	John xv.
45 The Holy Spirit and the Future ...	John xvi.

In addition to these *plain* discourses are a number of *parabolic* ones, which will be recognized by reference to the Table of Parables, on pp. 550, 551. Among the principal of these are: the Parables of the Kingdom (Matt. xiii.); the Talents (Matt. xxv.); the Pounds (Luke xix.); the Marriage of the King's Son (Matt. xxii.); the Two Debtors (Luke vii.); the Rich Man and Lazarus (?Luke xvi.); the Good Samaritan (Luke x.).

It should be observed that the Gospels of Matthew and John are pre-eminently the Gospels of Discourses, and in this are distinct from Mark and Luke.

QUESTIONS

1 In what three ways did Jesus accomplish His work as a Teacher, and what is the relation of these to one another?
2 What did Christ claim for Himself as a Teacher?
3 In what way or ways were people affected by Christ's teaching?
4 Where, for the most part, was Christ's teaching given?
5 Name and illustrate some characteristics of Christ's teaching.
6 What four teaching methods did Christ employ?
7 Name twenty objects which Christ employed for the purpose of illustration.
8 What was Christ's chief method of instruction, and why?
9 Approximately how many parables are there in the Gospels?
10 Name, from memory, twenty of the principal parables.
11 Name two parables in each of the Synoptic Gospels which are peculiar to these Gospels.
12 Name two allegories in the Fourth Gospel.
13 How many parables are recorded in all the Synoptics? Name twenty of them.
14 Distinguishing the generally admitted parables, and parabolic illustrations, name half a dozen of the latter.
15 In which three periods of Christ's ministry are the most parables found?
16 Explain the difference between interpretation and application in the use of the parables.
17 In which parables does Christ Himself appear, and in what aspects?
18 Name some of the ways in which men are represented in the parables.
19 How many parable-pairs are there? Name six of them.
20 In what parables is Christ's Second Advent taught, and for what purpose is it said that He will return?
21 Which are especially the Kingdom parables?
22 Of what times do the parables treat?
23 In what sense are the miracles parabolic?
24 How many times in the Gospels are there references to unparticularized miracles?
25 How many miracles are recorded in the Gospels?
26 Name two miracles in each of the Gospels which are peculiar to them.
27 Name four miracles which are recorded in three of the Gospels.

28 Is there any miracle recorded in all four Gospels, and if so, which?
29 How many miracles are there of raising from the dead, and which are they?
30 What is the spiritual significance of the miracles?
31 How could Christ teach by miracles what He could not by parables?
32 Name five principal discourses recorded in Matthew's Gospel.
33 Name four shorter discourses recorded by Matthew.
34 Name three discourses recorded only by Luke.
35 Name six discourses recorded only by John.
36 In what way or ways are the discourses in the Fourth Gospel distinguishable from those recorded in the Synoptics?
37 Is any problem raised by the discourses in the Fourth Gospel?
38 In what way did Christ teach other than by plain discourse?

LITERATURE

'The Land and the Book'	W. M. Thomson
'The Holy Land and the Bible'	C. Geikie
'The Master and His Method'	Griffith Jones
'Illustrative Texts and Texts Illustrated'	Canon Bardsley
'Models and Objects for Scripture Teaching'	J. G. Kitchin
'Our Lord's Illustrations'	R. R. Resker

Parables

'The Parables of Our Lord'	W. Arnot
'The Parabolic Teaching of Christ'	A. B. Bruce
'The Parables of Our Lord'	M. Dods
'A Study of the Parables'	A. Habershon
'The Parables of Jesus in Relation to His Ministry'	Robinson
'The Parables of Our Lord'	S. D. F. Salmond
'Parables of the Kingdom'	H. B. Swete
'Notes on the Parables of Our Lord'	R. C. Trench
'The Illustrative Teachings of Jesus'	Young
'Parables of the Kingdom'	Campbell Morgan

Miracles

'Our Lord's Miracles of Healing'	T. W. Belcher
'Notes on the Miracles of Our Lord'	R. C. Trench
'The Miraculous Element in the Gospels'	A. B. Bruce
'The Faith that Rebels'	D. S. Cairns
'Christ's Acted Parables'	Burton
'Nature and the Supernatural'	H. Bushnell
'Analogy of Religion'	Bp. Butler
'The Miracles in St. John's Gospel and their Teaching'	Gilbert
'Study of the Miracles'	A. Habershon
'The Miracles of Our Lord'	J. Laidlaw
'The Gospel Miracles in their Relation to Christ and Christianity'	W. M. Taylor
'The Miracles of Our Lord and Saviour'	W. M. Taylor
'Characteristics of the Gospel Miracles'	Bp. Westcott
'Meditations on the Miracles of Christ'	J. S. Howson
'Miracles: A Preliminary Study'	C. S. Lewis

Discourses

See the Literature of 'The Substance of Christ's Teaching,' pp. 567, 568.
    In addition to these works consult the Bible Dictionaries: Smith's, Hastings', International Standard. The Commentaries: Ellicott's, Pulpit, Bengel's, Plummer's, Swete's, Alford's, Matthew Henry's. Expositions: Spurgeon's, Parker's, Maclaren's, Expositor's Bible.

13

THE SUBSTANCE OF CHRIST'S TEACHING

THE study of Christ's imagery, parables, miracles, and discourses, lays the foundation for the consideration of His teaching on many themes. We do not know the Gospels well enough until we have learned, to some extent, what Christ has said about God, the Holy Spirit, Himself, His Death; about Man, Sin, Righteousness, Salvation, and the Kingdom; about Prayer, Judgment, His Second Advent, Destiny; about Injuries, Anxiety, Fear, Faith, and Forgiveness; about Money, Defilement, Law, Blasphemy, Ambition, and Angels; about Covetousness, Hypocrisy, Responsibility, Humility, Love, Neighbourliness; about Regeneration, Self-denial, Temptation, Truth, and Work; about Watchfulness, Worship, Repentance, Divorce, and Friendship.

    In illustration of this exercise, and to promote research, notes are here given on a dozen of these themes.

(1) GOD

He is Spirit (John iv. 24); Omnipotent (Matt. xix. 26; John i. 3); Omniscient (Matt. x. 29); Holy (John xvii. 11); Righteous (John xvii. 25); Loving (John iii. 16; xvii. 23); Good (Matt. vi. 26, 28-30; x. 29, 30).

    But the outstanding truth which Christ taught about God is that He is *Father*. This term, applied to Him, occurs 189 times —in Matthew, 44; in Mark, 4; in Luke, 17, and in John, 124. Is God the Father of all men? 'There is no passage in our sources in which Jesus explicitly speaks of God as the Father of all men.' (Stevens', *Theology of the New Testament*, p. 70). 'If the universal Fatherhood of God and the universal sonship of man are assumed, how is it that there is not a single clear instance of either truth in the New Testament?' (Griffith Thomas: *Principles of Theology*, pp. 498, 500). In a unique sense Christ is the Son of God (John v. 17-27; x. 30), and men can become God's sons only through Christ, and by faith (John i. 12; xiv. 6).

(2) THE HOLY SPIRIT

The chief source of Christ's teaching on this subject is His Upper Room discourse, and the continuance of it on the way to Gethsemane (John xiv-xvi). In these talks Christ teaches:

(i) THE PERSONALITY OF THE SPIRIT
  Terms of personality are employed of Him (xiv. 16, 17, 26; xv. 26; xvi. 7, 8, 13, 14).
  Qualities of personality are attributed to Him. He teaches, guides, and can communicate truth (xiv. 26; xvi. 13).
  Operations of personality are ascribed to Him. He leads, receives, glorifies, announces, assists (xiv. 16, 26; xv. 26; xvi. 13, 14, 15).

(ii) THE DEITY OF THE SPIRIT.
  Associations of Deity are His (xiv. 16, 26; xv. 26; xvi. 14, 15).
  Attributes of Deity are His (xiv. 17, 26; xvi. 7, 12, 13).
  Actions of Deity are His (xvi. 8-14).

(iii) THE CHARACTER OF THE SPIRIT.
  He is the Holy Spirit, the Spirit of Truth, the Comforter (xiv. 26; xv. 26; xvi. 13; xiv. 16, 26; xvi. 7).

(iv) THE ADVENT OF THE SPIRIT.
  (xiv. 16, 26; xv. 26; xvi. 7).

(v) THE MINISTRY OF THE SPIRIT.
  In the *World* (xvi. 8-11).
  In the *Church* (xiv. 26; xv. 26; xvi. 12-15).

(3) CHRIST HIMSELF

Our Lord's teaching concerning Himself is summarized in the section on His Divinity, pp. 535, 542. Study specially John v. 19-47; vi. 26-71; vii. 14-39; viii. 12-59; x. 22-38; xii. 20-50; and chapters xiii. to xvii.

(4) CHRIST'S DEATH

Jesus predicted the fact and manner of His death (Matt. ix. 15; xvi. 21; Luke ix. 22; xviii. 31-33). He also taught that His death was not inevitable, but that it had a universal significance (John xii. 32-33); that it had a bearing upon the spirit-world (John xii. 31); that for the purpose of death He came into the world (John xii. 27); that His death was vicarious (Matt. xxvi. 28; Mark x. 45); and that it glorified the Father (John xii. 27-28; xiii. 31; xvii. 1). 'The forfeiting of His free life has freed our forfeited lives.' (Denney, *The Death of Christ*, chap. I).

36

(5) MAN

Christ did not teach that 'God is slumbering in the heart of every man, and only needs to be wakened.' On the contrary, He affirmed that man's nature is 'evil' (Matt. xii. 34; Luke xi. 13); that he is capable of great wickedness (Mark vii. 20-23; Luke xi. 42-52); that he is 'lost' (Luke xv., xix. 10); that he is a sinner (Luke xv. 10); that he needs to repent (Mark i. 15; Luke xv. 10), and to be 'born again' (John iii. 3, 5, 7); that apart from Him, man will ultimately perish (Matt. xvi. 25; xviii. 3; John iii. 16); and that man's soul is of inestimable value (Matt. xvi. 26).

(6) SIN

The tragic fact of sin is involved in Christ's doctrine of man. Mostly He spoke of men as 'sinners' (Matt. ix. 13; xxvi. 45; Luke vi. 32-34; xiii. 2; xv. 7), and He spoke much about sin (John viii. 7, 34, 46; ix. 41; xv. 22; xvi. 8, 9; xix. 11). His metaphors illustrate the havoc wrought by sin. Sin is blindness, and sickness, and bondage, and darkness, and debt (Matt. xiii. 30, 41, 42; xxv. 41, 46; Luke xvi. 26; John iii. 19-21; v. 28, 29; viii. 12, 24, 43-46; xii. 35-46).

Christ teaches that this condition is universal, that all are in debt to God, whether it be to the extent of 'fifty pence' or 'five hundred pence' (Luke vii. 37-48). The Elder Brother is as much a sinner as the Prodigal Son. The ninety-nine sheep are as completely 'lost' as the one (Luke xv.). When Christ spoke of the 'righteous,' and of them that are 'whole,' He did not imply that any were righteous or whole, but only that some thought they were (Matt. ix. 12, 13).

All His teaching on salvation and judgment assumes the fact of sin, and of sinners (John iii. 16, 17; xii. 46, 47).

(7) RIGHTEOUSNESS

The root idea of this word is *right*, and it is so spoken of in Matt. xx. 4, 7; Luke xii. 57. In the teaching of Christ this word and its cognates are also translated: *just*, 5 times (Matt. v. 45); *righteous*, 18 times (Luke v. 32); *justify*, 4 times (Matt. xi. 19); *judge*, once (Luke xii. 14); and *righteousness*, 8 times (John xvi. 8, 10). Christ's employment of these words sets forth the following truths:

There is such a thing as *right*, implying *wrong* -	Matt. xx. 4, 7
God is the *Absolute Right* - - - - -	John xvii. 25
Our first duty is to pursue what is *right* in God's sight	Matt. vi. 33
Men are divided into two classes, those who are *right*, and those who are *wrong* - - - -	Matt. v. 45; xiii. 17, 41, 43, 49; xxiii. 28, 29, 35.
The Holy Spirit has come to convince the world of what is *right* - - - - - -	John xvi. 8, 10
Those who are *right* have already repented of their sins - - - - - - -	Matt. ix. 13
Our judgment of others should be *right* - -	John vii. 24
Wrong people often imagine they are *right* - -	Matt. v. 20; Luke xvi. 15; xviii. 9, 14
Christ's judgment in all things is *right* - -	John v. 30.
We should fulfil all that is *right* as Christ did -	Matt. iii. 15
They who yearn to be *right* can be *right*	Matt. v. 6; Luke xviii. 14
They who are *right* are likely to suffer - -	Matt. v. 10
Coming judgment will reveal who are *right* and who are *wrong* - - - - - - -	Matt. xxv. 31-46
Both the *right* and the *wrong* will be recompensed at last - - - -	Matt. x. 41; xxv. 46; Luke xiv. 14

An examination of these passages will show that righteousness embraces *morality*, that is, man's relation to man; and *religion*, that is, man's relation to God. (See further under 'Love,' p. 565).

(8) SALVATION

Christ uses the word 'to save' about 27 times, and 'salvation' twice, but what these words mean is integral in all His teaching, and is illustrated by His whole ministry. Salvation is a central idea in which many others meet, such as sin, repentance, faith, regeneration, justification, life, righteousness; and it stands in contrast to the ideas of lost, destruction, perish, and death.

Examine the following references: Matt. x. 22; xvi. 25; xviii. 11; Mark iii. 4; xvi. 16; Luke vii. 50; viii. 12; ix. 56; xvii. 33; xix. 9; xix. 10; John iii. 17; iv. 22; v. 34; x. 9; xii. 47; and mark what Christ says about the need, the nature, the condition, and the means of salvation.

This theme is illustrated by the parables of the Pharisee and the Publican, the Lost Sheep, the Good Shepherd, the Good Samaritan, the Great Supper, and the Wedding Feast.

(9) FORGIVENESS

This means to discharge, dismiss, acquit, let loose from; to remit a debt or sin, to pardon. On this subject Christ teaches two great lessons—one relates to God's forgiveness of men, and the other, to man's forgiveness of his fellows; and these two lessons are vitally related. They meet in Matt. vi. 12, 14, 15, where it is declared that if we do not forgive one another, God will not forgive us (Matt. xviii. 35; Luke vi. 37).

This introduces the important truth that forgiveness is conditioned on repentance (Luke xvii. 3, 4). Within this condition no limit should be put to forgiveness (Matt. xviii. 15, 21, 22).

At all times we should have the spirit of forgiveness, but we can actually forgive only where there are repentance and confession. If we have not this spirit, our prayers will not be heard (Mark xi. 25, 26). (Page 583).

The two great forgiveness parables are the Two Debtors, and the Prodigal Son (Matt. xviii. 21-35; Luke xv. 11-24).

We can forgive injuries, but only God can forgive sins (Mark ii. 7); and so, by forgiving sins, Christ revealed His Deity (Matt. ix. 2, 6; Mark ii. 5; Luke vii. 48). It is declared that there is one sin which can never be forgiven, and that is, charging Christ with being devil-possessed (Matt. xii. 31; Mark iii. 28-30).

(10) THE KINGDOM

No word, except *Father*, was more often on Christ's lips than this one. The single word, *Kingdom*, or with 'His,' 'My,' or 'Thy,' occurs in the Gospels between thirty and forty times; *Kingdom of God* occurs from fifty to sixty times; and *The Kingdom of Heaven* occurs thirty-three times, and in Matthew's Gospel only; thus the word occurs over one hundred and twenty times, so that what it stands for is of major importance.

'The idea as set forth in the Gospels is so complex, the phrase is used to cover so many and difficult conceptions, that it is practically impossible to frame a definition within which all the sayings of Jesus concerning the Kingdom can be included.' (*The Teaching of Jesus*: Jackson).

Comprehensively, the Kingdom is a spiritual commonwealth embracing all who do God's will. As the term 'Kingdom of

Heaven' occurs only in Matthew's Gospel, without doubt it has special significance, in keeping with the distinctive purpose of that Gospel, but elsewhere, the Kingdom, or Kingdom of God, is the equivalent of it (cf. Matt. vi. 10, 33; xii. 28; xiii. 31; xxi. 31, 43; Mark iv. 30).

The Jews expected Messiah to establish a visible earthly Kingdom, a manifested Theocracy, of which Jerusalem would be the capital, and that, by its establishment, the yoke of foreign domination would be thrown off, and Israel's enemies would be made to lick the dust.

But Jesus taught that His Kingdom is something new and distinctive (Mark i. 15); that it is moral and spiritual, and not political (Matt. v. 3-12; Luke vi. 20-23; John xviii. 36); that it is invisible and internal (Luke xvii. 20, 21); that it is silent, mysterious, and progressive (Mark iv. 26-29); that it is universal in its design and scope (Matt. xxi. 31, 43); that it is social (Matt. xx. 25-28); that by it we enter into a relation, not only to God, but also to men; that it can be entered only by regeneration (John iii. 3, 5; Matt. xviii. 3, 4); and that it is both present and future (Matt. xii. 28; Mark ix. 1; Luke xiii. 29; xvii. 21).

It is to be noted that the word 'Church' occurs only three times in the Gospels (Matt. xvi. 18; xviii. 17), and sixty-eight times in the Epistles; and that the terms 'Kingdom,' and 'Kingdom of God' occur eighteen times in the Epistles, and over one hundred and twenty times in the Gospels. Clearly then, the terms are not to be regarded as synonymous. The Church is in the Kingdom of God, but it is not that Kingdom. 'The Kingdom of the Son of His love,' is part of the Kingdom of God (Col. i. 13).

(11) LOVE

The love of which Christ speaks is not a sentiment, but a principle, and the substance of His teaching on the subject is— that God loves (Luke xi. 42; John v. 42; xv. 10); that God loves Him (John x. 17; xv. 9; xvii. 23, 24, 26); that God loves the disciples (John xvi. 27; xvii. 23); that God loves all men (John iii. 16); that He Himself loves God (John xiv. 31), loves the disciples in general (John xiii. 1, 34; xiv. 21; xv. 9, 10), loves individuals (Mark x. 21, 23, 24; John xi. 5, 36; xiii. 23), and expects men to love Him and God (John viii. 42; xiv. 23; xvi. 27), and to love one another also (Matt. v. 43, 44, 46; John xiii. 34, 35; xv. 12, 13).

The outstanding truth in Jesus' teaching on love is that it is the sum and substance of the law (Matt. xxii. 36-40; Luke x. 27); and that the law can be truly kept only as one loves God and his fellows (Exodus xx. 1-17).

(12) PRAYER

Christ's teaching on prayer is not limited to His direct instruction on the subject, but is to be looked for also in His recorded prayers, and in the fact that His own life was one of prayer.

(*a*) Christ's was a life of prayer. This is shown by many incidental references, especially in Luke's Gospel (cf. Matt. xiv. 23; xix. 13; Mark i. 33-35; xi. 11, 12; Luke iii. 21; v. 15, 16; vi. 12, 13; ix. 18; xi. 1; xxi. 37; xxii. 32; John xi. 41, 42).

(*b*) The few prayers of Christ which are recorded are full of instruction (Matt. xi. 25, 26; xxvi. 36-44; Luke xxii. 41, 42, 44; John xi. 41, 42; xii. 27-37; xvii. 1-26).

(*c*) Christ's teaching on prayer is extensive and profound. Prayer should be continuous (Luke xviii. 1); private and public (Matt. vi. 6; Luke xviii. 10); reverent and familiar (Matt. vi. 6; John iv. 24); sincere and earnest (Matt. vi. 7; vii. 7); definite (Matt. vii. 7-11); missionary (Matt. ix. 38); believing (Matt. xvii. 20, 21); united (Matt. xviii. 19, 20); watchful (Matt. xxvi. 41).

Collect from the Gospels all that Christ has said on prayer, and classify it to practise and teach it.

If the forty subjects here detailed (page 560) be studied in the way indicated in these twelve samples, our intellectual and spiritual enrichment will be great. And to these subjects may be added Christ's teaching on—Benevolence, Compassion, Confession, Defilement, Discipleship, Excuses, Fasting, Fellowship, Gratitude, Greatness, Heaven, Industry, Joy, Judging, Marriage, Meekness, Obedience, Peace, Persecution, Retaliation, the Sabbath, the Scriptures, Satan, Self-exaltation, Stewardship, Suffering, Talents, Trust, Truth, and Zeal.

QUESTIONS

1 Name twenty subjects on which Christ gave instruction.
2 What did Christ teach about God, and about His own relation to Him?
3 In what sense is Christ the Son of God?
4 Did Christ teach that the Spirit is a Person, and is Divine? If so, where?
5 What did Christ say about the Advent and Ministry of the Spirit?
6 What is Christ's teaching about Himself? Who did He claim to be? Give references.
7 How did Christ interpret His death?
8 What is Christ's teaching about Man, and how does it compare with man's view of himself?
9 What did Christ say about Sin? Give references.
10 Did Christ teach that some people were not sinners? If not, what is meant by: " came not to call the righteous," and, "he that is whole has no need of a physician"?
11 What did Christ mean when He spoke of Righteousness?
12 What do you understand by the terms 'right,' and 'wrong'?
13 What did Christ teach about the need, nature, and way of salvation?
14 Quote passages, both plain and parabolic, in which Christ speaks of Forgiveness. Detail some things which He says about it.
15 How is the word 'Kingdom' used in the teaching of Christ?
16 What is meant by the 'Kingdom of Heaven'? Answer in the light of what is said in Matthew xiii.
17 Is there any difference between the 'Kingdom of Heaven,' and the 'Kingdom of God's dear Son'? (Col. i. 13).
18 Is there any difference between the Kingdom and the Church?
19 What did Christ teach about Love? Give references.
20 In what parables does Christ enjoin Prayer? Name some of the lessons.
21 What evidence is there that Christ's was a life of prayer?
22 What prayers of Christ are recorded and where?

LITERATURE

'The Theology of the New Testament' - - G. B. Stevens
'The Teaching of Jesus' (2 vols.) - - - H. H. Wendt
'The Kingdom of God' - - - - - A. B. Bruce
'The Teaching of Jesus' - - - - - G. Jackson
'The Table Talk of Jesus' - - - - G. Jackson
'Our Lord's Teaching' - - - - - J. Robertson
'Ruling Ideas of Our Lord' - - - - C. F. D'Arcy

'Jesus and the Gospel'   -   -   -   -   -   J. Denney
'The Death of Christ'   -   -   -   -   -   J. Denney
'The Teaching of Christ' -   -   -   -   -   R. H. Horton
'The Mind of the Master'   -   -   -   -   J. Watson
'Keywords in the Teaching of Jesus'   -   -   A. T. Robertson
'The Words of Jesus'   -   -   -   -   -   Steir
'Studies in the Teaching of Our Lord'   -   -   H. B. Swete
'Principles of Theology'   -   -   -   -   -   Griffith Thomas
'The Central Teaching of Jesus Christ'   -   -   T. D. Bernard
'The Consciousness of Jesus'   -   -   -   -   Du Bose
'The Christ of History and Experience'   -   -   D. W. Forrest
'The Authority of Christ'   -   -   -   -   D. W. Forrest
'The Self-Portraiture of Jesus' -   -   -   -   Ross
'What Jesus Thought of Himself'   -   -   -   Stokes
'The Ethic of Jesus'   -   -   -   -   -   J. Stalker
'The Christian Experience of Forgiveness' -   -   H. R. Mackintosh
'The Teaching of Christ' -   -   -   -   G. Campbell Morgan
'Some Aspects of Christian Belief.'   Ch. iv   -   H. R. Mackintosh
'Lessons in the School of Prayer'   -   -   -   A. T. Pierson
'The Christian Experience of the Holy Spirit'   -   Wheeler Robinson
'The Prayer Life of Our Lord'   -   -   -   D. M. McIntyre
'The Prayers of Jesus Christ'   -   -   -   -   C. J. Vaughan
'The Holy Spirit of God'   -   -   -   -   Griffith Thomas
'The Parabolic Teaching of Christ'   -   -   -   A. B. Bruce
'Laws of Christ for Common Life'   -   -   -   R. W. Dale
'Christian Doctrine'   -   -   -   -   -   R. W. Dale

The literature on Christ's Teaching is vast, and the above is a small selection of useful books on the subject, to which should be added articles in the Bible Dictionaries.

14

THE DAY OF THE CRUCIFIXION

IN the 'Harmonistic Reading Outline of the Gospels,' presented
on pp. 68-81, as also in the 'Syllabus of the Gospel Story'
pp. 495-504), I have followed in the Last Week of our Lord's life,
the traditional time-reckoning of the Church from early times,
because the object of these Outlines is not to draw attention to
time so much as to *events*, and to have introduced the problem of
time without presenting explanatory notes would only have con-
fused the reader.

But the traditional view of the Last Week does not close the
inquiry, and if we come to the witness of the Gospels without
prepossessions and prejudices, I think we shall find that the
traditional view cannot be maintained, and, indeed, is contrary
to the recorded facts.

The accepted view is that Jesus was put upon the Cross at
9.0 a.m. on the Friday of Passion Week; that He died six hours
later, at 3.0 p.m.; and was buried before 6 p.m.; and that He
rose from the dead early on the following Sunday. This view
is perpetuated in the Christian Calendar by Good Friday and
Easter Sunday.

But the matter is by no means as simple as that. Against
such a view there are two fatal objections, namely, our Lord's
statement in Matt. xii. 40; and the number and nature of the
happenings between the death of Jesus and His burial.

(i) The 'Three Days and Three Nights'
(Matt. xii. 40, R.V.)

'As Jonah was three days and three nights in the belly of the
sea monster; so shall the Son of Man be three days and three
nights in the heart of the earth.'

To this statement must be added all the passages which speak
of '*after three days*' (Mark viii. 31; ix. 31, R.V.; x. 34, R.V.; Matt.
xxvii. 63; John ii. 19), and also all the passages which speak of '*the
third day*' (Matt. xvi. 21; xvii. 23; xx. 19; xxvii. 64; Luke ix.
22; xiii. 32; xviii. 33; xxiv. 7, 21, 46; Acts x. 40; 1 Cor. xv. 4).

That these two expressions were understood to mean the same thing seems clear from Matt. xxvii. 63, 64, which says: 'We remember that that impostor said, while He was yet alive, "*After three days* I will rise again." Command therefore that the sepulchre be made sure until *the third day*.'

Now, it is well known that the Jews reckoned any part of a day as a whole day. Rabbi Elazar ben Axaryah says: 'A day and a night are an *Onah* (Hebrew for a portion of time), and the portion of an *Onah* is as the whole of it.'

In this way it can be explained how Christ was three *Onoth*, or days, in the tomb between Friday evening and Sunday morning; a portion of the time on Friday before 6.0 p.m., the whole of Saturday, and a portion of the time after 6.0 p.m. on Saturday, the dawn of Sunday. But when the number of 'nights' is stated as well as the number of 'days,' the expression ceases to be an idiom, and becomes a literal statement of fact, and there were not three 'nights' between Friday evening and Sunday morning by any process of reckoning.

The expression, 'the third day,' which occurs twelve times (see refs. above) might be a part of three days, including two nights, but the expressions 'after three days,' which occurs five times (see refs. above), and 'three days and three nights' (Matt. xii. 40), cannot possibly be so reckoned, but must mean three days, each being preceded by a night; and so what our Lord said in Matt. xii. 40, cannot be explained by the Jewish use of the word *Onah*, but must mean just what it says, that He was to be in the tomb for three days and three nights, a period which the Friday theory does not allow of.

An early attempt to account for 'three nights' reckoned as a night the darkness from 12.0 to 3.0 p.m. on the Friday (Matt. xxvii. 45), a sorry strait to be put to. On the contrary Dr. W. C. Allen says: 'Matthew has, of course, rather forced his analogy.' But it was Christ, and not Matthew, Who said this!

Two simple diagrams will show that if the traditional time of the Crucifixion be correct, the references to it in the Gospels are inaccurate; but if this view be incorrect, and the outline in the summary on pp. 572, 573 be correct, the accuracy of the 'three days and three nights' of internment is established.

DIAGRAM I
The Traditional View

	14th	15th	16th	17th
THE MONTH NISAN (APRIL)				
JEWISH DAYS: SUNSET TO SUNSET	6 p.m.-6 p.m.	6 p.m-6 p.m.	6 p.m.-6 p.m	6 p.m.—
	Preparation	Crucifixion	Inhumation	Resurrection
	5th day	6th day	7th day	1st day
ROMAN DAYS: MIDNIGHT TO MIDNIGHT	Thursday	Friday	Saturday	Sunday

By this diagram it will be seen that the body of Jesus was in the tomb *only one night*, Friday-Saturday, as He rose after sundown on Saturday and before sunrise on Sunday; yet He said that His body would be there for *three nights*.

DIAGRAM II
The Reconstructed View

	14th	15th	16th	17th	18th
THE MONTH NISAN (APRIL)					
JEWISH DAYS: SUNSET TO SUNSET	6 p.m.-6 p.m.	6 p.m.-6 p.m.	6 p.m.-6 p.m.	6 p.m.-6 p.m.	6 p.m.
	Crucifixion	Passover Sabbath	Embalmment Anointing	Weekly Sabbath	Resurrection
	4th day	5th day	6th day	7th day	1st day
ROMAN DAYS: MIDNIGHT TO MIDNIGHT	Wednesday	Thursday	Friday	Saturday	Sunday
		"Three days and three nights in the heart of the earth" (Matt. xii. 40).			

(ii) *The Happenings between the Death and the Burial of Jesus*

If it be true that Jesus died at 3.0 p.m. on Friday, and was buried before 6.0 p.m. the same day—the latter event being necessary because the weekly Sabbath began at 6.0 p.m. on Friday, and lasted until 6.0 p.m. on Saturday—then, within those three hours the following events must have taken place:

1	The deputation of the Jews to Pilate - - -	John xix. 31
2	Pilate heard their request, and sent soldiers, or a messenger, from Jerusalem to Golgotha - -	——
3	Soldiers came and brake the legs of the two thieves, and pierced the side of Jesus - - - -	John xix. 32, 34
4	After this, Joseph of Arimathæa, went to Pilate and asked if he might take away Jesus' body	John xix. 38; Mark xv. 43
5	Pilate called a centurion and asked him if Jesus had been dead any while - - - - - -	Mark xv. 44
6	The centurion made inquiries, probably having to send to Golgotha, and reported to Pilate, who then gave a permit to Joseph to remove the body - -	Mark xv. 44, 45
7	Joseph went to the market, or bazaar, and bought fine linen, a transaction which would not be executed with speed - - - - - - -	Mark xv. 46
8	Joseph then went to Golgotha with the linen, and Pilate's permit, and presented the latter to the centurion on duty - - - - - - -	——
9	Having received the centurion's permission to take the body, Joseph, with the help of some of his friends or servants—for he could not do it alone—took down the body. They covered the body with a cloth, and tenderly carried it to Joseph's tomb -	Matt. xxvii. 59, 60 Mark xv. 46
10	Women from Galilee followed after - - -	Luke xxiii. 55
11	Joseph, with help, would remove the much soiled cloth, and wash the body of its bloodstains, after which it was wrapped in a single clean linen cloth, or sheet, without spices - Matt. xxvii. 59; Mark xv. 46; Luke xxiii. 53	
12	The body was then laid in Joseph's new tomb -	Matt. xxvii. 60; Mark xv. 46
13	During these operations the women watched, but did not help - - - - - - -	Matt. xxvii. 61
14	Joseph and his friends, or servants, rolled a great stone across the mouth of the tomb, and departed	Matt. xxvii. 60; Mark xvi. 4
15	The women returned to the city, having seen where and how the body was laid without embalming -	Luke xxiii. 55
16	Nicodemus, unknown to the women, procured a great quantity of very expensive spices, and with these made contact with Joseph - - -	John xix. 39
17	The women went to the market and bought raw materials for spices, which they prepared by grinding and cooking them - - - - -	Luke xxiii. 56
18	Joseph, Nicodemus, and servants no doubt, returned to the tomb, rolled away the stone, took off the single linen cloth in which the body was wrapped, and wound the limbs and the body in a number of bandages with spices - - - - -	John xix. 40
	They then wrapped the whole corpse in a single linen sheet, and the head separately in a napkin, and put the body back in its place - - -	John xx. 7
19	The stone was rolled again across the mouth of the tomb, and the men departed - - - -	——

20 The women having prepared the spices, rested on
the Sabbath, i.e. from Friday, 6.0 p.m., till Saturday, 6.0 p.m. - - - - - -   Luke xxiii. 56
On the first day of the week (Saturday after 6.0
p.m.), very early in the morning, the women came
to the sepulchre, bringing the spices which they
had prepared - - - - - -   Luke xxiv. 1

It must be admitted, surely, that all this could not have taken
place *within three hours*. No part of it can be relegated to Saturday
(i.e. Friday, 6.0 p.m. to Saturday, 6.0 p.m.), for that was the
Sabbath; the markets were all closed; linen and spices could
not be bought; no labour could be hired or engaged in after
the Sabbath had commenced; and after it was over would be
too late for these activities, as the women found, who came on
Sunday with their spices.

Unless we are to regard the Synoptics and the Fourth Gospel
as being in hopeless contradiction with one another, the Preparation of Matt. xxvi. 17-19; Mark xiv. 12-16; Luke xxii. 7-13,
must be the same as the Preparation of John xix. 31, and the
Sabbath in this last passage was not the weekly Sabbath, Friday
from 6.0 p.m., but another, earlier in the week, which is called
'*a high day*.' This 'high day' Sabbath, having been mistaken
from the earliest times for the weekly Sabbath, has led to all the
confusion as to when Christ was crucified.

We read, in Exod. xii. 3-8: 'In the tenth day of this month
they shall take to them every man a lamb . . . a lamb for a house.
Your lamb shall be without blemish . . . and ye shall keep it up
until the fourteenth day of the same month: and the whole
assembly of the congregation of Israel shall kill it in the evening.
And they shall eat the flesh in that night, roasted with fire.'

And in Lev. xxiii. 6, 7: 'And on the fifteenth day of the same
month is the Feast of Unleavened Bread unto the Lord; seven
days ye must eat unleavened bread. In the first day ye shall do
no servile work therein.'

On Monday, Nisan 12th, Jesus said to His disciples: 'Ye know
that after two days is the Feast of the Passover, and the Son of Man
is betrayed to be crucified' (Matt. xxvi. 1, 2; Mark xiv. 1). The
two days He mentions were Tuesday, the 13th, and Wednesday,
the 14th, and 'after two days' would be Thursday, the 15th.

The programme of these great and solemn days is as follows:

Day	Date	References	Events
SUNSET TO SUNSET	NISAN or ABIB		
THURS.-FRIDAY ...	9th	John xii. 1.	**Six Days before the Passover** Jesus came to Bethany.
FRI.-SATURDAY ... (*Sabbath*)	10th	John xii. 12-19; Mark xi. 1-11 (cf. Luke iv. 16); Zech. ix. 9.	**On the morrow**, the triumphal entry into Jerusalem. The lamb was chosen on Nisan 10th (Exod. xii. 3).
SAT.-SUNDAY ...	11th	Mark xi. 12-18.	**On the morrow**, fig tree cursed; Temple cleansed.
SUN.-MONDAY ...	12th	Mark xi. 20-25; xi. 27-xii. 44; xiii.	'**In the morning** . . . they come again to Jerusalem.' Fig tree incident recalled. Controversy with the authorities. Discourse on Olivet to the Apostles.
		Matt. xxvi. 1, 2.	Jesus' prediction: '**After two days the Passover cometh**'; that is on Thursday the 15th.
MON.-TUESDAY ...	13th	Matt. xxvi. 17-19; Mark xiv. 12-16; Luke xxii. 7-13.	Preparation made for the observance of the Passover.
		Mark xiv. 3-11; Matt. xxvi. 6-16; John xii. 2-8.	The Supper, and the anointing by Mary were probably on this day.
TUES.-WEDNESDAY	14th	John xiii. 1-20; Matt. xxvi. 20; Mark xiv. 17; Luke xxii. 14.	Jesus washes His Apostles' feet. He eats the Paschal Meal with His Apostles; points out the betrayer; and warns the Apostles against desertion.
		Matt. xxvi. 26-29; Mark xiv. 22-25; Luke xxii. 17-20; 1 Cor. xi. 23-26.	The Memorial of the Lord's Supper is instituted.

Day	Nisan	Scripture	Event
		John xiii. 21-xiv. 31.	The Upper Room Discourse.
		John xv-xvii. Matt. xxvi. 30, 36; Mark xiv. 26, 32; Luke xxii. 39, 40; John xviii. 1.	Discourse on the way to Gethsemane, and the Intercessory Prayer. The Agony in Gethsemane.
		Matt. xxvi. 47-68; Mark xiv. 43-65; Luke xxii. 47-65; John xviii. 2-24.	The Arrest and beginning of the Trials.
		Matt. xxvii. 1-30; Mark xv. 1-19; Luke xxii. 66-xxiii. 25; John xviii. 28-xix. 16.	Trials after dawn.
		Matt. xxvii. 31-56; Mark xv. 20-41; Luke xxiii. 26-49; John xix. 16-30.	The Journey to Calvary and the Crucifixion.
		Luke xxiii. 53, 54; John xix. 31-37.	The hasty entombment of the body at sundown, by Joseph.
WED.-THURSDAY ...	15th	Matt. xxvii. 62-66; John xix. 31.	The Passover Sabbath. 'The day of that Sabbath was a High Day,' which the weekly Sabbath never was.
THURS.-FRIDAY ...	16th	Mark xvi. 1; Luke xxiii. 56a.	Women bought spices with which to anoint Jesus' body, 'When the Sabbath was past,' i.e. the Passover Sabbath Nisan 15th, not the weekly Sabbath, which was the next day.
		John xix. 39, 40. Matt. xxvii. 62-66.	Nicodemus and Joseph embalm Jesus' body. The Tomb is sealed and a guard set.
FRID.-SATURDAY	17th	Luke xxiii. 56b.	The Jewish weekly Sabbath.
SAT.-SUNDAY ...	18th	Matt. xxviii. 1; Mark xvi. 2; Luke xxiv. 1; John xx. 1.	After sunset on Nisan 17th, our Lord rose from the dead, and the discovery was made by some women early on Sunday morning.

Just after sunset, on Nisan 17th, our Lord rose from the dead, and the discovery was made by some women early on Sunday morning, Nisan 18th (Matt. xxviii. 1-10 ; Mark xvi. 1-18 ; Luke xxiv. 1-49; John xx. 1-23).

By this calendar, instead of having three hours only, from 3.0 p.m. to 6.0 p.m. on Friday, for the twenty events tabulated on p. 572, there were the three hours, from 3.0 p.m. to 6.0 p.m. on Wednesday, and the whole of Friday. Thursday and Saturday could not be used, both being Sabbaths.

If this calendar is correct, Joseph hurriedly buried Jesus' body on Wednesday, before 6.0 p.m., and he, with Nicodemus, would embalm it on Friday. The markets being open on this Friday they and the women would be able to buy what spices they wanted.

Remarkable confirmation of the view that the embalming was not done at the time the body of Jesus was buried, but much later, is found in the exact use of two words. In the passages which record the taking of the body from the Cross and wrapping it in a 'linen cloth,' the word, *sindōn*, is used, which was one piece of linen, and not several pieces (Matt. xxvii. 59; Mark xv. 46 (twice); Luke xxiii. 53; cf. Mark xiv. 51, 52); but in the passages which tell of the embalming, the word *othonion* is used, which means a linen bandage, and in each occurrence it is in the plural, 'linen cloths' (*othonia*), and is associated with the aromatics (John xix. 40; xx. 5, 6, 7; Luke xxiv. 12). The procedure was as follows:

On the Wednesday, Nisan 14th, before 6.0 p.m., Jesus' body was taken from the Cross, wrapped in a linen sheet, and hastily buried. There it lay through Thursday, Nisan 15th, the Passover Sabbath. On Friday, Nisan 16th, Joseph and Nicodemus went to the tomb, removed the *sindōn*, and bandaged the limbs and body in linen cloths, *othonia*, with spices, with a separate piece for the head (John xx. 6, 7).

Some who reject the Friday theory hold that the crucifixion was on the Thursday, and not on Wednesday. As long as a matter is arguable it should be kept in view and its evidence examined, and not a little can be said for the Thursday view, but the Friday theory cannot be maintained.

It has been well said: 'However the tradition of Good Friday may have arisen, it has been thoroughly proved that it is quite incompatible with a due consideration of the Gospel narratives. Moreover, it provides much capital for many forcible infidel arguments, by introducing many apparent contradictions, the blows from which the traditionists try to parry by resorting to very unsatisfactory shuffling sophisms, which undermine confidence in the solidity of the truth of the Word of God. Therefore those who love the Lord, not only with all their heart, but also, as Jesus enjoins (Matt. xxii. 37, and Mark xii. 30), with all their mind, and are willing to have expounded unto them the way of God more perfectly (Acts xviii. 26), and thus become enlightened, are compelled by the Spirit of truth (John xiv. 17) to abandon the tradition of Good Friday being the day on which our Saviour was crucified.'

Of course, what matters first and last is that Jesus died for us, and the day of His death in no way affects its virtue, but as students of and believers in the Scriptures we should endeavour to know the facts of any given matter, especially when a tradition which has been held for centuries exposes the records to the charge of being historically unreliable.

QUESTIONS

1 On what ground is it claimed that Christ was crucified on a Friday?
2 Name a dozen events which took place between Christ's death and His resurrection.
3 What is meant by 'a high day' in John xix. 31?
4 When was the body of Jesus embalmed?
5 What is the significance of the words *sindōn* and *othonia*?
6 Could Jesus have been three 'nights' in the tomb?

LITERATURE

'What was the Day of the Crucifixion?' - Norman J. Denham
'The Hebrew Calendar Cycle' - - - Norman J. Denham
'The Harmony of the Last Week' - - E. C. Callaway
'Good Friday' - - - - - - James Gall
Hastings' Dictionary of the Bible. Articles: 'Jesus Christ,' 'Lord's Supper,' 'Passover,' 'Preparation Day.'
'Elements of the Jewish and Mohammedan Calendars' - - - - - S. B. Burnaby
Encyclopædia of Religious Knowledge—Article: 'Easter' - - - - - - Schaff-Herzog

37

15

THE SEVEN SAYINGS ON THE CROSS

(i) The Significance of the Sayings

LAST words are always important and are carefully stored in the memory, especially the last words of the dying, of the martyrs, of people who have been great leaders, inventors, discoverers, writers, and of our own loved ones. But all the greatest last words which have ever been uttered throughout all time are not of comparable significance and value with the Seven Sayings of Jesus on the Cross, and just because no one before or since can be compared with Him, no one before or since has been at once Perfect Man and Very God. It is His Divine-Human Personality that gives all that He ever said its value.

(ii) The Number of the Sayings

' That there should be exactly seven, the sacred and mystical number of Scripture, is itself not without its significance' (Trench) No Evangelist records all of them, but each Evangelist records some of them. Matthew and Mark have one; Luke has three, and John has three. They are:

Sayings	References
1 'Father, forgive them: for they know not what they do'	Luke xxiii. 34
2 'To-day shalt thou be with Me in Paradise'	Luke xxiii. 43
3 'Woman, behold thy son. . . . Behold, thy mother'	John xix. 27
4 'Eloi, Eloi, lama sabachthani?'	Matt. xxvii. 46; Mark xv. 34
5 'I thirst'	John xix. 28
6 'It is finished'	John xix. 30
7 'Father, into Thy hands I commend My spirit'	Luke xxiii. 46

It is strange that only one of these Sayings, the fourth, or central one, should be recorded by two of the Apostles, Matthew and Peter, from whom, no doubt, Mark got it. It was at Gethsemane, when Jesus was arrested, that 'all the disciples left Him and fled' (Mark xiv. 50; Matt. xxvi. 56); but they must have rallied again as, later, John and Peter are found in 'the Court of the High Priest' (John xviii. 15, 16), and, later still, Peter 'followed Him afar off' (Mark xiv. 54, et. al.), and John was at the Cross (John xix. 27). In all likelihood, therefore, the other Apostles, except Judas, were near the Cross, and must have heard more than one of Christ's Sayings as two of them were spoken in a 'loud voice' (Mark xv. 34; Luke xxiii. 46). Luke, who was not there at all, has three Sayings which the other Evangelists do not record, the first, second, and seventh. From whom did he get them? Probably from Mary the mother of Jesus. It is quite understandable that the Apostle John, writing at the close of the first century, and supplementing the Synoptic Gospels, would record the three sayings which were not already written, the third, fifth, and sixth.

(iii) THE ORDER OF THE SAYINGS

The order given above is agreed upon by most expositors, and an examination of it will reveal how eminently significant that order is. The first, fourth (central), and seventh are addressed to the Almighty, the first and seventh to Him as 'Father,' and the fourth to Him as 'God.' The first three relate to those around the dying Saviour, and the last four relate to Himself only. Christ's first consideration was for others.

(iv) THE TIME OF THE SAYINGS

Jesus was on the Cross for six hours. The 'third hour' (Mark xv. 25) was 9.0 a.m.; the 'sixth hour' (Mark xv. 33) was 12.0 noon; and the 'ninth hour' (Mark xv. 33) was 3.0 p.m.

These six hours were divided into two periods of three hours each by darkness coming over the whole land at noon (Luke xxiii. 44). The first three Sayings were uttered in the first three hours, in daylight; and the last four Sayings were uttered in the last three hours, in darkness. These facts are significant when it is observed that the last four Sayings only are dominated by the idea of Atonement.

(v) THE ROOTS OF THE SAYINGS

All these Sayings have their roots in the Jews' Bible, the Old Testament; some of them manifestly, and some of them inferentially.

THE SAYING	THE SOURCE
1 'Father, forgive them: for they know not what they do' (Luke xxiii. 34)	'He made intercession for the transgressors' (Isa. liii. 12)
2 'To-day shalt thou be with Me in Paradise' (Luke xxiii. 43)	'He shall see His seed; He shall prolong His days; He shall see of the travail of His soul' (Isa. liii. 10, 11).
3 'Woman, behold, thy son . . . Behold, thy mother' (John xix. 27)	Illustrating duty to parents (Exod. xx. 12; Mark vii. 10-13)
4 'Eloi, Eloi, lama sabachthani?' (Mark xv. 34; Matt. xxvii. 46). Spoken probably in Hebrew	Verbatim from Psalm xxii. 1
5 'I thirst' (John xix. 28)	'In My thirst they gave Me vinegar to drink' (Psa. lxix. 21)
6 'It is finished' (John xix. 30)	'They shall come, and shall declare His righteousness unto a people that shall be born, that *He hath done this*' (lxx. is *tetelestai*, meaning 'accomplished,' or 'finished') (Psa. xxii. 31). This is significant in a Psalm which begins as the 22nd does!
7 'Father, into Thy hands I commend My spirit' (Luke xxiii. 46)	'Into Thine hand I commit My spirit' (Psa. xxxi. 5).

Surely it cannot but impress us that in these hours of agony Jesus, breaking His silence, should express His deepest thoughts and feelings in words written long centuries before.

JERUSALEM

FORMS OF THE NAME:

Hierosolyma; Hierousalem; Hierusalem; Ierousalem;
Solyma; Urusale(i)m; Yerushalaim; Yerushalem.

DERIVATION: "Almost impossible to descry" (G.A.S.).
'Shalem casts the lot'; 'Secure lot'; 'Hearth of peace.'
(*Jerusalem*. Vol. I, Chap. ix. George Adam Smith).

OTHER DESCRIPTIONS:

Ariel. *City* of Judah, of God, of our God, of the Great
King, of Jahweh of Hosts, of David. The Holy City.
The City of Righteousness. *Daughter* of Zion, of Jeru-
salem, of My people. Virgin daughter of Sion.
(*Jerusalem*. Vol. I, Chap. x. George Adam Smith).

ELEVATION:

2593 feet above sea level.

GATES:

Damascus; Double; Dung; First; Fish; Fountain;
Garden; Golden; Herod's; Horse; Jaffa; Sheep; Single;
Sion; St. Stephen's; Valley; Water; Zion.

TEMPLES:

Solomon's, B.C. 970; Zerubbabel's, B.C. 520-516; Herod's,
B.C. 20-19—A.D. 27 (John ii. 20).

VALLEYS:

Hinnom; Kidron; Tyropoeon.

JERUSALEM

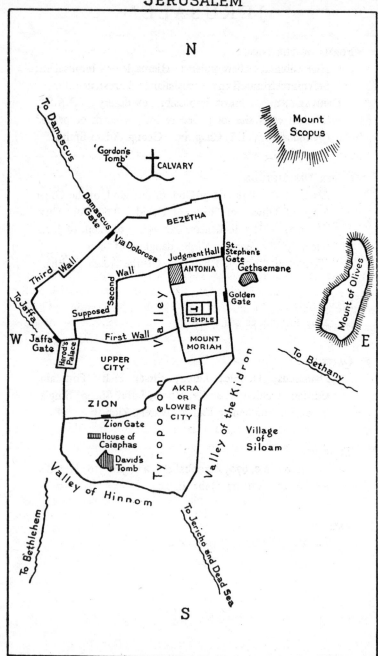

MAP VIII

(vi) AN ANALYSIS OF THE SAYINGS

These seven Sayings may be variously divided, and no legitimate classification is without its significance. We may say that the first three are characterized by *thoughtfulness*; the fourth and fifth, by *travail*; the sixth and seventh by *triumph*.

(a) Christ's Thoughtfulness

In the first three, which reveal Christ's consideration for others, three parties are in view: His cruel enemies; a repentant sinner; and His faithful followers. For the first He offers a prayer; to the second He gives a promise; for the third He makes a provision. In the first we see Him as Interceder; in the second, as Rewarder; and in the third, as Sympathizer.

(b) Christ's Travail

Here, in the fourth and fifth Sayings, two aspects of His unspeakable anguish are disclosed: His mental anguish in the cry: 'My God, my God, why hast Thou forsaken Me?' the central Saying of the seven; and His physical anguish in the cry, 'I thirst.' In these cries His Divine and human natures are revealed.

(c) Christ's Triumph

In the sixth and seventh Sayings the victory of the Cross is proclaimed. The sixth tells of Christ's satisfaction relative to the *past*. It was not, as the Jews supposed, that Christ was finished, but that the work He came to do was finished; the will of God had been perfectly done; man's redemption was now complete; salvation could now be offered to all, and already a sinner dying by Jesus' side had embraced it.

The seventh Saying is one of perfect and joyful resignation; a yielding up of Himself in death to His Father. It expresses Christ's satisfaction relative to the *future*. His first and last Sayings were addressed to His 'Father.'

We have called attention to the fact that there are *seven* Sayings, and like most, if not all, occurrences of this number, it is divided into three and four (see p. 314), and the substance, order, and relation of these two groups are of profound import (see p. 585).

DIAGRAMMATIC SUMMARY
Time of the Sayings

First Three Hours : 9-12 a.m.		Second Three Hours : 12-3 p.m.	
1 'Father, forgive them; for they know not what they do.'	Luke xxiii. 34	4 'Eloi, Eloi, lama sabachthani?' ...	Matt. xxvii. 4 Mark xv. 34
2 'To-day shalt thou be with Me in Paradise.'	Luke xxiii. 43	5 'I thirst'	John xix. 28
		6 'It is finished' ...	John xix. 30
3 'Woman, behold, thy son. . . . Behold, thy mother.'	John xix. 27	7 'Father, into Thy hands I commend My spirit' ...	Luke xxiii. 4

Centre of the Sayings

	4	
1 'Father, forgive them; for they know not what they do' ...	'Eli, Eli, lama sabach- thani?' (Matt.)	5 'I thirst.'
2 'To-day shalt thou be with Me in Paradise'	'Eloi, Eloi, lama sabach- thani?' (Mark)	6 'It is finished.'
3 'Woman, behold, thy son. . . . Behold, thy mother'	'My God, my God, why hast thou forsaken Me?'	7 'Father, into Thy hands I commend My spirit.'

Roots of the Sayings

Gospels		Old Testament
Luke xxiii. 34	1	Isaiah liii. 12
Luke xxiii. 43	2	Isaiah liii. 10, 11
John xix. 27	3	Exod. xx. 12; cf. Mark vii. 10-13
Matt. xxvii. 46; Mark xv. 34	4	Psalm xxii. 1
John xix. 28	5	Psalm lxix. 21
John xix. 30	6	Psalm xxii. 31
Luke xxiii. 46	7	Psalm xxxi. 5

Analysis of the Sayings

I. Christ's Thoughtfulness	1 A Prayer for Cruel Enemies	Luke xxiii. 34
	2 A Promise to a Repentant Sinner ...	Luke xxiii. 43
	3 A Provision for Faithful Followers ...	John xix. 27
II. Christ's Travail ...	4 His Mental Anguish	Matt. xxvii. 46 Mark xv. 34
	5 His Physical Anguish	John xix. 28
III. Christ's Triumph ...	6 His Satisfaction Relative to the Past ...	John xix. 30
	7 His Satisfaction Relative to the Future	Luke xxiii. 46

(vii) Notes on the Sayings

(1) 'Father, forgive them; for they know not what they do'
(Luke xxiii. 34)

'These words are missing in some of the oldest authorities. They are found, however, in the majority of the most ancient manuscripts, and in the most trustworthy of the old Versions, and are undoubtedly genuine.'—(Dean Spence).

'The words, of course, may well have been handed down in a genuine tradition, even if they were not recorded by Luke. . . . Absence from certain MSS. is not necessarily evidence of interpolation.'—(Canon Streeter).

'While it is not certain that it is a part of Luke's Gospel, it is certain that Jesus spoke these words, for they are utterly unlike anyone else.'—(Prof. A. T. Robertson).

Christ's first and last Sayings begin with 'Father.'

It is probable that this Saying was uttered as Jesus was being put on the Cross. There is difference of opinion as to who is meant by 'them.' The views held are: (a) the Romans (Dean Alford; Prof. A. T. Robertson): (b) the Jews (Dr. Plummer): (c) both Jews and Romans (A. Watson): (d) all mankind (Bishop How).

Can there be forgiveness without repentance? (Page 564).

By 'they know not what they do' is meant, 'they do not know *who* it is that they are crucifying.' Christ is speaking out of a Divine consciousness.

Ignorance mitigates the criminality of sin, but never exonerates it (1 Cor. ii. 8).

Was this prayer answered? The Jews are not forgiven yet.

(2) 'To-day shalt thou be with Me in Paradise'
(Luke xxiii. 43)

This is not to be read, as some have affirmed: 'Verily I say unto thee to-day, thou shalt be with Me in Paradise' (in the remote future). That the words were spoken to the man on that day is of itself evident. What Jesus declared was that He and the penitent sinner would be in Paradise that day, in a few hours' time. To hear this must have brought great consolation to His mother, the Magdalene, John, and other of His friends who were present!

'The promise implies the continuance of consciousness after death. If the dead are unconscious, the assurance to the robber that he will be with Christ after death would be empty of consolation'—(Plummer).

Prof. A. T. Robertson says that, 'Paradise is used here not for any supposed intermediate state, but the very bliss of heaven itself.' This, however, cannot be, for in resurrection the Lord said to Mary: 'Touch Me not; for I am not yet ascended to my Father' (John xx. 17), and from Psa. xvi. 10; Acts ii. 31, we learn that He descended into *Shēol*, the Hebrew for the Greek *Hadēs*, which is not *Heaven*. It appears that *Paradise* (*paradeisos*), was one part of Hades, that part to which the blessed went; the other part for the wicked, being *Gehenna* (*geenna*). That Paradise was in Heaven in Paul's time (2 Cor. xii. 2, 4) implies that at the resurrection a change took place, and that Hades was emptied of Paradise. Is not this the explanation of Eph. iv. 8-10? (See 1 Peter iii. 18, 19). (See Index IV).

This is the only instance we have of our Lord's using the word 'Paradise.' The New Testament writers, Luke, Paul, and John use it. Luke may have got this Saying from Jesus' mother, and, no doubt, John heard it at the Cross (2 Cor. xii. 4; Rev. ii. 7).

The promise distinguishes between the body and the spirit. The body of the robber was thrown into a hole, and the body of Jesus was laid in Joseph's tomb, but the spirits of both went, that day, to Paradise.

(3) *'Woman, behold, thy son . . . behold, thy mother'*
(John xix. 27)

Observe that Jesus uses the words 'mother,' and 'woman,' in this Saying, but not as we might have supposed. We would not have expected Him to speak of His own mother as John's mother, especially as Salome, John's mother was standing by (Mark xv. 40). And we would have expected Him to speak of His own mother as 'mother,' but He does not. He had spoken to her like this before (John ii. 4).

The view adopted by Luthardt, Alford, and others, that by addressing Mary as 'woman,' Jesus was separating Himself in His mediatorial character from all relationship with the mother who bore Him, is not to be entertained. No harshness and no disrespect attaches to the word 'woman'; indeed, it was a highly respectful and affectionate mode of address (cf. John xx. 13, 15).

Had Jesus called her 'mother' He would have exposed her to the mockery or persecution of His enemies who were standing by.

Mary was *the woman* whose *Seed* was now bruising the head of the Serpent (Gen. iii. 15).

'Thy son.' John was Mary's nephew, but he was to be a son to her. Mary had other sons, James, Simon, Joseph, and Jude, but they were not at the Cross, and they were not yet disciples; they had not accepted the claims of Jesus or believed in His mission. Jesus' cousin became His mother's son. The Romish idea, that the Lord commended all His disciples as represented by the beloved one, to the patronage of His mother, is simply absurd. 'Woman, behold, thy son.' Mary was committed to the care of John, and we read, 'from that hour the disciple took her unto his own home' (27).

When John went to Ephesus he must have taken Mary with him, if she were still living. 'How stupendous a legacy was this for divine piety to bequeath, and for human love to inherit!' The Divine Son was true to His Father in heaven, and to His mother on earth.

Dr. J. H. Bernard points out that in the first three Sayings is observable 'a narrowing of the circle of interest, as death draws near.' The first Saying is wide, the forgiveness of enemies. The second, is narrower, being addressed to a penitent thief. But at last His attention is fixed upon His relatives, and those of them who are dearest to Him, His mother, and 'the disciple whom He loved.' 'These are the stages of the approach of death, for the Perfect Man.'

(4) '*My God, My God, why hast Thou forsaken Me?*'
(Matt. xxvii. 46; Mark xv. 34)

This is the central of the seven Sayings, and the very heart of Christ's redemptive Passion.

This is the only one of the seven Sayings of Christ given by two Evangelists, and it is the only Saying given by these two, Matthew and Mark.

This is the only sentence of any length in Aramaic preserved in Matthew.

This is the first Saying uttered in the darkness of the second three hours, that is, after 12.0 noon (Matt. xxvii. 45), and it was uttered 'about the ninth hour,' about 3.0 p.m.

Dr. Fausset says of the darkness: 'This could not have been an eclipse of the sun, for the Passover was celebrated at the time of full moon, when the moon is opposite to the sun.'

Both Matthew and Mark give the Saying in Aramaic, with the interpretation in Greek, and the translation is that of the Septuagint (LXX). Mark more exactly follows the Greek of Psalm xxii. 1. (See Index IV).

Only this and the final Saying are said to have been uttered 'in a loud voice.'

The exact wording of the cry in Matthew and Mark remains a problem which cannot be solved with any certainty.

In Sayings one and seven, Jesus says 'Father,' but here He says 'God,' 'as being in a degree estranged.'—(Bengel).

'Forsaken,' is not in the *perfect* tense (A.V.), but in the *aorist*, the difference being between something that 'has been done,' and something that 'was,' at a certain moment, done. The implication is that during the three hours of darkness Christ had been in silence enduring this utter desolation, which had now come to its climax. If this is so, the coming of the darkness was the moment of the forsaking.

This fathomless utterance must be listened to from a great distance, for who can comprehend it? In this hour Christ was bearing the sins of the whole world. The LORD had 'laid on Him the iniquity of us all.' He was 'left' that He might bear man's sins in their full and crushing weight, and by bearing, save.

The so-called *Gospel of Peter* translates this Saying as: 'My power, my power, thou hast forsaken Me.' This seems to show that this Writing favoured the Docetic view that the *aeon* Christ came on the man Jesus at His Baptism, and left Him on the Cross, so that only the man Jesus died.

Though Jesus did not say 'Father' in this cry, He did say 'My God,' confident that in this most awful experience God was still His.

(5) 'I Thirst' (John xix. 28)

At the beginning of His anguish the stupefying draught, usually given to sufferers by crucifixion, Jesus had refused (Matt. xxvii. 34, 48), and now He has the torment of thirst caused by raging fever.

He who began His ministry by *hungering*, ended it by *thirsting*.

He who was the Rock whence Israel in the desert was refreshed (1 Cor. x. 4), and He who turned the water into wine (John ii.), now thirsts.

This was His last suffering, and was a fulfilment of Scripture (Psalm lxix. 21).

Although only John records the cry, yet the incident of the Lord's thirst being assuaged is given elsewhere (Matt. xxvii. 48; Mark xv. 36).

He, who, when once before He was thirsty, asked for water of a Samaritan woman (John iv. 7), now, at the hands of His enemies, receives vinegar.

The thirst of Jesus is a refutation of the Docetic doctrine that He only appeared to be man, but was not so in reality.

John sees in this part of Jesus' sufferings all the yearnings of His soul. He thirsts after the salvation of the world, after the glorifying of the Father. He thirsts after the song of redemption.

Because He thirsted for us, we should 'thirst after the living God,' and if we do so we shall be among those of whom it is said: 'They shall hunger no more, neither thirst any more,' for, 'the Lamb, who is in the midst of the Throne, shall feed them, and shall lead them *unto living fountains of waters*' (Rev. vii. 16, 17, A.V.).

(6) 'It is Finished' (John xix. 30)

Jesus had said: 'My meat is to do the will of Him that sent Me, and to *finish* His work' (John iv. 34). He spake of 'the works which the Father had given (Him) to *finish*' (John v. 36). In prayer He said: 'I have *finished* the work Thou gavest Me to do' (John xvii. 4). And He 'knowing that all things are now *finished*, said—' (John xix. 28). So at last He could say, 'It is *finished.*' All that the law required, all that prophecy forecast, all that the types foreshadowed, all that the promises proclaimed, all that all the ages had striven for, all was *finished.*

Krummacher well says: 'At these words you hear fetters burst, and prison walls falling down; barriers as high as heaven are overthrown, and gates which had been closed for thousands of years again move on their hinges.'

This was a cry of victory in the hour of seeming defeat. Redemption is accomplished. It would seem that in order to utter this word with a 'loud voice,' Jesus asked for an assuagement of His thirst; to speak this word of triumph His parched throat must be cooled. 'When He had, therefore taken the vinegar, He cried, "It is finished".'

(7) 'Father, into Thy hands I commend my spirit' (Luke xxiii. 46)

This is the last Saying, and reveals the voluntariness of Jesus' death. It asserts that the soul will exist apart from the body in the hands of God. Jesus' passing was tranquil and triumphant. He ended His ministry with a Scripture on His lips (Psalm xxxi. 5), even as He began it (Matt. iv. 4, 7, 10). Col. ii. 15 may refer to this cry.

By the *tree* Paradise was lost, and by the *tree* it was regained. Like His birth, Christ's death was the only one of its kind. Stephen also commended his spirit to God (Acts vii. 59).

Huss, on his way to the funeral pile, repeatedly said: 'I commit my spirit into Thine hands, O Lord.'

QUESTIONS

1 Write from memory the Seven Sayings on the Cross, in the order of utterance.

2 How many of the Seven Sayings are given by each of the Evangelists? and say which they are.

3 How are the Seven Sayings distributed in the six hours of Jesus' Passion?

4 Are the Seven Sayings related in any way to Old Testament Scriptures, and if so, to which of them?

5 What is the teaching of the Seven Sayings on Forgiveness, Immortality, Paradise, Human Affection and Obligation, being God-forsaken, the Work of Christ, and on Resignation?

16

THE DEATH OF CHRIST

THE Day of the Crucifixion is of historical interest, but what is of moral, spiritual, and eternal importance is the Crucifixion itself; not *when* Christ died but *that* He died is what matters. Dr. Denney has said that 'the death of Christ has not the place assigned to it, either in preaching or in theology, which it has in the New Testament.'

The contents of this Guide are largely factual, but it is necessary in this Christological part of the study to touch upon some of the mysteries of theology and religion, because the Gospels give much attention to these matters. This reference to the subject must be brief, and will be inadequate, but if it points out a line of thought, and encourages the pursuit of it, it will have been worth while. Space will not allow of an examination of modern critical views on the subject of Christ's death, nor is it necessary, as much has been written on this, but we assume the genuineness of the Gospels, and so it remains only to understand, as far as possible, what is meant by what is said on this subject. When Jesus spoke to His Apostles about His death, Mark says, 'they understood not the saying, and were afraid to ask Him' (ix. 32), and Luke is more explicit: 'It was concealed from them, that they should not perceive it' (ix. 45, R.V.), and although we are in a better position to understand, yet, like the women who were at the crucifixion, we, too, can behold only 'afar off' (Matt. xxvii. 55).

A vast library has been written on the subject of Christ's death, presenting now one aspect of it, and now another, but just because the finite cannot comprehend the infinite, the significance of this event cannot be stated in theological formulas. We pursue the theme, and yet it is ever beckoning us on.

Men of all schools of theological thought have stated what they have regarded to be the significance of that event, but what matters first and last is what Christ thought of His death, and if we would know this we must turn to the Gospels which, as Dr. Denney says, 'describe the sufferings and death of Christ with a minuteness which has no parallel in their narratives of other events of His life, and they all, to a certain extent, by references to the fulfilment of Old Testament prophecy or otherwise, indicate their sense of its meaning and importance.'

In the main, there are two views regarding Christ's attitude towards His death. One is known as the *historical* theory, and the other, as the *dogmatic*. According to the historical reading of the life of Jesus, 'He never looked for death, and least of all for crucifixion, so that in the end He passed away disillusioned, with words of despair on His lips, amid the darkness of physical nature, and with deeper darkness in His soul.'

According to the dogmatic reading Jesus came into this world in order to die, and from the very outset of His ministry consciously looked forward to death. In the one view the death was brought about inevitably by a recognizable series and sequence of events in Israel, and in the other view it was the historical precipitation of an eternal purpose, an eternal design materializing at a point of time.

It may be said at once that the *historical* view is rational and radical, and that the *dogmatic* view is Scriptural, and therefore true. It has been affirmed that the views expressed in the Gospels were derived largely from the teaching of Paul, but the opposite would seem to be the truth, namely that Paul's teaching is derived from the teaching of Jesus in the Synoptic Gospels, which include the Oral Tradition. The roots of the Pauline teaching are in these Gospels. Those who will not admit the Fourth Gospel as evidence of what Christ thought of His death, have still to reckon with the earliest of the Gospels, Mark's, which has many profound statements on the subject, with parallels in one or both the other Synoptics. (Pages 537-540).

All that we attempt here is to collect the material which shows how Christ regarded His death.

(1) **The Synoptic Gospels**

MARK ii. 18-20 (R.V.)	MATT. ix. 14, 15 (R.V.)	LUKE v. 33-35 (R.V.)
(18) John's disciples and the Pharisees were fasting: and they come and say unto Him, 'Why do John's disciples and the disciples of the Pharisees fast, but Thy disciples fast not?'	(14) Then come to Him the disciples of John, saying, 'Why do we and the Pharisees fast oft, but Thy disciples fast not?'	(33) And they said unto Him, 'The disciples of John fast often, and make supplications; likewise also the disciples of the Pharisees; but Thine eat and drink.'
(19) And Jesus said unto them, 'Can the sons of the bride-chamber fast, while the bridegroom is with them? As long as they have the bridegroom with them they cannot fast.	(15) And Jesus said unto them, 'Can the sons of the bride-chamber mourn as long as the bridegroom is with them?	(34) And Jesus said unto them, 'Can ye make the sons of the bride-chamber fast while the bridegroom is with them?
(20) But the days will come when the bridegroom shall be taken away from them, and then they will fast in that day.'	But the days will come when the bridegroom shall be taken away from them, and then will they fast.'	(35) But the days will come when the bridegroom shall be taken away from them, then will they fast in those days.'

Various attempts have been made to get rid of the obvious meaning of Mark ii. 20, and parallels. It has been said (*a*) that these are not the words of Jesus; (*b*) that they are displaced, and do not belong to this parable; (*c*) that they point to the passing apprehension of a possible sorrowful interruption of bridal joy; (*d*) that the utterance is conditional and not absolute; (*e*) that the words do not necessarily refer to a violent or premature or unnatural death, but merely to the parting which is inevitable in the case of all human relations.

Against all this is the fact that the words are in all the Synoptics, and that the word 'taken-away' (*apairō*) occurs in these three passages only, in the New Testament, and only in the *aorist passive*. If Jesus had meant to say that He would *go-away* from them, He would have said that, but what He does say points (for the first time) to His *violent death*.

MARK viii. 31 (R.V.)	MATT. xvi. 21 (R.V.)	LUKE ix. 22 (R.V.)
He began to teach them, that the Son of Man must suffer many things, and be rejected by the elders, and the chief priests, and the scribes, and be killed, and after three days rise again.	From that time began Jesus to show unto His disciples, how that He must go unto Jerusalem, and suffer many things of the elders, and chief priests, and scribes, and be killed, and the third day be raised up.	The Son of Man must suffer many things, and be rejected of the elders and chief priests and scribes, and be killed, and the third day be raised up.

MARK ix. 31 (R.V.)	MATT. xvii. 22, 23 (R.V.)	LUKE ix. 43, 44 (R.V.)
He taught His disciples, and said unto them, 'The Son of Man is delivered up into the hands of men, and they shall kill Him; and when He is killed, after three days He shall rise again.'	Jesus said unto them, 'The Son of Man shall be delivered up into the hands of men; and they shall kill Him, and the third day He shall be raised up.'	He said unto His disciples, 'Let these words sink into your ears; for the Son of Man shall be delivered up into the hands of men.'

MARK x. 32-34 (R.V.)	MATT. xx. 17-19 (R.V.)	LUKE xviii. 31-33 (R.V.)
(32) And they were in the way going up to Jerusalem; and Jesus was going before them: and they were amazed; and they that followed were afraid. And He took again the Twelve, and began to tell them the things that were to happen unto Him, saying,	(17) As Jesus was going up to Jerusalem, He took the twelve disciples apart, and in the way He said unto them,	(31) And He took unto Him the Twelve, and said unto them, 'Behold, we go up to Jerusalem, and all the things that are written by the prophets shall be accomplished unto the Son of Man.
(33) 'Behold, we go up to Jerusalem; and the Son of Man shall be delivered unto the chief priests and the scribes; and they shall condemn Him to death, and shall deliver Him unto the Gentiles:	(18) 'Behold, we go up to Jerusalem; and the Son of Man shall be delivered unto the chief priests and scribes; and they shall condemn Him to death,	(32) For He shall be delivered up unto the Gentiles, and shall be mocked, and shamefully entreated, and spit upon;
(34) And they shall mock Him, and shall spit upon Him, and shall scourge Him, and shall kill Him; and after three days He shall rise again.'	(19) And shall deliver Him unto the Gentiles to mock, and to scourge, and to crucify; and the third day He shall be raised up.'	(33) And they shall scourge and kill Him; and the third day He shall rise again.'

In these passages Jesus' teaching on the subject of His approaching death—about nine months distant—is quite unmistakable. Peter's confession at Cæsarea Philippi that 'Jesus is the Christ, the Son of the living God,' constituted a crisis alike for Christ and for His Apostles, for we read: 'From that time forth—' (Matt. xvi. 21), a phrase used to mark a previous crisis (Matt. iv. 17). The attitude of the Jews and their officials to Jesus led Him to turn from them and henceforth to devote Himself largely to the instruction of that small group of men who were the nucleus of the Christian Church; from now there is less preaching and more teaching, and His subject is less the Kingdom and more Himself, and in particular His death.

From the above references it will be seen that on three occasions Jesus solemnly informed this inner circle of the coming event. In the first instance, Peter made his presumptuous protest; in the second, the disciples remained silent; and in the third, they were overawed by the manner of the Master (Mark viii. 32; ix. 32; x. 32). The one point in which all the narratives agree is that Jesus taught that He *must* go up to Jerusalem and die (Mark viii. 31; Matt. xvi. 21; Luke ix. 22).

This *must*, as Dr. Denney says, may be one of 'outward constraint,' pointing to the inevitability of His death, or one of 'inward constraint,' pointing to the indispensability of His holy Passion. 'The Divine necessity for a career of suffering and death . . . belongs . . . to our Lord's consciousness of what He is and what He is called to do; it is not deduced from the malignant necessities by which He is encompassed; it rises up within Him, in Divine power, to encounter these outward necessities and subdue them. . . . The necessity of His death, in other words, is not a dreary, incomprehensible somewhat that He is compelled to reckon with by untoward circumstances; for Him it is given, so to speak, with the very conception of His person and His work.'—(Denney).

The disciples would have understood their Master's meaning if they had rightly understood Isaiah liii, and such-like passages.

Mark x. 35-40 (r.v.)	Matthew xx. 20-23 (r.v.)
(38) Are ye able to drink the cup that I drink? or to be baptized with the baptism that I am baptized with? (39) The cup that I drink ye shall drink; and with the baptism that I am baptized withal shall ye be baptized.	(22) Are ye able to drink the cup that I am about to drink? (23) My cup indeed ye shall drink.

That the 'cup' (*potērion*), and the 'baptism' (*baptisma*), are figurative terms pointing to Christ's death, and to His death in the aspect of tragedy, is not open-to doubt.

Matthew refers only to the 'cup,' and Jesus will return to this figure in Gethsemane (Mark xiv. 36; Matt. xxvi. 39; Luke xxii. 42). He had already used 'baptism' as a figure of death, in Luke xii. 50; and in this sense Paul employs the word (1 Cor. xv. 29; Rom. vi. 3-6; Col. ii. 12).

Bengel's exposition should be carefully pondered. 'To drink the *cup* was difficult (as often death itself is taken in the act of drinking). *Baptism*, also, among the Jews, was a thing to be shuddered at, inasmuch as the whole body was dipped in a stream, however cold. Accordingly, by both words the passion of Christ is denoted: by the *cup*, His inward passion; the cup is, therefore, placed *first*; by the *baptism*, chiefly His external passion. He was *distended* inwardly with His passion (referring to the *cup*; He was *filled* with the cup of anguish): He was *covered over* (as a person baptized is with water) with His passion.

'Moreover, both are appropriately employed; for they who take the sacraments, are partakers of the baptism and the cup of

38

Christ (1 Cor. xii. 13); and the baptism of Christ and our baptism, as also the Holy Supper, have a close connection with Christ's passion and death, and with ours also.

' "*Ye shall drink . . . ye shall be baptized.*"   James, when slain with the sword, drank the cup (Acts xii. 2); afterwards John was baptized in boiling oil, as Ecclesiastical History represents.   Boiling oil is in consonance with the term *baptism*.   Our Lord Himself, in Gethsemane, also calls His suffering of death *a cup*.   It is in consonance with this, that the *cup* is placed before the *baptism*.'—(*The Gnomon*, under Mark x).

With reference further to the *cup*, consider the institution of the Lord's Supper (Mark xiv. 22-25; Matt. xxvi. 26-29; Luke xxii. 15-20); and the Agony in Gethsemane (Mark xiv. 32-42; Matt. xxvi. 36-46; Luke xxii. 40-46).   These passages have no meaning at all if they do not signify an unnatural death, clearly anticipated.   The reference in the same passages to the partaking of *broken bread* as clearly points to Christ's violent death as does the drinking of the *cup*, and the *locus classicus* on the subject is John vi. 32-59.   In the light of this last passage writers who identify Christianity with the Sermon on the Mount, and the Parable of the Prodigal Son, have not only abandoned Paul, but Christ also.

The following passages disclose another important point.

MARK xiv. 24 (R.V.)	MATTHEW xxvi. 28 (R.V.)	LUKE xxii. 20 (R.V.)
This is my blood of the *covenant* which is shed for many.	This is my blood of the *covenant* which is shed for many unto remission of sins.	This cup is the *new covenant* in my blood, even that which is poured out for you.

1 CORINTHIANS xi. 23-26 (R.V.)

I received of the Lord that which also I delivered unto you, how that the Lord Jesus in the night in which He was betrayed took bread; and when He had given thanks, He brake it, and said:

'This is my body which is for you: this do in remembrance of me.'

In like manner also the cup, after supper, saying:

'This cup is the *new covenant* in my blood; this do, as oft as ye drink it, in remembrance of me.'

For as oft as ye eat this bread, and drink this cup, ye proclaim the Lord's death till He come.

EXODUS xxiv. 8 (R.V.)

Moses took the blood, and sprinkled it on the people, and said: 'Behold the blood of the *covenant*, which the LORD hath made with you.'

JEREMIAH xxxi. 31-34 (R.V.)

Behold, the days come, saith the LORD, that I will make a *new covenant* with the house of Israel, and with the house of Judah: not according to the *covenant* that I made with their fathers . . . which my *covenant* they brake . . . But this is the *covenant* that I will make with the house of Israel after those days, saith the LORD; I will put my law in their inward parts, and in their heart will I write it; and I will be their God, and they shall be my people: . . . I will forgive their iniquity, and their sin will I remember no more.

It must be plain that the covenants referred to in all these passages are *covenants of blood*, which was sacrificial blood; and surely it is equally clear that our Lord's reference to the *new covenant* (*kainē diathēkē*) has its roots in the passage in Jeremiah which associates it with the forgiveness of sins as its fundamental blessing.

Christ 'speaks as knowing that that blessing can only become ours through His death, and as the condition upon which it depends His death can be presented as a propitiatory sacrifice. It is as though He had pointed to the prophecy in Jeremiah, and said: "This day is this Scripture fulfilled before your eyes".'— (Denney).

There is another very important passage.

MARK x. 45 (R.V.)	MATT. xx. 28 (R.V.)
Verily, the Son of Man came not to be ministered unto, but to minister, and to give his life a *ransom* for *many*.	The Son of Man came not to be ministered unto, but to minister, and to give His life a *ransom* for *many*.

JOB xxxiii. 24 (R.V.)

Deliver him from going down to the pit, I have found a *ransom*.

PSALM xlix. 7 (R.V.)

None of them can by any means redeem his brother, nor give to God a *ransom* for him (for the redemption of their soul is costly, and must be let alone for ever).

ISAIAH liii. 12 (R.V.)

He bare the sin of *many*.

The principal word here is *ransom* (*lutron*), and we are confident that our Lord was familiar with the two passages in the Old Testament (above) in which the word occurs. Observe that in Job the word *deliver* occurs, and in Psalm xlix. *redeem* and *redemption*, and the thought is that for redemption or deliverance a ransom is required, but man cannot pay the ransom price. With these ideas we must associate what our Lord said about the soul or life:

'Whosoever would save his life shall lose it; and whosoever shall lose his life for my sake and the gospel's shall save it. For what doth it profit a man to gain the whole world, and *forfeit* his life? For what should a man give in exchange for his life?' (Mark viii. 35-37; Matt. xvi. 24-26; Luke ix. 23-25).

Dr. Denney says: 'A ransom is not wanted at all except where life has been forfeited, and the meaning of Mark x. 45 unambiguously is that the forfeited lives of "many" are liberated by the surrender of Christ's life, and that to surrender His life to do them this incalculable service was the very soul of His calling. . . . It is in the circle of such ideas that the words about giving His life a ransom for many must find their point of attachment, and it is not only for the simplest and most obvious interpretation, but for the most profound and the most consonant with the New Testament as a whole, that Jesus in this passage conceives the lives of the many as being somehow under forfeit, and teaches that the very object with which He came into the world was to lay down His own life as a ransom price that those to whom these forfeited lives belonged might obtain them again.'

But all the foregoing passages do not exhaust the evidence in the Gospels that Christ, regarding Himself to be the Messiah and the Son of Man, declared that He could bring deliverance to enslaved man, forgiveness to guilty man, and countless attendant blessings, and could do so only by His death, and that to accomplish such a death was the object of His coming to this world, and was the consummation of His ministry. To this effect are many other references.

MARK xii. 6-8 (R.V.)	MATT. xxi. 37-39 (R.V.)	LUKE xx. 13-15 (R.V.)
(6) He had yet one, a beloved son: he sent him last unto them, saying, 'They will reverence my son.'	(37) But afterward he sent unto them his son, saying, 'They will reverence my son.'	(13) And the lord of the vineyard said, 'What shall I do? I will send my beloved son; it may be they will reverence him.'
(7) But those husbandmen said among themselves, 'This is the heir; come, let us kill him, and the inheritance shall be ours.'	(38) But the husbandmen, when they saw the son, said among themselves, 'This is the heir; come, let us kill him, and take his inheritance.'	(14) But when the husbandmen saw him, they reasoned one with another, saying, 'This is the heir; let us kill him, that the inheritance may be ours.'
(8) And they took him, and killed him, and cast him forth out of the vineyard.	(39) And they took him, and cast him forth out of the vineyard, and killed him.	(15) And they cast him forth out of the vineyard, and killed him.

No one will doubt that the son of the parable is Jesus, who suffered a violent death at the hands of the Jews, for those who heard it 'perceived that He spake the parable against them' (Mark xii. 12).

MARK xiv. 27, 28 (R.V.)	MATTHEW xxvi. 31, 32 (R.V.)
(27) Jesus saith unto them: All ye shall be offended: for it is written, 'I will smite the shepherd, and the sheep shall be scattered abroad.'	(31) Then saith Jesus unto them: All ye shall be offended in me this night; for it is written, 'I will smite the shepherd, and the sheep of the flock shall be scattered abroad.'
(28) Howbeit, after I am raised up, I will go before you into Galilee.	(32) But after I am raised up, I will go before you into Galilee.

ZECHARIAH xiii. 7 (R.V.)

Awake, O sword, against my shepherd, and against the man that is my fellow, saith the LORD of hosts; smite the shepherd, and the sheep shall be scattered.

JOHN x. 11, 15 (R.V.)

(11) I am the good shepherd: the good shepherd layeth down his life for the sheep.

(15) I lay down my life for the sheep.

These passages make it plain that the violent death of Jesus was predicted, and that it was voluntary, motived by love, notwithstanding the fact that the Jews and the Romans acted freely.

The prediction of Christ's death is constantly emphasized by Him (Matt. xxvi. 53, 54, 56; Mark xiv. 49). Of special importance is what He said to the two disciples on the way to Emmaus (Luke xxiv. 25, 26), and to the Apostles later on (Luke xxiv. 44). Seeing that Christ's death was voluntary it may be asked how is it to be distinguished from that of a suicide. There are at least two distinctions: (a) His own hand did not accomplish His death, as in a case of hara-kiri, and (b) He did not die, as does a suicide, because He was tired of life, and in order to escape a fate worse than death.

Whether or not we can fathom the mystery, three things are plainly declared: first, that Jesus' death was predicted centuries before the incarnation; second, that the Jews were responsible for His death; and third, that He died voluntarily (Matt. xxvi. 53, 54, *et. al.*; Matt. xxvii. 25; John x. 17, 18; xix. 10, 11).

(2) The Fourth Gospel

We cannot deny that this Gospel presents difficult problems, especially with reference to the utterances which are attributed to Christ; but to say that the words ascribed to Him were 'put into His mouth' is not to solve the problems which are there, but only to create another one.

Here we do not go into critical questions (see pp. 135, 403), but, assuming the genuineness of the Gospel, would call attention to what is said, chiefly by Christ, concerning the death on Calvary.

It is difficult to understand how anyone can say—as has been said—that the death of Christ has no place in the Fourth Gospel corresponding to that which it has elsewhere in the New Testament. So far is this from being so, that at least eighteen passages make definite pronouncements on the subject. They are as follows: i. 29, 36; iii. 14, 15; iii. 16, 17; vi. 31-33; vi. 48-58; viii. 28; x. 11, 15; x. 17, 18; xi. 48-52; xii. 23, 24; xii. 27; xii. 32, 33; xii. 36; xii. 38; xiii. 31; xv. 13; xvii. 19; xix. 36; xiii-xix.

These passages present the profoundest teaching in the New Testament. Only one or two are expressions of men, and all the others are the words of Christ.

The word of the Baptist in i. 29, 36, is full of theological marrow. It speaks of *sin*, of universal sin ('*world*'); of Christ as *Lamb*, and *the* Lamb, and the Lamb *of God*; and of the Lamb as *bearing* and *bearing-away* (*airō*) the world's sin. This is the greatest thing the Baptist ever said. It connects Christ and His death with the whole sacrificial system of the Old Testament (Exod. xii; Leviticus; Isa. liii), and can leave no unprejudiced person in doubt as to the vicarious nature of Christ's death.

Chapter iii. 14, 15 is directly related to an Old Testament incident. It teaches that Jesus' death was to be a violent one; He would be 'lifted up' (cf. viii. 28; xii. 32, *hupsoō*), crucifixion being intimated, as xii. 33 reveals (cf. Ezra vi. 11, R.V.). This lifting-up on the Cross issued in Christ's being lifted up to the Throne (cf. Phil. ii. 5-11). This lifting-up of Christ is the way, for the sinner, to 'eternal life.'

In chapter iii. 16, 17, whether the words be Jesus' or the Evangelist's (and it is not possible to say which, p. 453), in addition to affirming the reference to the death as the way to life (14, 15), it is declared that Jesus' death was an expression of the love of God for sinful mankind; that Christ is God's gift to man, and must be received by faith.

The reference in vi. 31-33 must be linked with verses 48-58, if the whole truth is to be apprehended. In verse 33, the death is only vaguely hinted at, but in 48-58 it is declared that to be eaten, the 'Bread' must be broken (Mark xiv. 22; Luke xxii. 19).

In x. 11, 15, the voluntariness of Christ's death, and the love which motived it, are emphasized, and in verses 17, 18, in addition to these truths it is shown that 'Christ's death is not an incident of His life, it is the aim of it. The laying down of His life is not an accident in His career, it is His vocation; it is that in which the Divine purpose of His life is revealed.'—(Denney).

Chapter xi. 48-52 is a singularly impressive passage, if only for the reason that Divine authority attaches to the words of a bad man. Caiaphas predicted by the Holy Spirit that Jesus should die, not for Jews only, but also for Gentiles. There was no need for the Holy Spirit to make known to the Jews a purpose which was in their hearts, to kill Jesus, but the point of his pre-diction is the purpose of God in Christ's death, and its sacrificial significance.

The whole passage, xii. 23-38, is full of profound teaching concerning Christ's death. A principle of nature is made to illustrate a spiritual truth (24). A pronouncement is made relative to holding on to life, and yielding it up (25). Verses 27, 28, had better be read as 'What shall I say? (Shall I say) Father save me from this hour? (No) for this cause came I unto this hour, (but I will say) Father, glorify Thy name.' Here again it is declared that the purpose for which Christ lived was to die, and to die a violent death (32, 33; iii. 14; viii. 28), and that such a death, and for such a purpose was predicted long ago (38, Isa. liii).

In xiii. 31, Christ speaks of His death as a being 'glorified' (cf. Heb. ii. 9). Chapter xv. 13 tells of the uttermost length to which human love can go, but Christ's love, expressed by His death, goes infinitely beyond this (cf. Rom. v. 6-8, 10; John iii. 14, 16).

In chapter x. 36, it is said that the Father 'sanctified' Jesus for His work, and in xvii. 19, it says that He 'sanctified Himself' for it. In His death He was both Priest and Victim.

In addition to these specific references, there is the whole story of the Passion itself. Nearly half the Gospel is taken up with the events of a few days in a life of about thirty-five years.

This fulness of detail brings the whole story into its true perspective. What is of primary importance in the Gospels, and in Christian theology, is not the incarnation, nor the perfect life of Jesus, but His death and resurrection. The incarnation made the death possible, and the life made it worthy, but both could not save a soul. For salvation, redemption, justification, forgiveness, and all attendant blessings, the violent and voluntary death of Jesus, and His resurrection, were necessary. To grasp this is to understand the Good News.

QUESTIONS

1 What is the difference between the 'historical' and the 'dogmatic' theories of Christ's death?

2 What is Christ's teaching on His own death? Give references.

3 When did Jesus begin to instruct His Apostles about His approaching death, and what led to this instruction?

4 What did Christ mean by 'the cup,' and 'the baptism,' relative to His death?

5 What are Christ's references to 'the new covenant,' and what did He mean by them?

6 What did Christ mean when He spoke of His death being 'a ransom'?

7 In what parables did Christ speak of His death?

8 In what passages did Christ teach that His death would be both violent and voluntary?

9 Cite ten passages in the Fourth Gospel which speak of Christ's death.

10 Wherein does Christ's death differ from every other death?

11 Did Christ's death come to Him as a surprise and disappointment? What is involved in such a theory?

12 Which is the earliest reference to Christ's death.

13 Are all four Gospels in harmony on the subject of the Death?

14 Was Christ's death an example or an atonement?
15 If Christ had not died violently would He have died naturally?
16 Name six Old Testament predictions of Christ's death.
17 Name six Old Testament types of Christ's death.
18 Analyze John i. 29.
19 What is meant by Christ being 'lifted up'?
20 Does Christ's death throw any light on the age-long mystery of suffering?

LITERATURE

'Lessons from the Cross'	Brown
'In the Day of the Cross'	W. M. Clow
'The Death of Christ'	J. Denney
'The Cruciality of the Cross'-	P. T. Forsyth
'The Crucifixion from a Jewish Standpoint'	E. G. Hirsch
'The Trial and Death of Jesus Christ'	J. Stalker
'The Humiliation of Christ'	A. B. Bruce
'The Transcendence of Jesus Christ': Ch. iii	F. Cawley
'The Person of Jesus Christ'	H. R. Mackintosh
'Atonement in Modern Religious Thought'	P. T. Forsyth
'More than Atonement'	J. B. Champion
'Historic Theories of Atonement'	R. Mackintosh
'The Cross in Christian Experience'	W. M. Clow

For literature on the Atonement see works on Biblical and Systematic Theology; e.g., by Lindsay Alexander, Hodge, and Strong; and such works as, *The Atonement*, by R. W. Dale; *The Nature of the Atonement*, by McLeod Campbell; *History of the Doctrine of the Work of Christ*, by R. S. Franks; *The Doctrine of the Atonement*, by J. K. Mozley; *Law and the Cross*, by C. F. Creighton; *The Vicarious Sacrifice*, by Horace Bushnell; *Atonement and Personality*, by R. C. Moberly.

17

THE RESURRECTION OF CHRIST

THE fact that the New Testament is quite explicit as to
the resurrection of Christ has not prevented the challenge
of this fact and truth, not only outside of the Church, but also
within it. Let us, then, briefly summarize the evidence for this
miracle.

(1) THE IDEA OF CHRIST'S RESURRECTION

The literary sources of our information on this subject are the
Old Testament Writings, the Letters of the Apostles, the Records
of the Evangelists, and the final Apocalypse of Christ.

What claim is there made? Not that Jesus' spirit survived
death, nor that He spiritually manifested Himself to the spirits
of His disciples; but that He, in the totality of His personality,
came back to them; that His spirit, leaving Hades, again took
possession of His body, and raised it from the grave.

Three things are recorded with the utmost clearness and
simplicity, namely, that Jesus died on the Cross; that Jesus was
buried in Joseph's tomb; and that, three days later, the tomb
was empty, for Jesus had risen from the dead. These claims are
all on the same level of historical value; and their authenticity
is conclusive; yet, notwithstanding this, in times ancient and
modern, the fact of the resurrection has been denied. "The
history of the criticism of the resurrection narratives is one long
record of attempts to impugn their trustworthiness, and to form
hypotheses which are purely naturalistic."

But "why should it be thought a thing incredible that God
should raise the dead?" (Acts xxvi. 8).

It used to be said that Jesus did not die, but only swooned.
Then, in what physical state would He have appeared to His
disciples three days later? Many who do not deny the death and
burial try to explain away the empty tomb. The story is treated
as unhistorical.

Some have said that "an empty grave was never seen by any disciples of Jesus"; others, that the women and the disciples went to the wrong tomb (as though they were likely to do such a thing); and others again, that the body had been secretly removed from the tomb by the disciples, or by Pilate, or by the Sanhedrin, or by Joseph of Arimathæa.

But this denial of the fact of the resurrection is only part of the general disbelief in the supernatural. The resurrection is not denied because the evidence is regarded as insufficient, but the evidence is rejected and repudiated because the resurrection is denied.

A resurrection is regarded as impossible, and little attempt is made to explain away the evidence on which it rests. But the impossibility of supernaturalism is one of the most arrogant assumptions ever made. It takes for granted what still needs to be proved. Such a method is utterly unscientific. The true scientific method is to examine the facts and then form a theory; not first to form a theory and then flout and repudiate and deny the facts.

(2) THE EVIDENCE FOR THE RESURRECTION

This is manifold, direct and indirect, and altogether convincing.

(i) *Our Lord being what He was necessitated it.*

We can believe in His resurrection if we can believe in Him at all. In the light of His origin and character it is impossible to believe that He did not rise from the dead. With His resurrection everything else that has been revealed of Him assumes proportion, order and harmony; without it all is mystery; a lock without a key; a labyrinth without a clue; a beginning without a corresponding end.

(ii) *The Work which Christ came to do required it.*

The resurrection was an essential and integral part of His redemptive work. He said: 'I lay down My life that I may take it again' (John x. 17, R.V.).

The '*exodus*' of which He spake was more than decease; it was a '*way out*,' and only by His resurrection could there have been such a way! His rising from the dead was the complement of His incarnation, ministration, and crucifixion.

(iii) *Jesus Himself predicted it.*

This He did at first in vague terms, as in 'destroy this temple, and in three days I will raise it up' (John ii. 19, R.V.), and then plainly, always associating this event with His death and burial. Was He wrong? And if wrong, then what?

(iv) *The Empty Tomb demonstrated it.*

If His foes had taken His body, why did they not produce it, to silence for evermore those who were preaching that He had risen? If His friends had taken it, they were not deceived, but were deceivers, and on their deception the greatest Institution in the world, the Christian Church, has flourished for nineteen hundred years. Moreover, do we, can we, suppose that these men would have sacrificed liberty and life, would have been content to suffer, bleed, and die to proclaim a lie.

But the tomb was not empty. The clothes were there, and as He had worn them, for Jesus had sloughed them, and left them in perfect order. Had foes or friends stolen His body His clothes would not have been there.

(v) *The Primitive Belief is inexplicable if the Resurrection be not a Fact.*

Within twenty-five years of the event it was accepted as a fact by the whole Church, and in places as far removed from one another as Jerusalem, Galatia, Corinth, and Rome. Everywhere it was accepted as an historical fact, and the belief was based, in the first place, upon the testimony of eye-witnesses. It has been said that the story was started by Mary Magdalene, 'an imaginative creature,' and out of whom Jesus had cast seven demons; that she saw a man through the mist of the morning, and the miracle of love was accomplished, the resurrection was a fact; that she told it, and that others imagined it! This is utterly unsound psychologically. Is it likely that persons filled with disappointment, despondency, and despair, would see visions of Christ risen? Not a single disciple, man or woman, expected Jesus to rise from the dead. Had they done so they would not have embalmed the body. Their gloomy state of mind is reflected in that morbid word, 'we hoped that it was He who should have redeemed Israel' (Luke xxiv. 21). Yet, within six weeks of His death these disciples were declaring that they had seen their Master risen from the dead. The removal of the body would not explain the change; and three days is not long enough for a legend to spring up which should so affect them. The only rational explanation is that the resurrection is a fact.

(vi) *The Appearances of the Lord elaborate the certainty of it.*

There were ten of these within forty days, and they were made under a great variety of circumstances; to men and women; to individuals and to groups; in the house and on the street; to disciples joyful and sad; and on occasions momentary and protracted.

It is quite impossible that in all these circumstances all these people were mistaken.

(vii) *The Testimony of the Apostle Paul endorses it.*

It is impossible, except on the hypothesis of the fact, that a man of his intellectuality and education should have come to regard the resurrection of Jesus as absolutely irrefutable, and that, within six years of the supposed event. For twenty-five years he served and suffered as few have done; and the driving consciousness behind all was that his Lord was alive, and that he had seen Him in the body (p. 610).

His conversion is a mighty testimony to the reality of the resurrection. Nothing but a real objective appearance of Christ will satisfy the facts of the case.

(viii) *The Existence of the Christian Church points to it.*

But for the resurrection there could have been no Christian Church. The existence of this Society is the first and final proof of the historic truth of the miracle on which it was founded. The Church came out of the belief in the resurrection, and the belief came out of the fact. And what is true of the Church herself is true also of her Institutions. What was it that occasioned the distinction between the Jewish Sabbath and the Lord's Day, and the sudden change from the one to the other? Only one thing—the resurrection. A more powerful testimony to men's conviction of the truth of the event within a few weeks after it is said to have happened, it would be impossible to produce.

(ix) *The Convicting and Converting Power of the Christian Message Proves it.*

Faith in a dead man can save no one; only the living Christ can do that. And to all these evidences must be added:

(x) *The Experiences of countless Christians for nineteen hundred years.*

There is a knowledge which is independent of logical reasoning, and which constitutes an 'infallible proof' of the resurrection. Nothing on earth or in hell could induce millions of men and women to believe that Jesus had not risen from the dead. It is the best attested fact in history, and the rock from which all the hammers of criticism have never chipped a single fragment. Let them chant their mournful creed who will:

> 'Now He is dead! Far hence He lies
> In the lorn Syrian town;
> And on His grave, with shining eyes,
> The Syrian stars look down.'

But the Christian has a different song to sing, and one which simply throbs with confidence and joy:

> 'Up from the grave He arose,
> With a mighty triumph o'er His foes;
> He arose a Victor from the dark domain,
> And He lives, for ever with His saints to reign.
> He arose! He arose! Hallelujah! Christ arose.'

QUESTIONS

1 Can an argument for the resurrection be derived from the person of Christ?

2 Could Christ have accomplished His redeeming work by death only, without rising from the dead?

3 Did Christ predict His resurrection? If so, when? Give references.

4 Make a list of the supposed post-resurrection appearances of Christ. Do you think these could have been imagined, or invented?

5 Can the primitive belief in Christ's resurrection be accounted for apart from the fact?

6 What is the witness of the Epistles to the resurrection of Christ?

7 Name three other evidences of the resurrection which are not included in the answers to the preceding questions.

8 Wherein does Christ's resurrection differ from that of others who were raised, for example, Lazarus?

9 Can one deny Christ's resurrection and yet be a Christian?

10 Is the resurrection of Christ foretold or typified in the Old Testament; and if so, where?

LITERATURE

'The Risen Master'	H. Latham
'The Resurrection of Our Lord'	W. Milligan
'The Resurrection'	S. Cox
'The Gospel of the Resurrection'	Bp. Westcott
'The Historic Faith'	Bp. Westcott
'The Revelation of the Risen Lord'	Bp. Westcott
'The Glory and Joy of the Resurrection'	J. Paton
'The Resurrection of Jesus'	J. Orr
'The Crucifixion and Resurrection of Christ in the Light of Tradition'	G. H. Trench
'The Risen Christ'	J. B. Brown
'The Risen Redeemer'	F. W. Krummacher
'Theories of the Resurrection'	Marchant
'The Empty Tomb'	B. W. Randolph
'The Most Certain Fact in History'	Ring
'Studies in the Resurrection of Christ'	C. H. Robinson
'Our Lord's Resurrection'	W. J. S. Simpson
'The Resurrection and Modern Thought'	W. J. S. Simpson
'Pastor Pastorum': ch. xiii	H. Latham
'Foundations'	B. H. Streeter
'The Evidence for the Resurrection'	E. H. Day

Articles on the Resurrection of Christ in the standard Bible Dictionaries; and Expositions in the Critical Commentaries.

Also consult works on Theology: Hodge, Strong, Weiss, Dorner, Fisher, Stevens, and others.

18

THE APPEARANCES OF CHRIST

THE period between the Crucifixion and the Ascension of Christ is one of the utmost importance, and we can estimate its value to some extent by trying to imagine our loss if all that we are told of it were expunged. The period was, we are told, 'by the space of forty days' (Acts i. 3); and the 'not many days hence' (5) were ten, because the time between the Passover and Pentecost Feasts was fifty days. The word Pentecost means *fiftieth*, because the feast began on the fiftieth day after the second day of the Passover. During this six weeks momentous events occurred.

From the records it seems clear that our Lord made ten appearances, five of them being on the day of His resurrection; one of them a week later; three of them at times not stated; and one of them on the day of the ascension.

These appearances were made to different people, singly, in groups and companies, in public, and in private, in different localities, and at different hours of the day. All these particulars should be most carefully considered.

(1) The Record of the Appearances

This is found in Matthew, Mark, Luke, John, Acts, and 1 Corinthians; and the following are the passages:

Matt. xxviii. 1, 9, 10, 11-15, 16-20; Mark xvi. 9-11, 12, 13-14, 15-18, 19, 20; Luke xxiv. 13-32, 33-35, 36-43, 44-49, 50-53; John xx. 11-18, 19-25, 26-31; xxi. 1-25; Acts i. 3-8, 9-12; 1 Cor. xv.5, 6, 7.

From this it will be seen that the records are distributed, no Evangelist giving a full account; and the records are not made with regard to chronological sequence.

(2) The Number of the Appearances

These, as we have said, seem to have been ten; five on one day, and the other five on different days. The order of these, it may be assumed, is as follows:

(i) Appearance to Mary Magdalene ...	Mark xvi. 9-11 John xx. 11-18
(ii) Appearance to Other Women	Matt. xxviii. 9, 10
(iii) Appearance to Simon Peter	Luke xxiv. 33-35 1 Cor. xv. 5
(iv) Appearance to Two Disciples on the Way to Emmaus	Mark xvi. 12, 13 Luke xxiv. 13-32
(v) Appearance to Ten Apostles and Others	Mark xvi. 14 Luke xxiv. 36-43 John xx. 19-25

All these were on the day of the resurrection, on Easter Sunday, probably between 7 a.m. and 8 p.m.

(vi) Appearance to the Eleven Apostles ...	John xx. 26-31 1 Cor. xv. 5
(vii) Appearance to Seven Disciples in Galilee	John xxi. 1-25
(viii) Appearance to the Apostles, and over 500 Disciples in Galilee	Mark xvi. 15-18 Matt. xxviii. 16-20 1 Cor. xv. 6
(ix) Appearance to James, the Lord's Brother	1 Cor. xv. 7
(x) Appearance for the last time to the Apostles	Luke xxiv. 44-53 Acts i. 3-12 Mark xvi. 19, 20

It should be observed that the last appearance of the risen Lord to the Eleven 'began in Jerusalem, probably in the upper room; but it did not end there. As on the night before the Passion, in the midst of His discourse, the Lord had said: "Arise, let us go hence," and so saying had led the disciples out of the city towards the Mount of Olives; so now, we must suppose, at some point in the conversation which has not been indicated, He rose, followed by the Eleven, went through the streets of

Jerusalem for the last time, passed through the Eastern Gate, and crossed the Kidron valley. But on this occasion He did not stop at Gethsemane, but passed on in the direction of Bethany.' (Swete). This means that the record in Luke xxiv. 44-49; xxiv. 50-53, and in Acts i. 3-8, i. 9-12, refer to one event, though beginning in one place and ending in another.

(3) THE WITNESSES OF THE APPEARANCES

The Lord revealed Himself first of all to Mary Magdalene; then to a number of women; then to Simon Peter; then to two disciples on the Emmaus Road; then to ten of the Apostles, and, it would seem, the two Emmaus disciples, who had gone to the Apostles to report their experience, and perhaps others (Luke xxiv. 33); then to the Eleven Apostles, Thomas now being present; then to Peter, Thomas, Nathanæl, James, John, 'and two other of His disciples,' who may have been Andrew and Matthew, though, says Dr. Swete, 'the suppression of their names is against this identification'; then to the Eleven Apostles again, and five hundred other disciples; then to James, and finally to the Eleven again.

An analysis of this shows that Jesus appeared in order, to one, a group, one, two, twelve, eleven, seven, eleven, and five hundred, one, and eleven. Three times He appeared to eleven of the Apostles; once to ten of them, and once to five of them. Two of the appearances, the first two, were to women. Three of the appearances were to individuals, Mary, Peter and James. Six of the appearances were to non-Apostles; the women, the Emmaus disciples, the two disciples who were with the five Apostles, the five hundred disciples, and James, Jesus' brother. To so many was evidence given that Christ was risen from the dead, and so, as Bishop Westcott says, the resurrection is one of the best attested facts in history. Paul said, in A.D. 57, twenty-seven years after the resurrection, that over 250 persons were then living who had seen the Lord in Galilee, a statement he would never have made had there been any fear of contradiction.

(4) THE SCENES OF THE APPEARANCES

The appearances, one, two, three, five, six, and ten, were made in and around Jerusalem, that is, six out of the ten; one was made on the road from Jerusalem to Emmaus; and three were made in Galilee, if the meeting of Jesus with James is placed in the north, but it may have been in the south.

Three of the Jerusalem appearances, to Mary, other women, and Peter, were made out of doors, and three, to the Apostles, were made in the upper room, and on Olivet. Of the Galilee appearances, one was made on a mountain (Matt. xxviii. 16), and one by the Lake of Galilee (John xxi). The first six were made in the south, the next three, in the north (if that to James be included), and the last, in the south again. The distance from Jerusalem to Capernaum is about 80 miles in a straight line, but, of course, further to walk.

(5) THE TIMES OF THE APPEARANCES

The appearance to Mary Magdalene was in the early morning, probably about 7.0 a.m. (Mark xvi. 9); and to the other women not long after. It was probably in the morning also that Jesus appeared to Peter, but Bishop Westcott puts it at about 4.0 p.m. The journey to Emmaus with the two disciples would, in all likelihood, be between 4.0 and 6.0 p.m. The first appearance to the Apostles, ten of them, would be about 8.0 p.m. All these were on the day of the resurrection.

The second appearance to the Eleven was in the evening of Sunday, a week after the resurrection. The time of the appearance to the Seven was 'when the day was breaking' (John xxi. 4). The appearance on a mountain in Galilee must have been at a time which allowed of the five hundred disciples getting from their homes scattered all round the northern part of the Lake, to the appointed place, and getting back again before dark. We do not know when Jesus appeared to James. The last appearance must have been in daylight, because the Apostles saw Jesus ascend from Mount Olivet, a cloud receiving Him out of their sight (Acts i. 9).

(6) THE MANNER OF HIS APPEARANCES

The physical condition of Jesus in resurrection life is one about which little can be said, first, because more is concealed than is revealed about it; and second, because of our present ignorance of the properties of a body other than our own, a body on the borderland of flesh and spirit.

The following are the data in the Gospels:

(i) 'Mary turned herself back, and beholdeth Jesus standing, and knew not that it was Jesus. Jesus saith unto her, "Woman, why weepest thou? Whom seekest thou?" She, supposing Him to be the gardener, saith unto Him, "Sir, if thou hast borne Him hence, tell me where thou hast laid Him, and I will take Him away." Jesus saith unto her, "Mary." She turneth herself, and saith unto Him in Hebrew, "Rabboni," which is to say, Master (Teacher, *didaskalos*). Jesus saith to her, "Touch Me not; for I am not yet ascended unto the Father; but go unto My brethren, and say to them, I ascend unto My Father and your Father, and My God and your God"' (John xx. 14-17, R.V.).

The facts to note here are: that Jesus was visible; that He wore a human guise; that Mary did not recognize Him; that He was commonly clad; that He spoke to her in her language; that she did not know His voice; that when He mentioned her name there must have been something in the tone, and probably in a smile, which revealed Him; that He could be touched, but declined to be; that as He was He could ascend to heaven; that He left Mary, how and whither, we are not told. Mark these ten particulars.

(ii) 'Behold, Jesus met them, saying, "All hail." And they came and took hold of His feet, and worshipped Him. Then saith Jesus unto them, "Fear not; go tell My brethren that they depart into Galilee, and there shall they see Me"' (Matt. xxviii. 9, 10, R.V.).

Here, also, Jesus is visible, and is walking along the road; He speaks to the women and is at once recognized by them, and they clasp His feet. Again, we are told nothing of how Jesus left them or where He went.

(iii) As the third passage is a long one (Luke xxiv. 13-32) we will not quote it here, but it should be read with great care. As introductory to it, it is said in Mark xvi. 12, 13: 'He was manifested in another form unto two of them, as they walked on their way into the country.'

We cannot say what is meant by 'a different form' (*en hetera morphē*). Grotius, and the older commentators made the phrase refer to Jesus' dress, but we agree with Dr. James Morison, who says: 'It would serve no purpose but that of frivolity, to discuss the reciprocal limits of the subjective and the objective in the manner of the manifestation, and also the various ingredients of things that might enter into the determination of the "form." The Evangelist leaves the matter indefinite; and so should we.' The reason given in Luke's record for the disciples not recognizing Jesus, is that 'their eyes were holden' (16), not that the appearance of Jesus was different.

The salient features of Luke's account are: that Jesus was visible and human; that He walked some miles with the disciples, conversing with them; that He entered their house, and reclined at their table; that He took the bread of the evening meal, broke and distributed it; that as He did so, 'their eyes were opened, and they knew Him,' and that upon this, 'He vanished out of their sight.'

There was nothing 'docetic' about Jesus' body, yet there was something supernatural.

Even before the Cross He had a certain power which is strange to us. He could pass through the midst of His enemies, and go on His way; He could convey Himself away; He could hide Himself, and leave the Temple (Luke iv. 30; John v. 13; viii. 59). Dr. Swete says that such passages 'suggest that before the Passion the Lord's sinless human will possessed a power over His body which is wholly beyond our experience or comprehension.' Much more would this be so after the resurrection. At Emmaus the Lord remained visible to the two disciples just long enough to remove the last doubt of His identity, and then He withdrew Himself from their eyes.

It is noteworthy that the marks of the nails in His hands could not have been visible to the disciples, either along the road, or at the table, as that same evening they were visible to the Apostles!

    (iv) There is no record of how Christ 'appeared to Simon,' but he must have said something about it to his brother Apostles (Luke xxiv. 34).

    (v) The next manifestation, to the Apostles and others on Easter Sunday night, is profoundly important.

MARK xvi. 14 (R.V.)	LUKE xxiv. 36-43 (R.V.)	JOHN xx. 19, 20 (R.V.)
(14) He was manifested unto the eleven themselves as they sat at meat; and He upbraided them with their unbelief and hardness of heart, because they believed not them which had seen Him after He was risen.	(36) He Himself stood in the midst of them, and saith unto them, 'Peace be unto you.' (37) But they were terrified and affrighted and supposed that they beheld a spirit. (38) And He said unto them, 'Why are ye troubled? and wherefore do reasonings arise in your heart? (39) See, my hands and my feet, that it is I Myself; handle Me, and see; for a spirit hath not flesh and bones, as ye behold Me having. (40) And when He had said this, He shewed them His hands and His feet. (41) And while they still disbelieved for joy, and wondered, He said unto them, 'Have ye here anything to eat?' (42) And they gave Him a piece of a broiled fish. (43) And He took it, and did eat it before them.	(19) When therefore it was evening, on that day, the first of the week, and when the doors were shut where the disciples were, for fear of the Jews, Jesus came and stood in the midst and saith unto them, 'Peace be unto you.' (20) And when He had said this, He shewed unto them His hands and His side. The disciples therefore were glad, when they saw the Lord.

The natural and the supernatural are here strangely blended. The natural features are His visible, physical body, with the marks of the nails in His hands and feet; His references to His 'flesh and bones'; and His eating 'a piece of broiled fish.' Jesus first convinces the Apostles of His identity, and then, of His corporeity.

The supernatural features are His entrance to the upper room without opening the door; and the appearance which led His disciples to suppose that they were beholding a spirit. This record 'creates in many minds a difficulty which, in our present ignorance, cannot be wholly removed. How such properties as to be tangible, to bear the imprints of nails or a spear wound, to be able to partake of food, can be reconciled with the power of becoming invisible at will, or with any conception which can be formed of a spiritual body, we do not know.'

(vi) The appearance to the eleven Apostles a week after the resurrection, as on Easter Sunday, has the two features of the natural and the supernatural in conjunction (John xx. 26, 27).

(vii) Not much is said about our Lord's bodily appearance when He manifested Himself to seven disciples by the Lake of Galilee, but they knew that it was the Lord (John xxi. 7, 12).

(viii) Equally little is said about His appearing to that large crowd of His disciples on a mountain in Galilee. The statement, 'but some doubted,' would seem to mean, not that they doubted that Jesus was risen, but doubted if the figure they saw approaching them was Jesus (Matt. xxviii. 17).

(ix) We have no information of the manner of Jesus' appearance to James.

(x) Jesus' bodily reality is again demonstrated in His last appearance. 'He lifted up His hands and blessed' His Apostles, and bodily He 'was carried up into heaven' (Luke xxiv. 50, 51).

(7) THE TEACHING OF THE APPEARANCES

By this we mean what our Lord said to those to whom He manifested Himself. The passages to be read are: (i) John xx. 17; (ii) Luke xxiv. 25-27; (iii) John xx. 21-23; (iv) John xxi. 15-22; (v) Matt. xxviii. 18-20; Luke xxiv. 44-49; Acts i. 4-8. A detailed exposition of these profound passages would take us beyond the scope of this work, but the teaching is of sovereign importance.

(i) Jesus intimated to Mary that there could now be no tangible demonstration of affection. When soon after He allowed other women to touch Him it was not as an expression of affection, but an act of worship; and when later He invited Thomas to touch Him it was for the purpose of demonstration of His corporeal identity (an opportunity which Thomas did not embrace). Jesus, also, on this occasion, distinguished between His and His disciples' relation to God and the Father; 'My' and 'your,' twice; not 'our.' (Pages 537, 543).

(ii) Jesus demonstrated to two unknown disciples that He was the Christ, the Messiah of prophecy, and the fulfilment of all the Old Testament types.

(iii) Christ sees in the Apostles the future Church, and gives to them a mission which He places on the same level of importance and authority as the mission on which He Himself had been sent by the Father; and He bestows upon them the Power, the Holy Spirit, by Whom He had fulfilled His task. He also now granted to His Church the right and power to 'remit' and 'retain' sins (cf. John xx. 23, and Matt. xviii. 18).

(iv) In this great passage, which is concentrated on Peter, the Lord gives to His Apostle three progressive charges, which

include the whole duty of the pastoral office: 'feed my lambs';
'tend my sheep'; 'feed my sheep.' He also intimates to Peter
that his service would be crowned by a violent death.

(v) In some ways the Commission recorded in Matt. xxviii.
18-20, is the most wonderful of all Christ's post-resurrection
utterances; and it was given, not to the Apostles only, but to
over 500 other disciples. In these immortal words is outlined
the policy of the future Church, and is contained the inspiration
of all her missionary work from the first century until the
twentieth.

    (*a*) 'All authority hath been given unto Me in heaven and on earth.
    (*b*) Go ye therefore, and make disciples of all nations, baptizing
        them into the name of the Father, and of the Son, and of the
        Holy Spirit: teaching them to observe all things whatsoever I
        commanded you:
    (*c*) And lo, I am with you all the days, even unto the consummation
        of the age.'

The authority, the command, and the promise of Christ make
these words the greatest, perhaps, that He ever spoke.

Here are the 'all' of universal power, 'in heaven and on earth';
the 'all' of unbounded love, disciples are wanted; the 'all' of
unquestioning obedience, 'go,' 'make,' 'baptize,' 'teach'; and the
'all' of unending fellowship, 'lo, I with you Am: *egō meth'humōn
eimi*,' wherein we are placed between the two parts of the Divine
I AM (John viii. 58), 'unto the consummation of the age.'

(vi) Elements of previous utterances are in this one (Luke
xxiv. 44-49): Christ the fulfilment of the Old Testament Scriptures; preaching to all nations; and the enduement of the Holy
Spirit (cf. Luke xxiv. 25-27; Matt. xxviii. 19; Luke xxiv. 22,
23; Acts i. 4, 5).

These words derive added importance and value from the
fact that they are the last words of the risen Lord before He
ascended to the Throne of God, ending His prophetic, and
commencing His priestly ministry.

QUESTIONS

1 Why did Christ appear to people after His resurrection?
2 What is the significance of the fifty days between the resurrection and the descent of the Spirit?
3 In what books of the New Testament are post-resurrection appearances recorded?
4 How many times did Christ appear in resurrection life?
5 To whom did Christ appear, and where?
6 What was the manner of Christ's appearances, and from this what may we learn about the nature of the resurrection body?
7 Why did Christ forbid Mary to touch Him, and yet invite Thomas to do so?
8 What commissions did Christ give in resurrection life, and to whom?
9 How many men and how many women saw the risen Christ?
10 How many appearances were there on the day of the resurrection, and to whom?
11 To how many individuals did Christ appear, and who were they?
12 Where were the appearances made?
13 Do you suppose that Christ's resurrection body bears any relation to what ours will be?
14 Analyze and homilize Matthew xxviii. 18-20.

LITERATURE

'The Appearances of our Lord after the Resurrec-
    tion' -   -   -   -   -   -   - H. B. Swete
'The Forty Days of the Risen Life'   -   - Boyd Carpenter
'The Forty Days after our Lord's Resurrection' - W. Hanna
'The Revelation of the Risen Lord'   -   - Bp. Westcott
In addition to these consult the Bible Dictionaries,
    the Commentaries, and Lives of Christ.

19

THE ASCENSION OF CHRIST

L IKE all great facts and truths, the ascension of Christ is a subject of the Old Testament, the Acts, the Epistles, and the Revelation, by implication sometimes, but mostly by direct reference; but our present enquiry is limited to the testimony of the Gospels, in which there are more references than, perhaps, is commonly thought.

Our first business is to assemble these references, and then, to examine them.

(1) REFERENCES TO THE ASCENSION (R.V.)

Though it is commonly thought that Mark's Gospel ends at verse 8 of chap. xvi, we are still at liberty to quote verse 19, which is the record of a fact which is borne witness to elsewhere.

'So then the Lord Jesus, after He had spoken unto them (the Apostles), was *received up into heaven, and sat down at the right hand of God'*	Mark xvi. 19
'And it came to pass, when the days were well-nigh come that *He should be received up,* He stedfastly set His face to go to Jerusalem'	Luke ix. 51
'Behoved it not the Christ to suffer these things, and *to enter into His glory?'*	Luke xxiv. 26
'He (Jesus) led them (the Apostles) out until they were over against Bethany: and He lifted up His hands, and blessed them. And it came to pass, while He blessed them, *He parted from them, and was carried up into heaven*	Luke xxiv. 50, 51
'No man hath *ascended into heaven,* but He that descended out of heaven, even the Son of Man, which is in heaven'	John iii. 13
'What then if ye should behold *the Son of Man ascending where He was before?'*	John vi. 62
'Jesus said, Yet a little while am I with you, and *I go unto Him that sent Me.* Ye shall seek Me, and shall not find Me: and where I am, ye cannot come'	John vii. 33, 34
'I, if I be *lifted up from the earth,* will draw all men unto Myself'	John xii. 32
'Jesus knowing that the Father had given all things into His hands, and that He came forth from God, and *goeth unto God . . .'*	John xiii. 3
'*I go to prepare a place for you.* And if *I go and prepare a place for you,* I come again . . .' ...	———

'And whither *I go*, ye know the way' ...	John xiv. 2-4
'He that believeth on Me, the works that I do shall he do also; and greater works than these shall he do; because *I go unto the Father*'	John xiv. 12
'Ye heard how I said to you, *I go away*, and I come unto you'	John xiv. 28
'Now *I go unto Him that sent Me*; and none of you asketh Me, Whither goest Thou?'	John xvi. 5
'Nevertheless I tell you the truth; It is expedient for you that *I go away*: for if I go not away, the Comforter will not come unto you; but if I go, I will send Him unto you'	John xvi. 7
'*I go to the Father*'	John xvi. 10
'A little while and *ye behold Me no more*' ...	John xvi. 16-19
'*I leave the world, and go unto the Father*' ...	John xvi. 28
'I am no more in the world ... *I come to Thee*' ...	John xvii. 11
'Touch Me not; for *I am not yet ascended unto the Father*, but go unto My brethren, and say to them, *I ascend unto My Father*, and your Father, and My God, and your God'	John xx. 17
'As they were looking, *He was taken up; and a cloud received Him out of their sight*. And while they were looking stedfastly into heaven as *He went*, behold two men stood by them in white apparel; which also said ... this Jesus, which was *received up from you into heaven*, shall so come ... as ye beheld Him *going* into Heaven'	Acts i. 9-11

(2) MANNER OF THE ASCENSION

Not fewer than thirteen words are used to indicate the manner of the Lord's departure from this world into heaven.

ana-bainō	-	to arise, with *up* (John iii. 13; vi. 62; xx. 17).
ana-lambanō	-	to take, with *up* (Mark xvi. 19; Acts i. 11).
ana-lēpsis	-	to receive, with *up* (Luke ix. 51; only occurrence in the New Testament).
ana-pherō	-	to bear, with *up* (Luke xxiv. 51).
ap-erchomai	-	to go from one place to another, to return (John xvi. 7; cf. xx. 10); verb with *from*.
di-istēmi	-	to put apart (Luke xxiv. 51).
eis-erchomai	-	to come, or enter, with *in* (Luke xxiv. 26).
epairō	-	to lift or raise up (Acts i. 9).
erchomai	-	to come (John xvii. 11).
hupagō	-	to go away (John vii. 33; xiii. 3; xiv. 4, 28; xvi. 5, 10).
hupo-lambanō	-	to take from under, to receive up (Acts i. 9).
hupsoō	-	to raise on high, to elevate (John xii. 32).
poreuō	-	to depart, to journey (John xiv. 2, 3, 12; xvi. 28; Acts i. 10, 11).

These reflect shades of meaning of a stupendous event. In going forth from earth to heaven Christ was taken, was received, was borne, was lifted up, was taken up, arose, went, was raised, was separated. Other words are used outside the Gospels, but these are significant enough. That He went bodily is plainly declared, though the Gospels emphasize the fact rather than the mode, and think less of a transition from one locality to another than from one condition to another.

Christ's disciples did not see Him rise from the dead, but they did see Him ascend into heaven. For the confirmation of the certainty and reality of the resurrection it was not necessary that they should see Him rise, but only that they should see Him risen. But it *was* necessary that they should see Him ascend in order to be sure that He had ascended. In the one case they saw the effect, but not the act; and in the other case they saw the act, but not the effect.

All we are told is that Jesus left His disciples as He had never left them before, in leaving the earth. Up or down, indicating direction, will not bear scientific scrutiny, but that which matters is plain, that He who came to this world went from it, and never since has been physically in it.

(3) Necessity for the Ascension

The Ascension was the culmination of the Incarnation and the reward of Christ's redemptive work, and it is the point of contact between the Christ of the Gospels and the Christ of the Epistles. It proved the resurrection, and was demanded by it. The resurrection and the ascension stand or fall together. If Christ did not rise from the tomb He could not ascend bodily to heaven; but if He did rise, where has He been ever since? The ascension is congruous with Christ's whole career. Its relation to the laws of nature presents no greater difficulty than do the incarnation and resurrection. The whole of the Divine manifestation of God in Christ, in time and place, was supernatural; not contrary to nature, but above it. The ascension was the completion in history of the work which He came to do.

'I have glorified Thee on the earth, having accomplished the work which Thou hast given me to do.
And I am no more in the world. . . . I come to Thee' John xvii. 4, 11 (R.V.)

While Christ was here He was localized. He could not be in Jerusalem and Capernaum at the same time, but moved from one point to another. Had this continued He could not have been with His universal Church, which it was His intention to be; but, by the Ascension the local Christ became universal by the Holy Spirit's advent.

'I tell you the truth; it is expedient for you that
I go away: for if I go not away, the Comforter will
not come unto you; but if I go, I will send Him
unto you   ...   .   John xvi. 7 (R.V.)

The coming of the Spirit was dependent on the going of the Saviour, and yet His going was, spiritually and mystically, His coming again (John xiv. 3, 16-18, R.V.). The significance of Christ's earthly career could not be understood while He was here, so He departed, that the Spirit might interpret Him to His Church (John xvi. 7-15).

The 'all power' given to Him after the resurrection was to be exercised, not from the earth heavenward, but from heaven earthward (Matt. xxviii. 18-20). Then, it was necessary for Christ to ascend that He might 'prepare a place' for His people. The nature of this 'preparation' we are not told, but some light is thrown on the meaning of the word by its use in Mark x. 40; Matt. xx. 23; Mark xiv. 16; Luke ix. 52.

Then, it was necessary for Christ to ascend that the purpose for which He came might be accomplished in the world through His Church.

'Greater works than these shall ye do, because
I go unto the Father'   ...   .   John xiv. 12 (R.V.)

The spiritual conquests of the Church have been 'greater works' than the miracles performed by Jesus, for they were temporal, but these are spiritual; they were local, but these are universal.

These, then, are some of the reasons for the departure of Christ. There were things which could not be done while He was here. He could not save except by coming, and He could not keep except by going. The power of His eternal work in heaven was made possible by the accomplishment of His redemptive work on earth during thirty-five years.

His ascension, then, was the completion of His earthly mission; it made provision for His universal presence, and made possible the institution of the Christian Church. These facts emphasize, not Christ's physical remoteness, but His spiritual nearness.

QUESTIONS

1 In what terms is the Lord's ascension referred to in the Gospels, and what is the significance of them?
2 Name six words which are used to describe Christ's departure from this world, and give references.
3 What need was there for Christ to ascend to heaven?
4 What is the relation of the ascension to the crucifixion?
5 What references are there in the Acts and Epistles to Christ's ascension?
6 Where, do you suppose, is Christ now? Are we to think of Him as being in any sense localized?
7 What is Christ doing where He is?
8 What light does John xvii throw on this subject?
9 How can Christ be with us, seeing that He has gone from us?
10 What references are there to the ascension in John xiv.-xvi?

LITERATURE

'The Ascension and Heavenly Priesthood of Our Lord'	W. Milligan
'The Ascended Christ'	H. B. Swete
'The Heavenly Session of Our Lord'	Tait
'The Principles of Theology.' (Article IV)	Griffith Thomas
'Our One Priest on High'	Dimock
'The Historic Christ'	T. A. Lacey
'Studies in the Life of Christ'	A. M. Fairbairn
'The Apostles' Creed'	H. B. Swete
'Our High Priest in Heaven'	Perowne

Articles on the *Ascension* in the Bible Dictionaries.

20

THE RETURN OF CHRIST

IT is beyond the scope of this Guide to examine the doctrine of
the Lord's Return in general, because the studies are limited
to the Gospels, and even here no attempt can be made to deal
in detail with all the relevant passages, but only to assemble the
material for the construction of the doctrine, within these limits.
It should be understood, however, that what goes before, in the
Old Testament, and what follows, in the Acts, Epistles, and
Revelation, is vitally related to the teaching of Christ, and so
a full view of the truth can be obtained only by studying all that
the Bible has to say on the subject.

(1) WORDS WHICH SET FORTH SOME SORT OF A COMING

Of some seven words used in the New Testament to set forth
the Coming-again of Christ, four are found in the Gospels:

(1) *erchomai*	-	which denotes the act of coming, as, I am coming;
(2) *hēkō*	-	which denotes the result, as, I am come, and am here;
(3) *parousia*	-	which indicates presence, arrival;
(4) *apokaluptō*	-	which indicates exposure to view.

(A) *Erchomai*	'The Son of Man shall *come* in the glory of His Father'	Matt. xvi. 27
	'They shall see the Son of Man *coming* in clouds and glory'	Matt. xxiv. 30
	'Watch, therefore, for ye know not what hour your Lord doth *come*'	Matt. xxiv. 42
	'When He *cometh* in the glory of His Father'	Mark viii. 38
	'Lest *coming* suddenly He find you sleeping'	Mark xiii. 36
	'When the Son of Man *cometh* shall He find faith on the earth?'	Luke xviii. 8
	'I *come* again'	John xiv. 3 (R.V.)
	'If I will that he tarry till I *come* . . .'	John xxi. 22, 23

These are not all the occurences of this word, but these references reveal its force.

(B) *Hēkō* - 'Then shall the end *come*' ... Matt. xxiv. 14
'The lord of that servant shall
come' ... ... Matt. xxiv. 50

(c) *Parousia* - 'What shall be the sign of Thy
coming' ... ... Matt. xxiv. 3
'So shall be the *coming* of the
Son of Man' ... ... Matt. xxiv. 27, 39

(D) *Apokaluptō* 'The day that the Son of Man
is revealed.' Only occurrence Luke xvii. 30
in the Gospels relative to
Christ's advent.

(2) WORDS INDICATIVE OF TIME

(i) 'Then' (*tote*): Matt. xvi. 27; xxiv. 14; xxv. 31; Luke xxi. 27.
(ii) 'Till,' 'Until' (*heōs-an*): Matt. xxiv. 34; John xxi. 22, 23.
(iii) 'After' (*meta*): Matt. xxiv. 29; Luke xxi. 26.
(iv) 'Harvest' (*therismos*): Matt. xiii. 30, 39.
(v) 'Hereafter,' 'Henceforth' (*arti,* or *ap'arti*): Matt. xxiii. 39; xxvi. 64.
(vi) 'End' (*telos*): the fulfilment or completion of anything.   (Matt. xxiv. 14; Mark xiii. 7; Luke xxi. 9.
(vii) 'End of the Age' (*sunteleia tou aiōnos*): Matt. xiii. 39, 40, 49; xxiv. 3.
(viii) 'Time' (*kairos*):   a definite time with reference to some act or crisis (Matt. xiii. 30; Mark xiii. 33; Luke xxi. 8).
(*chronos*): time in general, duration (Matt. xxv. 19; Luke xx. 9).
(ix) 'Last Day' (*eschatē hēmera*): John vi. 39, 40, 44, 54; xii. 48.
(x) 'Day of the Son of Man' (*hē hēmera ho huios tou anthrōpou*): Luke xvii. 24, 30.
(xi) 'That Day' (*tēs hēmeras ekeinēs*) 'and the hour' (*kai tēs hōras*): Mark xiii. 32; Luke xvii. 31.

(3) OTHER IMPORTANT WORDS

(i) KINGDOM (*Basileia*).
Of God (Luke xi. 2; xxii. 14-18; xxiii. 51).
Of the Father (Matt. xiii. 43 (context); xxvi. 29).
Of David (Mark xi. 10; Luke i. 32, 33).
Of the Son of Man (Matt. xvi. 28-xvii. 8; xiii. 41).
(ii) SON OF MAN.
This designation appears to have special reference to Christ's association *with the earth* (Matt. xvi. 27, 28; xix. 28; xxiv. 27, 30, 37, 44; xxv. 31; xxvi. 64; Mark viii. 38; Luke xvii. 30).
(See under 'Son of Man,' p. 521).
(iii) RESURRECTION (see under 'Last Day').
(iv) TRIBULATION (Matt. xxiv. 21, 29; Mark xiii. 24).
(v) RETURN, *hupostrephō*, to turn back (Luke xix. 12).

All these, and other words and phrases in the Gospels, clearly show that all events are leading to a consummation which will be cataclysmal. But the evidence that there is to be a Second Advent of Christ is not confined to these words and phrases, but is found in the warp and woof of His teaching.

Whatever we may think about Christ's views concerning the *last things*, there can be no misapprehension as to what they are. His teaching, both parabolic and plain, speaks of a future *coming* as an event in history which will close one age, and open another; and, having regard to who Christ was, it will not do to speak of such teaching as though He held a private view of the course of events which is entitled to no more consideration than the opinions of other people on the subject, or that He simply promulgated the Jewish conception of an earthly kingdom, the perpetuation of a theocracy on a Davidic basis.

No theory of His 'Self-emptying' (Phil. ii. 7, *Kenosis*) can in the least degree invalidate His pronouncements on this or any other subject. We must either accept the teaching of Christ as infallibly true, or we must reject His claims for Himself, and by so doing challenge the whole New Testament revelation.

(4) CHRIST'S PARABOLIC TEACHING

It is difficult to understand how anyone who reads the parables with any care can doubt that our Lord taught that He would come again.

The message of some of these parables gathers around the *period of His absence*, with its necessary boundaries, His *departure* and His *return*, so that if there is to be no Second Advent these parables lose their significance.

(i) THE LORD AND HIS SERVANT ... ... Matt. xxiv. 45-51
The servant says: 'My lord delayeth his coming,' which implies that the lord went away, is away, and intends to return.

(ii) THE BRIDEGROOM AND THE VIRGINS ... Matt. xxv. 1-13
That 'the bridegroom tarried,' implies that he intends to come.

(iii) THE LORD AND THE TALENTS ... ... Matt. xxv. 14-30
The lord is 'as a man travelling into a far country' (14); this tells of his *going away*. 'After a long time' (19), tells of his *absence*. 'The lord of those servants cometh' (19), tells of his *return*.

(iv) THE MASTER OF THE HOUSE ...   .   Mark xiii. 34-37
    Here Christ says that 'the Son of Man is as
    a man taking a far journey.' This journey
    implies his *absence*; and, Christ continues:
    'Ye know not when the master of the house
    cometh,' that is, when the Son of Man will
    return.

(v) THE GOOD SAMARITAN   ...   .   Luke x. 30-35
    Incidentally the same three particulars are
    here also. Having helped the wounded
    man, we read that 'on the morrow (the
    good Samaritan) *departed*'; but, before doing
    so he said to the innkeeper: "Take care of
    him, and . . . when *I come again* I will repay
    thee.'"

(vi) THE NOBLEMAN AND THE POUNDS ...   ...   Luke xix. 12-27
    'A certain nobleman went into a far country'—
    there is the *going away*; 'to receive for
    himself a kingdom'—there is the purpose
    of his *absence*; 'and to return'—there is his
    intention to *return;* and he bids his servants
    'occupy' until he does return.

All these parables refer to Christ Himself. He is the Lord,
the Bridegroom, the Master, the Good Samaritan, and the
Nobleman; and surely language could not state more clearly
the triple fact that He who was here, went away, is now absent,
and is pledged to return; and the last of these is not less certain
than the other two.

One great object of the parables was to make the disciples
understand that their Master was about to leave them, and
would return; and the exhortation throughout to faithfulness
and watchfulness loses its force and sense if He is not to come
back.

(5) CHRIST'S PLAIN TEACHING

Twenty-one times, at least, Christ speaks of His second
advent, and these references are made on the eve of His departure.
It was in the shadow of the Cross that He foretold His advent
in glory.

The following are some of His words:

'The Son of Man shall come.' 'They shall see the Son of Man coming.' 'Your Lord doth come.' 'When the Son of Man shall come.' 'When He cometh in the glory of His Father.' 'Ye shall say: "Blessed is He that cometh in the name of the Lord."' 'When the Son of Man is revealed.'

These declarations are made in terms which present shades of His meaning; terms which signify,

To expose to view (*apokaluptō*)	...	...	Luke xvii. 30
The act of coming (*erchomai*) ...	...	...	Matt. xxiv. 30
Presence, or arrival (*parousia*) ...	...	...	Matt. xxiv. 27, 39
To be here, to have come (*hēkō*)	...	...	Matt. xxiv. 50

In addition to these are such passages as refer to

'the time of the harvest'; 'the end of the age'; 'the day'; 'that day'; 'the last day'; 'the regeneration,' and 'rewards.'

Such references in Christ's teaching point almost always to that crisis which is precipitated by His second advent. It is perfectly clear that Christ said He would come again, and said so both before His death and after it.

Towards the construction of a doctrine of Christ's return, one or two matters claim attention.

(a) *The Manner of the Return*

This, we are told, will be *personal* and *visible*.

References to this are taken by many to mean that Christ is always coming. We are told that He came in A.D. 70, at the Fall of Jerusalem; and when the massive fabric of Roman civilisation fell before the attacks of Goths and Huns; and at the birth of modern Europe in the 13th century; and when Martin Luther shook and shattered the edifice of the Papacy, and brought reality back to religion; and at the time of the Evangelical Revival, when Wesley and Whitefield aroused a torpid and dead England to spiritual life; and in the time of the American Civil War.

Now, whatever may be said about these and other Divine visitations, by no fair handling of Scripture can they be in any way related to Christ's predictions of His second advent.

Referring to such interpretations Dr. James Denney has said: 'But all these admissions, giving them the widest possible application, do not enable us to call in question what stands so plainly in the pages of the New Testament—what filled so exclusively the minds of the first Christians—the idea of a personal return of Christ at the end of the world. *If we are to retain any relation to the New Testament at all, we must assert the personal return of Christ as Judge of all*' (the italics are mine).

Let it not be denied that great crises in history may be regarded in some sense as a coming of Christ, nor that there is a coming which is spiritual and progressive. Christ teaches this quite plainly in the words: 'I come again, and will receive you unto Myself' (John xiv. 3, R.V.) Not, 'I will come again and receive you.' The first tense is the *present*, not the future, and the second is the *future*, 'I will receive you.' This rendering includes the second advent, but embraces much more, as does verse 18 also, which likewise has the present and future tenses: 'I will not leave you orphans; I come to you.'

His 'coming,' in this latter verse cannot refer to His second advent, for that would mean that His people have been left orphans until now. Both verses 3 and 18 have a progressive meaning. Christ came again when He rose from the dead, and also on the Day of Pentecost, and He has been coming to His people in many ways since then, and all these comings will be consummated when in person He returns from heaven at the end of the age.

We do not need to deny one truth in order to affirm another, and so we must reject the view which denies Christ's personal and visible coming, on the ground that He is always coming.

Our Lord teaches that His advent will be *sudden*, as well as personal. In His Olivet discourse He employs three illustrations to set forth the suddenness and visibility of His advent.

It will be 'as the *lightning* cometh out of the east, and shineth even unto the west.' It will be as the *flood* in the days of Noah, which came swiftly 'and took them all away.' It will be as the *thief*, who is not expected to come (Matt. xxiv. 27, 39, 43). These figures of lightning, flood, and thief, cannot be applied to any past coming, but, in their context, must refer to an advent yet future, which will be personal, visible, and sudden.

And again, our Lord teaches that His return will be in *glory*.

'The Son of Man shall come in the glory of His Father, with His angels.' 'The tribes of the earth shall see the Son of Man coming on the clouds of heaven with power and great glory.' 'When the Son of Man shall come in His glory, and all the holy angels with Him, then shall He sit upon the throne of His glory' (Matt. xvi. 27; xxiv. 30; xxv. 31).

Such affirmations should not leave one in any doubt as to the manner of the second advent; yet it has been said that for Christ to come again would be derogatory to His majesty. But surely the fact of a past coming should predispose us to expect a future one! Surely He who once came in weakness, can and will come again in power! Surely He who once came to suffer, can and will come again to reign! Surely He who once came in humiliation, can and will come again in glory! And surely this earth, which was once the scene of His apparent defeat, will one day be the scene also of His unquestionable triumph! If nineteen hundred years ago it was not derogatory to His majesty to become incarnate, to be born in a stable, and to work at a carpenter's bench, to die on a cross, and be buried in a borrowed grave, how can it be derogatory to His majesty to come with 'flaming advent feet,' to come with shining hosts of angels, to come with regal authority and power, to come to judge and rule the world?

(b) *The Time of the Return*

Christ's teaching on this point is clear, and may be summarized in three statements:

First, that the period of His absence would be protracted;
Second, that certain signs would herald the approach of His advent; and
Third, that the precise time of His coming will not be known.

That the period of His absence would be protracted is intimated in the parable of the Talents, where it is said: 'After a long time, the lord of those servants cometh' (Matt. xxv. 19); and also, in the parable of the Pounds, where it is said that the nobleman went into a far country 'to receive for himself a kingdom,' a mission which would require time (Luke xix. 12).

The protraction of His absence is indicated also in passages which speak of wars and rumours of wars; of nation rising against nation, and kingdom against kingdom; of famines, and pestilences, and earthquakes; and of all these as being 'the beginning of sorrows'; and in that passage which says that the 'Gospel of the Kingdom shall be preached in all the world for a witness unto all nations, and then shall the end come' (Matt. xxiv. 6-8, 14).

Christ also intimated that certain signs in the physical and moral realms would herald His return (Matt. xxiv. 15, 16, 23-26, 29-33); but He plainly taught that no one could know just when He would come (Matt. xxiv. 36-44).

When Christ said: 'There be some standing here who shall not taste of death till they shall see the Son of Man coming in His kingdom' (Matt. xvi. 28), the context makes it clear that He was referring to the Transfiguration which took place a week later (Matt. xvii).

A more difficult passage is Matt. xxiv. 34: 'This generation (*genea*) shall not pass till all these things be fulfilled.'

Now, as the 'things' referred to in the preceding context did not occur before the destruction of Jerusalem, in A.D. 70, our Lord cannot be pointing to that event; and that He did not mean that the people to whom He was speaking, that 'generation,' would be alive when He returned from heaven, is evident in the fact that He has not yet come.

The passage, however, must mean something. It has been influentially held that 'generation' here means 'race,' and that what is affirmed is that the Jewish race would be preserved till the second advent. If this be the meaning, the promise has been wonderfully fulfilled.

But the passage may also mean, not the generation *to* which Christ was speaking, but the one *of* which He was speaking; which interpretation would cast the event into the distant future.

Whether these and other interpretations are, or are not correct, we must assume that Christ did not speak ignorantly, and did not contradict Himself.

(c) *The Purpose of the Return*

Here, also, Christ's teaching is plain. He will come to 'reckon' with men; to judge, to reward, and to rule. In the Talents parable the lord returned 'and reckoneth with' his servants. In the time of the harvest the darnel is separated from the wheat. At the end of the age the good fish are gathered into vessels, and the bad are cast away; 'the wicked are severed from among the just' (Matt. xiii).

There is a profound ethical and spiritual reason for all the Divine actions; they are rooted in God's holy character, and in the necessity of things. The Apostles' Creed says He shall return 'to judge the quick and the dead.' 'There is an inherent fitness,' says Dr. Orr, 'if not a moral necessity, about such a return of Christ at the end of the world, as the New Testament uniformly asserts.' This fitness is found in the necessity for judgment; a necessity which is witnessed to alike by the human conscience (Rom. ii. 15), man's sense of justice (Acts xxiv. 25), the declarations of Scripture (Heb. ix. 27), and the nature of God (Gen. xviii. 25).

Belief or disbelief in this matter of whether Christ will return to this earth will determine one's whole philosophy of history. If Christ is not coming back, and if there is any future for the world, then, men must work out their own destiny, as indeed, they have been attempting to do by the League of Nations, and the United Nations Organization. But the failure of men to work out a high and noble destiny for themselves should have convinced us that an impossible task is attempted.

The words of Dr. Thomas Chalmers to the Rev. Edward Bickersteth, in 1836, are in harmony with the teaching of Christ as recorded in the Gospels. He said:

'I utterly despair of the universal prevalence of Christianity as the result of a pacific missionary process, under the guidance of human wisdom and principle. But without slackening in the least our obligation to help forward this great cause, I look for the conclusive establishment (of Christianity) *through a widening passage of desolating judgments, with the utter demolition of our present civil and ecclesiastical structures.*'

Christ was not, as Dr. Schweitzer supposes, an apocalyptic dreamer, but 'The Truth,' and what He declared was the expression of infallible knowledge.

There is an end, a goal for creation, a purpose to be fulfilled, a will to be accomplished. History is not an aimless succession of changes. By the revelation of the final judgment we are enabled to see that for mankind, as for men severally, there is an appointed close to earthly work. All the currents of human history are setting in to the Judgment. All generations of men out of Christ are moving on to the Great White Throne; and the infallible justice of that Judgment is guaranteed by the fact that Christ will be the Judge, Whose are majesty, authority, knowledge, justice, and power, and Who also is Love. From His verdict there can be no appeal, for His own character is the criterion of judgment.

The Husbandman will thoroughly purge His floor; the House-holder will bind the tares in bundles for the fire; the Fisherman will cast away that which is bad; the Bridegroom will shut the door upon the foolish; the Shepherd will separate the sheep from the goats; the Nobleman will consign the unprofitable servant into outer darkness, and the Judge of all the earth will do right.

When Christ will come from heaven to earth 'to judge the quick and the dead' we do not know, but *that* He will do so is a revealed fact, and a moral necessity. Christ has declared what He will do, and unbelief will make no difference, except to the unbelieving.

The matter of the Return of the Lord Jesus is in the warp and woof of the Church's history. It can be traced from the time of the Apostles, through that of the Apostolic Fathers and Ante-Nicene Fathers. Then follows the history of the rejection of this truth by the Roman Catholic Church, and the suppression of it for a thousand years. Yet, though persecuted, the faith was held by such as the Waldenses, the Pauliciaus, and the Cathari, until the Reformation in the sixteenth century; since when it has been and is held by individuals in every section of Christendom. In Theologies, Creeds, and Hymns this truth is borne witness to; and yet there is not a Denomination which, as a Denomination, accepts this article of the Faith.

The influence of the belief upon the Missionary Enterprise cannot possibly be estimated, and in our time there is a con-siderable revival of interest in the subject.

QUESTIONS

1 What four words are used in the Gospels of the Lord's Return, and what do they mean?
2 What other words are used in the Gospels which imply that the present age will be concluded by the Coming of the Son of Man?
3 What is the significance, respectively, of the terms 'Kingdom,' 'Son of Man,' and 'Tribulation,' in the Gospels?
4 Do any of Christ's parables teach that He will return to earth; and if so, which of them?
5 In what passages does Christ plainly declare that He will return?
6 How, according to some, has the promise of the return been fulfilled?
7 Is there any sense in which Christ is continually coming?
8 Do any of the claims that Christ has already come satisfy His predictions on the subject?
9 What, according to the Records, will be the manner of Christ's return?
10 What may we learn from the Gospels as to the time of the return?
11 Do world-conditions to-day agree with the predicted signs of the Second Advent?
12 What do you suppose is the meaning of Matt. xxiv. 34?
13 What is the revealed purpose of Christ's return, and what necessity is there for it?
14 Trace the history of the doctrine of Christ's Return from the Apostolic age to the present time.

LITERATURE

'The Teaching of the Lord, by the Twelve Apostles, to the Gentiles,' called the 'Didache': first century. Chapter XVI
'The Coming of the Kingdom of the Lord Jesus'   H. Bonar
'The Approaching End of the Age'   -   -   H. G. Guinness
'The Last Times'   -   -   -   -   -   J. A. Seiss
'Ecce Venit'   -   -   -   -   -   A. J. Gordon
'Christianity and Antichristianity in their Final Conflict'   -   -   -   -   -   -   S. J. Andrews
'Prediction and Fulfilment'   -   -   -   S. H. Kellogg
'Jesus is Coming'   -   -   -   -   -   W. E. Blackstone
'The Lord's Return'   -   -   -   -   -   J. F. Silver
'At Hand'   -   -   -   -   -   W. Scott
'The Second Coming of Christ'   -   -   -   M. Matthews
'The Return of the Lord Jesus'   -   -   -   R. A. Torrey
'Four Prophetic Periods'   -   -   -   -   E. W. Bullinger
'Sermons on the Second Advent'   -   -   -   E. W. Bullinger
'Christ's Prophetic Teaching'   -   -   -   E. W. Bullinger
'Sermons on the Second Coming'   -   -   -   J. M. Haldeman
'Lectures on the Second Coming and Kingdom of the Lord Jesus Christ'   -   -   -   -   -   W. Kelly

See also the Bible Dictionaries under *Parousia, Millennium, Eschatology*.

*'Now of the things which we have spoken this is
the sum'* (Heb. viii. 1)

WHEN I survey the wondrous Cross
   On which the Prince of Glory died,
My richest gain I count but loss,
   And pour contempt on all my pride.

Forbid it, Lord, that I should boast,
   Save in the death of Christ, my God;
All the vain things that charm me most,
   I sacrifice them to His Blood.

See! from His head, His hands, His feet,
   Sorrow and love flow mingled down;
Did e'er such love and sorrow meet,
   Or thorns compose so rich a crown?

Were the whole realm of nature mine,
   That were an offering far too small;
Love so amazing, so divine,
   Demands my soul, my life, my all.

ISAAC WATTS

'How shall we escape, if we neglect so great salvation?' (Heb. ii. 3)

INDEX I

SUBJECTS

INDEX II

PERSONS

(referred to in the text of the Guide).

For another list of Authors see Index III.

BIBLIOGRAPHY

The following is only a skeleton bibliography, and could
be indefinitely expanded.

1. Historical and Religious Background

ANGUS, S. 'Environment of Early Christianity.'

CHARLES, R. H. 'Religious Development between the Old and the New Testaments.'

DÖLLINGER J. J. I. 'The Gentile and the Jew' (2 vols.).

FAIRWEATHER, W. 'Background of the Gospels.'

FAIRWEATHER, W. 'From the Exile to the Advent.'

FARRAR, F. W. 'The Herods.'

FARRER, J. A. 'Paganism and Christianity.'

FORDE, G. M. 'Between Malachi and St. Matthew.'

FOWLER, W. W. 'Roman Ideas of Deity in the Last Century before the Christian Era.'

GLOVER, T. R. 'Conflict of Religions in the Early Roman Empire.'

GREGG, D. 'Between the Testaments.'

HENDERSON. 'The Age of the Maccabees.'

MAHAFFY, J. P. 'The Story of Alexander's Empire.'

MANLEY, G. T. (Editor. I.V.F.) 'The New Bible Handbook.'

MORRISON. 'The Jews under Roman Rule.'

MOSS, R. W. 'From Malachi to Matthew.'

NOLLOTH, C. F. 'The Rise of the Christian Religion.'

PETRIE, W. M. F. 'Personal Religion in Egypt before Christianity.'

REDFORD. 'Four Centuries of Silence.'

RIGGS, J. S. 'History of the Jewish People in the Maccabean and Roman Periods.'

STREANE, A. W. 'The Age of the Maccabees.'

WENLEY, R. M. 'The Preparation for Christianity in the Ancient World.'

WOOLF, B. L. 'The Background and Beginning of the Gospel Story.'

ZAHN, TH. 'The Greek Language Among the Jews.' Vol. I of Introduction to the New Testament.'

WHEELER, J. T. 'Alexander the Great.'

The Apocryphal Books of the Old Testament.

2. Old Testament Christology

ALEXANDER, Bp. 'The Witness of the Psalms to Christ and Christianity.'

CASE, S. J. 'The Messianic Hope.'

DELITZSCH, F. 'Messianic Prophecies in Historical Succession.'

EDERSHEIM, A. 'The Witness of Israel to the Messiah.'

FAIRBAIRN, P. 'Typology of Scripture.'

GLOAG, P. J. 'Messianic Prophecy.'

GREENHOUSE. 'The Messiah in Jewish History.'

HABERSHON, A. 'The Study of the Types.'

HENGSTENBERG, E. W. 'Christology of the Old Testament' (4 vols.).

HODGKIN, A. M. 'Christ in all the Scriptures.'

LEATHES, S. 'The Witness of the Old Testament to Christ.'

LIDDON, H. P. 'The Divinity of our Lord (Lect. II).'

OESTERLEY. 'The Evolution of the Messianic Idea.'

PIERSON, A. T. 'Many Infallible Proofs.'

RIEHM, E. 'Messianic Prophecy.'

WESTCOTT, Bp. 'Introduction to the Study of the Gospels.'

3. Sacred Geography

ANGUS and GREEN. 'The Bible Handbook.'

CLAPHAM, J. W. 'Palestine.'

DALMAN, G. 'Sacred Sites and Ways.'

GEIKIE, C. 'The Holy Land and the Bible' (2 vols.).

GLUECK, N. 'The River Jordan.'

HODGE. 'Historical Atlas and Chronology of the Life of Christ.'

SANDAY, W. 'Sacred Sites of the Gospels.'
SMITH, G. A. 'Historical Geography of the Holy Land.'
STANLEY, A. P. 'Sinai and Palestine.'
THOMSON, W. M. 'The Land and the Book' (3 vols.).
'A Companion to the Bible.' Edited by T. W. MANSON. (pages 133-156)

4. Ancient Tradition Relative to the Gospels

ANTE-NICENE CHRISTIAN LIBRARY: Translations of the Writings of the Fathers down to A.D. 325.
BACKHOUSE and TYLOR. 'Witnesses for Christ.'
BARTLET (and others). 'The New Testament in the Apostolic Fathers.'
EUSEBIUS. 'Ecclesiastical History' (2 vols.).
FARRAR, F. W. 'Lives of the Fathers' (2 vols.).
GURNEY, T. A. 'The Church of the First Three Centuries.'
LATOURETTE, K. S. 'The First Five Centuries.'
LEIGH-BENNETT, E. 'Handbook of the Early Christian Fathers.'
LIGHTFOOT, J. B. 'The Apostolic Fathers.'
MOFFATT, J. 'The First Five Centuries of the Church.'
MOSHEIM. 'Ecclesiastical History.'
SCHAFF. 'The History of the Church' (2 vols.).
SWETE, H. B. 'Patristic Study.'
WAKE and BURTON. 'The Apostolic Fathers of the Second Century.'

5. Introducing the New Testament

ALFORD, H. 'The Greek Testament' (4 vols.).
ANGUS and GREEN. 'The Bible Handbook.'
BENGEL, J. A. 'Gnomon of the New Testament' (5 vols.).
DODS, M. 'Introduction to the New Testament.'
FARRAR, F. W. 'Messages of the Books.'
GLOAG, P. J. 'Introduction to the New Testament' (4 vols.).
GODET, F. 'Introduction to the New Testament.'
KELLY, W. 'Lectures Introductory to the New Testament' (3 vols.).
MANLEY, G. T. (Editor. *I.V.F.*) 'The New Bible Handbook.'
McCLYMONT, J. A. 'The New Testament and its Writers.'

MEYER, H. A. W. 'Critical and Exegetical Commentary on the New Testament' (20 vols.).
MILLIGAN, G. 'The New Testament Documents.'
MILLIGAN, G. 'The New Testament and its Transmission.'
MOFFATT, J. 'Introduction to the Literature of the New Testament.'
MOFFATT, J. 'The Approach to the New Testament.'
NICOLL, W. R. 'The Expositors' Greek Testament' (5 vols.). (Editor).
SALMON, G. 'Introduction to the New Testament.'
SELWYN, E. C. 'The Oracles in the New Testament.'
STRONG, A. H. 'Popular Lectures on the Books of the New Testament.'
WEISS, B. 'A Manual of Introduction to the New Testament' (2 vols.).
WESTCOTT, Bp. 'The Canon of the New Testament.'

6. Harmonies of the Gospels

BROADUS, J. A. 'A Harmony of the Gospels' (1921).
GOSPEL PARALLELS. Revised Standard Version (1949).
HILL, J. H. 'The Diatessaron of Tatian' (1894).
HOBSON. 'The Diatessaron of Tatian and the Synoptic Problem.'
KERR. 'A Harmony of the Gospels in the American Standard Version' (1903).
LYTTON, The Earl of. 'Love Incarnate. A Continuous Narrative of the Gospels, based on the Authorised Version' (1945).
PIERSON, A. T. 'The One Gospel.' A combination of the Narratives of the Four Evangelists in one Complete Record.
PONSONBY, R. 'The Life and Teaching of Christ.'
ROBERTSON, A. T. 'A Harmony of the Gospels for Students of the Life of Christ' (1923).
ROBINSON-RIDDLE. 'A Harmony of the Gospels in Greek' (1885).
SECRETT, A. G. 'A Combined Analysis of the Four Gospels' (1927).
STEVENS and BURTON. 'A Harmony of the Gospels for Historical Study, in the Revised Version' (1910).
TOLSTOY. 'The Gospel in Brief.'
WRIGHT, A. 'A Synopsis of the Gospels in Greek.'
WRIGHT, A. 'The Composition of the Four Gospels.'
ZAHN TH. 'Tatian's Diatessaron.'

644 BIBLIOGRAPHY

For Harmonies as Interwoven Gospels, see the Bibliography in the New SCHAFF-HERZOG Encyclopædia of Religious Knowledge. Vol. V., p. 154.

For Harmonies in Parallel Arrangement, see the Bibliography of the SCHAFF - HERZOG Encyclopædia (above). Vol. V., p. 155.

7. The Synoptic Gospels

ABBOTT and RUSHBROOKE. 'The Common Tradition of the Synoptic Gospels (R.V.),' (1884).

BURTON and GOODSPEED. 'A Harmony of the Synoptic Gospels in Greek' (1920).

BURTON and GOODSPEED. 'A Harmony of the Synoptic Gospels for Historical and Critical Study.'

GLOAG, P. J. 'Introduction to the Synoptic Gospels.'

RUSHBROOKE, W. G. 'Synopticon.' The Common Matter of the First Three Gospels (1880).

TISCHENDORF. 'Synopsis Evangelica.'

8. The Text of the Gospels

BURGON and MILLER. 'The Traditional Text of the Holy Gospels.'

BURKITT, F. C. 'The Gospel History and Its Transmission.'

DRUMMOND, J. 'The Transmission of the Text of the New Testament.'

GREGORY, C. R. 'Canon and Text of the New -Testament.'

HAMMOND, C. E. 'Outlines of Textual Criticism.'

KENYON, F. G. 'Handbook to the Textual Criticism of the New Testament.'

KNOX, R. A. 'The New Testament Newly Translated' (1946).

LAKE, K. 'The Text of the New Testament.'

MILLIGAN, G. 'The Expository Value of the Revised Version.'

MILLIGAN, G. 'The New Testament Documents.'

NEWTON, B. W. 'Remarks on the Revised Version of the New Testament.'

NICOLSON, W. M. 'Critical Revision of the New Testament.'

ROBERTSON, A. T. 'An Introduction to the Textual Criticism of the New Testament.'

——. 'Revised Standard Version of the New Testament' (1946).

SCRIVENER, A. 'Plain Introduction to the Criticism of the New Testament.'

SOUTER, A. 'The Text and Canon of the New Testament.'

S.P.C.K. 'Addresses on the Revised Version of the New Testament.'

VAUGHAN, Dean. 'Authorized or Revised?'

VINCENT, M. R. 'A History of the Textual Criticism of the New Testament.'

WESTCOTT, Bp. 'Some Lessons of the Revised Version of the New Testament.'

WEYMOUTH, R. F. 'The Resultant Greek Testament.'

WARFIELD, B. B. 'An Introduction to the Textual Criticism of the New Testament.'

9. The Synoptic Problem

ABBOTT and RUSHBROOKE. 'The Common Tradition of the Synoptic Gospels.'

BACON, B. W. 'The Beginnings of the Gospel Story.'

BLACK, M. 'An Aramaic Approach to the Gospels and Acts' (1946).

BRUCE, F. F. 'Are the New Testament Documents Reliable?'

BUCKLEY, E. R. 'An Introduction to the Synoptic Problem.'

BURKITT, F. C. 'The Gospel History and Its Transmission.'

BURKITT, F. C. 'The Earliest Sources of the Life of Jesus.'

BURTON, E. D. 'Some Principles of Literary Criticism and their Application to the Synoptic Problem.'

CARPENTER, J. E. 'The First Three Gospels.'

HAWKINS, Sir John. 'Horæ Synopticae.'

HOBSON, A. A. 'The Diatessaron of Tatian and the Synoptic Problem.'

HOLDSWORTH, W. W. 'Gospel Origins.'

JAMESON. 'The Origin of the Synoptic Gospels.'

McINTYRE, D. M. 'Some Notes on the Gospels.'

MONTEFIORE. 'The Synoptic Gospels.'

NICOL, T. 'The Four Gospels in the Earliest Church History.'

PATTON. 'The Sources of the Synoptic Gospels.'

PETRIE, Sir Flinders. 'The Growth of the Gospels as Shown by Structural Criticism.'

REDLICH, E. B. 'The Student's Introduction to the Synoptic Problem.'

ROBERTSON, A. T. 'The Christ of the Logia.'

RUSHBROOKE, W. G. 'Synopticon': The Common Matter.

SALMON, G. 'The Human Element in the Gospels.'

SANDAY, W. (Editor). 'Oxford Studies in the Synoptic Problem.'

SCOTT, E. F. 'The Making of the Gospels.'

SMITH, R. 'The Solution of the Synoptic Problem.'

STANTON, V. H. 'The Synoptic Gospels. Part II: The Gospels as Historical Documents.'

STREETER, B. H. 'The Four Gospels.' A Study of Origins.

TAYLOR, V. 'The Formation of the Gospel Tradition.'

TAYLOR, V. 'Behind the Third Gospel'

TAYLOR, V. 'The Gospels.' A Short Introduction.

TORREY, C. C. 'The Translations Made from the Original Aramaic Gospels.'

WERNLE. 'The Sources of our Knowledge of the Life of Jesus.'

WRIGHT, A. 'Some New Testament Problems.'

WRIGHT, A. 'A Synopsis of the Gospels in Greek.'

WRIGHT, A. 'The Composition of the Four Gospels.'

10. The Old Testament in the Gospels

GOUGH. 'New Testament Quotations (compared with the Hebrew and the LXX).'

JOHNSON, F. 'The Quotations of the New Testament from the Old.'

McFARLAND. 'Jesus and the Prophets.'

McNEILE, A. H. 'Our Lord's Use of the Old Testament' (Cambridge Biblical Essays).

SCOTT, E. F. 'New Testament Quotations.'

TOY, C. H. 'Quotations in the New Testament.'

TURPIE, D. C. 'The Old Testament in the New.'

TURPIE, D. C. 'New Testament View of the Old Testament.'

11. The Four Gospels

ABBOTT, E. A. 'The Fourfold Gospel.'

ALEXANDER, Bp. 'Leading Ideas of the Gospels.'

ANGUS and GREEN. 'The Bible Handbook.'

BIRKS, T. R. & H. A. 'Horæ Evangelicæ.'

BADHAM, F. P. 'Formation of the Fou. Gospels.'

BURTON, E. D. 'A Short Introduction to the Gospels.'

CHASE, F. H. 'The Gospels in the Light of Historical Criticism.'

COHU, J. R. 'The Gospels in the Light of Modern Research.'

DA COSTA. 'The Four Witnesses.'

DEANE, A. C. 'How to Understand the Gospels.'

GODET, F. 'Biblical Studies.'

GODET, F. 'The Collection of the Four Gospels.'

GREGORY, D. S. 'Why Four Gospels?'

JONES, M. 'The Four Gospels.'

JUKES, A. 'Differences of the Four Gospels.'

LUCKOCK, H. M. 'Characteristics of the Four Gospels.'

MOREHEAD, W. G. 'Studies in the Four Gospels.'

McINTYRE, D. M. 'Some Notes on the Gospels.'

NORTON, W. 'Genuineness of the Gospels.'

ROBERTSON, A. T. 'The Christ of the Logia.'

ROBINSON, J. A. 'The Study of the Gospels.'

SCOTT, E. F. 'The Making of the Gospels.'

TAYLOR, V. 'The Gospels.' A Short Introduction.

TISCHENDORF. 'Origin of the Four Gospels.'

WESTCOTT, Bp. 'Introduction to the Study of the Gospels.'

WILSON, J. M. 'The Origins and Aims of the Four Gospels.'

WORK, E. W. 'The Fascination of the Book.'

12. Mark's Gospel

ALFORD, H. 'The Greek Testament': Vol. I.

ALEXANDER, Bp. 'Leading Ideas of the Gospels.'

BACON, B. W. 'The Gospel of Mark: Its Composition and Date.'

BACON, B. W. 'The Beginning of the Gospel Story.'

BENGEL, J. A. 'Gnomon of the New Testament': Vol. I.

BRUCE, A. B. 'The Expositor's Greek Testament': Vol. I.

CHADWICK, C. A. 'The Gospel of Mark' (Expositor's Bible).

ERDMAN, C. R. 'The Gospel of Mark.'

GLOAG, P. J. 'Introduction to the Synoptic Gospels.'

GOULD, E. P. 'St. Mark' (International Critical Commentary).

HASTINGS, E. (Editor). 'The Speaker's Bible' (2 vols.).

JONES, J. D. 'Commentary on St. Mark.' (Devotional Library: 4 vols.).

JONES, M. 'The Four Gospels.'

LINDSAY, T. M. 'St. Mark's Gospel' (Handbooks for Bible Classes).

LUCKOCK, H. M. 'Footprints of the Son of Man as Traced by St. Mark.'

MANSON, T. W. 'The Beginning of the Gospel' (1950).

MANSON, T. W. ʿ A New Translation of Mark's Gospel.'

MENZIES, A. 'The Earliest Gospel.'

MEYER, H. A. W. 'Critical and Exegetical Handbook on the Gospels of Mark and Luke.'

MORISON, J. 'St. Mark.' A Practical Commentary.

PLUMMER, A. 'St. Mark' (Cambridge Greek Testament).

PLUMMER, A. 'St. Mark' (Cambridge Bible for Schools).

ROBERTSON, A. T. 'Studies in Mark's Gospel.'

ROBERTSON, A. T. 'Making Good in the Ministry': A Sketch of John Mark.'

ROBERTSON, A. T. 'Word Pictures in the New Testament': Vol. I.

SALMOND, S. D. F. 'St. Mark' (The Century Bible).

SWETE, H. B. 'The Gospel According to St. Mark.'

TAYLOR, V. 'The Gospels.'

TAYLOR, VINCENT. 'The Gospel According to St. Mark.'

VINCENT, M. 'Word Studies in the New Testament': Vol. I.

WESTCOTT, Bp. 'Introduction to the Study of the Gospels.'

13. Matthew's Gospel

ALEXANDER, Bp. 'Leading Ideas of the Gospels.'

ALLEN, W. C. 'St. Matthew' (International Critical Commentary).

ALFORD, H. 'The Greek Testament': Vol. I.

ANDERSON, E. E. 'St. Matthew's Gospel' (Handbooks for Bible Classes).

ANGUS and GREEN. 'The Bible Handbook.'

BENGEL, J. A. 'Gnomon of the New Testament': Vol. I.

BRUCE, A. B. 'The Expositor's Greek Testament': Vol. I.

BULLINGER, E. W. 'The Companion Bible.' Part V.

CARR, A. 'St. Matthew' (Cambridge Greek Testament).

CHRYSOSTOM. 'Homiletical Discourses.'

ERDMAN, C. R. 'The Gospel of Matthew'

FINDLAY, J. A. 'Jesus in the First Gospel.'

GIBSON, M. 'The Gospel of St. Matthew' (Expositor's Bible).

GLOAG, P. J. 'Introduction to the Synoptic Gospels.'

HASTINGS, E. (Editor). 'The Speaker's Bible' (3 vols.).

JONES, M. 'The Four Gospels.'

KILPATRICK, G. D. 'The Origins of the Gospel According to St. Matthew' (1947).

McNEILE, A. H. 'The Gospel According to St. Matthew.'

MEYER, H. A. W. 'Critical and Exegetical Handbook on the Gospel of St. Matthew.'

MORISON, J. 'A Practical Commentary on the Gospel According to St. Matthew.'

PEMBER, G. H. 'The Great Prophecies of the Centuries Concerning the Church.'

PLUMMER, A. 'Exegetical Commentary on the Gospel According to St. Matthew.

ROBERTSON, A. T. 'Word Pictures in the New Testament': Vol. I.

SLATER, W. F. 'St. Matthew' (The Century Bible).

TAYLOR, V. 'The Gospels.'

VINCENT, M. 'Word Studies in the New Testament': Vol. I.

WESTCOTT, Bp. 'Introduction to the Study of the Gospels.'

14. Luke's Gospel

ADENEY, W. F. 'St. Luke' (The Century Bible).

ALEXANDER, Bp. 'Leading Ideas of the Gospels.'

ALFORD, H. 'The Greek Testament': Vol. I.

BENGEL, J.A. 'Gnomon of the New Testament': Vol. II.

BICKERSTETH, C. 'The Gospel of an Artist and Physician.'

BRUCE, A. B. 'The Expositor's Greek Testament': Vol. I.

BURTON, H. 'The Gospel of St. Luke' (Expositor's Bible).

CADBURY, H. J. 'Critical Studies in the Gospel of Luke and the Book of the Acts.'

CARR, A. 'Notes on the Greek Testament: St. Luke.'

ERDMAN, C. R. 'The Gospel of Luke.'

FARRAR, F. W. 'St. Luke' (Cambridge Greek Testament).

GELDENHUYS, N. 'Commentary on the Gospel of Luke' (1950).

GLOAG, P. J. 'Introduction to the Synoptic Gospels.'

GODET, F. 'Commentary on St. Luke's Gospel' (2 vols.).

HARNACK, A. 'Luke the Physician.'

HAYES. 'The Most Beautiful Book in the World.'

HOBART, W. K. 'The Medical Language of St. Luke.'

JONES, M. 'The Four Gospels.'

LINDSAY, T. M. 'St. Luke's Gospel' (Handbooks for Bible Classes).

LUCKOCK, H. M. 'The Special Characteristics of the Four Gospels.'

MACKINLAY, G. 'Recent Discoveries in St. Luke's Writings.'

McLACHLAN, H. 'St. Luke, Evangelist and Historian.'

MEYER, H. A. W. 'Critical and Exegetical Handbook on the Gospels of Mark and Luke' (2 vols.).

PLUMMER, A. 'St. Luke' (International Critical Commentary).

RAMSAY, W. M. 'Luke the Physician.'

ROBERTSON, A. T. 'Luke the Historian in the Light of Research.'

ROBERTSON, A. T. 'Word Pictures in the New Testament': Vol. II.

ROBERTSON, A. T. 'A Translation of Luke's Gospel with Grammatical Notes.'

ROSS, J. M. E. 'St. Luke' (3 vols. Devotional Commentary).

TAYLOR, V. 'The Gospels.'

VINCENT, M. 'Word Studies in the New Testament': Vol. II.

WESTCOTT, Bp. 'Introduction to the Study of the Gospels.'

WRIGHT, A. 'Some New Testament Problems.'

WRIGHT, A. 'St. Luke's Gospel in Greek.'

15. John's Gospel

ABBOTT, E. A. 'The Johannine Vocabulary.'

ALEXANDER, Bp. 'Leading Ideas of the Gospels.'

ASKWITH, E. H. 'The Historical Value of the Fourth Gospel.'

BENGEL, J. A. 'Gnomon of the New Testament': Vol. II.

BERNARD, J. H. 'St. John' (International Critical Commentary: 2 vols.).

BERNARD, T. D. 'The Central Teaching of Jesus Christ.'

CAWLEY, F. 'The Transcendence of Jesus Christ' (Ch. V.).

DODS, M. 'The Gospel of John' (Expositor's Bible: 2 vols.).

DOREN, VAN. 'Suggestive Commentary on St. John' (2 vols.).

DRUMMOND, J. 'Character and Authorship of the Fourth Gospel.'

ERDMAN, C. R. 'The Gospel of John.'

FARRAR, F. W. 'The Messages of the Books.'

FARRAR, F. W. 'The Early Days of Christianity': Vol. II.

GAIRDNER, W. H. T. 'Helps to the Study of St. John's Gospel.'

GLOAG, P. J. 'Introduction to the Johannine Writings.'

GODET, F. 'Commentary on St. John's Gospel' (3 vols.).

JONES, M. 'The Four Gospels.'

McCLYMONT, J. A. 'St. John' (The Century Bible).

MEYER, H. A. W. 'Critical and Exegetical Handbook on the Gospel of St. John' (2 vols.).

MOFFATT, J. 'Introduction to the Literature of the New Testament.'

NOLLOTH, C. F. 'The Fourth Evangelist.'

NUNN, H. P. V. 'The Son of Zebedee.'

PLUMMER, A. 'St. John' (Cambridge Greek Testament).

REITH, G. 'St. John's Gospel' (Handbooks for Bible Classes: 2 vols.).

REYNOLDS, H. R. 'St. John' (Pulpit Commentary: 2 vols.).

ROBERTSON, A. T. 'Word Pictures in the New Testament': Vol. V.

ROBERTSON, A. T. 'The Divinity of Christ in the Gospel of John.'

ROBINSON, J. A. 'The Historical Character of St. John's Gospel.'

TAYLOR, V. 'The Gospels.'

TEMPLE, WM. 'Readings in St. John's Gospel.'

THOMAS, W. H. G. 'The Apostle John.'

VINCENT, M. 'Word Studies in the New Testament': Vol. II.

WESTCOTT, Bp. 'Introduction to the Study of the Gospels.'

WESTCOTT, Bp. 'Gospel of John.'

16. Authorship of the Fourth Gospel

(i) *In favour of the Johannine Authorship*

ABBOT, E. 'The Fourth Gospel and its Authorship.'

DRUMMOND, J. 'The Character and Authorship of the Fourth Gospel.'

GODET, F. 'Commentary on the Fourth Gospel.'

LEATHES, S. 'The Witness of St. John to Christ.'

LUTHARDT, C. E. 'St. John the Author of the Fourth Gospel.'

MEYER, H. A. W. 'Critical and Exegetical Handbook on the Gospel of St. John.'

NOLLOTH, C. F. 'The Fourth Evangelist.'

NUNN, H. P. V. 'The Son of Zebedee and the Fourth Gospel.'

ORR, J. 'The Authorship of John's Gospel.'

REYNOLDS, H. R. 'St. John': Vol. I: Introduction (Pulpit Commentary).

REYNOLDS, H. R. Hastings' Dictionary of the Bible: ii, 680-728.

SANDAY, W. 'The Authorship and Historical Character of the Fourth Gospel.'

SANDAY, W. 'The Gospels in the Second Century.'

STRACHAN, R. H. Hastings' Dictionary of Christ and the Gospels; i., 869-885.

WESTCOTT, Bp. 'Introduction to the Study of the Gospels.'

WESTCOTT, Bp. 'St. John.' Commentary.

(ii) Against the Johannine Authorship

BACON, B. W. 'The Fourth Gospel in Research and Debate.'

MOFFATT, J. 'Introduction to the Literature of the New Testament.'

STREETER, B. H. 'The Four Gospels.' Most German Critics.

(iii) A Mediating Position

BERNARD, J. H. 'St. John' (International Critical Commentary. Vol. I: pp. xxxiv-lxiv).

17. The Apostles

BAUR, F. C. 'The Apostles.'

BRUCE, A. B. 'The Training of the Twelve.'

GREENOUGH, J. G. 'The Apostles of Our Lord.'

EDERSHEIM, A. 'The Life and Times of Jesus the Messiah.'

ELLICOTT, C. J. 'Historical Lectures on the Life of Our Lord.'

HAUSRATH, A. 'History of New Testament Times: The Apostles.'

JONES, J. D. 'The Glorious Company of the Apostles.'

LATHAM, H. 'Pastor Pastorum.'

LUCKOCK, H. M. 'Footprints of the Apostles.'

PATRICK, W. 'Apostles' (Hastings' Dictionary of Christ and the Gospels: Vol. I.).

SELWYN, E. C. 'The Christian Prophets.'

Consult also the Commentaries and Books on Bible Biographies.

18. Lives of Christ

ANDREWS, S. J. 'The Bible Student's Life of Our Lord.'

BORCHERT, O. 'The Original Jesus.'

EDERSHEIM, A. 'The Life and Times of Jesus the Messiah.'

FAIRBAIRN, A. M. 'Studies in the Life of Christ.'

FARRAR, F. W. 'The Life of Christ.'

GARVIE, A. E. 'Studies in the Inner Life of Jesus.'

GEIKIE, C. 'The Life and Words of Christ.'

GLOVER, T. R. 'The Jesus of History.'

HANNA, W. 'Our Lord's Life on Earth.'

HEADLAM, A. C. 'The Life and Teachings of Jesus Christ.'

HUNTER, A. M. 'The Work and Words of Jesus' (1950).

MATHESON, G. 'Studies in the Portrait of Christ' (2 vols.).

MORTON, H. V. 'In the Steps of the Master.'

NOEL, Conrad. 'The Life of Jesus.'

PAPINI, G. 'The Life of Christ.'

PARKER, J. 'Ecce Deus.'

PATERSON-SMYTH. 'A People's Life of Christ.'

PRESSENSE, E. de. 'Jesus Christ, His Times, Life and Work.'

ROBERTSON, A. T. 'Epochs in the Life of Jesus.'

SANDAY, W. 'Outlines of the Life of Christ.'

SANDAY, W. 'The Life of Christ in Recent Research.'

SEELEY, Sir John. 'Ecce Homo.'

SELBIE, W. B. 'Aspects of Christ.'

SMITH, D. 'In the Days of His Flesh.'

STALKER, J. 'The Life of Jesus Christ.'

TAYLOR, Jeremy. 'The Great Exemplar of Sanctity and Holy Life.'

WATSON, J. 'The Life of the Master.'

WEISS, B. 'The Life of Christ' (3 vols.).

WHYTE, A. 'The Walk and Conversation of Jesus Christ.'

WILSON, W. 'The Christ that We Forget.'

Radical Works

BOUSSET. 'Jesus.'

EWALD. 'History of Christ and His Times.'

HOLTZMANN. 'The Life of Jesus.'

KEIM. 'The History of Jesus of Nazara.'

RENAN. 'The Life of Jesus.'

SCHMIDT. 'The Prophet of Nazareth.'

SCHWEITZER. 'The Quest of the Historical Jesus.'

STRAUSS. 'The Life of Jesus Critically Examined.'

19. Christology

BORCHERT, O. 'The Original Jesus.'

BRUCE, A. B. 'The Humiliation of Christ.'

BUSHNELL, H. 'The Character of Jesus' (in Nature and the Supernatural).

CAWLEY, F. 'The Transcendence of Jesus Christ.'

CHADWICK, Bp. 'Christ Bearing Witness to Himself' (Donnellan Lectures).

DALE, R. W. 'Christian Doctrine.'

DENNEY, J. 'Jesus and the Gospel.'

DORNER, A. 'History of the Development of the Doctrine of the Person of Christ' (5 vols.).

DORNER, A. 'System of Christian Doctrine.'

FAIRBAIRN, A. M. 'The Place of Christ in Modern Theology.'

FORREST, D. W. 'The Christ of History and of Experience.'

FORREST, D. W. 'The Authority of Christ.'

FORSYTH, P. T. 'The Person and Place of Jesus Christ.'

GARVIE, A. E. 'Studies in the Inner Life of Jesus.'

GORE, C. ' The Incarnation of the Son of God.'

HARNACK, A. 'History of Dogma.'

HODGE, C. 'Systematic Theology.'

ILLINGWORTH, J. R. 'Personality: Human and Divine.'

LACEY, T. A. 'The Historic Christ.'

LIDDON, H. P. 'The Divinity of Our Lord.'

MACKINTOSH, H. R. 'The Person of Jesus Christ.'

NOLLOTH, C. F. 'The Person of Our Lord in Recent Thought.'

PEARSON, J. 'Exposition of the Creed.'

SANDAY, W. 'Christologies Ancient and Modern.'

SHEDD, W. G. T. 'Dogmatic Theology.'

SIMPSON, P. C. 'The Fact of Christ.'

SMITH, D. 'The Historic Jesus.'

STALKER, J. 'The Christology of Jesus.'

STREATFIELD, G. S. 'The Self-Interpretation of Jesus Christ.'

STRONG, A. H. 'Systematic Theology.'

DIGGES LA TOUCHE, E. 'The Person of Christ in Modern Thought.'

WARFIELD, B. B. 'The Lord of Glory.'

WARFIELD, B. B. 'The Person of Christ.'

WILBERFORCE, R. J. 'Doctrine of the Incarnation.'

20. The Birth of Christ

BERNARD, J. H. '*Studia Sacra*': Ch. vii.

BOX, G. H. 'Virgin Birth' Hastings' Dictionary of Christ and the Gospels: vol. II.

BRUCE, A. B. 'The Humiliation of Christ.'

CHAMPION, J. B. 'The Virgin's Son.'

GORE, C. 'Dissertations on Subjects Connected with the Incarnation': D. I.

KNOWLING, R. J. 'Our Lord's Virgin Birth.'

MACHEN, J. G. 'The Virgin Birth of Christ.'

MACKINTOSH, H. R. 'The Person of Jesus Christ' (Appendix, p. 527).

ORR, J. 'The Virgin Birth of Christ.'

RAMSAY, Sir W. M. 'Was Christ Born at Bethlehem.'

SWEET, L. M. 'The Birth and Infancy of Jesus Christ.'

SWETE, H. B. The Apostles' Creed.'

TAYLOR, V. 'Historical Evidence for the Virgin Birth.'

THOMAS, W. H. G. 'Christianity is Christ.'

THORBURN, T. J. 'A Critical Examination of the Evidences for the Doctrine of the Virgin Birth.'

Consult also Commentaries on Matthew and Luke; Articles in the Bible Dictionaries and Encyclopædias, and in theological magazines.

21. The Ministry of Christ

(i) DISCOURSES

BERNARD, T. D. 'The Central Teaching of Jesus Christ.'

BRUCE, A. B. 'The Kingdom of God.'

BRUCE, A. B. 'The Galilean Gospel.'

DALE, R. W. 'Laws of Christ for Common Life.'

DALE, R. W. 'Christian Doctrine.'

DALMAN, G. The Words of Jesus.'

D'ARCY, C. F. 'Ruling Ideas of Our Lord.'

DEANE, A. 'Rabboni.'

DENNEY, J. 'Jesus and the Gospel.'

DENNEY, J. 'The Death of Christ.'

DU BOSE, W. P. 'The Consciousness of Jesus.'

FORREST, D. W. 'The Christ of History and of Experience.'

FORREST, D. W. 'The Authority of Christ.'

HEADLAM, A. C. 'The Life and Teachings of Jesus Christ.'

HOGG, A. G. 'Christ's Message of the Kingdom.'

HORTON, R. H. 'The Teaching of Jesus.'

HOYT, W. 'The Teaching of Jesus Concerning His Own Person.'

JACKSON, G. 'The Table Talk of Jesus.'

JACKSON, G. 'The Teaching of Jesus.'

KENNEDY. 'The Self-Revelation of Jesus Christ.'

MONTEFIORE, C. G. 'Some Elements in the Religious Teachings of Jesus.'

MORGAN, G. C. 'The Teaching of Christ.'

ROSS. 'The Self-Portraiture of Jesus.'

SAMPEY, J. R. 'The Ethical Teaching of Jesus.'

STALKER, J. 'The Ethic of Jesus.'

STALKER, J. 'The Christology of Jesus.'

STEVENS, G. B. 'The Theology of the New Testament.'

STIER, R. 'The Words of Jesus' (8 vols.).

STREATFIELD, G. S. 'The Self-Interpretation of Jesus Christ.'

SWETE, H. B. 'Studies in the Teaching of Our Lord.'

VOS, G. 'Teaching of Jesus Concerning the Kingdom and the Church.'

WATSON, J. 'The Mind of the Master.'

WENDT, H. H. 'The Teaching of Jesus' (2 vols.).

ZENOS, A. C. 'The Teaching of Jesus Concerning Christian Conduct.'

On The Sermon on the Mount

BACON, B. W. 'The Sermon on the Mount: Its Literary Structure.'

BOARDMAN, G. D. 'Studies in the Mountain Instruction.'

CARPENTER, W. B. 'The Great Charter of Christ.'

FINDLAY, J. A. 'The Realism of Jesus.'

GORE, C. 'The Sermon on the Mount.'

GRIFFITH-JONES, E. 'The Sermon on the Mount.'

HOGG and WATSON. 'The Sermon on the Mount.'

JONES, J. D. 'The Way into the Kingdom.'

LUTHER, Martin. 'Commentary on the Sermon on the Mount.'

STALKER, J. 'The Ethic of Jesus.'

TAIT, A. 'The Charter of Christianity.'

THOLUCK, A. 'A Commentary on the Sermon on the Mount.'

TRENCH, R. C. 'Exposition of the Sermon on the Mount.' Drawn from the Writings of St. Augustine.

VAUGHAN, C. J. 'Characteristics of Christ's Teaching Drawn from the Sermon on the Mount.'

VOTAW, C. W. 'The Sermon on the Mount' (Hastings' Bible Dictionary: vol. V, pp. 1-44).

WESLEY, John. 'Discourses on the Sermon on the Mount.'

(ii) PARABLES

ARNOT, W. 'The Parables of Our Lord.'

BROWNE, L. E. 'The Parables of the Gospels in the Light of Modern Criticism.'

BRUCE, A. B. 'The Parabolic Teaching of Christ.'

CALDERWOOD, H. 'The Parables of Our Lord.'

DODS, M. 'The Parables of Our Lord' (2 vols.).

DRUMMOND, J. 'The Parabolic Teaching of Christ.'

GOEBEL, S. 'The Parables of Jesus.'

GRESWELL, E. 'Exposition of the Parables.'

GUTHRIE, T. 'The Parables.'

HABERSHON, A. 'The Study of the Parables.'

MORGAN, G. C. 'The Parables of the Kingdom.'

MURRAY, G. 'Jesus and His Parables.'

RESKER, R. R. 'Our Lord's Illustrations.'

SALMOND, S. D. F. 'The Parables of Our Lord.'

SWETE, H. B. 'The Parables of the Kingdom.'

TAYLOR, W. M. 'The Parables of Our Saviour.'

THOMSON, W. H. 'The Parables and their Home.'

WESTCOTT, Bp. 'Introduction to the Study of the Gospels' (Appendix F).

(iii) MIRACLES

BELCHER, T. W. 'Our Lord's Miracles of Healing Considered in Relation to Some Modern Objections and to Medical Science.'

BRUCE, A. B. 'The Miraculous Element in the Gospels.'

BUSHNELL, H. 'Nature and the Supernatural.'

BUTLER, Bp. 'Analogy of Religion.'

CAIRNS, D. S. 'The Faith that Rebels.'

CAMPBELL, G. 'A Dissertation on the Miracles.'

HABERSHON, A. 'The Study of the Miracles.'

HEADLAM, A. C. 'The Miracles of the New Testament.'

HOWSON, J. J. 'Meditations on the Miracles of Christ.'

HUTCHINSON, J. 'Our Lord's Signs in St. John's Gospel.'

ILLINGWORTH, J. R. 'The Gospel Miracles.'

LATHAM, H. '*Pastor Pastorum*.'

LAIDLAW, J. 'The Miracles of Our Lord.'

LEWIS, C. S. 'Miracles: A Preliminary Survey' (1947).

LIAS, J. J. 'Are Miracles Credible?'

LYTTELTON, A. T. 'The Place of Miracles in Religion.'

MOZLEY, J. B. 'Eight Lectures on Miracles.'

MURRAY, J. O. F. 'Spiritual and Historical Evidence for Miracles' (in Essays on Some Theological Questions: Ed., H. B. SWETE).

STEINMEYER, F. L. 'The Miracles of Our Lord in Relation to Modern Criticism.'

TAYLOR, W. M. 'The Miracles of Our Lord and Saviour.'

TAYLOR, W. M. 'The Gospel Miracles in their Relation to Christ and Christianity.'

WENDLAND, J. 'Miracles and Christianity.'

WESTCOTT, Bp. B. F. ' Characteristics of the Gospel Miracles.'

22. The Trial of Christ

BUSS, S. 'The Trial of Jesus: Illustrated from Talmud and Roman Law.'

BUSS, S. 'Roman Law and History in the New Testament.'

CHANDLER, C. W. 'The Trial of Jesus from a Lawyer's Standpoint' (2 vols.).

HALL, J. 'Contemplations' (Bk. IV, xxx, xxxi).

INNES, T. 'The Trial of Jesus Christ: A Legal Monograph.'

ROSADI, G. 'The Trial of Jesus.'

STALKER, J. 'The Trial and Death of Jesus Christ.'

WILSON, T. F. 'The Trial of Jesus.' Historical and Legal Standpoint.

23. The Death of Christ

ALEXANDER, W. '*Verbum Crucis*.'

ANSELM. '*Cur Deus Homo*.'

ARMOUR, J. M. 'Atonement and Law.'

BRUCE, A. B. 'The Humiliation of Christ.'

BUSHNELL, H. 'Vicarious Sacrifice.'

BUSHNELL, H. 'Forgiveness and Law.'

CAMPBELL, McLeod. 'The Nature of the Atonement.'

CAVE, A. 'The Scriptural Doctrine of Sacrifice.'

CAWLEY, F. 'The Transcendence of Jesus Christ' (Ch. III).

CLOW, W. M. 'The Cross in Christian Experience.'

CREIGHTON, C. F. 'Law and the Cross.'

DALE, R. W. 'The Atonement.'

DENNEY, J. 'The Death of Christ.'

DENNEY, J. 'Studies in Theology.'

DENNEY, J. 'The Atonement and the Modern Mind.'

DENNEY, J. 'The Christian Doctrine of Reconciliation.'

FAIRBAIRN, A. M. 'The Place of Christ in Modern Theology.'

FAIRBAIRN, A. M. 'The Philosophy of the Christian Religion' (Ch. V).

FORSYTH, P. T. 'The Cruciality of the Cross.'

FRANKS, R. S. 'History of the Doctrine of the Work of Christ.'

HIRSCH, E. G. 'The Crucifixion from a Jewish Standpoint.'

MABIE, H. C. 'Under the Redeeming Aegis.'

MABIE, H. C. 'How Does the Death of Christ Save Us?'

McDOWALL, S. 'The Evolution of Atonement.'

MOBERLEY, R. C. 'Atonement and Personality.'

MOZLEY, J. K. 'The Doctrine of the Atonement.'

POTEAT, E. McNeill. 'The Scandal of the Cross.'

SABATIER, A. 'The Doctrine of the Atonement and its Historical Evolution.'

STEVENS, G. B. 'The Christian Doctrine of Salvation.'

STEVENS, G. B. 'The Theology of the New Testament.'

TYMMS, V. 'The Christian Idea of Atonement.'

WESTCOTT, Bp. B. F. ' The Victory of the Cross.'

For further literature on the Death of Christ see works on Biblical and Systematic Theology, e.g., by LINDSAY ALEXANDER, HODGE, and STRONG. Also articles in Bible Dictionaries and Encyclopædias on Atonement, Redemption, Reconciliation, Ransom, Forgiveness, Propitiation, Gospel, Sacrifice, Vicarious Sacrifice, Mediator, etc.

Also the many 'Lives of Christ' (see Sec. 18), and the standard Commentaries.

24. The Resurrection of Christ

BROWN, J. B. 'The Risen Christ.'
COX, S. 'The Resurrection.'
DAY, E. H. 'The Evidence for the Resurrection.'
KRUMMACHER, F. W. 'The Risen Redeemer.'
LATHAM, H. 'The Risen Master.'
LATHAM, H. '*Pastor Pastorum*' (Ch. xiii).
MARCHANT. 'Theories of the Resurrection.'
MILLIGAN, W. 'The Resurrection of Our Lord.'
ORR, J. 'The Resurrection of Jesus.'
PATON, J. 'The Glory and Joy of the Resurrection.'
RANDOLPH, B. W. 'The Empty Tomb.'
RING, T. 'The Most Certain Fact in History.'
ROBINSON, C. H. 'Studies in the Resurrection of Christ.'
SIMPSON, W. J. S. 'Our Lord's Resurrection.'
SIMPSON, W. J. S. 'The Resurrection and Modern Thought.'
STREETER, B. H. 'Foundations.'
THOMAS, W. H. G. 'The Principles of Theology.'
THOMAS, W. H. G. 'Christianity is Christ.'
WESTCOTT, Bp. B. F. 'The Gospel of the Resurrection.'
WESTCOTT, Bp. B. F. 'The Historic Faith.'
WESTCOTT, Bp. B. F. 'The Revelation of the Risen Lord.'

25. The Appearances and Ascension of Christ

CARPENTER, W. Boyd. 'The Forty Days of the Risen Life.'
HANNA, W. 'The Forty Days after Our Lord's Resurrection.'
MOBERLEY, G. 'Sayings of the Great Forty Days.'
SWETE, H. B. 'The Appearances of Our Lord after the Passion.'
WESTCOTT, Bp. B. F. 'The Revelation of the Risen Lord.'

DIMOCK, N. 'Our One Priest on High.'
FAIRBAIRN, A. M. 'Studies in the Life of Christ.'
LACEY, T. A. 'The Historic Christ.'
MILLIGAN, W. 'The Ascension and Heavenly Priesthood of Our Lord.'
PEROWNE, T. T. 'Our High Priest in Heaven.'
SWETE, H. B. 'The Ascended Christ.'

SWETE, H. B. 'The Apostles' Creed.'
TAIT, A. J. 'The Heavenly Session of Our Lord.'
THOMAS, W. H. G. 'The Principles of Theology' (A. IV).

The monographs on these subjects are sadly few, but in addition to the above titles consult the many 'Lives of Christ,' the Commentaries, and works on the Apostles' Creed.

26. The Second Advent of Christ

ANDREWS, S. J. 'Christianity and Anti-Christianity in their Final Conflict.'
BERG, J. F. 'The Second Advent of Jesus Christ: Not Premillennial.'
BLACKSTONE, W. E. 'Jesus is Coming.'
BONAR, H. 'The Coming of the Kingdom of the Lord Jesus.'
BROOKES. 'Maranatha.'
BROWN, D. 'Christ's Second Coming: Will it be Premillennial?'
BULLINGER, E. W. 'Christ's Prophetic Teaching.'
BULLINGER, E. W. 'Sermons on the Second Advent.'
BULLINGER, E. W. 'Four Prophetic Periods.'
BULLINGER, E. W. 'The Apocalypse, or the Day of the Lord.'
GORDON, A. J. '*Ecce Venit.*'
GUINNESS, H. G. 'The Approaching End of the Age.'
HALDEMAN, I. M. 'Sermons on the Second Coming.'
HEAGLE, D. 'That Blessed Hope: the Second Coming of Christ.'
KELLOGG, J. H. 'Prediction and Fulfilment.'
KELLY, W. ' Lectures on the Second Coming and Kingdom of the Lord Jesus Christ.'
MATTHEWS, M. 'The Second Coming of Christ.'
MERRILL, S. M. 'The Second Coming of Christ. Considered in its Relation to the Millennium.'
SCOTT, W. 'At Hand.'
SEISS, J. A. 'The Last Times.'
SEISS, J. A. 'Lectures on the Apocalypse' (3 vols.).
SILVER, J. F. 'The Lord's Return.'
TORREY, R. A. 'The Return of the Lord Jesus.'

The Second Advent: Will it be before the Millennium? Discussion in the *British Weekly* in 1887.
Affirmative: Canon FAUSSET; Dr. and Mrs. H. G. GUINNESS; Prof. GODET.

Negative: Prof. AGAR BEET; Prin. T. C. EDWARDS; Prin. D. BROWN.

In the above list books are named on the Pre-Millennial and the Post-Millennial views relative to the Lord's Return.

Articles should be consulted in the Bible Dictionaries under Eschatology, Millennium, and Parousia.

27. General

(a) DICTIONARIES

Hastings' Dictionary of the Bible (5 vols.).
Hastings' Dictionary of Christ and the Gospels (2 vols.).
Hastings' Dictionary of the Apostolic Church (2 vols.).
Smith's Dictionary of the Bible (4 vols.)
Encyclopædia of Religion and Ethics (13 vols.).
International Standard Bible Encyclopædia (5 vols.).
New Schaff-Herzog Encyclopædia of Religious Knowledge (12 vols.).
Universal Bible Dictionary. Buckland.
A Dictionary of the Bible. Davis.
A Standard Bible Dictionary. Jacobus.
The Jewish Encyclopædia (12 vols.).
Expository Dictionary of New Testament Words. W. E. Vine (4 vols.).

(b) COMMENTARIES

Pulpit Commentary. The Gospels (8 vols.).
People's Bible. The Gospels (4 vols.).
Speaker's Commentary. The Gospel (2 vols.).
Ellicott's Commentary. The Gospels (1 vol.).
Matthew Henry's Commentary. The Gospels (2 vols.).
Bengel's Gnomon of the New Testament. The Gospels (2 vols.).
Meyer's Critical and Exegetical Handbook. The Gospels (6 vols.).

(c) EXPOSITIONS

Maclaren's Expositions. The Gospels (10 vols.).
Speaker's Bible. The Gospels (11 vols.).
Companion Bible. The Gospels (1 vol.).
Expositor's Bible. The Gospels (5 vols.).

(d) CONCORDANCES

Strong's Exhaustive Concordance.
Young's Analytical Concordance.
Cruden's Complete Concordance—(Revised).
Walker's Comprehensive Concordance.
Gall's Interpreting Concordance.
The Treasury of Scripture Knowledge.
The Topical Bible Concordance (1947.
Student's Concordance to the New Testament (Revised Version).
Critical Greek and English Concordance. Hudson.
Critical Lexicon and Concordance to the English and Greek New Testament. Bullinger.

(e) EDITIONS OF THE ENGLISH NEW TESTAMENT

American Standard Version.
American Revised Standard Version.
Twentieth Century New Testament.
New Testament in Modern Speech. Weymouth.
The Scofield Bible.
The Chain Reference Bible. Thompson.
The New Analytical Bible. Kaye.
New Translation of the New Testament. Moffatt.
The New Testament Newly Translated. Knox.
The Literary Man's New Testament. Courtney.
Student's Chronological New Testament. Robertson.
The Modern Reader's Bible. Moulton.
Goodspeed's New Translation of the New Testament.
The New Testament in Braid Scots. Smith.

(See other titles at end of Index IV.)

This bibliography includes books which are conservative, liberal, and radical, and many of them do not represent the standpoint of this Guide.

GREEK AND OTHER WORDS

(which occur in the text of the Guide).

PAPYRI and ostraca discoveries have shown that the Greek of the New Testament is not the classic Attic, but a 'common' Greek, or world-speech which dates from the conquests of Alexander, and which is called the *Koinē*. This became the *lingua franca* of the world of Alexander and his successors, and also of the Roman period which followed.

This *Koinē* was the language not only of letters but also of commerce and everyday life, and the appearance of such a world-speech at the period when Christianity was about to dawn is a very significant fact, for, says A. T. Robertson, 'it is just in the first century A.D. that the *Koinē* comes to its full glory as a world-language,' and Deissmann says, 'in the period which gave birth to Christianity there was an international language,' and Hope Moulton calls attention to the remarkable fact that the new religion which was to master the world began its career at the very time when the Mediterranean world had one ruler and one language.

In the Gospels the Greek spoken by the people makes its entry into literature, and Rothe has spoken of the *Koinē* as 'a language of the Holy Ghost.' This from Deissmann is important:

'Until the papyri were discovered there were practically no other contemporary documents to illustrate that phase of the Greek language which comes before us in the LXX and New Testament. In those writings, broadly, what we have, both as regards vocabulary and morphology, and not seldom as regards syntax as well, is the Greek of ordinary intercourse as spoken in the countries bordering on the Mediterranean, not the artificial Greek of the rhetoricians and literateurs, strictly bound as it was by technical rules. This language of ordinary life, this cosmopolitan Greek, shows unmistakable traces of a process of development that was still going on, and in many respects differs from the older dialects as from the classical Attic' (*Bible Studies*,' p. 81).

Before this fact was apprehended the older lexicons and commentaries had much to say about words which, it was supposed, Christianity had found it necessary to coin in order to express the richness of its thought, but it is now known that all such words were in the vernacular *Koinē* of the time, so that, as Moulton puts it, 'the Holy Ghost spoke absolutely in the language of the people' (*Prolegomena*, p. 5). Because of this the older works need to be checked by the more modern.

In the *Koinē* of the New Testament, various linguistic streams intermingle, as they do in the English language, and to trace and disentangle these for the purpose of study is as fascinating as it is a necessary pursuit. These streams may be classified as Hebraisms, Aramaisms, Latinisms, and a few other sources. The following lists do not claim to be complete, but they must be nearly so.

A

		PAGE
aganakteō	...	221
agapaō	...	414
agapē	...	414
aggelia	...	129
agra	...	200
agrauleō	...	347
agreuō	...	200
agros	...	347
agō	...	50
adēlos	...	362
adikia	...	339
aidōs	...	347
airō	...	598
aiteō	...	347, 414
aichmalōtizō	...	362
aiōn	...	214, 414
aiōnios	...	414
akribōs	...	345
alētheia	...	414
alēthēs	...	414
alēthinos	...	414
alēthōs	...	414
allogenēs	...	348
allos	...	348
amēn	...	414
amnos	...	460
ampelos	...	348
ampelourgos	...	348
amphi	...	199
amphiballō	...	199
amphiballontas	...	199
ana	105, 200, 347, 348, 619
anabainō	...	619
anathema	...	362
anaideia	...	347
anakuliō	...	199
analambanō	...	347, 619
analēpsis	...	347, 619
analiskō	...	362
analuō	...	362
anapēdaō	...	199
anapēros	...	348
anastenazō	...	200
anastenaxas	...	200
anapherō	...	619
anaphōneō	...	347
anachōreō	...	277
anthomologeomai	...	347
anthrōpos	...	540, 624
anoētos	...	362
anomia	...	339
anti	105, 107, 347, 347, 348
antiballō	...	348
antikaleō	...	348
antiparerchomai	...	347
apairō	...	591
apaiteō	...	347
ap'archēs	...	456
apelpizō	...	347
aperchomai	...	619

		PAGE
apo	105, 106, 116, 347, 619
ap'arti	...	624
apokaluptō	...	623, 624, 627
apoluō	...	369
apostellō	...	116, 414
apostolos	...	116, 144
apostomatizō	...	347
argurion	...	201, 275
arguros	...	275
arnia	...	460
arnion	...	460
arti	...	624
archē	...	456
architriklinos	...	47
archōn	...	47
augeō (with tēle)	...	200
aulē	...	347
aphiēmi	...	369

B

		PAGE
bainō	...	348, 619
ballein	...	207
ballō	...	199, 348
baptisma	...	593
basileia	...	624
belonē	...	378
belonēs	...	378
bios	...	414
biōtikos	...	362
blepō	...	220, 414

G

		PAGE
geenna	...	584
genea	...	630
genos	...	348
ginōskō	...	414

D

		PAGE
daktulos	...	168
de	...	413
despotēs	...	520
dia	49, 105, 107, 143, 348, 378, 619
diaireō	...	362
diapragmateuomai	...	348
diaspora	...	49
diatessaron	...	143, 174
didaskalos	...	520, 612
didachē	...	175
didrachmon	...	274
Didumos	...	63
diistēmi	...	619
diōkō	...	199
dokeō	...	526
doxa	...	204, 414
doulos	...	202
dunamesin	...	204
dunamis	...	203, 204, 547

E

		PAGE
egō meth'humōn eimi	...	616
eidon	...	414
eipen	...	195

ARAMAIC WORDS

Increasing attention is being given to the Aramaic background of the Gospels, and in this field much remains to be done. The reason for and importance of this will be clear when we realize that Jesus spoke in Aramaic as well as in Greek, and read the Hebrew and the Septuagint Old Testament. Dalman affirms that 'Aramaic was the mother tongue of the Galileans' (*The Words of Jesus*, p. 10), and, no doubt, the Oral Gospel was spoken in both Aramaic and Greek as occasion required. It is held by some that there was a primitive Aramaic *Mark*, and, it will be recalled, Papias said that Matthew wrote his *Logia* in Aramaic. Thrice Mark uses Aramaic quotations from the words of Jesus (v. 41; vii. 34; xiv. 36), and he has an Aramaic adaptation of one of Jesus' Sayings on the Cross (xv. 34). It would seem then that there is a strong Aramaic influence in the Greek of the Gospels. The following words are evidence of this.

Abba, Father: Mark xiv. 36, only occurrence in the Gospels. The words are both Aramaic and Greek, and not one a translation of the other. Jesus may have used both words as Paul did (Gal. iv. 6; Rom. viii. 15).

Bariōna   -   Bar-Jonah, with Simon; Matt. xvi. 17. 'The Apostle's full patronymic (Aramaic) name. —Robertson.

Beelzeboul   -   Matt. x. 25: *lord of dung*, or' *lord of flies*. This is the form of the word in most Greek MSS. The etymology is unknown, but the term is one of reproach.

Bēthesda   -   John v. 2. House of Mercy.

Gabbatha   -   John xix. 13. Or, Gab Baitha, meaning 'the ridge of the house,' that is, the Temple Mound. It is the same place as the Pavement (lithostrōton) just referred to.

Geenna   -   (Hell), Gehenna; Valley of Hinnom; not Hades. Matt. v. 29, 30 (see page 584). In Jewish thought a symbol of the supposed place of future punishments. The word is used exclusively in a figurative sense in the Gospels, and only in the Synoptic reports of Christ's Sayings. 'Hell,' which is used also for 'Hades,' is our ambiguous rendering of the word.

Golgotha   -   Matt. xxvii. 33; Mark xv. 22. Not 'place of skulls.' but the place of a skull-shaped mount. The Latin Vulgate has 'Calvariæ, whence our Calvary.

The fourth and central of Christ's Sayings on the Cross.

Mark xv. 34 *Elōi Elōi lama sabachthanei.*

Matt. xxvii. 46. *Eli Ēli lema sabachthanei.*

The only Word from the Cross recorded by Mark and Matthew.

Plummer says: 'In both Gospels it is given in the original Aramaic, but texts vary somewhat as to the transliteration.' Eli, Eli, Elei, Elei, 'Elōi. Whether Jesus uttered the first word in Aramaic or Hebrew is not clear. Dalman things it was in Hebrew. He says: 'It is conceivable that, to secure greater uniformity, one copyist corrected *ēlei* to *elōei*, so that the whole should be Aramaic, while another changed *lema sebachthanei* into *lama (a)zaphthanei*, so as to have the whole in Hebrew' (*Words of Jesus*, p. 54). Allen thinks: 'It is difficult not to believe that Christ quoted the Psalm (xxii. 1) in Hebrew, *Ēli Ēli lama azabhtani*' (*Studies in the Synoptic Problem*, p. 305); 'in which case,' says Plummer, 'the Aramaic form in Mark is given for the sake of those to whom Aramaic was more familiar than Hebrew' (Cambridge Greek Testament: Matthew, p. 357).

Ephphatha	-	'Be opened,' Mark vii. 34.
Kēphas -	-	Cephas; John i. 42. Rock. cf. Matt. xvi. 18. Greek *Petros*.
Korbanas	-	Treasury; Matt. xxvii. 6: cf. *Korban* in Mark vii. 11. In Mark is Aramaic with a translation. Korban, a gift (*dōron*, LXX), an offering to God. Exod. xxi. 17; Lev. xx. 9.
Mamōnas	-	Mammon: Matt. vi. 24.
Messias	-	Messiah; John i. 41; iv. 25, only occurrences in the New Testament. Elsewhere translated Xristos, Christ, Anointed One.
Pascha	-	Passover; Matt. xxvi. 2. Hebrew and Aramaic.
Pharisaios	-	Pharisee; Mark ii. 16. 'From an Aramaic word *peras* (found in Dan. v. 28), signifying *to separate*, owing to a different manner of life from that of the general public' (W. E. Vine, *Expository Dictionary of New Testament Words*).
Rabbōni	-	(Rabbounei); Rabboni; Mark x. 51; John xx. 16. Here the Aramaic is preserved. Matthew and Luke have *Kurie*. The word is practically the same as Rabbi(ei), from *rab*, denoting Master in contrast to slave (W. E. Vine).
Raka -	-	Raca; Matt. v. 22 (only occurrence). A term of contempt, from a Hebrew root signifying *emptiness*, or *vanity*. 'Empty intellectually rather than morally, empty-headed' (W. E. Vine).
Sabbaton	-	Sabbath; Matt. xii. 5; Mark ii. 27. 28. The root idea of the word is 'cessation from activity.'
Satanas	-	Satan; Matt. iv. 10. Adversary.
Saton -	-	Measure; Matt. xiii. 33; Luke xiii. 21 (only occurrences). A Hebrew measure, about a peck and a half.
Sikera -	-	Strong drink; Luke i. 15 (here only in New Testament). An Aramaic word transliterated into Greek.
Talitha -	-	Talitha; Mark v. 41; meaning *maiden*.
Koum -	-	Cumi; Mark v. 41; meaning *arise*.
		Mark interpreted the words into Greek for those who did not know Aramaic.

HEBREW WORDS

Amēn	-	Amen; Matt. v. 18, 26; John i. 51. In John's Gospel the word is always double; occurs thus 25 times, and only in the words of Jesus. A Hebrew word transliterated into Greek, and then into English.
Batos -	-	Bush; Mark xii. 26, cf. Exod. iii. 3-6.
Boanērges	-	Boanerges; Mark iii. 17. A Hebrew nickname, 'sons of thunder.'
Bussos -	-	Fine linen; Luke xvi. 19 (here only in the New Testament). *Bussinos* in Rev. xviii. 12.
Hebraisti	-	'In Hebrew'; John xix. 13, 17, 20. Robertson says that strictly it is 'in Aramaic,' as in v. 2; xx. 16; Rev. ix. 11; xvi. 16.
Hussōpos	-	Hyssop; John xix. 29; Heb. ix. 19 (only occurrences).
Hōsanna	-	Matt. xxi. 9, 15, means, 'save we pray thee.'
Ēli -	-	'My God'; Matt. xxvii. 46. From the Hebrew *El* (see under Aramaic Words).
Kamēlos	-	Camel; Matt. iii. 4.
Ioudaios	-	Jew; Matt. ii. 2.
Kuminon	-	Cummin; Matt. xxiii. 23 (only occurrence).
Libanos	-	Frankincense; Matt. ii. 11; Rev. xviii. 13 (only occurrences).
Manna -	-	John vi. 31; lit. 'what is this?'; cf. Exod. xvi. 1

Pascha   - Passover; Matt. xxvi. 2.   Hebrew and Aramaic.
Rabbi   - Matt. xxiii. 7.   (See under Aramaic Words, Rabbōni).
Sabbaton   - Sabbath; Matt. xii. 5.   (See under Aramaic Words).
Silōam   - Siloam; Luke xiii. 4.
Sukaminos   - Sycamine; Luke xvii. 6 (only occurrence).
        The Hebrew and the Aramaic are not distinguished on page 417, last para.
The words are sometimes used interchangeably, though incorrectly.   *Aram* is
the Hebrew word for Syria, and so the Aramaic is sometimes called the Syro-
Chaldaic.

LATIN WORDS

Assarion   - Farthing; Matt. x. 29; Luke xii. 6 (only occurrences).   Diminu-
                tive form of the Roman *as*, slightly more than half an English
                penny; one tenth of a *drachma*; one-sixteenth of a Roman
                denarius.
Dēnarion   - Penny; Matt. xviii. 28.   *Denarius.*   A Roman coin of value 9½d.
                to 1/- English money.
Kenturiōn   - *Centurio*; centurion; Mark xv. 39, 44, 45.   Only here in the New
                Testament.   Elsewhere the Greek *hekatontarchos(ēs)* is employed
                (Matt. viii. 5, 8, 13, *et al*).
Kēnsos   - Tribute; Matt. xvii. 25.   *Census*, registration.   A poll-tax (pp.
                247, 275).
Kodrantēs   - Farthing; Matt. v. 26; Mark xii. 42 (only).   The Latin word is
                quadrans, the quarter of an *as (Assarion*, which see; p. 275).
Koustōdia   - Watch; Matt. xxvii. 65, 66; xxviii. 11 (only).   *Custodia.*   The
                word occurs in an Oxyrhynchus papyrus of A.D. 22.
Krabattos   - (*Krabbatos*); bed; Mark ii. 4, 9, 11, 12.   Latin, *grabatus.*   Com-
(W. H.)   pare *Klinē* in Matt. ix. 2.   A word common in the papyri.   A
                mattress or small couch.
Legiōn   - (Legeōn); legion; Matt. xxvi. 53.   *Legio.*   A full Roman legion
                had 6826 men, foot and horse, in the time of Augustus.
Lention   - Towel; John xiii. 4, 5 (only).   Latin, *linteum*, linen cloth.
Litra -   - Pound; John xii. 3; xix. 39 (only).   Latin, *libra*, of twelve ounces
                weight.   Cf. Mark xiv. 3; Matt. xxvi. 7.
Milion   - Mile, Roman; Matt. v. 41 (only).   *Mille.*
Modios   - Bushel; Matt. v. 15; Mark iv. 21; Luke xi. 33 (only).   *Modius.*
Xestēs -   - Pot, vessel; Mark vii. 4 (8) (only).   *Sextus, sextarius.*   A small
                measure of about a pint and a half.
Praitōrion   - *Prætorium*, Palace; Matt. xxvii. 27; Mark xv. 16.
Spekoulatōr   - Executioner; Mark vi. 27 (only).   *Speculator.*   A looker-out, a
                spy; sometimes an executioner (p. 198).
Titlos -   - Title; John xix. 19, 20 (only).   *Titlon.*   'The technical Latin
                word for the board with the name of the criminal and the crime
                in which he is condemned' (A. T. Robertson).
Phragellion   - Phragelloō; noun and verb; scourge.   The noun is in John ii.
                15 only.   The verb, in Matt. xxvii. 26; Mark xv. 15 only.   *Flag-
                ellum; flagello.*   In John xix. 1, the word *mastigoō* is used.
        In addition to these words there are a few Latin phrases in the Gospels, for
which consult Robertson's 'Greek Grammar in the Light of Historical Research,'
pp. 109, 110.
        The names of two Roman Emperors are found in the Gospels, both in Luke
—*Augoustos*, Augustus; Luke ii. 1; and *Tiberios*, Tiberius; Luke iii. 1; and the
surname *Kaisar*, Cæsar, is applied to them both.   (See Acts xxv. 21, 25; *Sebastos*,
referring to Nero (cf. Acts xxvii. 1).

OTHER WORDS

Aggareuō   - Compel; Matt. v. 41; xxvii. 32; Mark xv. 21 (only).   'The word
                is of Persian origin and means public couriers or mounted mes-
                sengers (*aggaroi*) who were stationed by the King of Persia
                at fixed localities, with horses ready for use, to send royal messages
                from one to another.   So if a man is passing such a post-station,

an official may rush out and compel him to go back to another station to do an errand for the King. This very thing was done to Simon of Cyrene who was thus compelled to carry the cross of Christ' (A. T. Robertson).

Baïon - - Branch; John xii. 13 (only). Apparently a word of Egyptian origin, which occurs in the papyri. Cf. 1 Macc. xiii. 51.

Biblos - - Book; Matt. i. 1, et al. "Egyptian or Semitic" (Robertson).

Bounos - Hill; Luke iii. 5; xxiii. 30 (only). A Cyrenaic word; so called by Herodotus.

Zizanion - Tares; Matt. xiii. 25, 26, 27, 29, 30, 36, 38, 40 (only). 'A word of Semitic origin' (Grimm-Thayer). 'Possibly Arabic' (Robertson).

Kuminon - Cummin; Matt. xxiii. 23 (only). The word may be Hebrew or Phœnician.

Mna - - Pound; Luke xix. 13, 16, 18, 20, 24, 25 (only). 'A word of Eastern origin' (Grimm-Thayer).

Chitōr - Coat; Matt. v. 50; Mark xiv. 63. Oriental.

Paradeisos - Paradise; Luke xxiii. 43; 2 Cor. xii. 4; Rev. ii. 7 (only). A Persian word used by Xenophon for an enclosed park or pleasure ground.

Rhumē - Street, lane; Matt. vi. 2; Luke xiv. 21 (only, in Gospels). Contrasted with the *plateiai* or broad open spaces in an Eastern city.

Sandalion - Sandal; Mark vi. 9; Acts xii. 8 (only). Persian.

Sinapi - - Mustard seed; Matt. xiii. 31. Thought to be of Egyptian origin, but uncertain (Grimm-Thayer).

Sindōn - Linen cloth; Mark xv. 46. May be of Egyptian or Sanskrit origin (Grimm-Thayer). See page 576, 'Crucifixion.'

A few book titles are here given for the benefit of those who would pursue this line of study.

LITERATURE

BLASS, F. 'Philology of the Gospels.'

CREMER, H. Biblico-Theological Lexicon of New Testament Greek.

DEISSMANN, A. 'Bible Studies'; 'Light from the Ancient East'; 'New Light on the New Testament.'

GRIMM-THAYER. A Greek-English Lexicon of the New Testament.

HAWKINS, J. C. 'Horæ Synopticæ.'

KENYON, F. G. 'Evidence of the Papyri for Textual Criticism of the New Testament.'

MILLIGAN, G. 'Selections from the Greek Papyri.' 'The Greek Papyri with Special Reference to their Value for New Testament Study.'

MOULTON, J. H. 'A Grammar of New Testament Greek' (Vol. I: Prolegomena). 'From Egyptian Rubbish Heaps.' 'The Christian Religion in the Study and the Street.'

MOULTON and MILLIGAN. 'The Vocabulary of the New Testament.' Illustrated from the Papyri and other Non-Literary Sources.

ROBERTSON, A. T. 'A Short Grammar of the New Testament.' 'A Grammar of the Greek New Testament in the Light of Historical Research.'

THOMSON, J. E. H. 'The Language of Palestine during the Time of Our Lord.'

VINE, W. E. 'Expository Dictionary of New Testament Words.'

ZAHN, T. 'On the Language of Palestine.' Introduction to the New Testament. Vol. I, pp. 1-72.

In addition to these, relevant articles should be consulted in

Hastings' Bible Dictionary.

Hastings' Dictionary of Christ and the Gospels.

The International Standard Bible Encyclopædia.

The Encyclopædia Biblica.

The International Critical Commentary.

The Expositor's Greek Testament.

APPENDIX A

MIRACLES IN LUKE'S GOSPEL

IN LUKE ONLY (7)

First Miraculous Draught of Fishes	v. 1-11
A Widow's Son Raised	vii. 11-17
A Dumb Demoniac Healed	xi. 14
A Woman's Infirmity Cured	xiii. 10-17
A Man with Dropsy Healed	xiv. 1-6
Ten Lepers Healed	xvii. 11-19
The Ear of Malchus Healed	xxii. 49-51

IN ONE OTHER GOSPEL (2)

A Demoniac Liberated	iv. 31-37
A Centurion's Servant Healed	vii. 1-10

IN TWO OTHER GOSPELS (10)

Healing of Peter's Mother-in-Law	iv. 38,39
A Leper Cured	v. 12-16
A Paralytic Healed	v. 18-26
A Man with a Withered Hand Healed	vi. 6-11
Stilling the Storm	viii. 22-25
Two Demoniacs Liberated	viii. 26-39
A Woman's Issue of Blood Staunched	viii. 43-48
The Daughter of Jairus Raised	viii. 41, 42, 49-56
Cure of an Epileptic Boy	ix. 38-43
Two Blind Men Healed	xviii. 35-43

IN THREE OTHER GOSPELS (1)

Five Thousand Fed	ix. 12-17

Thirty-five specific miracles are recorded in the Four Gospels of which twenty are in Luke's Gospel.

To these must be added recorded groups of miracles:—iv. 40 f.; v. 15, 17 f.; vi. 17-19; vii. 21 f.; ix. 11. (See pages 203, 286, 287, 553-556).

APPENDIX B

MIRACLES OMITTED BY LUKE (16)

(*Chronological Order*)

Water Made into Wine.
A Nobleman's Son Healed.
Impotent Man at Bethesda Healed.
A Blind and Dumb Man Cured.
Two Blind Men Healed.
A Dumb Demoniac Exorcised.
Jesus Walking on the Sea.
A Syro-Phœnician Girl Healed.

A Deaf and Dumb Man Healed.
Four Thousand Fed.
A Blind Man Healed.
Tribute Money Provided.
Healing of a Man Born Blind.
Lazarus Raised from the Dead.
Cursing of the Fig Tree.
Second Miraculous Draught of Fishes.

(See pp. 553-555).

APPENDIX C

PARABLES IN LUKE'S GOSPEL

In Luke Only (19)

The Two Debtors	vii. 41-43
The Good Samaritan	x. 30-37
The Friend at Midnight	xi. 5-8
The Rich Fool	xii. 16-21
The Waiting and Watching Servants (?)	xii. 35-40
The Faithful and Evil Servants	xii. 41-48
The Barren Fig Tree	xiii. 6-9
The Chief Seats	xiv. 7-11
The Great Supper	xiv. 16-24
The Unfinished Tower	xiv. 28-30
The Unwaged War	xiv. 31, 32
The Lost Piece of Silver	xv. 8-10
The Prodigal Son and Elder Brother	xv. 11-32
The Unrighteous Steward	xvi. 1-13
The Rich Man and Lazarus (?)	xvi. 19-31
The Unprofitable Servants	xvii. 7-10
The Unjust Judge	xviii. 1-8
The Pharisee and the Publican	xviii. 9-14
The Pounds	xix. 11-27

In One Other Gospel (6)

The Two Builders	vi. 46-49
The Unclean Spirit that Returned	xi. 24-26
The Inward Light	xi. 34-36
The Master and the Thief	xii. 39, 40
The Leaven in the Meal	xiii. 20, 21
The Lost Sheep	xv. 3-7

In Two Other Gospels (10)

The Bride and the Bridegroom	v. 34, 35
The New Cloth on an Old Garment	v. 36
The New Wine in Old Wine-skins	v. 37-39
The Sower and the Soils	viii. 4-15
The Lighted Lamp	viii. 16, 17; xi. 33
The Mustard Seed	xiii. 18, 19
The Savourless Salt	xiv. 34, 35
The Wicked Husbandmen	xx. 9-16
The Rejected Stone	xx. 17-19
The Sprouting Fig Tree	xxi. 29-33

To these must be added:—

PARABOLIC ILLUSTRATIONS (10)

Fishers of Men	v. 10
The Physician and the Sick	v. 31, 32
The Blind Guiding the Blind	vi. 39
The Mote and the Beam	vi. 41, 42
Good and Bad Fruit Trees	vi. 43-45
The Children in the Market Place	vii. 31-35
The Strong Man	xi. 17-22
The Light of the World	xi. 34-36
Birds and Flowers	xii. 22-31
The Strait Gate and the Shut Door	xiii. 23-30

This Table shows that in Luke's Gospel there are 35 parables proper, and 10 parabolic illustrations, 45 in all. Luke's record is pre-eminently pictorial. In the Four Gospels there are approximately 70 parables and parabolic illustrations. (See pp. 278, 279, 549-553).

664

APPENDICES

APPENDIX D
PARABLES OMITTED BY LUKE

The Wheat and the Tares.
The Hidden Treasure.
The Pearl of Great Price.
The Fish Net.
The Householder.
The Unmerciful Servant.
The Labourers in the Vineyard.

The Two Sons Called to Work.
The Marriage of the King's Son.
The Ten Virgins.
The Talents.
The Sheep and the Goats.   (?)
The Seed Growing Secretly.
The Householder and the Porter.

PARABOLIC ILLUSTRATIONS

The Salt of the Earth.
Dogs and Swine.
Doomed Plants.
The Broad and Narrow Ways.

The Offending Members.
About Satan's Kingdom.
Good and Bad Treasures.
On Defilement.

(See pages 549-551)

APPENDIX E
DISCOURSES IN LUKE'S GOSPEL

THE SERMON ON THE MOUNT ... ... **vi.** 20-4c

About this Dr. A. T. Robertson says:

"There is little doubt that the discourses given by Matthew and Luke are the same (Matt. v-vii), Matthew locating it on 'the mountain,' and Luke 'on a level place,' which might easily be a level spot on a mountain. Observe that they begin and end alike, and pursue the same general order. Luke omits various matters of special interest to Matthew's Jewish readers (e.g., Matt. v. 17-42), and other matters that he himself will give elsewhere (e.g., Luke xi. 1-4; xii. 22-31); while Luke has a few sentences (as verses 24-26, 38-40) which are not given by Matthew." 'Harmony of the Gospels for Students of the Life of Christ' (p. 48, note).

Commission of the Seventy and Words on their Return   x.   1-20
Words in Reply to the Demand for a Sign... ... ...   xi. 29-32
Indictment of the Pharisees ... ...   xi. 37-52
Discourse to the Disciples on Several Topics ... ...   xii. 1-12
Discourse on Anxiety ... ...   xii. 22-34
Discourse on Being Saved ... ...   xiii. 22-30
On the Future Coming of the Son of Man ... ...   xvii. 22-37
Discourse on the Destruction of Jerusalem and the End
of the Age ... ...   xxi. 5-36
Words to the Disciples on True Greatness ... ...   xxii. 24-30

This list does not include parables which were spoken in the course of instruction (for which see Appendix C), nor the shorter utterances of our Lord in this Gospel (see page 366).

APPENDIX F
PARABLES OMITTED BY MATTHEW (21)

The Seed Growing Secretly.
The Householder and the Porter.
The Two Debtors.
The Good Samaritan.
The Friend at Midnight.
The Rich Fool.
The Waiting and Watching Servants.
The Barren Fig Tree.
The Great Supper.
The Unfinished Tower.
The Unwaged War.

The Lost Piece of Silver.
The Prodigal Son and Elder Brother.
The Unrighteous Steward.
The Rich Man and Lazarus (?)
The Unprofitable Servants.
The Unjust Judge.
The Pharisee and the Publican.
The Pounds.
The Strait Gate and the Shut Door.
The Chief Seats at Feasts.

(See pages 550, 551)